# The RAF Britannia and its people 1959 to 1975

by Squadron Leader David Berry

This history has been written in appreciation of the comradeship of all my past Britannia compatriots in the air and on the ground.

It is also dedicated to all those who, whilst we were engaged in our worldwide tasks, kept the 'home fires burning' - in particular, to a certain Valerie who has maintained that support to the extent of proof reading this book!

By the same author:

*'The Motorcaravan Handbook'*

*'Tales from the Crewroom'*

*'The Whispering Giant in Uniform'*

*'RV in UK'*

*'Specialist Aircrew'*

*'The Recreational Nomad'*

CDs:

*'A Cute Little RV'*
*How to travel the USA in your own motorhome*

*'Ireland'*
*A CD-ROM Guide for Motorhomers*

# The RAF Britannia and its people 1959 to 1975

by

Squadron Leader David Berry

**The history of the Bristol Britannia in Royal Air Force service is also that of RAF Lyneham and RAF Brize Norton for those years**

Keyham Books

First edition published in 1996 by
Keyham Books
Startley
Chippenham SN15 5HG
www.keyhambooks.co.uk

This second, revised and expanded edition
published in 2005.



ISBN 0 9527 715 4 3

Layout by Keyham Books
Printed and bound by Antony Rowe Ltd

# Contents




The author is indebted to the late Flight Lieutenant Bill Robinson for the many fine photographs he took during his time on the RAF Britannia fleet. Also, a thankyou to Air Vice Marshal N E Hoad CVO CBE AFC. As Wing Commander Norman Hoad he was a CO of 216 Squadron and in that time completed a number of paintings of the RAF Lyneham scene. The pen and ink drawings in this book are from his sketches for a Britannia painting.

# Foreword

## by Air Chief Marshal Sir Thomas Kennedy GCB AFC

I have to confess that I was with the Brit force for only about 16 months as a Squadron Commander although I retained links with the transport force subsequently as Gp Capt Ops at Transport Command, Station Commander at Brize Norton and Director of Ops at the MOD. I also had the background experience of a few years on Hastings and then on Dakotas in the Pacific area. So I knew a little about the problems facing a fleet of large aircraft. I recall that we used to set off for Singapore secure (?) in the knowledge that the staging post would look after us as far as anything untoward was concerned. The problem arose off-route where communications were difficult or non-existent and if the aircraft had some unserviceability beyond the capacity of the crew to fix, inordinate delays were inevitable.

With the introduction of larger, technically more complex aircraft the problem was exacerbated. Another aspect was that the number of RAF bases was reducing with the passing of time. The introduction of slip services added to the difficulties of command and control. And in terms of sheer numbers Transport Command had many times more aircraft than say BOAC. By the late 1960s onwards we had 23 Britannias, 13 VC10s, 10 Belfasts, about 40 Argosys, about 20 Andovers and some 60 odd Hercules on the horizon. At any one time there would be well over a 100 aircraft flying all over the world.

The Ops Controllers at Upavon were rarely experienced with the requirements of many of these aircraft and in any case they had almost no means of rapid communication with them.

One of the first things to be done was to get aircraft captains into the Ops Controller seats. This was not too popular initially but it soon proved its worth. David Berry and Tony Cullum were two of the first incumbents. Then better communications were now available on the civil net and, after much MOD procrastination, Wg Cdr D'Oliveira got us linked into OFTS which was a rapid worldwide network available at almost every airfield. This meant that aircraft captains could contact Upavon from the other side of the world in minutes rather than days and latterly, with the advent of the 'Dispatch Drop', could speak direct to the controller from the cockpit

wherever they might be around the world. A good example of this was when we spoke to the captain of a VC10 on the New York flight to divert him to Washington because of a bomb scare. We actually spoke on a VHF frequency from an office at Upavon. Later, on another network, SITA came on line. As we came to rely on these systems more and more, it became apparent that we needed to co-operate with the civil aviation authority when it came to off-route operations and we split the world into three slices. From UK east to Singapore we worked with updated RAF systems, from Singapore to San Francisco, with Qantas and from San Francisco to UK with BOAC. Contractual arrangements were made with each of these organisations. Not an easy task to arrange with the civil servants in MOD. Well done Basil D'Oliveira. Updating the RAF communications from UK east to Singapore was done through the old Area of Responsibility centres which were subsumed into a flight watch area with direct communication to Upavon initially and direct to aircraft latterly.

The next step was to develop a full Flight Watch system globally. This became vital as the financial squeeze on the Air Force began to bite to the extent that hours of operation of many of our airfields were reduced and it became necessary to time the arrival of aircraft to the published opening hours. Weather became more important too, yet the Met system at Upavon was archaic to say the least. For a start the Met Office was away across the north airfield so that up to date forecasts were always delayed and the controller could not always get hold of the duty forecaster to discuss whether he should bring an aircraft in from, say Cyprus, or whether to hold him there for several hours or whether to arrange for a diversion in the UK. It took a double diversion of a VC10 casualty evacuation aircraft into London Airport to convince the financiers that we were serious about our business and that we needed investment in facilities. To be fair we got one of them down to Upavon for a day and he spent most of it in the Ops Room; then he was convinced and we got the funding to improve the weather reporting system and to bring it in to the Ops Room. Another communications system was ASMA, an administrative network which was developed to be used by the operators and, I believe, the air support of the Falklands War was largely dependent on it. With all these changes it was vital that aircraft captains were persuaded of the benefits of the new system and that operations staffs were up to date with all the necessary procedures; so we started a series of courses at Upavon to spread the word. Also they were introduced to the OCUs where aircrews converted on to new aircraft.

A small but important aspect was the attitude of the MOD Finance staffs who were becoming increasingly worried about the extent and the size of the claims from Transport Command/Air Support Command. Gp Capt Freddie Hazlewood, ex-Station Commander Lyneham 1965/67, was on the Ops(AT) staff in MOD and he found the woman who was responsible. She had no idea of the expansion of the Command and was trying to balance her account against the increasing costs coming from Upavon. He invited her down to HQTC/ASC where we explained the set up. From then on we got nothing but splendid co-operation from her and her colleagues. Another example of the importance of 'communication'.

But all these improvements were in their infancy during the Oil Lift. I first went down to Nairobi in January 1966 just as the crews were arriving from Dar-es-Salaam and there was indeed some tension in the atmosphere caused almost totally by the lack of information of what was going to happen. However things soon settled down and a regular pattern of flights to Lusaka and Ndola became the order of the day - and night. It continued until October 1966. The strain on RAF Eastleigh was quite considerable. The sudden administrative burden looking after some 200 seasoned transporters and groundcrews more or less overwhelmed the small Station. We required most of the available MT on a H24 basis and much of their engineering and supply support to say nothing of the signals capacity and the routine administration of people coming and going to and from the UK. I had a series of strained interviews with the Station Commander but with a bit of goodwill on both sides we came to agreements on most problems.

The limitations of parking space at Lusaka and Ndola meant that strict attention had to be paid to the arrival/departure times to tie in with the civil movements. Once this was fully appreciated by the crews, it ceased to be a problem and the flow of aircraft proceeded smoothly.

My second detachment covered the period of the introduction of the rubber seal drums. Filling them was one problem, then loading them into the aircraft was another. Then we found that the odd one leaked. A representative of the manufacturing company was summoned post haste. He flew in and we tested a number of the drums for leaks. Unfortunately, too many of them did and whilst it was OK for tactical operations in the field it was quite unacceptable for carriage in strategic aircraft. So it was back to the standard 50-gallon metal drums. The Oil Lift is covered in Chapter 20 but I must say that the ground crews - and the aircrews - were quite splendid. It was just another job for them. They worked extremely hard but the whole experience was fun and most of them managed to see a bit of East Africa while they were at it.

I commend this book to all transporters wherever they may be. I'm sure I speak for most of them in saying that we thoroughly enjoyed our years of flying round the world doing a good job and having, in the main, a great deal of fun too.

December 2004

# Preface

Nine years ago, in the Preface to the first edition of my history of the RAF Britannia I described it as a 'labour of love'. With this revised and expanded edition having 350 more pages and hundreds of additional photographs, it perhaps could be described as an orgy! For those of you with a copy of that first edition, it can be regarded as the skeleton for this book - to those bones a lot of flesh has been added.

Again, I previously wrote of my determination to see that the history of the RAF Britannia era was duly recorded. With, in the intervening years, so much more material becoming available then it seemed right and proper to see that it was added. One source has been copies of '*The Lyneham Globe*', the Station newspaper, and my improved software skills to make those photographs reasonably presentable. Perfection from such sub-standard material is not possible but as they are the only record of typical and momentous times then it is a pity not to include them.

But one of the major sources of new content is articles that have appeared in The Britannia Association magazine, which I have edited and produced for 20 years. I am extremely grateful to the authors of these for their agreement to them being reproduced here. I am also indebted to the suppliers of other material, particularly photographs. I have made all this thanks general and unidentified as it would be impossible to list individuals. In the book I have done my best to identify the contributors. My apologies to any that I have missed.

In that first Preface I did make the point that this is an individual view of RAF Britannia history and the interpretation of facts. Some readers might have a different view. I will leave them to challenge mine in their own book!

There are many people who consider their time with the Britannia as the best years of their lives. I'll say 'Hear, Hear' to that and hope that this book will bring back happy memories.

*David Berry*
*August 2005*

# The Author

Squadron Leader Berry gained his Private Pilots' Licence at the tender age of 17 under the Air Training Corps' Flying Scholarship scheme; a year on he joined the Royal Air Force as a pilot. Forty years and 10,000 flying hours later he retired. In his time he was a fighter pilot and flying instructor but the bulk of his service was occupied with world-wide transport flying and a large part of that with the Britannia. Joining the fleet in 1962, just two years after its inception, he was one of the last to leave on its demise some 13 years later. He received a commendation from the C-in-C, Air Support Command in 1969 and was awarded The Queen's Commendation for Valuable Service in the Air in 1974. His connection with the Britannia recommenced at the Aeroplane and Armament Experimental Establishment, Boscombe Down which continued to operate one until 1984. Indeed, David was the last military pilot to fly the Britannia.

An interest in writing stems from completion of an education degree course as a mature student. With two books conventionally published, David decided to try self-publishing and the first edition of this book was his initial project. For that, and the subsequent three books he completed all the lay-out etc himself and subsequently marketed them. A topic for some of the books (and CDs) is provided by his interest, in retirement, in travel - in particular motorcaravanning.

CHAPTER ONE

# The Birth of the Britannia

For an aircraft that looked so right and served the Royal Air Force so faithfully and efficiently for many years, the story of the evolution of the Britannia might be considered perverse. It certainly reflects the turmoil of the immediate post-war aviation years and the difficulties generated by the explosive nature of technological development of that time. Interwoven is chance, creating on the one hand triumph ... and on the other disaster. To tell the whole story of those development years would exceed the scope of this book; however some part needs telling for it would not be right to reflect on a life without musing on the conception and birth.

**Sir Archibald recalls**

That whole story is a complex one and my simplification might distort the truth. However, I am able to avoid this with a personal summary contributed by Sir Archibald Russell. As Dr A E Russell CBE FRAeS FIAeS, he was Technical Director and Chief Engineer of Bristol Aircraft Limited, and as such can be considered the '*Father of the Britannia*'. His work at the time was beyond compare and, it must be true to say that, had all the other components that go to make up an aeroplane matched the excellence of his airframe, then the Britannia, despite the thrusting development of jet air transport aircraft, would have been a world beater. As it was, there were tremendous setbacks and these, coupled with what can now be seen as poor decisions, resulted in its less than moderate commercial success.

Sir Archibald writes of '*The Britannia Genesis*' thus:

'*Through the critical days of the Second World War it was essential that this country should devote its total resources towards immediate means of base survival. Then, when the United States of America became directly involved, as part of a combat sharing policy, it was agreed that they would supply the total requirements for transport aircraft. Consequently and subsequently, in respect of postwar Civil Aviation, it was obvious that the British aircraft industry had been placed at a singular disadvantage. So, in 1943, when the outcome of the war was no longer in doubt and new military developments were most unlikely to be used in anger, a top level committee was formed, with Lord Brabazon as chairman. He was charged with defining the future requirements of the two major airlines, British Overseas Airways and*

Sir Archibald kindly provided a hand written, 14-page account especially for this book.

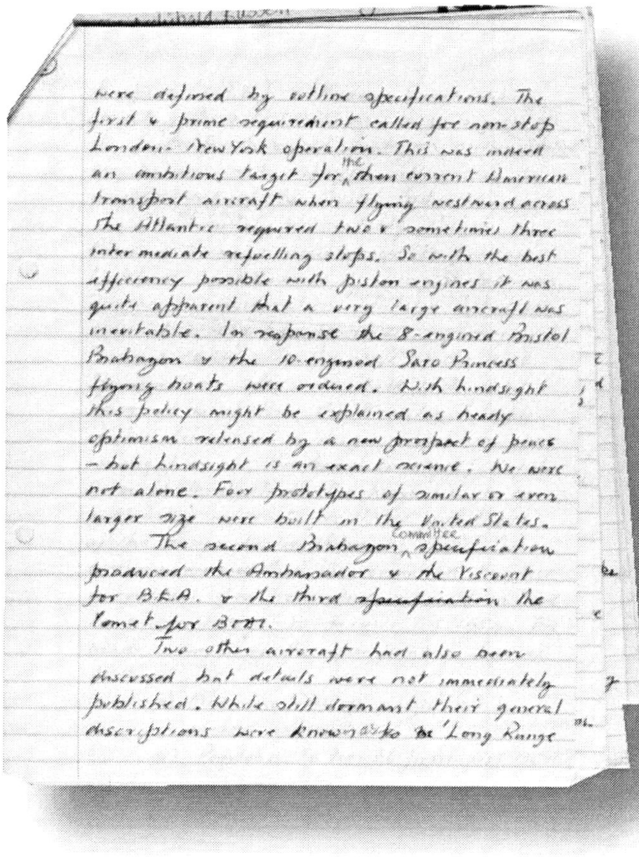

were defined by outline specifications. The first & prime requirement called for non-stop London - New York operation. This was indeed an ambitious target for the then current American transport aircraft when flying westward across the Atlantic required two & sometimes three intermediate refuelling stops. So with the best efficiency possible with piston engines it was quite apparent that a very large aircraft was inevitable. In response the 8-engined Bristol Brabazon & the 10-engined Saro Princess flying boats were ordered. With hindsight this policy might be explained as heady optimism released by a new prospect of peace - but hindsight is an exact science. We were not alone. Four prototypes of similar or even larger size were built in the United States.

The second Brabazon Committee specification produced the Ambassador & the Viscount for B.E.A. & the third ~~specification~~ the Comet ~~for~~ BOAC.

Two other aircraft had also been discussed but details were not immediately published. While still dormant their general descriptions were known to be 'Long Range

*British European Airways.*

**Future air liners**

*'After discussions in depth with individuals and institutions seeming to have relevant experience, five types of aircraft were defined by outline specifications. The first, and prime requirement, called for nonstop London to New York operation. This indeed was an ambitious target, for the then current American transport aircraft, when flying westwards across the Atlantic, required two, and sometimes three, intermediate stops. So, with the best efficiency possible with piston engines, it was quite apparent that a very large aircraft was inevitable. In response, the eight-engined Bristol Brabazon and the ten-engined Saro Princess flying boat were ordered. With hindsight, this policy might be explained as heady optimism, released by the prospect of peace ... but hindsight is an exact science! We were not alone. Four prototypes of similar or even larger size aircraft were built in the United States. The second Brabazon Committee specification produced the Ambassador and the Viscount for BEA and the third, the Comet for BOAC.*

*'Two other aircraft had also been discussed, but details were not immediately published. While still dormant, their general descriptions were known as Long Range Empire and Medium Range Empire. In a*

Dr. Russell at his desk in October 1965. (*British Aerospace*)

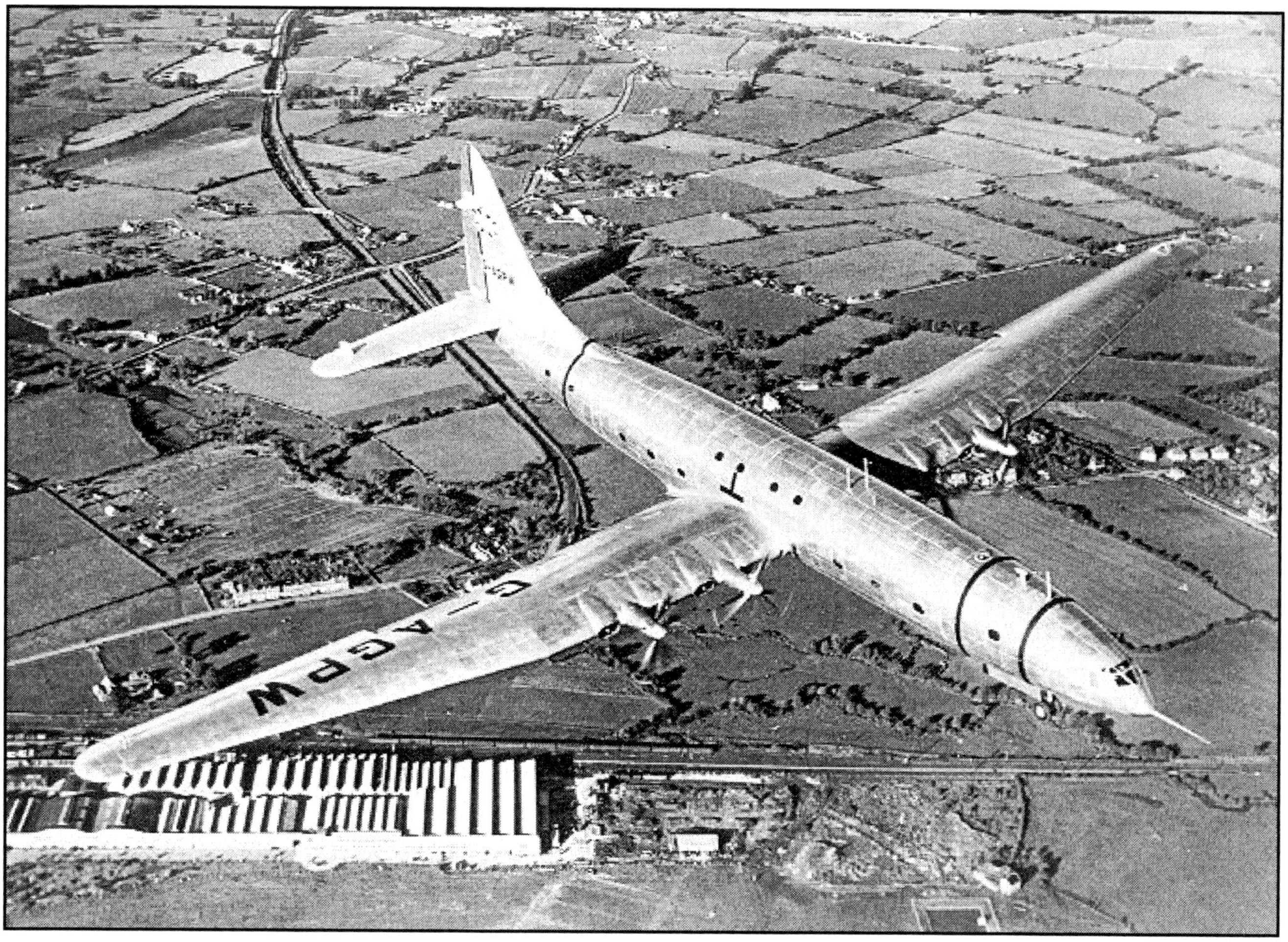


Sensational in its day - the Bristol Brabazon. (*British Aerospace*)

*tortuous way, and in regressive order, the fifth, fourth and first of the Brabazon recommendations can be seen, with reflected influence, in the development of the Britannia.'*

**The Medium Range Empire**

*'At first, and inevitably, British Overseas Airways were forced to purchase Lockheed Constellations and Boeing Stratocruisers. Financial considerations then dictated that these aircraft would have to remain in service until the mid 1950s. So the issue of the MRE specification was held back until 1947, at which time the Ministry of Supply invited tenders in a design competition open to any firm in the Society of British Aircraft Constructors. The prize was to be a Ministry contract for three prototypes of the design to be chosen by BOAC. The airline would then be committed to place a contract for production aircraft in time to allow entry into service by 1954. The main clauses of the specification were:*

*1. Maximum take-off weight not to exceed 100,000lbs.*
*2. Payload to be 36 first class passengers.*
*3. Four air-cooled engines.*
*4. Service intended on the main routes to the Far East, Australia, and South Africa.*
*5. Stage length, with full payload, 1200 miles.*

*'As a first impression, it might seem that the chief influence in fixing these conditions stemmed from nostalgic ex-crews of Imperial Airways, with fond memories of the romance in pre-war aviation, especially with the old Empire flying boats. The second impression could be that Specification 2/47 had, in fact, been lifted from Lord Brabazon's bottom drawer, without noting that postwar traffic was already different. The first false assumption was that civil airports and runways would place a limit on future airline potentials. Then again, the number of passengers, fixed at 36, had been determined by the seating capacity of a standard airport bus! Any greater number would require doubling the bus fleets throughout the network.'*

**Prototype contract**

*'After the Bristol Type 175 had been declared the winner of the Ministry of*

The Saro flying boat. (*British Aerospace*)

*Supply competition, it was considered safe to question the specification. There was no alternative choice to the 3000hp Centaurus, but with that power available and both airport limits and airworthiness requirements satisfied, there could be a modest increase in take-off weight. The 100,000lbs would be slightly exceeded, but the higher payload offered 48 instead of 36 passengers. The immediate response from the Ministry was that they could not place an order for prototypes with a specification so different from that which had been so recently the basis for an official competition.*

*'For a while it seemed that the rest of the industry would have to be offered a*

The first flight of the first prototype. There were a few initial anxious moments as the elevators proved over responsive. (*British Aerospace*)

The Argus maritime aircraft. (*British Aerospace*)

*second chance. But the point was successfully made, that the consequential delay would make the required operational date of 1954 very difficult to meet. So the prototype contract was placed in 1948, BOAC following in 1949 with a production order for 25 aircraft.'*

**The engine**

*'With design work and component manufacture under way, unquestioned confidence in the project was still lacking. One typical point was that BOAC had conceived a British version of the Lockheed Constellation with built in obsolescence. Another emphasised inconsistent policies regarding gas turbine engines. Thus the Comet and the Viscount were totally dependent on particular successful engine developments - and the Bristol cupboard was not bare. A turboprop power plant had recently begun bench development tests. That engine, the Proteus, started in 1944, was designed as a replacement for the Centaurus engines in the Brabazon 1 and Saro Princess flying boat. Its unusual dimensional feature of reduced length at the expense of an increased diameter, originally arranged to allow mechanically coupled pairs to be installed completely within the wing leading edges, had no obvious disadvantage when installed singly in a conventional wing nacelle. With a change near the top of BOAC management a reversal of policy was promoted. There was no problem making this official.'*

**The 100 Series is born**

*'So as to take proper advantage of the different turboprop power characteristics, and not forgetting that, with a new engine, more power was sure to come with time, a major redesign was necessary. The main alterations included an increase in wing span from 120 feet to 140 feet, with the all up weight raised to 140,000lbs. This*

A RCAF Argus Mark II photographed at RAF Lyneham in 1966. (*Ken Guest*)

*greater payload gave 74 seats, now six abreast, and fuel tanks sufficient for 2500 miles, with reserves. An obvious economy gain was achieved with stops now only necessary at major cities en route, and these were centres that generated the great bulk of the traffic.'*

This version became the Series 100 Britannia.

*'An unaccustomed calm settled for the next two years, unfortunately unbroken by serious enquiries from potential new customers. Quite vigorous sales tours had found keen interest if only the aircraft had more range. This was not the usual story of finding it easy to sell something you haven't got! Bristol was unable to finance what would have to be a major programme but at least the design work was prepared.'*

**The Series 200 evolves**

*'A sequence of events then came about that made the way. Firstly BOAC asked for an investigation to examine the possibility of producing a freighter version. The essential targets being a 40,000lbs payload with transatlantic capability. Two loading doors would be required, one forward of the cabin and one aft; to make this possible the length of the cabin had to be increased by 10 feet.*

*'At least a part of the answer had already been schemed. There was no serious problem in finding sufficient space for fuel; that part of the spar box, beyond existing*

The forlorn sight of the second prototype on the muddy banks of the River Severn. (*British Aerospace*)

G-ANCA, the aircraft which later crashed due to an autopilot fault, on the approach to Filton. It is carrying part of Capital Airlines livery.

*flexible bag tanks, could be converted to integral tanks. The weight of the additional fuel located outboard, along the span, gave a relieving bending moment so avoiding the need for extensive wing structure modifications. So it was shown that the defined requirement could be offered at an all-up weight of about 180,000lbs. The means would be extensive but not difficult.'*

This design was given the Series number 200.

**And then the Series 300**

*'Early in 1953 BOAC placed an order for three aircraft with an option for another five. The Ministry of Supply looked*

The Brabazon airborne in company with a Bristol Freighter. A scaled down version of the Britannia's dramatic tail was flight tested on a modified Freighter. (*British Aerospace*)

*after development costs. Obviously, parallel studies were made on a passenger version with the extra length of cabin accommodating up to 110 seats. The first sign that we now had something to see came with an order for six aircraft from Quantas.'*

The Series 300 was born

**Comets grounded**

*'But outside effects now took control. In 1954, after three disasters in flight, the Comet was grounded. The only way BOAC could see to get back into the airline business was to buy Douglas DC7s. These were fairly quickly available. HMG gave permission to order ten aircraft with a condition that the DC7s must be sold as soon as long range Britannias were available. Top priority had to be given to the 300s.'*

**Flight testing**

*'So much depended on a smooth flight test programme. First flight of the first prototype came in mid-1952 but the total value of that aircraft was limited to establish flight handling and general characteristics; too many detail features had been left some way behind in the modification scene.*

*'One major encouragement however did follow. Pilots from the Royal Canadian Air Force carried out their own flight handling tests with conclusions recommending that the aircraft was suitable for conversion to a maritime reconnaissance role. This conversion was engineered by Canadair in Montreal. The Argus, re-engined with American turbo-compound engines, served in a NATO function over the Western Atlantic. Later a freighter version was also produced with significant sales in the USA.'*

This was the CL44.

**Second prototype force lands**

*'Alas a real crisis was not far away. The second prototype, an up-to-date version of the Britannia 100, was lost after a short life of two months. This was when the Dutch airline KLM was showing signs of real interest and two of their directors were taken on a test flight. Cruising altitude had not been reached when the turbine in No.3 engine burst. Flames of the fire from the ruptured oil tank reached the tail plane. With a bright glow persisting in the nacelle, it seemed wisest to land in the soft mud of the banks of the River Severn, which, after some splendid cockpit work, duly happened some 22 minutes later. KLM was not the only airline left visibly daunted.'*

Sir Archibald omits to say that he too was on board the aircraft!

**Engine icing strikes**

*'Flight testing then suffered a double setback. The first production aircraft, planned to replace the lost aircraft, had to be diverted instead to a water tank fatigue test devised at Farnborough to establish the*

The tide inexorably advances on the stricken prototype.

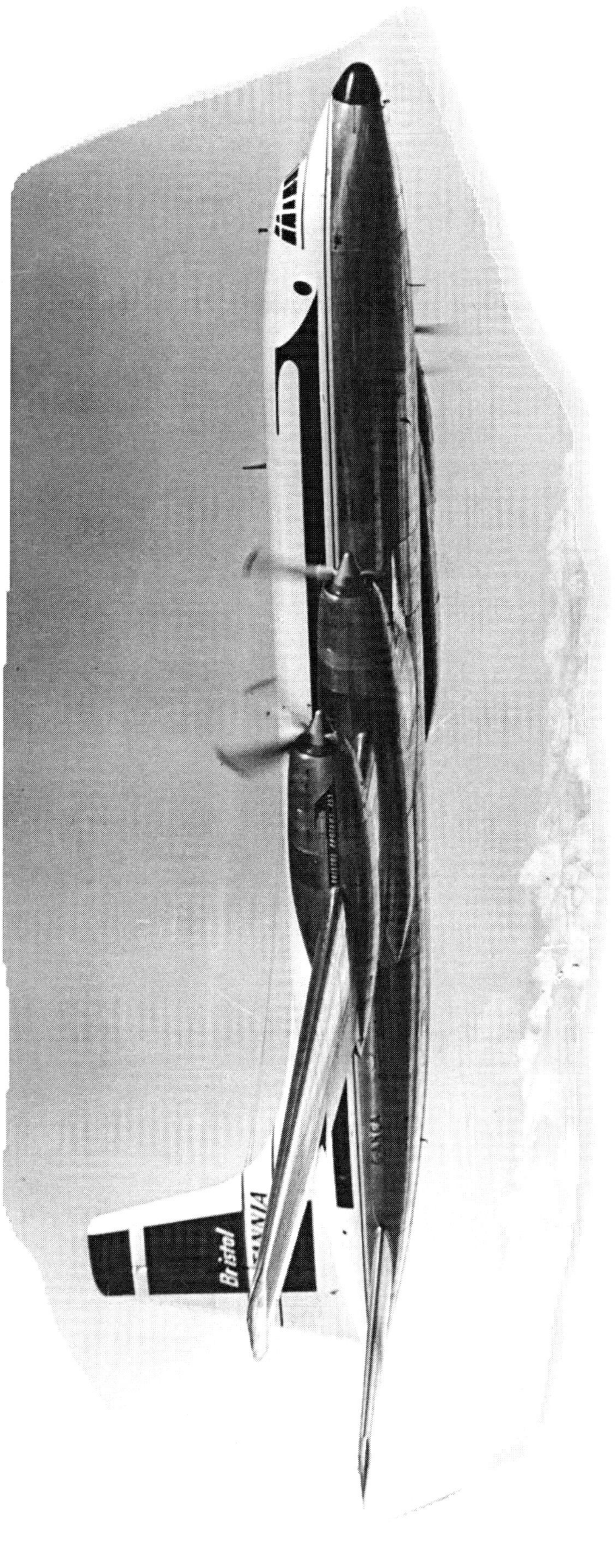
Bristol

*cause of the Comet disaster. After completion of the fatigue loading schedule, the Britannia was cleared for full airline life without any structural alteration.*

*'At last, in 1956, it seemed that clear weather had been reached, no obstacle was apparent that might prejudice an unrestricted Certificate of Airworthiness and aircraft had been delivered to BOAC for route proving. Very soon there was that second setback. When flying in monsoon conditions in Central Africa, engine flame-outs occurred, on one occasion to all four engines!*

*'The cause was found to be wet ice accumulating at the back of the reverse flow intake and then releasing in a quantity sufficient to extinguish the flame in the combustion chambers. Of course the Proteus had successfully passed the official de-icing tests as prescribed. Unfortunately it was shown that over a narrow temperature band around freezing, and in monsoon conditions at 20,000 feet, the measured water content was four times greater than that defined in those tests. At so late a stage this was indeed a difficult problem.'*

**Two more aircraft lost**

*'The whole spectrum of potential trouble during aircraft development was finally covered with the loss of two more aircraft. Firstly, a BOAC captain on a crew training flight, misread his altimeter (and this of a type and presentation chosen by the airline). His last contact with the air traffic control reported his altitude at 13,000 feet, continuing descent. He was in fact at 3,000 feet and in dense fog. About three minutes later a swathe was cut through a copse of semi-mature trees.*

*'Lastly, another aircraft was lost on an approach to land at Filton with a test pilot and flight crew aboard. An extremely sophisticated investigation by the Royal Aircraft Establishment, Farnborough established that an electrical failure in the autopilot had caused the controls to be locked in, with full aileron displacement.*

**The eclipse by the 707**

*'When seen alongside the Comet, the total picture of the British aircraft industry was not one to inspire confidence among the world's airlines. With the Britannia, the potential commercial appeal had been severely damped by a two-year delay in availability for service, bringing the Boeing 707 that much closer behind.*

*'For this last reason, and with the first deliveries of the 707 directed towards the major international airlines, opportunities for the Britannia in world markets were confined to the smaller operators. Customers included El Al Israel, Canadian Pacific, North East Airlines, Compania Cubana, Aironaves de Mexico and Hunting Clan Air Transport. But there was still to be a near miss with Capital Airlines of America. During a visit by their president to England a demonstration flight to Copenhagen was arranged - but the Britannia had to turn back, en route, with engine trouble.'*

**Conclusion**

This ends Sir Archibald Russell's account, which gives such an honest insight into the birth of the Britannia. It has been seen that it was a project plagued with the vagaries of aeronautics and business.

We, resting back in our '*armchair of hindsight*', might see a better way. But what concerns us here is that the efforts of Sir Archibald, and the Bristol Aeroplane Company, produced the Royal Air Force Britannia.

CHAPTER TWO

# Buy Britannias!

To put a precise date on the beginning of the Royal Air Force Britannia is difficult. Partly to support production development, the Ministry of Supply took an early interest in the aircraft, and to justify this, anticipated that eventually these aircraft would be leased to civil operators for air trooping. Thus we see, from June 1955, Development Progress Reports on Civil Aircraft, issued by the Directorate of Civil Aircraft Research and Development, Ministry of Supply, featuring the Britannia. It can be appreciated from samples of these reports, the agonising struggle to produce the aircraft on time, up to specification and last, but by no means least in the case of the Britannia, with a full Certificate of Airworthiness.

**The Bingley Committee**

If a conception date has to be determined for the totally military Britannia then it might be seen as July 1956 when the Chiefs of Staff set up the Bingley Committee (chaired by Rear Admiral A N C Bingley, the then Fifth Sea Lord and Deputy Chief of Naval Staff (Air)), to make recommendations on the inter-service requirements of the future air transport force.

In a MOD narrative published by The Stationery Office (©Crown Copyright MOD), T C G James has written on the subject of '*Defence Policy and the Royal Air Force, 1956-1963*'. This clearly sets out the climate which existed to prompt the Chiefs of Staff to consider the future composition and facility of Transport Command:

'*Total resources available in mid-1957 for a major peacetime emergency comprised 20 Hastings, 10 Beverleys, 5 Comet 2s, 11 Valettas, 30 Shackletons and 29 civil aircraft diverted from routine trooping. Such a force had some obvious inadequacies. Its variety of types was inherently inefficient; it was, in general, technically inadequate; the Beverley was proving a disappointing heavy lift aircraft over long distances; and its medium range component of Valettas and civil Vikings could make little or no contribution to some of the more taxing contingency tasks. Overall, however, it had a substantial and reasonably flexible capability and provided a solid base of experience and organisation for future improvements in air mobility which were*

The expansion of the Transport Command fleet would see the demise of the troopship. (*Jim Aitken*)

*regarded as crucial to the success of the White Paper policies.*

*'The report of the Bingley Committee, coming as it did at the end of 1956, was a timely focus for the extent and character of these improvements. The report is notable, not only for its substance, but as one of the few attempts by the Chiefs of Staff at this time to produce an inter-service answer to a question of future force structure and capability.'*

**The 1950s World**

It is worth considering the backdrop to these deliberations. The Royal Air Force was concerned with the emergence of the thermo-nuclear bomb and acquiring its delivery system, the V-Force. Military emphasis had changed from the post-Korea threat of major war to the prospect of a prolonged period of maintaining delicately balanced forces to secure peace. There were clear signs that, with a continuing commitment to global affairs, conflicts of a lesser nature were to be our concern. Mau Mau in Kenya and terrorism in Malaya and Cyprus were but precursors of problems to come. Suez had demonstrated the sensitivity of world affairs and the Hungary uprising clearly showed the substance of the Iron Curtain. It was in this atmosphere that the Bingley Committee was making its recommendations on an air transport force that would allow us to meet our possible commitments far and wide, and that with an intended smaller, but more mobile Army. They completed their task in January 1957. Mr James continues his account:

*'The Committee's analysis of the air transport task and its recommendations for the future size of the air transport force showed an appropriate realism about the resources that were likely to be available. The report set out the ideal air transport requirements, though these were based on a sober view of likely, as distinct from theoretical, tasks and then proceeded to recommend what it considered could be afforded and at what risk. It was assumed that the country would not become involved in limited war in*

A publicity shot of 519 over Mount Kilimanjaro. (*Rolls Royce*)

All engines running at The Aeroplane and Armament Experimental Establishment, Boscombe Down. It was normal for all aircraft entering the Royal Air Force to be fully flight tested at Boscombe Down. This was almost entirely eliminated in the case of the Britannia where the civilian test results were 'read across'. (*J Howell*)

*more than one area at one time and accordingly defined the determining requirement as the ability to move specified forces from all three Services to the Far East within seven days.*

*'These were, for the Army, a Spearhead Brigade with its light equipment and a number of specialist reinforcements, which would require 54 Britannia sorties for the move to Singapore; for the Navy, a modest reinforcement of officers and ratings for the Far East, requiring 12 Britannia sorties; for the RAF, equipment and accompanying technical personnel to support the move of four V-Bomber squadrons (or a force of similar size), requiring 34 Britannia sorties. Calculated on this 'idea' basis, a force of 64 Britannias would be needed to complete the task within a week.*

*'The committee's view was that so large a force could not be afforded and proposed one of half that size. This would be able to move about half the reinforcing elements of each Service within a week but would take up to a month to complete the task. The assumption that heavy equipment for Army reinforcements would be prestocked was important because this involved a change in current Army policy. The choice was made clear: pre-stocking would be expensive but much less than the aircraft that would be needed if smaller overseas garrisons were to be effectively reinforced.*

*'A similar analysis was made of the air transport required to move reinforcements to deal with a serious internal security problem in the Far East, as distinct from a limited war. If the latter contingency was ignored, the Committee estimated the required force as 26 Britannias. This allowed for part of the force to be retained for some of the normal transport tasks which it would be sensible not to abandon in an internal security emergency: air trooping, medical evacuation, operational exercises, support of GW and nuclear tests, VIP flights and numerous other occasional commitments. The Committee stressed the need for the earliest possible introduction of the Britannia as the only aircraft in prospect with the necessary range for strategic movement; otherwise it accepted the need to make do with aircraft already in service or about to come into service.'*

**A civil consortium?**

At this time civil aviation was on the threshold of an expansion which has resulted in the market that we know today. The dawn of a new age was about to break with the development of pure jet airliners, a factor that was to contribute to the demise of the Britannia as a commercial success. The importance and usefulness of a flourishing 'home grown' airline business was being recognised. This, possibly combined with expediency, led to the rather dramatic further recommendation of the Bingley Committee as related in the commentary on RAF Policy of those years.

*'... a novel feature of the Bingley Committee's recommendations ... (was that)*

Some of the agony of the those early days can be sensed from these '*Development Progress Reports on Civil Aircraft*' prepared for the potential Service purchasers of the RAF Britannias.

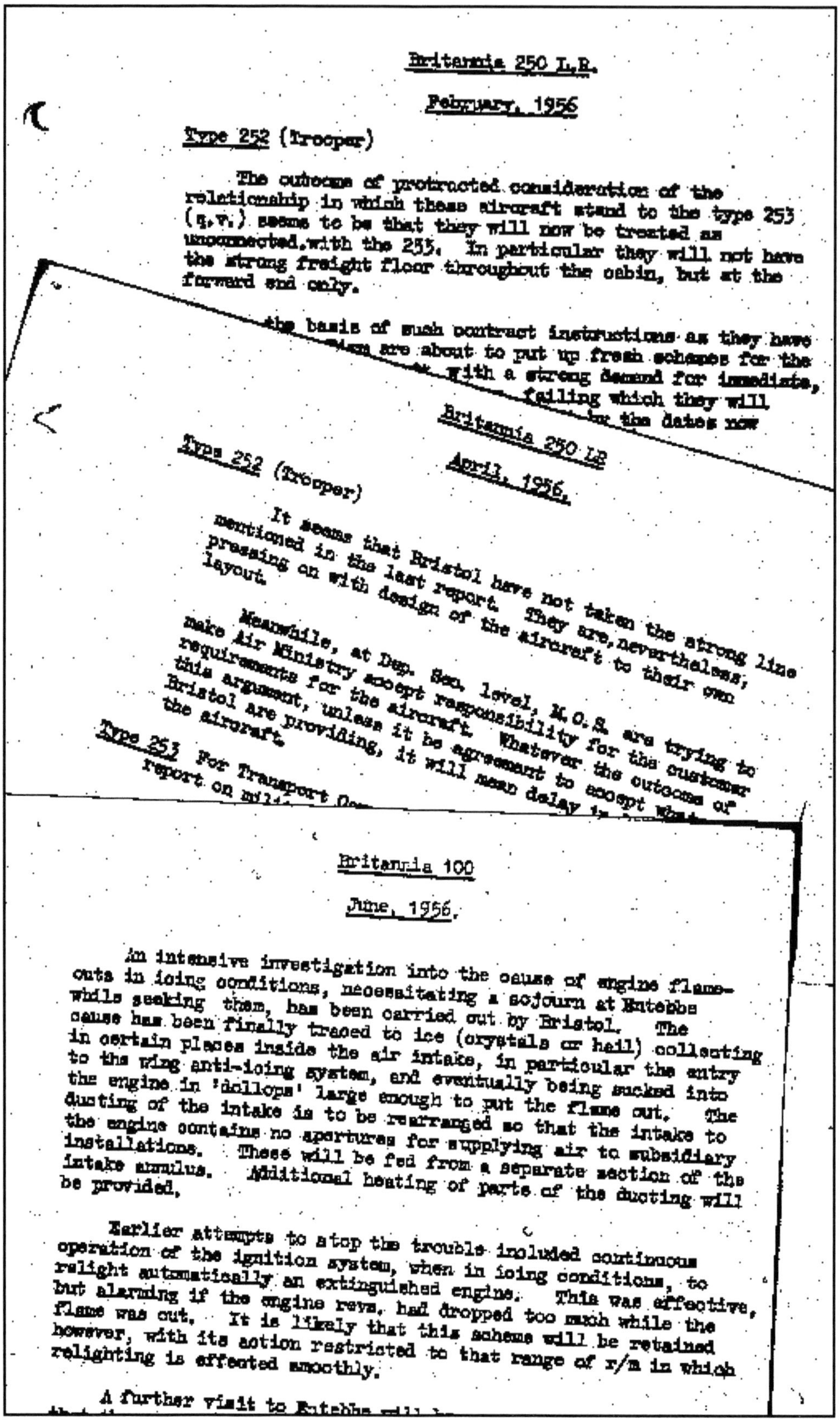

Britannia 250 L.R.

February, 1956

Type 252 (Trooper)

The outcome of protracted consideration of the relationship in which these aircraft stand to the type 253 (q.v.) seems to be that they will now be treated as unconnected with the 253. In particular they will not have the strong freight floor throughout the cabin, but at the forward end only.

… the basis of such contract instructions as they have … are about to put up fresh schemes for the … with a strong demand for immediate, … failing which they will … for the dates now

Britannia 250 LR

April, 1956.

Type 252 (Trooper)

It seems that Bristol have not taken the strong line mentioned in the last report. They are, nevertheless, pressing on with design of the aircraft to their own layout.

Meanwhile, at Dep. Sec. level, M.O.S. are trying to make Air Ministry accept responsibility for the customer requirements for the aircraft. Whatever the outcome of this argument, unless it be agreement to accept what Bristol are providing, it will mean delay in … the aircraft.

Type 253 For Transport Com… report on mil…

Britannia 100

June, 1956.

An intensive investigation into the cause of engine flame-outs in icing conditions, necessitating a sojourn at Entebbe while seeking them, has been carried out by Bristol. The cause has been finally traced to ice (crystals or hail) collecting in certain places inside the air intake, in particular the entry to the wing anti-icing system, and eventually being sucked into the engine in 'dollops' large enough to put the flame out. The ducting of the intake is to be rearranged so that the intake to the engine contains no apertures for supplying air to subsidiary installations. These will be fed from a separate section of the intake annulus. Additional heating of parts of the ducting will be provided.

Earlier attempts to stop the trouble included continuous operation of the ignition system, when in icing conditions, to relight automatically an extinguished engine. This was effective, but alarming if the engine revs. had dropped too much while the flame was out. It is likely that this scheme will be retained however, with its action restricted to that range of r/m in which relighting is effected smoothly.

A further visit to Entebbe will b…

On a damp day, 'Roll Out' of one the Mk 1s. Note how black propeller blades are a feature of these early models. (*Arthur Mitchell*)

*... only part of the total force should be within the RAF, the rest should be operated by a civil consortium. The Air Staff favoured a concept of military air transport designed to achieve a rapid response from a force of given size to any emergency demand that may be placed upon it. This postulated a mode of peacetime activity which continuously left something to spare for continuous operations with crews trained to operate at the extremes of airmanship and thus needing an allocation of aircraft time and resources for this purpose. Such a concept was difficult to reconcile with the optimum achievement of routine air transport tasks, air trooping in particular where the test of efficiency is maximum use of the minimum number of aircraft. It was the difference which had led increasingly in the 1950s to the use of civil aircraft for most of the air trooping task; yet such aircraft could, in an emergency, be used to assist in the movement of reinforcements. The Bingley Committee had, therefore, to consider the extent to which the air transport force might in future be provided respectively by the Royal Air Force and civil agencies. Clearly, theatre operations had to be wholly military. The question of how long range, inter-theatre transport might best be organised turned on the Air Ministry's assessment of the size of Transport Command, on the assumption that it was not used for regular trooping or any other routine tasks that would provide suitable work for civil companies. The Air Ministry's answer was two squadrons of Britannias, each with 16 aircraft. This, in fact, was the long range component of Transport Command that had been in mind for some time. It was related more closely to the re-equipment needs of Transport Command than to a precise assessment of the tasks which could only be undertaken by a military air transport force. It was, however, acceptable to the Bingley Committee*

The demise of the troopships would see the disappearance of the passenger's duty postcard!
(*Jim Aitken*)

*as a force of substantially improved capability which could fulfil all normal tasks demanding military as distinct from civil aircraft and many contingency requirements as well. Moreover it took into account the objections to the use of civil aircraft and crews in the sensitive nuclear and GW areas, including the transport of the V-Force and other front-line squadrons, and the difficulties that could be encountered in flying civil aircraft into airfields that might come under attack.*

*'Otherwise there was much to be said for continuing to use civil aircraft for the bulk of the routine air trooping, and it was on this basis that the Committee recommended that a civil consortium should be formed to operate up to 16 Britannias, making up the total of 32 aircraft which would meet the determining limited war contingency ...*

**Ministry of Supply aircraft**

*'Three Britannias built to civil, not RAF, standards and already on order for use by the Ministry of Supply ...'*

... these aircraft were destined to eventually become fully RAF aircraft, XN392, XN398, XN404 ...

*'... were seen as the first element of the consortium fleet. The formation of the consortium and the proposal to divert the three Ministry of Supply Britannias were to run into difficulties. Nevertheless the Bingley Committee's report, which the Chiefs of Staff Committee endorsed in February 1957, registered some important and enduring necessities of air transport policy.*

*'One was the importance of a long range component of high quality aircraft for strategic movement, complemented by civil aircraft for much of the routine air trooping task, and another was integrity of control of the strategic air transport force and the air transport force within overseas theatres.'*

**Britannia the RAF winner!**

In fact, sufficient aircraft for one Royal Air

XN404, one of the three 'Mark 2' aircraft.
(*Geoff Chandler*)

Force squadron had been ordered in January 1956 after the abandonment of the purpose-built strategic air transport project, the Vickers 1000. Nevertheless, the choice of the Britannia was debated again by the Air Council when it considered the Bingley findings and set them alongside the alternatives of Comet 4s and Vanguards. The Britannia came out a clear winner with its ability, in the military version, to carry freight or passengers (or a combination of both). What may come as some surprise is that the RAF came close to having Orion-engined aircraft as opposed to the Proteus. An extra £9m cost was involved which bought an additional range of 500 to 800 miles and an increase in cruising speed of 50 knots. It was decided, however, that the extra cost could not be justified. So, the difference that the Orion would have made remains a matter of conjecture. The reason for such comment will be lost on readers not familiar with the problems of the Proteus engine. These difficulties will be revealed as the story of the RAF Britannias is told.

After the collapse of the consortium idea, it was clear that, whilst civil air trooping would certainly be used and the facility to call upon civil aircraft in the event of an emergency kept in reserve, some potential for response to a situation had been lost. It was out of this that the final decision emerged early in 1958 that a plan to keep some of the ordered aircraft in store was scrapped and the two squadrons would be equipped with ten aircraft apiece. It was the intention that the first squadron should be formed by April 1960 and both be operational by the end of the year. The final fleet total of 23 aircraft evolved as the result of the decision to add the three Ministry of Supply aircraft, ostensibly just for crew training. In fact, even though the recorded number of landings for these aircraft always exceeded the number of flying hours, a measure of much training use and an exhausting airframe life, they were eventually to take a real place in the fleet and were used fully, in spite of their limited role flexibility. These three aircraft, originally sponsored by the Ministry of Supply, were designated the 252 Series and served in the Royal Air Force as C Mk2s. The C Mk1s were the 20 specifically ordered for military service and carried the tag of the 253 Series. The essential difference between them was the freight carrying capability. The former were only intended essentially as passenger aircraft although they were fitted with a freight door and the first 12 feet of the floor was stressed to take high density cargo. The rest of the flooring was high impact balsa with a coating of phenolic resin. The 253s had a fully strengthened metal 'floating' floor capable of supporting cargo loads over its entire length. Seat rails were integral; it too had a freight door.

**The long range transport force**

By way of ***conclusion*** it is apt, if a little odd, to quote the ***introduction*** to *'Defence Policy and the RAF, 1956-1963'*:

*'The force as a whole has to be seen as the Air Council's response, and a very adequate response as the later achievements of the Britannia Squadrons were to show, to the Bingley Committee's recommendations for the long range movement of personnel and freight. With support from the Comet 2s of 216 Squadron, it was capable, without reinforcement, of meeting the contingency that was the agreed determinant of the long range transport force i.e. the movement of a brigade group at light scales from Britain to Singapore in seven days. If the associated Naval and RAF forces had to be moved as well, the task could be completed in about 15 days. ... For what was at least as likely a contingency - the protection of Kuwait - the introduction of the Britannia greatly eased the problems of the planning staffs. As events turned out, the force was required for this operation less than a year after its build up had been completed.'*

And a final extract gives a measure of what had been acquired:

*'At the time of Suez, RAF transport aircraft, assuming 75% serviceability, were capable of moving 2,400 passengers or 375 tons of freight in a single lift. By 1962, on the same basis of calculation, the corresponding figures were 5,600 passengers and 1,000 tons of freight. Set against what was involved in the air movement of a brigade group (2,600 men, 100 trucks and trailers and 70 tons of freight) the general improvement in air lift capability speaks for itself.'*

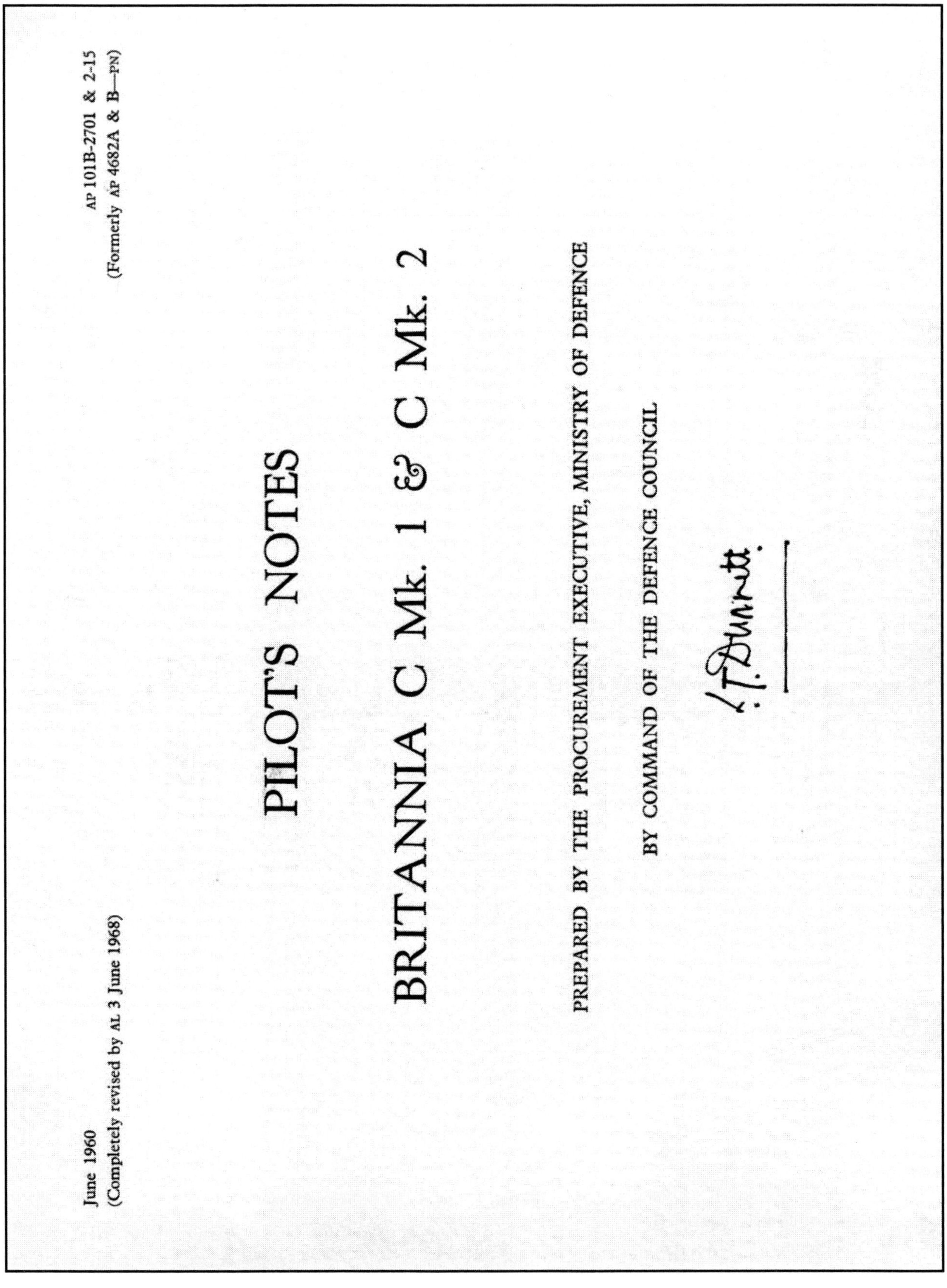

June 1960
(Completely revised by AL 3 June 1968)

AP 101B-2701 & 2-15
(Formerly AP 4682A & B—PN)

PILOT'S NOTES

BRITANNIA C Mk. 1 & C Mk. 2

PREPARED BY THE PROCUREMENT EXECUTIVE, MINISTRY OF DEFENCE

BY COMMAND OF THE DEFENCE COUNCIL

CHAPTER THREE

# The RAF Makes Its Start

Sir Archibald Russell has referred to the crash of the Type 301, G-ANCA, at Downend, Bristol. The fatal accident occurred on 6th November 1957 as the aircraft was returning to Filton after a test flight. It was making a left turn on to the final approach at about 1500 feet, when it suddenly banked steeply to the right and turned through some 270°, losing height in the turn until it struck the ground. All the occupants of the aircraft were killed.

**RAF copilot**

The copilot was Squadron Leader D M Hunter, who had been at Filton only a few months, undergoing ground training on the airframe and engines and had flown some 16 hours as copilot, all this to prepare him for his role as the Royal Air Force representative during the building of the RAF Britannias.

An aside to this sad accident is the fact that a master switch was later fitted to the Britannia auto-pilot to enable all power supplies to it to be totally isolated, if necessary, for it was concluded that:

'*Whilst the reason for the pilot not being able to control* (Continued page 30)

A newspaper photo of some of the devastation at the scene of the crash. (*Richard Randall*)

# BRITANNIA CRASH: DISASTER 'A TERRIBLE BLOW TO BAC' SAYS CORONER AT INQUEST

ARRIVING at Filton House for the opening of inquest on the Britannia crash victims today are: Left, the Coroner, Mr Seymour Williams; (centre) Ft.-Lt. Harris of the RAF; (right) Supt. F. A. Statham and PC John Hammond carrying official documents.

**All 15 victims of the Britannia crash disaster at Downend died "simultaneously and instantaneously," a doctor told the South Glo'shire Coroner, Mr. J. A. Seymour Williams, today.**

The inquest on the men was adjourned provisionally until January 10 after the Coroner had heard evidence of identification and the cause of death.

One man aboard the plane, Frederick Charles Walsh, of the Redifon Electronics company, could not be identified.

**Said Mr. Kenneth Benton, an electronics engineer for Redifon: "His injuries were too bad."**

More than 50 heads of departments at BAC and representatives of de Havilland Propellor Company and Redifon Ltd. crowded into the BAC conference hall at Filton.

In the front row was Mr. Peter Masefield, managing director of Bristol Aircraft Ltd.

## 'A Court of Grief'

They heard the Coroner say: "A coroner's court is always a court of grief. This tragedy has cast a cloud over the neighbourhood

"It is a terrible blow to the Bristol Aeroplane Company."

Mr. Michael Baker, representing BAC, added: "This has been a personal tragedy to the relatives of these men and also a personal loss to all the many who make up the vast organisation of the company."

Dr. Ronald Duncan Brown, of Frampton Cotterell, said he had examined the 15 bodies at Staple Hill mortuary.

"The cause of death in all cases was multiple injuries," he said.

The bodies of all 15 men were identified separately by Mr. Walter Gibb, chief test pilot of BAC; Mr. Keith Turner, the company's chief flight research engineer; Mr. Richard Ross-Hall, aircraft engineer of de Havillands; and Mr. Benton.

Seven of the men on board the plane were BAC employees. Three were from de Havillands, four from Redifon, and one from the RAF.

## The Crash Death Roll

The dead men were:

**Ernest Hugh Statham** (46), pilot, of Rivermead, Bitton-road, Keynsham;

**S/Ldr. Donald Matthew Hunter** (35), co-pilot, of Cogswell, Tytherton Lucas, Chippenham, Wilts (R.A.F. liaison officer on the Britannia project with the Air Ministry);

Radio Operator **William James Todd** (32), of 3, Gore-road, Ashton, Bristol;

Flight Engineer **Donald Charles Cameron** (28), of 70, Brentry-lane, Brentry, Glos., whose father lives at Southover, Bromley, Kent;

Systems Engineer **John Harold Parry Jones** (40), of 1, Upper Belgrave-road, Clifton;

Junior Technical Engineer **Frederick William Mycroft** (24), of 5, Lansdown-road, Clifton, whose father lives at Peterborough;

Photographer **Nigel Morris Thorn** (27), of 37, Richmond-road, Mangotsfield, Glos.;

Senior technical engineer **Philip Norman E. Hewitt** (27), of 3, Elton-road, Bishopston, Bristol, whose father lives at Rock-road, Trowbridge, Wilts.

The three de Havillands' employees killed were:

**John Edward Burton** (40), of 19, Manor Park-crescent, Edgware, N.W. London, a section leader in the strain gauge department;

**Albert Edward Ebling** (33), of 61, Wellcroft-rd., Welwyn City Herts., a tester in the same department; and

**Dudley Neville Stephen Moynihan** (37), of 18, Havenscroft-road, Patchway, near Bristol, a development engineer.

The Redifon employees killed were:

**John Kenneth Barker** (35), **Frederick Charles Walsh** (31), and **Kenneth Graham Lucas** (28), electronics engineers, and **Bernard Francis Waite** (39), photographer and writer. All lived at Crawley, Sussex.

## PROVING FLIGHT GOES ON

**A BRITANNIA 312 long-range airliner of BOAC took off from London Airport today for a non-stop proving flight to New York. The flight is expected to take about 11 hours.**

**It was postponed from Thursday because of the Britannia crash, but a BOAC spokesman said investigations into that accident had revealed no obvious reason why the Atlantic proving flights should not go on.**

BRISTOL EVENING WORLD, SATURDAY, NOVEMBER 9, 1957.

Flight Lieutenant Harry (Jock) Harris was an early member of the Britannia fleet - No.1 Britannia Course, in fact. Amongst his papers he found the newspaper cuttings opposite ... and with them goes his story:

*'Attached are cuttings from the Bristol Evening News of November 9th 1957. How did I come to be at the inquest of the Britannia crash? Well I really do not know for certain but here is my tale of how I became connected with the Britannia.*

*'I was posted a as a nav tutor to the RAF Flying College at Manby in 1954. There were five tutor navs and the boss man was Sqn Ldr Douglas Bower. Amongst other things we were doing long distance flights in Canberras, proving their capabilities as long range aircraft using cruise climb techniques. On 13th October 1954 Wg Cdr Humphrey, with Douggie Bower and another nav flew from Bardufoss in Norway to the North Pole and back to Bodo. I was nav of the accompanying Hastings. We continued with our long distance flights and I flew with the Commandant, Air Commodore Gus Walker, to the Pole on December 13th the following year, from Bodo.*

*'Meantime the College had visited the Bristols factory to see the Britannias being built and I got the expected performance data from one of the men. I realised that the data was similar to the Canberra performance. Later we visited Smith's Instruments and persuaded them to fit one of their gyro compasses into Canberra Aries V. It was a tremendous improvement and I found they were to be installed in the RAF Britannias. From then on I wanted to be on the Britannia. I had a choice of posting on leaving Manby and after a conversation with Gus I was posted to Hastings and on to 99 Squadron, where I became nav leader.*

*'Sqn Ldr Hunter visited Lyneham from time to time and he and I got on well, discussing the probable possibilities of the Britannia in Transport Command. When he was killed I was appointed to look after his affairs. I was at Bristol from time to time and took his car to his wife, accompanied the coffin to London, went to the memorial service in Bristol Cathedral and went through his papers he had at Bristol. It was when I went through his RAF history that I found out it was very similar to that of John Owen. I had known John when we were on 48 Squadron in Singapore from 1947-1950 and when he was on a jet conversion unit in 1953. John became Don's replacement.*

*'Then, as promised by Gus Walker, I was on the first Britannia Course ...'*

G-ALBO, the first Britannia to fly, would have still been gracing Filton skies during those early days. (*British Aerospace*)

*the very steep descending turn could not be determined, the possibility existed that it had occurred as a result of the auto-pilot malfunctioning.'*

**Squadron Leader John Owen**

Don Hunter had gone to Bristols from RAF Benson, where he had commanded the Ferry Training Squadron. On posting to Filton, he was replaced by Squadron Leader J S Owen. By a strange chance it transpired that John Owen was the most suitable officer to fill the gap at Bristols. Squadron Leader Owen recalls the sadness of this coincidence and how, having been summoned for an interview with the AOC-in-C Transport Command, Air Marshal A McKee CB CBE DSO DFC AFC, he was charged with the task of becoming the leader of the RAF liaison team. In his words:

*'My unwritten brief was to monitor the progress of the aircraft as a military transport, to keep the planning staffs informed, to formulate a syllabus of conversion training for HQ Transport Command and, eventually, to train two squadrons of aircrew at Lyneham to operate the Britannia in a global role. All this was a considerable challenge and, in retrospect, I consider it the biggest job I ever tackled and it made a most satisfying peak, as well as culmination, of my RAF career.'*

After his rather nervous interview with 'Square' McKee, he joined the Bristol Aircraft Company on 30th November 1957 and completed a course on the aircraft and its engines. Two months later he started flying and at that time was invited by test pilot Walter Gibb to join the party proceeding to Darwin for engine icing trials.

**That engine icing**

The potentially disastrous engine flame-outs that had occurred in tropical clouds in 1956, on BOAC route proving flights, have already been mentioned. This problem was to dog the Proteus engine for many years and resulted in delayed availability of the Britannia on the aviation market. Sir Stanley Hooker, the brilliant and dynamic Chief Engineer of the Bristol Engine Division relates, in his autobiography '*Not Much of an Engineer*':

*'It took us a little while to identify what the problem was. With the aid of TV cameras mounted inside the engine cowlings, we were able to see that ice could adhere to the inner walls. When it reached sufficient thickness, it would break away and enter the engine compressor. The quantities were so large as to produce a compressor stall, or extinguish the flame in the combustion chambers, or cause both these effects simultaneously.*

*'It proved difficult to locate the atmospheric conditions under which the ice could build up in this way. The conditions were not the same as those under which ice formed on the aircraft wings, so that the test aircraft was not always successful in locating an ice ladened atmosphere. In the tropics, where the sea level temperature is about 45°C, the ambient temperature reduces to zero at about 20,000 feet. At this altitude, the ice crystals can be found in the air because of the enormous amount of water evaporation at sea level. BOAC could easily have avoided these conditions by choosing to fly at a different altitude but we were unable to persuade them to do so.*

*'We quickly devised glow plugs which were fitted in a number of combustion chambers. These were heated by the burning gases and, when the flame was momentarily extinguished, the plugs continued to glow long enough to re-ignite the fuel/air mixture, thus the engine suffered only a momentary bump, and full cruising power was restored at once.*

*'These glow plugs were entirely effective and never failed to relight the engine. The aircraft was totally safe, and the only evidence of severe icing was a brief flicker of the cockpit instruments. However, we were unable to persuade BOAC to put the Britannias into service with this palliative. The major flight test programme thus continued for two years to find a means of preventing the build up of ice inside the cowlings. Eventually a series of modifications to the cowling ducts overcame the problem, and the aircraft had a long and profitable life.'*

**Bumps in the night**

Any passengers who have experienced these 'auto-relights', from that glow plug solution, might question their acceptability as they witnessed the flame that belched from the tailpipe or were wakened by the disquieting sound of the 'bumps', as they occurred. However, some sympathy has to be felt for the Bristol Engine Division and

Sir Stanley Hooker in particular.

With the operating altitudes and latitudes of the Britannia, they had run into conditions which no one, up to that time, had realised existed. Furthermore, these conditions would have been of no consequence if it had not been for the legacy of the reverse flow design of the Proteus from the Brabazon and Saunders-Roe Flying Boat plans - the ice accumulated on the 'bend' in the engine.

An appropriately sympathetic note was struck by Sir Stanley's son-in-law, Mr Stephen Greensted, a number of years later:

'*... SGH was never really happy with the engine, and counted it among one of the unhappiest periods in his otherwise distinguished life. It should be said, however, that he inherited the design when he joined Bristol, and that he found himself in a time-box owing to the need to supply engines to Saunders-Roe for the Princess Flying Boat, which meant that a major redesign was effectively ruled out.*'

**B-Skin Jets and Cowl Heat**

The modification referred to by Sir Stanley was the installation of hot air jets to prevent the ice accretion in the rogue areas. These went by the designation, of the abstruse style to be constantly found in aviation, of 'B-Skin Jets'. An alternative method was also devised which went by the less obscure appellation of 'Cowl Heat'. With this system, the areas were heated internally by a supply of hot gases bled from the turbine casing. The means of routing these gases was tortuous and led to the description of this method having the 'rabbit warren' intake. How all this affected the Britannias of the Royal Air Force will be discussed later; meanwhile, to return to John Owen's narrative, the team flew to Darwin to test and compare both these systems, the engines of G-AOVA representing each of them.

**Trial by tropics**

These trials proved a valuable experience for him, if only on how *not* to handle the Britannia in the tropics, as the flight test crew deliberately sought out adverse conditions to put the systems to the full test. In this they were aided by the

A very shiny XN404 is manoeuvred. In later years, during a fleet repaint programme, the reflective under surfaces were painted grey. (*Arthur Mitchell*)

A cartoon from an early edition of 'The Lyneham Globe' which gives a hint of the old attitude towards copilots!

*Off we go into the wild blue yonder ...' 'Which Command did he come from?'*

device intended to help the crew avoid such areas, the Cloud Collision Warning Radar (CCWR). This radar displayed clouds with high water content which the laws of physics dictates are extremely turbulent and should be avoided at all costs. These deliberate attempts to encounter such conditions proved useful in demonstrating to him, for later use, how to avoid them! The drama of the tests can be judged by his words:

*'I think we altered the propulsive capabilities of a couple of engines! The final trial flight culminated in a rather Wagnerian traverse of the Duty CuNim over Melville Island, north of Darwin. It was so big it filled the whole of the radar screen! We experienced seven lightning strikes and did £50,000 worth of damage to the cowlings - a considerable sum in those days. The hail modified the shape of the tailplane to the extent that the whole leading edge profile had to be restored with filler before we could depart for the UK. An interesting, but hairy, experience!'*

On return to Filton, he completed his captain's check out and attended an invaluable simulator course at BOAC. He comments that there he was taught to use the aircraft's instrument flight system and the pilot interpreted navigation aids in a more disciplined way than hitherto; a subject he is to return to later.

In May 1958, he moved from Filton and joined the development production team at Belfast at Short Brothers and Harland Ltd, where the three Series 252s and 15 of the 20 253s were to be built. With the part he was playing in the production test flying, Squadron Leader Owen was becoming a very experienced Britannia operator and was able to start formulating ideas for operating procedures, training requirements and check lists, in preparation for his training commitment at RAF Lyneham.

**A training philosophy**

John's story, which can be seen as a pathfinder for training considerations and methods which are now, perhaps, taken for granted, continues:

*'It didn't take any gift of clairvoyance to appreciate some of the difficulties that might arise during the Britannia's introduction and the training programme at Lyneham. One of the problems already identified was that, with the pilot and crew training, the flight simulator would play a major role in crew conversion, and both the flying and simulator programmes would*

*have to be well thought out and would, indeed, be complementary. Also that the aircraft was too costly to use 'ad lib' as a training vehicle and, moreover, training accidents would be most expensive and unthinkable. I was later informed by the Directorate of Flight Safety that they expected 2½ Britannias to be broken in the first two years. I am glad to say they were proven wrong.'*

We now know, with the benefit of hindsight, that the safety record of the RAF fleet was to be quite remarkable, a legacy, maybe, from this thorough groundwork done by Squadron Leader Owen and his team. I will allow his story, which so neatly covers those early days, to continue. An apology is due to non-fliers for some of the terminology used. A glossary of terms is provided as an appendix. Those who know him will recognise that this is a transcript of a verbal account, which he kindly provided on tape. I will not spoil the style with Sassenach editing!

*'I formed a very good liaison with the flight simulator team, Flight Lieutenants Vic Colwell and Jackie Whelan. They were totally dedicated and together we were able to try out a number of crew drills long before the aircraft entered service. It was evident to everybody that this was the biggest, most complex and expensive aeroplane ever to enter the Service, with the possible exception of the Vulcan or, in terms of sheer electronics, maybe the Lockheed Neptune. I did have some experience of the Neptune and it did stand me in good stead. The Neptune had to be operated by a completely proficient and trained crew and the copilot was no longer the 'hewer of wood and drawer of water'.*

*'The same thing was going to apply to the Britannia; the copilot's handling and airmanship had to be equal to that of his captain and he had to share in the management, handling and monitoring duties - share in a meaningful manner - that is to say.'*

It will be touched on later, but indeed the copilot did have his hands full. Apart from having a share of half the flying, he also handled the fuel panel, which required careful management and the pressurisation, which called for juggling!

The captain (left) is operating the engine starting controls whilst the engineer monitors the engine instruments (centre low). Here he is glancing at the electrical control panel behind the copilot's seat. Note the bulbous black headsets; they are a later topic. (*Bill Robinson*)

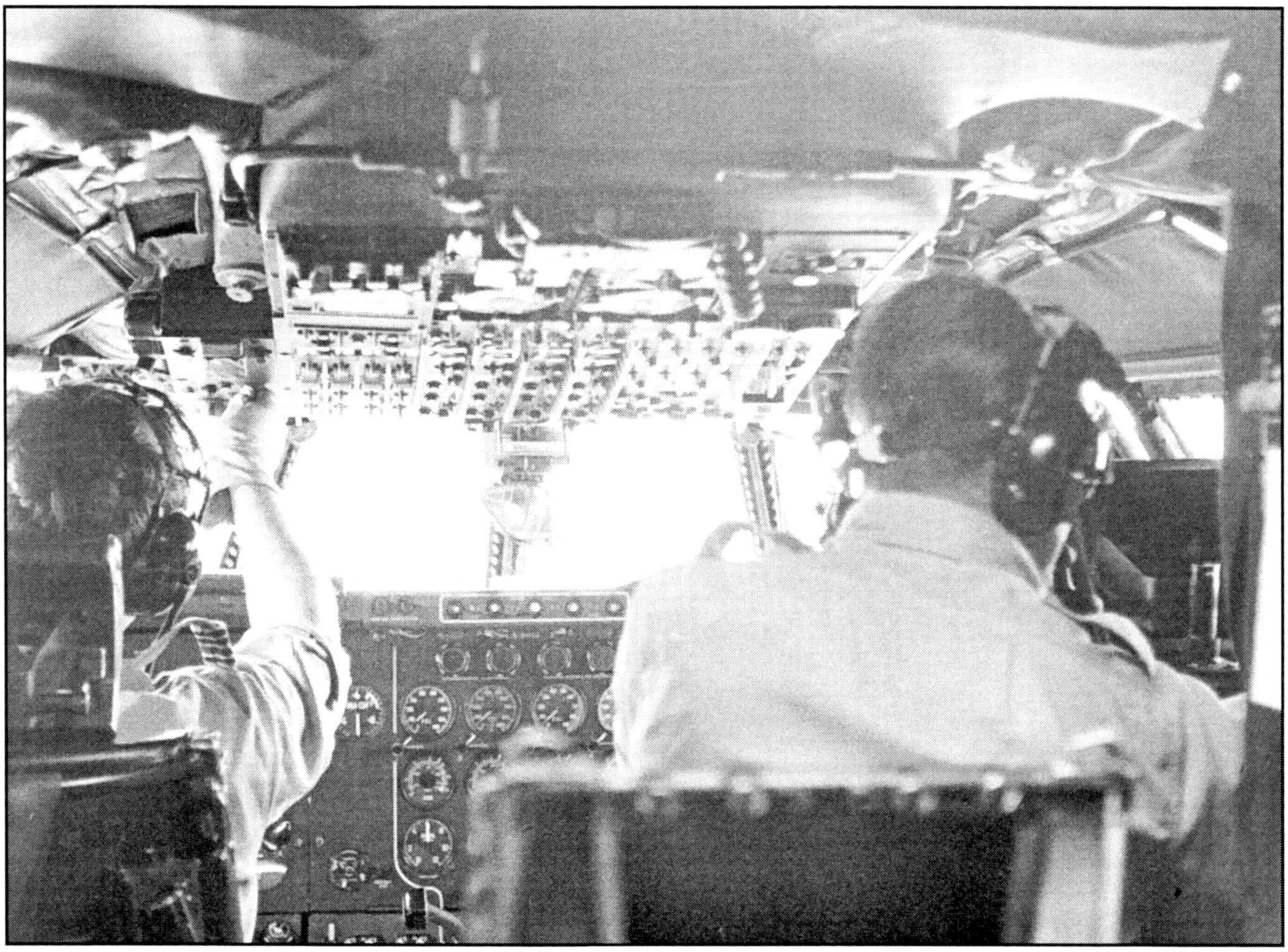

**The flight engineer's lot**

John Owen's account continues:

*'The flight engineer, of course, was no longer welded to his set of throttles and gauges and he had to know a hell of a lot more than was the case say on the Hastings or Beverley. The flight engineer, indeed, became an active partner on the operational scene as well as being a first class flying spanner during route troubleshooting.'*

To break from J.O.'s account, it perhaps should be explained that, with most contemporary multi-engined aircraft, and those that preceded, it was usual for the flight engineer to have his own instrument panel and separate set of engine controls including, obviously, throttles. Not so the Britannia - the original plan of the designers was to make the aircraft capable of two-pilot operation, a system that was to anticipate what was to become the norm many years later. This proved unacceptable to the potential Britannia customers and it perhaps has to be agreed that the plan was a little premature. Whilst all the controls and panels were so located that they could be reached or seen by one or other of the two pilots, one had to be something of a long armed contortionist with binocular vision! Furthermore, the systems, advanced as they were for their day, still did not possess the sophistication which was eventually achieved to make two-pilot operation satisfactory. So the idea was dropped, but too late for drastic redesign of the flight deck. Thus, it was something of a compromise between a two-pilot layout and a three-man operation. It can be said that the RAF version went the least way in this compromise. In other variants, at least the fuel and pressurisation panels and controls were moved so that they could be operated by the engineer. As already indicated, in the 252/253 the copilot controlled them.

**Old dogs - new tricks**

Squadron Leader Owen continues on the standing of copilots:

*'In those days, '57 to '59, the transport force was fortunate in being able to set a standard of experience and ability in the recruitment of copilots. This certainly paid off, as many of the original ones progressed, quite naturally, into the left-hand seat. A further training challenge was that existing long range captains would have to be indoctrinated into the concept of pilot interpreted navigational aids, airways, VOR, ILS, ADF etc. instead of just sitting back and flying the headings and heights provided by the navigator. In the new procedures the navigator would, of course, perform a vital monitoring role. It was anticipated that the idea of coupled auto-pilot approaches would also take a lot of selling to old hands, and it did indeed.*

*'In all training matters, I was fortunate in having the stalwart support in court, that is to say in HQTC, of Group Captain 'Black Jack' McKay, God Bless His Soul, and Wing Commander R C Scott, good old Scottie, ex-Queen's Flight. They were Group Captain and Wing Commander Training, respectively. Later Wing Commander Johnson took over from Scottie. He was equally staunch in his support.*

*'The next matter which made me sit up was that of Performance.'*

**Performance criteria**

Aircraft Performance covers the whole area of the calculated behaviour of a transport aircraft from take-off to landing. Civilian safety standards had reached the point that, providing the aircraft weight was correctly calculated and adjusted in relation to runway dimensions, meteorological conditions and terrain clearances, then an engine failure at any stage of the flight would not precipitate an accident. It had been decided that this criterion would be adopted by the new Royal Air Force transport force.

*'With the advent of the Britannia, gone were the days when the crew and the movements staff would not be over concerned with the effects of weight, altitude, temperature, take-off and landing distance etc. In the past it had been a question of just filling up to maximum take-off weight. Those days were gone. It was indeed a new concept, not easily accepted by quite a few in high places, that every take-off had to be made at a total weight which was scheduled on the supposition that an engine would be lost somewhere on the take-off run or whilst on route. Moreover, the normal handling procedures by the crew would be based on this assumption. I had a rough time trying to explain this to the C-in-C, who just wanted to fill her up to the gunwales, gross performance, you know, the lot. 'By the way, what can you drop from this airframe?'*

A Type 300 on the approach into Filton. This was to become a familiar sight to RAF Britannia crew's over the years. Ahead was the runway specially built for the Brabazon. It was one with an extremely uneven surface. The road lights by the garage are significant - a Vulcan took some of them out on a misjudged approach! (*British Aerospace*)

*Thank heavens I had a staunch partner in Squadron Leader Pat Burgess who was my navigator and thinking counterpart during this preparatory phase and was responsible for route planning and performance analysis.'*

**Squadron Leader Burgess**

Pat Burgess has written too on those early days. He was very much amongst the founders of the transport force of the late 50s through to the 70s. He spent 1954 to 1956 at Transport Command, acting mainly as liaison officer with de Havillands introducing the Comet 2s into the RAF. Through this, he was the original advocate of Transport Command operating its aircraft to the standards of the British Civil Airworthiness Requirements (BCARs). As if to test him out, he was asked to look at how the Beverley would fare if these BCARs were applied. He found that, according to those standards, it would descend in the event of an engine failure after take-off. The exercise was abandoned! This aside, it is a fact that from the Comet 2 onwards, all RAF transport aircraft were capable of conforming to the performance safety rules applicable to civil ones.

After this spell, Squadron Leader Burgess completed the Bracknell Staff College course which usually leads to a promotion worthy staff appointment. It was not to be. In his words, '... I was disappointed to find that I was destined to go directly to Filton, in January 1958, to be the start of the Britannia Force. In the event, it was the best thing that happened to me!' That sentiment was to be echoed so often by so many others down the years.

He and John Owen were joined by navigator Bill Hickox and Pat and Bill prepared the cruise control and performance manuals, '*... which Bristols later published, unaltered!*'

Pat, in his recollections, comments on the previously mentioned idea of

498 on the move on a grey day. The black propeller blades are in evidence. (*Arthur Mitchell*)

powering the military Britannias with Orions:

*'Whilst it seemed an attractive idea, it was expensive and generated the need for an 'auto-feather' system for the outboard engines. It was one of the attractions of the Proteus that, with the propeller and its turbine being entirely independent of the engine, windmilling drag was greatly reduced.'*

**A new era**

We return to John Owen's account:

*'The whole concept of hitherto accepted patterns of long range operations would indeed change dramatically. Instead of, say, Lyneham to Malta or El Adem, North Africa on the first day then on to Aden on Day Two and perhaps Karachi on Day Three, the aircraft could do Aden or Nairobi nonstop, and the following day go on to Singapore via Gan. Also, for such operations and navigational accuracy the auto-pilot was no longer a luxury but a necessity. A new era had indeed dawned. Notwithstanding the experience gained on the Comet operation, I think it can well be said that 'Boffins' had removed the guess work and sporting instinct out of flying. Another circumstance arose during the final approach to the aircraft's entry into service, and this concerned the Service Trials and the CA release.'*

The subsequent silver anodised propeller blades. (*Bill Robinson*)

**CA Release**

It should be explained - a country that is going to license a new civil aircraft to fly, requires a 'Certificate' that the aircraft is airworthy and technically satisfactory. The UK licensing organisation these days is the Civil Aviation Authority and the licence to fly is the 'Certificate of Airworthiness', (C of A). Service aircraft have a parallel system. They are tested by an agency that stands between the customer, the RAF, and the manufacturer. This organisation was the Ministry of Supply at the time of the Britannia, to become the Ministry of Aviation. The present equivalent is the Ministry of Defence (Procurement Executive). The equivalent military certificate to the C of A being the Controller of Aircraft (CA) Release to Service.

*'When the Britannia was selected for military service it was understood it would already be a going concern. It already had a civil C of A by the time the*

*military version was built. Little difficulty was thus anticipated with its acceptance into the Service, the major differences being the beefed up floor, the cargo door, different engine intakes, slightly different electrics and, perish the thought, the radio navigation aids were somewhat below its civil counterparts. One difficulty did arise, particularly at Belfast, where it became obvious that, although the civil ARB personnel and inspecting team were well acquainted with the civil aircraft and its systems, the same could not be said of their military equivalent, the Aeronautical Inspection Directorate (AID). By the way, AID has been well and truly described as 'the contraceptive on the prick of progress'! There were some embarrassing delays at Shorts resulting from AID's lack of technical knowledge of the aircraft, during the period following the 'roll-out' of the prototype at Belfast. This was quite astonishing, and it tended to reflect the view that this was just another aircraft. How wrong they were.*

*'After the initial flight trials on the 252 and 253 variants, the CA Release conference was rather a tense occasion. At the last moment, for instance, civil servants from the Ministry of Supply emerged with odd sorts of objections. For example, they were unhappy about the interior trim and its flame resistant qualities. My question was, what had they been doing for the last two years? Another bone of contention was the VOR equipment. 'Oh it can be jammed, you know.' So, for that matter could MF beacons and in this respect the Air Ministry Operational Requirements (OR) Branch put their faith in Tacan, which was a military point source aid of which, at that time, there were precious few. It was difficult to convince a number of people in policy making positions that this aircraft would be used mainly on civil air routes, along airways and advisory routes, and in controlled air space, as well as being able to operate in transoceanic 'long grass' navigational mode. The 'powers-that-be' also wanted to remove the existing VOR equipment in the 252s. These were equipped to Civil Air Navigation Order standards as they were originally intended for civil charter from the Ministry of Supply.*

*'I also found it difficult to convince OR that the military Britannia would not conform to the minimum regulation navigation aid equipment scale for flight in controlled air space in the UK, with all due respect to Green Satin etc., to say nothing of navigating along US air space with its Victor Airways network, which required basically VOR/DME. As you might guess, after about 12 months in squadron operations the message sank in, but it was a hard slog trying to convince them.'*

**Black props**

*'The next saga was the black propeller story. The civil Britannias were equipped with propellers with a hard clear anodised finish which was remarkably resistant to the shot blasting from dirty, gritty runways, especially when you were in reverse pitch. The Service variants, however, were to be fitted with a matt black finished propeller and the first time they were used was early in the New Year of 1959 at Belfast on an icy runway. You can imagine the effect of landing on the sanded surface. The propellers were noticeably pitted through the black surface and this was going to create a corrosion problem. It would prove even worse at sand strewn locations such as El Adem. Now, the M of S was advised of this potential problem but they were adamant that the specification of a matt black finish should be adhered to. I then asked them why such a 'spec' was insisted upon, and eventually I was told by someone in St. Giles' Court, following much research, of course, that the requirement that all military aircraft were to have black propellers, originated from about 1940. This was to minimise the reflection from the engine exhausts! I do believe this was eventually changed a few years later.*

*'A new idea was introduced during this programme - I hasten to say that it was stolen from BOAC - the role of the supervisory copilot. The first of this new breed was Flight Lieutenant Tony Davies who was my copilot, and also being a QFI shared the brunt of copilot training in the simulator as well as the aircraft. His main role being to supervise pre-flight checks, in-flight monitoring procedures, in conjunction with the flight engineer, whilst the training captain and his navigator were otherwise engaged with the trainee crew. This idea proved highly successful and it was a fertile training ground for future captains. Tony Davies was joined later by Peter Hill, Peter Gray, Geoff Shipway and John Brown.*

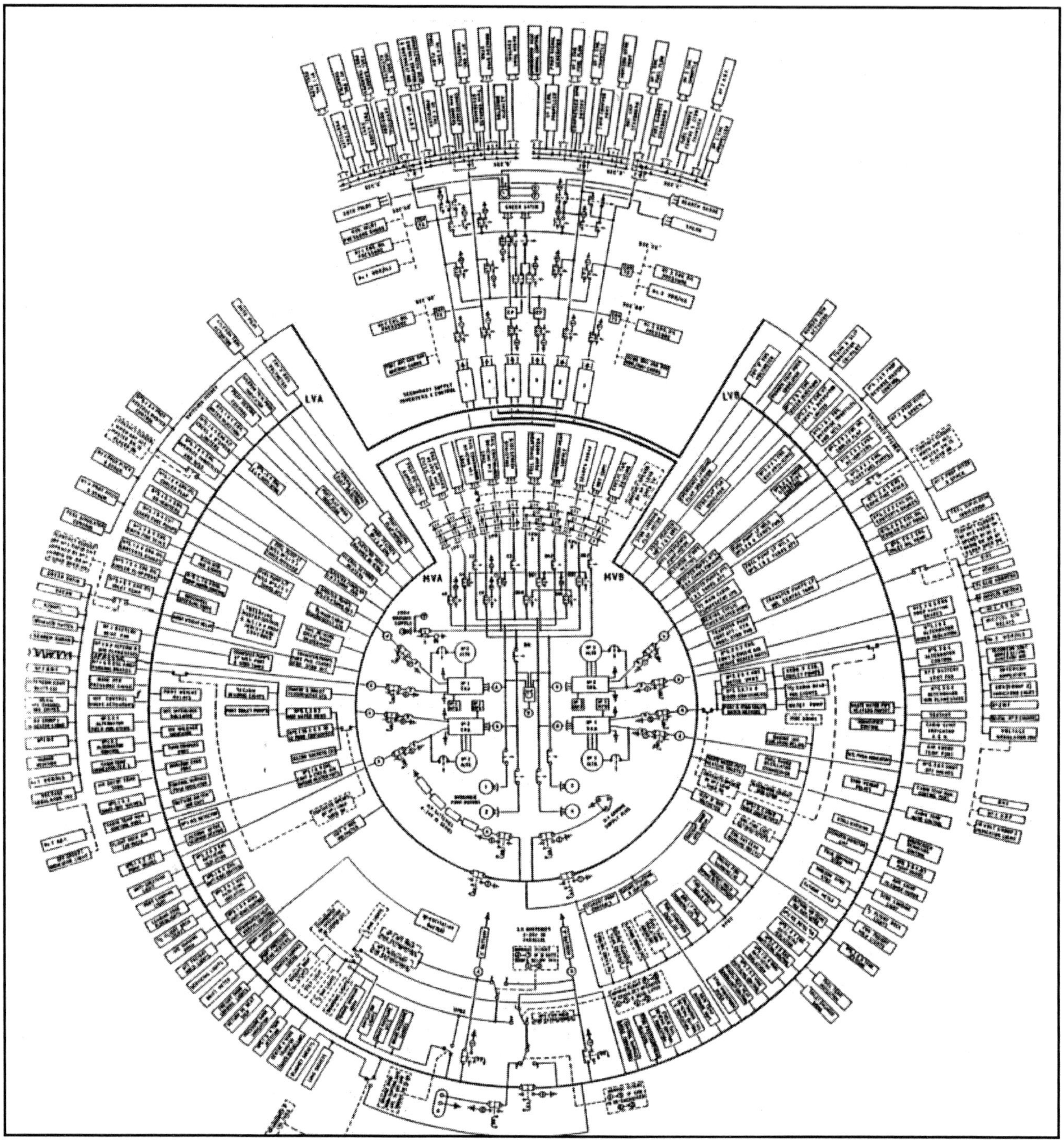


The Britannia was ahead of its time, relying heavily on electrical control of systems. This is the cleverly arranged electrical schematic diagram from Pilots' Notes. A 6ft x 6ft representation of it greeted the aircrew students of the Bristol Aircraft Training School where it hung in the entrance hall.

*'As the training programme gathered momentum, the original training staff were joined by Training Captains Rip Kerbey, Nobby Hall and John Loveridge, who incidentally, had at last decided to join the commissioned ranks after much prevarication. The navigators in ATS(B) were Bill McCreedy, Ken Jenkin and Pip Moules. The flight engineers were headed by the one and only Titus Oates, who was later commissioned. His team was Master Engineers Duffield and Jerrum, aided and abetted by the other living legend, who alternated between the aircraft and the flight simulator, Jackie Whelan. I can always remember his famous war cries, about, say, an 'On or Off?' situation. 'It's your decision Captain; you've got a fifty-fifty chance of getting it right!' Master Signaller Wood kept the communications department in good order and maintained the highest standards of professionalism. Sergeant Robby Robinson arrived to take charge of AQM training and from henceforth his sovereign service was the norm in the cabin throughout the whole fleet. This*

*was indeed a formidable and highly competent team of superb professionals whose efforts were reflected in the subsequent safety record and achievements of the whole Britannia force for years to come. They also provided a standard of excellence, probably not fully recognised by those who followed in the Comet 4, the VC10 and the Belfast.'*

**Comparisons**

*'This exceptional standard was probably not fully appreciated by me until I left the Royal Air Force in 1962. The gap was absolutely immense and it took quite a while to adjust to the accepted norms of civil aviation, which, whilst being undeniably safe by international standards, seemed to lack the polish and dedication of those of their underpaid Service counterparts. This feeling became more entrenched during my subsequent 18 year stint as an AIB Inspector of Accidents. This was an experience which, unfortunately, added fact and substance to a view I originally accepted as being emotionally or emotively based on prejudice and professional nit picking.'*

**'Britannia Task Force'**

This is the title quoted by ex-Chief Technician Ron King for the ground crew element of the RAF representation at Filton during the development and construction of the RAF Britannias.

*'Formed in 1957, the Officer Commanding was Sqn Ldr W Berry and his deputy, Flt Lt M Mould. The NCO i/c was Flt Sgt F Venables (Airframe Fitter) and the rest of the team was:*

| | |
|---|---|
| *Chief Tech R J King* | *(Aircraft Fitter)* |
| *Flt Sgt B Travers* | *(Electrician)* |
| *Sgt J Shearer* | *(Electrician)* |
| *Sgt L J Smallwood* | *(Instrument Navigational)* |
| *Sgt C Bonner* | *(Instrument General)* |
| *Sgt A Wardrop* | *(Avionics)* |

*Joining later was Sgt T Tate (Airframe Fitter) whose speciality was 'Ancillary Structures'.*

*'This last study covered the complex structures of the 'floating cargo floor'. The team was involved in the 'Pain in the Arse' phase when we had two types of propellers, steel and aluminium, each*

636 was destined to be the first Mk1 (the full military version) to be delivered. (*British Aerospace*)

Ex-Crew Chief Ron King maintained his enthusiasm for Britannia aircraft maintenance into retirement. He plays a major part in the care at Kemble of the last Britannia to fly - XM496. A later chapter is devoted to this aircraft (*Ron King*)

*with a different critical speed. Aircraft G-ANCA, apart from the Redifon (Simulator) trials, was also involved with Propeller Phase Sync trials. This was later abandoned but at least it resulted in the replacement of the steel bladed airscrews - although we went through that hybrid phase where we had two types of propeller on the aircraft. This rendered control, to avoid the forbidden speeds, quite difficult and a lot of skill was needed to control the prop RPM on landing with it passing through the transition phase, avoiding the critical prop rpm and still keeping the services on-line as the speed sense zone was very adjacent to the PRPM to be avoided. There were two plastic engraved labels stuck to the centre console displaying the prohibited figures.*

*'We were experiencing difficulty with flap area damage and various coverings were experimented with, mostly on XN392 at Boscombe Down. We were also experiencing trouble from the vortex induced by the Green Satin radome stripping the flap protection and there was a lot of soul searching for a suitable adhesive.*

*'The Downend crash occurred during the finalisation of those 'Redifon Flight Simulator Trials' and the 'Propeller Phase Sync Trials'. I too would have gone down that road but Don Hunter had given me the weekend off to attend my brother's wedding; so I was lucky not to be on board. It was the only propeller trial that I had not been on - so there was a stroke of luck.*

*'The original flight engineers were sent on an 'Advanced Electrics Course', before embarking on the 'Flight Engineers' Course' at Filton. It was quite a step forward in aircraft electrics, being basically the first 'Fly by Wire' AC/DC system in the world. It needed a complete grounding in AC systems. They were away for some considerable time. I embarked on the Ultra throttle, Napier spray mat and DH propeller courses. I was then detached to two airlines, having Britannia aircraft, for air and ground handling experience, finally joining the flight engineers at Bristol for the major electrical phase. I then went to Short and Harlands for their production line, and the dreaded 'Britannia Freight Lift Platform' that they were developing. That is another story. I then moved on to be a member of the ferrying crews for acceptance and delivery flights.'*

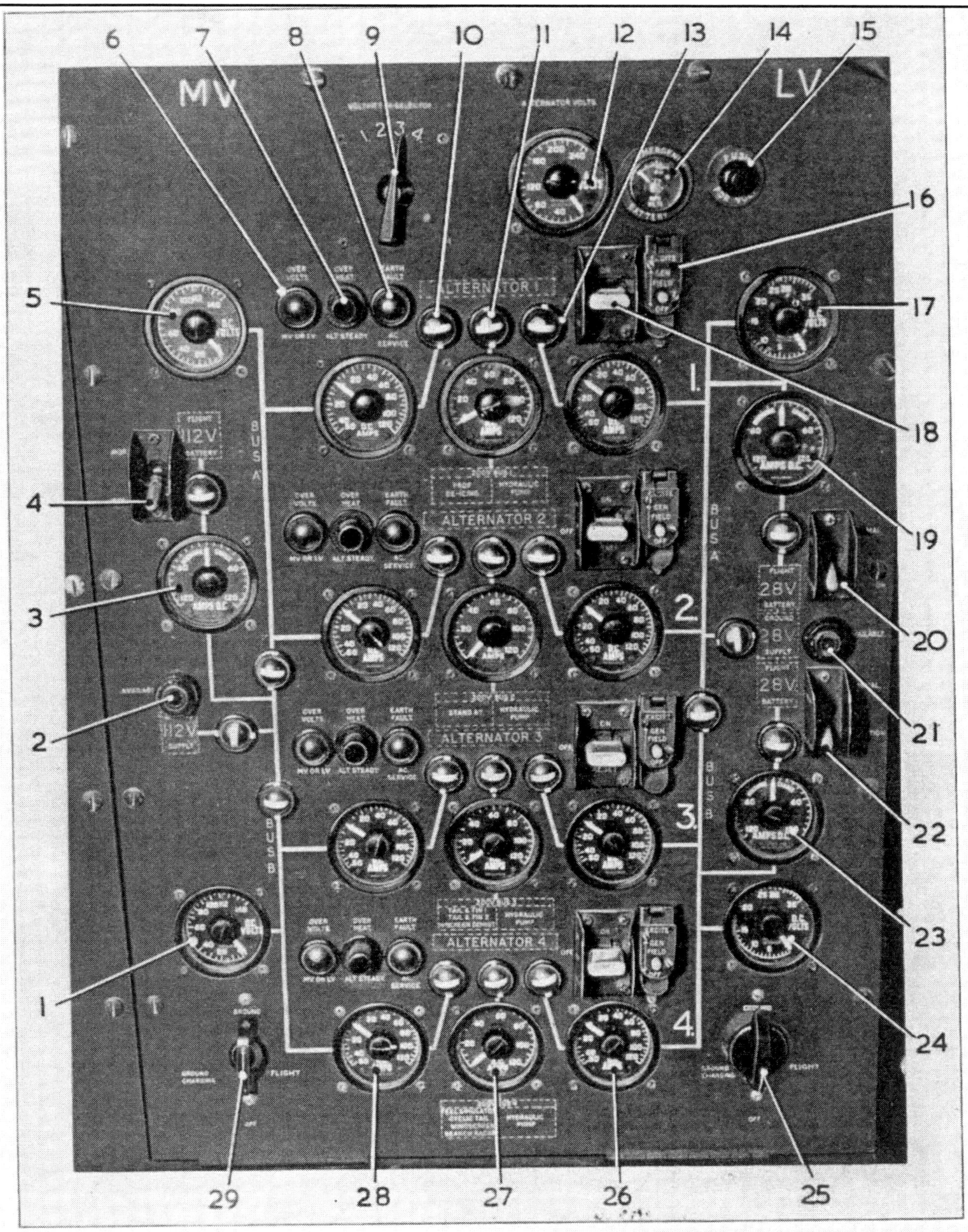


Fig. B Main electrical panel E1

The engineer's electrical panel, which was awkwardly situated on the wall behind the copilot's seat.

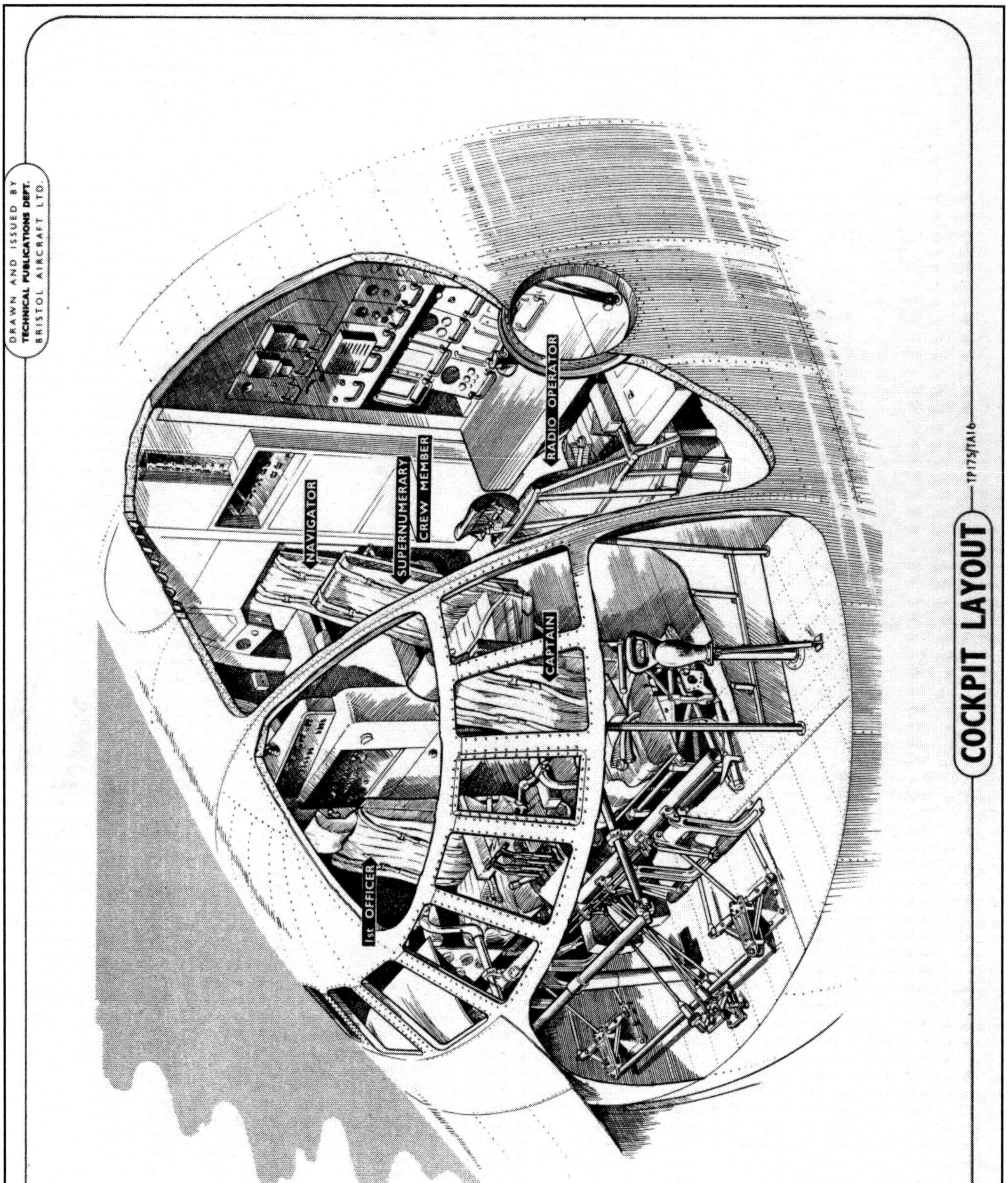


A diagram from a Bristol's publication.

CHAPTER FOUR

# The Pre-Britannia Era

At this point, it is appropriate to reflect on the historical setting for the delivery of the first Britannia for service in Royal Air Force Transport Command. Here, I am indebted to Wing Commander G F Bowles who first served the Britannia fleet as a Flight Lieutenant navigator in the 1960s. Later, as a staff officer at Air Support Command, the successor to Transport Command, he wrote a history of the roots of the Command. In his introduction he neatly summarises the events in Transport Command, and its forbears, that preceded the entry of the Britannia.

A Vickers Vernon.

**Those early days**

*'British Military air transport and supply squadrons began long before any official 'Transport' Command existed. In 1916, food and ammunition were dropped by 70 mph 'pusher' biplanes to the beleaguered garrison of Kut-al-Imara, Mesapotamia. RAF communiques, during the closing months of World War I in 1918, reported the parachuting of ammunition, rations and other supplies to the advancing infantry on the Western Front. In Trans-Jordan, a Handley Page bomber carried a servicing party to enable fighter aircraft to operate from a forward base. The first regular British air mail and passenger services in 1918-19 were flown by RAF Communications Squadrons, with crudely converted de Havilland and Handley Page bombers, from London to France and Germany. Nearly 3,000 such flights were made, carrying some 1,000 passengers and 100 tons of mail. In 1921 RAF aircraft inaugurated the Cairo - Baghdad mail service which operated until 1927. Soon after World War I, the Air Ministry evolved a requirement for a dual-purpose bomber-transport aircraft, and in the inter-war years such aircraft as the Vernon, Victoria, Valentia and Bombay undertook this role in the Middle East.'*

The Liberator.

RAF Kai Tak, Hong Kong, would have been familiar to many early transport aircraft fliers. It is believed that this photograph originates from the early 1950s. (*Len Moore*)

**Bomber-transports**

*'The first substantial troop airlift was in February 1923 when Vernons of Nos 45 and 70 Squadrons flew 480 Sikhs from Kingerban to Kirkuk in Iraq during tribal disorders. Later nearly 200 patients suffering from dysentery were flown out. In 1928-29 bomber-transports flew the first major emergency airlift in history - the evacuation of nearly 600 civilians from Kabul, Afghanistan, following a revolt against King Ammanullah. During the early part of World War II military air transport requirements were partly met by the RAF bomber-transports. It was soon apparent, however, that not only were specialised aircraft required, but also some organisation for their control.'*

**Ferry Command**

*'The direct history of Transport Command can be traced to the Anglo-Canadian agreement for the delivery of American built aircraft across the Atlantic. The first arrived in November 1940 and the Atlantic Ferry Organisation was formed in March 1941. Four months later this became RAF Ferry Command,*

The Avro York, with which 511 Squadron, destined to become a Britannia squadron, was equipped. (*Len Shout*)

A Handley Page Hastings of 99 Squadron, which was also destined to be a Britannia squadron. (*Len Shout*)

*controlling a network of air routes over the North and South Atlantic, and later across Africa to India. Among the aircraft used were converted Liberator Bombers, with passengers lying on mattresses in the bomb bays. Specialised transport squadrons were forming in all overseas theatres of war. The Dakota entered RAF service in 1942, and by the end of the war nearly 1,900 such aircraft equipped 25 squadrons. Ferry Command's squadrons operated with great distinction everywhere. In 1942, for example, unarmed Hudsons of 24 Squadron made 323 flights to Malta carrying 6,000 passengers and 1,000,000 pounds of freight. During the advance from El Alamein, Hudsons flew fuel, rations and other supplies several hundred miles inside enemy lines in order to maintain a Hurricane wing. Expansion continued and by the Spring of 1943 Ferry Command aircraft were flying approximately 66,000 hours per month, and the demand for air transport was still growing. It was then decided that there must be a revised organisation to standardise and coordinate the expanding air transport operations at home and abroad.'*

**Transport Command**

*'On 25th March 1943, therefore, Transport Command was formed under the command of Air Chief Marshal Sir Frederick Bowhill. Initially it contained two groups (Nos 44 and 45) and 80 aircraft. By the end of the war it was the largest of all Commands with 12 groups and 58 squadrons. Its 3,000 aircraft flew about 24 million miles a month from 36 regular stations and through 100 staging posts all over the world. Some groups operated with the airborne forces, and others operated scheduled passenger and freight services. The Avro York, developed from the Lancaster bomber, flew many of the longer schedules as well as carrying out many notable VVIP sorties. Transport Command aircraft headed the great airborne assault on 6th June 1944, which heralded the liberation of Europe. They later flew in the Arnhem operation during which Flight Lieutenant David Lord, flying a Dakota, won posthumously, the Command's only Victoria Cross. The Command delivered thousands of tons of ammunition and stores to the Continent for advancing land forces and more than 300,000 battle casualties were flown to UK hospitals in 1944 alone. During the Burma Campaign, most of the supply work could only be undertaken by air, and from January 1944 until March 1945, one group alone flew 11 million miles carrying 100,000 troops together with supplies, and also carried out such operations as 'Birdcage' and 'Mastiff' when airborne medical teams and supplies were dropped to released prisoners of war in Burma and Siam.'*

**Berlin Airlift**

*'In the immediate post war period, Transport Command maintained a substantial*

Two images of the Transport Command Hastings era. The one above is probably a very early publicity shot as there is no Command livery. (*Peter de Frère*)

Hangar work at RAF Lyneham.
(*Peter de Frère*)

A somewhat over-glamourous publicity photograph. (*British Aerospace*)

A Comet 2 at RAF Changi in the late 1950s ...

... In later years the Comet 2s were joined by Mk4s.

A Comet 2 of 216 Squadron. This photograph was taken on the last flight of the aircraft on 1st April 1967. (*Lyneham Globe*)

*network of European services, but these gradually disappeared as the civilian airlines returned to business. The long range schedules continued and the Hastings started service in 1948. Its introduction coincided almost precisely with the biggest peacetime air supply operation yet undertaken - Operation 'Plainfare', the Berlin Airlift. The operation started on 28th June 1948. The blockade was officially raised on 11th May 1949, by which time the RAF had flown 281,000 tons of supplies and 67,000 passengers into Berlin in a total of nearly 50,000 flights. The resupply of the city continued until October 1949, and by then the Command had flown nearly 25 million miles and increased its carriage of supplies to 400,000 tons. At the peak of the operation, 40 York, 40 Dakota and 14 Hastings aircraft of the Command were used. In the 1950s Transport Command was frequently called upon for urgent overseas troop deployments, for example Cyprus, Kenya and predominantly the Suez Canal, where culminating action took place in November 1956, when British and French troops were flown from Cyprus to be dropped over Egypt.'*

**The modern force**

*'The middle of the 1950s marked the start of a major re-equipment of the Command, albeit mainly due to partial failure of British civilian transport aircraft projects. The Comet 1, after early promise with BOAC, failed disastrously and only after intensive testing and research was the basic fault found. Modifications produced the Comet 2 which was never to see civilian service. Ten of these aircraft were, however, pressed into service with 216 Squadron of Transport Command, who thus became the first major users of jet military transport aircraft. During the following decade, they operated these aircraft worldwide with an absolutely unsurpassable safety record. The Britannia followed in 1959.'*

Thus concludes Wg Cdr Geoff Bowles' account.

My contributor, Wing Commander Geoff Bowles, writing here of the noble history that ushered in the Britannia, was to ultimately play a part in its demise. He was the last commanding officer of one of the two Britannia Squadrons, No.99. He is photographed here (right), for the occasion, with the last 511 CO, Wing Commander Dickie Robertson.
(*JB*)

## Leading Particulars

**Airframe data**

| **Main plane** | |
|---|---|
| Dihedral | 3° |
| Incidence | 3° |
| Wash-out | 2·4° |
| Root section | NACA 25017 |
| Tip section | NACA 4413 modified |
| Area (gross) | 2,075 sq. ft. |
| Flaps (total) | 401 sq. ft. |
| Ailerons (each, including tabs) | 70 sq. ft. |
| **Fuselage** | |
| Gross surface area | 3,802 sq. ft. |
| **Tail plane and elevators** | |
| Dihedral | Nil |
| Incidence | Nil |
| Area (gross) | 588 sq. ft. |
| Elevators (each, including tabs) | 85 sq. ft. |
| **Fin and rudder** | |
| Area, clear of fuselage (including rudder and dorsal fin) | 356·4 sq. ft. |
| Rudder (including tabs) | 92·2 sq. ft. |
| Dorsal fin | 41 sq. ft. |

**Main undercarriage**

| | |
|---|---|
| Type | Four-wheel bogie, rearward retracting main u/c UC 1000, Mk 2 or UC 1016 |
| **Shock absorber** | |
| Type | Messier oleo-pneumatic |
| Fluid | OM 15 |
| Fluid capacity | 2·8 gall. approx. |
| Air pressure | Refer to graph in Vol. 1 |
| Max. extension | 15 in. |
| Extension | 2·1 in. to 13·4 in. (all-up weight 185,000 lb.) |
| Bogie wheel base length | 4·0 ft. |
| Bogie track, forward wheels | 20·2 in. |
| rear wheels | 29·8 in. |
| **Wheels** | |
| Type | Dunlop AH 51809 or AH 51090, Ref. No. 27A/4235 |
| Tyre | Dunlop DC 7521T, Ref. No. 27A/3974, dimpled tread, nylon 16-ply rating |
| Size | 40 × 12·18 in. |
| Tyre pressure | $145^{+10}_{-0}$ psi |
| Brakes (4) | Dunlop AH 51293 with Maxaret 12636-40 anti-skid units |

'Leading Particulars' from Pilot's Notes.

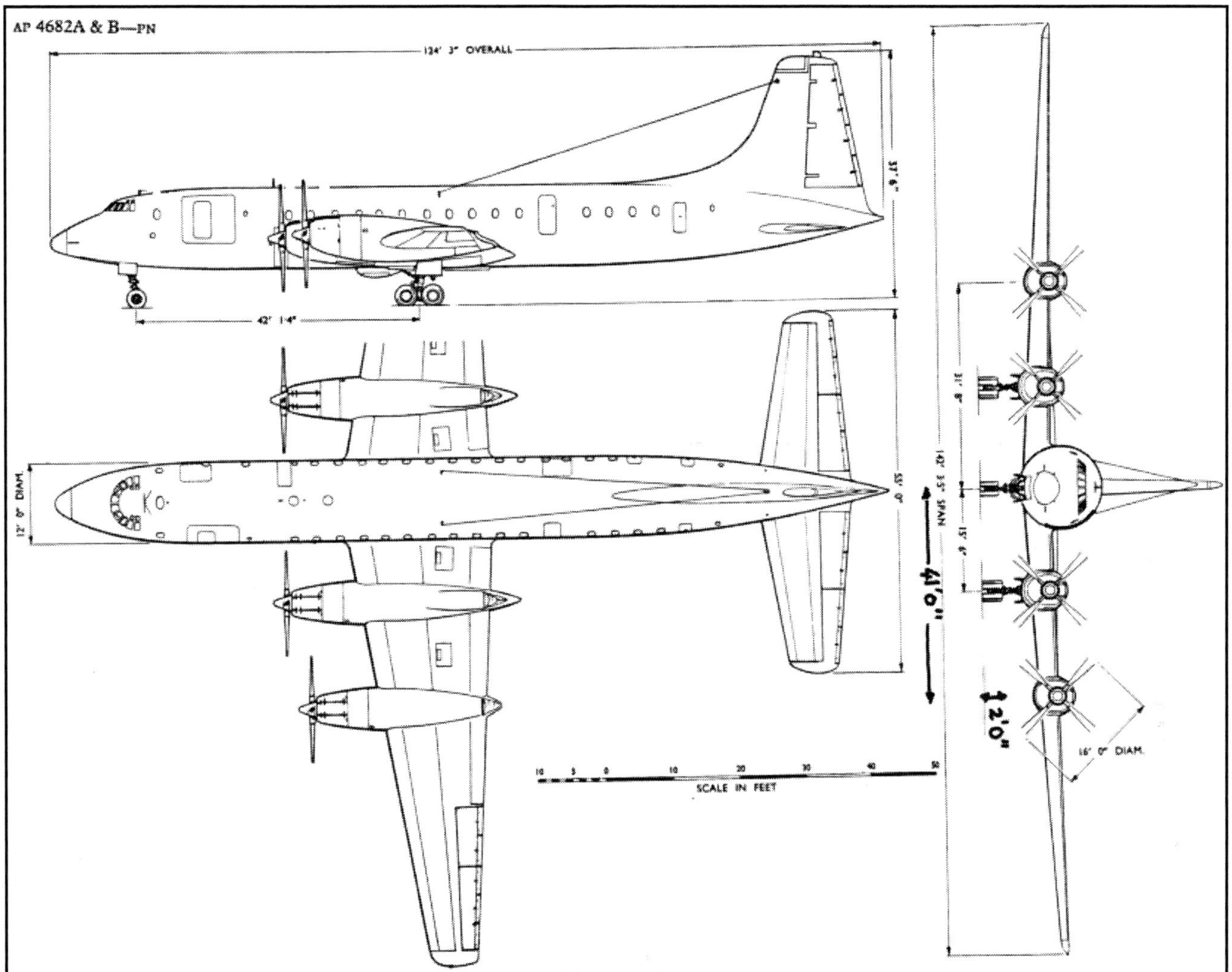


**Fig. B Britannia C Mk. 1 General arrangement**

**Nose undercarriage**

| | |
|---|---|
| Type | Twin-coupled wheels, steerable, forward retracting |

**Shock absorber**

| | |
|---|---|
| Type | Messier oleo-pneumatic |
| Fluid | OM-15 |
| Fluid capacity | 1·45 gall. approx. |
| Air pressure | Refer to graph in Vol. 1 |
| Max. extension | 16 in. |
| Extension | 5·45 in. to 11·1 in. (all-up weight 185,000 lb.) |
| Steering angle | 50° either side of centre line |

**Wheels**

| | |
|---|---|
| Type | Dunlop AH 50916, Ref. No. 27A/3951 |
| Tyre | Dunlop DC 7666T, Ref. No. 27A/3975, dimpled tread, nylon 12-ply rating |
| Size | 32 × 8·8-16 in. |
| Tyre pressure | $145 \pm {}^{10}_{0}$ PSI |

**Hydraulic system**

| | |
|---|---|
| Fluid | OM-15, Nato Code No. H-515, American Spec. MIL-H-5606A |
| Total system capacity approx. | 16 gall. |
| Tank capacities— | |
| Main (with main accumulators empty) | 2·29 gall. |
| Emergency | 2·06 gall. |
| Total | 4·35 gall. |
| Main system pressures— | |
| Cut-in | 3,500 ± 100 PSI |
| Cut-out | $4,000 \pm {}^{50}_{100}$ PSI |
| Relief valve | 4,800 ± 100 PSI |
| Nosewheel steering operating pressure | 2,000 ± 50 PSI |
| Wheel brakes operating pressure | 1,700 ± 50 PSI |
| Control surface locks operating pressure | $4,000 \pm {}^{50}_{100}$ PSI |
| Alighting gear emergency system pressure— | |
| Cut-in | $3,500 \pm {}^{100}_{50}$ PSI |
| Cut-out | 4,000 ± 50 PSI |
| Accumulator pressure (air with hydraulic off-load) | |
| Supply system | 2,500 ± 50 PSI |
| Wheel brakes | 1,800 ± 50 PSI |
| Control surface locks | 2,500 ± 50 PSI |
| Bogie door locks | 2,500 ± 50 PSI |
| Emergency system | 2,500 ± 50 PSI |

**Feel simulator system**

| | |
|---|---|
| Tank capacity | 0·875 gall. |
| Simulator accumulator pressures | HP 500 ± 10 PSI<br>LP 60 ± 5 PSI |
| Elevator damper accumulator pressure | 20 ± 5 PSI (air) |

**Freight door system**

| | |
|---|---|
| Tank capacity | 0·75 gall. |

The RAF Britannia's vital statistics from a diagram in Pilot's Notes. Note the hand-written amendment showing that the out-board propellers had only a two foot ground clearance at a distance of 41 feet from the aircraft centre line. This was quite a critical factor when taxying on some airfields.

Further details from Pilot's Notes.

In the Britannia Association magazine the question was asked, 'What, exactly, does the Transport Command motto, 'Ferio ferendo' mean?'

There was the ideal person to ask, Squadron Leader David Court-Smith, an ex-511 navigator of Classical bent. He didn't disappoint.

**FERIO** is the **1st person singular**, **present** tense, **active** voice, **indicative** mood of the 4th conjugation verb **ferire - to strike. FERENDO** derives from the irregular verb **ferre - to carry**. It could be the dative or the ablative case (both of which have an **-O** ending) of the gerund, which is a neuter singular verbal noun. It can be translated as **carrying**. Dative is the **to** or **for** case. Ablative is the **from**, **by**, **with**, **in**, **on**, **at** case.

As Latin is a rather economical language, one has to arrive at the meaning by inspection. In this instance, the only sensible translation is **by** - one of the variables offered by the ablative case.

The final translation of this (fortunately) simple motto therefore is:

**I STRIKE BY CARRYING**

This is the literal translation, and it makes absolute sense and is completely appropriate, so one doesn't have to render it in a colloquial version, as is so often the case.

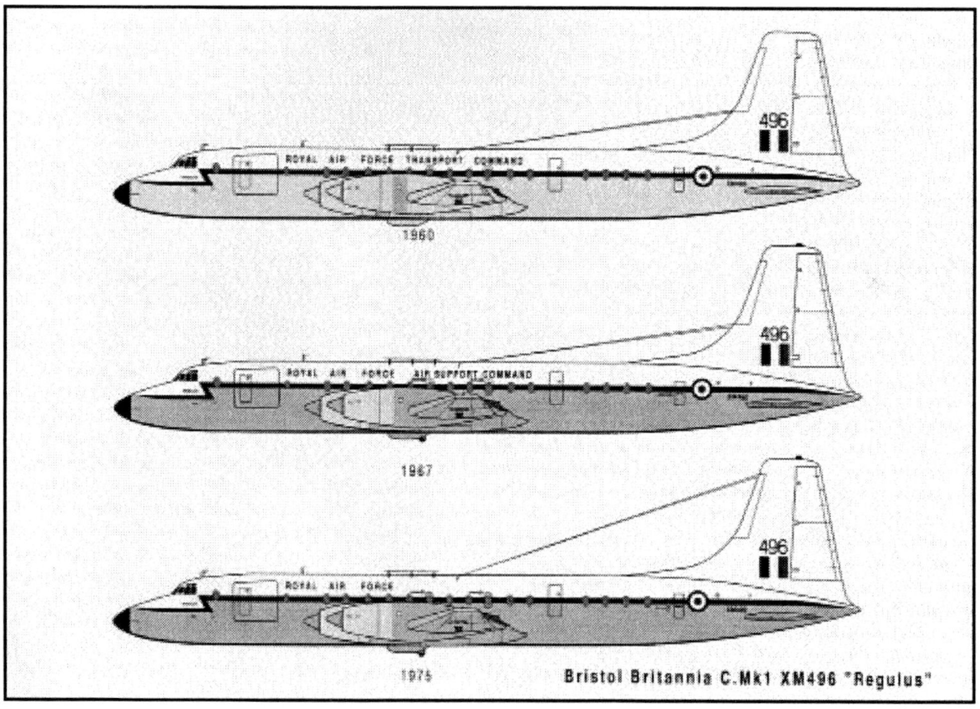


In its lifetime, the lettering on the RAF Britannias was to change three times reflecting reorganisation of the Command structure. The other major appearance change was from a shiny, bare metal lower fuselage to a painted 'battleship grey' one. Roger Carvell worked with his computer on these variations. (*Roger Carvell*)

CHAPTER FIVE

# Delivery

All that precedes is but a preface to 19th March 1959. On that day, at Royal Air Force Lyneham, in the County of Wiltshire, at 1752 hours, Britannia XN398 landed. This opened a chapter in Royal Air Force history that was not to close until January 1976, (although there was to be a single military representative of the aircraft, in the Boscombe Down Britannia, until February 1984.)

**The Britannia's era**

This chapter covered a period that was to see the demise of the Commonwealth, as it had been, and the UK's increasing commitment to NATO and Europe. The Britannia was introduced to support a smaller but more mobile Army and provide an ability to respond rapidly to global demands. It was terminated as our sphere of influence contracted and defence cuts became the order of the day. The chapter included involvement, in some way or other, in the majority of the events in the Free World of that time and the maintenance of the fragile peace through the regular exercise of our military plans. Contingency plans, continually revised and held in reserve in case of some international crisis, relied heavily on the Britannia fleet

Whilst Bristol is considered to be the home of the Britannia, a not often acknowledged fact is that 18 of the 23 RAF Britannias were built by Short Brothers & Harland Ltd at Belfast. Here 635 lands at the Queen's Island airfield, Belfast. *(Stu Bailey)*

and were put into action on many occasions, because of natural disasters, political unrest and the like.

The prestigious stature of a fleet of 23 'shiny' aircraft must not be underestimated, so that chapter also included many 'showing the flag' flights and the Britannia completed its considerable share of the associated VIP flying.

Underlying all this was training and practice; so successfully completed that the fleet never suffered a flying accident which involved the loss of life or serious injury in the whole of its operations.

**The early days**

What follows, covers four components of the story of those crucial early days. Firstly, there is the delivery of the aircraft to Lyneham and the wary steps along the first routes, the aircraft being flown by those crew members, who had gained their experience at Filton. Secondly, to supplement these, there was the immediate training of a chosen few, before the third stage, the establishment of a full blown training system. Last, but not least, was the training of, and gaining experience by, the ground staffs. All these strands were inexorably interwoven which means that the description that follows is not straightforward.

**The first aircraft**

XN398 was flown into RAF Lyneham by Squadron Leader Owen with his first crew, Flt Lt Tony Davies, copilot, Sqn Ldr Pat Burgess, navigator, Flt Lt Johnny Holf, engineer. Chad Hannah was the signaller. The delivery flight was not without incident as the crew had, unwittingly, violated Irish airspace. Many countries, including Eire, require that diplomatic clearance is obtained for over-flights by military aircraft. XN398 did not have this permission. During its pre-delivery flying by the RAF the aircraft flew under civil registration and it was quite acceptable for it to overfly Eire. But the situation changed on 19th March, when it became a military aircraft. The subsequent comment of Sqn. Ldr. Owen was:

*'... it wasn't until some time later that the Wg Cdr Operations at Lyneham was rather put out and he mentioned that we had committed a 'faux pas', but apparently our Irish friends weren't too upset. I was too busy to worry anyway!'*

**First aircraft date disputed**

In later years Flight Lieutenant Bill

The stage is set for the official handover ceremony. (*Maurice Flynn*)

Mr Cyril Uwins, Managing Director of Bristol Aircraft Ltd., formally handed over the technical documents of the aircraft to Wing Commander J O Barnard OBE, the Officer Commanding No.99 Squadron. On the extreme left is the Station Commander, RAF Lyneham, Group Captain R E Craven OBE DFC and on the right Air Marshal Sir Denis Barnett KCB CBE DFC MA, AOC-in-C Transport Command. (*Maurice Flynn*)

Hickox was not happy with the declaration that 19th March 1959 marked the date of the 'first' flight into Lyneham and wrote to Editor of The Britannia Association magazine:

*'I felt it incumbent upon me to remind others, particularly those who write histories of the Britannia, or of 99 Squadron, that by 19th March, as Navigation Leader Britannia Force, I had already been flying the Britannia at Filton for nine months and, in between flights, I had produced the Flight Planning Tables, Sector Fuel and Payload Tables and the RTOW charts for the aircraft. As it happened, on that great day, I was in Rangoon with G-APPE, later XN392, having taken out a servicing party to rescue a BOAC Brit 100 which had overshot the runway, collapsing the nose gear. Thus, it was not until 2nd April that I first flew XN398 at Lyneham - and a week later that I watched John Owen performing his rope trick out of the freight door.'*

The Editor (who is, coincidentally the author of this book!) replied:

*'As someone not a complete stranger to RAF Britannia history writing or, indeed, contributing the Britannia bit of a history of 99 Squadron, I too felt some 'incumbency' to reply. I have to say that I have always had some doubts about the veracity of saying that the 'first' was on*

Many events in Britannia life were recorded in '*The Lyneham Globe*', the RAF Lyneham station newspaper. Some unique photographs are contained in those records and, whilst the quality leaves something to be desired, it does seem a pity not to include them in this comprehensive history. This is the Globe's depiction of the handover. Note the highly polished underside of the aircraft. This was the delivery livery. Many years later a dull grey finish was applied.

JULY 1959

Britannia handover at Lyneham. Logbook handover of 636 by Mr. Unwin of Bristols. (Photo by courtesy of Evening Advertiser)

IT'S UP TO

*19th March 1959. With the aircraft ordered and you guys at Filton, there must have been many occasions when a Britannia visited Lyneham before that date. Possibly what happened was that it was decided that the arrival on 19th March would be regarded 'Officially' as the 'First'. My authority for using this date in my Britannia book is the 99 Squadron Form 540, which I studied at the Air Historical Branch. Obviously 99 regarded the flight on that day as the arrival of their first aircraft and as they were the first Britannia squadron then QED! I don't think it does any harm to peg a particular time and date - it has a nice historical sense. But then so do the facts that you have presented in your letter and I shall use them in the next magazine to 'put the record straight'.'*

**That 'Rope Trick'?**

Part of RAF Britannia legend is the story of an unusual exit from the aircraft by John Owen - like many legends, it probably only bears a passing resemblance to the truth! It is alleged that, with their training detail complete, the Owen crew are waiting for some steps so that they can leave the aircraft. The minutes tick by. John is quietly stewing. Suddenly he says, 'We'll practise an emergency exit using the escape ropes!' Each door was equipped with such a rope. Without more ado, he grabs the rope for the forward passenger door, set in the freight door, and swings out over the sill. But, the end of the rope is not attached to the aircraft and he crashes the 10+ feet to the ground - but landing on his feet. A measure of the guy is that he then walks to the waiting crew bus - with, it subsequently turns out, two broken ankles!

**Steady flow**

Britannia XN398 was closely followed, on 8th April, by another member of the 252 Series, XN404. It is interesting to reflect on the delivery pace from there on. Seventeen aircraft were delivered in that first year and the total of 23 aircraft was completed in well under two years. A

'Prop Change' by Junior Technician Alan Warner. (*Bill Robinson*)

review of the memoranda circulating in high places in the Air Ministry reveals, however, that the Air Council was not satisfied with this rate. But with the financial constraints on Bristols, due to their small order book, the production line could not be speeded up.

**The official handover**

The first 253 Series, designated the Britannia CMk1, was XL636. It was flown to Lyneham on 4th June and was the centrepiece, flanked by 404 and 398, for the official handover to 99 Squadron on a breezy 9th June 1959.

**The Ninety Ninth**

No.99 Squadron first arrived at Lyneham in late 1947. Peter Jordan provides the squadron's previous history:

*'Until it reformed at Lyneham in November 1947, as a Long Range Transport Squadron flying Yorks, No.99 was predominantly a bomber squadron. Even in its bomber days it specialised in long range work, initially in France flying DH9s towards the end of WW1, as part of Lord Trenchard's Independent Air Force,*

*which was demonstrating for the first time the strategic use of air power. Between the wars No.99 retained its bomber role flying the Avro Aldershot and Handley Page Hyderabads, Hinaidis and Heyfords before converting to Wellington Mk 1s shortly before the outbreak of WW2 in October 1938. During the first three years of WW2, No.99 operated mainly against German naval and port targets until moving to Ambala in India in June 1942, when it became the first heavy bomber squadron to operate in the Far East. There, most of its operations were against the Japanese in Burma using Wellington Mk IIIs and Xs until August 1944, when the Wimpy was superseded by Liberator Mk IVs. Continuing its Long Range Heavy Bomber role, No.99 progressively increased sortie lengths from eight hours through 12½ to 15, and eventually to 16 hours - a round trip of 2500 miles. The Squadron's final location was in the Cocos Islands, when it was commanded by Wg Cdr A Webster DSO DFC, and it was disbanded in November 1945. I wonder if the aeroplanes finished up at RAF Pegu, which this contributor commanded for a short time in 1946.'*

On its arrival at Lyneham, the aircraft flown was the York which could carry 20 passengers or 8000lbs of freight and operated to such places as Habbaniya, Mauripore, Fayid, Tengah and Nairobi. Wunsdorf also featured largely in the Squadron's history, which points to its participation in Operation 'Plain Fare', the Berlin Airlift.

In August 1949, the then squadron CO and crew went to Dishforth and converted to the Hastings. September 1949 saw the delivery of the Squadron's first new aircraft and the postings out of some York crews and in of Hastings crews. It is interesting to note that the Squadron never ceased to operate on the routes in this period. A reduced number of Yorks operated whilst the Hastings found their feet, and then finally took over all the Squadron's route flying commitments in October 1949.

Jumping ahead, it will transpire that 99 Squadron was disbanded in 1976 with the demise of the Britannia. But it was reformed in 2001, at RAF Brize Norton, to operate Boeing C-17 Globemasters. (*Stu Bailey*)

The Hastings carried about 40 passengers or 12,000lbs of freight and initially flew the same routes as the Yorks. However, by 1951 they were taking their first tentative steps westwards into the Americas, and to Cyprus in association with the mounting political turbulence in the Eastern Mediterranean. By 1952 the Hastings had expanded their sphere of operations to cover Japan and Australia and flew relief to the disaster victims of Belem in Brazil.

In 1953, the Hastings took on the new role of Air Transport Support, dropping troops and supplies at Nicosia and Shallufa. Subsequent historical highlights illustrate the course of 99 Squadron for those years: squadron detachments to the Canal Zone and Singapore, to assist RAF deployment into those areas - ammunition to Nairobi for the fight against Mau Mau - supply drops in the UK in severe weather - the award of the Berlin Airlift Gold Cup as Transport Command's most efficient squadron - troops and armoured cars to Aden and Cyprus - Suez - schedules to Woomera and Christmas Island - detachments to Bahrain in support of operations in Oman - reinforcements to Cyprus, Aden and Amman.

As if to restart the cycle, in December 1958 Hastings crews were posted out of 99 Squadron to 24 and 36 Squadrons to make way for their Britannia trained replacements awaiting arrival of the new aircraft.

**Training the aircrew**

The training they were receiving was quite unlike any aircrew instruction that had been experienced before. It has already been emphasised that the Britannia was seen as a far more complex aircraft than its predecessors; it was indeed the first aircraft to use electrical systems so extensively. Gone were the levers, cocks and other manual devices. They were replaced by switches, operating relays to activate and control the various systems.

The conduct of the fire drill neatly illustrates this. In the past, the action in the event of an engine fire required some considerable exercise and coordination of the hands over various controls which, through the necessities of engineering, were situated in what seemed to be random location on the flight deck. Not so the Britannia - with the use of electrics the actual disposition of the final components was no longer a controlling factor. Thus the fire drill was reduced to closing a throttle, pushing an illuminated propeller feathering button and then going up a column of five switches and one button, set out in the required order. The column was clearly designated by another illuminated red light.

This is a simple example of Britannia electrics, as many a flight engineer would be quick to point out. Because of these technical advances it was considered necessary for the engineers to do an electrical 'lead-in' course at Melksham before they joined the pilots and navigators for a manufacturer's course at the Bristol engine factory at Filton and then an airframe course at the nearby Bristol Aircraft Training School.

An indication of how the entry into service of the Britannia had been anticipated is the diary of one of the first 99 Squadron flight engineers, Master Engineer Arthur 'Mitch' Mitchell:

*26 Jun 57* *Electrical Lead-in Course*
*6 Jan 58* *Filton Course Pt I*
*6 Oct 58* *Filton Course Pt II*
*2 Mar 59* *Commenced 20 hours flying with BOAC at Hurn*
*1 Jul 59* *Started screened flying at Lyneham on XN404*

Two years plus, training!

The follow-up to the Filton course was the flying element provided at Lyneham by Air Training Squadron (Britannia) - ATS(B), the aircraft distinction was necessary as there was also an ATS(C), the Comet trainers. OC ATS(B) was, of

Arthur Mitchell photographed many years later at a Britannia Association committee meeting. He was the stalwart secretary for many years. *(Joy McArthur)*

course, Squadron Leader John Owen.

**First route**

To return to the delivery of XN398 on 19th March, 11th April saw it on the first training flight to El Adem, near Tobruk. This was to be the beginning of the aircrew and ground crew becoming accustomed to operating the aircraft.

A second flight to El Adem took place on 16th April and a third took in Nicosia as well. An early example of the interest that the Britannia was to arouse during its service came from an unusual quarter. Their Majesties, The King and Queen Idris of Libya inspected the aircraft at El Adem on 13th June.

**Paris Air Show**

Twice during the third week in June a Britannia paid a visit to the Paris Air Show at Le Bourget. On the first occasion it was flown by a Lyneham crew and was demonstrated in the Aeromedical (casualty evacuation) role. The second visit was organised by the Bristol Aeroplane Company and was flown by Bristol's Chief Test Pilot, Walter Gibb. An invitation was extended to Air Ministry and Transport Command officers to fly to the show in the aircraft. On this occasion it was operated in the trooping role.The aircraft routed from Bristol to Le Bourget via Heathrow to pick up its full complement of passengers. All this is an indication of the aura that was surrounding the Royal Air Force's latest, substantial - and graceful - acquisition.

**Bill Smith's early Britannia memories**

*'My first recollection is probably libellous, but I will tell it anyway. When I was on my Changi tour in 1953-56, we were still using the old airfield at Kai Tak, which then had two runways, 07/25 and 13/31. The new airfield came under construction at that time and work was going on night and day on the new runway 32, with which most of us became more familiar in later years. This was of course just at the beginning of the jet-age and the Comet and 707 were in competition, but the Britannia was coming on to the scene and was then proving itself as a very long range aircraft and Bristols were keen to sell it everywhere. As you well know, the Brit had its towing difficulties with the nosewheel between 45° and 90°; when being demonstrated on the West coast of America, they managed to tear off the inboard main wheel when towing it. The FAA refused it a licence!*

*'The 707 was still a little underpowered and take-off performance was quite restricted. The proposed runway at Kai Tak was a bit short and the Americans offered to fund additional length but, so the story goes, on account of the Brit incident the offer was turned down and the runway remained at its designed length. It was probably lengthened in later years when that reasoning was abandoned. It's just one of those stories!*

*'My next encounter with the Brit was on 8th June 1959 to get airborne in my Hastings from Colerne to photograph a Britannia and a Comet in formation. Formating was quite a struggle with the difference in speeds; they were not very comfortable to fly clean at the Hastings normal speed and they didn't want pictures with the flaps down. This was followed on the 9th to take the same Hastings to Northolt to pick up a load of photographers for Lyneham where we landed them to take part in the handing-over of the first Brits to the RAF. After the ceremony, we got airborne, followed by the Britannia, carrying favoured guests, who, it appeared were stuffing themselves on board as again we were taking pictures. We landed to pick up those photographers who had been on board the other aircraft, took them back to Northolt and returned to Colerne. I think John Owen was flying the Brit.*

*'Then came the glorious Monday, 30th May 1960, when Jack Hailey called me into his office and asked me if I would like to be posted to Lyneham to go on the course. How could I refuse? So I was out of there by Thursday and started the course alongside Nogger Norris and Ken Bick at Filton, but it was 21st October before flying started with Butch Loveridge as our instructor. He also did our route trainer, to Singapore of course, and we were catted just before Christmas. I can remember taxying out on 21st December to do our Cat III and John Owen saying, 'You can smoke if*

*you want.' As all of us had come off non-smoking types, this was a bit unexpected, so none of us did. Then he said, 'Don't any of you buggers smoke?' He must have been dying for one. I have many more memories, a couple of which Wyndy Deere has recounted . One is of a cockpit full of smoke when I was down the back talking to the passengers. Happy days!'*

**... and this prompted further recollections**

Peter Jordan, a 'senior' signaller of the Britannia fleet, was reminded ...

*'Reading Bill Smith's nostalgic letter about his earliest encounter with the Brit. had me diving for one of my log books and yes, there it was! Hastings WJ327, Flt Lt Smith, Duty - Press Liaison, 1.40 day - amongst all the Britannia entries.*

*'I had known Bill on and off since his Changi days, although I don't remember how we became friendly because we had never been stationed together until he joined the Brit. Force full time in 1960. I expect it was because he was just a nice friendly old Transporter and I was a poor lost and lonely TCEU Examiner away from home so often - signals, I hasten to add, not pilot for those of you who don't know. Anyway, although Signals Leader on 99 at the time I had somehow got lumbered with the Station Press Liaison job hence my escort duties for those press photographers in the back of Bill's Hastings. The images are a bit hazy (and I didn't have a camera with me) but I do recall some excellent close formation flying on the part of both captains - the Hastings and the Brit.*

*'And my log book also tells me that I flew twice more on that day doing my usual bout of circuit R/T for Alfie Musgrove and Joe Barnard in 404; this was in the days when pilots were just drivers airframe before we gave them H/F SSB to keep them busy all the time. And talking of being busy I notice that I went with Alfie to the Paris Air Show at Le Bourget eight days later on 17 June 1959 in 636, which had been the subject of Bill's photocall. It was the first of the 253s to be received at Lyneham and was, therefore, the subject of the official handover to the RAF.'*

**Ground crew's part**

Ex-Chief Technician Brian Kneen describes the ground crew's introduction to the Britannia at El Adem. He was posted there in 1957 as part of the start of the Transport Aircraft Servicing Specialist (TASS) teams along the trunk route to Singapore. Their initial training was on Comet 2s, Hastings and Beverleys. They were then trained on the Britannia by the specially formed Transport Command Britannia Aircraft Servicing Demonstration Party.

Flight Sergeant Larry Smallwood describes the formation of this party. The need was anticipated in 1957 and during January 1958 technicians were invited to apply to be members of the team and such was the importance attached to it that they were interviewed several times at Upavon before the final composition was decided upon.

They were posted to Lyneham and introduced to their 'Boss', Squadron Leader Bill Berry, DFC, an ex-flight engineer, turned ground engineering officer. He was a considerable personality who was to feature in Britannia operations for many years. Each member of the embryo demonstration party was sent to the various manufacturers for specialist training. Three months later they reassembled at RAF Lyneham and proceeded as a team to the Bristol Aircraft Company factory at Filton. For a period of three months, they had free access to any department they wished, to improve their knowledge of the aircraft. There was then a move to RAF Uxbridge to work daily at London Heathrow with BOAC in the Flight Servicing Hangars. By these means the

Snapped by a colleague, an historical moment for ex-Chief Technician Brian Kneen as he marshalls the first Britannia to land at El Adem. (*Brian Kneen*)

team learned at first hand the Britannia servicing requirements. With the completion of this experience they moved to Short and Harlands, Belfast to come into contact, for the first time, with the military variant, the 253 Series.

On return to Lyneham each member of the team produced, for his trade, servicing schedules, the recommended establishment levels required for first and second line servicing and for the major servicings. They considered the range of spares required at each level of servicing and at the staging posts. The quantity of special materials, tools and test equipments was decided, as was the preparation of technical training aids, instructions, handouts and guidelines. All this was achieved by the considerable dedication of the demonstration party members inspired by their talented leader, my namesake, Squadron Leader Berry.

This different and inspired approach to the technical aspects of the introduction of a new aircraft does seem to have stemmed, in part, from lessons learned from previous new types. There is a hint that the process could be overborne by the technical hierarchy that existed and that an aircraft so different needed a more dynamic and specialised approach.

With the arrival of the first few aircraft at Lyneham, the Transport Command Britannia Aircraft Servicing Demonstration Party was able to start proving the worth of its considerable preparation for the event. The aircraft were readied by them for their early route flights and members of the team travelled with the aircraft to lend their expertise on the ground. One such trip was a 'showing-off' of the new toy at the Paris Air Show on 17th June 1959. The aircraft was demonstrated in the Aeromed role. It was a great day, remembered well by the then Sergeant Smallwood - it was his 38th birthday!

Their next task was to train the servicing crews who were to meet the Britannia at their airfields. These obviously included the staging posts along the route to the Far East; El Adem in North Africa; Khormaksar, Aden; Gan in the Indian Ocean; Changi on Singapore Island. Their net also included Nicosia in Cyprus; Bahrain in the Persian Gulf; Mauripur, Pakistan; Katunayake, Ceylon and Edinburgh Field by Adelaide.

This training and travelling accomplished, the time had come for the instruction to start at the source and a Transport Aircraft Servicing Specialist Training School was established at Lyneham obviously under the influence of the original experts. To quote Larry Smallwood:

'*So ended three wonderful years from the cradle, so to speak, right up to cutting the mustard!*'

I am sure there were many others who found this period an extremely challenging and satisfying time and much of the subsequent success of the aircraft is due to them.

**Another pioneer recalls those days**

A strange feature of RAF Britannia life was that many of the very experienced people who first joined the fleet were posted having completed their 2½ year tour. It was only subsequently that it was seen as crazy to lose valuable experience and tours were extended - some into infinity (Bob Henderson?)! One of the early captains was Jack Hayley and he writes:

'*... it struck me that I have read very little recently of the early days of the introduction of the Britannia into RAF service. ... I (was) among the group of flight crews who were on the first ground training course at Bristol for the squadron crews. We followed the conversion training team, headed by John Owen, and including Jim Munro, Alf Musgrove and Harry Liddell. I think that the two squadron commanders, Wally Gray and Wing Commander Barnard, and Pat Burgess (the Performance expert) were also on that first course. Others pilots on our course, as far as my memory from over 40 years ago permits me to recall, were Danny Thomas, John Earland (known to us as Mike), Robbie Robertson ('Big Robbie'), Len Whiteight and Alec Wicks, the New Zealander. Most of us were from Hastings and Beverley squadrons of Transport Command, and the language of 'V1 and V2' and 'Performance Tables', was quite new to us, and we needed the navigators along side us to help interpret them and carry out the calculations! The flight engineers in particular, as well as us pilots, were faced with an aircraft with an electrical system of such complexity not previously experienced, and turbine engines which had no direct mechanical connection with the propellers,* *and an induction system that twice went round 180° degrees with the consequent liability to the build up of ice on the first bend. Pressurisation and air conditioning were also foreign to us and added to the complexity of the knowledge we were required to absorb. Of the navigators on the course, I have little recollection, but I do remember the name of Maurice Avery, who used to fly with me fairly regularly, together with Norman Hargreaves as copilot. I started my flying conversion training in August 1959, and by the beginning of November I had my 'C' category, and started operating as a fully qualified passenger-carrying captain.*

*'One of my earliest and most memorable flights, for which I was tasked, was to fly a group of SAS personnel direct from Lyneham to Bahrain, a flight of nearly 11 hours! A flight of such endurance and distance was a new experience to all of us. We were due to depart in the early morning of 13 January 1960. There had been heavy snow and frost overnight and the aircraft, 636, had been outside all night. The poor ground crew having defrosted the tail and having moved forward to the fuselage and wings, found that by that time the tail was frosted up again. This procedure carried on until they decided that they would have to put the aircraft into the hangar and delay our departure until the following day. In the meantime the SAS group had been billeted at the transit accommodation at Clyffe Pypard. There was no transit accommodation at Lyneham at that time.*

*'To digress for a moment, my first flight ever was from Clyffe Pypard in June 1942 in a Miles Magister when it was 29 EFTS. I was on what was called a Grading Course, to decide whether I had the potential ability and aptitude to become a pilot. The criterion was to be able to fly solo within 12 hours flying training. This I just managed to do. Other memories of Clyffe Pypard were positioning at Lyneham on Hastings schedules the day before, and having to stay there overnight. The pickled eggs in the bar were very popular, but the resultant aromas on the flight deck the following day were quite atrocious!*

*'To return to our SAS group, Clyffe Pypard is about seven miles from Lyneham, and is situated at the top of a steep hill. In the weather conditions that prevailed there was no way that motor transport could get to Clyffe Pypard. Nothing daunted, our SAS friends marched all the way to Lyneham, only to find on arrival that we had to delay our departure until the following day. So back they marched to Clyffe Pypard, and as the conditions were the same the next day, that meant another seven miles trudge through the snow and ice! Needless to say they arrived in good time, and we were away spot on our amended scheduled time. The flight was quite uneventful, and from those extreme winter conditions at Lyneham we arrived to a typical Persian Gulf temperature and humidity at Bahrain. Our SAS friends were immediately transferred on to a waiting Beverley to be transported to one of the Trucial States to do battle in the desert with some troublesome tribes. My admiration for the guts and determination of those SAS soldiers has never ceased.*

*'Another Middle East adventure was on a flight from Aden to Bahrain, when we were diverted to the new international airport at Kuwait. The airfield had only just been completed and had not been officially opened. Consequently there were no approach aids available, and I have recollections of being talked down, through a severe sandstorm, by, I believe, Brian Weatherehead - or was it Weatherall? - (Author: Weatherly?) from a beacon about 10 miles from the airfield. We were, by this time getting low on fuel, and were desperate to get down safely. Thanks to Brian's ingenuity we managed to do so. I can recall, after landing, being driven from our dispersal to the Air Traffic building in an open Landrover, and the air was so hot and dry, that the faster we went, the hotter it felt. The air was literally burning.*

*'My time on Britannias sadly came to an end in February 1962, when I was told that we 'oldies' had to vacate the left hand seat to allow the frustrated young copilots to be able to move over! I then spent 2½ years in the operations section at Benson, from where I was sent, for my sins, on a 12 months unaccompanied tour in Aden, in the Operations section of HQ Mid East. I was there from September 1964 to September 1965, just before we pulled out of Aden, when the local Arabs were tossing bombs all over the place, a couple, of which, at least, landed in the Officers' Mess at Steamer Point. One redeeming feature was meeting up with Ian Lawson who was the Station Commander at Lyneham during my tour on 99 Squadron. He was the Senior*

*Air Officer Administration at HQ Middle East. My final 18 months were spent at Odiham, in the Operation Section of 38 Group before retiring from the RAF in March 1967.'*

**That Goddamned Airplane**

Bill Hickox, the very first RAF Lyneham Britannia navigator, found this excerpt from an unknown American book. To what aircraft can it possibly refer? It is suggested that if you are totally 'Britannia Loyal' then you skip to the start of the next chapter!

*'Pan Am, who had done much in the way of providing technical assistance to budding, as well as established airlines of foreign countries, had more than a casual interest in Aeronaves de Mexico, a Mexican airline. In 1958 this carrier was in the process of establishing a route between New York and Mexico City, utilising newly obtained British built airliners equipped with British built turbo-prop engines. Along with instructors from Pan American's Miami base, Jack Ryan and I were sent to Mexico to assist in the crew training and implementation of this new airplane. At the same time it was intended that we gain familiarity with the new turbine engines and their operation, in as much as Pan American had very recently placed an order for the first 707s in the airline industry and there were only a few on the airline, and no one in pilot training, with any turbine experience ... Prior to the beginning of our flight training, Jack and I were given, in ten days, the same preparatory ground schooling on this new airplane, its systems and its engines, that others previously sent to England had been scheduled for a programmed 30 days to complete. Our subsequent flight training required many weeks before completion, with many interruptions because the airplane simply would not survive much more than an hour's flying, nor more than three or four landings in a row without having to be returned to the hangar for another week or ten days of repair, or design modification.*

*'Our flight instruction was hit and miss and could occur on a moment's notice any time the airplane was declared ready to fly. With a few interruptions from 'Montezuma's Revenge' and the Mexican 'tourista', our haphazard qualification was finally judged complete and we then began a period of qualifying Aeronaves pilots an the airplane while en route on the Mexico City, New York run. This airplane was equipped with probably the world's worse instrumentation, and radio and navigation equipment. If we were fortunate enough to leave Mexico City with all components operating, we would seldom arrive in New York with half of them remaining, because one by one they fizzled out in puffs of smoke in the radio rack. To interpret, then fly, the instruments of flight and navigation on the airplane's panels was an exercise similar to patting your head and rubbing your stomach as you stood on your head. In addition to all this, it just was not a good flying airplane, having little dihedral in the wings and therefore devoid of lateral stability.*

*'It was, by any standard, a big*

Aeronaves de Mexico Britannia.

*airplane and one of the first of its generation with a double bogied landing gear, necessary to support its heavier weight without damaging paved surfaces of airports. As a result, moving the airplane around on the ground precipitated some very interesting problems, because, by design, to avoid tyre scrunching and high twist loads on the landing gear, the amount of deflection of the steerable nose wheel was greatly limited. Thus, short radius turns on to narrow taxi strips, and on to ramp areas, were impossible. It was often necessary, when clearing a runway to position a man with his head and shoulders out of the opened navigator's astrodome in the ceiling at the rear of the flight deck. From this position, by tapping the pilot's left and right shoulders with his feet, the observer would signal as the pitch of the propellers reversed and the airplane backed up, often cutting the other way before making another try.*

*'To compound the airplane's taxying problems, with the propellers in their normal low (fine) pitch setting, at taxying low thrust settings the engine and generator rpm's would be too low to keep the engine driven generators operating at speeds sufficient to power the airplane's critical buses, and if rpm's were increased in compensation you taxyed like a madman and in turn badly overheated the brakes in order to keep the airplane slowed down. To alleviate this unworkable situation, the propellers were ingeniously equipped with an additional 'superfine' pitch setting for ground operation, which produced the desirable high rpm's but with very little forward thrust. An often encountered problem would occur when attempting to cancel 'superfine' prior to takeoff. This cancellation process required about 20 seconds on the runway itself due to very high thrust settings and engine rpm's involved. The cancellation was done two props at a time, first outboards, then inboards with very high thrust settings required to supply electrical needs as the propellers resumed their more coarsely pitched takeoff settings. The airplane shook and shimmied and roared as the procedure was performed. Often, the cancellation process was unsuccessful because one or more props would fail to change from superfine to fine pitch. This necessitated taxying down the active runway to a clearing taxy strip, and return to the ramp, with much gnashing of teeth by the control tower and pilots of other aircraft that had been in line waiting for take-off.*

*'Regarding the airplane's flight controls. When in flight, the ailerons for lateral control, elevators for longitudinal control, and rudder for yaw control, were all caused to be 'flown' to the desired deflected position by small 'flying tabs' on the trailing edge of each of the surfaces. The cockpit controls were cable connected to these flying tabs ONLY, at no time on the ground or in the air could movement of the pilot's controls directly cause positioning of the controls themselves.*

*'This brought up operational difficulties when preparing for take-off. When the flight control gust lock was released, as part of the pre-take-off procedure, the ailerons on each outer wing fell down, both elevators fell down, and the rudder flopped over if any cross wind existed, regardless of cockpit control positioning, which only moved the small flying tabs. Until enough speed could be attained on take-off for the controls to be lifted to the faired position, in addition to the drag of the wing flaps extended for take-off, the pilot was also dragging down the runway two drooping ailerons, two drooping elevators, and with the rudder full over in crosswinds, whether he wished it there or not.*

*'The control surface gust locks were applied when groundborne by a pedestal actuated gust lock control, which caused hydraulically actuated jackscrews on the control surface itself, to centre and lock each control. In the cockpit there were five red warning lights on the glareshield over the instrument panel directly in front of the pilots which illuminated and confirmed that the surfaces were locked, two lights, one for each aileron, two lights, one for each elevator, and one additional light for the lonesome trailing rudder. In cruising flight, it was not at all unusual for one or more of these lights to occasionally come on, perhaps signalling 'left aileron LOCKED' or, 'right elevator LOCKED'. A frantic grab for reactuation of the gust lock would be made by interested crew members in order to extinguish the lights.*

*'The foregoing certainly should have foretold the kind of problems that were certain to be encountered as this mixed up airplane entered the rigors of everyday airline service. (There then follows a long tale*

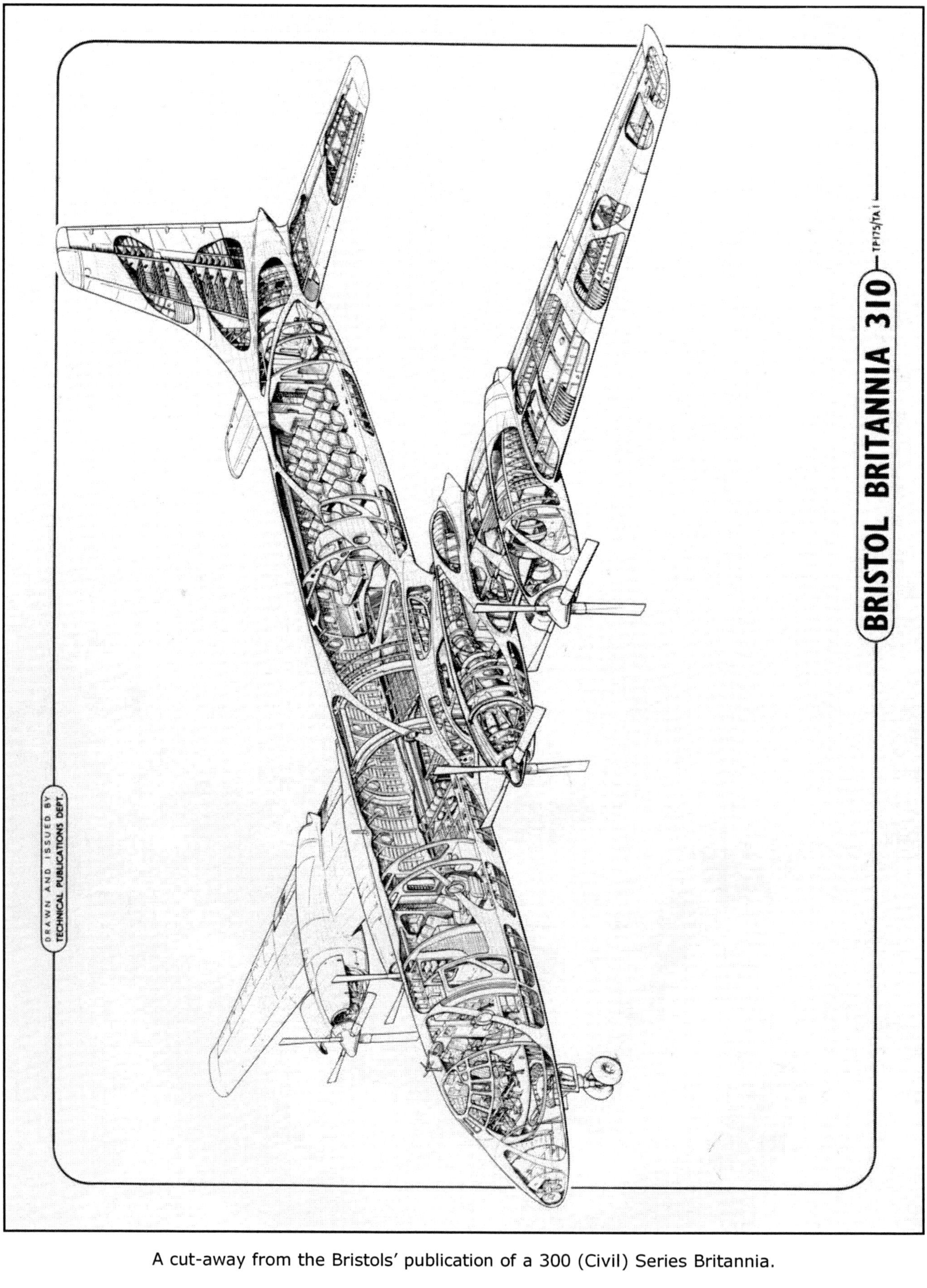


A cut-away from the Bristols' publication of a 300 (Civil) Series Britannia.

*of loss of pressurisation due to the ground conditioning inlet valve being left open.) We requested clearance back to New York and removed our oxygen masks. New York Centre read us our new clearance routing and altitudes while from my manuals I withdrew charts and adjusted to our new navigation situation. Many thoughts whirled through my head. We switched on a landing light to check for precipitation and cloud and saw we were now flying in heavy wet snow. Engine cowl and guide vane heat, wing heat and electric propeller de-icers were hastily turned on.*

*'In the airplane's short history it had shown great susceptibility to engine icing and as we flew I felt in the rudders, and the instruments also showed, the airplane suddenly pulling hard to the left. A quick check of the engine instruments showed No.2 engine tailpipe temperature lower than the others and dropping fast, with the engine's compressor rpm also dropping. No.2 engine had flamed out and we quickly prepared to do an in-flight engine relight procedure.*

*'For each engine, on the cockpit overhead panel between the pilots, were rows of many toggle switches that were normally utilised for ground engine starts. Using these same switches, we began the in-flight relight countdown. 'One, two,' actuate a switch, -'three, four,' actuate another, 'five, six, seven,' actuate another, 'eight, nine,' another, and at the count 'ten,' the last switch, the engine ignitor was actuated, which was supposed to light off the fuel flowing to the engine. Halfway through our countdown the airplane pulled in the opposite direction and to my dismay I saw that No. 4 engine had also flamed out, but No. 2 engine was spinning up and running again as we began a new countdown for No.4 engine.*

*'My cockpit companion, with his strong Spanish accent, tried with little success to explain to traffic control what our problem was, so I picked up my mike and requested a no-delay approach, while explaining our engine flameout problems. We were immediately cleared to a lower altitude and in the process had to relight No. 2 engine again. I was very concerned that we might end up gliding with no engines into the Atlantic Ocean below us because the airplane's scanty operating manual cautioned, 'If a flamed out engine cannot be relit in fifteen seconds it is to be drained of fuel for five minutes. If this is not done, high temperatures in the tailpipe can cause severe structural damage to the airplane's wings spars.' Those writing the manual knew what they were talking about because during an engine relight over England as part of the airplane's certification, a wing had been badly damaged. Between the required ten-second relight countdown procedure and the fifteen second restriction within which to do a relight, or drain for five minutes, flight crews only had five short seconds to, first, determine which engine had flamed out, and second, get under way with the relight countdown procedure.*

*'We had several radio frequency handoffs as we were vectored out over Long Island, unseen below us in the storm, while the approach controllers, intent on their radar blips, gave us steers toward the runway 22 ILS final approach course. At about 600 feet we were happily under the clouds and the airport lights ahead, and automobile traffic on the rain slicked parkway paralleling us below, could be seen through the rain-streaked windows. The storm continued buffeting us as we touched down in a strong wet crosswind ...*

*'This was a big airplane and its cockpit was supposedly designed and laid out so, if necessary, it could be flown and its systems also managed by only two cockpit crew members. Operating in high density areas in itself can be very demanding, then add to this the operation of a complicated airplane's complex systems, saturating two men to the point where something sooner or later gets neglected, or omitted. In our case failure to pressurise went un-noted for far too long in a very busy cockpit.*

*'The following evening we again originated the south-bound flight to Mexico City flying the same airplane with many of our passengers of the night before. It had been thoroughly inspected, engines tested and run up, and the airplane released for flight with confirming signatures in the log books. Full commissary was aboard, lavatories spotless and the fuel and water tanks topped off.*

*'The storm of the night before was not far off Newfoundland. Its passage through the New York area had thoroughly cleansed seaboard skies and it was a sparkling night as we again climbed to cruising altitude. In a short while coffee*

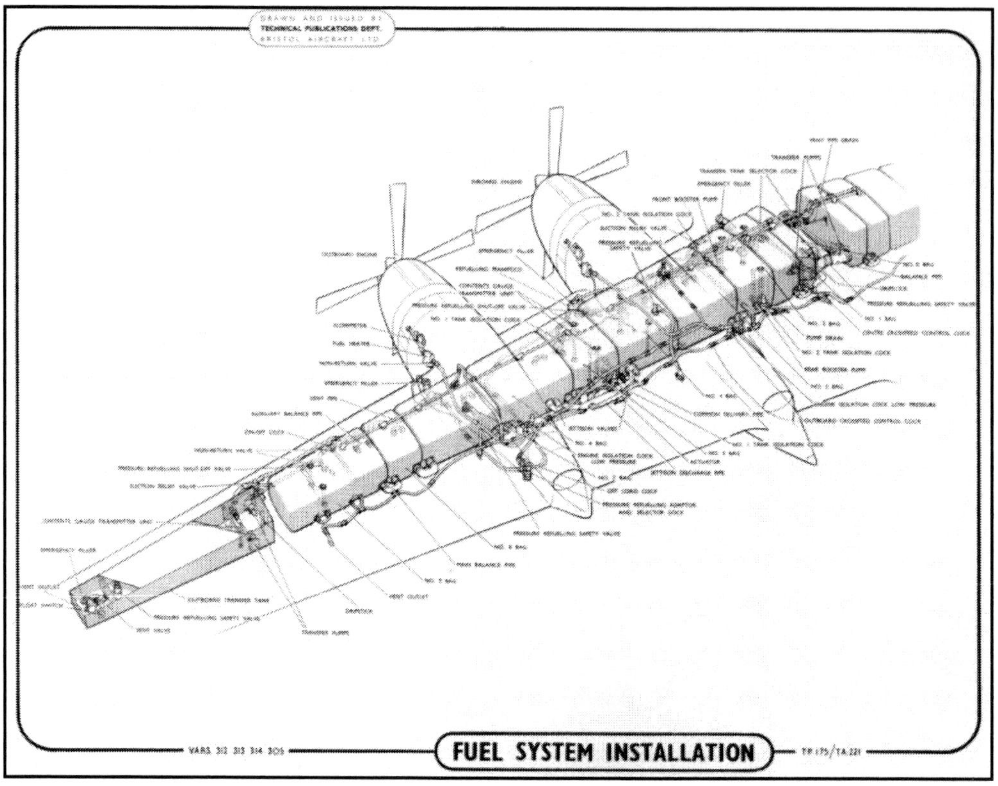


*was delivered to the cockpit. We were far above the low-level turbulence associated with the clearing weather and snug and warm as the lights of Philadelphia, beneath the huge wings, growling engines and throbbing propellers.*

*'My companion, sitting across from me, occasionally turned up his map light as he referenced his charts and flight computer and we were both enjoying the evening in the dimly illuminated cockpit. Suddenly he turned to me and cried, 'Look!', as he pointed to the indicators showing the positions of the airplane's fuel supply valves on the cockpit side wall adjacent to his position. By design, the engine's supply valves and fuel crossfeed valves were positioned electrically in response to inputs from switches on the copilot's fuel control panel, with the position of the valves being displayed on small indicators, one for each valve, and adjacent to its controlling switch. The indicators were designed to display, 'ON', 'OFF', or a 'CROSSHATCH' indication if the valve was in transit from one position to another.*

*'I was dumbfounded and alarmed to observe these fuel valve position indicators, despite no cockpit inputs, clicking in a random pattern across the four engines from 'OFF', to 'CROSSHATCH', to 'ON'. 'It must be the indicating circuits,' I announced, and to confirm my hopes quickly checked the fuel pressure warning lights on the engine instrument panel in front of us because these fuel system lights operated from entirely different circuitry, but they too were blinking 'ON' and 'OFF', in the same random pattern as the valve position indicators.*

*'New Orleans, our last land point prior to heading across the Gulf of Mexico, was not far ahead. It was midnight and we didn't know with this crazy fuel system whether we could keep the engines running, or not. We eased over toward the shoreline and quickly called New Orleans traffic control appraising them of our problems. If it became necessary to ditch we would put the airplane down close to the sandy beach, rather than in the Louisiana swamps.*

*'One thing was sure, after our engine icing problems of the preceding evening, should engines now flame out due to lack of fuel, as the fuel supply valve went through their crazy cycle, we were at least now well acquainted with the necessity for relight within 15 seconds, the ten second countdown procedure and the penalties involved should we not adhere to the five minute drain requirement. We were at 28,000 feet and the lights of New Orleans at last appeared far ahead, then crept ever so slowly toward us.*

*'We were spring loaded for the engine relight procedure and watched tail pipe temperatures and the fuel valve indicators very closely, while trying to dig out New Orleans airport and approach charts. Neither of us had ever landed there. Twice the airplane pulled hard to the left, but before we could get under way with the relight countdown procedure the engine relit itself as fuel supply was luckily restored by the opening and closing valves. We clung to our altitude and we were both very busy and the cockpit and main cabin got very hot because the air conditioning panel near the copilot was not receiving its required normal attention.*

*'At last we pinpointed the lights of the airport far, far below with the runways outlined in white, green and red lights. The airplane was positioned directly over the field before gingerly reducing power and starting a spiralling descent, keeping the airport in sight close on the left and within no engines gliding range. The valves and lights of the fuel system continued their crazy cycle and as we descended she pulled softly to the right and the tail pipe temperatures indicted No. 4 engine was flaming out, but as we began the engine relight countdown she came back in as fuel was re-supplied.*

*'As we got lower we could see that all of the airport runway lights were now on and the tower cleared us to land unrestricted on any runway. The evening winds were light as we lined up for a steep power off approach to the longest runway and delayed flap and gear extension until certain we could make it even should all four engines flame out. I was scared and ready for anything and totally unsure of what might happen next.*

*'As we neared the runway threshold, ahead in the night alongside the runway flashed the lights of the airport's waiting emergency equipment and fire trucks. As we touched down they sped up, trailing close behind us down the runway as I reversed the pitch of the big propellers and applied the wheel brakes. Should there be any flameouts now, we were at least safe on the ground, and let the engines quit.*

*'Except for the airplane's very warm cabin we were all right and their job done, we dismissed the emergency trucks and thanked them. As we taxied to the ramp area, and then past the tower, the men silhouetted there peered down on us. Which radio voice that we had been communicating with, went with which of the figures silhouetted up there, I did not know, but I opened the cockpit side window as we rolled past and waved while radioing our thanks for their help during the last many hectic minutes.*

*'Our sweltering passengers were off-loaded as we finished our cockpit chores. A few minutes later as we left the cockpit and stepped into the main cabin I was most disturbed to find a soaking wet forward cabin floor with streams of water dripping from the airplane's ceiling. Then, as we descended the stairway to the airport ramp, large puddles could be seen beneath the airplane just aft of the nose landing gear, glistening in the glare of the ramp floodlights, where water was dripping heavily from the plane's belly.*

*'The airplane's forward drinking water supply tank was located in the main cabin ceiling and unfortunately positioned directly over the main electronic bay although far below in the forward belly. The tank had sprung a leak and shorted out the fuel system operating circuitry located in the electronic bay.*

*'Following our night glide from 28,000 feet a platoon of factory technical people were flown up to New Orleans, and then after two days of very extensive checking the airplane was ferried back to Mexico City where it was bedded down in the hangar for another ten days of tests and modifications.*

*'At the completion, and for in-flight evaluations, a combined test and training flight was scheduled and because I had been there at the time of the fuel feed problems, I was asked to accompany them as an observer. For a couple of hours, the fuel system, its shutoffs and its crossfeeds were carefully and systematically wrung out, and under all possible conditions the system now functioned perfectly.*

*'As the tests progressed we worked our way northward to Brownsville, Texas, at that time the nearest airport to Mexico City with an instrument landing system. The fuel tests completed, it was planned to then do some badly needed ILS training with several Aeronaves pilots that were aboard. The first approach, however, was to be an auto-coupled approach during which the autopilot automatically tracked the ILS glide slope and localiser beams.*

*'As we had just done with fuel system, the auto-pilot also was to be thoroughly tested prior to release of the airplane back to the line, because up until the night preceding there had been a long-standing restriction against its use at altitudes below 10,000 feet, the reason being that the autopilot was strongly suspect in an earlier accident in Britain. At the factory extensive changes to the autopilot circuitry had been made, with the modified unit arriving in Mexico City the night preceding our flight. Slipping this new black box into the radio rack and connecting the electrical Cannon plugs removed the 10,000-foot restriction.*

*'In the autopilot section of the Aircraft's Operating Manual, was a statement in big black letters, 'WHEN ENGAGED, THE AUTO-PILOT CAN NOT BE OVERPOWERED BY THE PILOTS.' I must say that such design philosophy was different from Yankee thinking on this subject.*

*'Following our fuel system evaluations I left the cockpit. In a few more minutes, as the training crew in the cockpit prepared for the planned auto-pilot controlled ILS descent to the runway, the airplane was turned outbound on the ILS system at 1500 feet. When it was time to engage the autopilot the autopilot switch was positioned to 'Engage', but I learned afterward that the switch would not stay in the engaged position. After a few checks were made it was tried again, but to no avail because preventative circuitry continued doing its job. A third try was then made and this time it seemed to say, 'OK boys, if that's what you want!' and applied full left aileron and locked it there.*

*'In response, the airplane quickly rolled into a very steep bank causing a sideslip at a very high rate toward the fast-rising ground. In the cockpit, the combined strength of the two pilots at the controls was unable to overpower the displaced and locked ailerons in order to level the wings, and actuation of the auto-pilot disengage buttons on the control wheels and the engage/disengage switch on the auto-pilot pedestal control module had no effect. Aft, in the main cabin I was unable to imagine what was happening and hung on for dear life.*

*'Bill Daniels, a Miami-based instructor with more schooling and experience on the airplane than any of us, had been observing the training in progress from the rear of the cockpit. From this position Bill clawed his way over other observers and crew, cutting the master electrical gang bar on the overhead panel, thereby, completely removing electrical power from all of the airplane. The autopilot at last released the locked controls and a wobbly recovery was effected a few hundred feet above the trees.*

*'As things simmered down, explanations made, and brows mopped in relief, a representative of the auto-pilot company moved to the radio rack, loosened the retaining screws and removed the 'new and improved' unit. He then walked aft to where I was sitting and placed it on the main cabin floor. At this point I suggested, and he agreed, perhaps we should heave it out the back door.*

*'Nobody now felt like doing any more training so the airplane was headed back to Mexico City. We landed and taxyed up to the airline's hangar where a stairway was rolled to the forward entry door and at this juncture, I picked up my battered flight bag, strode the length of the cabin, out the main cabin door, down the stairway, across the hangar ramp, then trudged a mile and a half across the airport, its runways, and its taxy strips in the hot sun to the airline terminal building.*

*'I never looked back once, I had had enough of this crazy airplane in the past few weeks and with my own money bought a ticket for a flight that night back home to New York, aboard a good old Eastern Airlines Yankee built Douglas DC-7.*

*'Although the airline eventually possessed three of these airplanes, they just couldn't keep them in the air. Operations were later resumed but with a Douglas DC-7 leased from Pan American and I was asked to come back and flew several months in this Yankee-built, wonderful flying airplane, which did the work of three airplanes. Over the years I have done considerable training with British airline pilots and I have often heard them state that no one can build an airplane like the Americans, and they are right!*

Author: I get the feeling that this guy was not too impressed with our beautiful Whispering Giant.

CHAPTER SIX

# Settling In

The major routine task for the Britannia fleet was going to be the support of our garrisons in the Middle and Far East; an aircraft would leave Lyneham daily to fly to Singapore. To begin with, this was via Libya, Aden, the Maldive Islands in the Indian Ocean and then to the Royal Air Force station on Singapore Island, adjacent to the notorious wartime gaol - Changi.

**Proving flight**

It was, therefore natural, that one of the first proving flights should be along this 'Changi Route'. This took place from 6th to 17th July 1959, combining aircrew training with the familiarisation of ground crew. One difference from previous aircraft, commented on by Chief Technician Brian Kneen, waiting at El Adem to be indoctrinated into the mysteries of the new

Captain Bill Robinson, heavily disguised, manipulates the starting controls. The helmet and mask are discussed later. (*Bill Robinson*)

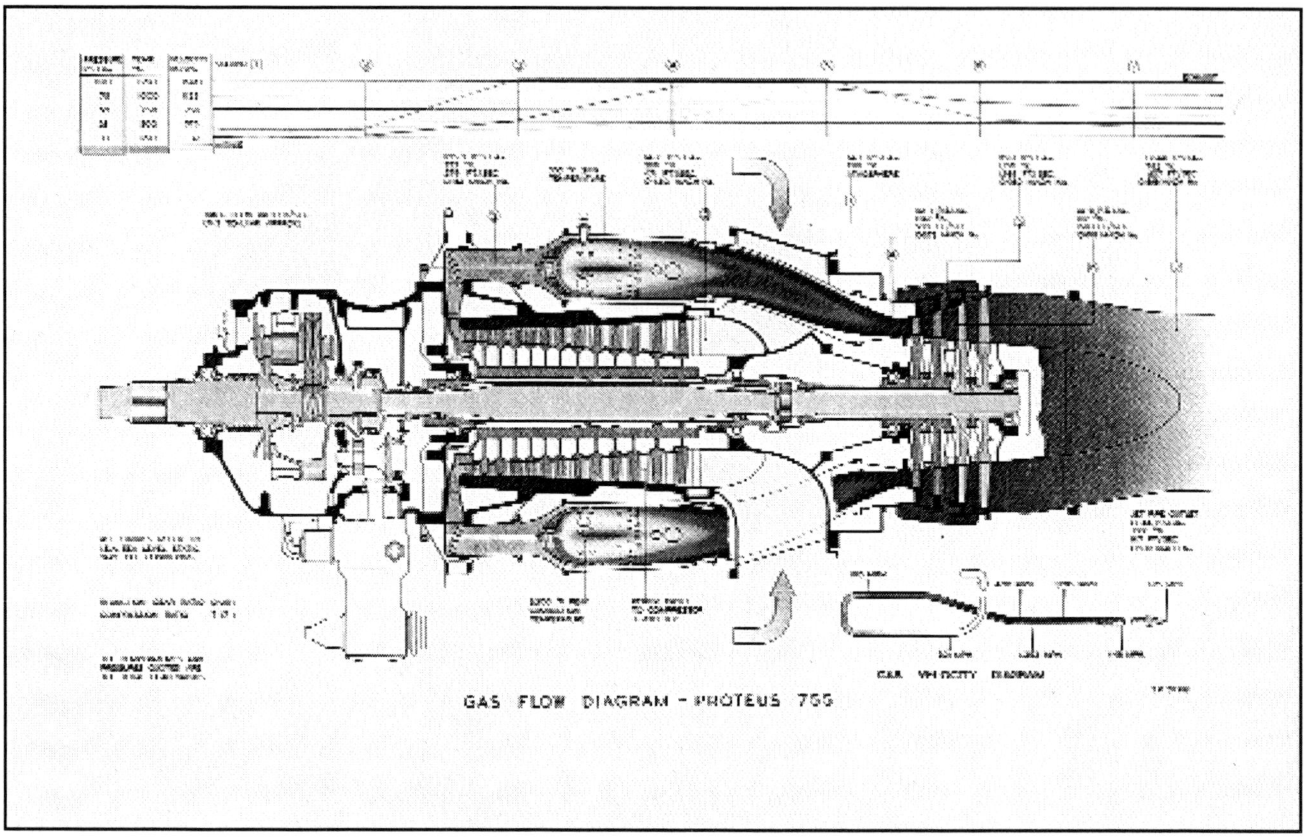


The Proteus gas flow diagram.

machine, was the start-up procedure where, contrary to all previous propeller practice, the starter crew had to hold them until the start sequence had been initiated.

**The free turbine Proteus**

It perhaps should be explained that the Proteus was a free turbine engine, the propeller and its turbine were completely independent of the engine and its turbine. This was achieved by the shaft of the former rotating within that of the latter. Thus, when the propeller brake had been released, the propeller (and its turbine) could rotate entirely independently of the engine compressor. This situation could cause a problem with a strong wind from behind the aircraft, for it was possible, with the propeller acting just like a windmill, for it to rotate in the wrong direction prior to the engine starting. This could give rise to a failure of a quill shaft in the starter motor. The ground crew, therefore, were trained to hold the propeller stationary until the starting sequence had commenced. This gradually led to ‘macho’ performances of really hanging on until the compressor well and truly ‘bit’! Interpreting the remarks of one of my correspondents, some airmen believed that the longer they held on, the bigger the flame that would belch from the tail pipe of the engine. I am sorry to disappoint them after all these years. That flame was due to over enthusiastic ‘blipping’ by the captain on the fuel starter pump during the start.

It is interesting to reflect how much manual manipulation there was in the starting sequence in the Britannia. Sophistication in later aircraft meant ‘Press the button, sit back and wait’!

In this period, Lyneham was a considerable centre of attention. A party of Peers and MPs visited the station on 7th September 1959.

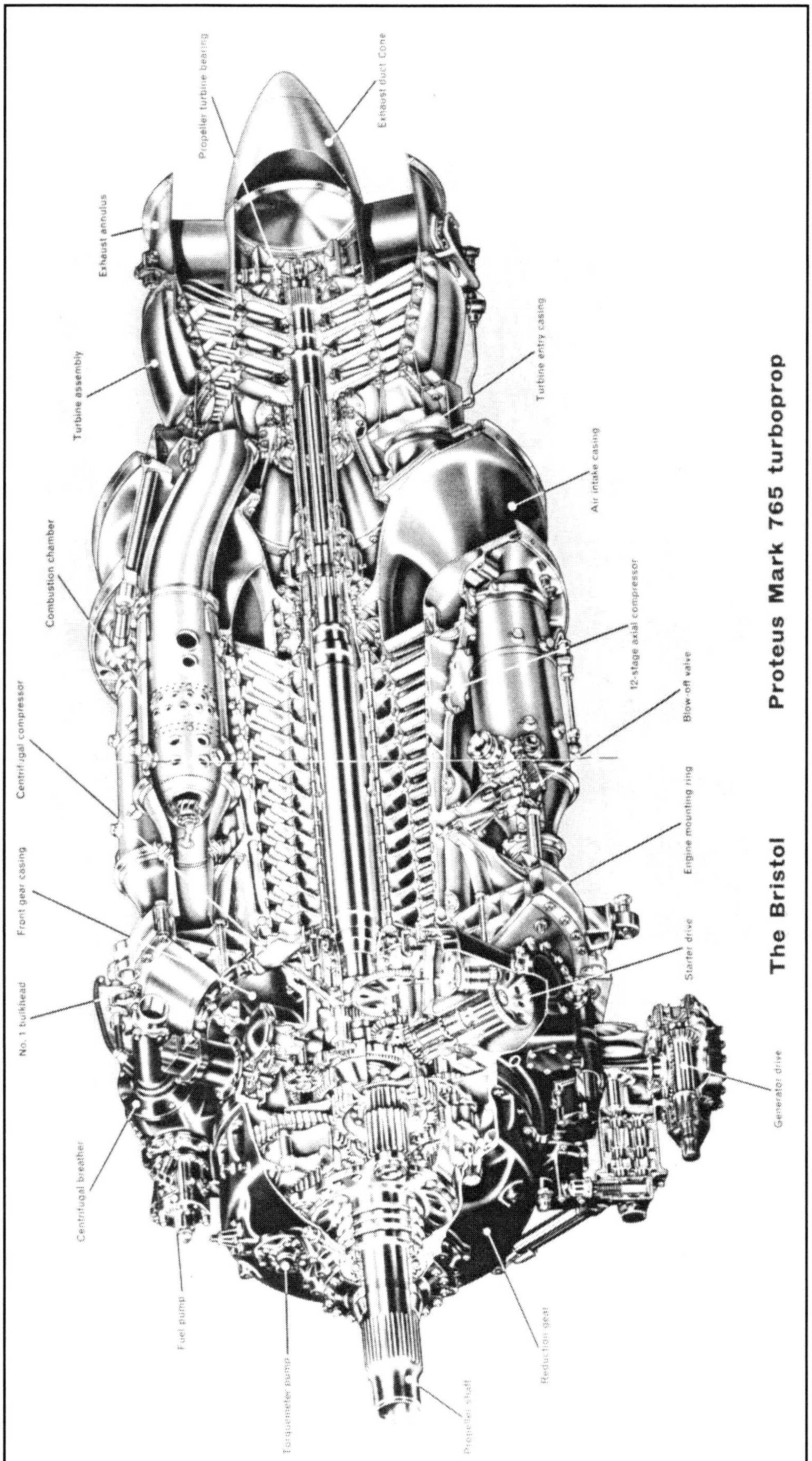


**The Bristol Proteus Mark 765 turboprop**

**Viewed by Lord Louis**

Factory delivery continued through the summer of 1959, XL637 and XL638 followed their pathfinding brother 636. A measure of the novelty (and pride?) in the RAF's new acquisition can be assessed by the events of 3rd September. XL638, especially cleaned and polished, flew to Cranwell to be present for the Chief of Staffs of the Commonwealth Forces' annual conference.

The aircraft inspection was led by Admiral of the Fleet, Lord Louis Mountbatten of Burma, the chairman of the committee. (Some years later he was to complete his last official duty with the assistance of a Britannia). Lord Louis was followed by a train of generals, admirals and air marshals of Britain, Canada, Ghana, Australia, Pakistan, Malaya and others. In all, 125 very senior officers inspected the aircraft and questioned the crew. This perhaps can be seen as the prologue to the drama that was to be enacted in the next 16 years which, in some way, would involve the Britannia and all those countries - and many others.

It is an insight into the pressure of those times that, after the visitors had departed, the aircraft left for Lyneham to carry out a night flying training detail.

**New Zealand saga**

XL637, not to be outshone, was slipping away to Australia under the command of Squadron Leader Peter Gray. The purpose was to support, in some style, the Valiant bombers from RAF Wittering attending the Queensland centenary celebrations. Antipodean excursions continued with another Britannia XL638 flying to New Zealand in support of three Vulcans for the opening of the new International Airport, Rongati. The aircraft was captained by Flight Lieutenant Harry Liddell who was to have a long standing training role on the aircraft. He has described, in great detail, this most memorable of trips:

*'Early in the morning of 21st October 1959 Britannia XL638 climbed slowly away from Darwin's damp heat, setting its nose south eastwards for the long haul to Ohakea in New Zealand's North Island. A euphoric mood pervaded the flight deck, and not only because Darwin was a good place to leave; we were on the final stage of our long flight from the UK to NZ,*

The interest that a Britannia visit generated can be judged by these photographs. The Britannia captain is Flt Lt Chick Adams. (*Bill Robinson*)

Wellington Airport November 1959 - XL638 plus Beverley. (*Harry Liddell*)

Author: It is appropriate to reproduce Harry Liddell's comment accompanying his photographs, which appear in this chapter and elsewhere:

*'The two NZ photos have not aged as well as the others, probably because they were Agfa rather than Ektachrome and also were in cardboard frames, which had fallen apart; the Ektachrome ones were in plastic frames which kept them sealed between the glass sandwich.'*

Nevertheless, they have been used in this book, enhanced as much as possible, as have other less than perfect images. In spite of this, they do provide a useful and interesting record - sometimes a social one viz the 1950s' Air Day dress of the gentleman above!

*a leisurely schedule wished on us by the 617 Squadron detachment whose ground crew we carried on this first global flight by a RAF Britannia. Already the original three Vulcans had dwindled to two following an absurd attempt by one of their pilots to land at Karachi without using his drag 'chute. The consequent bogie fire right outside the terminal provided a Peter Sellers type comedy act as the local fire brigade attempted, unsuccessfully, to extinguish the blaze, eventually doused by a crew chief using a hand extinguisher.*

*'Scenically the route was boring; long hours of desert followed by the Tasman Sea, so first sight of Mount Egmont's volcanic cone above the horizon gave glad tidings of journey's end. Ohakea is situated on a rich agricultural plain about 100 miles south east of the mountain, not far from the west coast, and is one of the RNZAF's main bases; the weather was gin clear, and so it was not long before we touched down on its lengthy runway. Unusually, it appeared to be made of hexagonal concrete panels neatly fitting into each other in the manner of parquet flooring, a form of construction I have never encountered elsewhere; however, it was less satisfactory than it looked, being incredibly bumpy.*

*'During the approach there had been comment on the countryside's lush appearance, and on leaving the aircraft one's nostrils were assailed by a powerful aroma of fresh cut grass with more than a hint of clover; delicious almost beyond belief, and giving some reason as to why the country's meat and dairy products are so toothsome. On the personal level we were greeted in an equally welcoming manner, receiving profuse apologies for the accommodation offered and being given a rundown on the programme for our 12-day stay. Now the primary reason for our visit was attendance at the forthcoming grand opening of Wellington's new airport, in addition to Vulcans and our Britannia there was an RAF Comet 2, a Beverley from Singapore, a contingent from the USAF and (I think) the RAAF also. As for accommodation, due to the large number of visiting crews it was necessary to house us, dormitory-style, in huts; not ideal but the weather was fairly benign and anyway in those days we were younger and less particular. There was little alternative, as the area was very rural and hotels virtually non-existent.*

*'At this distance of almost 35 years I cannot recall the exact chronological sequence of events, but my log book tells me that two days after arrival the entire RAF contingent boarded Beverley XN104 (Captain Flt Lt John Grobler) for the brief flight to Wellington. Officially this was for the formal greeting by the mayor and corporation at the town hall, but it also afforded a valuable preview of the airfield for those of us who were to partake in the display a couple of days later. For me there was a further attraction; my parents were on a world cruise, and their ship the 'Southern Cross' was due to sail from Wellington that very day. Taking a taxi from the airport direct to the docks I was disappointed to find the Blue Peter hoisted and visitors streaming ashore; however the officials kind-heartedly allowed me on board for half an hour or so, time enough for a happy reunion over some stiff gins, and as I finally stepped off the gangplank, dockworkers were waiting to pull it away. Unable to see the ship depart as I was already late for the town hall beano, it was another taxi for an event of which I remember next to nothing (memory failure not booze). Climbing away in the Beverley sometime after dark, I noticed a large ship well down the harbour*

Flight Lieutenant Harry Liddell, the captain of the New Zealand flight. There are a couple of things to note in this photograph - apart from the subject! Behind Harry's head there are four switches which control the propeller turbine over-speed limiters. These were fitted after the incident with the prototype G-ALRX which resulted in it force-landing on the banks of the River Severn. This photograph must have been taken above 10,000 feet as the switches are in the 'Down' position! This selection reduced the sensitivity of the system. Also note Harry's headset - the bulbous sort, which is discussed later. (*Harry Liddell*)

*inlet on its way to the open sea; probably the 'Southern Cross' again.*

*'Next day we positioned XL638 to Wellington for the Open Day and its associated flying display, and perhaps this is a convenient point to say something about the city's rather unique airport. The local topography can only be described as hostile to all forms of transport: the harbour, although an excellent natural shelter, has a tricky entrance from the dreaded Cook Straight with no shortage of jagged rocks on the way in; early railway builders had great difficulty in laying out workable grades, and in later years much track alignment became necessary; local motorists get plenty of practice in hill climbing; while providing an airport was so difficult that for decades there was none, and the country's capital had to make do with Palmerston North, many miles distant.*

*'With the development of air transport this became an insupportable nuisance, and eventually a small general aviation airfield was increased to its maximum permissible dimensions and dubbed 'Wellington International'. Situated on an isthmus connecting the city to a lumpy island jutting into the harbour, the runway was a bare 6,000ft long or perhaps even a shade less; further extension would only have been possible by building into the harbour, a ruinously expensive project as the runway is about 50ft above mean sea level anyway. Indeed, on my only subsequent visit many years later nothing had changed but whether or not it has since been lengthened I do not know. So what with the surrounding high ground, steep drops immediately off both thresholds of an undesirably short runway plus Wellington's notoriously wet and windy weather, it bid fair to rival the old Kai Tak as one of the world's less enticing airports. All this is of some significance in view of events to follow.*

*'For the night of the 24th our crew was lodged with various families, and I found myself in an attractive modern house overlooking the city where I was pampered and over-fed by my hospitable middle-aged*

638 with nose art courtesy of RNZAF, (*Harry Liddell*)

*hosts. Next day our sequence was due fairly early in the day's events and had already been cleared with the airport authorities. As I recall, we made flypasts at low level, one slow with everything hanging down and one fast; this latter at Vne and then throttles to idle approaching the airfield, thus providing a silent passage in contrast to the din of the jets. Aided by low all-up weight the landing was satisfyingly short, and by remaining in reverse after coming to rest the Britannia's backwards taxying capability was convincingly demonstrated to the appreciation of a large crowd.*

*'With this over I was free to watch the larger part of the programme yet to follow. For the locals, one of the highlights was to be the Vulcan display which it was hoped would terminate with a full stop landing. Normally the runway would have been considered a bit on the short side, but given the aircraft's low fuel load and the typically Wellington weather itself, a gusty breeze, fortunately from the north and straight down the runway, no problem was anticipated in stopping the aircraft with the aid of a drag 'chute.*

*'The Vulcan duly appeared, following its sequence with a couple of roller landings; the second of which was nicely judged and could easily have become a full-stop had the 'chute been streamed. But rather to my surprise the throttles went forward again and the B1 climbed away for a third arrival, the PA system announcing that this would be the final landing. Right from the start the approach looked wrong, very draggy and far too flat, and I watched with increasing unease, well aware that the vertical distance between the pilot's eye level and his main wheels was far greater than usual given the very high angle of attack; a dangerous trap in view of his excessively flat approach. It became patently obvious that even if he made the runway it would be a very close run thing, and I willed him to take remedial action before it was too late; in vain, for a shower of dirt flew up as the main wheels touched in the short under-run and as the aircraft decelerated it tilted increasingly to the left, the main leg's drag link fractured due to the bogie impacting the runway's raised lip.*

*'With nil support on the port side the stricken Vulcan continued its leftward's veer, which I saw to my horror would take it into the public enclosure. Just in time, with wing tip almost scraping the hard stuff, one correct decision was taken and the throttles slammed forward so that it roared back into the air with fuel streaming from a ruptured tank. Apprehensively I watched clouds of kerosene swirl about in the jet efflux, and waited for the seemingly inevitable explosion which thankfully never came; however had the fuel been JP4 rather than Avtur it might well have been a different story.*

*'The display continued, in fact the RNZAF seemed determined to provide the crowd with further thrills when one of their Sunderlands made an extremely low pass; pushing his luck somewhat I thought, watching it disappear momentarily behind a low building between me and the runway. However its tail fin remained visible, and I was intrigued to notice that it suddenly dipped out of sight and then reappeared a second or two later. There followed some rather excitable comment from the PA, which I failed to pick up, but subsequently I learned that the flying boat had encountered what old timers would call an air pocket and thus scraped its keel on the runway. This had somehow started a fire in the bilges, and following futile in-flight attempts at extinguishment during the flight back to its Auckland base the pilot alighted as near*

Interest in the RAF Britannia warranted a picture postcard! (*Ian Lansdowne*)

*to the shore as possible in hope of reaching a slipway before foundering; in which he was unsuccessful, thus depleting his air force of one of its few remaining Sunderlands. Altogether the airport's opening could only be considered somewhat inauspicious, although the crowd had the benefit of some unscheduled thrills at no extra cost (to them).*

*'At the end of the day we ferried XL638 back to Ohakea where the crippled Vulcan squatted ignominiously on the grass, its pilot having to some extent redeemed himself by carrying out a well executed arrival on nose and right legs only. Six days retained of our sojourn in NZ, however I cannot remember why so much time had been allowed but fancy that the delayed arrival of a replacement Vulcan might have had something to do with it; for them the whole global flight was some sort of exercise. We had no complaints, for there was a pressing invitation from a local farmer we had met at some local function.*

*'I think we were first introduced to Pat Gilebrist at some hospitality function in the local farmers' club, to which we were later invited to return on a more casual basis. This was of course long before the Antipodean nations liberalised their drinking laws, the basic and very dismal pub offering only the horrors of the notorious 'six o'clock swill'; thus the facility of a private club was more than welcome. To comply with the law it was not possible to order individual drinks over the bar; instead, members had their private lockers (it was of course a male only club) in which were kept such bottles as they themselves supplied, the barkeep's sole function being to provide glasses and ice. Again, memory fails me as to how we managed to stand our round under such a system, but suspect that bottles were obtained from the officers' mess and passed on (probably illegally) to our friends.*

*'Anyway, Pat invited several of us to stay overnight on his sheep farm some miles away. Fairly remote, with only a couple of other farms distantly visible, by UK standards of those days the house was luxurious to a degree and the farm itself looked very well equipped. Some friends had been invited to the evening meal and we were promised a good feast of local produce, but in the event pre-dinner drinking went on so long that the excellent joint of meat was done to a frazzle by the time we got to the table. Local hospitality being what it was, this was unfortunately not the only occasion when similar waste of good food took place; I fear that New Zealand women of that era had to put up with a lot!*

*'As a gesture of appreciation for all that had been done for us, on the 28th, XL638 provided a two hour tour of local sights that included Mount Egmont and Lake Taupo among other attractions; it also enabled us to thoroughly check the aircraft and its equipment prior to the long flight home via the Pacific and USA. For all but a very few of our passengers this was their first flight in a turbine-engined aircraft of any description, so they were much taken*

*with the Britannia's smoothness and relative silence. Particularly impressive was the demonstration of standing a coin on edge in order to show the lack of vibration, however it did help to use a coin with a good edge; we also ensured a slight and surreptitious increase of the prop rpm prior to the demo!*

*'Our final event was to be part of the static line-up at Ohakeal's own open day, where XL638 attracted much interest and favourable comment as the largest and newest aircraft on show; all day long a straggling queue waited for their turn to have a look inside. The flying display was without incident, although the only thing I do recall was one of the USAF visitors going supersonic by request, which shows how long ago it was. It was less exciting than might be imagined, because in those far off days very few aircraft were able to exceed Mach 1 in level flight and so it was necessary for him to climb to a vast height and then dive towards us from afar; all we knew of it was a loud double bang, the aircraft remained invisible!*

*'Bidding farewell! to me on the first day of November, the Station Commander bade us to return 'at any time; you guys are always welcome, but for pity's sake leave that other ...'*

Harry Liddell's copilot, Flt Lt Pete Burgess. He later converted to the left-hand seat and subsequently became an instructor/examiner on Air Training Squadron (Britannia), ATS(B). (*Harry Liddell*)

Author: The 'Blue Pencil' has been used here but it is by a mutual agreement between Harry and myself. It is not for us, certainly at this distance in time, to denigrate another organisation.

*'... This was not only the first proper route trip for any of us in a Britannia, it was also the first lengthy flight of any description undertaken by a RAF specimen. The aircraft performed flawlessly, the only problem that I recall being one with flap selection that was rectified outbound at Akrotiri. At that time the familiar rigid procedure for use of cowl heat had not yet been formulated, and the only guidance we had was to use it (as I recall) in 'visible icing conditions'. Luckily we encountered no such conditions during the entire circumnavigation, which was probably just as well; even EGV heat had only been used once or twice. Also, the engine problems that were to come in the New Year lay in the future, so we were spared having to drag our way round the world at a miserable 11350 rpm even if we were limited to 11500. The crew were:*

Gp Capt Joe Barnard,
Flt Lt John Holf (Eng),
Flt Lt Pete Burgess (Co),
F S McCarthy,
Flt Lt Cyril Lougheed (Nav)
Sgt Kierney (Paddy?),
Flt Lt Pete Jordan (Sig),
Sgt Taylor

*'I apologise if I have missed anyone, but these are the only names in my logbook. Joe Barnard (the first CO of 99) had been in post so long awaiting the aircraft's delayed introduction into service that he was by this time virtually tour ex, and had anyway recently been promoted to Group Captain; this was, I think, his only proper route flight on the Britannia!'*

In all this can be sensed the pride of possession of these new aircraft and the Britannia, with its good looks, would certainly have sustained such feelings.

**More memories of the NZ flight**

Publication of Harry Liddell's account in the Britannia Association magazine prompted responses from other members. Signaller Ian Lewis wrote:

*'I was fascinated to read the article 'A New Zealand Saga' ... At that time I was a Corporal Fitter based at Travis Air Force Base, theoretically servicing RAF aircraft transiting through California on the*

*way to and from Christmas Island on the 'Grapple' atomic bomb tests. In fact there was very little to do and I spent seven months acclimatising, working as a migratory fruit picker, serving gas and, finally, endeavouring to sell the most unbelievably expensive sets of stainless steel and copper pots and pans. It was clear in November 1959 that our operation at Travis was coming to an end and since my first child had been born a month or so previously in the UK, I was itching to get home.*

*'Imagine my delight, therefore, when my CO said, 'Put down your soldering iron and hitch a lift on that Britannia.' It was the one on the journey back from NZ. The article describes some of the frustrations and delays of working back to the UK, through Offut, Goose Bay and Scampton but it was, nevertheless, a most impressive flight as far as I was concerned. Little did I imagine that, six years later, I would be operating as a signaller on the same aircraft. 'New Zealand Saga' brought back a host of pleasant memories which had lain dormant for many years and is yet another example of the tremendous impact of this brilliant magazine!'*

By a coincidence yet another person recalls that very flight. Corporal David Taylor was serving at RAAF Butterworth at the time:

*'I was with 110 Squadron. When the circus arrived I, naturally, wandered over to look around, the Britannia and Vulcan being much more interesting than the Whirlwind HAR1. It was aboard the Britannia that I encountered an ex-colleague of 18th Entry, Cosford, who was carrying out the instrument checks. We got talking, and it was then that I first learnt of Mobile Servicing Flight, Lyneham. This is for me, thought I, so when repatriation came around, I listed Lyneham as my first choice. My aim being successful, I then set out to wangle my way on to this unique flight and was again rewarded with success. Who says it never pays to volunteer! Now followed the most rewarding three years of my service and a better bunch of guys you couldn't hope to meet anywhere. Not just MSF but also the crews we flew with.'*

**The Five Eleventh**

So far, 99 Squadron had carried the Britannia flag alone, but now it was to be joined by the resurrected 511 Squadron, their companions-to-be in Britannia flying for the next 15 years.

*'511's history commenced at RAF Lyneham on 10th October 1942, equipped with Liberator transport aircraft engaged in the carriage of passengers and freight to and from Gibraltar, Malta and the Middle East.'* A Britannia of 511 follows that tradition. *(David Berry)*

On 15th December 1959, 511 Squadron was reformed. There was a parade at which the Managing Director of the Bristol Aircraft Company formally handed over XM517 to the new Squadron Commander, Wing Commander A W G Le Hardy OBE.

Eighty year-old Air Chief Marshal Sir Frederick Bowhill who had, 15 years previously, as AOC-in-C Transport Command, presented the squadron with its badge on behalf of HM The King, bestowed it again. It is reported that he gave a stirring address during which he reminded members of the restored squadron of some of the unit's past.

511's history commenced at RAF Lyneham on 10th October 1942, equipped with Liberator transport aircraft engaged in the carriage of passengers and freight to and from Gibraltar, Malta and the Middle East. There then followed a distinguished war record in the transport role. Post-war saw the squadron continuing in this work with their Yorks. Following the Berlin Air Lift, 1948-49, they converted to Hastings.

Their history is then marked with such occurrences as Shallufa in the Canal

German Officers leading advance party:— (*left to right*) — Capt. Smidt Rosemann (German Navy), Lt. Klaus Neumann, Capt. Horst Naumann, Capt. Helmuth Panter, Capt. Kurt Altenburger and 2nd Lt. Klaus Steuer (Interpreter).

Wing Commander Le Hardy, acting Station Commander, greeting Capt. Helmuth Panter.

Wind Commander A W G Le Hardy OBE was the first CO of 511 Squadron on it being reformed. Here he is seen with two German officers on a visit to Lyneham. (*Lyneham Globe*)

Zone for the bomber squadrons annual bombing exercises - schedules to the Far East - Fayid on standby connected with the Abadan oil situation - re-deployment of Middle East land forces resulting from Egypt's abrogation of the 1936 treaty - Mau Mau Kenya - airlifting ex-POWs from Korea - Suez 1956 - EOKA 1957 - Jordan and Lebanon crises - Christmas Island. All this, of course, punctuated with the normal features of air transport work - mercy missions, casualty evacuations, VIP flights and the like.

In May 1957, the squadron moved to RAF Colerne where, on 1st September 1958, it was renumbered No.36 Squadron. So 511, as such, had hibernated for a while, to be aroused and equipped with an aircraft that would enable its members to match the squadron motto, '*Surely and Quickly*'!

**Large lift**

In an aircraft's early days, breaking of new ground is going to be a newsworthy item. The Britannia was to be no exception. Thus it was that '*The Lyneham Globe*', the station's newspaper, had the headline, '*Large Lift by Britannia*':

'*During the period 8th to 14th December 1959, a Britannia (Spec 6040), captained by Flying Officer Whiteight and Pilot Officer Haley, transported 1,231 passengers between Lyneham - Luqa - Idris - El Adem - Alconbury. An interesting feature of this operation was that 1,179 of those passengers were moved in 11 flights.*'

This news item speaks volumes, demonstrating the intention of using the potential of the Britannia to the full. Arithmetic gives that 107+ passengers must have been carried on each of the flights. The capacity of the cabin is given, in the

Some 'technical difficulty' down the route. (*Peter Hobson*)

Britannia Pilots' Notes, as 108 passengers at 39 inch pitch (distance between the seats, fore and aft) and 113 troops at 36 inch pitch. So this operation was done on or near to limits.

Imagine how loads like this must have seemed after the Hastings.

**Around the world**

The first round-the-world (in eight days!) took place between 16th and 23rd December. XL638 was captained by Flight Lieutenants 'Rip' Kerbey and Tom Goddard. The latter established a reputation over the years for taking a teapot on route with him and, if it was a bit chilly, flying in his raincoat ! The route was Nicosia, Karachi, Changi, Darwin, Fiji to Christmas Island. Here, happy tour-ex servicemen, from this nuclear bomb test site, boarded with the prospect of being home in time for Christmas. The aircraft was suitably decorated for the occasion by the crew! The route home was via Vancouver, Montreal, to Lyneham. All this done in eight days - another example of using the aircraft to its limits, acknowledged by the media, as its return to base was covered by TV and the national press.

**A significant year ends**

So concluded 1959, the inauguration year for the Royal Air Force Britannia. In it can be detected the difficulties and the challenges. But it can be sensed that there was a real pride in the Service of its new possession. But underneath the glamour was a gritty intention to use this new tool to the maximum.

The next year was to see that determination being put to the test.

From Harry Liddell's album - four photographs taken on a Far Eastern route trainer, August 1959.

404 is at Gan.

Alf Musgrove and Don West boarding.

The newness of 404 is evident from this view of the galley.

Elegant passenger step provision had not kept up with shiny aircraft acquisition!

CHAPTER SEVEN

# The Start of the 60s

The year 1960 commenced with appropriate anticipation of what was to come. Work started on the new Terminal Building at RAF Lyneham (to cost what can seem a curious figure now, £135,000!). It housed, under one roof, Operations, Customs and passenger handling. The Station Commander, whose office on RAF stations had, traditionally, been in the administrative area, was to be put on the 'Ship's Bridge', on the upper floor overlooking the aircraft.

This was all part of a rebuilding programme at Lyneham. A new Officers' Mess and Airmens' Restaurant had already been completed, as well as new Barrack Blocks, revolutionary for their day with single rooms. Planned for the future were a new Sergeants' Mess, Medical Centre and Passenger Hotel. This activity, and the way it ceaselessly continued over the years, prompted the regular comment that, '*Lyneham will be great - when it's finished!*'

**Lyneham Airfield**

The seed of Lyneham as an airfield was sown back in the late 1930s when the area was surveyed for possible use as storage for the increasing number of Royal Air Force aircraft. This came to fruition in May 1940 with the completion of the buildings and the establishment of No.33 Maintenance Unit. It subsequently became the lodger unit as flying units moved in. The first of these was No.14 Service Flying Training School, with Airspeed Oxfords, in 1941, for the advanced flying training of

POINTER TO PROGRESS

The nose of "Pegasus" points towards the new £135,000 Passenger Terminal. Work on this building, which began early this year, is expected to be completed by March, 1961.

*The Lyneham Globe* updates readers on the progress with the Terminal Building construction. (*Lyneham Globe*)

A remarkable photograph - Lyneham with not an aeroplane in sight! (*Lyneham Globe*)

RAF and Commonwealth pilots. The stay was short-lived with a move to Ossington and their replacement by various Ferry Training Units. This started Lyneham in its role of being a gateway to the world with the ferry units operating out of and into the UK. This overseas involvement was strengthened with the arrival of BOAC in 1943. They used Lyneham as a terminal from then until 1945. As a result, Mr Winston Churchill was a frequent visitor, to be flown by BOAC or by 511 Squadron, who were now present with their Liberator aircraft. The transport tradition became firmly established in 1944 with the arrival of 525 Squadron with Vickers Warwick transports and on the transfer of the Ferry Training Unit to Pershore.

After the war, the transport role continued with the delivery of Avro Yorks for the squadrons and it was with these that a full part was played in the Berlin Airlift. The next generation of transports, the Hastings, duly appeared, along with additional

Until the move to RAF Brize Norton in 1970, the Britannias shared RAF Lyneham with 216 Squadron. One of their Comet 4Cs is pictured outside the new Terminal Building. (*Bill Robinson*)

The atmosphere of the preparation of a Britannia for a route departure has been totally captured here. 520 occupies the spot, to the west of the Terminal Building, traditionally reserved for the daily 'Changi Slip' (Singapore) aircraft. Note the aircraft's raised freight door and the load on a 'scissors truck'. Black propellers indicate that this is an early photo as does the absence of barrack blocks in the far background. The second Britannia is being loaded using a Britannia Freight Lift Platform (BFLP); this is a later topic. *(Peter Hicks/Rolls Royce Heritage Trust, Bristol Branch)*

squadrons and by 1951, Nos.99, 242, 24 and 53 Squadrons were all present, playing their part in the world events of that time, which included Suez and Korea.

216 Squadron arrived in 1955 with its Vickers Valettas which were replaced the following year by the Comet 2s. 53 and 511 moved out in 1957 which just left 99 Squadron alongside 216 - and the still surviving 33 MU. This was the situation which saw the re-equipment of 99 Squadron with Britannias in 1959.

**Kenya standby**

Returning to the Britannia story, in the 1960s the 'Wind of Change' was blowing and the demand for independence from the African States was gaining a momentum which had not been totally anticipated. Humble countries, such as Somalia, were amongst the first to gain this independence. So it was not surprising that a country like Kenya with a forceful, charismatic leader in Jomo Kenyatta, but still racked by the political divisions that had caused Mau Mau, should be pressing to be rid of the 'Shackles of Empire Rule'. However, unlike other countries in the area, our stake in Kenya was considerable. We had been using it, for many years, as a military reservoir and springboard for the volatile Middle East proper. It took strain away from those over burdened stations, provided a base for units of the Strategic Reserve and was a relief, both logistically and psychologically, from trying conditions in Aden and the Gulf stations. So it was a hope that we could retain some facilities in Kenya, an anticipation that can be seen in retrospect to have been naive. Through these years, which culminated in the independence of Kenya, the Britannias were in Nairobi for one reason or another.

Some signs of unrest in this situation led to the C-in-C, British Forces, Arabian Peninsular, calling for the 1st Battalion Duke of Wellington's Regiment. Seven Britannias with 12 crews took them to Nairobi and they were then placed on a 24-hour standby at the disposal of the C-in-C. 99's Operational Record Book (Form 540) records that 'operational flying was not required and little was done except continuation training'.

OBE—No. 33

NIGERIAN INDEPENDENCE CELEBRATIONS — Our photo shows H.R.H. Princess Axelandra with a group of Royal Air Force Officers who attended her private cocktail party at Government House, Lagos, during the Nigerian Independence celebrations. On the right of Princess Alexandra is Air Vice Marshal M. H. Dwyer, A.O.C. 3 Group, Force Commander of the R.A.F. Aircraft which took part in the fly-past over Lagos racecourse on 29th September.

HRH Princess Alexandra with the RAF officers who attended her private cocktail party at Government House, Lagos, during the Nigerian Independence celebrations. Amongst the group is Wg Cdr Le Hardy who captained the attendant Britannia. (*Lyneham Globe*)

**Operations**

So the Britannia's first 'Operation' turned out to be a bit of a damp squib. It perhaps should be pointed out, for future reference, that an 'Operation' is the real thing in military parlance. Assistance is required somewhere for something and it is given the utmost priority. If the event or situation can be anticipated then a 'Contingency Plan' may well have been prepared for it. 'Exercises' might specifically practise these contingency plans or similar.

Reading between the lines, one can picture the typical aircrew individual's situation in the Nairobi standby circumstance. He did not know in advance, but it was to end up that he would be in Kenya for, say, a fortnight - initially tired and under some commitment (and eagerness!) to do a job. The days drift by and nothing happens and before he knows it, the problem has passed by and there is talk of going home - and then the stay is over. Analysed by his family and friends back home he has done nothing - not even any sightseeing!

**Nigerian independence**

In 1960, much further West but still in Africa, a Britannia featured in supporting and being partner in the Royal Air Force representation in Lagos for the Nigerian Independence celebrations. Three Valiants of No 7 Squadron, Wittering, a Comet from 216 Squadron and the Britannia, crewed by 511 Squadron, made this grand gesture. HRH Princess Alexandra represented Her Majesty The Queen.

**More flag waving**

It must be some wonder, as the account continues of these dizzy events, that there were any aircraft remaining for the more mundane work. Yet another Britannia was 'spared' to fly students from the Royal Air Force College Cranwell to visit their

American compatriots at the USAF Academy at Colorado Springs. The navigator was of some esteem; he was Squadron Leader Pat Burgess: it has been outlined how he had played the major part in establishing the performance aspects of the Britannia for RAF use. The combination of this expertise, a relatively light payload and a most unusual meteorological feature, an EASTERLY jet stream across the North Atlantic, prompted an attempt to fly from Cranwell to Peterson Field, Colorado DIRECT!

Flight Lieutenant Peter Jordan was the signaller and is our raconteur:

*'It was not to be: about half way across, around 40 West, the fickle winds did a smart 180 back to their normal westerly direction and we only just crept into Montreal in the gathering gloom and that after much number crunching and great persuasion (backed by, literally, original performance data) from said navigator, who reluctantly forewent his dream and settled for matters more earthly ...*

*'... Eastern seaboard fog prevailed, the Montreal stack was full (after we landed, not because of us) and there was a 1½ hour delay for an outbound slot. This delay and the onward flight to Peterson would take the crew out of crew duty time (even the 19 hour day) so a night stop was enforced, much to the chagrin of 'OC Troops', a certain dynamic little Group Captain. The 'troops', however, enjoyed their unexpected visit to Montreal, as did the crew. The following day's flight was uneventful apart from repeated requests, through a variety of channels, from the Academy for our ETA!'*

**The Cable Route**

It perhaps can be assumed that it was not entirely unassociated with signs of the advancing independence of the Third World, that the first 'Cable Route' was flown in October 1960. This route was so called because it followed, in its initial concept, the necessary path of the underwater Cable and Wireless lines of communication. It was initiated and regularly exercised in order to provide an alternative, albeit a lengthy one, to routes which required the acquiescence of countries which might not be willing to co-operate in a particular operation or exercise. This first one, flown by 511 Squadron, routed from Lyneham to Sal, Cape Verde Islands. Ascension Island was next, then on to Luanda, Angola, then Salisbury, Rhodesia. There were further developments in the 'Cable Route' which will come later.

**A Cable Route story**

I am fortunate in being allowed to use the writings of some of my past compatriots in this book and I am grateful to them. They are mostly contributions to the magazine of The Britannia Association. Harry Liddell has already been introduced and there will be further from him. This is the first appearance of Wyndham Deere - and, again, there will be more. Windy was one of the first navigators to be recruited to the Britannia fleet. After serving for eight years, he decided that civil flying and Canada called and he joined Air Canada. Eventually navigators were no longer required and Windy retrained as a pilot and then flew Air Canada's 747s for many years. He has demonstrated his writing skills in a number of magazines; this naturally led him to a book. *'A Brat's Progress'*

tells the story of his childhood, life as a RAF Apprentice, a short spell as a student pilot before finding his niche as a navigator. The story takes us through his aircrew years up to the time he retired from the RAF. It is a very amusing and interesting read.

Copies of the 230 page softback can be obtained for £12.50 from:

W. Deere, 4095 Peach Tree Court, Vineland, Ontario, Canada L0R 2C0.

Now for that Cable Route story. Windy recalls the route trip, which he relates, in his inimitable style - lost teeth, donkeys, turtles ...

*'Once in a while we 'won' a trip that was out of the ordinary, as well as being off the beaten track of the Changi Slip, or the standard routes to the Middle East. One such trip was known as the Cable Route; an exercise apparently intended to demonstrate to friend and foe that if overflying rights in Africa or the Middle East were denied, we could jolly well find our way around the Dark Continent and onward to the Far East without infringing on anyone's idea of sovereignty. It also served as a 'Show the Flag' trip, which meant that we were often greeted by someone higher in status (but not necessarily in importance) than the sergeant i/c duty crew. Apart from the novelty of such a journey, there was the additional benefit of generous hospitality from the various officials who greeted us throughout the journey, - the only implicit stipulation being that we dressed up posh, and left the host's premises unassisted and in an approximately upright posture. I am pleased to report that among our crew there was only one minor infringement of this unwritten rule, and I shall touch on that a little later in the narrative.*

*'To be honest, I haven't the slightest idea of the location of the Cable and Wireless submarine cable around Africa, or indeed whether there is one at all, but if one uses our own planned route as a rough guide, it passes Aden, goes around the horn of Africa and down to Mauritius and beyond. Our own route took us from Mauritius to Pretoria, where we spent a pleasant day of sightseeing, followed by a very jolly party at the house of the British Air Attache. We followed the tradition of Transport Command crews of being first to arrive and last to leave, but I would hasten to add that this had the enthusiastic approval of our host. Bill Smith tells me that one of our fellow revellers subsequently made a name for himself as an Astronaut.*

*'Only slightly the worse for wear, the following morning we set forth once more in pursuit of the elusive cable, this time in a north westerly direction over southern Africa and the South Atlantic, towards the tiny island of Ascension Island. There were few navigation aids, and not a great deal of help from the Met man as to winds, so it was a case of cobbling together Least Improbable Positions using sun shots and a dodgy Green Satin, backed up with Dead Reckoning - such was the lot of the Royal Air Force Britannia navigator.*

*'However, with incredible skill and uncanny accuracy I guided the aeroplane to the somewhere within a hundred mile radius of our destination, at which point the pilots were nudged wide-awake, so to speak, to commence the business of landing at Wideawake Field (Note: Some years later I was regularly flogging the Atlantic with navigational ease, producing frequent accurate fixes using Loran Sets purchased for the grand sum of ninety Canadian dollars apiece - and I sometimes wonder why our Royal Air Force 'procurers' were not privy to such open-market bargains - oh well, that's outside the scope of this tale.)*

*'To most of us, Ascension Island was well and truly the back of beyond, and we really had no idea what to expect. We were warmly greeted by a Major of the USAF, as well as representatives of Pan American, who were contracted to supply airport services. The Major kindly offered Bill the loan of a jeep for the duration of our stay, the only stipulation being that Bill literally kept on the straight and narrow, and did not venture up the winding mountain road.*

*'Shortly after our arrival we received a message from the local manager of Cable and Wireless, in his capacity as Governor (Acting, Unpaid), inviting the commissioned part of the crew to dinner that evening. It turned out to be a small but rather formal affair, with the two ladies present retiring to the drawing room with the arrival of the port - a tradition I had thought had been put out of fashion by Clem Atlee and his fellow iconoclasts - Not in the remnants of the Old Empire, apparently.*

*'Whilst all this circumstance and minor pomp was going on, the NCOs of the crew were being royally entertained in the PanAm mess, where they were given a fine meal, and offered an apparently unlimited quantity of alcohol. This is when the minor indiscretion previously mentioned, occurred. One idiot member took it as a challenge when he discovered that one of*

Royal Air Force Lyneham: 24 hours a day, 365 days a year. (*Bill Robinson*)

*our chaps was effectively a teetotaller, who imbibed the odd glass of sherry at Christmas, and occasionally on St.David's Day with his leek soup. Anyway, poor old Taff became the victim of 'spiked' lemonade, and spent much of the evening entertaining them with renditions of Sospan Fach and 'We'll keep a welcome' before succumbing to a form of oblivion. When he came round he had not only lost his smile, but also the teeth that went with it. Needless to say, he woke with a dreadful hangover, and was not in the least bit amused. Neither should he have been.*

*'Anyway, our 'hungover' Welshman managed to find his teeth in time for a full day of sightseeing activity. Some Royal Navy personnel had volunteered to take us on a tour. One might have thought that on such a small island we could see all there was to see, and be back in the bar by lunchtime. Not a bit of it. First we were taken to see the old buildings and various bits and pieces of left-over ironmongery that had been undisturbed since the demise of Napoleon, who had spent his final years on nearby St.Helena. After that we were shown the turtle breeding grounds, and toured the moonscape terrain that covers much of the island.*

*'From there we progressed by stages up the mountain. Bill honoured his pledge not to drive the major's jeep further than the first stage, beyond which the road was quite hazardous. We transferred to RN Land Rovers in which we were taken as far as the 2000 feet level, at which point the road becomes a footpath. Here, the arid lower elevations of the island give way to fertile soil and lush foliage. This area had been developed as an experimental farm by Kew Gardens. From there we trudged in line astern up the narrow track to the summit of the mountain, with Tommy and myself risking life and limb as we attempted to record all this excitement on 8mm film. By this time we had exhausted the tourist possibilities, and it was time to beat a hasty retreat back to base, for we didn't wish to insult our hosts by being absent at opening time.*

*'The reason Pan American Airways had a station on Ascension Island was that the company was contracted to operate a rocket recovery station for Cape Canaveral. This was at a time when the good old U.S.of A. were throwing money in huge quantities at their space programme, and the PanAm employees stationed there were highly paid and well provisioned. That second night we were on our own for dinner, which we took in the mess, and we noted one particular fellow on whose plate was at least three pounds of fried chicken. From each piece of meat he took but a single bite, before throwing the remainder into a nearby garbage bin. He replenished his plate from time to time until he could*

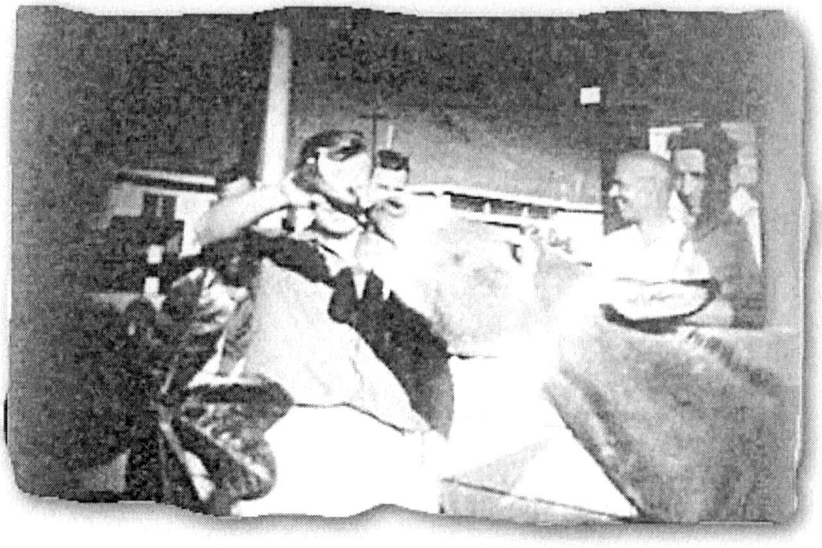

Windy obtained this picture of the beer-drinking donkey by photographing the projected 8mm film image! (*Wyndham Deere*)

*eat no more, with a considerable quantity of perfectly good chicken completely wasted. To this day I have not seen a more wanton display of indiscriminate gluttony.*

*'It was shortly after dinner that we witnessed a rather bizarre but amusing incident. The members of the mess had adopted a donkey as a mascot. As far as I can remember, and I must confess I can get no corroboration, this ass answered to the name of Lester. Lester arrived outside the mess shortly after dinner, and was clearly making a bit of a fuss about something - hee-hawing and stamping its hooves on the ground. 'What's going on?' one of us asked. 'Oh he's just waiting for his evening drink,' replied another onlooker. Then someone appeared carrying a bucket and a case containing a dozen or so beer bottles, and commenced to fill the bucket from the bottles. The ass immediately stuck its head in the bucket and eagerly gulped down the lot, then looked around expectantly in the hope of a refill.*

*'That is where I got into the act, and offered it a full bottle, which it disposed of without a drop being wasted. We were told that it was equally proficient with beer cans. Lester lingered for half an hour or so after his final drink, at which point its thoughts appeared to stray to matters of the flesh, as what could have been mistaken for a fifth limb appeared in the region of its rear undercarriage. In fact another leg would have come in handy, 'cos the four on the corners were not doing too good a job of keeping the beast upright. However, it managed to stagger away and out of sight, but had it been lucky enough to find an unsuspecting mare it is doubtful if it presented a serious threat, for we were witnessing. I think, a rather impressive case of 'brewers droop'. As Shakespeare said 'Liquor provokes the desire, but takes away the performance'. Many years later I learnt that there is in fact a herd of feral donkeys on the island, and it is entirely reasonable to assume (excuse the pun!) that some of them can boast a drunken ass as an ancestor. Not a lot different from some of us homo sapiens!*

*'Some time ago I reminisced on the various souvenirs sitting in odd corners of our humble dwelling that were obtained during my days on 99 Squadron. One object I neglected to mention was Barrabas - the stuffed baby turtle given to me by a friendly member of the Pan Am staff at Ascension Island.*

'... applied his amateur taxidermy skills, and nailed the poor buggers to wooden plaques by their little legs ..'. (*Wyndham Deere* )

*'Life on the island could get a little tedious, and one needed a hobby or pastime. This chap had taken up Turtle Stuffing, which must surely rank as one of the World's strangest hobbies. Any turtle fancier can tell you that Ascension Island is a well known breeding ground for these creatures. During the period when the turtle eggs are hatching and the little blighters are making a mad dash for the oggin, this fellow would be there among the predators, and bag a number of them. He then applied his amateur taxidermy skills, and nailed the poor buggers to wooden plaques by their little legs. A coat of varnish, and he had solved his Christmas Gift problem. Presumably he didn't send them to members of the RSPCA or what passed for Greenpeace in those days.*

*'The final couple of legs of our journey around the African Cable Route were the least interesting of the trip, consisting of two longish flight legs with a refuelling stop at Sal, in the Cape Verde Islands. Throughout the whole flight we had not caught even a glimpse of the putative cable, but the trip was flown exactly according to plan, and presumably struck the right note with both friend and foe. They were in no doubt that if things got a little dodgy over that troubled continent, Bill Smith and his merry men could get around Africa without too much trouble. - But next time Taff would hang on to his teeth.'*

**The Cyprus time bomb**

A reminder that Cyprus had been a trouble spot for many years is given by an item in the Lyneham Globe. In February, an RAF Britannia transported the Colonial Under-Secretary, Mr Julian Amery, for his talks with Cypriot leaders. The tenseness of the situation can be judged by the fact that the departure for Gatwick was delayed twice, due to last minute attempts at mediation.

Cyprus was to be a constant port of call for the aircraft. Cries from the Greek Cypriots for 'Enosis' (Union with Greece) and from the Turkish element for partition, had resulted in many years of terrorism, mostly aimed at British servicemen. Now, agreement was being reached on granting of self-government. The Republic of Cyprus was to be formed with British sovereignty being retained over the two military base areas at Dhekhelia and Akrotiri. The maintenance of this foothold in the Eastern Mediterranean would require a considerable amount of air lift. Also, Akrotiri became firmly established as our staging post to the East. Additional activity came from the failure of the formation of the Republic to provide a peaceful settlement between Greek and Turk and there were many occasions, over the subsequent years, when peace-keeping forces were required and action to protect our Servicemen and other British Nationals. All in all, Britannia crews were to spend a lot of time on the island.

**A big test**

In March 1960, the Britannias contributed towards the largest RAF/Army exercise ever to take place outside the United Kingdom, a sign of the newly acquired potential. Exercise 'Starlight' was a Strategic Reserve air mobility trial. Transport Command air-lifted the 1st Guards Brigade Group and ancillary units nearly 2000 miles to El Adem in North Africa. Four Britannias of 99 Squadron and 17 Hastings of Nos.24, 36 and 114 Squadrons, from Colerne, operated a shuttle service between Lyneham and El Adem. On 10th March, 'D-Day', the strategic lift of troops, equipment and vehicles began. Daily, until 20th March, three Britannias, each carrying 110 men and two Hastings loaded with vehicles, touched down in North Africa. The Britannias slipped crews there, illustrating the intention of keeping on the move an aircraft of such newly acquired lift potential.

The summary of the Britannia effort for this demanding test was that 4000 troops were moved; there was one sortie every eight hours outbound. For the return, 39 sorties were flown in less than five days with only 12 crews and 10 aircraft. This was a fine demonstration of the new capabilities of the Strategic Transport Force and its powerful new tool - the Bristol Britannia.

**Mercy flight**

Flag waving continued when a contingent, led by the then Secretary of State for Air, the Rt Hon George Ward, attended the 150th Anniversary Celebration of Argentine Independence; how subsequent events put another colour on occurrences of the past! The detachment consisted of a Comet from 216 Squadron, two Vulcans

Stores for the Chile mission being offloaded. (*Lyneham Globe*)

m Man in Display Team

STORES FOR THE CHILE MERCY MISSION BEING OFF LOADED FROM BRITANNIA 659. SEE FULL STORY ON PAGE 3.

A photograph to make ex-Britannia mouths water! Open air eating at Bedok Corner, Singapore - a favourite gastronomic haunt for Britannia slip crews. Note the empty egg shells! (*Harry Liddell*)

from 101 Squadron, all supported by a Britannia of 99. There was, however, another aspect to this flight, and of a sort for which the Britannia was to establish a noble record, best described as 'Mercy Flights'. Just prior to the Argentine celebrations, the Chileans suffered a devastating earthquake. British firms in Argentina joined together to provide help and collected clothing, medical supplies and food. It was then decided to make it a totally UK effort and use XL659, on the ground having arrived for the celebrations still to come, to transport the supplies to Santiago. Two flights were carried out. These completed and the festivities over, the aircraft proceeded to Montevideo, Rio de Janeiro, Bogata and Caracas - heady days!

Another example of how it seemed to be 'hang the expense' times, was the air-lifting, by six Britannias, of a 550-strong inter-service team to partake in the Tattoo associated with the British Exhibition in New York.

Meanwhile a less glamourous task was being completed by Flight Lieutenant 'Rip' Kerbey and crew at El Adem. This was a 'heat trial' involving 100 soldiers in an attempt to break the aircraft air-conditioning system - or them - or both!

**Chaos in the Congo**

This chapter on 1960 concludes with a return to the starting topic of Africa. The Belgian Government granted independence to the Congo at the end of June 1960. Very shortly chaos reigned, Katanga Province declared itself an independent state; there was a mutiny by many members of the Congolese Army, tribal friction and looting. The new Congo Government called for United Nations' help to restore order. Ex-99 AQM, Sergeant Peter Phillips describes how the Britannias then contributed:

*'A detachment of two aircraft, four crews, ground servicing party and an Ops Officer operated at Accra. The task was to take Ghanaian troops and police of the UN Force into Leopoldville and bring refugees out. These included European missionaries who had fled for their lives from their stations in the interior. My log book tells me that Ted Millson took 491 to Accra from Lyneham on 18th July, Accra - Leopoldville - Accra on 19th July and 518 Accra - Nairobi on the 25th to join the 99 Squadron detachment already at Embakasi.*

*'Incidentally, there was a Comet 2 operating at Accra also and books on the events of that time refer to the Comet taking Patrice Lamumba to New York to the United Nations. Ted's crew was called out to undertake this task but the Nav had 'gone to ground' downtown! I recall being driven around the night-spots of Accra trying to locate him, without success. The Comet was used, so a chance to put the Britannia on that page of the history books was lost!'*

As with many UN operations, their essence is persistence and the Britannias were back in Accra in November to assist with the evacuation of European civilians from Leopoldville and again in January and June 1961, to transfer UN troops. So 1960 left an African legacy for 1961.

The flavour of these flights is given by Squadron Leader John Bourn who recalls one of them:

*'We were on a UN lift from Dar-es-Salam to Kamina, in the Congo, and ran into low cloud. The controllers at Kamina only spoke French. Luckily my copilot was Flt Lt George Cristinacce, a French speaker, and he drew on a pad the directions given by Air Traffic Control. We broke cloud 200 feet above primary jungle!'*

**Behind the scenes**

The acquisition of 23 large, modern, sophisticated aircraft presented challenges which had not been met before in the Service. Not the least of these was the keeping of technical records and facilitating the action required by them. An article in the *Lyneham Globe* outlined the enormity of this task - in pre-computer days:

Service humour! The way one contributor to the *Lyneham Globe* responded to the Congo situation.

*'As a sequel to 'Operation Paper Weight', in the course of which three tons of 'bumf' were brought onto the station, RAF Lyneham now has in operation the planned maintenance system for Britannias - a project which kept a section of the Service Department at Filton busy for seven months.*

*'The Air Ministry contract for the maintenance system involved 6,000 cards, a master reference index, and an index dividing the system into the various trades of the RAF structure. Then came the blow. The number of copies needed totalled 480,000! A SOS went out to Ilford, the photographic firm, who supplied a prototype Azoflex automatic printing machine, which eliminated laborious hand-feed printing. Squadron Leader Bill Berry, Officer Commanding Aircraft Servicing Squadron, recommended the adoption of a maintenance schedule broadly based on that supplied to civil airline operators. It was he who put forward*

The help in 1960 given to Chile was later acknowledged at the residence, in London's Eaton Place, of the Chilean Ambassador. Four members of the crew were presented with diplomas. They are (L to R) Flt Lt Don West, Flt Geoff Shipway, Flt D A Hancock and Master Signaller Les Bennett. (*Les Bennett*)

*the idea to have such a maintenance system for military Britannias. This was, of course, a unique procedure for RAF aircraft, and, by taking advantage of this opportunity, Transport Command now have a servicing system which will give them full safety and economy.*

*'In addition to the mammoth printing job, a vast amount of typing, compiling and checking has been carried out by the section's staff of 12. When pressure of work became overpowering, extra typing was farmed out to various other sections of the company. In the master reference index all the maintenance cards are cross-referenced, and a major task was completed in the compilation of the index, channelling the servicing into trades. The initial printing of cards will last for 12 months, but master cards have been supplied to Lyneham, who now have their own printing facilities. The station will also be responsible for the amendment of its own documents, as modifications and changes are made to the aircraft.*

*'Briefly, the system works in this way. A master reference index has been compiled from the civil maintenance schedule, which lists all the components, systemwise, in the aircraft. This utilises, for reference purposes, the existing civil schedule code detailing, under the RAF servicing periods, all the work and inspections which have to be carried out on each system and component up to the fourth progressive major servicing. This may take six years to achieve and completes the servicing cycle. Under each servicing period in the master reference index any applicable cards are quoted. The cards themselves have a logical code which, at a glance, tells the user what precise sub-zone of the aircraft, trade and type of work is involved. In addition, thought has been given to rudimentary data processing (punched card control), and each card has control spaces provided, giving the foregoing information and the servicing periods at which each card is needed.*

*'There are cross-references to other trades involved in the work and to the length of time it would take. All this makes the controlling of the system and planning of manpower and equipment simple. Separate sets of indexes cover the work loading for each servicing period grouped under trades. It is perhaps the most comprehensive servicing system that the RAF has ever had.'*

**A collection flight remembered**

An appropriate note to start to leave 1960 on is the delivery of XM497 on 2nd December; the Britannia fleet was now complete. As the number of aircraft grew, the task of collecting the new ones from the factory fell to 'lesser mortals'.

Flight Lieutenant Dinger Bell recalls his turn:

*'It was 4th May 1960 when, summoned to the presence, I received orders to collect a new Britannia from the factory. Together with the rest of my crew we were deposited at Aldergrove by kind permission of the 'Country Club'. A battered Service bus, driven by a broad Irish driver, left us an hour later, somewhat bemused, in the middle of Short and Harlands shipyard! That should have been a clue to the rest of the day's events.*

*'Eventually we found the aircraft factory and, after signing my life away on a sackful of paper, the Form 700 was signed and we took possession of 489 which then had a total flying time of 6 hours and 25 minutes.*

*'Start up and taxy were no problem; we then entered the runway to back-track. About halfway down we came across a very large electric cable, protected by sloping duckboards, crossing the runway at ninety degrees. This cable supplied the entire power supply to the factory and the shipyard! A board beside the runway requested pilots to exercise caution when taxying over it. This we duly obeyed and arriving at the take-off end, commenced the checks only to have two 'limiters' fail to arm. A slow taxy back to the buildings followed, with a plea for help over the radio.*

*'At the shed a figure in a white coat appeared, shouted something, probably rude, and taking a large hide faced hammer from his pocket, proceeded to beat hell out of the two offending engines. Closing the cowlings again he rapidly disappeared into the shed with a backwards thumbs up. At least that's what we thought it was!*

*'We taxied out again, eased over the cable, turned at the far end and, at last, started the take-off run. What followed is still not terribly clear. We hit the aforementioned duckboards somewhere between V1 and V2 and were thrown instantly skywards followed by a lurching weaving climb over the shipyard cranes. The short trip back to Lyneham was something of an anti-climax*

The Britannia was often used as the backdrop for a news photo. Here the South African cricketers pose in front of 639. They were nearing the end of their 1960's tour and on a visit to Filton during their match against Gloucestershire. (*Lyneham Globe*)

Farewell to Springboks — The South African cricketers, who will shortly be leaving us after their summer tour, seen here in front of Britannia No. 639. (Picture taken on their visit to Filton during their match against Gloucestershire).

IN MEMORY OF LORD TRENCHARD

*until downwind when all our hydraulics failed; but that's another story.*

*'A considerable time later some saucy sailor at Farnborough claimed to have invented the ski jump - typical!!'*

**G-ALBO also remembered**

By an odd coincidence, on the same day that the last RAF Britannia was delivered, the original Britannia prototype, G-ALBO, which first flew on 16th August 1952, was officially transferred to No.4 School of Technical Training, RAF St Athan to be used for ground instructional purposes. It served in this role until broken up in May 1969. An ex-Lyneham Britannia ground engineer, 'Tiny' Livingstone, was posted to St Athan to instruct the Boy Entrants, using the aircraft. He has memories of that time:

*'The prototype Britannia was really something; unpressurised, 12 feet shorter than the production model and with a mixture of Proteus and Orion engines. The flight deck was non-standard.*

*'Having bored the pants off everyone talking about the biggest and best aircraft the Royal Air Force had at the time, the Wingco decided that I should run the engines - preferably in the near future when he was away on a course!*

*'I need to point out that, at that time, I was a rigger and the closest I came to ground runs at Lyneham was being on the headset outside the aircraft. I lived on that flight deck for three days and built up a starting check list of sorts. Secretly I hoped that fire, flood or pestilence would strike the aircraft in the night!*

*'Come the day of the start, I had kept it to myself; the Boy Entrants had been sent to lunch and the Fire Section called to stand-by. It was time. Through the check list I went. All set, fingers crossed, I pressed the*

in-C. AT LYNEHAM

A.O.C.-in-C. INSPECTING GUARD OF HONOUR

Sir Denis Sees Progress of New Building During Tour Of Inspection

In much later years a different view was taken of the time-consuming nature of large parades. But in the 1950/60s, in spite of Lyneham's hectic task, a full blown AOC's Inspection was carried out each year with the whole of the station on parade. Here, on 27th May 1960, the AOC-in-C, Transport Command, Air Marshal Sir Denis Barnett inspects the Guard of Honour. (*Lyneham Globe*)

Each aircraft had a name. Here 518's - Spica - just manages to get into shot. See 'Postscript' below for more on this naming system. (*Bill Robinson*)

*button and the starting cycle commenced - and the engine came to life! There was a lot of smoke! I had done it - only to idle, mind you - and only the Proteus!'*

**Postscript**

As they had come off the production line, as well as the necessary registration number, each aircraft received a name:

XM489 Denebola
XM490 Aldebaran
XM491 Procyon
XM496 Regulus
XM497 Schedar
XM498 Hadar
XM517 Avior
XM518 Spica
XM519 Capella
XM520 Arcturus
XL635 Bellatrix
XL636 Argo
XL637 Vega
XL638 Sirius
XL639 Atria
XL640 Antares
XL657 Rigel
XL658 Adhara
XL659 Polaris
XL660 Alphard
XN392 Acrux
XN398 Altair
XN404 Canopus

The statement is often made that the RAF Britannias were named after stars. If this is said in the presence of Squadron Leader David Court-Smith then the speaker will be corrected:

*'XL636 was named after Argo, which is not a star. Argo Navis, to give its correct name, was a large constellation in the Southern Hemisphere between Canis Major and Southern Cross. In the middle of the 18th Century an astronomer called Nicolas de Lacaille decided that it was actually four separate constellations. The name Argo Navis meant 'Argonaut's Ship' (you remember Jason pursuing the Golden Fleece in his Argo) so de Lacaille called the new constellations Carina (the keel), Puppis (the stern), Vela (the sail) and Pyxis (the compass).*

*'The intriguing questions which come out of these facts are, therefore, why was one Britannia not named after a star*

*and why was the constellation name chosen one of such astronomical antiquity?'*

Well?! What do you have to say about that!

**Farewell 1960 - a Christmas message**

In its rather stilted way, the *Lyneham Globe* reported the following:

*'Flt. Lt. Adams and crew, whilst operating Special Flight 6328 with Britannia XL660 en-route McGuire NJ to Lyneham on 23rd December 1960, were surprised when invited by Gander Air Radio to broadcast from the air (for recording by Canadian Broadcasting System) a Christmas message of greeting. This opportunity was too good to miss and accordingly the captain authorised Master Signaller Aindow to pass the following message:*

*'Royal Air Force Prop. Jet 6328, a Britannia en-route McGuire New Jersey to Lyneham UK, flying at 23,000 feet at a speed of 420 mph. The captain, officers and men of the crew extend their heartiest greetings for Christmas to our Canadian friends and also from the officers and men of the Royal Air Force to all ranks of the Royal Canadian Air Force with best wishes for the New Year."*

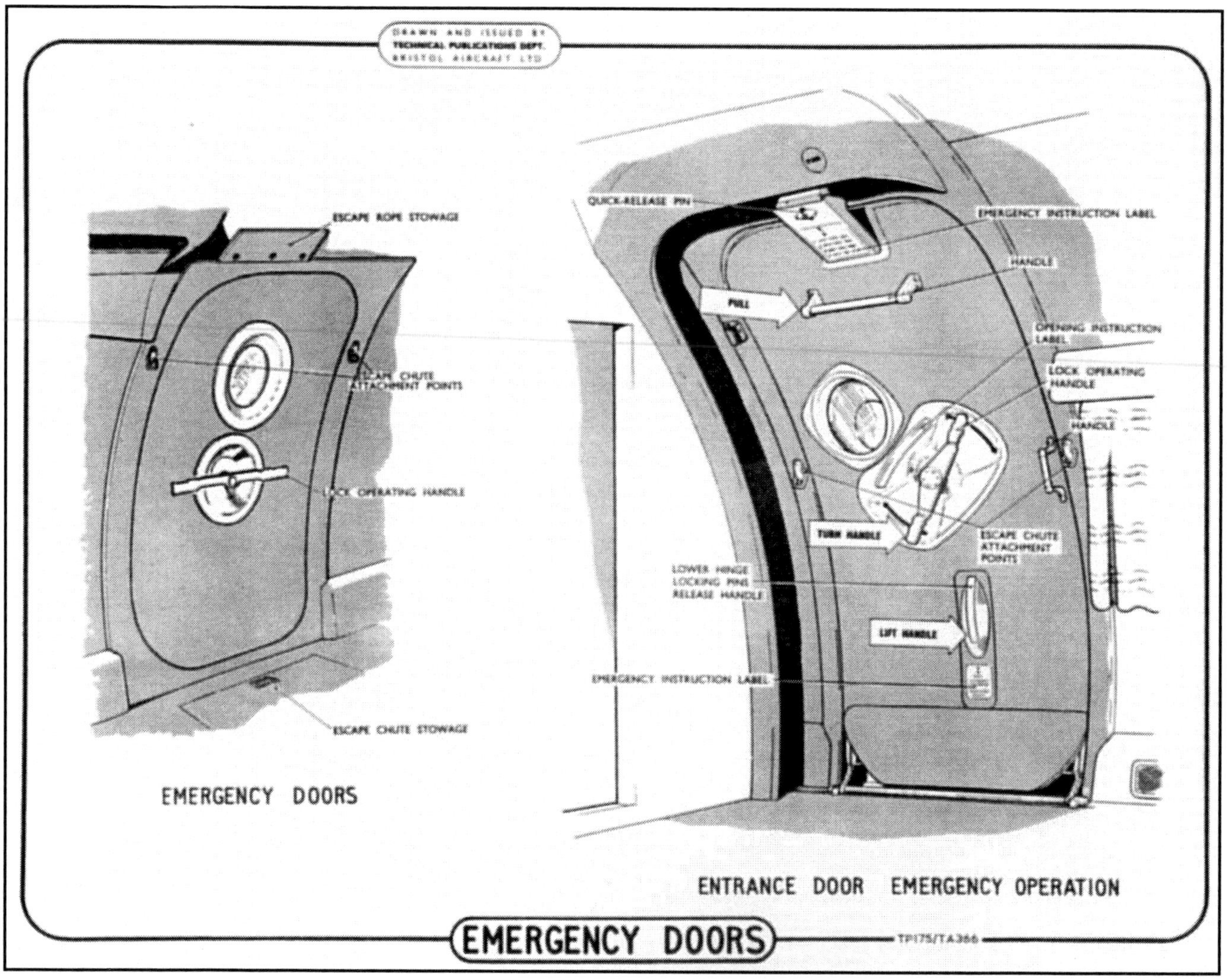

CHAPTER EIGHT

# Kuwait - The First Real Thing

A good way to open this new year of 1961 is to report that Squadron Leader John Owen was awarded the Air Force Cross in the Honours List for his considerable efforts in shepherding the Britannia into service.

As mentioned in the previous chapter, the Congo situation continued into 1961. This extract from '*The Lyneham Globe*' perhaps gives a good insight into the atmosphere of such operations:

*'... The hotel accommodation was a little primitive but the food was good and the bar open 24 hours a day, so there were few complaints on that score; entertainment took the form of an almost continuous procession of airline passengers, natives, cats, dogs and lizards across the hotel verandah. Squadron Leader Wickes took the first aircraft round the route Accra - Leopoldville - Luluaborg - Accra on 24th January. At Leopoldville the crew had to wear the blue berets of the United Nations to meet the requirements of the Congolese authorities. Flight Lieutenant Hayley joined the detachment on 25th January with a spare engine to replace the one feathered by Squadron Leader Wickes on his return to Accra. Again, on 29th January, Flight Lieutenant Chamberlain stopped at Accra on his way through to Nairobi to drop off another engine to replace the one lost by Flight Lieutenant Goddard at Luluaborg.*

This photograph of Sqn Ldr Ted Millson might have been clearer if there had not been the cloud of cigar smoke! There is an interesting social comment here. In the 1950s/60s smoking on the flight deck was totally acceptable - in fact there were more smokers than non-smokers. The roof lining used to be stained brown! Things did gradually change over the years to the point where, in the 1970s, it became unacceptable to smoke at all on the flight deck. (*Bill Robinson*)

*Despite these difficulties, one or two sorties were flown each day and the lift completed on 29th January. Aircraft operations into Accra were complicated by the detachment having to compete with other operators for ground power and steps and also to use the only two jet refuelling pans.*

*'Most of those present suffered from tummy trouble at some time ... ... Late on January 31st, Squadron Leader Wickes took off for Luluaborg with Major General Alexander, CIGS of the Ghana Army as passenger. The landing at Luluaborg was made at dawn, minutes before rising ground mist blotted out the approach. The commander of the Guard of Honour valiantly stood his ground while the Britannia nose passed over his head due to the very restricted taxying area. After unloading the engine for Flight Lieutenant Goddard's aircraft, Squadron Leader Wickes returned to the UK, night stopping at Kano on the way. Flight Lieutenant Goddard followed four days later, after praiseworthy efforts by Flight Sergeant Holt and his ground crew in changing the engine ...'*

**A Junior Technician remembers**

Peter de Frère was a young J/T and around this time he was detached from Colerne to Ghana in support of two Hastings.

*'It was a mere four years since Ghana had gained independence from Great Britain and, in 1960, its fledgling army still relied heavily upon British Officers and NCOs under secondment. At the time, Ghana had no air force. When the Ghana Army was selected for duty in the Congo under the UN banner, it had to use the services of the seconded British personnel. It also called upon Britain to provide air transport between Accra and Leopoldville, later to include Luluaberg, for its troops. Some of the Ghanaian troops in Leopoldville mutinied and attacked their superiors. I believe an officer died and an NCO was wounded in the incident which was sparked by rumours of the poor treatment the soldiers' families were receiving back in Accra. The decision was made to replace the mutineers as quickly as possible, a task that was too great for the small detachment already there with the Hastings aircraft.*

*'It must have been early evening, because I was still sober, when Paddy Murtagh called me over He instructed me to take one of the lads down to the airfield where we were to meet a RAF Britannia. Our job was to marshal it into the parking area, chock it, put up some passenger steps, then clear off into the night like will-o'-the-wisps. We were told not to tell anybody or even to speak to anybody. The whole operation was to be hush hush.*

The photograph of the engine instruments from Pilots' Notes.

*'I have mentioned, the groundcrew of 1960 were paid very poorly. When you had bought your beer and fags, there was nothing left for luxuries such as the 'Flight' magazine, so neither my colleague that night nor I had any idea what a Britannia aircraft looked like. To us, it was just a name. Remember too, we were the poor relations stuck up on the hill at Colerne, defending ourselves against the IRA, and not living in luxury like the bods at Lyneham who had all the latest information and gear.*

*'The airport at Accra, in those days, had only a single runway, one end of which housed the civil aircraft dispersal and the other the military. On landing, the pilots had to turn their aircraft on the runway and taxi down to the appropriate dispersal. My colleague and I had been driven to the airfield by a Ghanaian Army Corporal who had been placed at our disposal for the duration of the detachment. He was a most obliging chap with a very pleasant nature and was liked by us all. However, due to the relationship between Army and RAF personnel at the time, he was known to us all simply as Corporal. If he ever did know that we 'Sergeants' were imposters, he never showed it. We arrived at the airfield around 10pm, expecting our secret 'plane to land about half-an-hour later. We asked our driver to wait in area away from the dispersal, so that he would not be witness to the secret goings-on, and took up our positions with marshalling wands and wheel chocks at the ready.*

*'It must have been near to 11pm before we saw the distant landing lights of an approaching aircraft, and we watched as it landed and begin to taxi back along the runway towards us. When it was within manoeuvring distance I held up the illuminated wands and marshalled it towards the parking area. It turned off the runway and followed my waved instructions closely until I had it nicely in line ready for engine shutdown. The pilot then turned off the landing lights and, for the first time, I saw the words on the tailplane. It simply said 'PANAM.' I realised immediately that I had captured a PanAmerican DC8 without firing a single shot.*

*'I distinctly remember, after all these years, that I did not panic. I simply turned off the wands, grabbed my assistant by the scruff and dived for cover. We waited round a dark corner for a few minutes whilst the DC8 sat on the dispersal with its engines still running while, I suppose, the pilot was talking to the control tower on the radio. Then it began to move back onto the runway and disappeared from our view on its way to the civil aircraft dispersal. What blessed relief, for us at least. So, if you are in Accra or have visited there and have heard the story of the phantom marshaller, you now know the truth. It was me, or*

The ubiquitous fork lift, at the Britannia's freight door, somewhere down the route. The height of the freight door sill was a continual loading challenge. (*Bill Robinson*)

*probably more correctly, it was I.*

*'I do not believe, after all these years, that the RAF Britannia ever arrived in Accra on its secret mission. I am basing this on the fact that I was not asked to go to the airfield to greet it.*

*'Looking back on this episode, I can see where I made two significant errors. First I should have realised that an aircraft with no propellers could not possibly be a Britannia and, secondly, I should have known that no RAF pilot could have followed my marshalling instructions so closely.'*

**Proteus problems**

It perhaps is not difficult to perceive that all was not well with the Proteus engine. Troubles in 1960 had been of the magnitude to prompt the Form 540 comment, 'Engine failures persist.' Cruise power was reduced from 11500 rpm to 11350 in an attempt to extend turbine life. More trials had been conducted, this time out of RAF Changi, Singapore to test the efficaciousness of the continuing modifications being devised for the persistent engine icing problem. Someone at Bristol Siddeley Engines had used a lot of imagination in selecting the name of the Greek sea-god for this revolutionary reverse flow turbo-prop engine. The mythological Proteus possessed the power to assume different shapes. Unfortunately, in the engineering world, such change can obviously lead to unexpected difficulties.

Harry Liddell recalls the tedious times at the lower rpm settings:

*'I believe (though cannot be certain) that the dreary period of operation at the restricted limit commenced in August 1960 following a spate of turbine failures. I am fairly certain that the first aircraft fitted with a set of modified engines appeared early the next year, but conversion of the rest then had to await the trial results. Given the passage of time actual dates elude me, but I think that full fleet modification was achieved by the end of '62. There is also the point that, prior to the spate of troubles resulting in imposition of the 11350 rule, we had anyway never been permitted the higher cruise setting of 11650 - 11500 was the top limit, So, the advent of the modified engines enabled us, for the first time, to utilise the Britannia to its full design capability; indeed, it was like entering a whole new world.'*

**News items**

Mentioned now, to emphasise the wide range of Britannia operations is a stand-by that was manned at Changi, Singapore three months later, to take troops to Laos and, around the same time, a ceremony that took place at the Chilean

Norman Rose (centre front) with his crew in Aden in December 1961. Some of these featured in the Kuwait story - and/or later ones:

Back row: M. Sig John Beardon AFM, M. Eng Bob Anstee, AFM, Flt Lt Dickie Thornborough, Sgt Smith.

Front row: Fg Off Tony Boardman DFC, Flt Lt Norman Rose AFC, Sgt Geoff Pearce. *(Norman Rose)*

Embassy when the crew of the aircraft which had flown relief supplies to Santiago after the earthquake were made honorary members of the Chilean Air Force. Building back at base continued. The new Terminal Building was officially opened by the Chief of the Air Staff, Air Chief Marshal Sir Thomas Pike KCB CBE.

**Suspicious Russia**

The Britannia's first flight behind the Iron Curtain took place in May 1961. The Regimental Band of the Argyll and Sutherland Highlanders was flown to Moscow for the British Trade Fair. The Russians decreed that for all such flights, the aircraft had to stage through an airfield outside their border, Copenhagen in this instance, and pick up an English speaking Aeroflot navigator and radio operator to monitor their progress. No chances were taken! The aircraft was only on the ground at Moscow for two hours.

**'Vantage'**

By now, both Squadrons were operational, fully equipped and manned. As they had grown, their potential had been partially tested by the various events over the past 18 months. Now, in July, was to come, as if ordained by an unseen hand, their true 'Baptism by Fire'. This was Operation 'Vantage', the provision of military aid to Kuwait.

The escape chute in use on a less serious occasion. Gurkhas put the evacuation method through its paces.

A photograph taken in later years but clearly illustrating the challenge, with limited facilities, of getting the freight on board the aircraft. The load is oxygen bottles on a trolley.

As early as 1899, Kuwait had entered into treaty relations with Great Britain and, in 1914, was recognised as an independent state under British protection, a situation that was maintained until 1961. These treaties were of importance to us to safeguard the main source of our oil supplies. Kuwait's northern border with Iraq was agreed in 1923. In 1961, the standing of Kuwait, internationally, clearly indicated that it should be independent and this was agreed on 19th June. In this agreement a close relationship was to be maintained and Kuwait requested, and Great Britain agreed, that if assistance should be required, it would be provided. Only six days later such help was needed! Iraq claimed that Kuwait belonged to them and started to move forces towards the border. Operation 'Vantage' was launched.

The first Britannia involvement was the commandeering of an aircraft on the Singapore route, as it passed through Khormaksar, Aden to immediately assist the Air Forces Middle East's Beverleys and Valettas, which were hard pressed with the preparatory moves. The operation called for the movement of troops and other personnel, tanks and armoured cars into Kuwait to secure the airfield. Two Hunter Squadrons would also fly in. The Britannia role would be the long range work from Cyprus, Aden and Kenya.

**One crew's story**

Flight Lieutenant Norman Rose captained the Britannia that was plucked from its Changi Slip. He tells of how the news of what was to come was broken to him:

*'During the approach to RAF Khormaksar, just as the crew were looking forward to a few ice-cold beers in 'Neddy's Bar', we were told that the flight would now terminate in Aden. We were astonished at this as we expected to hand the aircraft over in the usual way for its onward flight to the UK. This would be done expeditiously, in this case, as we were an Aeromed aircraft and amongst the patients was one serious case, a pregnant lady - with a broken back!*

*'On landing we were briefed, 'Kuwait - Operation Vantage - go to bed as soon as possible and we will call you when you are needed.''*

The crew retired to bed at around 1am, Aden time, and only four hours later Norman was awakened to be told that they were to be on their way to Kuwait immediately. He had considerable difficulty convincing his crew, particularly the copilot, Flying Officer Tony Boardman, that, having just worked a 19 hour day, and with only four hours sleep, they had to get going again. One can picture the scene with the captain having to say to the copilot, 'I am ordering you to get up - this is like war - all the rules go out of the window!' With this difficulty over, the crew were briefed on their mission, to take fully armed Paras to Kuwait - not the fully mapped old Kuwait Airport, for which the normal aeronautical information was available, but to Kuwait

Clearly an anxious loading moment for the chap in charge?

New, the partly completed, modern replacement for the old airfield. All that existed was the runway and dispersal areas. There were more rules to be thrown away, along with their crew rest ones! They had no information on the airfield, no diplomatic clearance to overfly the countries en route and no weather forecast for their destination. But the message was clear - ' Go!' They flew along for five hours, with no navigation lights and maintaining radio silence until in Kuwait itself and in contact with the controllers at the airport. They had to ask them the position of the new airfield! 'From our overhead steer 180 for 18 miles.' They were also given the weather. 'Strong wind, blowing sand, visibility about one mile, temperature 40°C'! They did find the airfield, just a strip of concrete, and little else, in the middle of the desert. It was then necessary to carry out a low level circuit to land - an exercise practised constantly to this day in all transport aircraft, which to many seems a pointless activity. The Rose crew were very glad they had rehearsed it!

Communications, in a situation like this, are a key factor but always a difficulty. Thus it was that the Parachute Regiment Lieutenant Colonel on board was advising Captain Rose that they were not sure what situation they were to meet on arrival and they may have to leave the aircraft fighting. In the event, the first thing that the crew spied through the swirling sand was the line of Royal Air Force Hunters! Gritty action, however, was still required of the Paras. Obviously there were no passenger steps available, so they were required to vacate the aircraft down the escape chute, briefed on and deployed by the petite WRAF air quartermaster, Sergeant Sylvia Wapen!

**Not perfect**

It is apt, with the immediate foregoing in mind, to consider the Britannia in the circumstance it had so soon found itself. It would perhaps be discordant, in this eulogy, to suggest that the Britannia might not have been the best choice as a military transport, but the situation that presented itself in Kuwait was one to be constantly met, though perhaps not to such an extreme. We have this aircraft, designed to carry 100+ passengers, on business and pleasure, between civil airports with all the implied facilities. It is converted to a military transport for the carriage of passengers and/or freight by the addition of a strengthened floor and a large freight door. Such modification does not adjust a basic dimension of the aircraft - the height of that floor, and the associated door sills, above the ground - more than ten feet. When one contemplates the RAF's present day transporter, the Hercules, with its low-bodied profile, enabling loading and unloading without the help of any outside agency, it is astonishing that the Britannia withstood the onslaught to its gentle breeding and coped over the years. It has to be said that it never again quite met the conditions that were encountered in Kuwait. Therefore all self-congratulation on its success over the years really needs tempering with the thought that it was fortunate that this was so, and that the situations met could be overcome in one way or another.

**Battery start**

Perhaps to crown this moment of self-denigration, it is mentioned that the Britannia had no self-contained electrical power source, prior to starting the engines, other than its batteries. This may be all very well for a car, but for an aeroplane it represents a vulnerable situation. If no external ground power source is available, then as soon as power is applied from the batteries to use the electric start motors, then the starting sequence has to be commenced immediately, otherwise the batteries will be flattened by the loads that are inevitably present as soon as the aircraft is made 'live'. If that start is unsuccessful then there could be a real problem.

The 'Battery Start', as it was known, became the eternal first hurdle to many Britannia operations where a suitable ground power unit was not available. For planned events such units could be pre-positioned. They could be carried on the first Britannia of the exercise or whatever - providing there was a means of off-loading it from its giddy height of ten feet up! This brings us full circle, back to that vertical chasm that had to be bridged. There will follow, in this story, the variety of ways this was achieved.

**A sinking feeling**

But the content of this digression is minor compared with the next problem that was going to beset our first crew into Kuwait New. The passengers having been off-loaded, preparations were being made for the immediate return of the aircraft - but that was almost not soon enough for the flight engineer, who suddenly noticed that the aircraft was sinking into the so-called concrete dispersal. This was another difficulty to be met over the years, the relatively high wheel loading of the Britannia - relative, that is, to the strengths of the runways, taxiways and aprons of some of the airfields into which it was to operate.

What he had seen was a neat square crack around each of the two main wheel bogies and that piece of concrete slowly descending like a very slow motion lift! Slow motion it might have been in a lift context but it was a rapidly approaching disaster in aircraft terms! The crew rushed into the aircraft and immediately started the inboard engines and Norman used full power to pull the Britannia out of the holes. Fearing that worse was to come, they kept moving towards the runway, starting the outboard engines as they went. The poor navigator, steeped in the new fangled subject of 'Performance', was concerned about the take-off criteria. But it was clear that, in spite of the temperature, which had now soared to 45°C, with an 'eye ball' assessment of the runway length and an empty aircraft, all would be well - as it was!

As soon as they were airborne they reported what they had experienced back to Aden, where more Britannias were gathering and Flight Lieutenant Rose suggested that the turning areas at the ends of the runway would be strong enough to take the aircraft. It did indeed transpire that for the subsequent Britannia movements during Operation 'Vantage', only these loops were used.

Sergeant Curly Beauchamp has good reasons to remember those loops. He headed the ground crew turnround team there. They had to scrounge everything. He 'acquired' a coach which was used for their accommodation. At the end of the operation they had to spend days in hospital recovering from fatigue and dehydration.

**Taking stock**

Returning to the Rose crew: settled now at height, the aircraft air conditioning starting to take effect, and reversing what they had just endured, sending a chill through their bodies, they took stock. In the captain's words:

'*We had left Singapore 30 hours previously and in that time we had flown for seven hours, spent 90 minutes on the ground at Gan, then flown for a further eight hours on to Aden. We then had four hours sleep! Then up and to Kuwait - and the traumatic arrival and time on the ground there. Now we were on our way to Bahrain to refuel and then on back to Aden.*

'*At Khormaksar, the massive nature of the operation was evident. Britannias were arriving from the UK and Kenya, Hastings and Beverleys were there, playing their part. Where to sleep was a problem. We were only too pleased to climb into the still warm beds of our compatriots who were taking our aircraft back to Kuwait with another load.*'

**Diplomatic problems**

Nine hours later they were off again back to Kuwait. By now the long range airlift from UK, Cyprus, Aden and Kenya was under way, but not without major difficulties. Overflights of foreign countries are always something of a problem, one minor example has already been given. They reach their peak of difficulty in times of tension. In this instance, just as all was set to establish the force in Kuwait by 2nd July, Turkey and Sudan banned flights over their territory by aircraft supporting the Kuwait operation. The motives for such action are always hard to anticipate as they stem from unpredictable international behaviour. This obstruction by the two countries necessitated considerable changes of intention. Changes of changes then occurred as Turkey conceded a little and permitted overflights providing they were by night!

**Praise from on high**

It can be imagined what this meant for the operating crews. Communications were swamped, and what did come through altered previous instructions. Facilities in Cyprus and Aden were over-stretched and, as already described, the final destination presented the most atrocious conditions. Air Chief Marshal Sir David Lee GBE CB wrote later in his book '*Flight from the Middle East*':

'*The flexibility shown by Transport Command in switching aircraft and routes to suit the changing circumstances was quite outstanding with the result that, by 4th July, the maximum number of transport aircraft had been concentrated where needed and committed to the airlift.*'

This 'flexibility' is illustrated by a comment from Squadron Leader John Bourn:

'*We flew El Adem - Aden - Bahrain - Aden - Nairobi - Aden without relief. Someone kept moving the slip crews!*'

**Objective achieved**

The final object was achieved in that the ground force was established in time to deter, it is believed, the potential invaders. We return to Norman Rose's account for some insight as to how this was achieved:

'*On our second run to Kuwait, we knew more what to expect! I was able to pass on this information to the Operations Staff we had on board. We once again arrived at Kuwait New in blowing sand, 40°C - and at night. With our passengers disgorged - at the end of the runway - we were pleased to be on our way again in 30 minutes, to Bahrain to refuel. Here chaos reigned with so many aircraft to be turned round. Devious ways had to be used to secure a refuelling bowser. Through fair means or foul, we got our fuel and were airborne for Aden. On landing we learnt that the major effort was just about over and that we were now required to take an aircraft to the haven of Nairobi.*

'*There we relaxed and I was able to reflect on what we had done, under the most demanding conditions, and the wonderful support I had received from my crew - little Sylvia Wapen and her compatriot Air Quartermaster, Sergeant Geoff Pearce, had been fantastic. I knew that, over the last few days we had shown ourselves as real fighters - prepared to have a go when the challenge arose.*'

**Airman killed**

Back at Kuwait, the conditions on the ground did, sadly, take their toll. A

Britannia was being marshalled by Corporal Bob Frost, who had been hastily detached from the Lyneham Electrical Bay as part of the ground servicing party at Kuwait. He must have been blinded or confused by the blowing sand and was struck by one of the propellers and killed outright.

Corporal Frost was 27 years-old and had been at Lyneham since November 1957, being posted in from Germany. He worked first in the electrical bay and then on the Comet and Britannia servicing teams. Bob joined the Royal Air Force in 1952 in the electrical trade group. He was always a very keen sportsman and took great interest in station sports. He played soccer for the station and was largely responsible for organising the inter-section soccer league; he also played cricket for his section. A full military funeral was held at the Kuwait Christian Cemetery on July 5th.

**Withdrawal**

Having achieved its deterrent aim, it was considered diplomatically unsound to retain such a large force in Kuwait and, from 20th July onwards, withdrawal commenced and standby situations created in Bahrain and Cyprus to establish the necessary vigilance.

**A less serious version of events**

'Windy' Deere was also engaged in Exercise Vantage and this is his story:

*'In May of 1991 Audrey and I travelled across the Pond to greet our son who was returning to R.N. Rosyth after having spent six months angling for mines in the Persian Gulf. The two small minesweepers were being accorded full pomp and circumstance, and we were lucky to be granted the privilege of observing much of the ceremony from what appeared to be a converted herring boat rather grandly referred to as 'The Admiral's Barge'. The one incongruous note was that in a sea of red, white and blue my wife and daughter-in-law were enthusiastically waving what passes in this part of the world as the Canadian flag. This caught the Admiral's attention, and he came across and politely offered to lend us his Union Jack to wave. An aide explained to him about exchange officers, thereby saving the ladies from being lashed to the mast. Being flagless, I decided to gain a bit of this VIP's attention by mentioning that I had been involved in the previous Iraqi fracas, and WE didn't need half a million troops, an armada and a thousand aircraft. It took just a few squadrons of transport aircraft and a few battalions of British Brown-Jobs to kick the Iraqis up the Euphrates and home to Baghdad. 'My dear chap, I was in that 'do' too', he replied.*

*'I can't remember the details, but there was the usual 'Flap' as they called out the crews and did mysterious things with flow charts whilst we hung around the crew room drinking coffee and patiently waiting for the chap with the Big Picture to put in an appearance. He never did, of course, and later in the day we were dispatched in the direction of Cyprus on spec. with a couple of crews plus some yeomanry in the back. At Cyprus they also were trying in vain to contact the keeper of the Big Picture, but by now the Brits. were arriving thick and fast they had to do something, and what better way than to send us in the direction of the conflict. The only minor problem was the little matter of diplomatic clearance to overfly hostile Arab and sundry other countries. That problem was quickly solved - 'don't tell 'em!!' We were briefed to fly to Bahrain over Turkey and Iran on the normal airways route, NOT to contact anyone and show NO lights. My minor concern had something to do with aeroplanes flying legally (i.e. with bands playing and bayonets fixed) on the same route, and the chances of all death and no bloody glory. 'Don't worry', said the presiding Wing Commander as he fondled his Little (and unfinished) Picture, 'The chances of hitting something are statistically infinitesimal.' He was just showing off his big words, but we went anyway, maintaining a healthy space between us and the centre-line of the airway.*

*'Well, we didn't hit anything (or I wouldn't be here telling tales) or even see anything, and after about five and a half hours arrived over Bahrain, where, after a bit of explaining about our unexpected and undocumented appearance, were allowed to land. By this time it was well over the nineteen-hour crew duty limitation, but with no prospect of an imminent kip. Instead, we were ushered into the Movements Office whilst the search continued for the fellow with the Big Picture. After about an hour the only sign of movement was, appropriately enough I suppose, the duty Movements*

*Officer. He was an amiable Scotsman, but with a bit of a nervous twitch. I can remember it well. There we are, the five of us, sitting in rather uncomfortable chairs. Ernie Steele, puffing away on his sixtieth cigarette that day, and Taff Richards gently snoring, with just the occasional fart to add a bit of pungency to the proceedings. At the counter in front of us is this Scotsman humming away at some Gaelic ditty. All was peace. The Scotsman starts to fish in his pocket, and after a few moments smiles as he produces on the counter - a spider. A large bloody spider! This was no ordinary Arachnid - the little beasty had had the advantage of a bit of training. We were treated to a remarkable exhibition as our twitchy Jock put the thing through a full repertoire of multi-legged tricks. It climbed his arm, jumped on his nose, did interesting things on the wall and then, after about ten minutes, when no doubt it was a bit clapped out, was gently replaced in the owner's pocket. Throughout all this Tommy Atkins sat transfixed, in open-mouthed astonishment. He did not move a muscle until the show was over, and then exclaimed in disbelief. 'Are they all like you in this part of the world?' 'Och no,' the Movements Officer replied, 'The others only think they've got a spider.'*

*'We eventually went to the operations cum flight planning premises and were instructed to prepare to depart for Kuwait. By this time things were getting into gear, with important looking chaps working on flow charts and a general air of efficiency, giving us the impression that the fellow in charge was privy to at least a significant part of the Big Picture. It was therefore with some confidence that we took off for Kuwait with reasonable expectation of a few beers and a good sleep at the other end. From this point my memory is rather hazy with just vague impressions of Noddy Nursaw, Dinger Bell, heat and sand, Pongos and military hardware, and a slanderous story that the crew of a Britannia had spent some time looking for a marshaller, a ground crew, or at least some sign of life, before deciding that it would be wise to get back in the air a bit sharpish and find the right airfield. I seem to remember that we were treated to a crew meal before being ushered once more on to the aeroplane for the return to Bahrain, where finally we were shown to a rude hut in which were five beds and little else, and where we were assured we could lay our weary heads for seven hours. At that point it had been 53 hours since we had left Lyneham.*

*'The crew call was in the form of a loud banging on the door and for some reason, which I can't explain, we all responded with alacrity, leaping out of bed and abluting in record time, no doubt looking forward to a hearty breakfast before continuing on our way to the next planned destination - Khormaksar. We were washed, shaved and looking dapper in our Changi Khaki when someone glanced at his watch. We'd been in bed all of three hours! A few inquiries revealed that the wrong crew had been called, and we resumed our slumber, all feeling rather foolish.*

*'Apart from that incident there is little else to report of that operation, except that we somehow got lost in the flow chart shuffle and spent the remainder of the trip as passengers, ending up at Lyneham with nothing to show except a bottle and two hundred and a deep scepticism as to the existence of ... the BIG PICTURE.'*

**Summing up**

A suitable postscript to 'Operation Vantage' is provided in Air Marshal Lee's book:

*'The crisis over Kuwait produced what could be described as 'the operation that never was. The plan ... was fully implemented but not a shot was fired and in the event it turned out to be perhaps the most, comprehensive, realistic and valuable movement exercise ever carried out by the three British Services ... In retrospect, intervention in Kuwait ... was highly satisfactory in that it complied fully with the terms of Britain's agreement with Kuwait and brought assistance to the Ruler quickly and efficiently. It may have prevented the annexation of Kuwait by Iraq, although this will never be known with certainty.'*

He also provides a post postscript in that, describing the atrocious conditions, he *alleges* that one Britannia pilot landed in the open desert thinking that it was Kuwait New runway!

*'... undismayed and doubtless contrary to all Transport Command regulations, he took off again and landed in the right place!'*

These words say it all about the Britannia's 'Baptism by Fire'. Though the aircraft was to serve nobly for its many years, it was fortuitous that it was never to meet the conditions and demands of the like of Kuwait again. Hindsight tells us that it was not equipped to do so and for that sort of operation another type of aircraft was required.

The Hercules was not to be purchased for a number of years to come.

CHAPTER NINE

# Behind the Scenes

After the headiness of the description of the Britannia on the front line it is as well to return to earth and consider some of the essential activities being pursued by the 'back room boys'.

**The Brit Sim**

Amongst these can be counted the simulator technicians. Reference has already been made to the provision of a Britannia simulator and its important role in training. This, indeed, was the heralding of a new era. Simulators are now common place, no commercial aircraft of any size is operated without the backing of simulator training and the Royal Air Force has them for its 'fast jet', training and maritime aircraft as well as the transport aircraft that have followed in the Britannia's footsteps. Although they are now taken for granted, their sophistication is not and each new generation amazes as advantage is taken of the cascade of technological development.

The Britannia simulator was an 'early model' in every sense. Its inception was planned alongside the building of the Service aircraft. During the first half of 1958, seven Electrical Fitters (Ground),

490, perhaps typically at night, loaded with the freight and awaiting crew and passengers. Many people contributed to this state of readiness. (*Bill Robinson*)

Here is a 'back room girl'! In the early 60s, Pilot Officer (W) Anne Ibbotson was the personal assistant to Lyneham Station Commander, Group Captain Alasdair Steedman. She married 511 captain Mike Joyce whose subsequent civilian aviation career took him to Canada and, eventually, to Australia. Some 30 years later, on a visit to the UK, Anne met her former boss at a Britannia Association reunion. He was then retired Air Chief Marshal Sir Alasdair Steedman, a patron of the Association. (*Bill Robinson*)

Chief Technician Bradley, Senior Technicians Lockhart, Bristow, Dallas and Cook and Cpl Technicians Ewan and Mills were called to HQ Transport Command for interview by the Command Electrical Officer. They were informed they were to be a new breed - Simulator Technicians. During the summer of 1958 they completed a basic electronics course at RAF Melksham and in September they gathered at the simulator manufacturer's school for a six month course. They then returned to Lyneham and found a new building awaiting the machine. A pilot, Flt Lt Colwell and a flight engineer, Flt Lt Whelan had completed the Bristol aircrew course and were now with the simulator makers advising and checking progress. All came together as the simulator was manoeuvred through the open roll-up door, which occupied the whole of one wall of the purpose built building.

There followed many months of hard work getting the device ready for the important role it was to play and on 21st May 1959, just two days after the delivery of the first aircraft, the first training sortie

Following the demise of the Britannia fleet, the old simulator ended up in Norfolk in a military museum known as the Muckleburgh Collection. It was discovered by Peter Jordan. The author visited the museum some years later and the simulator had disappeared. There was some talk of it having fallen off a lorry when being moved! (*Peter Jordan*)

was flown. A pattern of use was established. For crews on initial training, 20 hours were 'flown' before the aircraft itself. A further 30 hours simulator was then intermingled with the flying to complete the training. When on the Squadrons, pilots and engineers completed six hours continuation training each month. Ground crew found themselves with considerable responsibilities in their handling of the aircraft and full use was made of the simulator for their training in engine starting and checking. All this added up to the target of use of 300 hours per month. The working day was 0600 to 2359 hours.

**5000 hours**

On 2nd March 1961 the 5000th hour was completed. Since installation the simulator had only been unserviceable for

The simulator interior seemed to have survived well - and not a sign of student blood! (*Peter Jordan*)

The incredibly clever structure - the Britannia Dock.
(*David Hamshire*)

30 hours when required for training - a 99.4% availability record! All this achieved by keeping in order 2000 relays each with numerous contacts, 400 amplifiers and over 2000 valves: a far cry from the computer technology of today.

The Britannia simulator, in spite of the rapid dating of its technology, was to last the lifetime of the aircraft. An acknowledgement of its delicate nature in later years was made when it was decided that it should not be moved when the Britannia fleet was transferred to RAF Brize Norton in 1970. Crews travelled back to Lyneham for their valuable training.

**Don't trust Fred**

Behind the scenes is the theme and the technicians working at Embakasi, Nairobi's international airport, who serviced the RAF aircraft staging there, would have considered this very much their venue. Ron Bath writes:

Copilot, Flying Officer Bob Henderson and captain, Flight Lieutenant Bill Robinson 'getting themselves together' for their BEA Viscount training.
(*Bill Robinson*)

'*I was in charge of the shift at Embakasi and so met most flights passing through. I remember one particular Britannia occasion. Very early one morning, during a lift of troops back from Kuwait, a Brit duly landed, parked and disgorged its passengers. We set to on the QTR (Quick Turn Round), refuel, servicing, cleaning. The galley sink was blocked. My airframe ace, Fred, with quick thinking, put an air line plus HP bottles on the outlet horn beneath the aircraft. Fred 'I know everything about Brits' rushed up the steps saying, 'When I shout, give a burst of air.' Always one to do as requested - well nearly - I did as instructed. When I turned the air off there was a sound of wailing. Up the steps I went, to the galley. There was Fred covered in tea leaves, as was most of the back of the aeroplane. We did clean up the mess but what a job. Taught me a lesson - never trust a Fred - he who knows everything!*'

**Operation Dart**

That example of behind the scenes ground crew activity is followed by an aircrew one. The roles of 99 and 511 Squadrons and, indeed, RAF Lyneham in the Berlin Airlift has already been acknowledged in these pages. With road and rail links with West Berlin cut, the only line of supply was by air and the Allies saw to it that this was maintained and succeeded in playing out the Russian challenge. The immediate threat stifled, there had to be an ongoing demonstration of the West's determination to see the air corridors to Berlin maintained. A part of this was to be a clear intention of their continual use. The most obvious way this would be done, and a necessary one to provide links, was civil airline use. It was seen however that, should there be a serious military threat, then the situation would be untenable for civilian crews. It therefore became part of the Cold War scene to have RAF crews qualified to take over and fly civilian aircraft, should the need arise. In the year reached, 1961, crews of 99 and 511 took on this commitment, receiving training and route experience from British European Airways on their Viscount aircraft. It was a task that was to continue for many years and subsequent types of aircraft.

**The Dry Dock**

More background activity, and a sign that the Britannia history is moving along, is the fact that airframe 638 had been with the fleet long enough to require a Major Inspection, the first. This was successfully completed by June 1961. For these inspections, the Britannia Dry Dock had been constructed; a cleverly designed series of platforms and ladders that enabled every part of the aircraft to be reached easily, quickly and safely. With the inspection complete it could be moved aside to allow the aircraft to be towed out of the hangar. It would not be long before the space was refilled and another thorough 'Major' commenced.

**Paris Air Show**

The place held on the world's aviation stage by the Britannia, in spite of its rather chequered civilian career, was indicated by the previously reported invitation for a Royal Air Force Britannia to attend the 1961 Paris Air Show. XL660 was on display in the aeromedical role. That was the story 'in front'. But 'behind the scenes' the preparation of the aircraft prompted the calculation by Tech Wing that there was three times the area on the Britannia to polish compared with a Comet! It is reported that the outside shone like a mirror and the inside looked brand new. It is estimated that 90,000 people passed through the aircraft during the ten days.

At the risk of conveying an impression that the 'Shiny' fleet was all show and no grit, a further mention of 'bull' is extracted from '*The Lyneham Globe*'. On 26th June at 2030 hours the Senior Technical Officer was charged with the task of converting the rear compartment of Britannia Mk2 XN398 into a VIP stateroom complete with two beds. A bulkhead was constructed and covered, beds obtained and secured with manufactured brackets. The job was completed in 17 hours. Who the

Lyneham's hangars had to be modified to accommodate the Britannia's 37½ feet high tail.

A very youthful John Hunting at the Britannia's radio installation. (*John Hunting*)

VIP was needing such a facility at this short notice is not recorded.

**Airborne cinema**

The Lyneham of these years was a prime target for prestige visits. The sight of a proportion of the 23 Britannias and their sister Comets sitting on the apron would surely stir the hearts of MPs, overseas dignitaries, Staff College students, local councillors, career advisers - there was an endless stream of visitors. Some of the more important ones would be taken on a local flight. Not all of this might be magical; on the wrong day it could take place entirely in cloud!

Out of this came the idea of being able to show a film of Lyneham's activities whilst airborne. Peter Jordan was told to investigate:

*'The stipulation was that neither aircraft nor projector were to be modified. The available projector was a 16mm talkie with a 750 watt bulb and 110 volt, 50 c/s motor mounted on a tripod. It stood five feet high and weighed in at 60lbs. Ground tests showed that equipment stability could be guaranteed and adequate sound would be available from the loudspeaker without recourse to the aircraft's passenger address system, use of which had been tentatively suggested. The height of the seats would restrict viewing to a limited number of carefully positioned passengers but that was thought acceptable; there could always be two 'houses'.*

*'It only remained to provide a suitable electrical input and at that point the whole scheme foundered. It was not possible to match the projector requirement with any of the aircraft supplies without some modification. No medals for the originator; no promotion for the investigator. I sometimes wonder what traumas the civvy airlines experienced before airborne films became commonplace.'*

**John Hunting**

Ex-Chief Technician John Hunting was very much part of the Britannia scene for almost all its years of service. Joining the Royal Air Force as a Boy Entrant, he completed 18 months training as an Air Wireless Mechanic and was posted to RAF Lyneham in August 1960. John remembers those early days:

*'I spent the first nine months in Air Radio Servicing Flight; this was a wooden hut at the top of the main road, facing down the 'Calne Strip'. While there, I discovered that little of what I learnt at Cosford could be applied to what was fitted to the Brits and Comet 2s. At this time, I remember the new Brits arriving and was delighted when, in May '61, I was posted to Brit Servicing but spent quite a while on the infamous Handling Flight. Here I mastered the arts of 'moving parties', 'starter crews' and countless re-crystalisations. A break from work at this time was a Brit Wireless course at*

*Filton. Later in 1961, as a result of the then Kuwait crisis, I was sent as part of a servicing team to Nairobi. June '62 saw me off to the wilds of Yatesbury for my Fitter's course. Despite the wooden huts, I survived the horrendous winter of 62/63 and 'passed out' in July '63 complete with an upside-down, single J/T's stripe. It was then back to the Brits at Lyneham, working for Flt Sgt 'Jan' Purbrick and a Flt Sgt whose name escapes me but he called everyone 'dear'.*

**Many Detachments**

*'During the next couple of years I was on many detachments with the Brits. I well remember spending four weeks at El Adem - and Bermuda!*

*'The Britannia radio installation was not the best and would be considered crude by modern standards, but, in general, it was pretty easy to work on. Worldwide flying must have presented many comms problems with the rather limited facilities. The original STR 18B HF could be a pig when there were many Westabout crystal changes to be done; why did the faults occur just when the last crystal was being tuned? The three Mk2 Brits were even worse because they had twin STR 18C HFs; these had up to 100 channels. These three aircraft, and some of the Comet 2s, also had a mysterious and little used Standard SR 32/33 VOR installation. It was just as well that it was either not used or maybe it was extremely serviceable because nobody knew how to fix it. The introduction of the Collins HF was a great improvement but the replacement of the old ten channel TR1998 VHF T/R by the 44 channel TR13046 caused many a headache on crystal changes, although the transmitter autotune facility was much better than doing it by a light bulb.'*

**More behind the scenes**

There is a danger, in highlighting people and sections that contributed to the whole Lyneham effort, that some will be omitted. The risk is being taken!

The MT Section supplying passenger transport, crew buses, catering vehicles, equipment and stores movement, refuellers ... and much more.
(*Lyneham Globe*)

The Air Cargo Section which handled all the incoming and outgoing freight - from boxes of biscuits to aircraft engines ...
(*Lyneham Globe*)

The RAF Police provided airfield security, control of entry to the station, the guarding of special loads ...
(*Lyneham Globe*)

A vital member of the team was the Met Office. Its forecasters and observers had to provide a 24 hour service supplying local forecasts and those for the overseas flights. This is the Senior Met Officer, Mr A Lumley.
(*Lyneham Globe*)

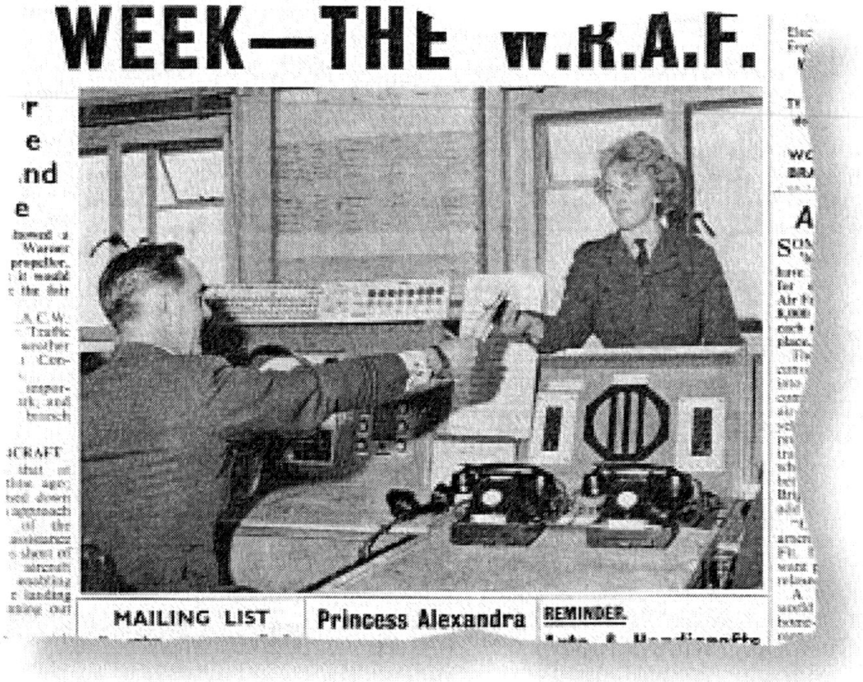


'We Never Close!' Apart from controlling the day and night departures and arrivals of route aircraft, the local training and visiting aircraft and those wishing to transit the Lynham area, Air Traffic Control provided a 24 hour service as a Master Diversion Airfield. Aircraft operators knew that, whatever the time or day, ATC facility were available. The *Lyneham Globe* informs us that LACW Maureen Sutton is passing the daily weather report to Flt Lt Ian Burgess, the Approach Controller.
(*Lyneham Globe*)

Not always the most popular members of the team but, nevertheless, doing a vital job were the Lyneham HM Customs men. They were led for many years by Mr Don Pearce. He established a reputation with crews who alleged that his scale of Customs' Duties was influenced by the Swindon Town football result!

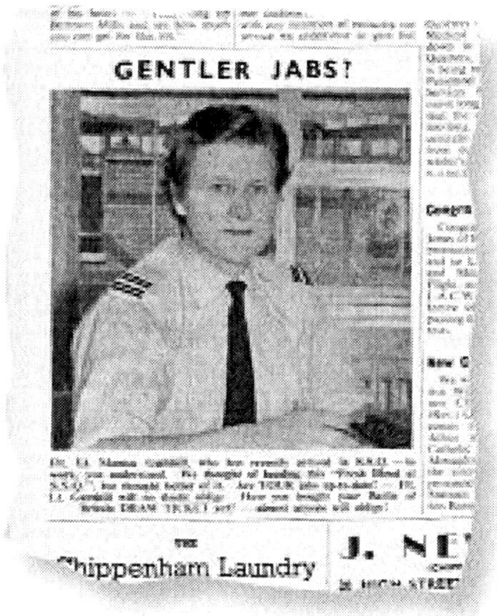

GENTLER JABS?

A vital component of community living is health. Lyneham's Station Sick Quarters (later more sympathetically called the Medical Centre) staff took good care of that. Apart from attending to ills of the servicemen and their families, there was a daily inoculation parade. Aircrew annual medicals were required and there was the safety cover for the airfield and an aeromedical commitment. A busy section! Flt Lt Monica Gurnhill is the representative doctor.
(*Lyneham Globe*)

THEY KEEP 'EM FLYING

Movements Miscellany

... by keeping 'em fed! The Catering Squadron had a mammoth task. Apart from feeding the servicemen in the three separate messes there was the requirement to provide in-flight meals for the departing passengers and crews.
(*Lyneham Globe*)

**The station carpenter**

Ken Guest wrote this article for the Britannia Association magazine:

*'I have recently been passed four copies of 'The Whispering Giant' and reading them brought back many happy memories of RAF Lyneham, and the Britannia. Indeed, I was able to associate with some of your Association members' recollections. I was neither aircrew or a front-line fitter, in fact I arrived at Lyneham in August 1963 as a 17 year-old LAC and was employed in the Station Workshops as a Carpenter, fresh out of Boy Entrant training at St Athan.*

*'No doubt some of you will recall walking past the Carpenter's Shop on your way to the Britannia simulator - who was the officer-in-charge? I upset him one day whilst working on the external door to the flight-deck. He had asked for the door to be hung the opposite way round. For whatever reason, this involved moving the steps out of the way, and whilst positioning the door (without its hinges) he walked through. Did he fall out, or was it just the door that went flying? Either way he was not best pleased with me. The incident must have been well impressed on his mind, for a couple of years later I was back in the simulator block carrying out other work for him and he said to me 'I hope you're not like that other idiot who worked here before.' 'That was me Sir.' 'Oh!'*

*'As a schoolboy I was always interested in aircraft, and whilst in the Air Training Corps, gained flying experience in various aircraft. You will perhaps understand therefore that whilst at Lyneham I was keen to work in areas associated with aircraft whether it be repairing the roof of the red and white chequered PAR hut on a sunny day, in the Control Tower where I could watch you being 'talked down' by one of the Controllers or up in the Operations Room where the map of the world fascinated me with the many destinations that I had never heard of let alone be able to pronounce.*

*'I thought the announcements over the Station tannoy system to alert all staff of an incoming overseas flight were quite a novelty, 'The aircraft now in circuit is Britannia / Comet flight No..... inbound from Akrotiri / Idris ...'*

*'My 'big day' came about 18 months after arriving at Lyneham when Gerry Ormston - my Sergeant, entrusted me with carrying out the monthly maintenance on each of the Britannias as and when they came into the 'dock' in hanger J1. The element of work wasn't that glamorous: removing the toilet bulkheads for inspection and repair, (these were constructed from a spruce timber framing and skinned with 2mm plywood), and taking out the galley worktop and making a new one. I would take these back to the workshop to carry out repair then, at the right time, return to J1 to install. Strange as it may seem I enjoyed this work, because it provided me with a tangible link with the Britannia.*

*'I expect you all remember the wooden glazed 'shed' with one open side, used for lowering aeromed patients from the aircraft via a fork lift truck. It was made by the civilian carpenter, Jack Webb.*

*'My first flight in a Britannia was not planned, as it resulted from a job I had carried out for Flt Lt McGregor, a 99 Sqn captain. When thanked for what I had produced, he said, 'If there is anything I can do for you just let me know', and before he could get out of the door, 'There is one thing Sir, can you fix me up with a flight?' 'Come and see me in my office.' The upshot of it all was that I found myself in baggy KD waiting to be picked up by the crew bus on the main 'drag' outside the NAAFI. I didn't realise it at the time, but Flt Lt McGregor had organised everything for me, as I found out later when I applied for other overseas flights. I will always be grateful for the way he looked after me on my first flight as a Supernumerary Crew member under the watchful eye of Sgt AQM Brian ????.*

The fork lift device constructed by the carpenters to facilitate the transfer of an aeromedical patient from the aircraft to a helicopter or ambulance. An alternative was a covered ramp. (*Lyneham Globe*)

*'It was Friday 22 May 1964, a month before my 18th birthday, when we took off in Britannia XM517 on a four day trip to Malta, Aden and Bahrain. After leaving Luqa we flew over Benghazi and on down through the Sudan and around what I was told was Nasser's Corner across Ethiopia into Khormaksar for an overnight stay prior to flying on up to Muhurraq, returning to Khormaksar the following morning. The next day we returned to the UK via Luqa bringing back wounded soldiers of 40 Commando who I believe had been fighting up in the Radfan.*

*'An amusing point on this flight, or so I thought, was when Brian asked me to make the sandwiches for the captain and crew. Easy, two pieces of bread, bit of butter on each, slap a piece of beef in between and cut in half. Not so! I had obviously forgotten what company I was with. Brian said, ' They're no good, you can have them,' and he proceeded to prepare those for the crew. Out came a tray with serviettes laid over, then the sandwiches were made in much the same way as I had made them, (without the fat on the beef). All the crusts were removed prior to cutting the sandwiches diagonally making little triangles, which were then laid one behind the other on the tray. Ten out of ten for presentation, but what was wrong with what I had produced? They tasted the same!*

*'Once I had 'learnt the ropes', it wasn't too long before I was up in 'Operations' to arrange further Supernumerary Crew trips on both Britannias and Comets. My next Britannia flight was in XL658 to Changi via Akrotiri, Muhurraq and Gan. We left Lyneham on a Thursday 8th July 1995, returning home Monday 12th July on XM497.*

*'One of the articles in the magazines refers to the formation flying for the original 'Freedom of Swindon' parade. I was on that parade, as a member of the Ceremonial Flight. Rehearsals began one cold morning in February 1964 on a wind swept apron. Being in the Ceremonial Flight we were continually practising rifle drill using the .303. Two days before the parade took place, we were joined by the 'Queens Colour Squadron' who were using the newly introduced SLR. Now, although the commands were the same, the movements were not. Chaos! For example the*

Demonstration of troops loading into a Britannia. Brave, and chilly, spectators in the background.

Troops board Britannia 519. This is something of an artificial scene in that the boarding was arranged as a demonstration for HRH Princess Marina, Duchess of Kent on a visit to RAF Lyneham. (*Lyneham Globe*) *slope with the SLR was up to the right shoulder, whereas with the .303 it was up and across the chest to the left shoulder. After spending three months' rehearsing, we had two days in which to relearn at a speed which would allow us to complete each rifle movement at the same time as the Colour Squadron. Quite simply this was achieved by those with the .303 moving a darn sight quicker!*

*'One of my regrets whilst at Lyneham was that I didn't take more photos. The same old story, you think that the present is going to last for ever. I have quite a good selection taken during my two tours (1963-66 and 1968-70). Occasionally, in my dinner hour I would go down to the old boiler house adjacent to the taxi-way to the main runway, and photograph whatever was about at the time. Sunday afternoons were always a good time to wander around the 'pan'. Do you remember the Canadian 'Yukon' - a stretched Britannia with, I believe, Tyne engines, also the Canadian 'Argus' which was a derivative of the Britannia. One Sunday afternoon in 1965 or '66 there was an unusual arrival, the Grumman Goose - at the time the only amphibian to land at Lyneham, I wonder if there have been others since? I remember taking my younger brother Dave to Lyneham when he was still at school and introducing him to my 'Chief ', Johnny Gilkes. The next time Dave was to meet him, Johnny had to salute. One of my proudest moments was when I too had to salute Dave when I met him outside the Squadron Offices. At the time he was with 511 Squadron (I believe), waiting to go on an advanced flying course at Oakington. He went on to become a Hercules pilot at Lyneham, and later returned as CO of No.30 Squadron.'*

**A tailplane story**

There are many 'behind the scenes' stories which never come to light. The majority of Britannia people would be unaware that there was a mid-life crisis with the elevators. In an article for the Britannia Association magazine Warrant Officer Derek (Dicky) Bird BEM told the story:

*'I have been motivated into writing an engineering story that I feel should be recorded in the annals of the 'Life of the Britannia', a previously unsung, enormous effort carried out by many aircraft engineers and supporting trades during a particularly difficult period at RAF Lyneham. What better medium than 'The Whispering Giant'. Hopefully it may ignite some interest among the many readers of this excellent publication.*

*'This may come under the heading of 'Not Many People Knew That' or perhaps even 'When the Brit Was Nearly Grounded'. Some may not find this as interesting as 'A Happening' on the Changi Slip, culminating in a dozen prawns at Lims, and others I can hear saying, 'Didn't Dicky have something to do with the Sergeants' Mess?' So be it! So, it wasn't all fun!*

*'For close on eight years before enjoying the Britannia 'Down Route' at Muharraq VASF and the Hong Kong Airport Unit, I had the privilege of heading a group of magnificent engineers situated in the Airframe Components Bay in the depths of J1 Hangar, alongside the all-embracing Britannia Dock. This is the time when a well organised, logistically efficient and well-manned engineering set-up supported all servicing of the Britannia. Among many airframe and engine components overhauled and tested in the bays, the Britannia flying controls were 'in depth' serviced. The focus of this story centres on the Britannia elevators. To understand the events leading up to a major problem for the Britannia, without being patronising I hope, I must explain, as simply as I can, quite a complex aerodynamic problem - my apologies to the enlightened. 'Flutter' is a dangerous feature of an out of balance control surface, particularly if the system of control should be, as in the design of the Britannia, servo operated. If flutter develops, structural failure will occur. Accordingly, an important feature of servicing a control surface, is the weighing and balancing; the balance is adjusted by a number of weights situated forward of the hinge line of the elevator; they are positioned in the elevator horn. The quantity of weights will affect the all up weight of the control surface. What will affect balance? Modifications, repairs and paint!*

*'During the mid 60s, beavering merrily away, modifications were incorporated with gay abandon and it became difficult to fit the now many balance weights required in the horn aperture. It was also noticed that the elevator 'all up weight' was getting close to the Vol VI limits. BAE were*

*informed and, what was considered to be, a simple request made for an increase in the all up weight of the elevators. This request was met with disapproval, derisory comments and criticism of our RAF methods of weighing and balancing. BAE Filton records showed that the elevators were nowhere near the max all up weight. Eventually our quality methods were proved to be absolutely accurate.*

*'It was about this time, that the Fleet was being painted, with that almost indestructible polyurethane paint - pretty expensive and very heavy. The first painted elevators were sent to be serviced - weighing the components, the all up weight was considerably exceeded. Accordingly, with urgency in our voices, the cry went up, 'What now?' Grave faces, worn by senior quality and weights engineers from Filton, appeared in the flying control bay. It was admitted that Filton had been using inappropriate balancing methods and, more importantly, had neglected to maintain accurate weight records with the incorporation of modifications to the elevators. Heads rolled. It was determined that it was impossible to increase weight allowance due to the insufficient strength of the structure. Significantly it was suggested that the cause of the Britannia crash in the Avon Gorge might have been the breaking off of the elevator horn. To add to the flow of adrenaline, I had to point out that a quite intensive repair programme was in full flow, and I produced wonderful x-rays of damaged trailing edge structure taken from many of the Britannias.*

*'We must all be aware that the Britannia burnt its own tail - the corrosive exhaust gases flowing over the horizontal stabiliser and elevators wreaked havoc with the 32 swg Dural, reduxed structure. Many repairs were carried out to the elevators - particularly at the trailing edge. A few ounces of repair material fitted at the trailing edge, a large distance from the hinge line, required significant weights to balance it out a short distance from the hinge line i.e. situated within the elevator horn. By now, we had determined that the effect of painting the fleet gave us lots of overweight elevators and significantly second thoughts were given to repairs. What to do? High power meetings, MOD etc, realised the impact of the problem. New strengthened elevators were required with haste. Not possible, says BAE, all the elevator jigs have been removed and destroyed to accommodate the Concorde build. It will take a year to start up an assembly line and a further two years to build 22 sets of elevators. There was no alternative! What to do in the meantime! Full emergency measures required - this is our strategic force in jeopardy - Cold War and all that. To minimise this story, it was decided to:*

*1. Remove the paint from elevators (with great difficulty) and only spray with a light coat for protection and cosmetic purposes.*

*2. Examine all elevators by x-ray and determine which elevators were suffering from minimum damage and could be allowed to fly with limited hours. (Red line entries).*

*3. Remove all elevators and use lightest components as 'light sets'.*

*4. Use four spare sets held at Quedgley with limited modifications.*

*'With this situation now urgently receiving attention, it was suggested that a recovery exercise was carried out to bring home the set of undamaged elevators from the pranged Britannia in Aden. This was carried out successfully, I believe by a special task force under dangerous conditions. All this gave us a quantity of elevators to*

THEY KEEP 'EM FLYING

Chief Technician John Westlake (Non-Destructive Test Section) closely studies a Radiograph of part of a Britannia tank bay. All Britannia and Comet aircraft based at Lyneham are systematically X-rayed for corrosion and metal fatigue by the Non-Destructive Test Team.
(Photograph by S.A.C. Harris, N.D.T. Sect.)

The 'back room' job to end all 'back room' jobs? Chief Technician John Westlake of the Non-Destructive Test Section, closely studies a radiograph of part of a Britannia tank bay. All Comet and Britannia aircraft were systematically X-rayed for corrosion and metal fatigue by the Non-Destructive Test Team. (*Lyneham Globe*) *work on and hold in reserve.*

*'I cannot begin to itemise what these subsequent procedures meant in effort and man-hours; the exercise to maintain few selective flying aircraft was enormous. Continuous unscheduled removal and selective fitment of elevators night and day, and sometimes after very limited route trips, became the order of the day. This enormous additional tasking was carried out by A and B Lines personnel ably supported by the Servicing Teams, Rectifications, the various Bays and of course the MT Section. The non-destructive test (NDT) programme was extensive; the study of internal damage was essential. Decisions to repair or to allow aircraft with damaged elevators to continue to fly had to be made. The lads in the Flying Control Bay were on call night and day with continuing repairs and weighing and balancing. A major task was to remove the polyurethane paint, and to this end a dozen or more young WRAFs and lads were posted in as a reinforcing team to complete this unenviable task. The enormous contribution by the ground crews kept the Britannia flying until eventually the whole fleet was fitted with new strengthened elevators. The modification programme did take longer than the predicted three years - and so this story can be told with some pride.*

*'If you knew nothing about this, we* ***were*** *told to 'Keep Mum' - after all it was our* ***only*** *strategic transport force!'*

**Epitome of a Station Warrant Officer**

Warrant Officer Bill Baird will not need any introduction to anyone who served at RAF Lyneham between 1958 and 1966. Mr Baird was the, high profile, Station Warrant Officer for those years. On 31st October 2000, Jack Moore, one of the Britannia Association's welfare staff, organised a return visit for the old SWO. It was hosted by Lyneham's Community Relations Officer, Sqn Ldr Christopher Bartle, who later published this press release:

*'A 90 year old former RAF Warrant Officer recently paid a nostalgic visit to his old station at RAF Lyneham - 34 years after he left it. The position of Station Warrant Officer is the highest non-commissioned post available in the RAF, and Warrant Officer William George Baird MBE held the post at Lyneham from 1958. He returned to the scene of nearly nine*

*years of his RAF service to see the changes that had taken place since he retired from the RAF there in 1966. The visit was arranged by Mr Jack Moore of the Britannia Association, and several other members accompanied Mr Baird in the visit. All of them were contemporaries of the ex-SWO, and all flew on the Britannia aircraft at Lyneham in the 1960s.*

*'Bill Baird joined the RAF on an impulse when passing the headquarters at Adastral House in London in 1930. He and a friend decided to pop in, and within a couple of hours they had done a few tests and passed a medical, and five weeks later they were wearing light blue uniform. Enlisting as a physical training instructor, Mr Baird won awards in many sports over the years; he played both football and cricket for the RAF, and he was the welterweight boxing champion for both the RAF and the Imperial Services. On his return visit Mr Baird was shown round Lyneham by the Station's Community Relations Officer, Christopher Bartle. He recognised some of the buildings that had been opened during his time there, but confessed himself lost at times amongst the many new buildings that have gone up in the intervening years. The visit ended with tea in the Sergeants' Mess, which was opened during Bill's time at Lyneham. Reminiscences with his old comrades produced many memories of the Station. These included the big development programme of the late 1950s and early 1960s; the time an engineering officer got airborne by mistake*

'KEEP OFF THE GRASS!!' Station Warrant Officer Bill Baird on the occasion of his visit to RAF Lyneham. With him are Britannia Association members Brian Jordan, Ann Bihan and Jack Moore. (*David Berry*)

*in a supersonic Lightning fighter that he was servicing; the years he spent coaching the Lyneham boxing team to victories in national competitions; and a Sergeant who worked for him, but who never came in on the last Thursday of the month because that was the day he got drunk. Prime amongst his recollections, however, was the fact that he had been among the first Station Warrant Officers to introduce a gentler, more human approach to the job, rather than the then traditional way of shouting at people. He liked to think that this contributed to the happy atmosphere on the Station during his time there.*

*'Since his retirement Mr Baird has been living in the Moredon area of Swindon, just 12 miles from where he spent one quarter of his RAF career.*

*He hopes to visit Lyneham again when he reaches the age of 100!'*

A fork lift truck handling freight in the cargo shed.

Motor Insurance

JONES'

Three *Globe* photographs to round off this 'Behind the Scenes' chapter. Here a fork lift handles freight in the cargo shed. (*Lyneham Globe*)

The Route Hotel was an essential part of passenger handling. Here they could be assembled and fed, if necessary, prior to a flight. Overnight accommodation was also available for departing and arriving passengers. (*Lyneham Globe*)

.OBE—No. 163 (2)

J FIT AMP?

PADR

Churc

Free Cl

Passengers for the 2 o'clock Comet West Med schedule arrive at the Route Hotel, Lyneham for lunch. They have been brought by bus from Swindon station.

The Operations Room, located on the upper floor of the Terminal Building, controlled all the tasks that contributed to safe and punctual departure and arrival of route aircraft. A plot was kept of the location of the aircraft around the world. (*Lyneham Globe*)

Operations control scan the world—bringing up to date the place and E.T.A. of Lyneham aircraft.

St. Mic

Parish

RADIO PADRE

CHAPTER TEN

# The Changi Slip - and Icing

Proof that the Britannia was a 'World Shrinker' came on 9th October 1961 when XM497 returned to Lyneham having circumnavigated the globe in 15 days covering 33,000 miles, landing at Gibraltar, Ascension Island, Waterkloof (Pretoria), Mauritius, Cocos Island, Changi (Singapore), Guam and Midway in the Pacific, Fairbanks (Alaska), Thule (Greenland) then on to Lyneham. It will be noted that this was very much a 'sea' route and the land overflown belonged to nations sympathetic to our cause. It is another example of the previously mentioned 'Cable Route' and needed keeping in reserve for the worst diplomatic situation in which we could find ourselves - at least that was the excuse for a very pleasant trip!

But meanwhile what were the more menial tasks?

Ascension Island used the Britannia on a stamp to mark the 50th Anniversary of the Royal Air Force. (*Roger Carvell*)

**The Changi Slip**

Whilst members of the 'Country Club', as were known those whose experience and influence gravitated them towards the more exotic tasks, flew such routes as the one just described, what occupied the average squadron member? The major continuous task of all the Britannia years was known as the 'Changi Slip' - Changi being the terminal airfield in Singapore and 'Slip' indicating that the aircraft was kept on the move by changing, or slipping, crews along the route. The Britannia saw the height of our postwar global commitment when we had garrisons all over the world but principally in the Middle and Far East. All these needed a constant supply of men (and their families) and materials and it was this that was the purpose of the 'Changi Slip'. A Britannia departed every day from Lyneham and by slipping, i. e. changing crews en route, it was in Singapore in 30 hours. There it was unloaded and reloaded and on its way back to the UK within eight hours. Thus, an aircraft would be in use for around three days. The crews, however, would be away for two to three weeks. So the 'Changi Slip' was very crew intensive and Mr (and Miss) Average spent a lot of their time somewhere in the Middle or Far East.

**The route**

That somewhere changed over the years. The original route flown was Lyneham - RAF El Adem in Libya - RAF Khormaksar, Aden - RAF Gan, on one of the southernmost Maldive Islands in the Indian Ocean - RAF Changi, Singapore. They were all refuelling stops but the crews only normally slipped at Khormaksar and Changi.

Over the years, with altering circumstances, the route changed. RAF Brize Norton became the UK departure airfield and RAF Akrotiri, Cyprus the first stop. With the evacuation of Aden, RAF Muharraq, Bahrain was the staging post for

Not a warning to the Middle and Far East of Britannia crew activity but a notice on the slipway of the RAF Marine Craft Unit at Gan. (*David Berry*)

a while. This changed again to RAF Masirah on Masirah Island off the East coast of Oman. Throughout the years, Gan remained constant. Towards the end of our Far East era, the terminal airfield on Singapore Island became RAF Tengah.

**Those airfields**

An attempt will be made to paint a picture of these staging posts. A start is made with RAF El Adem. Extracts from '*The Lyneham Globe*' would not win a major literary prize! But they are being used here to give a feel for the times. El Adem was a woeful airfield in the middle of an unattractive desert - but there was spirit:

'*RAF El Adem is situated about 18 miles from the Libyan town of Tobruk of World War II fame. The airfield was originally built at that distance by the Italians to be just outside the range of the guns of British battle cruisers. There is an acute shortage of accommodation suitable for Royal Air Force families and the Station has had to control not only hirings, but also even the private accommodation to curb the likelihood of inflation. These precautionary measures have been very successful but, unfortunately, it does mean that there just is no accommodation available to anyone until his name comes up on the waiting list. However, there are approximately 300 service families living in Tobruk and it is this that has resulted in a spate of building and an increase in the local population's eagerness to get in on the boom. Right now, the face of the station is changing at a fabulous rate. Self-help labour has enabled the preparation of flowerbeds in the vicinity of Station HQ and there is the intention of raising two beds of grass on the approach from the guardroom. If this project is a success, the largest 'KEEP OFF THE GRASS' notices in the world will certainly be employed. During the coming year there will be the beginning of the building of married quarters outside the camp which will ease the strain on Tobruk. Also, the almost legendary El Adem swimming pool will open. Much of El Adem's difficulties have come about because of the advent of larger aircraft and more frequent flights from Lyneham. The workload on the Station outgrew the building programme but it is beginning to catch up. Before Christmas the new El Adem Transit Hotel is to open and it will really streamline the Station's primary function. Additional transit accommodation has already been prepared and, dare it be suggested, El Adem could face up to an unserviceable Britannia with a full passenger load, without the Duty Air Movements Officer having a heart attack.*'

**The 'Changi Slip' aircraft configuration**

The aircraft flew mainly in the PCF role, Passenger cum Freight: there must have been a Latin scholar around when this term was created. More prosaic

ROBINSON ON ROUTE—1

A passenger's view of the French Alps, seen from a southbound Britannia flying at 19,000 feet. It was over terrain such as this that the Comet 4 of King Ibn Saud of Saudi Arabia was recently lost.

Bill Robinson was a regular provider of photographs for the *Globe*. This is the view *en route* to the first stop on the Changi Slip - over the French Alps. (*Lyneham Globe*)

folk would have had the abbreviation PWF handed down the years: Passengers With Freight. This role met a demand; most families travelled, on posting, by civil charter aircraft, typically British Eagle (which will have left an indelible and painful memory of the Britannia with many) but there were always a few to travel in between those flights. Add to these personnel travelling for various temporary duties and there was enough demand for 30 seats at the back of the aircraft.

Forward of this would be the freight. This could be anything from, say, a jet engine to a box of stationery. The aircraft were always full. This may have been more in proof of a Parkinson's Law of Military Air Transport, (if space is available on aircraft then someone will find a way of filling it) than of real demand! With their eyes averted from the cargo, our passengers would have happy memories of the RAF Britannia. There was room to move around and they had the attention of our air quartermasters who took great pride in their service.

**Windy Deere with Changi Slip stories**

*'I was lucky enough to be posted on to the Britannia in the days when one did the maker's course at Bristol, followed by the OCU at Lyneham and, for navigators, a short course on Green Satin at Gaydon, a total period of about six months after which we should have been able to build our own Brit. Apart from gaining a fairly comprehensive knowledge of the aeroplane, the course served to cement the relationships that were later to be the foundation of three closely knit and well trained crews. The industry was just beginning to become preoccupied with cutting down crew complement in order to avoid high wage bills, but the RAF was getting five for the price of three, and in any case Transport Command had one of the safest and most efficient systems in aviation.*

*'Our course consisted initially of Bill Smith, Nogger Norris, Ken Bick, Kel Thomas, Tommy Atkins, Graham Bayliss, Pete Barnett, Barry Wildin and yours truly. I was crewed up with Bill and Tommy. We were joined by the engineers and signallers during the OCU phase, and unfortunately I cannot recall who joined the other two crews but our own team was completed with Taff Richards and Ernie Steele. And so began three of the most enjoyable and eventful years of my flying career.*

*'The main task was of course the Changi Slip, although I seem to recall that we did spend a fair number of days in Aden.*

*Ernie enjoyed Aden. I think that was because he knew most of the Arabs there. At least I think he did. He certainly knew their names. Without exception they all answered to the name of George, which was convenient for Ernie but must have been a mite confusing for the indigenous folk. Taff didn't care too much for the Arabs. It was his opinion that if we transported them anywhere they could travel in the F-F-F-F-F-F-Freight Bay. Come to think of it, that's where he thought Pongos and all other lesser beings should be. Taff was never short of an opinion. After completing his pre-flight cockpit check he would spend any remaining time giving us the benefit of his point of view of the various topics of the day, in his lilting Welsh accent coloured by his occasional tendency to stutter when he became excited.*

*'There was one famous occasion when we were being treated to a particularly venomous diatribe. There he stood, blocking the access to the pilots' seats, facing Ernie and myself, who were really more interested at that moment in logs and charts and high frequencies, when in walks Tommy, who had no doubt been chatting up the AQM, and commences to do his cockpit check. So there's Taff in full V-V-V-V-Voice going on about some political bother, one hand on his seat and the other resting comfortably on a convenient handhold on the cockpit wall, when he suddenly became over-excited and started raving. 'What the F-F-F-F-F-...' at the same time as the fire bell started ringing. It quickly became apparent that his excitement was due to the transmission of a fair number of volts through Taff - via the fire bell. Ernie and myself didn't get the gist of what followed; well it's difficult when you're doubled up in the aisle, but I seem to remember Tommy remarking to Taff that he really shouldn't say that to a 'hociffer'.*

*'I am sure there are many members of our Association who remember Air Vice Marshal Craven, ex-Station Commander of Lyneham. I can't remember what his subsequent appointment was, but we saw quite a lot of him during our first year or so on 99 Squadron. He always showed a keen interest in the Britannia operation. I often wondered if some senior officers did not rue their promotion from the plebs to exalted rank, leading to rather dull ivory towers. On one of our early Slips he joined us at Lyneham and accompanied us as far as Singapore. We were unlucky, for on each leg we suffered some sort of mechanical snag. By the time we arrived at Gan, Taff had decided where the problem lay, and that night in the bar of the Transit Mess he gave full vent to his theory. 'It's*

6356 29 " MWBJH

FLIGHT ROLE: To be notified by MOD (RAF)

ITINERARY

| STATION | CHOCKS IN | TURNAROUND TIME | CHOCKS OUT | CHOCK TO CHOCK TIME |
|---|---|---|---|---|
| Lyneham | | | D1/1810 | 06.30 |
| Akrotiri | D2/0040 | 1.30 | D2/0210 | 06.15 |
| Muharraq | D2/0825 | 1.30 | D2/0955 | 07.00 |
| Gan | D2/1655 | 1.30 | D2/1825 | 07.05 |
| Changi | D3/0130 | 6.00 | D3/0730 | 06.50 |
| Gan | D3/1420 | 1.30 | D3/1550 | 07.00 |
| Muharraq | D3/2250 | 1.30 | D4/0020 | 06.25 |
| Akrotiri | D4/0645 | 1.30 | D4/0815 | 07.00 |
| Lyneham | D4/1515 | | | |

A circa 1965 schedule for a Changi Slip. There are several points to note. Crew duty time was calculated from the reporting time for the flight - two hours before departure time. So the planned day for Lyneham to Muharraq is 16 hours and 15 minutes - starting at 1810. Hope the kids weren't making too much noise for that day sleep! The Changi departure time looks a little better - 0730 - but that's GMT. The local time is 1500 for a 17 hour 20 minute day! So it's go to bed a normal time and try to sleep on during the heat of the morning.

*that B-B-B-B --- AVM - he's a jinx, that's what he is a J-J-Jinx.' Unfortunately for Taff, the jinx was sitting just a short distance away and possibly within earshot. (One could have been within earshot of Taff on other side of the island!) In the interests of diplomacy and career prospects we managed to cool the rhetoric and change the subject, and apparently no harm was done.*

*'We proceeded on to Changi complete with Air Vice Marshal and yet another snag, and of course this was further proof that we were carrying a high ranking jinx, and that night we were again treated to a short but vehement lecture over our pints of Tiger. The next leg was to Hong Kong, and we set forth the following morning, this time without our distinguished passenger. Once we were nicely settled in the cruise, Bill took leave of us for the greener pastures of the galley area, where one could have a friendly chat with Betty Fendley whilst enjoying a cup of 'instant' and a fag. Shortly after that the firebell went off, woke up Ernie and Tommy and startled me. There seemed to be no clear indication of where the fire could be, until smoke began to arise from the left side of the vacant captain's seat. Check lists were quickly being consulted, but things seemed to be getting worse, and I decided it was time the Boss was put in the picture. Putting on my 'everything's just dandy and I'm just popping down for a leak' expression, I proceeded down the aisle past the passengers at a leisurely 25 knots to where Bill and Betty were in amiable conversation. 'Bill, we've got a small problem up front.' 'Oh yeah, what's that then,' says Bill, drawing contentedly on his Woodbine. 'Well, Bill, I think we're on fire, and they can't put it out.' It takes a lot to shake Bill, and give him his due, it took him a few microseconds to douse fag and return to the sharp end. By then there was a fair old cloud of acrid smoke in the cockpit, and I could only just see Tommy's bleak expression as he stared anxiously rearward from behind his oxygen mask. Taff was still at it, isolating electrical circuits and so forth, and eventually the smoke began to dissipate. The weather radar had burnt out. We did a 180 and returned to Changi and after a quick shower and change of clothes reported to the bar at Changi Creek for a medicinal pint to settle the old nerves. Who should be there but our faithful engineer's favourite scapegoat, Air Vice Marshal Craven, who promptly left his seat, came up to Taff, and with a sardonic smile remarked, 'Well, Master Engineer, you can't blame me this time!!'*

Group Captain R E Craven OBE DFC was the Station Commander of Lyneham when the Britannias first arrived. (*Lyneham Globe*)

**The challenge**

The average squadron member would probably do at least one Changi Slip a month. It might well be that before the end of that month he would be part way into another

*'The tumult and the shouting dies, the captains and the kings depart ...'* But the beast still has to be unloaded and here an awkward box is tackled on an autumn evening. (*Lyneham Globe*)

The Britannia provided new standards of comfort for Service passengers. With the RAF commitment to rear-facing seats, then the flight deck must be the bright area in the background of this photograph.
(*Bill Robinson*)

one. So it was a route with which we became very experienced; this was as well for it did offer its challenges.

Obviously there were the vagaries of the UK, European and Mediterranean weather to contend with and then, as the route progressed, the tropics threw up their challenge. Cumulo-Nimbus clouds, with their associated turbulence (with aircraft breaking potential) and icing, reach their greatest intensity in this region. There was a device for giving information on these for avoidance action, the Cloud Collision Warning Radar (CCWR), but this was not always the answer. Firstly, it was not completely reliable and secondly the occurrence of these clouds could be so widespread that there was no real way of totally avoiding them. If flying in such a situation could have been stripped of its discomfort and apprehension then the scale of the clouds and the lightning flashes provided 'the greatest show on earth'!

**The engine icing problem**

Of course, all aircraft flying in that region would experience the same risks (saying that, it was not an area that generated much commercial air traffic). However, the Britannia had an additional problem which has already been mentioned a number of times - engine icing.

Devices and procedures had been devised in an attempt to eliminate this

Changi was typical of many RAF airfields: expanding and expanding from small beginnings. Britannias had to cross a public main road to reach their dispersal area. Here one does so beneath a blackening sky. (*David Court-Smith*)

difficulty but they did not provide the whole solution. Sometimes, no matter that the correct drill was being carried out, conditions could be so severe that the devices were unable to cope. Secondly, the procedures were so critical that it was not always possible to follow them. For whatever reason, possibly a combination, engine icing would occur.

**EGVs on**

The first line of defence was heating of the engine entry guide vanes (EGVs). Air entering the nacelle met these vanes whose purpose was to suitably adjust the flow to meet the next engine component. The heating of these vanes had to be switched on if the aircraft entered cloud at any temperature. Two questions might cross the mind. One: why not have them on all the time? Answer: there was a fuel penalty; consumption was increased by 5%, which could be critical. Two: what's the problem? You can see cloud. At night? That is why visitors to the flight deck in the dark might have found one or both of the pilots, sitting on the edge of their seats peering through the windscreen, possibly with a torch.

A photograph from Pilots' Notes of the overhead control panel with de-icing controls to the right. The left is concerned with engine starting and in between are the four engine fire control channels.

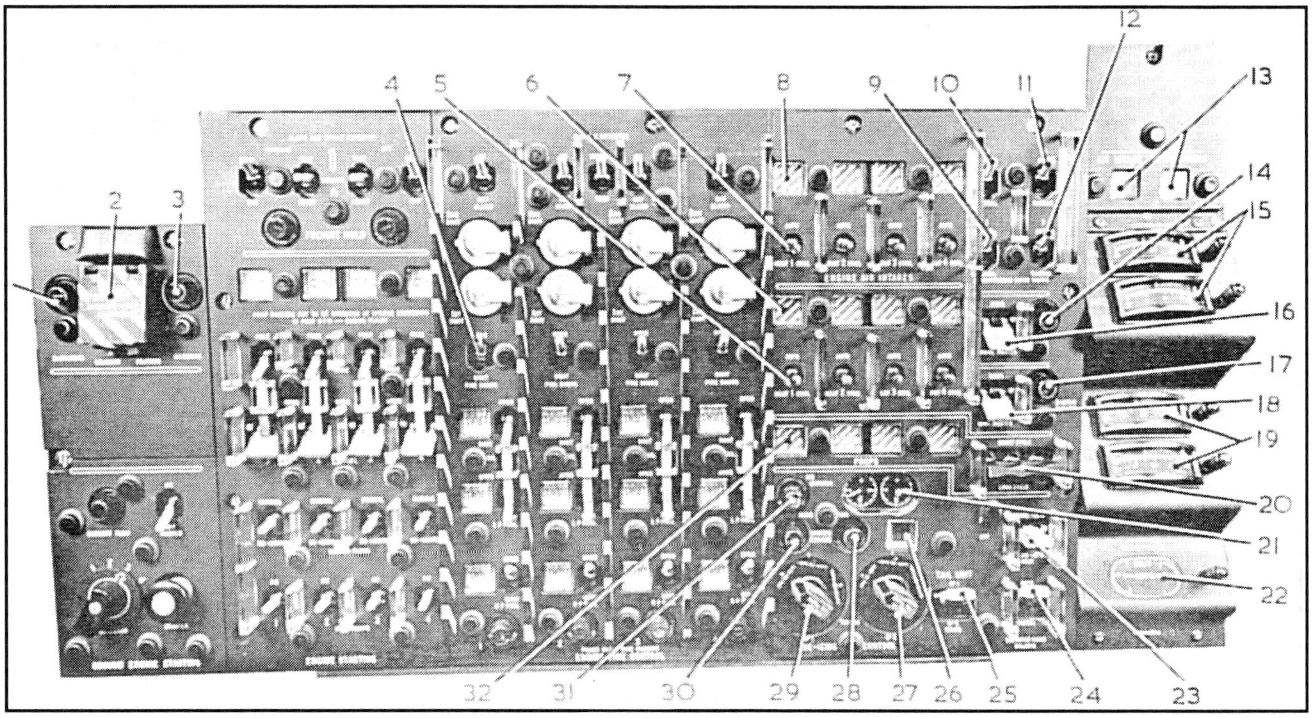

**Cowl Heat on**

The EGVs went on, no matter what the temperature. The next protection device was very temperature, and speed, sensitive. This was known as the Cowl Heat and was designed to combat the problem caused by the reversing of flow in the engine of air with a high water content at particular temperatures, such as are met in the tropics. It has been mentioned how the Britannia development met bad luck here in that it was not previously realised that such sensitive conditions existed.

**Lumps of ice**

Cowl Heat did just what its name implies. The outer surface of the engine air intake was heated as well as the rear walls and corners of the individual ducts by hot air bled from the engine. All this to stop the wet cold air depositing ice on the bend where the flow reversed. If ice was allowed to accumulate there, then when it reached a certain volume, it would detach itself and pass down the engine. The finely engineered components there were intended for the flow of gases, not lumps of ice, so damage could occur, the engine be temporarily stalled and, in the extreme, the flame of combustion extinguished.

**Critical temperatures**

One can imagine crews under training, learning of this deficiency, being somewhat relieved to hear that this icing phenomena was only critical at certain temperatures. Such relief would be dashed when it was discovered that those temperatures were just the ones met at the aircraft's normal cruising altitudes in the tropics. It was a real problem.

The Cowl Heat HAD to be switched on, in cloud, between indications on the outside air temperature gauge of +2°C and +12°C. However, if the temperature was between +2°C and +6°C, then the speed had to be reduced to 200 knots first and the temperature rechecked to see if it was still in the 'Cowl Heat On' range of +2° to +12°. Just its use carried a large fuel penalty and if slowing down was also required, the result could be critical.

All this concentrated the minds of crews at the Meteorological Briefing and the subsequent pre-flight planning. Choosing the height at which to fly was like

Time in the right-hand seat was a valuable learning experience for copilots. The degree of help given from the captains in the left-hand seat was variable. Here captain Bill Robinson gives his copilot a few tips. (*Bill Robinson*)

some aeronautical brain teaser; flying at the optimum height for fuel flow, airspeed and range could have the temperature right in the critical range. Lower height and the temperature would be alright but the fuel flow too high; as high as possible might bring the temperature below +2°C but the airspeed might be unacceptably low to cover the distance with the fuel available. It was certainly a nightmare situation for crews.

**Fly Low/High**

Strangely, it was a number of years into the life of the aircraft before a system evolved which largely beat the problem; this was known as the 'Low/High Technique'. Initially the aircraft was flown low, typically 12,000 feet, with temperature well above the dreaded band. Good progress would be made but at the cost of high fuel flows.

After two or three hours, with the weight now reduced by the amount of fuel burnt, the aircraft was climbed and was comfortably able to achieve a level, at a good airspeed with low fuel flows, where the temperature was below +2°C.

It worked, although initially it took a lot of nerve as the fuel tank contents seemed to sink so rapidly. Remember, on the legs into and out of Gan, this was taking place over a predominantly ocean route.

**Bumps**

Trouble with engine icing would be heralded by no more than a flicker of a compressor RPM (CRPM) gauge. This would be a small piece of ice being released into the engine. The momentary movement of the needle would only be apparent to the experienced, and perhaps anxious eye, of a pilot or flight engineer. The next stage, as a larger piece of ice became dislodged, would be noticed by everyone. There would be a

Many loading trials had to be completed, with the height and dimensions of the door presenting a particular problem. The Sid James look-alike on the right seems pleased with the progress so far! *(Ian Berry)*

positive needle deflection accompanied by a jolt through the airframe. There might even be a slight yaw because power was being lost, albeit only for a moment, as critical fuel/air ratio was upset by the ice.

**Flame-out**

The crew would be double checking that they had carried out the correct actions and if so, whether there was any way of escaping from this dilemma. If not, then things were likely to worsen. The lurches would increase in intensity and perhaps the next level of trouble would be reached where so much ice passed into the engine that the flame in the combustion chambers was extinguished.

Into play would then come the engine manufacturer's crude solution; two plugs were located in two of the chambers and they would glow white hot whilst the engine was running normally. If the flame went out, because of the passage of ice, the plug would reignite the fuel. This would have continued to flow during the extinction, so when the relight took place there would be a huge tongue of flame from the jet pipe. There must have been many a Britannia passenger who thought that the end was nigh as he sat in the dark witnessing this spectacle.

**Relight drill**

There was even a further degree of

It could be that ingenuity often solved a loading problem. (*Ian Berry*)

seriousness. It might be that the fuel was not reignited and the engine would start to totally wind down. It was then up to one of the crew to go through a rapid engine restarting procedure. It did not have to be too quick though; it would be unsuccessful if it was commenced at too high a CRPM. Nerves of steel were indeed required.

All these engine 'bumps' were recorded by the navigator and the number and severity reported to the technicians on landing. Internal engine damage could have been caused and a check on this would have to be made.

A device known as an introperiscope was passed into the air intake and around bends and, through an eyepiece, the condition of the entry guide vane and the rotor blades of the first stage compressor could be checked to see if they were damaged.

From all this it can be seen that the Britannia's engine icing problem was a continual potential hazard and constraint. But, having said that, it was amazing how crews came to terms with it and, with skilful management, kept the hazards to a minimum.

**A 'people' aside**

The title of this book claims that it is, in part, about Britannia people. With that in mind, it is worth returning to that example of a Changi Slip itinerary that appeared above. The reason that it is preserved is that it was used as scrap paper. On the reverse are notes by a struggling Flying Officer - one trying to pass the 'B' Promotion Examination to qualify him for promotion to Flight Lieutenant. There were a number of very senior Flying Officers on the Britannia fleet who had missed out on taking/passing the exam earlier in life. Now, with route flying commitments it was a real struggle. There was also the deadly boring and irrelevant nature of the syllabus. The notes on the scrap paper are for 'Military Studies'. One example is that the examinee is asked to define 'Air Superiority' - '... can be defined as a condition in which we are able to make use of the air for our own purposes and the enemy air forces are unable to operate effectively against us.' ... Really! Yawn ... eyelids droop ... another fail!

*'Specialist Aircrew'* is published by and is available from Keyham Books, Startley, Chippenham SN15 5HG for £10.99, UK p&p free.

It is curious to reflect on why it was thought necessary for a Flight Lieutenant to possess the knowledge required to pass the exam. Indeed, common sense did eventually prevail and it was abolished - but not soon enough for these sufferers of the 1960s. When it did go then the promotion only depended on an approval from the Flying Officer's commanding officer. This was, more or less, a 'rubber stamp' process - except in the case of one charismatic 511 navigator - whose aura and charm obviously did not embrace his CO. But we move away from the core of this book. Perhaps for more of this theme you should read another of the author's books, '*Specialist Aircrew*'!

**Gan**

Returning to the main scene of that icing angst, the Changi Slip, it was seen from the start that there would have to be a full infrastructure to support the continual and intensive operation of sophisticated aircraft along this military lifeline to the Far East.

These facilities were to be shared with the Comets in their trooping role and later the VC10s and Belfasts. Perhaps the largest project was the construction of the staging post airfield on the island of Gan.

A very early photograph, as indicated by the almost total lack of vegetation, of the completed Gan. This was soon to regrow. The runway was a dazzling white.

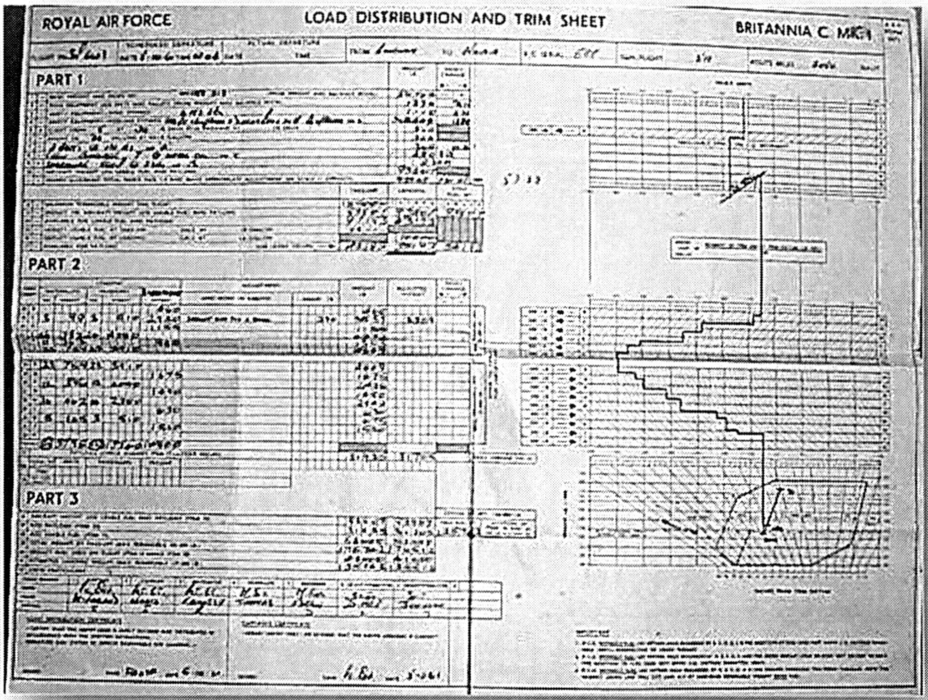


Ex-Movements corporal Jim Aitken preserved this record of the Britannia trim sheet which taxed many minds over the years!. (*Jim Aitken*)

A regular and popular feature of '*The Lyneham Globe*' was the cartoon strip '*Ad Minn and Org*', drawn by 511 captain and talented artist, Flt Lt Malcolm Fraser with the story line by 511 navigator, Flt Lt Dicky Thornborough. Apart from amusing, it often provided 'social comment' from 'the workers'! Malcolm and Dicky's work has been preserved in a booklet which was published and contained all the past 'strips'. These are reproduced in the pages that follow to provide a little light relief at the end of a 'heavy' chapter!

## INTRODUCTION

ON a Cotswold pimple, near Bradenstoke-cum-Clack and in the vicinity of Wootton Bassett, spreads the huge, ugly and now famous Royal Air Force station at Lyneham —once called "Steptoe and Son in Cinemascope." Based there is the Long-Range Force, fleets of Britannias and Comets. This complex route terminal publishes its own newspaper fortnightly—*The Lyneham Globe*, largely in self-defence.

In the autumn of 1962, two earnest and high ranking officials of the Ministry of Watsit, Mr. Ad Minn and Mr. Org, began a search which makes the Holy Grail affair look like "hunt the thimble." The *Globe* despatched two reporters to cover the investigations of these two gentlemen (and also to clear office space). Flight Lieutenant Richard ("Dicky") Thornborough wrote the epic story, chapter by chapter, while Flight Lieutenant Malcolm ("Drac") Fraser drew pictures. This he did (a) because he can't write, (b) the Editor sat on our cocoa-tin camera, (c) the average *Globe* reader NEEDS pictures.

Dicky "deserted" after our distinguished pair reached the Antipodes, and retired to a Northumbrian fastness, there to contemplate among other things, a somewhat chilly navel; but the indefatigable "Drac" remains a faithful if slightly sardonic chronicler of the heroes' pilgrimage through the military air transport world. In his spare time he flies Britannias, for a small fee.

People may consider that the adventures of Messrs. Ad Minn and Org at Wootton Lynestoke bear a resemblance to events, people and routine current at R.A.F. Lyneham and on its associated trunk route (Lyneham — Tobruk / El Adem — Aden / Khormaksar — Gan Island — Singapore / Changi), and that beyond this sphere of activity there would be no interest in their doings.

We ask you to turn the pages, look closely at the superb illustrations and see just how wrong these people can be.

Once upon a light year . . .

3

The adventures of Messrs. Ad Minn and Org at Wootton Lynstoke commence ...

CHAPTER ELEVEN

# Oh Island in the Sun ... and other staging posts

The stirrings of the need for an Indian Ocean staging post began as plans were being made to equip the Royal Air Force with a modern air transport fleet. The story of Gan's closing told by the last Station Commander, Group Captain W Edwards AFC RAF, in an article for a 1976 edition of Air Clues, provides information on its beginnings:

*'On 29 March 1976, the RFA Sir Percivale embarked the last of the rear party, weighed anchor, headed through the Gan Channel bound for Cyprus, and with a farewell blast on the ship's siren, signalled the end of the RAF presence in the Maldives ...'*

**The beginning**

*'The final withdrawal was the closing, not perhaps of a chapter but a footnote in Royal Air Force and British military history. The association with Addu Atoll, on which Gan is the most southerly island, goes back to 1941 when the then highly secret Port T was built as a Safe Fleet Anchorage in anticipation of war in the Far East. A short airstrip was subsequently constructed on Gan and the lagoon was used by flying boats operating over the Indian Ocean. At the end of the war the naval, military and*

Strangely it has fallen to a Victor captain to provide a good aerial photo of Gan. Visiting the island was something of a novelty for Squadron Leader Tony Cunnane - so he used his camera. We regular visitors rather took things for granted. (*Tony Cunnane*)

*air installations were closed and all service personnel withdrawn.*

**The return**

*'The year 1956 saw the return of the RAF to Gan in small numbers while preparations were made for the construction of a staging and communications centre as components in the strategic air route to the Far East. Internal Maldivian political troubles caused some delay in the work but by 1960 the construction was complete. The role of Gan and the Signals Unit conclave on Hittadu over the 15 years to 1975 is well known ...'*

A return will be made to Group Captain Edwards' account of those last days at an appropriate point in this Britannia history. For now, more detail is given of that 15 year role.

**Paradise station**

Gan was a contradiction. It was as if a complete RAF flying station had been parachuted into a tropical paradise. There was the long modern runway, large aircraft parking areas, workshops, offices, accommodation and messes. A profusion of trees and grass took the harsh edge off all this and, as it was only a small island (the runway occupied its whole length), the white sand and turquoise water of the lagoon were always close at hand. Temperatures were high, as was the humidity but these were abated to some extent by the gentle sea breezes. But it could rain! Gan was frequently attacked by horrendous thunderstorms but they were mostly short-lived.

**Men only**

However, all was not perfect for the serviceman in this tropical paradise. It was an unaccompanied tour - wives and children were left behind for 12 months. But it seemed that most people cheerfully resigned themselves to this situation for the spirit on Gan was terrific. There was always that general air of comradeship and helpfulness - it was a happy, lively place.

**Quick turn round**

The whole *raison d'etre* for Gan was the aircraft staging through. There could be as many as six in a day which

Chief Technician 'Dave' David, far right with his team on the Staging Aircraft Servicing Flight, Gan, 1970. The photograph was prompted by an historic moment; it was the first time, on the island, that a Britannia had been fully jacked up for undercarriage retraction tests. (*'Dave' David*)

would mean that the relatively small number of men would be very busy. Each aircraft would be on the ground for 1½ hours. In that time the passengers would be disembarked and taken to the Transit Mess for refreshments. Refuelling would immediately commence, as would any routine servicing. Added to this there might be a 'snag' which had to be fixed if the aircraft was to proceed. For many of the movements this was vital because it was undesirable for passengers to be delayed, though there was contingency accommodation. So a lot rested on the shoulders of the specialist tradesmen and their ingenuity. Gan's pride was in giving each aircraft a speedy and efficient turnround.

**Search and Rescue**

With its remoteness, safety was a concern. A Search and Rescue Shackleton was permanently detached from the squadron stationed in Singapore and its crew on constant standby to cover the thousands of miles of the western and eastern approaches to Gan. Close range cover was provided by the Marine Craft Unit with their high speed launches. Another service they provided was manning the lighters for unloading the regular supply ships which could not negotiate the shallow waters to the jetty. Finally there was a Signals Unit which contributed towards the worldwide military communications cover.

All this generated people who had to be cared for so there were the administrators, caterers, doctors and nurses, all of whom felt very much part of this team that was RAF Gan.

**John at Gan**

One person to 'do' his year was the previously met ex-Chief Technician John Hunting:

*'My year at Gan ('67/'68) involved working with many ex-Lyneham bods who ended up, like me, on the SASF; people such as Steve Stokes, 'Nobby' Clark, 'Mitch' Mitchell and Pete Gibbs etc. After my spell on the RAF's own aircraft carrier, guess what? September '68, back to Brit Line at Lyneham.'*

**The locals**

A component of the success of RAF Gan, not to be ignored, was the local labour force. There were a number of Pakistanis employed on contract and it was a six monthly role of the Britannia to exchange these workers with a trip from Gan to Karachi and return. Many Maldivians were also employed as labourers, cleaners, waiters and the like. They were cheerful people, although there was an element of their lives that could have made this not the case. It was the rule that none of them was to remain on the island overnight so they 'commuted' - by rowing boats. One of the sights for visitors was to see the work force departing as the evening sun went down. From the shore the dhows would be rowed out; around 20 men to each and all with an oar apiece. It could be that on a bad day some of them would be rowing for two hours; to be repeated on the return journey the following morning.

There should be some guilt about what we did to these people. They gave willing service and in return their standard of living was raised. A measure of this was that the women bore larger babies and the RAF medical staff regularly had to provide assistance. Then we left. One reads of the Maldives establishing itself as a tourist spot but this is largely centred to the north around the capital island of Male. Only those wanting to get even further away than this remote spot, travel to Gan. No doubt time has healed and the present generation of islanders has largely returned to natural ways.

**Crew break**

For the Britannia crews, Gan was often a hot and sticky break, usually in the middle of the night, and part of a long duty day. Seven hours will have already been

The proximity of the runway threshold to the sea can be judged from this photo ... (*Tony Cunnane*)

The sign outside 'The Blue Lagoon' which provided a sitting area for passengers whilst their aircraft was being refuelled. In the event of a delay then food would also be provided - and even accommodation, if the worse came to the worst. One of its important functions was a social centre for crews in transit. (*Tony Cunnane*)

flown with the prospect of another seven to go. In the 1½ hours on the ground Met Briefing and flight planning for the next leg would need completing and there might be time for a quick meal in the Transit Mess. Alternatively, arriving at Gan could be the start of a very pleasant two or three day break with the prospect of lazing in the sun, swimming, snorkelling amongst the most exotic fish in the lagoon, perhaps an outing on one of the Marine Craft and generally enjoying the considerable social atmosphere. Did we ever have it so good?

**Weather hazards**

As the Britannias flew eastbound or westbound into Gan they would enter an area within which it was impossible, because of distance, to divert to another airfield. Clearly, crews had to be sure of the Gan weather before proceeding beyond their Last Point of Diversion (LPD). In the early days of HF AM communications this was not always easy. The introduction of

Ron Wheatman, PB fitter, spent his year on Gan 62/63. One day a helicopter needed some assistance. Having fixed it, Ron was taken for a flight when he took this aerial photograph. Note the lack of trees. They had been felled during the construction phase but the young replacements rapidly grew. (*Ron Wheatman*)

'B' Shift - 24 January 1964.
(*Dave Davies*)

Some ground crew
memories of Gan

Awaiting an aircraft arrival.
(*Ron Wheatman*)

Boxing Day regatta -
the Royal Navy being overhauled.
(*Dave Davies*)

Hussein - room boy.
(*Dave Davies*)

Someone took some time making the point that Gan was a long way from everywhere! (*Tony Cunnane*)

HF SSB improved matters. But what could they be told? The weather pattern was such that there could be clear sky one moment; an hour later torrential rain. From weather data gathered over the years, it could be shown that these storms passed through and only exceptionally lasted more than an hour. So the solution was to carry extra fuel to be able to hold off until the weather cleared.

But the general practice was to 'have a go', down to the specified height limits. Although this could be like flying down a tunnel of water on the final approach, the runway, with its powerful approach lights, was invariably seen.

Some caution was necessary. A rain-soaked Britannia windscreen could produce an optical illusion of the aircraft appearing to be higher than it actually was. Add to this, perhaps, some slight nudging down below limits and an undershoot situation could be created. Could this have been the reason for a civil Britannia, on a Service families' charter flight, landing short of the Gan runway one day? Undershooting at Gan meant being in the sea. Luckily it is shallow and this aircraft ran up on to the beach and then the runway.

Another hazard with so much rain was a flooded runway surface. At the high tyre speeds of landing a thin film of water can be retained between the tyres and the runway surface. The effect, known as aquaplaning, is just like landing on ice. One victim of this phenomena, about which little was known at the time, was an RAF Britannia at Gan. After touchdown it slid gracefully off the runway on to the golf course that lay alongside. Little damage was done to the aircraft; a few extra bunkers were created for the golfers.

**Gan ground crew remember**

By a coincidence a number of people, at the same time, sent information and material to the Britannia Association magazine on the Gan of yesterday ... and today. This was launched by John Hunting 'paddling the Internet'. He found a Maldives site with a guest book. An entry in the book mentioned RAF Gan and a recent visit. He e-mailed the writer (George Bell) who turned out to be an ex-Gannite living in

The C-in-C FEAF's Hastings at Gan. (*Tony Cunnane*)

In the dining room of the RAF Brize Norton Officers' Mess there are a number of excellent oil paintings by Penelope Douglas of aircraft that have been based at Brize. The Britannia is represented by this scene at Gan. (*David Berry*)

Abu Dhabi. After exchanging messages, George sent John some of his writings on the Gan of 1962 and how it looked when he holidayed there in 1996. At the same time another Gannite, Ron Wheatman, joined the Association and sent the editor some excellent b&w photographs. He recruited an old compatriot of his, 'Dave' Davies, who also delved into his album. Suddenly the '*The Whispering Giant*' office was awash with Gan material! Some of this has been assembled here.

George Bell was an air radar fitter who found himself enjoying Singapore and working on the Shackletons. This idyll was ended when he was told that he was posted to Gan on the 205 Squadron detachment. He settled in and found that looking after two old Shackletons did not completely fill his day. He joined the Go-Cart club, learnt to dive, walked around the island most afternoons ... and, in his words, '*A large part of life on Gan was competitive drinking!*' He recalls bicycle races on the jetty walls. These were three feet across; with a rider on each they would race to end:

'*It didn't seem to matter too much that it was impossible to stop because the sensation of flying through the air to land in the warm Indian ocean was not such a bad one.*

'*... A favourite venue for the hard drinkers was the RAFA Club. It was way down the end of the island beyond ASF and the power station. It had a huge old gas fridge with the imprints of countless cans moulded into the ice which never completely melted from its cavernous interior. The Orderly Sergeant closed the club down regularly every night and then rode away on his bike, knowing that as soon as he had gone the place would be swinging again within five minutes. The Fire Section Landrover used to make a run down to the end of the island about 2.00 am and pick up any stragglers who couldn't make it back to their billets. Anyone who wandered off the road and was not noticed, invariably woke up with their hangover compounded by millions of mosquito bites. Drink was very cheap. I remember gin being sixpence a tot. I ended up drinking pink gin. This, I consumed in ever increasing quantities, until one day, at work, I actually had to practise the finer art of miniature soldering. My hand was shaking so badly that I could not do it. I made a resolution there and then to drink only beer, where the sheer volume of the stuff was enough to limit consumption to 'reasonable' levels.*

'*... All the equipment that went wrong in 'my' Shackletons either had to be sent back to Singapore for repair or, if I thought I could do it or it was urgent, I used to take it to the Radio Servicing Flight. This* *is where I used to go, if there was not much happening down the road at ASF. We had a delightful Warrant Officer in charge, who knew there was not really much to do and we never felt guilty doing something that was not really work. I used to keep my bait in the RSF fridge, and the only Maldivian I really got to know used to keep the place tidy and make coffee etc. there. He must have been about 16 years-old and, because of exposure to a lot of English, had managed to get a good grasp of it. The only problem was that he could not pronounce his S's correctly and if I asked him to say 'spoon' he would say 'espoon'. I made it one of my good deeds for the tour on Gan to help him out in this and every time I saw him tried to get him to say spoon. He never did learn, however and I count it as one of my life's failures that I never achieved this.*

*It was fascinating to discuss things with him as his outlook was so incredibly narrow, and yet he was wise beyond his years. He had been born on the neighbouring island of Hittadhu and had never done anything but come to Gan to work for the RAF. He was always ready to talk about anything under the sun and had absorbed some surprising things from the airmen to whom he had been exposed. He had a great fear of the 'Male Men' from the Northern capital of which he must have heard ghastly tales ... I heard tell of one of the helpers in another section, who, on being shown the picture of some stately home in the UK, sagely pronounced that it must be 'many lockers having'.'*

Gan leaves an indelible impression.

**Gan revisited**

George Bell returned to the island for a holiday in 1996 ...

*'I could not believe how grown over the place was. It was really only possible to see the runway and on both sides of it hardly anything but Coconut palms. If one looked carefully there were buildings in the trees and the old Aircraft Parking Area stuck out like a sore thumb. A minibus took us to the east end of the island and all the way I was craning my neck to see all the things I still recognised. Apart from the general dilapidation and prolific vegetation not much had changed at all. I was very pleased. The Ocean Reef Resort was a very open and airy place and the little chalets were perfectly acceptable, not being lavish, but having a shower, etc., a big double bed, a quite adequate air conditioner and a ceiling fan and a small patio outside every room with a table and two chairs, from which we could watch the sea and the sun go down. It still had the air of a NAAFI about it, although no one but me would have noticed it ... (we set off round the island) taking the road west to the end of the runway and continued on to the south and then east past the old Pakistani camp, which, if it remained at all, was hidden in the prolific vegetation that had grown up in the 40 years since the island had been cleared by members of the Airfield*

The swaying palms of Gan. (*David Berry*)

The Strategic Transport Force was by no means the sole user of Gan ... (*Tony Cunnane*)

*Construction Squadron.*

*'... After our experience on the bikes, the next day we decided to walk for a change. It had rained at night; the heavy tropical downpour that had ruined the sound at the ASTRA cinema so many years before. It was windy but not cold and we had one umbrella between us, so we set out across the causeway that now connected Gan and Fedhu. I had never been off Gan before, so this was a new experience for me too. Once across the causeway we found a matrix of straight sandy lanes running between small cottages constructed with the only building material that was plentiful - lumps of coral - all cracked to approximately the same size and stuck together with cement. Surrounded by neat walls of the same material and topped by corrugated iron sheeting (like most of the buildings remaining on Gan) these houses were surprisingly well kept and often boasted little gardens too with mango trees and the inevitable coconuts. People were very friendly and the cute local kids all wanted their photos taken. Grown-ups were more reserved, especially the women who often were very shy and dressed in typical Muslim dress, but they obviously did not see many tourists walking through their village, and were very interested in us.*

*'Most of the other guests at the Ocean Reef Resort were there for the diving, which was superb, and did not venture out on foot. There were the odd shops dotted about too. General stores and clothes shops mostly and prices were not competitive ...*

*'The last night I got talking to the manager of the Ocean Reef, Ajith. He too was very interested in the old photos and treated us to a few free drinks while we discussed the possibility of publicising the ex-RAF nature of Gan to attract a new class of clientele to holidays on the island. I told him how much I personally had enjoyed re-exploring the place, but that there was a lot of urgent maintenance needed to a lot of the old structures if they were to survive much longer. The tall boat shed especially is really a historic building and the steel frame is falling apart, with rusty struts hanging in*

... these Vulcans were engaged in a 1966 Far East exercise labelled 'Spherical'. (*Tony Cunnane*)

*the breeze. Roofs are starting to curl up on other places and the next really strong wind will demolish many of them. The place is crying out for a bit of attention. Everywhere I looked I could see things that needed to be done. I really wish I had taken some tools. I wonder if enough expertise still exists amongst the former residents to get to grips with the repairs urgently needed. I would imagine that local labour would be fairly cheaply available and what a wonderful project such a thing would be. All it needs is a bit of a grant from the Ministry of Tourism and someone to organise it. Is anyone interested ? I can't do it on my own.'*

**Too much sun?**

A year of all male company, too much sun - too much beer! It would not be a total surprise if this didn't topple some 'over the edge'. Vic Merrill served in many Britannia ground crew roles and there will follow a number of recollections of those days. Here he recalls a particular event during his year on Gan:

*'The night is one of those that can only be read about in a Mills and Boone novel - but is real. The warm, gentle, breeze blows off the Indian Ocean and rustles the Coconut Palm tree leaves. In the distance is the soft murmur as the rollers break on the reef. Stars shine down and seem no more than arm's length away. The moon shines so brightly as to make it possible to read a newspaper outside, in the middle of the night, and I can - I tried! Things could be perfect, or as perfect as they can get on Gan, but the situation has gone horribly 'pear-shaped'.*

*'It's like this: manpower on the Transit Aircraft Servicing Flight dictates a permanent three shifts system each twelve hours 'On' and twenty-four 'Off'. No weekends, no Bank Holidays, no leave, nothing but 'Time Ex' to relieve the repetition. We have two/three Airframe trades, two/three Engine, two Electricians, two Instruments*

One intention of this book is to bring tears to the eyes of ex-Britannia people! Just a picture of unexceptional content might do this - the entrance to The Blue Lagoon 'Hotel'. (*Norman Rose*)

None of the locally employed Maldivians were allowed to remain on Gan overnight. Each morning and evening they rowed from and to their home islands in their dhows. This could be some distance and conditions were not always idyllic. (*Ken FitzRoy*)

A fleeting glimpse of a sorry Hastings from the window of a landing Britannia at Gan. (*Harry Liddell*)

*and one 'Electronics' man, plus a Boss, on each shift. The usual total of thirteen is definitely unlucky for some.*

*'At the moment we have a problem. Due to sickness and family difficulties back in the UK we are down to just one 'Electronic' representative, Cliff, among the three shifts. He can't work a 24 hour day, so he is not on any one shift, but available at any time. 'Available' in Cliff's language means that you have to search the right watering hole in order to catch him for work when he is required. We need him tonight because we have received a 'Tech Warning' from a Brit coming in from Singapore, 'No returns on CCWR'. This means the crew cannot use Radar to see tropical storms ahead. They won't be happy with a 'Turnaround' servicing and take-off again. Gan has to increase its population from around 300 to 400, with all the feeding and shelter for crew and passengers this entails, until the aircraft is fit to fly once more. No one is happy at the prospect. Cliff must be found!*

*'Everything that can be done is done and we are ready for the arrival. As the aircraft comes to a halt and shuts down, we go through the turn-round procedure. Cooler, oxygen/air bottle/bog trolleys, ground power unit, fuel bowsers etc. are brought into position and the inspection starts and finishes as far as we are concerned, radar excepted.*

*'Excuses are found to go onto the aircraft to see how the shift boss is getting on with the navigator. The 'Rover' arrives - the driver has found Cliff. Mixing him and the navigator is likely to be a problem. Cliff looks and smells like someone who hasn't showered, eaten or slept for some time. The nav is immaculate; for someone who has just flown a leg from Changi, he is a walking miracle. SD hat TDC, creases only where required in trousers. No sweat streak down the middle of the shirt back above a ramrod spine, tie straight and matt black. Shoes with no marks to mar the high polish and not a pinpoint of a sweat on his brow. A regulation picture.*

*'Cliff gets down to business; that is, he sits at the nav's station and closes his eyes. Electricians hover with AVO and lamp and batteries at the ready. 'Check resistance between 'D' and 'F' on No.3 plug'; the check is made and the result passed back to Cliff. 'Check between 'A' and 'K' on No.2'. The assistants down in the 'Forward Freight' carry out further instructions as requested, the shift boss anxiously consults his watch, the nav stands waiting. Why doesn't he sit, go away, or at least, lean.*

*'Time passes, Cliff sweats even more, brow furrowed, heads peek out from the forward freight, every one is at the ready, waiting for him to work his magic. Our meagre store of spare 'boxes' etc. for the CCWR system are gathered and we are ready to change, repair as far as we can or just thump the item that Cliff indicates is U/S, but he seems stuck.*

*'Everything is back to the way it was when we started. We are going round in circles. The aircraft is cleared of equipment, except for ground power and the cooler, ready to go when it's fixed. We await Cliff ...*

*''Run it' said Cliff. In no time I have three and four going in superfine and the radar 'ON'; we wait. Time seems to stand still, no one moves. The roar of the GPU intrudes above the engines and they are the only sounds in the world, apart from the thump, felt rather than heard, of the oscillating scanner. Suddenly, Cliff surges to the front of the cockpit, crying, 'Let me see that f*****g display.' He stares at the screen, turns to me and says 'Stop it'. He stays there as the engines stop and the steps come in. We wait for Cliff to say something.*

*'He turns and says 'Who snagged this f*****g thing?' 'I did,' states the Nav. Cliff looks at him and, apparently, sees him for the first time. He puts his face close to the nav's, breathes out and tries to focus. Everyone stays frozen in impossible positions, thinking he has finally cracked. You?'*

*'Cliff hangs on to the nav's tie, flows round him and then pulls him, by the tie, to the top of the steps - we follow. He swings his spare arm in a gesture that covers the star-spangled firmament and declares. 'Can you see any f*****g clouds?' Then, How do you expect to get any f*****g returns?'*

*'The nav enters the cabin while Cliff stumbles down the steps and into the back of the Rover, shouting 'Get me back to*

The map opposite shows the Changi Slip staging posts that featured over the years. It was drawn by 'Holly' for the author's first book *'Tales from the Crewroom'*.

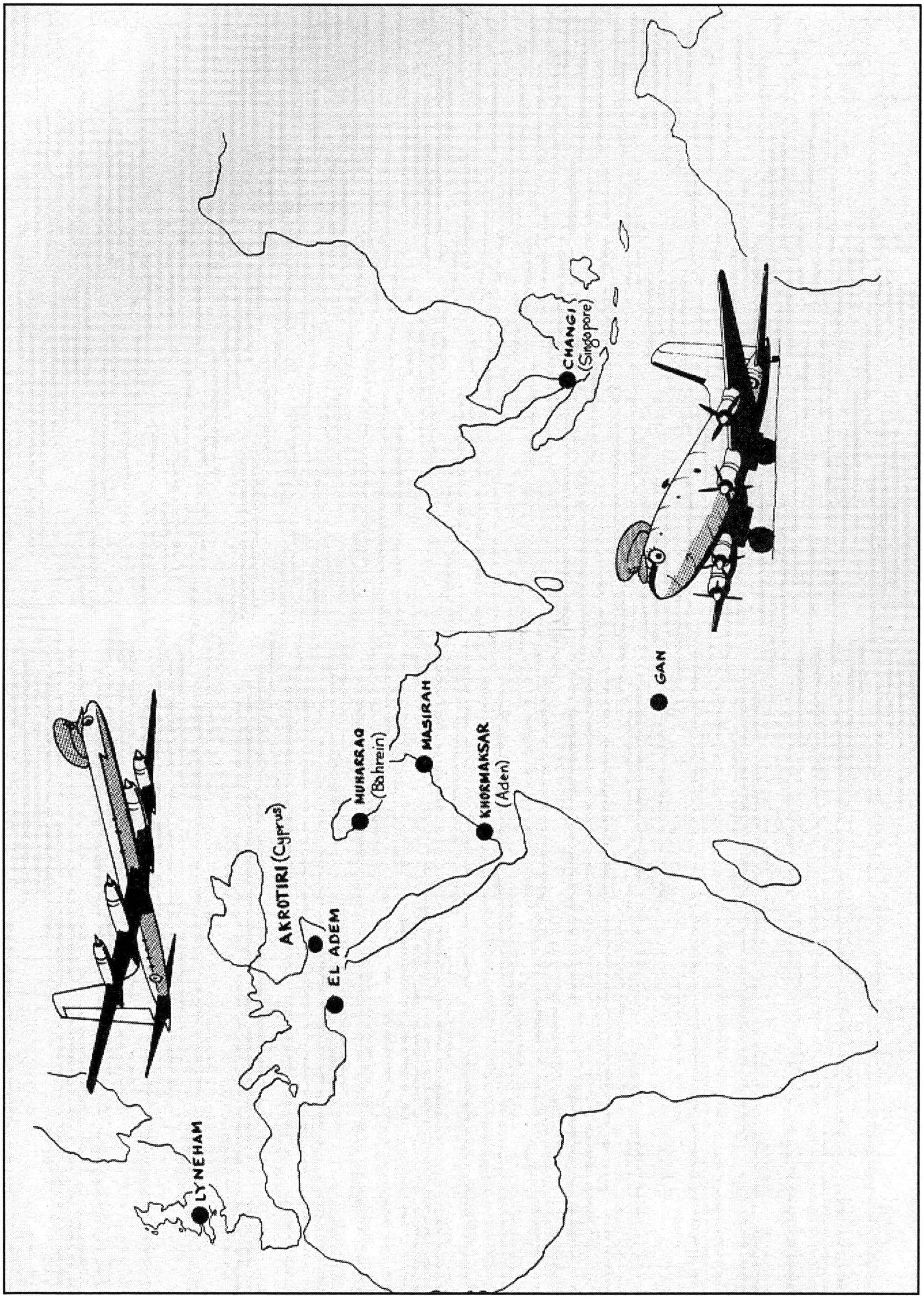
LYNEHAM
EL ADEM
AKROTIRI (Cyprus)
MUHARRAQ
(Bahrein)
MASIRAH
KHORMAKSAR
(Aden)
GAN
CHANGI
(Singapore)

El Adem airfield is situated about 18 miles from the Libyan town of Tobruk of World War II fame and was built at that distance, by the Italians to be just outside the range of the guns of the British battle cruisers. Its desert location is evident. (*TEARS website*)

Air Traffic Control - and to the right the scene of some of the crew's turnround activity - Met and Flight Planning. (*TEARS website*)

Images of RAF El Adem

This photo illustrates how El Adem tried to make the best of what they had - which wasn't a lot! Note the popular lettering style of the 1960s and the garden layout - without any garden! (*TEARS website*)

*the 180'. It goes off. So do we, fast.*

*'No one but the shift boss and the nav is on the aircraft. Everyone is back on the Flight veranda, gazing back at the Brit and wondering what will happen now. After a few minutes the shift boss comes in and calls 'Ops'. 'The Brit is finished, Form 700 cleared, and it's ready to go'.*

*'I suppose we never will find out what happened after we left the aircraft, or what was said - unless one of the readers of TWGIU ... ?'*

**A Gan book**

A trip down 'Memory Lane' is available for those with recollections of Gan. These can be shared with Michael Butler who, as a National Serviceman, spent a year on the island in 1960. His recall is very detailed. He was able to check on the current Gan situation with a holiday visit in 1998. His book, '*Return to Gan*', is published by Woodfield Publishing - ISBN 1-873203-52-7.

**... and other Staging Posts**

When the Britannia came into service and the supply route to Singapore was established, RAF El Adem was the first staging post. On the Changi Slip, it was only a 90 minute refuelling stop during which the crew prepared for the next leg. The pilots, navigator and signaller would get a new Met briefing and then attend to flight planning matters. The flight engineer would monitor the turn-round servicing and refuelling whilst the AQM would see to any offload/onload of freight and the stocking of any required food and drinks.

This gives a feel for the surrounding El Adem 'countryside'! (*TEARS website*)

**RAF El Adem**

The airfield is situated 18 miles from the Libyan town of Tobruk. In 1934, Italy adopted the name 'Libya' as the official name of its colony. King Idris led Libyan resistance to Italian occupation between the two World Wars. Following the desert campaign of WWII, parts of Libya were under British administration from 1943 to 1951, the French controlling the remainder. In 1944, King Idris returned from exile in Cairo but declined to resume permanent residence until the removal in 1947 of some aspects of foreign control. Under the terms of the 1947 peace treaty with the Allies, Italy relinquished all claims to Libya.

On 21st November 1949, the UN General Assembly passed a resolution stating that Libya should become independent before 1st January 1952. King Idris represented Libya in the subsequent UN negotiations and Libya was declared independent on 24th December 1951. King Idris was overthrown in a military-led coup on 1st September 1969. The new regime, headed by the Revolutionary Command Council (RCC), abolished the monarchy and proclaimed the new Libyan Arab Republic. Colonel Gadafi emerged as leader of the RCC and eventually as *de facto* chief of state. An early objective of the new government was withdrawal of all foreign military from Libya. Following negotiations, British military installations at Tobruk and El Adem were closed in March 1970.

Royal Air Force El Adem, in the north east corner of Libya, was an airfield frequently visited by the Britannia being the first staging post in the original 'Changi Slip' and was much used as an exercise airfield and area. It was the home of nearly 2,000 airmen and their families and had been occupied by the Royal Air Force ever since its capture from the German Afrika Corps in 1942. It was originally built in 1935 by the Italians to provide air defence for their naval base at Tobruk.

**Memories**

El Adem generally only featured briefly in Britannia lives. On the 90-minute turnrounds there was an awareness of the station personnel doing everything to keep the Britannia rolling. On the odd occasions when a night stop was planned or required, one was able to relate more closely to the environment that the permanent staff 'enjoyed'! El Adem was a sorrowful place, surrounded by scruffy desert. It could be hot, which influenced building design, so when it was cold, which it could equally be, things were uncomfortable. One abiding memory is that, in spite of its desert location, there was a

RAF Khormaksar.

pervading smell of dampness in the accommodation. The other lasting impression of the setting is the intense blackness surrounding the airfield on our, inevitable, night arrival. It was not one of our favourite places and we were pleased to mostly see it only in transition; our tactical compatriots (the Argosys and Andovers) were welcome to their longer term acquaintance.

**RAF Khormaksar**

Military involvement with Aden goes back to 1839 when Royal Marines landed to deal with pirates who were threatening British shipping. Aden's big leap forward occurred when the Suez Canal was opened in 1869 and the port became a bunkering station on the route to India. There was a need to protect this and the Canal so a British garrison was established. This was maintained through the years and after the seizure of the Canal by the Egyptians, Aden became the hub for our interests in the Middle East. The 1960s brought Arab unrest and a call for the overthrow of British rule. This unrest grew into a full guerrilla war in the newly formed Yemeni Republic and a call for Aden to join that republic. After many years of fighting in which RAF Khormaksar played a major role, plans began to be formulated for the withdrawal of British troops. The date originally set was in January 1968. This date moved slightly to 29th November 1967. A full description is given later of this operation to which the Britannias contributed.

**Facelift for Khormaksar**

RAF Khormaksar was an intensely busy place in the 1960s and had rapidly outgrown itself. Under the headline 'Facelift for Khormaksar', the 5th January 1962 edition of the Lyneham Globe reproduced what appears to be a press release which describes new developments and conveys the intense activity of this RAF station:

*'Less than four years ago a fighter squadron and a communications flight were the only flying units permanently based at RAF Khormaksar, Aden. Today the station has five squadrons and a helicopter flight, a strength that will be increased still further by a Hunter squadron when No.208 completes its move to Aden from Nairobi, Kenya, on 30th December. Khormaksar, which has existed for 33 years, is already the permanent home of the following*

'd like to mention that these pictures were taken in Canada by J/T Selkirk.

"I dreamt I dwelt in . . ."

Aircrew in transit at Khormaksar, Aden, leave the new transit accommodation while a crew bus waits to pick up a departing crew.

"PADDY and DUFFY"

Tel. 3365

The architecture of Merrifield House was not particularly awe inspiring! Left are Sgt Paddy Hoy and Cpl Duffy, the stalwart staff. (*Lyneham Globe*)

Aden was a blighted place, constantly blasted with the heat of the sun - although it did very occasionally rain. Then the water would be very slow to drain away. (*Bill Robinson*)

NEW DEAL FOR ADEN

Bill Robinson contributed this view of the port of Aden to the *Globe*. (*Lyneham Globe*)

The badge of RAF Khormaksar.

*squadrons: No.5 (Hunters); No.78 (Twin Pioneers); No.84 (Beverleys); No.37 (Shackletons) and No.233 (Valettas). The development of the Station is in step with the growth of Aden as a whole, brought about by the establishment there, in 1958, of Britain's first peacetime unified command headquarters.*

*'Khormaksar is the Middle East Command's main flying station responsible for defending Aden and the Protectorates from external attack, for maintaining law and order within the territory and for operating scheduled air services within the Command from East Africa to the Persian Gulf. It is also the RAF's main staging post between the United Kingdom and the Far East.*

*'Close on £4,000,000 has been spent on developing the station during the past two years. An £800,000 powerhouse is nearing completion and a £274,000 air-conditioned school for 1,000 children has been opened. Just over a year ago accommodation at Khormaksar was so tight that airmen were obliged to sleep on balconies. Today, three fully air-conditioned blocks each accommodate 150 men. A new Airmens' Mess and Club and a NAAFI shop are among other amenities. A large housing estate with air-conditioned bedrooms has been developed at a cost of £897,000, to accommodate 156 airmens' families. A smaller scheme provides additional accommodation for 48 officers' families.'*

**What was Khormaksar really like?**

The environment of the Station has not been conveyed. It might be best done with an extract from the author's '*Tales from the Crewroom*':

*'... and we land at Khormaksar at 0800 local time. The heat, even at that time of the morning, is searing. And the cruel sun bounces off the concrete and the sand into our tired red eyes. If you imagine that the deserts of such places are sandy, as in beach, then this is far from the case. In fact it is difficult to distinguish between 'sand', tarmac and concrete. On this inhospitable surface are perched our unimaginative concrete military buildings, seemingly designed with no thought to minimise the harshness of the environment. Although there was the impression that every grain of sand had been compacted, there was still enough at liberty to create, at times, an eye-irritating and obscuring sandstorm.*

*'Ignoring the local time, it's the end of a long working day for us, so it's time for a few beers in Neddy's Bar. This facility was one of the first recognitions that slip crews required special arrangements if they were to lead any sort of reasonable way of life. Wing Commander 'Neddy' Pearson, an early OC Flying at Khormaksar, decided that there should be a bar facility at the airfield for crews when they landed, no matter what time of the day or night. This watering hole was affectionately named Neddy's Bar, a name that was transferred to similar facilities, elsewhere, in later years.*

*'Refreshed at Neddy's we move to our accommodation at Merrifield House, another early effort that acknowledged the difficulties of route flying and fatigue. It was at Khormaksar that the first signs appeared that special accommodation arrangements were required for slip crews. They could not just be pushed into any old transit block. They needed reasonable comfort in air-conditioned rooms to help alleviate the transition between climes and time zones and flying all hours of the day and night. They needed the opportunity to eat and rest at all times of the day and night and they needed the facility to be 'social' at non-standard times. At Khormaksar the special accommodation built was named Merrifield House after a past Station Commander. I remember well the first enthusiastic Sergeant Steward who ran the*

*place. One of his dreams was to have a grass area between the buildings, not an easy objective in the middle of a desert. His enthusiasm at organising exceeded his horticultural talents for he had, flown out in a Britannia, the only lawn mower in Aden before a blade of grass had grown there.'*

There was no doubt that such an accommodation facility did alleviate much of the discomfort, certainly for a short stop where obtaining an adequate amount of sleep was at a premium. However, for longer stays, there was perhaps a reverse effect where the accommodation took on a prison-like quality, the restraint being the air conditioning. It made it a real effort to venture out!

**Moving on**

The Changi Slip aircraft has been flown from the UK to Khormaksar via El Adem by the same crew - this would amount to nearly a 16-hour day, counting the two hours pre-flight briefing time at Lyneham. They now hand over to a fresh crew who had flown the previous aircraft into Khormaksar. That crew would operate to Gan and then on to Singapore. Gan has been studied.

**RAF Changi**

The military history of Changi dates from 1927 when the decision was made, in the light of the perceived increasing Japanese threat, to build a Singapore naval base and a protective heavy artillery battery, the latter to be located in the area which would eventually become RAF Changi. It took three years to clear the forest and swamp, and building commenced. However, in 1930 the Great Depression hit and the order was given for no fresh building to be started. The place was put under 'Care and Maintenance'. But the Japanese threat increased and construction was recommenced in 1933 and went on to 1941. In December 1941 HMS Prince of Wales and HMS Repulse sailed into the naval base to leave later and be sunk. The Japanese land forces were moving south towards the island and there was bombing in February 1942. On 7th the invasion began and on 15th the 50,000 British forces surrendered. Changi became a prison camp. By September the number of prisoners had been halved by death and transfer to the notorious working parties.

In September 1943 the building of an airfield commenced using the prisoners as labour. Conditions were appalling. Flying commenced in latter part of 1944. May 1945 saw the surrender of Germany and the concentration now on the Far East war. On 15th August Japan surrendered.

Changi was in a mess which took three years to clear. It became clear that, with the increasing size of aircraft that a better airfield was required on the island. One of the Changi unpaved runways was strengthened with PSP. It was eventually seen that a permanent runway was required and work commenced. Changi now grew and grew. Apart from it becoming the main RAF headquarters it had three transport

A totally recognisable, to past inmates, Changi Creek Hotel survived as a Country Club. (*Keith Govey*)

The old part of the Changi Creek Hotel ... (*David Berry*)

squadrons: Nos.48 and 52 and Far East Communications. No.41 RNZAF Squadron arrived. The major effort was the support of operations associated with Confrontation. 215 Squadron joined the fleet. At various times the skies above Changi were filled with Dakotas, Valettas, Hastings, Bristol Freighters, Shackletons, Argosys, Hercules etc. Also, it being the terminus of the long range transport force, there was a constant stream of Britannias, Comets, Belfasts and VC10s.

But an axe fell in 1971 - withdrawal would be complete by December.

... and the new. (*David Berry*)

**The Slip Crews' Changi**

Royal Air Force Changi had been like a Mecca for transport crews for all the post-war years. It was the terminus; the place to take a deep breath and ready oneself for the return journey. It had atmosphere. This was heightened for the aircrew in that the transit accommodation was located on the water's edge - Changi Creek Hotel.

**A history of Changi Creek Hotel**

In 1962, as the pace of route flying quickened, *The Lyneham Globe* reported on this transit accommodation:

*'Before the War, a well-to-do Chinese merchant built a house near the eastern end of Singapore Island. If he could return to see it now, he would he surprised to see it as the central portion of the RAF transit hotel, surrounded by the town, which comprises RAF Changi. Although accurate information about the early pre-war years is necessarily scarce, it is understood that the house became an Officers' Mess shortly before the war until the Japanese occupation, and was then taken over as a residence for the local Japanese Army Commander.*

*'At the end of the war, largely because the Japanese had built an airfield with POW labour, Changi changed owners from Army to RAF, and it is known that some of the occupants of Changi Creek in the years immediately after the war were Nos.48 and, it is believed, 215 Squadrons.*

*During 1948 the house became an Officers' Mess once more, this time for Air Headquarters Malaya, and remained thus until it became a transit centre. In its present form the house remains as the centre portion of the hotel, and contains a reception lobby, lounges and bars for passengers and crews, while accommodation is provided in chalet blocks on either side of the main building. Dining arrangements have been greatly improved by the recent building of a separate dining block and in-flight meal preparation has been allotted another new building which separates it from day-to-day catering.*

*'For the transient, the hotel need never be dull, as clock golf and croquet are available to absorb the energy (if any) of its visitors, and the swimming facilities of the officers and airmens' clubs are only a short distance away. In the other direction, the shopping facilities of Changi village are literally at the door, and any requirements from a car to a bunch of orchids can be obtained after suitable negotiation from the enterprising businessmen who make it their creed to sell something - anything to every visitor. 'Car coat? Transistor radio? Yasshicamat? New suit? Toy Telephone?' - the shopkeepers of the village can sell you several things you don't want in five minutes, and obtain the most outlandish requirement in another five - and remain open until 8.30pm to do it.*

*'For an inbound Lyneham crew, usually arriving in the early hours of the morning, the first requirement is a glass of cold beer. This appears as if by magic and, after a chat, bed is usually sought, except by the really hardy. The hotel will soon have air-conditioned rooms for its transit crews, and then one of the main grouses of UK-based aircrews will disappear. Up to now, the sudden transition from England to the Far East with the large climatic change and a 7½ hour time difference has made sleep difficult, if not impossible, but this trouble will soon be a thing of the past.*

*'The pernickety among the Lynehamites would also appreciate the murder of the Chinese fisherman who sails slowly past using the shrillest outboard motor in the world, always five minutes after they have dropped off to sleep, but this is unlikely to be achieved on the grounds that local colour must be preserved. Looking ahead, the hotel seems in for a busy future - 100% air trooping has put upon its shoulders all passenger movements through Payar Lebar and Changi, with the responsibility for the preparation of the in-flight meals for the appropriate RAF flights out of Changi. Although numbers vary from month to month, the hotel staff expect to cater for up to 15,000 meals and 4,500 'night- stops', all of whom arrive at short notice. An item such as 10,000 paper cups would cause no surprise on the Creek's*

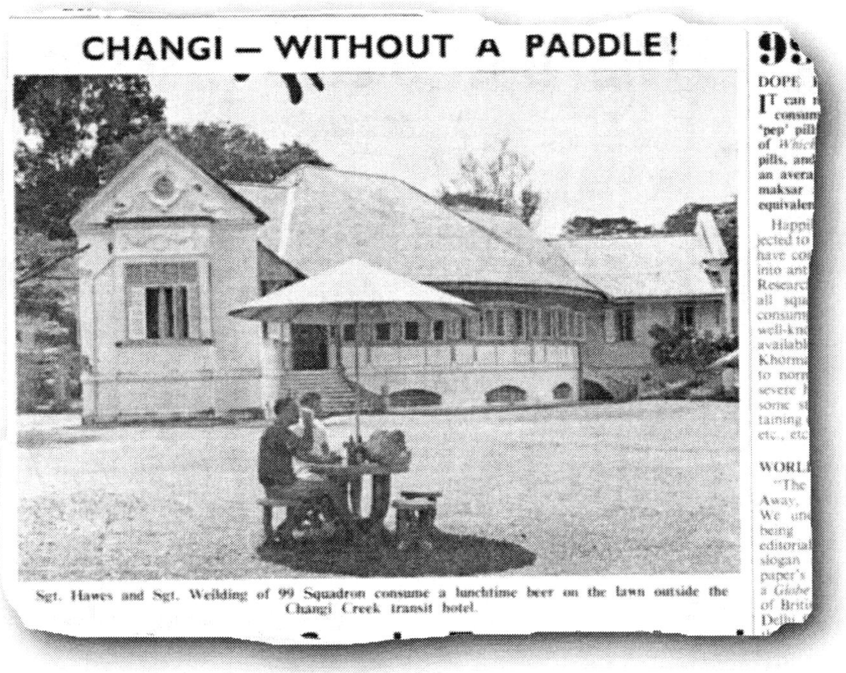

CHANGI — WITHOUT A PADDLE!

Sgt. Hawes and Sgt. Welding of 99 Squadron consume a lunchtime beer on the lawn outside the Changi Creek transit hotel.

A lunchtime beer on the lawn outside the Changi Creek transit hotel. (*Lyneham Globe*)

Not Changi Village but Hong Kong. ALM Sergeant(W) Donnelly, known to everyone as 'Smiley', tries to strike a bargain. The eventual scrapping of the Britannias meant the parting of the ways. Smiley left the WRAF and joined the Metropolitan Police, rising to the rank of Detective Sergeant. (*Ralph Dexter*)

*'Shopping List'. While the staff are quick to admit its limitations, the Creek nevertheless fills admirably a need for transit accommodation in a very pleasant spot and with its proposed improvements completed, will doubtless prove to be the most popular stop on the route.'*

**Britannia authors!**

Perhaps coincidentally or, maybe there is some perverse psychological reason, the Britannia fleet has produced a number of authors and they will continue to be highlighted as the story unfolds. Unashamedly, their books will be given a plug! We authors need to stick together. David Taylor was a member of Mobile Servicing Flight, which will be a later topic, as will another book he has written which covers his RAF career and subsequent one. His second book is mentioned here as it is Singapore-based. It was reviewed in the Britannia Association magazine:

*'The book is entitled 'Seletar' with two sub-titles - 'Crowning Glory' - 'A History of the RAF in Singapore'. The latter gives the key to the book's content. Whilst it gives an extremely comprehensive and well researched history of RAF Seletar, in so*

*doing it covers the turbulent and varied times of Singapore Island. This is a very readable book. The author has a way of providing all the historical facts but not as a boring list - he succeeds in weaving them into a story to which he adds some of his own experiences.'*

The book details are: ISBN 1-903953-16-2, published by Woodfield Publishing, price £15.

**More staging posts**

It has already been stated that the version of the Changi Slip just described (Lyneham - El Adem - Khormaksar - Gan - Changi) was not going to last forever. Akrotiri, Muharraq, Masirah and Tengah featured and these places will be 'visited' later.

The story of 1961 now continues.

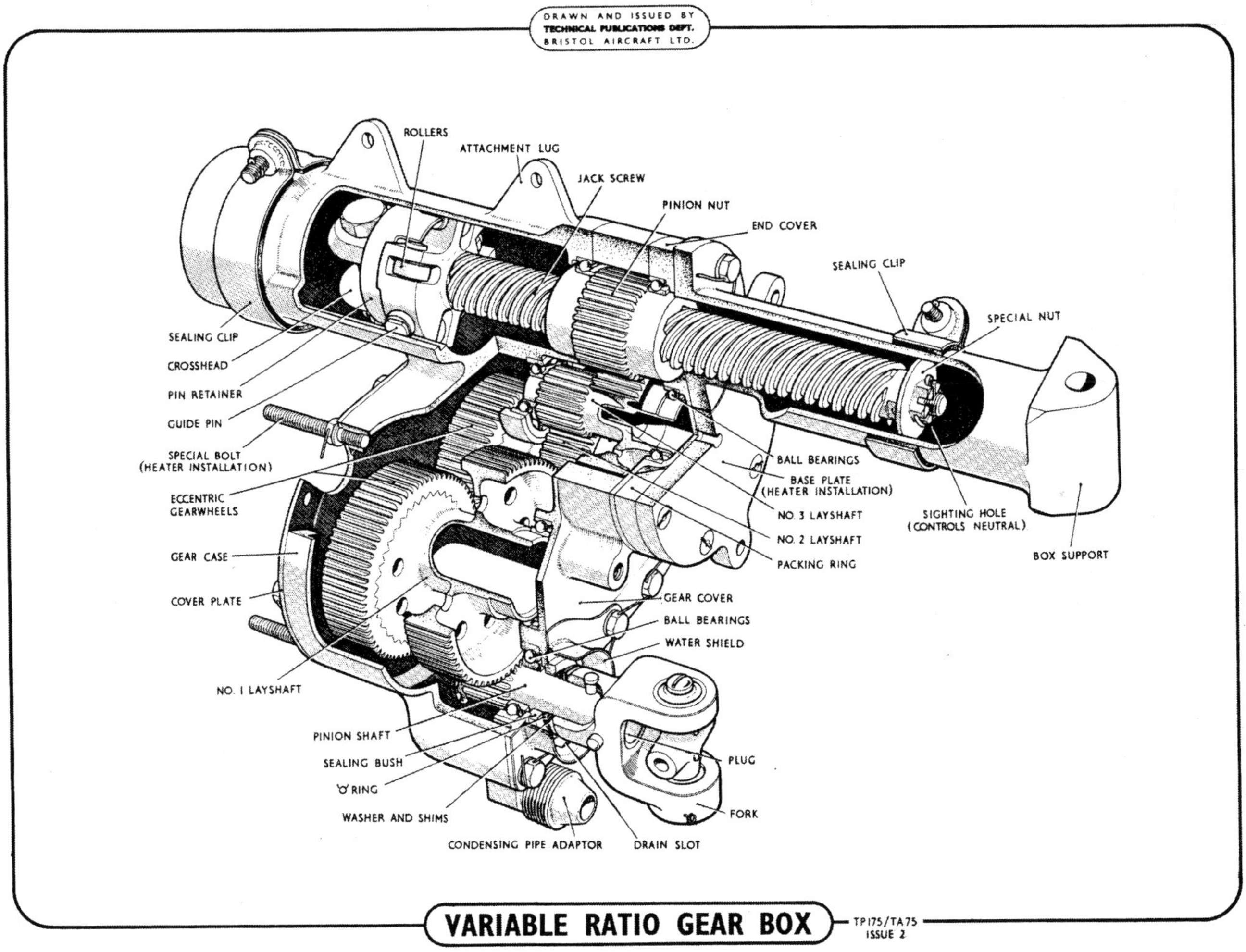


VARIABLE RATIO GEAR BOX

For general interest these diagrams will appear occasionally. Unbelievably they are taken from the 'Aircrew Lecture Notes' issued to students attending the course at the Bristol Aircraft Training School prior to starting their flying training at Lyneham. One has to admire the skill of the artists.

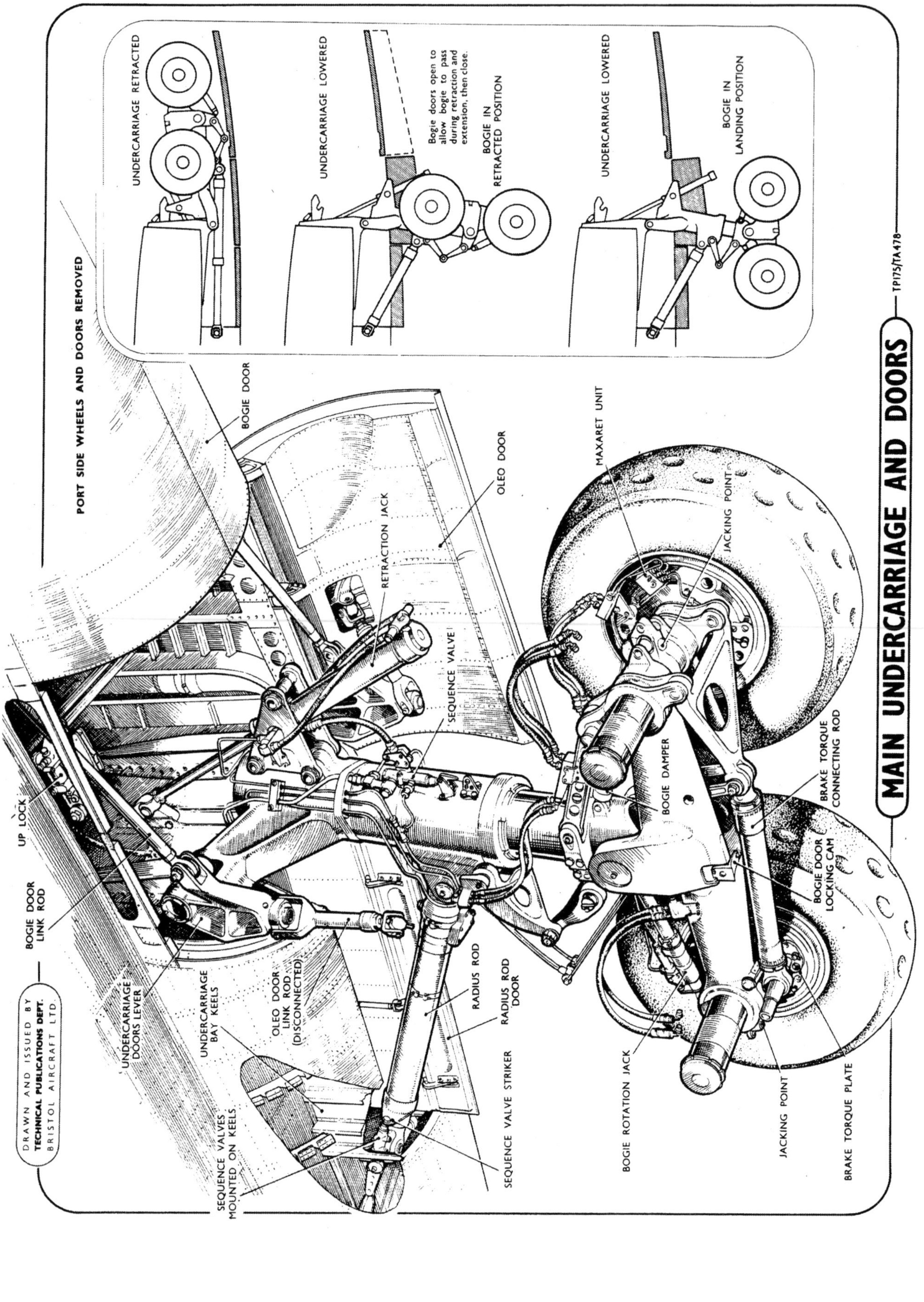
MAIN UNDERCARRIAGE AND DOORS
PORT SIDE WHEELS AND DOORS REMOVED
UNDERCARRIAGE RETRACTED
UNDERCARRIAGE LOWERED
Bogie doors open to allow bogie to pass during retraction and extension, then close.
BOGIE IN RETRACTED POSITION
UNDERCARRIAGE LOWERED
BOGIE IN LANDING POSITION
TP175/TA478
BOGIE DOOR
OLEO DOOR
MAXARET UNIT
RETRACTION JACK
JACKING POINT
SEQUENCE VALVE
BOGIE DAMPER
BRAKE TORQUE CONNECTING ROD
BOGIE DOOR LOCKING CAM
UP LOCK
BOGIE DOOR LINK ROD
UNDERCARRIAGE DOORS LEVER
UNDERCARRIAGE BAY KEELS
OLEO DOOR LINK ROD (DISCONNECTED)
RADIUS ROD
RADIUS ROD DOOR
SEQUENCE VALVES MOUNTED ON KEELS
SEQUENCE VALVE STRIKER
BOGIE ROTATION JACK
JACKING POINT
BRAKE TORQUE PLATE
DRAWN AND ISSUED BY TECHNICAL PUBLICATIONS DEPT. BRISTOL AIRCRAFT LTD.

The adventures of Messrs. Ad Minn and Org at Wootton Lynstoke continue ...

"'ERE THEY ARE CORP, THEIR UNIFORMS 'AS BEEN BLACKENED BY FLASH"
DECONTAMINATION
"WHAT'S THIS AD ?"
"LOOKS LIKE A RACE"
BUT THE CHRISTMAS BREAK FREEDOM RUSH TRAPS OUR HEROES
(THINKS) WHY RUSH TO GET OUT — THERE'S BOUND TO BE ANOTHER BY-ELECTION SOON
R.T. & DRAC WISH ALL GLOBE READERS A MERRY CHRISTMAS
THE MINISTRY OF WHATSIT BREAK OVER (JAN 5th) AND ADMIN & ORG RETURN TO WOOTTON LYNESTOKE
BUT ON PASSING S.S.Q.
SQN.LDR. LEFT JABB
FLT.LT. RIGHT LUVLY
"WE CAN'T JUST HAVE THEM WALKING ABOUT WITHOUT MEDICAL SANCTION"
AND SO...
OVERWEIGHT
...HIGH TONE DEAF.....
... REFLEXES POOR.....
...LILY-LIVERED SHORTSIGHTED OVERWEIGHT PIGEON-TOED CLOTH-EARED OVERWEIGHT ..... SEEMS ALL RIGHT...
-A1G1"
9

CHAPTER TWELVE

# Truly Established

The end of 1961 marked the Britannia fleet having been at full strength for two years and now, being a vital cog in the country's defence machine, ready to answer all manner of calls. There are a number of examples for the year.

**Cranwell cadets to the USA**

A lovely new shiny aeroplane was just the vehicle to carry a group from a prestigious British establishment to an American one. A *Lyneham Globe* correspondent spells out the details:

'*The annual tour of the United States by a party of some 75 cadets from the RAF College was this year made in a Britannia of No.511 Squadron (Captains: Wing Commander Le Hardy and Flying Officer McLaren). The party left Cranwell on Sunday, 9th April and, after staging through Harmen AFB because of a heavy snowstorm at Gander, the aircraft arrived in Washington the same evening. Here the cadets (and the crew) were able to see the famous places in the capital. A visit was also paid to the United States Naval Academy, Annapolis. On 12th April, the aircraft flew on to the Headquarters of Strategic Air Command at Arthur, in the geographical centre of the USA and then to Colorado Springs in the Western Mountain Region, where the new USAF Air Academy is situated.*

'*The Air Academy is a truly fantastic establishment. The site consists of 17,900 acres and is set 7,000 feet above sea level in the foothills of the Colorado Mountains The buildings are all of ultra-modern design, and the college is entirely self-supporting with its own hospital, shops and hotels. By next year it will have 2,400 cadets!*

'*The course lasts four years and at the end of this period, successful cadets pass out with a university degree and are commissioned as first lieutenants. Unlike the system at Cranwell, cadets at the Air Academy are not trained as members of aircrews - this training is given after cadets leave the College. The system of nomination is also very different. Of the 772 cadets who will enter the College in June this year, 637 were nominated by members of the US Congress and 22 by the President of the United States - the latter are reserved for the sons of serving or retired members of the Armed Forces. A further ten nominations are reserved for the sons of deceased veterans.*

'*Whilst at Colorado Springs members of the Britannia crew were entertained royally by the Academy staff - every moment of each free day (and the nights too, in many cases!) was covered with fine*

The captain's seat! (*Harry Liddell*)

Major overhauls being undertaken at the Bristol Aircraft Company works at Filton ... (*Lyneham Globe*)

*American efficiency and thoroughness. The party left Colorado on 16th April for New York, and returned to the United Kingdom on 19th April.'*

**Exercise Fabulist**

Later there was a more mundane task. Exercise Fabulist involved five crews, captained by Wg Cdr Le Hardy, Flt Lts Adams, Lowe, McFarland and Salter, transporting members of the 16th Independent Parachute Brigade and their equipment to Cyprus. During the stay the troops were involved in the largest exercise staged in Cyprus since independence. The Le Hardy crew also flew the Air Secretary, Air Chief Marshal Sir Theodore McEvoy, to Nicosia on 1st May and returned the next day with the MPs and press party who had been observing the transport phase of the exercise.

**Operation Bedstead**

The following account illustrates what goes on behind the scenes of a VIP trip:

*'Accustomed as Tech Wing is to the sudden and seemingly impossible calls for VIP aircraft, at short notice, the night of 26th June will remain, we hope, an all time record. The task given to the STO at 2030 hours was to prepare a Britannia Mk2 to VIP standard, converting the rear compartment into a Stateroom complete with two beds. The STO marshalled his forces and under the guidance of WO Taylor (i/c Gen. Eng. Flight) the problem was tackled. There was just 20 hours in which to complete the task. This included the designing, manufacture and fitting of bulkhead and attachment fittings for the two beds.*

*'Cpl. Lewis, of the Carpenters' Shop, was called in and set about the task of designing and making the bulkhead. He traced the contour of the passenger door guard and from the template thus made, he fashioned the bulkhead. Meanwhile WO Taylor raided Role and Loose Equipment Section found some freight guards, which suited the job admirably. Sgt. Norman, Cpl. Bithell and SAC Read of the Metal Workers' Shop fitted the beds with substantial brackets. Naturally the beds required had to be up to Lyneham VIP standard, so Mr. Nolan of Barrack Stores was called in and procured, via Hullavington, two brand new officer-type beds.*

*'Work proceeded steadily throughout the night and by 0530 the bulkhead was made and the beds fitted. At 0730 hours ACs Alexander and Purdy, Fabric Workers, commenced covering the bulkhead with 'Vynide'. These two airmen had been at Lyneham only a few days, coming direct from training school and they did a splendid job on their first important task. The problem of providing a pelmet and curtains was solved by WO Taylor who 'robbed' XN392 of the fitted items attached to the centre bulkhead. The pelmet was recovered in 'Vynide' and adapted to the new bulkhead in XN398, thus providing a completely separate stateroom. By 1330 hours the conversion was complete, reflecting great credit on all concerned and a perfect example of team spirit.'*

**Accra and Lagos**

In the now established light-hearted style of the *Lyneham Globe*, the 511 Squadron correspondent reports:

*'The middle of June saw elements of four Squadron crews with two Britannias in Accra. This detachment, led by the Squadron Commander with 'Sir Percy' (we seek him here - we seek him there) Wickes, Major Cook, USAF and Flt. Lt. Eglington as the other captains, was due to have returned to the UK after five days. However, on completion of the lift of a Ghana Battalion from Luluabourg in the*

"She wore an Itsy-Bitsy Teeny-Weeny Polka-dot Bikini"

*Congo to Accra, the detachment was transferred to Lagos to undertake a similar task for the Nigerian Army. In two days operations, from Accra the detachment moved 388 passengers and 16 tons of stores. We then moved to Lagos and in six days transported 589 troops and 43 tons from Lagos to Kamina and 524 troops and 56 tons in the reverse direction. The lift was completed two hours ahead of schedule. Fortunately (or unfortunately?) the CO is no stranger to Lagos - having captained the Britannia, which took part in the Nigerian Independence Celebration in October last year. Ever mindful of the importance of morale in such circumstances, he was instrumental in discovering (or would 'uncovering' be the better word) a notable local attraction - this week's pin-up refers.'*

**Mercy flight 1**

Throughout their lifetime, the RAF Britannias were called upon to assist with emergency situations. One of these came on 31st October 1961. Hurricane Hattie and the accompanying tidal wave, devastated Belize, the capital and principal sea port of British Honduras on the Caribbean coast of Central America. Its houses were mostly built of wood, with verandas, raised on piles for coolness and roofed with corrugated iron. All this was turned into a tangled mass

... and with the overhaul complete, 636 lifts off from the Filton to return to Lyneham. (*Rolls Royce plc, Bristol*)

To assess the damage to Belize by Hurricane Hattie and tidal waves, two Valiants from No.543 Squadron, RAF Wyton carried out photographic reconnaissance for the Colonial Office. This is one of the photographs of the town from 30,000 feet.

by the force of the wind and the water.

**Weekend callout**

It did always seem that calls such as this would come just as a weekend or stand down period was approaching. This was no exception; on Friday 3rd November came the summons that an emergency air lift was required to Kingston, Jamaica from where the loads would be flown, by smaller aircraft, to Belize. By 9.30 the next morning, the first aircraft, captained by Wg Cdr Le Hardy, OC 511 Squadron, was on its way via Lajes in the Azores and Kindley, Bermuda. This was followed by four other aircraft at six hourly intervals. A sixth aircraft left on the Tuesday. In all, 450 personnel and 3½ tons of supplies were uplifted to Jamaica. The airfield at Belize was unsuitable for sustained Britannia operations so the loads were transferred to Hastings, Shackleton and civil charter aircraft. The Britannia had done its considerable bit by speedily transferring such a large load over the long distance.

**Social comment?**

This book not only tells the story of an aircraft; inevitably, it has also to be a reflection of those times. In looking back, it is quite surprising the way it is revealed how different life was in what some of us will see as only a few years ago. Some recollections appeal - others jar. An instance of the latter is illustrated opposite with an extract from '*The Lyneham Globe*'. It is unbelievably patronising and the tone of it would be totally unacceptable in this day and age.

**The Belfast approacheth**

A report in the November issue of

(continued on page 174)

A threequarter-front view of the full-scale mock-up of the Short Belfast military freighter.

The full-scale wooden mock-up of the Short Belfast military freighter. (*Lyneham Globe*)

**THE GLORIOUS ERK The Power Behind The Force**

Banished from the front page are the usual pictures of shiny aeroplanes and VIPs dripping with gold braid. Instead, we pay tribute to the erk, the man or woman who wields spanner, typewriter, spoon or syringe, the 'bod' who actually does the work.

In the past, the Globe has been accused of becoming something of an aircrew preserve, with lots about the glamorous side of transport flying - 'travel abroad - wild blue yonder' sort of stuff. While we think this criticism unjustified, we wish to avoid any taint of preferential treatment, hence the big spread about erks.

The general impression among non-erks is that an erk is a lazy, ignorant, immoral, dishevelled figure, who performs the minimum amount of duty he possibly can with the utmost reluctance, and with a cynicism that would make a Lord Chesterfield wince. Of course, there are erks like this - we can think of illuminating occasions when they have been encountered.

**Loyalty**

But, let's face it, the average erk is just an average person with normal tendencies towards bad habits as well as flashes of good ones. The squalid description above is assiduously cultivated by the mass of erks, to observe the conventions of the Service, but occasionally, very occasionally, the other side of the coin is presented to the baffled onlooker. The reaction of the Nuclear Disarmers at Brize Norton, for instance, has to be imagined as one of utter incredulity that blokes who have given the impression for months of the most virulent discontent with the Royal Air Force in general, and Lyneham in particular, should behave with the greatest loyalty and devotion to an unpleasant duty, all in the most morale-sapping environment.

Another instance was the great efforts made by erks in the vilest weather conditions recently, when the most natural reaction to what had just been done to them was mutiny.

So, here is our tribute to the Erk of Lyneham; he or she would undoubtedly prefer us to buy him or her a drink, but luckily this is impossible. This screed is written from the point of view of your Editorial Staff, who, if you care to check, you will find to be officers (and gentlemen, of course).

Is anyone prepared to challenge our assessment of erks, or to expand it? If we know anything about erks, almost certainly not, but we could be proved wrong, couldn't we?

THE GLORIOUS ERK

The Power Behind The Force

BANISHED from the front page are the usual pictures of shiny aeroplanes and V.I.P.s dripping with gold braid. Instead, we pay tribute to the erk, the man or woman who wields spanner, typewriter, spoon or syringe, the "bod" who actually does the work.

In the past, the *Globe* has been accused of becoming something of an aircrew preserve, with lots and lots about the glamorous side of transport flying—travel abroad, "wild blue yonder" sort of stuff. While we think this criticism unjustified, we wish to avoid any taint of preferential treatment, hence the big spread about erks.

The general impression among non-erks is that an erk is a lazy, ignorant, immoral, dishevelled figure, who performs the minimum amount of duty he possibly can with the utmost reluctance, and with a cynicism that would make a Lord Chesterfield wince. Of course, there are erks like this—we can think of illuminating occasions when they have been encountered.

Loyalty

But, let's face it, the average erk is just an average person, with normal tendencies towards bad habits as well as flashes of good ones. The squalid description above is assiduously cultivated by the mass of erks, to observe the conventions of the Service, but occasionally, very occasionally, the other side of the coin is presented to the baffled onlooker. The reaction of the Nuclear Disarmers at Brize Norton, for instance, has to be imagined as one of utter incredulity that blokes who have given the impression for months of the most virulent discontent with the Royal Air Force in general, and Lyneham in particular, should behave with the greatest loyalty and devotion to an unpleasant duty, all in the most morale-sapping environment.

Another instance was the great efforts made by erks in the vilest weather conditions recently, when the most natural reaction to what had just been done to them was mutiny.

So, here is our tribute to the Erk of Lyneham; he or she would undoubtedly prefer us to buy him or her a drink, but luckily this is impossible. This screed is written from the point of view of your Editorial Staff, who, if you care to check, you will find to be officers (and gentlemen, of course).

Is anyone prepared to challenge our assessment of erks, or to expand it? If we know anything about erks, almost certainly not, but we could be proved wrong, couldn't we?

ERK AT W(E)RK

J/T Alan Warner tightening the retaining nut on a Britannia propellor in the Propellor Bay.

It being the heyday of the V-Force, a Vulcan was often a companion of the Britannia and many exercises were flown in their support. (*Bill Robinson*)

The Rock Hotel, Aden which would have been the accommodation for the crews away for Christmas. This establishment was thus used until Merrifield House, the on-base transit accommodation, was built. (*Lyneham Globe*)

'*The Lyneham Globe*' gave a portent for the future. For loading trials, a wooden mock-up of the cargo compartment of the proposed Belfast freighter had been constructed at the Fighting Vehicles Research and Development Establishment at Cobham, Surrey. The Belfast was destined to become a route companion of the Britannia.

**Mercy flight 2**

From helping a nation to helping an individual:

*'The wife of an airman flown into Lyneham on 29th November wishes to thank everyone concerned at Lyneham, for their efforts on behalf of herself, her children, and her injured husband. The airman was J/T Kenneth Davis of Halifax. He broke his neck in Aden when he dived into shallow water. He was flown home in an iron lung, in Britannia 637 of 99 Squadron, Captain Flt. Lt. L. Simpson and went from here to Stoke Mandeville Hospital by helicopter. Mrs. Davis and her two young children were very grateful for all that was done for them here, so we would like to congratulate all those who are responsible for eliciting such a pleasant and favourable mention.'*

There are two points that strike one here. Diving into a swimming pool's shallow water - or indeed no water at all - was quite a common serviceman accident. Secondly, how dated the term 'Iron Lung' now seems! The Britannia did have the electrical facility built in to supply what would now be called a life support machine.

**Record breaking**

The potential of the return flight with an empty aircraft and prevailing tail winds was realised by the Le Hardy crew who accomplished a record breaking non-stop flight from Jamaica to the UK. With the full fuel load of 68,000lbs, the aircraft took off from Kingston at 1300 hours (local) on 6th November and completed 4,100 nautical miles in 12 hours and 40 minutes, the longest single stage distance completed at that date by an RAF Britannia. The fuel, as it was burnt off, was eked out with constant increases in cruising level. The final height reached was 33,000 feet. In the latter stage, descent was refused because of a Boeing 707 below! But it was not to Lyneham that it was to come to roost. Thick fog shrouded the airfield and the aircraft was diverted to St Mawgan in Cornwall, a rather ignominious end for a record breaker.

**A proud year**

1961 had been a good Britannia and Lyneham year. The Station Commander, Group Captain I D N Lawson, summed things up in his Christmas message:

'*I am convinced that we can all look back on the year now ending with much pride and with a sense of considerable achievement. This has been a particularly busy year, calling, at times, for much extra effort. We have handled, and handled well, the Kuwait operation ... All the many tasks connected with the operation of our transport fleet have placed a heavy burden on you all. You have not let me down and for this I offer you my most sincere thanks and appreciation. Let us look forward to 1962 with all that it has in store, with confidence*'

**Christmas away**

But 1961 was not to lay down yet for the Britannia. Aden was to provide many a call for years to come as attempts were made to unify Aden itself and the tribal states of the Aden Protectorate surrounding it. One such call came, with that uncanny timing, on 17th December when crews flew out to Khormaksar and were there for Christmas and the New Year.

Flt. Lt. B. D. Weatherley is seen relaxing at the Officers' Club, Changi, Singapore. His unusual attitude is caused by the gyrations of the "Twist." Flt. Lt. Weatherley was formerly with 99 Squadron, Lyneham, and is now based at Headquarters, F.E.A.F.

As we have reached Christmas and party time, here is a reminder of the 60s - The Twist! Brian Weatherley, ex-99 navigator is in full swing! (*Lyneham Globe*)

Group Captain I D N Lawson (*Mike Joyce*)

Smart looking troops board a smart looking aeroplane (*Peter de Frère*)

The adventures of Messrs. Ad Minn and Org at Wootton Lynstoke continue ...

THEY RING THE MINISTRY OF WHATSIT – DIRECT.
"YES FRED! COVERS, RAIN, CIVIL SERVANT PROTECTING, BLACK, WHANGEE HANDLED, NON -REVERSIBLE, DENOM EA, QUANTITY TWO -MOST URGENT, MAKE IT C.S.O.G.!"
... AND WITHIN 3 HOURS THE ITEMS ARRIVE AT WOOTTON LYNESTOKE.
C.S.O.G.
TO HAVE AND TO HOLD AND HOLD AND HOLD AND HOLD ........
"PER VOUCHER AD ASTRA"
"HOW CAN YOU KEEP A STORES GOING IF YOU ISSUE IT ALL — YOU'LL HAVE NOTHING TO STORE!"
CLOTHING STORES
"GOOD MORNING GENTLEMEN I HAVE TO TAKE YOU TO SHQ. STRAIGHT AWAY."
"WHAT'S THAT SPLENDID BUILDING OVER THERE DRIVER?"
"OH THATS THE NEW SERGEANTS MESS...
...MARVELLOUS INSIDE, SIR. GLASS ALL ROUND, CENTRAL HEATING, HOT AND COLD ....TELEVISION.... PARQUET FLOORS....."
"IT SOUNDS VERY COMFORTABLE"
"YES BUT IT'S ONLY FOR SHOW SIR — I DON'T THINK THEY'RE GOING TO LET THE SERGEANTS LIVE IN THERE"
TURN RIGHT
SHQ
8

CHAPTER THIRTEEN

# 1962 - A Significant Year

Other history books may well overlook a significance of 1962; it was the year that the author joined the Britannia fleet!

**Recruits**

In the first two years of its service, crew members selected for Britannia training had, almost without exception, previous air transport experience, the most obvious source being the Hastings squadrons. But this pool was drying up and the net needed casting wider. So, for instance, pilots with two or three flying tours, no matter the type of aircraft, were now deemed suitable for Britannia training. I was one of these having completed two years on a Meteor day fighter squadron, the flying instructors' course at the Central Flying School and four years as a basic stage flying instructor on Piston Provosts. Out of the blue came a posting to RAF Lyneham.

**Training**

With this break with tradition, our lack of transport experience cast us as a very low form of life! Nevertheless, our training proceeded. The first phase of this was at the engine and airframe manufacturers, the Aero Engine School of Bristol Siddeley Engines Ltd and the Bristol Aircraft School, both located at Bristol. These totalled a whole four months. In that time the most incredible detail was covered. At times we felt we were being instructed to a level to allow us to construct the aircraft rather than just fly it! It was very difficult for us, with our lack of relevant experience, to sort out what was necessary knowledge. The general effect, therefore, was that we staggered out at the end without any really clear ideas.

This was confirmed at the next stage of training, the simulator. Experience with these devices over the years has led to them being incredibly useful TRAINING tools, but in those early days they were totally misused and became machines for subjecting crews to emergency upon emergency until they cracked up.

The same bitterness creeps into my memories of the flying phase. It seemed that the majority of those set to teach us had neither the ability or inclination to do so. They were capable themselves but found no way of conveying that knowledge. So, 'instruction' consisted of us having our pathetic 'go' which would be scathingly criticised. It certainly was a very strange feature of those early days.

**Captain Graham Bayliss**

Eventually our pitiful standard was considered to be just acceptable enough for us to proceed to a squadron, 'providing an eye was kept on us'. It was policy then for a new copilot to fly with just one captain for his first six months on the squadron. My captain, on 99 Squadron, was a very experienced transporter. Flight Lieutenant Graham Bayliss was a New Zealander who had a

An intrepid band! No.65(F) Squadron in front of one of their Meteor 8s at RAF Duxford, 1954. The author is second from the right. *(David Berry)*

Flt Lt Graham Bayliss

distinguished career in the RNZAF before joining the RAF. He had been stationed at RAF Changi, Singapore flying Bristol Freighters at the height of the Communist guerrilla warfare in Malaya. Graham's flying, parachuting men and stores into remote and hazardous dropping zones, earned him the Distinguished Flying Cross. The opportunity to leave RNZAF provided him with the chance to fly bigger and better transport aircraft, a prospect not then available in New Zealand, by joining the Royal Air Force. This he duly did obviously impressing on the hierarchy his motives for so doing as he found himself at Lyneham as one of the first copilots on the new aircraft. When I came under his kind and helpful wing he had just obtained his captaincy.

After a few years as a Britannia captain, Graham's talents were needed elsewhere when the VC10 fleet was being established and eventually he became their senior instructor and examiner. Sadly, he was grounded for a minor medical condition (now considered acceptable for continued flying) so he left the RAF as Squadron Leader G G Bayliss DFC AFC, the Air Force Cross awarded for his outstanding training efforts, and returned to New Zealand. For many years he headed the staff of Air New Zealand simulators and, in that time, master minding the introduction of new types of simulator to match ANZ's changing aircraft fleet.

Graham will be remembered by many as being the quintessence of professionalism and expertise which was the quality of the best of the 1960s Britannia captains.

After Graham's initial assistance, I progressed from my dubious start to eventually feel qualified to write this history - 13 years Britannia flying, 5000+ hours on type, 'A' Cat, last RAF pilot to fly a Britannia - if you stick to one thing long enough you might get good!

**ATS(B) to 241 OCU**

To return to the Britannia training scene, using the manufacturers' courses continued until these closed down in the late 1960s when the civilian airline training requirement dried up. The ground training then joined the air side at Lyneham - Air Training Squadron (Britannia). With the move of the fleet to Brize Norton in 1970, Britannia training became an element of the organisation that already existed for the VC10 and Belfast training, No 241 Operational Conversion Unit.

**One of many Adens**

The Aden standby, started just before Christmas 1961, continued into 1962. By April the dissident tribesmen were temporarily quietened; so the Britannia crews came home.

**Windy Deere remembers Aden**

'Dinghy Drill' was one of the crosses that Britannia crews had to bear. It was a requirement to attend, periodically, the survival school at RAF Mount Batten, near Plymouth, and put to sea to practise inflating, boarding and operating one of types of dinghy that were stored in the Britannia's wings. There were four in total. Windy's captain, Bill Smith, hatched a plot to overcome having to do the drill in the cold water of Plymouth Sound. Windy wrote about it for *The Whispering Giant* (*TWG*):

*'I have been searching through my log book entries to see if I noted when it was that Bill Smith and his merry men did the 'Dinghy Exercise'. I cannot find any reference to it, but it must have been in the early 60s. I wish now that I had kept a diary (don't we all!) for there are a thousand and one snippets of amusing little stories but it's often difficult to link them as to time and place. Anyway, the facts of this little tale are reasonably accurate, but before I submit this for publication I will check the detail with Bill Smith, who has a remarkable memory and can often relate events as*

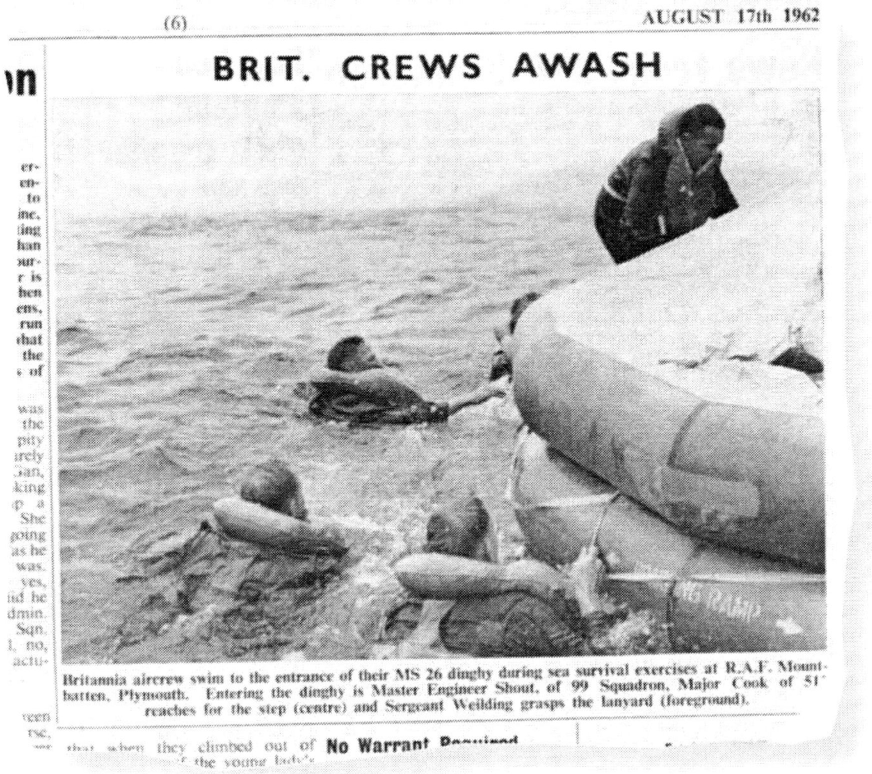
(6) AUGUST 17th 1962

BRIT. CREWS AWASH

Britannia aircrew swim to the entrance of their MS 26 dinghy during sea survival exercises at R.A.F. Mountbatten, Plymouth. Entering the dinghy is Master Engineer Shout, of 99 Squadron, Major Cook of 51 reaches for the step (centre) and Sergeant Weilding grasps the lanyard (foreground).

No Warrant Required

The *Lyneham Globe* caption reads: Britannia aircrew swim to the entrance of their MS26 dinghy during sea survival exercises at RAF Mount Batten, Plymouth. Entering the dinghy is Master Engineer Shout of 99 Squadron. Major Cook of 511 reaches for the step (centre) and Sergeant Weilding grasps the lanyard (foreground). (*Lyneham Globe*)

*if they happened the day before yesterday. If there are some significant discrepancies I will add a postscript. In the meantime bear with me as I relate the story of our day out on the Oggin.*

*'I don't know if we were low in the pecking order for the Far East runs, but that particular winter we seem to have spent rather a lot of our route days in Aden. We were all nicely tanned, and were feeling rather guilty, having to spend our days on the beach; sipping cold beer, swimming in the warm sea and ogling the 'marine life'. One morning, after breakfast, Cap'n Bill said, 'Chaps, I have a suggestion. Let's have a break from all this boring old laying around under the warm sun on Tanchine Beach and drinking cold beer and ogling the b**ds - er, I mean marine life. Why don't we do a dinghy drill?' In the interests of any grandchildren who may be idly leafing through this magazine (under the misapprehension that the silly old geezer reads only dirty books), I will not relate the rest of the conversation, but it can be summed up in the pithy phrase, 'Sod Off!' But then he offered a persuasive argument. If we did it here, we wouldn't have to do it there - 'there' being the English Channel in January in a Force 9 gale.*

*'And so it came to pass that early one morning, just as the sun was rising our motley Britannia crew plus ten or so fighter pilots boarded the Air Sea Rescue launch, which then set off at about fifty knots in the*

Two of our heroes prepare themselves for a day in the sun at Tanchine Beach, Aden Officers' Club - Alec Wickes and John Baxter. (*Malcolm Fraser*)

*direction of Bombay. About an hour later, out of sight of land, the vessel came to a grinding 'alt and us Transport Command wallahs were invited to step into a largish inflatable life-raft. The fighter jockeys were each issued with a single seat dinghy into which they got comfortable after an imaginary hurried exit from their high flying machines. From the outside, our dinghy looked quite large. Once we were gathered in the interior of the thing, sitting in a circle under the canopy, facing the centre, there wasn't a lot of spare room. The little flotilla of dinghies was distributed over about ten acres of ocean, on a fine, warm morning, with little wind and just a gentle sea swell. Not a bad day to do the exercise. As soon as we were all aboard our flimsy craft there was a mighty roar and the launch buggered off home for breakfast.*

*'I don't quite remember what was the order of business, but we had a variety of survival equipment to play with, as well as water and rations, so there was a reasonable prospect of surviving for a few hours, but we rather hoped the navigator of the launch had noted our position on his chart. For about an hour we practised installing the radio, worked out the mysteries of the heliograph, messed about with lanyards, made water! - yes, that too, but I mean with a distillation device that on a good day could convert salt water into fresh at the rate of about a gill a week. The brains behind the whole operation was Sailor Bill who in a previous life had been a lifeboat wallah, and knew of what 'e was er-doin'.*

*'The planned time for the oceanic portion of the exercise was about four hours. After about an hour we had more or less exhausted the entertainment possibilities within the craft and were getting a mite bored. Also, what had seemed such a gentle sea swell was beginning to have an adverse effect on my stomach. I was sitting opposite Taff and he was looking positively green about the gills, his normally good natured countenance replaced by a fixed and determined grin. By taking the occasional breather through one of the two openings I managed to keep a check on my queeziness, but Taff wasn't so fortunate, and he eventually succumbed to a rather noisy bout of sea-sickness. Once he had suffered his first spell of illness, Taff had to spend much of the time with his head stuck outside the canopy and his generously endowed rear end aiming at the rest of us; not a particularly attractive view, but this could be forgiven - until the aforementioned arse began to suffer a reaction to what was going on at the other end. To paraphrase Isaac Newton - 'To every Flatulance there is an equal and opposite Flatus'. The result of this was that the view our Fighter Pilot colleagues had of our dinghy was of Taff's head protruding from one opening and four heads, gasping for air, at the other.*

*'Things were not quite tickety-boo with the fighter jocks. Whilst we were enjoying ourselves grinding away at the Gibson Girl, being in single-seaters they had only themselves to play with, and were likely to do themselves an injury. Also, one of them periodically complained that his dinghy was leaking air. What was he worried about? He surely had a supply of those magical conical stoppers that Pete Smith had taught me years before would plug any leak. After about an hour, his dinghy did indeed look a little low in the water. However it still looked safe enough, but as a precaution he activated his ration of shark repellent. This was indeed a wise move, for these waters have a reputation for the ferocity of the sharks therein.*

*'Half an hour later the leaky dinghy was a sorry sight, as was the expression of its occupant, and fighter pilots being what they are he was not getting a great deal of sympathy from his comrades. At the exact moment it happened, I was under the canopy, but suddenly Tommy shouted 'Jesus Christ!', and I immediately looked out to to see what had caused this uncharacteristic outburst. The pilot in the leaking dinghy, having weighed up all the possibilities; the idea that a tiny slick of brightly covered repellent could thwart a 200 pound Great White Shark, the fact that there were only five of us in a seven-man dinghy, and the possibility that if he hurried there was an even chance he could reach us 'limbus intactus', had decided to abandon ship, and was at that moment proceeding towards us at a remarkable speed, and one could certainly get the impression that the chap was running towards us upon the surface of the sea! It is therefore reasonable to suppose that Tommy was not so much uttering a blasphemy as for a moment wondering if this was the real thing! A few moments later we had hauled the hapless survivor aboard,*

HM The Queen leaving the Britannia at the conclusion of her flight. (*John Bourn*)

*and just to be on the safe side spent the time after that sitting at his feet.*

*'About an hour later a distant 'whop, whop, whop' heralded the arrival of the rescue phase. Two choppers appeared overhead (perhaps guided by our smoke signals) and commenced the task of plucking people from the dinghies. Once the fighter pilots had been dealt with, it was our turn. Taff, who judging from his semi-comatose state was still rather ill, was the first to go, then it was my turn. I had drawn the helicopter flown by the pilot who, with one hand on the controls and the other holding the 'How to Hover' section of Pilots' Notes, was having trouble keeping the retrieval equipment in one position. Salvation hung in equal balance with decapitation. After a few desperate lunges I eventually managed to grab the harness and was finally deposited on to the deck of the launch*

*'The following lunchtime, we were back in our accustomed positions at Steamer Point beach, under a warm sun, sipping cold beer and taking in the er ... 'marine life'. Bill took a sip of beer, and then said meditatively, to no one in particular, 'Well, it seemed like a good idea at the time!"*

**Tarmac lifter**

Squadron Leader John Bourn was one of the early Britannia pilots. Promotion in 1962 took him into a Flight Commander spot on 99 Squadron. He describes one of his route trips in March/April:

*'On 30 March we departed Lyneham for Bermuda, California (March AFB), Christmas Island and thence to Changi via Fiji and Australia. En route we diverted into the old Pago Pago airfield, on American Samoa, to drop some freight. The surface of the parking area rolled up behind the Britannia's wheels!'*

**The Queen's only flight**

John Bourn also contributed, as escort officer, towards the one and only occasion when Her Majesty The Queen flew in a Royal Air Force Britannia. On 1st May 1962, XN404 conveyed Her Majesty, accompanied by HRH Princess Marina and HRH Princess Alexandra, to Amsterdam to attend the celebrations in connection with the Silver Wedding of Queen Juliana of the Netherlands and Prince Bernhardt. HRH

(7) JUNE 8th 1962

Here is the only photograph we could obtain of Her Majesty the Queen and H.R.H. Prince Philip arriving at London Airport after being flown from Amsterdam by 99 Squadron, as reported in our Edition No. 70. We would like to thank Associated Press for their permission to use the photo, and the L.A.P. Press Relations Office for their help in tracing it for us.

THE

The *Lyneham Globe* photograph of HM The Queen leaving the Britannia after the flight from Amsterdam. (*Lyneham Globe*)

Prince Philip joined the party for the return. JB records that the aircraft suffered complete radio failure shortly after take-off in the London Control Zone!

**Aircrew status**

In May 1962 a new flying brevet was introduced. It bore the letters QM. This was overdue recognition of the important aircrew role of the air quartermaster. From the earliest days of transport aircraft there had been ground crew who were co-opted on to flights to 'give a hand down the route'. This gradually developed from certain personnel unofficially specialising to it being given formal status with recruitment of corporals and sergeants from the Supply Trade Group; a natural choice as the developing

The caption to this photo, which appeared in the '*Lyneham Globe*', read: *'At Tafuna Airport in American Samoa a Lyneham-based Britannia is seen parked outside the air terminal. Although the airport has at present only one runway 6080 feet long, leading towards the hills seen in the background, a new runway is under construction and is expected to be ready in July 1962.'* (*Bill Robinson*)

A newspaper photo of a 1970's recruit to the ranks of the AQMs (by then renamed airloadmasters) - Sgt (W) Joan Hisbent. A female crew member on board was a great reassurance to women and children passengers. (*The Gateway Gazette*)

Air Movements organisation was manned by Equipment Branch personnel. In 1957, corporals and sergeants from any trade were permitted to volunteer. Employment was for 2½ years with a possible extension of a year before they returned to their original ground trades. Their responsibilities were recognised by the award of an extra 2s.3d per day. Corporals were given the acting rank of sergeant whilst fulfilling these duties. This was the state of affairs as the Britannia came into service although the aircraft's status was acknowledged in a strange way with the posting in of some Master Pilots (Warrant Officer rank) to AQM duties.

The ground tradesmen, turned fliers, were a great bunch. They were there because they wanted to be. They had to be something of a 'Jack of all Trades' - but most of them were certainly also 'Master of Many'. Checking and advising on the load, completing the 'Trim Sheet' which ensured that the aircraft was to fly within its weight and centre of gravity limits, care of the passengers during the flight and guarding them against potential danger with a full knowledge of emergency procedures. In the more remote locations, they had also to be capable of taking on the total responsibility for the loading, the physical as well as the 'numbers' side.

**Food! Food!**

Each one developed a style that established him as a true crew member. The area that perhaps drew the greatest admiration from his compatriots was facility with food! There were constraints, the standard crew meal would be similar to a passenger's, prepared on a plastic tray. Our enterprising AQMs escaped from this as often as possible. To 'bulk ration', i. e. drawing basic ingredients from the kitchens along

Les Stables: *'Group Captain Steedman presenting me with my Air Quartermaster brevet. The two other AQMs with me are Pete Smith (511) and Bob Ogilvy (99). When this picture was taken I was a Corporal, acting Sergeant (paid). Moments later I was informed that I was a substantive Flight Sergeant! Promotion almost as rapid as wartime!'* (*Les Stables*)

the route rather than the standard meals, would be their target. Then the crew would be served such delights as 'Honker's Soup' - a hot and tasty delight, one certainly more tempting than the tray meal. If this had to be used then it would be 'humanised'. Your meal would be served on the AQM's table at the back of the aircraft. This would have a 'table cloth', sauces and seasoning would be provided and many carried their own stainless steel cutlery to replace the provided ghastly plastic.

Gastronomic achievements reached their greatest heights when we escaped from the standard routes and the AQM went 'shopping' locally. Over the middle of the Pacific Ocean, I have filled my plate from a buffet which would have done justice to a Hunt Ball. Those early AQMs certainly confirmed that, 'The way to a man's heart is ...'

Air Ministry Order A115/62 introduced the new aircrew category of air quartermaster. Many of those in the role qualified for assimilation and the door was opened for full career recruits, more from within the Service and fresh faces from civilian life. Sex was no barrier. The debate as to whether AQM members of the WRAF were thus the first females to wear an aircrew beret will not be entered into here. There were a few previous claimants resulting from special circumstances.

One anomaly did arise out of the creation of this scheme in that many of the existing incumbents were corporals holding acting sergeant rank. But non-commissioned aircrew promotion was 'time in the Service' based and there were several cases of men stepping straight from corporal to Master Aircrew (Warrant Officer) rank.

So the air quartermasters took their full place alongside pilot, navigator, signaller and flight engineer and, as the years passed by, it was proved that this was an

(3) JULY 6th 1962

Soldiers of the Royal Welch Fusiliers deplane from a Lyneham-based Britannia of Transport Command at Gander Airport, Newfoundland. En route to Edmonton, Alberta, the soldiers had sufficient time for a meal and to send a postcard home before boarding the aircraft again.

Soldiers of the Royal Welsh Fusiliers deplane from a Britannia at Gander Airport, Newfoundland en route to Edmonton, Alberta. The soldiers had sufficient time for a meal and to send a postcard home before boarding the aircraft again. (*Lyneham Globe*) entirely rightful position.

**AQM Les Stables**

Les Stables was one of that band of air quartermasters; older than some, an ex-air gunner. He was Yorkshire born and bred - Darfield near Barnsley - August 1920. They were hard times. His father had a small business that fell victim of the 1926 General Strike and by the early 30s he was trying to raise a family of four on the 'Means Test'. Les felt that he had to get a job to help out. Fourteen was the school leaving age and he left, without his parents' permission, and obtained a job as a pony driver in a local coal mine, at 'two shillings and tuppence halfpenny' a day!

He first became interested in aircraft at about the age of nine when Alan Cobham brought his flying circus to a field about two miles from his home. He was hooked. At the outbreak of the War he was still in the mines, now at the coal face. Mining was a reserved occupation and his mother was pleased that he would not have to go to war.

But Les Stables could not resist the call - or aeroplanes - and found himself, on his 21st birthday, being told to report to Blackpool in three weeks to start initial training. His first air experience was in a Beaufighter on an air test by pestering a Flight Commander on 29 Squadron at West Malling. He was then Flight Lieutenant Gibson, later to lead the Dam Busters and earn the VC. Les did his air gunnery training on Blackburn Bothas. Squadron service followed, typically 36 Squadron in Algeria, on Wellingtons, engaged in daylight convoy escort duty.

The war over, he left the RAF to go back to the mines in South Yorkshire. He missed the Service, and aeroplanes, enormously and a few years later he found

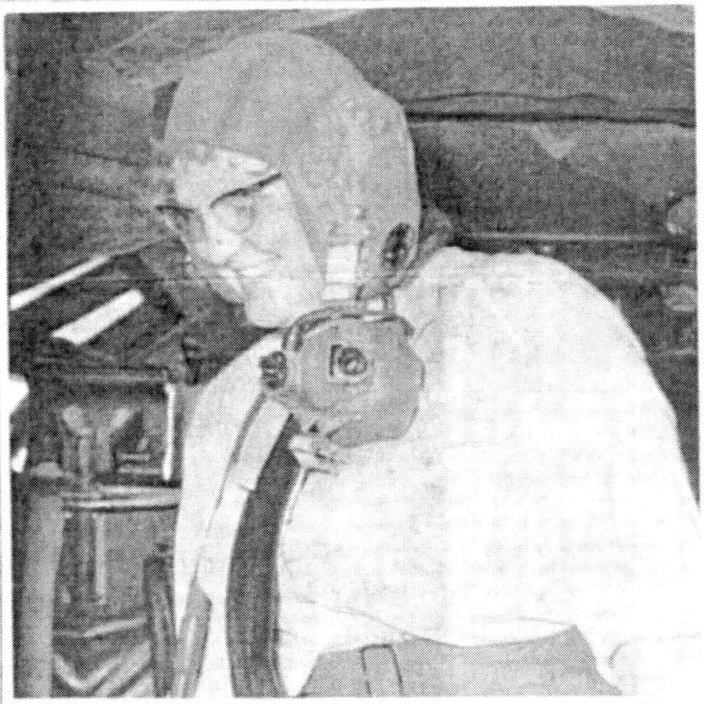

LYNEHAM L.A.C.W. GETS THE MESSAGE

(Photographer's 'Tammy'—Ed.)

During Exercise Berengaria L.A.C.W. Joyce Wilson, who normally works in General Office, was one of the helpers who assisted in looking after the 'return load' wives and children. Here she is seen taking time off to listen to the aircraft's VHF messages to the airways controller

During Exercise Berengaria, LACW Joyce Wilson, who normally worked in the General Office at Lyneham, was one of the helpers who assisted in looking after the 'return load' of wives and children. (*Lyneham Globe*)

himself back in the RAF as a corporal in Air Traffic Control. But he still had that urge to fly and Les saw the chance of applying to do a tour as an AQM. It was the days just described when AQMs were ground tradesmen who just did one tour, as acting sergeant (paid), before reverting to their previous trade and rank.

He did his training on Hastings and Beverleys but then, at the end of the course, was sent to Lyneham for conversion to Britannias and went to 99. He had been there about a year when the trade of AQM was made permanent and the first brevets presented. Les could not believe his luck. He completed five years on 99 before being sent to Belfasts, and then to return to Britannias, this time 511, for his last few years before retirement.

Asked for a story of his Britannia years, Les Stables recalls:

*'We were taking the Duke and Duchess of Kent on the first two legs of their return to Hong Kong after the wedding of Princess Alexandra. Crowds had gathered at the terminal, including a lot of top brass. When I got them on board, the other AQM showed them to their seats and I closed the passenger door. We already had 3 & 4 engines running and I was just about to call up the captain, Pete Gray, to give him the 'All Clear' for 1 & 2 when there was a tap on my shoulder. It was the Lyneham Movements Officer. His responsibilities were firmly on the ground not in the air with us! It was a rather sheepish Flight Lieutenant who descended the repositioned steps!'*

The first VC10 about to land at Wisley ...

.10—PRESENTATION AT LYN

The first VC10 proves that it DOES fly—coming into land at Wisley, with leading edge slats and large Fowler flaps akimbo, to say the least.

**A helping hand**

On many occasions the Britannia was able to give assistance to aircraft and ships in distress. An instance of this occurred on 1st May. Early in the morning a Britannia crewed by 99 Squadron, headed by Flt Lt 'Nogger' Norris, was ready for take-off at El Adem, when they were informed by Air Traffic Control that there was a Viscount aircraft in the vicinity lost with total compass failure, unreliable radio compasses and short of fuel. El Adem could not offer a haven as it was fog bound and ATC were doing their best to guide the aircraft towards Benina airport, near Benghazi on the North Libyan coast. After the Britannia had taken off, it closed in on the Viscount's track and established radio contact. The navigator, Flt Lt 'Tommy' Tomlinson, established its position and the relief was evident in the radio response to this information. A little while later a thankyou came from the safely landed aircraft. Only minutes of fuel remained.

**Army to Canada**

To this day a summer commitment exists for the air transport force to airlift elements of the British Army to Alberta, Canada. Close by Edmonton there is an exercise area along the style of Salisbury Plain but of a size to swallow that 'blasted heath' many times over. The annual lift of 900 men and 41,000lbs of freight went by the title of Exercise Pond Jump, which showed a little more imagination than that normally associated with such exercise namings. Outbound the aircraft routed via Gander, Newfoundland for Namao, close by Edmonton. With empty aircraft for the return, many made it back direct.

**... then Cyprus**

With hardly time for a breath to be drawn, Exercise Berengaria was under way, air lifting a brigade group of 19 Brigade to Cyprus. Twenty flights flew out 1,600 men and 162,000lbs of freight. With the recovery planned for several weeks later, advantage was taken of the empty aircraft flying to and fro to offer the Service families in Cyprus a holiday at home. A number of Lyneham's WRAF were recruited as temporary AQM's assistants for these family loads.

**A good boss!**

One of the considerable personalities

other interested parties who feel they should have a finger in the pie.

Maybe we should have left a sample? After a presentation of information on the VC 10, two members of the B.A.C. team pack up their projector. They are Pat Burgess (left), of Sales and Service Engineering of B.A.C., formerly of 99 Sqdn., and Roger White-Smith, Sales Manager.

... a BAC team gave a presentation to Lyneham personnel on the VC10. One member was Pat Burgess (left), of BAC's Sales and Engineering, ex-99 navigator and RAF Britannia pioneer. (*Lyneham Globe*)

LYNEHAM "STEELY-E

At the show at Upavon recently commemorating '50 years of military a from Fighter Command's book with precision formation flypasts. Despite quite close enough to [illegible] all the nice things said about them. In t

Three Britannias, in line astern, overfly Upavon at the display to celebrate 50 years of military aviation. (*Lyneham Globe*)

of the Britannia scene appeared in 1962. Wing Commander John Lewis AFC RAF took command of 511 Squadron.

Joining the Royal Air Force in 1939, he served with 604 Squadron on Blenheims. Then it was Blenheims again and later Beaufighters in nightfighter and intruder roles with 25 Squadron of the Desert Air Force and 255 in Malta. When peace was declared he was with 575 Squadron in Italy opening up the transport routes.

Still in the transport business he commanded the Levant Communications Squadron after serving as the Flight Commander on 78 Squadron (Kabrit). Leaving Aqir in the Transjordan in 1948, he completed the Central Flying School (CFS) course and took up flying instructional duties at the RAF College, Cranwell. 1950 was the year that Dr Vivian Fuchs made his first incursion into the wastes of Antarctica. Wg Cdr Lewis was seconded for a year to the Expedition. He returned to Cranwell and then went back to CFS as an instructor. Time came for a ground tour and he served on the Permanent Commission Selection Board at the Air Ministry.

John Lewis had clearly made an impression in the Antarctic, for he was now recalled there and served for three years with Fuchs flying Beavers, Otters and Austers. After this, a desk in the Air Secretary's Branch must have seemed dull. From that he completed the Latimer Staff College Course and then went to Lyneham to take command of 511 Squadron - a post he filled with some style.

A reunion of ex-511 COs. John Lewis is 5th from the left, beneath the clock. (*Lyneham Globe*)

**Another 'Shiny' on its way**

Reports on the Belfast's progress towards entering the Service were a regular feature of RAF news of this time. This was now joined with word of another future addition, the VC10. These were indeed heady days for the Royal Air Force Strategic Transport Force.

**50 year display**

The Force was able to show off its present 'shiny' aircraft at a display to commemorate 50 years of military aviation. Aircraft upon aircraft flew by RAF Upavon on a glorious summer's day. I was there with a weekend break from my Britannia course and my heart stirred as the line astern formation of three Britannias flew by!

**Mishaps**

It is only in later years that some stories leak out about 'incidents'. The author recalls that when he visited Edinburgh Field, South Australia, in September 1963, the locals talked of a RAF Britannia that had done a little exploring of the 'bundoo' the year before. The story is now told by Tony Harrison:

*'My introduction to the Britannia was a test flight in G-ANBB with Mr E. Statham on 21st April 1955 when I was converting on to Sycamore helicopters at Filton. The culmination of the flight was landing using full reverse on all four to simulate complete brake failure. Seven years later I was to be very grateful that the system operated successfully.*

*'By that time I had completed a chopper tour in Cyprus and a home tour at Acklington and was nearing the end of a 'Ground Tour' as AQM Leader on 511 Squadron. We had left Lyneham on UAB 6103 in XM490 for Edinburgh Field, South Australia on 6th April with a scheduled departure of 14th April from Edinburgh. At 0800hrs that morning we lined up for departure direct from Edinburgh to Changi a flight time of some 10hrs 45 minutes. We had a fuel load of 68,000lbs and a 'Hot' load of 30,400lbs including 700lbs high explosive and just for good measure a tail component wind factor.*

*'Given take-off clearance the clock was punched, taps were opened, brakes off and we started to roll - Changi here we*

JULY 20th 19

## RUNWAYS TOO HIGH?

Cpl. Tech. Heath assisted by S.A.C. Jones doing a final check on the "three thousandth wheel" before "issuing out" to Britannia XL 636.

**Mechanical Engineering Squadron**

*'Cpl. Tech. Heath assisted by SAC Jones doing a final check on the 'Three Thousandths wheel' before 'issuing out' to Britannia XL636.' (Lyneham Globe)*

*come or do we? At full throttle and a fair number of knots on the clock over the head-set came the voice of the Engineer, 'Loss of power No.4, Captain.' 'Check it, Engineer.' 'Confirm power loss four Captain.' 'Throttle 4.' The Engineer throttled all four as the Navigator called 'V-One'; the Captain ordered 'Full reverse all engines.'*

*'In that condition, with full braking, we ran out of runway and it got rough in the overshoot area and rougher still when we ran out of overshoot, went through a metal post and wire fence, over a ditch across a dirt road, another ditch through another fence and finally came to a halt some forty to fifty yards into a paddock with four curly props and a smoking port bogie.*

*'I went forward and opened the crew entrance door and put the emergency ladder down. The Crew Chief, armed with a* $C0^2$ *extinguisher, and I went out. He sprayed the over-heated port bogie to cool it as a fire precaution whilst I went to check the starboard bogie which I found to be hot but not hot enough to be a fire hazard.*

*'It was then I saw the old Holden pick-up roaring down the dirt road towards us hotly pursued by a rolling cloud of billowing red dust. Without slowing he shot through the hole we had made in the fence, the water bags on his 'roo bar' thrashing around like Dolly Parton doing a hundred metres dash and slewed to a stop by the tailplane.*

*'I moved towards him to warn him out of a potential explosion area. As I approached he got out of the pick-up, pushed his hat to the back of his head,*

The Britannia did not take kindly to its wheels running over grass and there were, over the years, a number of instances like the one above. An aircraft enthusiast took this photograph of 518 from the perimeter fence of RAF Northolt. (*Internet*)

*scratched his temple and greeted me with: 'Strewth mate that's a hell ova thing to leave in a place like this!"*

**That sinking feeling**

The aircraft enthusiast who took the Northolt photograph above added this comment:

*'There must have been a very red-faced pilot on this a/c when he tried to use the triangle of taxiways on the NE side of the 26 threshold to turn around (The centre of the triangle was concreted over soon after, to give the current configuration). I was lucky enough to be there when this happened, although the photo was not taken by me. To add to the embarrassment,I believe the aircraft was filled with ATC cadets on their way to the USA on an annual exchange visit. A replacement Britannia was flown in a few hours later with a very marginal wingtip clearance when it landed. All other flights that day had to use runway 31, but presumably the Brit was too large for that.'*

Social comment continues - an advert from '*The Lyneham Globe*' aimed at a new breed of serviceman - one who might buy his own house. Note the price!

Many years later, at a Britannia Association reunion, the full details emerged. Ex-99 captain Dave Ray was a new recruit to the Association ranks. He revealed that he was the copilot on the doomed flight:

*'The date was 9th August 1962 and we were engaged in an International Air Cadet exchange scheme. The captain had his air cadet son on the jump seat and our passengers were American cadets. We were making a tight turn on a narrow taxiway - the picture shows the rest. The Duty Crew from Lyneham turned up with XN404 and, to our surprise, handed it over to us to complete the task while they sorted out 518!'*

**The lucky ones**

Away from the Changi Slip and the like, two crews sampled something a little different. Flt Lt Dave Nursaw and team circumnavigated the world in just 12 days -

first stop, off the standard eastbound route, was Darwin. There followed Townsville, Guam, Midway Island, California, Thule in Greenland and home. Meanwhile Flt Lt Ken Bick and crew flew what was to become a regular task - the tour of the capitals of Northern Europe for the NATO Defence College students. The tour took in Oslo, Copenhagen, Bonn, Brussels, The Hague and Paris.

**National Service**

A section on 1962 cannot be complete without a mention of the end of National Service. As with all parts of the Service, the Britannia fleet had its share of those young men forcibly removed from their home environment - and like those other 'parts' we were appreciative of what they contributed.

Not the least of that 'contribution' is the fact that many stalwart members of the fleet, both air and ground, started life as National Servicemen and 'stayed on'.

During these years, this photograph was a popular presentation gift.

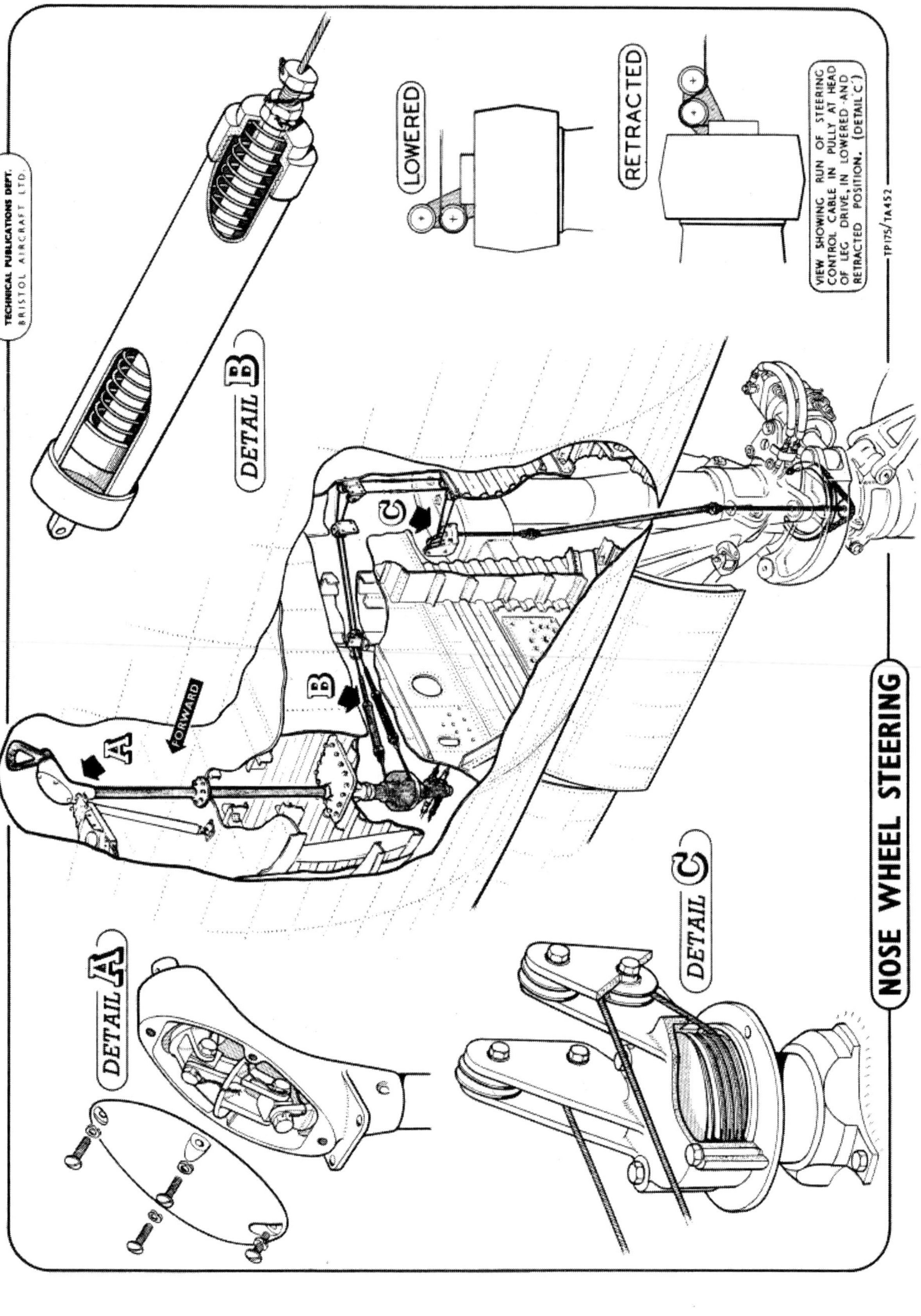
NOSE WHEEL STEERING
DETAIL A
DETAIL B
DETAIL C
FORWARD
A
B
C
LOWERED
RETRACTED
VIEW SHOWING RUN OF STEERING CONTROL CABLE IN PULLY AT HEAD OF LEG DRIVE, IN LOWERED AND RETRACTED POSITION. (DETAIL 'C')
TP175/TA452
DRAWN AND ISSUED BY TECHNICAL PUBLICATIONS DEPT. BRISTOL AIRCRAFT LTD.

The adventures of Messrs. Ad Minn and Org at Wootton Lynstoke continue ...

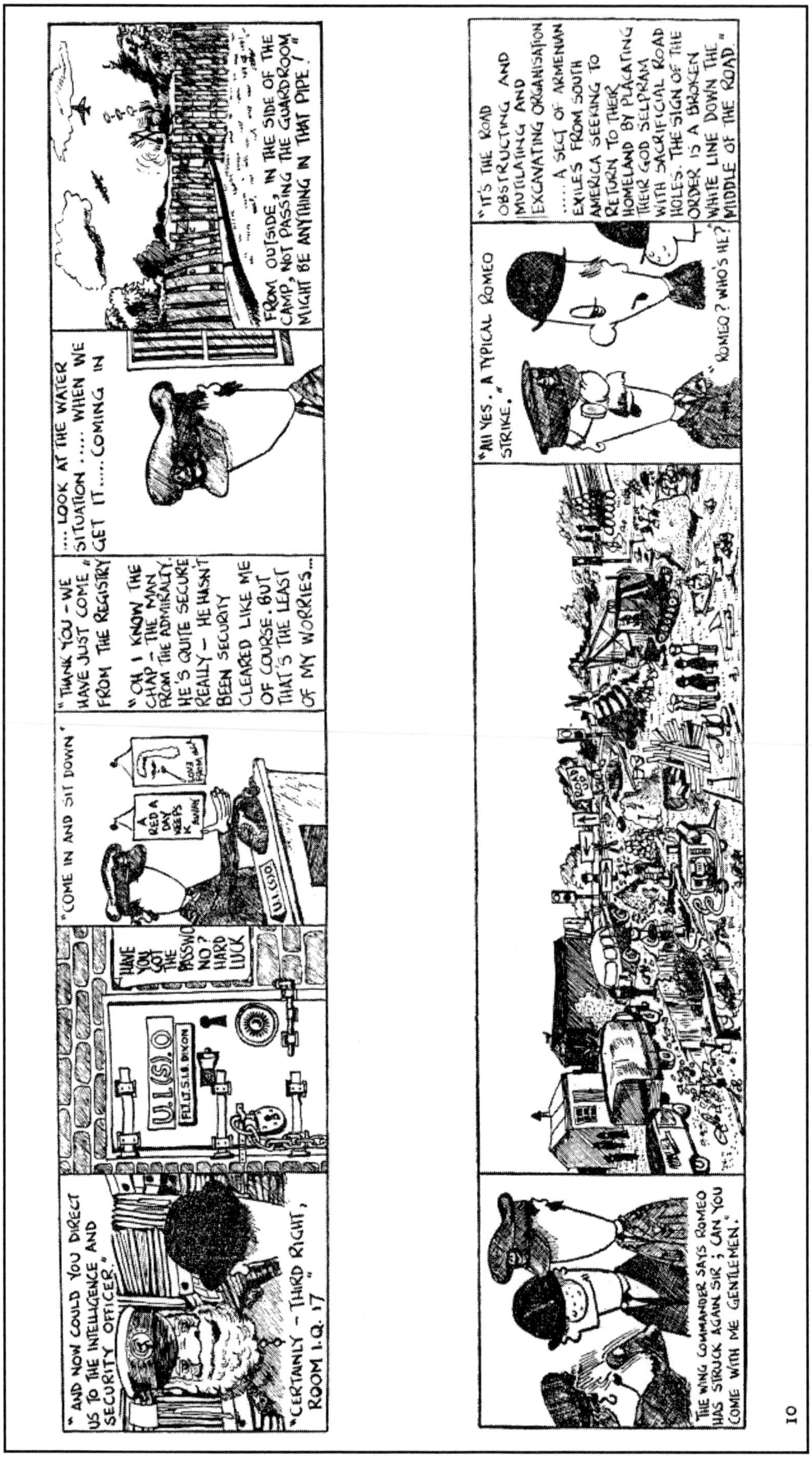
"AND NOW COULD YOU DIRECT US TO THE INTELLIGENCE AND SECURITY OFFICER."
"CERTAINLY - THIRD RIGHT, ROOM I.Q. 17"
U.I.(S).O
FLT.LT.S.I.B. DIXON
HAVE YOU GOT THE PASSWORD? NO? HARD LUCK
"COME IN AND SIT DOWN"
U.I.(S).O
"THANK YOU - WE HAVE JUST COME FROM THE REGISTRY"
"OH, I KNOW THE CHAP - THE MAN FROM THE ADMIRALTY. HE'S QUITE SECURE REALLY - HE HASN'T BEEN SECURITY CLEARED LIKE ME OF COURSE. BUT THAT'S THE LEAST OF MY WORRIES...
.... LOOK AT THE WATER SITUATION ..... WHEN WE GET IT..... COMING IN
FROM OUTSIDE, IN THE SIDE OF THE CAMP, NOT PASSING THE GUARDROOM MIGHT BE ANYTHING IN THAT PIPE!"
THE WING COMMANDER SAYS ROMEO HAS STRUCK AGAIN SIR; CAN YOU COME WITH ME GENTLEMEN."
"AH YES. A TYPICAL ROMEO STRIKE."
"ROMEO? WHO'S HE?"
"IT'S THE ROAD OBSTRUCTING AND MUTILATING AND EXCAVATING ORGANISATION ..... A SECT OF ARMENIAN EXILES FROM SOUTH AMERICA SEEKING TO RETURN TO THEIR HOMELAND BY PLACATING THEIR GOD SELPRAM WITH SACRIFICIAL ROAD HOLES. THE SIGN OF THE ORDER IS A BROKEN WHITE LINE DOWN THE MIDDLE OF THE ROAD."
10

CHAPTER FOURTEEN

# Busy 1962 Continues

VIPs featured large in the life of the Britannia, especially in the early days when the aircraft was very much a prestige symbol. Great pride was taken by the ground crew in the preparation of the aircraft. On the route they were represented by the crew chief, an experienced Chief Technician or Flight Sergeant who had been trained (plus much self taught) in all aspects of Britannia servicing; this involved study and practice way outside his own specialist trade. The aircraft taxying in and shutting down would be the start of his work with refuelling, routine servicing and rectification. If all went well he would probably be finished and securing the aircraft in two to three hours. But his rest would be short for he would have to be first to the aircraft to unlock and get everything prepared for the departure. With many en route faults, much ingenuity was required and a common sense to distinguish between what was an acceptable unserviceability and what was not; the cry from above would be, 'Keep the aircraft moving, and on time.'

**Crew Chief memories**

Some insight of this can be gained from some of the memories of, larger than life crew chief, Ron King:

*'There were two types of electrical relays for services, the original Pullins and the replacement Plesseys. It was nothing to change 15 Pullins to keep a route going. The Plesseys solved most of these problems. When the spares ran out, I have had to bridge the contacts in flight to get the gear down. The final resort with reluctant undercarriage relays was to lift the nav's astro step (a height adjustable platform to enable the navigator eye to reach the flight deck roof mounted sextant) and jump on it. This used to retract the platform very quickly! As the platform was situated directly over the undercarriage relays it never failed to provide the needed impetus to 'dangle the Dunlops'!*

*'A thorough knowledge of the electrical circuitry was essential to maintain an aircraft off route. In this, the flight engineers sure earned their keep and the respect of associated tradesmen with their expertise. The tech de-brief after a route was something to be seen and often went on for an hour.*

*'One of the many hazards was implosion of the humidifier water tank as the vent pipe lines were prone to blockage. It used to make it 'rain' in the passenger cabin and the tank had to be 'stabbed' to stop the monsoon. Another impressive snag was if someone left the bog drain cap insecure. Pressurisation would be lost. A remedy to try and stop the escaping air was to put the library box lid on the bog seat with all the towels the 'Q' could find. Another use for the lid was when a flight deck window cracked in flight. The lid was placed over it; this eliminated the possibility of one of the crew's rapid exit through the failed window.*

Ex-Crew Chief Ron King (right) is photographed, in later years, in an appropriate location. He and fellow ex-Crew Chief Ted Sharpe are in the control room of the old Proteus engine test bay at Filton. It became the home of the museum of The Rolls Royce Heritage Trust (Bristol Branch). Members of the Britannia Association were guests of the Trust. (*David Berry*)

The success of 'off the normal route' trips depended heavily on the crew chief - an experienced ground technician. Such people had their own trade but crew chiefs had additional training in all the other trades so that they could tackle any of the faults occurring on a route trip away from normal servicing facilities. This was the cover photo for the Winter 1990 edition of the Britannia Association magazine. It was taken on Tutuila Islands, American Samoa and shows Sgt Geordie Morpeth checking the fuel for any water contamination. (*Bill Robinson*)

*'Then there was the 'Dance of the Seven Veils' over Spar 178 to return the JPT servo pots to the null position for start up. I was performing this ritual on 398 and forgot it was a balsa floor and went through it up to my shins, right in front of a Group Captain, 'Does this happen often, chief?' he enquired. When we got to Le Bourget I mended the hole with a sheet of 18g aluminium but had to take a lot of stick about stress components and overweight crew chiefs.*

*'The use of 'Le Knocking Stick' technique was required on a number of components - flap relays under the main spar panel centre floor, prop parking brake actuators, hot gas override actuators, firetech boxes and relay panels (that's if you couldn't lose the induced warning with a twitch on the igniter switch). An adage of those days, 'a knock to the brute saved many a route!'*

*'I was lucky, I think if a Brit went, I went. I will always be grateful to such a real good ship and the wonderful friends I made amongst the special people who flew and operated them.'*

**VIP care**

Timings on VIP flights were a great pride of aircrew and their accompanying crew chief. The aim would be to board the VIP and close the door at the precise moment dictated by the itinerary and arrive and open the door for the VIP to disembark to the second - and that is not loose wording. Speed, height, route, taxy pattern would all be adjusted to ensure timing to that second.

In the cabin, the important persons would receive every attention and quality of service from the VIP air quartermasters. This would rival any standard reached in the easier conditions on the ground.

**European tour**

A VIP trip could be centred around one person or several, expanding, as often happened with the capacity of the Britannia, to a considerable number. April 1962 provides an example of the latter with what became a recurring commitment, to convey staff and students of the NATO Defence College on their tour of Southern Europe. On the 3rd, XM398 positioned at Le Bourget for VIP Flight 1051.

The 72 students from 14 nations were flown to Lisbon, Malta, Istanbul, Ankara, Izmir, Athens, Naples, Rome, Turin and back to Paris. To quote the Lyneham Globe:

*'Thanks to the sterling efforts of Chief Tech Ron King and his servicing party plus some excellent spares backing by the chaps at Lyneham the whole tour was completed on schedule. Everywhere it went the aircraft left an excellent impression ... Finally a word of thanks to Aircraft Prep. for the standard to which the aircraft was turned out. It did much to enhance the prestige in which the Royal Air Force, and Transport Command in particular, is held by many high ranking officers of NATO.'*

**Home from home Brit**

A smaller party, but making up for lack of numbers with their high rank, was conveyed on a tour in August/September 1962. Fourteen staff and students of the Imperial Defence College (IDC) visited 14 major cities in East and West Pakistan, India and Ceylon.

With such a small number it was

An anonymous photographer has some fun with his wide angle lens.

When this photo of the Uganda VIP crew was published in *TWG* there was some memory loss with regard to names. 'Squire' Morecombe came to the rescue in the next edition:

*'Further to the photo from Nick Carter. I have a copy of the same photo, but have a slight advantage in that mine obviously came from 'The Lyneham Globe' of the day, and I have the info that went with it.'*

**MY KNEES ARE KILLING ME!**
Sergeant Leslie Dipper (centre front), AQM of the 511 Squadron Britannia which went to Uganda for the Independence Celebration, was clearly disinterested when an East African Airway's hostess visited the crew at Entebbe. Could it have been professional jealousy? Or was he afraid that the rest of the crew would start making unfavourable comparisons?
L to R (back row): M/E W. Sneddon; Co-pilot Flt. Lt. N. Carter; 'Norah' an East African Airways' hostess; Flt. Lt. L. Morecombe, Navigator; F1t. Lt. W. Eglinton, Captain; (Front) Ch. Tech. Williams, Crew Chief; Sgt. L. Dipper, AQM; M/Sig. L. Manning.

(*Nick Carter*)

possible to divide XN392 into a sitting room, dining room and cocktail area. For this IDC party, the tour was a very strenuous one, their time on the ground being completely occupied with visits, presentations and receptions. Therefore they came to regard the flying time as a very welcome breathing space. For this, their needs were catered for by the two AQMs, Sgt Rick Hahnfield and Sgt Newman. To quote a report:

*'At this point it is appropriate to pay tribute to AQMs on a trip of this nature. Working off route without the familiar ground organisation, calls for a great deal of ingenuity and initiative to procure everything that might be needed.'*

**Royal VIP**

Another VIP flight for the year was 'Royal'. Their Royal Highnesses, The Duke and Duchess of Kent were flown to Kampala for the Uganda Independence celebrations.

511's Flt Lt Bill Eglinton was the captain for this Uganda VIP trip. He left the Service some time later and ended up as something of a 'Bush Pilot' in Australia. He wrote an amusing article for *TWG*.

Nick Carter, the copilot for this trip had a rather alarming experience in 'former life'. He was a Meteor fighter pilot, and whilst engaged in a 'tail chase' his aircraft went into an uncontrollable spiral dive, forcing him to eject. Obviously he survived but was badly injured. He has written of this experience in his book, '*Meteor Eject!*' (see later). In the course of correspondence with the magazine, Bill Eglinton wrote: '*I was interested to read about Nick Carter's book, 'Meteor Eject'. I got first hand account of his amazing escape from the Meteor. He flew with me on several occasions - one of them to attend the Uganda independence celebrations. I wonder if he remembers that? Ask him if he remembers the hand of bananas presented to each member of the crew?*'

The Editor did ask Nick: '*How nice to hear from Bill again. Yes, we did fly together quite often and I well remember attending the Uganda celebrations. We flew out to Entebbe via Luqa, Khormaksar and Nairobi. On arrival we were told there would be a day of pageantry in Kampala Stadium, culminating in the lowering of the Union Jack. We were told to fly a low level route around Uganda beating up towns and villages on the way and finish with a flypast over the stadium. A Vulcan and four Hunters were to do the same but following different routes. Then, about 10 miles from Kampala, we had to join up in formation for the flypast. The planners, obviously thinking it had the making of a enormous cock-up, said we could do three rehearsals. On our first practice we soon discovered that with no NDBs, wind information, landmarks, navigation was a bit of a challenge. The next day's practice was cancelled due to weather but the second went OK with Bill and I doing a lot of pilot navigation. On the big day we bought our first issue stamps at the post office and off we went. All went well and somehow we managed to form up with the Vulcan and Hunters to complete the flypast more or less on time. After a quick shower and a meal, we were taken by car to the stadium to witness the evening celebrations. We were given seats in the VIP stand and it was all very entertaining especially the arrival of an Allouette helicopter with a searchlight on the nose making it look like the arrival of a space ship - most impressive. I seem to recall a slight feeling of apprehension at being in this stadium with 25,000 Africans. This feeling wasn't helped by the arrival in the arena of Kenya's Jomo Kenyatta waving his flywisk to celebrate the British departure from another African state. But, on the stroke of midnight, the flag came down and the rest is history, as they say. Yes, when we left we were each presented with a hand of bananas, each being about 4 feet high with enough bananas to last a lifetime, most of which had to be given away when we got home. To record this historic event we had our photograph taken (with a stewardess from East African Airways) by an Air Ministry PR man.*'

**Another 'Britannia Author'!**

Here is a review that appeared in the Britannia Association magazine of the aforementioned book, '*Meteor Eject!*' by Nick Carter:

'*It was Britannia policy for many years to recruit experienced pilots as copilots. They brought with them know-how from a variety of fields, in which many carried specialist qualifications - QFI, IRE, Weapons Instructor, V-Force and Maritime categories. Accompanying this policy was a Britannia feature - such experience was*

Nick Carter's book with the sub-title, 'Adventures of a cold war fighter pilot'.

Our 216 compatriots took delivery of their first Comet 4 on 15th February 1962. Here the Station Commander, Group Captain Lawson is speaking to Sqn Ldr D'Oliveira and Mr Pat Fillingham of de Havillands, who delivered the first aircraft. Basil D'Oliveira was a 216 Flight Commander at the time. Later he commanded the squadron. As Wg Cdr Ops, HQ Transport Command he was instrumental in the introduction of the Flight Watch system, which is described later. On his retirement from the RAF he had a distinguished career with the Civil Aviation Authority. Yachting was an enthusiasm and, apart from being a major contributor to yachting magazines, he had the enormous task of annually editing Reeds Nautical Almanac. (*Lyneham Globe*)

MARCH 2nd 1962

Group Captain Lawson speaking to Mr. Pat Fillingham of de Havillands, and Squadron Leader d'Oliviera, upon the arrival of the Comet 4C.

Seven-Week Course

J. R. COC

*largely dismissed by the established transporters! But I digress - before even starting!*

*'Nick Carter was such a copilot on No.14 Course, subsequently serving on 511 Squadron. He didn't make it into the left hand seat as he had insufficient time to serve and he chose to leave the Service having completed his 12 years. His background was 'Day Fighters' - Meteor and Hunter. The book opens by going straight into the action - a dramatic description of the event that gives the title. Nick was lucky to survive*

One of the new acquisitions outside the Terminal Building. (*Lyneham Globe*)

Outside the Air Terminal at Lyneham a Comet 4C of 216 Squadron starts its engines, while the 'follow-me' vehicle waits to lead it out of dispersal.

*this ejection but was seriously injured. This incident has obviously concentrated his mind on the Meteor accident record. The chilling dedication of the book says it all: '... to the 434 RAF pilots and 10 navigators who lost their lives flying the Gloster Meteor.' Following the 'eject' introduction, Nick then takes us along the path that led him to RAF pilot training. As an apprentice in the aircraft industry, we get a worm's eye view of the huge variety of post-war aircraft development. Faced with National Service, he opted for a four year aircrew engagement. His pilot training was different to most in that it was on the Balliol. His descriptions of the Meteor training phase are really quite hair raising and it does not surprise that the accident rate was so high.*

*'The story must not be spoilt with too much detail. In brief, Nick progresses to his Meteor squadron - ejects - Hunters follow and a tour with the Royal Jordanian Air Force - then the Britannia. If you served in his years then you will enjoy relating to the incidents in his life. I found it a fascinating and very readable account. DB'*

... is not as bad as it seems from the background.

Cases of automatic rifles depart in Indian Army trucks after being unloaded from an R.A.F. Britannia at Palam Airport, Delhi. In the background can be seen U.S.A.F. C130 transports and a commandeered civil Dakota.

Cases of automatic rifles in Indian Army trucks after being unloaded from a RAF Britannia at Palam Airport, Delhi. (*Lyneham Globe*)

'*Meteor Eject*' is published by Woodfield Publishing, ISBN1 873203 65 9, price £9.95.

**Russia once more**

In November, John Bourn captained an aircraft to collect His Excellency, The British Ambassador, Sir Frank Roberts, from Moscow. John recalls:

*'In order to over-fly Russia, two Russians were taken on at Copenhagen! A navigator and signaller. They 'route checked' the crew thoroughly and acted as interpreters. Doing a radar approach with height information being given in metres using an altimeter graduated in feet was a bit tricky! ... The 'Ukraine Hotel' needs a special mention. Looking somewhat of a wedding cake design from outside, it stood 29 storeys high and contained nearly 3,000 rooms. An extremely efficient central heating system was balanced by an equally inefficient plumbing system. Some of us spent quite a while looking for the plug hole!!! The lift was operated at high speed and was in need of a pressurisation system ...*

*Unfortunately Snr. Tech. Jose and Cpl. Tech. Fryer, our untiring crew chiefs, had to spend an uncomfortable night guarding the aircraft - with no heaters and the temperature at minus 4°C ...'*

**And 'Down Under'**

In the same month a Britannia carried the support party for the Vulcans participating in the flypast at the opening of the British Empire and Commonwealth Games at Perth, Australia. The Britannia was certainly being proudly used.

**Not so glamorous**

Away from the glory, more down to earth activities were in progress; in the case of one, 'down to mud' would be a more suitable phrase. This was the 16 Para Brigade Group joint Greek exercise at Larissa, midway between Athens in the south and Thessaloniki to the north. There were many Britannia lifts required for this exercise and one on 4th October via Wildenrath, West Germany, marked my first 99 Squadron trip. Part way through the detachment, a two day downpour completely washed out the tented RAF Detachment and a lot of ingenuity was required by the Britannia ground servicing party to secure a dry bed.

This report in the *Lyneham Globe* gives an insight into what such detachments could be like for the ground crew:

On 2nd November 1962 Group Captain A McK S Steedman DFC took over command of RAF Lyneham from Group Captain Ian Lawson on the latter's posting to Aden and promotion to Air Commodore. (*Lyneham Globe*)

*'During the recent joint exercises in Greece, in which Lyneham's Britannias were involved, a servicing party was positioned at Larissa. On arrival, ready for the last phase, members of the party were somewhat dismayed to discover that the RAF Domestic Site, situated in a cornfield, under canvas, had been completely washed out by the severe downpour of a couple of days previous, and that the 'resident' RAF personnel had been hastily and soggily evacuated to various dry buildings scattered around the airfield.*

*'As accommodation for the Lyneham Detachment had not been arranged, there were thoughts of 'snagging' the last Britannia of the day in order to provide the necessary overnight accommodation, but luckily, a Recce Party returned with the welcome news that they had found a room in a grain store, whereupon, with all speed, all concerned collected their scattered effects, their camp beds and their blankets, and proceeded to their newly acquired quarters. Then began the task of making the place habitable.*

*'Firstly, the place had to be swept out and the beds erected. This chore was just finished as darkness fell, bringing with it the first setback - no lights! This was overcome by sending a foraging party, armed with Boots, Knee, Rubber, into the nearby washed-out RAF 'tent-town' with instructions to appropriate as many hurricane lamps as they could lay their thieving hands on. This was soon done, and light became available. At this time it began pouring with rain, and it was found that the 'vacant' grain store was already occupied - by king-sized centipedes. After a fierce battle, victory went to the British who suffered only one casualty, S/Tech. Shaw who later found stowaways in his bed. At this point it was decided to raise the beds off the floor by placing them on top of some tables which were found in a corner. Willy had the bright idea of slinging his safari bed on ropes to form a hammock, but found next morning that this was impractical with the highly flexible, safari bed, so the idea was abandoned.*

*'When the 'salvaged' hurricane lamps had been lit the previous evening, Mick Ortega, the 'Do-It-Yourself' king of the party, being dissatisfied with the lights, acquired from sources unknown, some power cable and began fixing up electric lighting. Whilst outside, tramping around in the mud, Mick lost one of his gum-boots, which Willy found several feet away deeply embedded in the mud. During another foraging expedition, looking for the bulbs and fittings for the lighting system, several tins of camp rations were found; these being heated over the hurricane lamps, a long and frustrating operation, eventually provided a welcome meal. Thus was conceived the idea of acquiring a couple of field kitchen burners. This operation, however, was delayed by the arrival of a series of Britannias, whose captains seemed to be of the opinion that the lads were there merely to service their flying machines, and not to convert a grain store into some semblance to a three star hotel. The burners were 'found' that evening.*

*'The next necessity was a water supply, this being obtained by running a length of plastic hose from a tap in the nearby Greek Station Workshops. According to the Medics, this had to be boiled prior to drinking, which caused Mick to ruminate, and very soon peculiar sketches began appearing on odd scraps of paper. The secret was out - he was devising, with the aid of an old tank, length of hose and reels of adhesive tape a hot water system; a*

*system, which would provide boiled drinking water and hot showers, no less! The heat was to be provided by one of the kitchen burners. This scheme was actually in operation by the following evening, although a later mod. providing a somewhat cooler shower was not quite so successful.*

*'Willy meanwhile, was fixing up a dartboard which mysteriously appeared, complete with overhead lighting and a shade. This rather upset the i/c, a Master Engineer, as the board being erected at the foot of his bed, deprived him of the light. Also, I suspect, he objected to being in the line of fire. Therefore, the board had to be re-sited before play could be resumed.*

*'Within two or three days the conversion from a barn into comfortable living quarters was complete, all work being carried out during the evenings. Dave Taylor's suggestion that tins of Pom be used to plaster the walls caused some merriment, but was not acted upon. Some apprehension was felt when the 'hotel' was inspected by various officers, who seemed envious of the set-up, the lads fearing that a Requisition Order would be forthcoming and the whole shebang transformed into an Officers' Mess. However, these fears, were groundless.*

*'The new Station Commander of Lyneham looked in on the lads during his visit to Larissa, and seemed favourably impressed by these efforts. A few days previous to this visit, the OC 511 called in, and although thinking highly of the set-up, lost some of his enthusiasm after accepting a cuppa, only to be told that it had been brewed for three hours. This in fact was not so, it was only two hours old! A reet good brew! Part of the recreational facilities was an occasional game of soccer on the pan against members of the Greek Air Force, the games being played during the time that the lads were not required to service the Britannias. It was during one such session that Tony Birchenough slipped and damaged his knee; from then on he became known as Chester. There is a fear that he may fully recover.*

*'All personnel of the detachment would like to give their thanks to those AQMs (and there were many of them) for their help in varying the diet. Special thanks go, too, to Mrs. Mitchell for the hours spent baking those beautiful apple pies and for sending out the other foodstuffs, all of which were most welcome.'*

**Gun running**

Two world trouble spots caused the Britannia to adopt its aggressive role. In October, a conflict arose between Chinese and Indian troops on the North East frontier and the Indian government requested a supply of small arms. So some legalised gun running was done to Palam Airport, Delhi by two Britannia aircraft. The arms arrived rapidly as a crew slip was established through Sharjah, in what is now the United Arab Emirate. This was repeated at the end of November.

I participated, flying from Lyneham to Sharjah via Nicosia. This was one of my first experiences of how long a Britannia day could be. From reporting time at base to landing at Sharjah - 16 hours and 10 minutes. This was probably why I did not notice that the Sharjah runway was unusually narrow which upset the perspective for the landing flare. The aircraft hit the runway when I thought we were still at 50 feet!

The second problem occurred in, what was in those days, the British Protectorate of Brunei, North Borneo. Rebels had seized hostages and the Shell oil refinery at Seria was under threat. Flexibility was the byword and two aircraft were pulled off the Changi Slip, at short notice, to fly personnel and equipment to Labuan.

**There, but for the Grace ...**

... of God, go I. Many pilots might say that after reading this honest tale from Harry Liddell:

*'As yet another course drew on, ATS staff and students looked forward to the final treat (or trial, depending on one's viewpoint) of the route trainer. Globals lay in the future, so the expected routing would normally have been the standard Hong Kong via Changi in both directions. On this occasion however, one of the periodic Middle East crises erupted shortly before the due date, with the inevitable result that all available aircraft were required for area reinforcement.*

*'Given a sudden urgent need for airlift capacity, the accustomed normal leisurely progress was now out of the question and so our commitment was slotted in as part of the operation; having shed our passengers at Bahrain, we would then proceed*

OUR 'F——D FRIENDS

THE MORNING CONFERENCE. To show that not everything goes to plan *all* the time, here aircrew and ground crew confer before the feathered propellor of their No. 3 Proteus engine, on the tarmac at El Adem. The Britannia was obliged to return to El Adem through this unserviceability.

A big headache for a VIP or 'off the normal route' aircraft? In fact, this photograph was taken at El Adem where there would have been permanent staff with specialist Britannia knowledge. (*Lyneham Globe*)

*onwards in a normal instructional role. Staff crew would be reduced to one per aircraft, but trainees would not be reduced pro rata and thus I found myself saddled with four u/t copilots plus the usual other variegated crew members; plainly my workload would be enhanced as compared with normal tasking, especially so since our young hopefuls were prohibited by ASIs from carrying out take-offs or landings with pax on board.*

*'The op. was fairly intensive, with flights departing every few hours. Drawing a short straw I was allocated a late evening departure, the prospect leaving me distinctly unchuffed; commencing a maximum duty period at a time when the body would normally expect rest, we could only look forward to a condition of living death prior to final destination. As expected, afternoon sleep proved a lost cause, so that the flight planning stage found me at least in an even less alert condition than normal.*

*'Out on the ramp the Station Commander (Alasdair Steedman) hovered around, proof of pressure from high places that all must go well. Off blocks on time, everything looked good until the very last moment; but the spring of '64 had been fairly lush, and with the airfield mowers having been hard at work the loose grass bogey struck yet again - one engine well down on torque.*

*'Taxying back in I prayed we might be granted a night's rest but it was not to be. Already XL640 was parked in the next bay, ready and waiting; all hands set to with a will to transfer our load, even Alasdair lending his services as a baggage*

Harry Liddell on a happier occasion! It is interesting to try and date such photographs. The shiny underside of the aircraft is a guide - and look at that tractor! Harry's uniform is a misleading clue. He must have been one of the first with a barathea working blue. The rest of us were still in the 'hairy' variety! (*Harry Liddell*)

Flt Lt Bill Robinson, whose excellent photography graces these pages, was Highly Commended in the 1962 RAF Arts and Handicrafts Exhibition for this photograph of 'A Britannia Navigator'. (*Lyneham Globe*)

*handler and then finally pushing us up the steps. This time all was well and soon we were climbing into the, now dark, sky, feeling more ready for bed than for the interminable hours confronting us.*

*'Of the long drag to Akrotiri I remember little, other than total time off flight deck amounting to the few minutes necessary for a dash to the toilet and back. The sun was well up when Cyprus came into view, and arrival presented no problems despite our general exhaustion, but by the time onwards flight planning had been completed I felt like a zombie and awaited the next stage with some apprehension in so far as my fitness for duty was concerned. On the other hand, barring further delay we would just be within the legal duty time limit, and so there was little option but to proceed and hope that nothing testing occurred. Recalling the cryptic saying that an aviator of superior ability is one who uses that ability in such a manner as not to have to make use of it, we climbed back aboard, but in my head was an uneasy feeling that I, at least, was already functioning in autopilot mode; while a certain prospect of the morning sun blazing into our eyes during the run east further degraded morale.*

*'Acknowledging the marshaller's farewell wave, I noticed a 3-ton truck parked on slightly rising ground to the left of the short taxyway leading to Runway 29. Although closer than either desirable or necessary, I judged clearance to be adequate; a*

*judgement reinforced by the lack of any visible sign of alarm from the truck's passengers, plus a distinct impression that the curve of the taxyway would take us well clear. A second or two later the aircraft lurched sickeningly to the left, and although it then continued normally I braked to a halt at once, enquiring if anyone knew what had happened; incredibly, my addled brain refused to deduce the obvious. Reality was restored by the signaller pointing out that our port wing tip was 'sticking up out of that 3-tonner'. Unwillingly craning my head round, the grisly sight told me everything - every pilot's nightmare, the unforgivable sin, was there right in front of my eyes, and it was all my own work.*

*'But even accidents sometimes have redeeming features; by a stroke of fortune the lorry's tilt frame had taken the tip off dead clean, all retaining rivets having sheared neatly and leaving the mainplane's virtually undamaged stub end ready to receive replacement. This arrived only hours later in a back-up aircraft, while I was already facing a hastily convened inquiry.*

*'It did not take long; the cause of the accident was only too plain, and having been in sole control at the time it was both impossible and unreasonable to try and duck my responsibility for what had occurred. However, a lot of flak landed on the MT section; not only was the truck in flagrant disregard of MT standing orders by being parked where it was, the driver had no airfield driving permit and had not even signed his section order book. As for me, the board's president was kindly and sympathetic, finding something to say about our ludicrous scheduling as a mitigating circumstance (although obviously not in so many words), but his conclusion was nonetheless inevitable; my fault, open and shut case.*

*'Five days later we flew our now repaired Britannia back home, the students soon to depart again on a proper Hong Kong trainer but this time without me. Weeks passed, the administrative mills ground as slowly as ever, but sure as fate came the expected summons to a formal interview with the Station Commander. As I listened to Alasdair politely deliver a formal admonishment I unworthily wondered if he too was thinking of his episode at Gan some months before, but soon realised that the words were not his. He was only acting under orders in relaying a bollocking from on high.*

*'Although the C-in-C had chosen to ignore anything the Board said in mitigation concerning fatigue, scheduling and so on, it was a lesson I did not forget and in the years to come did what little I could by way of sundry reports etc to moderate the severity of excessive and poorly planned crew duty times often wished on us by those above; I like to think something was achieved thereby, even if not very much. But given the economic imperative for large transport aircraft to be flown round the clock, plus the human body's natural limitations, this is a problem, which will surely remain with aviation so long as there are aeroplanes.'*

**Special effort**

1962 had been quite a year but it was not to end quietly. Who better than the then Station Commander of RAF Lyneham, Group Captain Alasdair Steedman DFC RAF, to provide a contemporary postscript extracted from the Lyneham Globe:

*'On Tuesday 11th December, as you all know, we made a special effort with the Britannia force. Your ordinary efforts are pretty good by any standards and your special efforts over the years have worked wonders; but this effort was prodigious. Every Britannia not on major servicing or manufacturer's modification was in use on a wide variety of jobs, and despite the foul weather were hustled on to the top line and the tasks were completed on time. All sections of the Station were involved and it was truly a hectic day. A magnificent effort; well done all of you.'*

It was asked, in later years, what demanded this 'special effort' on 11th December 1962? This reached the ears of the past Station Commander, by then, Air Chief Marshal Sir Alasdair Steedman GCB CBE DFC, who responded:

*'I have done a little research with the Air Historical Branch. It seems that my message in the Lyneham Globe was well justified. Exercise Cross Channel Express, involving 600 troops and 200,000lbs of freight was taking place between December 6th and 12th and the recovery phase occupied 13 Britannias. On the evening of December 10th we suddenly received an emergency requirement to move 400 troops*

A flypast on an unidentified occasion at an unidentified place - but it was an air display, viz the static aircraft display.

*and 40,000lbs of freight for the Royal Welsh Regiment to Brunei and this took five Britannias with two diverted from Singapore. You will recall that we always had one aircraft in the 'Dock' undergoing a major inspection and, as it happened, we were also preparing two aircraft for a VIP flight on the 12th. Simple arithmetic shows that we needed 20 aeroplanes from the 23 and the whole programme was completed without delay.*

*'I think this remarkable effort epitomises the professionalism, spirit and dedication of all ranks at Lyneham and is a tremendous compliment, in particular, to the ground crews who worked wonders to produce the goods. I had only been a short two months in command at this stage and I was to learn that this effort was typical of Britannia operations and the remarkable levels of serviceability which were maintained. Moreover, the aircrew took it all in their stride - it just added to the interest of the job.'*

On that fitting note, the curtain on 1962 is lowered.

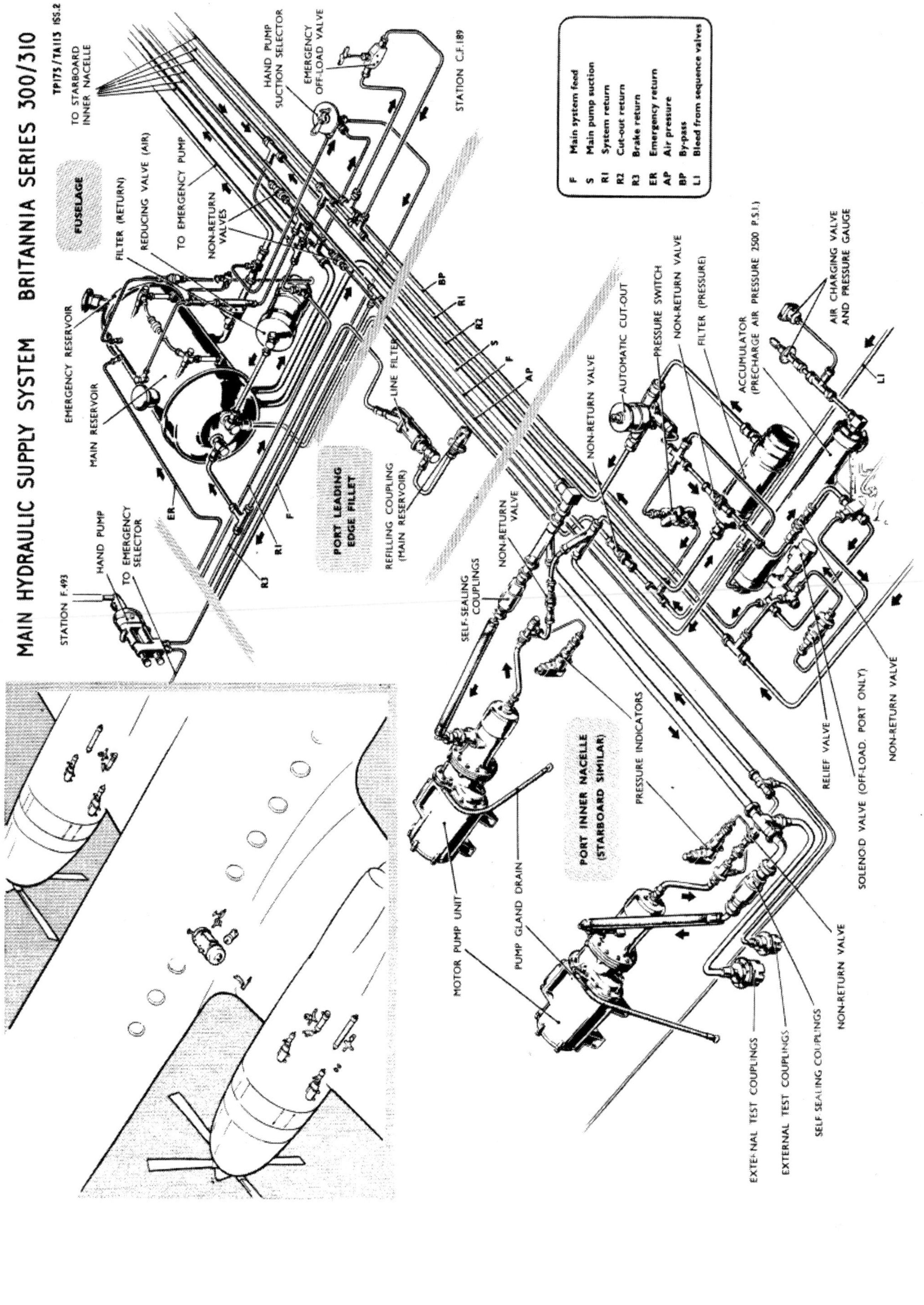
MAIN HYDRAULIC SUPPLY SYSTEM
BRITANNIA SERIES 300/310
TP173/TA115 ISS.2
TO STARBOARD INNER NACELLE
FUSELAGE
HAND PUMP SUCTION SELECTOR
EMERGENCY OFF-LOAD VALVE
STATION C.F.189
FILTER (RETURN)
REDUCING VALVE (AIR)
TO EMERGENCY PUMP
NON-RETURN VALVES
EMERGENCY RESERVOIR
MAIN RESERVOIR
STATION F.493
HAND PUMP
TO EMERGENCY SELECTOR
ER
F
R1
R3
PORT LEADING EDGE FILLET
REFILLING COUPLING (MAIN RESERVOIR)
LINE FILTER
BP
R1
R2
S
F
AP
F Main system feed
S Main pump suction
R1 System return
R2 Cut-out return
R3 Brake return
ER Emergency return
AP Air pressure
BP By-pass
L1 Bleed from sequence valves
NON-RETURN VALVE
AUTOMATIC CUT-OUT
PRESSURE SWITCH
NON-RETURN VALVE
FILTER (PRESSURE)
ACCUMULATOR (PRECHARGE AIR PRESSURE 2500 P.S.I.)
AIR CHARGING VALVE AND PRESSURE GAUGE
L1
SELF-SEALING COUPLINGS
NON-RETURN VALVE
PRESSURE INDICATORS
PORT INNER NACELLE (STARBOARD SIMILAR)
MOTOR PUMP UNIT
PUMP GLAND DRAIN
RELIEF VALVE
SOLENOID VALVE (OFF-LOAD. PORT ONLY)
NON-RETURN VALVE
NON-RETURN VALVE
EXTERNAL TEST COUPLINGS
EXTERNAL TEST COUPLINGS
SELF SEALING COUPLINGS

The adventures of Messrs. Ad Minn and Org at Wootton Lynstoke continue ...

DULY DOCUMENTED AD MINN AND ORG GO TO THE AIR BOOKINGS CENTRE TO GET THEIR TICKETS FOR THEIR OVERSEAS FLIGHT IN SEARCH OF PURE WATER.
more or less REGULAR SERVICE to (nearly) all parts
BARBAIR & LEWAIR
BIG AND FAST GET YOU BACK FOR CHRISTMAS !! BOOK NOW !!
BRITISH RAILWAYS ?
WINTER SPORTS? TRY THULE (R.I.P.)
HARPAIR
INCORPORATING BASAIR & YEOAIR
HIGHEST FASTEST (WHEN THEY GO)
THE SHORT HAUL LINE WITH THE BEST RECORD
Fed up with the wife and kids? GET AWAY FROM IT ALL ON SUNNY GAN
HAVE YOU SEEN THE CHESTS IN HONG KONG
WHILE AWAY AN HOUR (OR MORE) IN FRIENDLY EL ADEM
CHANGI for a CHANGE with real CHINESE CHOW
TAKE THE NIGHTLY SPECIAL TO TEMPLE HILL AND BEDOK
BAHREIN!!
CARPETS THE ALL AMERICAN TRANSPORTATION
TRAVEL? BY CHARTAIR
INDULGE YOURSELF AND GO COMET TO THE SUN
THERE ARE SOME QUAINT OLD CUSTOMS AT DARWIN
NAIROBI FOR FUN
SLIP WITH US TO
ENJOY A RIOT IN ADEN
NO TEAR GAS ON THE AIRFIELD
VISIT NEDDY'S BAR
STAY A WHILE AT PADDY'S
WHILST AD MINN AND ORG ARE GETTING THEIR AIR TICKETS THE AIRCRAFT IS BEING PREPARED FOR ITS FLIGHT .....
.... THE CREW GO TO MET BRIEFING ....
CHRISTINE SQUEALER MADE WARD OF COURT
W.V.S. EXPELS DANDY NICE-BABY
"THE WEATHER'S ON THE NEXT PAGE BUT THIS IS MORE INTERESTING."
.... AND THE 'OPS' STAFF EXERCISE FIRM CONTROL OF THE SITUATION...
LATER ... AT THE AIRCRAFT
"FORGOT TO REFUEL IT DID WE ? — RIGHT I'LL GET A BOWSER."
AVNU
NATO
"SORRY MATE THIS ONE SEEMS TO BE EMPTY, I'LL HAVE TO GET ANOTHER ONE."
12

CHAPTER FIFTEEN

# Squadron Leader Norman Rose AFC & bar

The end of 1962 was a significant time for a crew of 511 Squadron. Twice they were to endure severe airborne emergencies, the second of which must rate as the worst that the Britannia experienced in the whole of its military career.

**The story so far**

On each occasion, the crew was headed by Norman Rose. He joined the Royal Air Force in 1942 at the age of 18 and after training he was posted to No.6 Squadron in the Middle East flying

Norman Rose retired from the RAF with an entry in the Guinness Book of Records as the longest serving RAF pilot: 47 years. This photograph was taken when he presented to the Imperial War Museum his medals, log book and a collection of scale models he had made of the 54 types of aircraft he had flown. (*Imperial War Museum/Norman Rose*)

*'It was the early hours of the morning and behind the darkened flight deck ...'* (*Norman Rose*)

Hurricanes. Meteors followed with Nos.56 and 245 Squadrons and then to the Central Flying School. He was a flying instructor on the Overseas Ferry Unit at Benson for four years. Commissioned in 1954, he became a fighter controller in Singapore later transferring to the Far East Comms Squadron, Changi as a jet flying instructor. It was during this time that Norman was awarded the Air Force Cross. Two years test pilot work preceded joining No.511 Squadron, as one of the few pilots to go straight into the captain's seat, in the early days of the Britannia.

**One dark night**

The story of the Kuwait operation has been related through Norman's experiences. Now, 18 months later, there was another tale to be told. On a routine trip, the Rose crew were inbound to the UK in XL636 from the Mediterranean. It was the early hours of the morning and behind the darkened flight deck, 100 passengers slept. About 100 miles North of Rome, approaching the radio beacon on the island of Elba, the peace was shattered by the sound of fire alarm bells. Anxious eyes moved rapidly to the relevant indicator; there was a fire in the below floor forward freight bay.

**Smoke!**

The crew swung into action with the drills so often practised in the simulator. There were now signs of smoke on the flight deck. They donned their oxygen masks and the aircraft was put into a descent for a diversion to Rome. As much of the electrical and radio equipment that was not essential was switched off in an effort to isolate the cause of the overheating. This included the Hobson feel simulator, a hydraulic device that compensated for the lack of natural 'feel' in the Britannia's floating flying control system.

**Crew cooperation**

All this required maximum crew effort and cooperation. The copilot, Flt Lt

*'... 100 passengers slept'* (*Richard Ling*)

Roy Johnson, took over the flying of the aircraft, leaving the captain free to oversee the handling of the emergency. The navigator, Flt Lt George Dobson, provided the necessary information for the diversion and, with the check list, monitored the crew's actions. The signaller, John Beardon, kept the important communications going as the flight engineer, Master Engineer Bob Anstee, prepared to go down into the freight bay to investigate the source of the fire and attempt to extinguish it.

Down below there was a good deal of smoke and the engineer had to hack his way, with an axe, through an obstructing cargo net. He found that the tube provided for the smoke mask he had donned was too short to allow him to move far enough into the compartment so he had to discard it and survive on gulps of air taken in at intervals at the trap door entrance.

**Carbon dioxide attack**

Bob reported that the smoke was so thick that he was unable to locate the source and, as the smoke on the flight deck continued to increase, the diversion to Rome continued. The engineer once again went below and now believed that the smoke was emanating from the feel simulator. He attacked it with a carbon dioxide extinguisher.

**All clear**

And, indeed, as rapidly as it had appeared, the smoke now started to dissipate and with things so returned to normal, the diversion was cancelled and the flight continued to the UK. Gradually, as required, equipment was brought back into use but the offending feel simulator remained isolated.

**Further assault**

The threat of weather ahead caused the captain to switch the Cloud Collision Warning Radar (CCWR) back on - and then it all happened all over again - bells, lights, smoke! Down went the engineer once again, this time with the extinguisher aimed, well and truly, at the CCWR which was adjacent enough to the feel simulator to have been subdued by the previous attack. The smoke once again dispersed.

When he reappeared, Bob Anstee was on the point of collapse through smoke ingestion. But the fire was out. The CCWR remained well and truly isolated.

An Indian Ocean view? (*Bill Robinson*)

**Praise**

Norman Rose sums up:

*'The efforts of the engineer were particularly praiseworthy. He is a big man and it was not easy for him to move about in the confines of the hatchways and amongst the freight. He displayed great tenacity and strength of character and undoubtedly prevented a bad situation getting much worse.'*

**To Gan**

The Rose crew was to get some respite from such excitement but only until 16th December 1962, when they were winging their way from Aden to Gan Island on Flight No.6323 in Britannia XM519. All was the usual transoceanic routine as they cruised along at 17,500 feet. There were just three passengers on board, the main load being Sea Slug missiles destined for Borneo. Also on board was a 'route checker', John Loveridge, an instructor/examiner giving Norman a periodic check. Four hours into the flight they passed the 'Point of No Return' (PNR). This is an important position, always calculated on such a sea leg. Beyond it, the aircraft must continue to the destination; there would be insufficient fuel for a return to the departure airfield.

**Routine**

It was a typical Indian Ocean day. A fair bit of cumulus cloud bubbling up, some of it blossoming into full blown cumulo-nimbus. The navigator worked away steadily, ensuring, with the minimum of navigational information, that the aircraft remained on track. The pilots took it in turns to supervise the flight, monitor the autopilot and the weather up ahead. The

Coincidentally, there was, in Bill Robinson's collection, a photograph of a No.4 engine at Gan! (*Bill Robinson*)

engineer completed a log on each hour, noting all the engine gauge readings, the fuel flows and the fuel tank contents. The latter would be passed to the navigator for plotting on a 'Howgozit' graph. From this, the future fuel state could be calculated and action taken if the prediction did not look good. The signaller passed regular position reports with the Morse key to distant Air Traffic Control Centres. Amid this calm routine the air quartermaster would appear regularly with tea and coffee. Conversation was sporadic; professional calm prevailed.

**Pitch lock**

Just ten minutes after passing PNR there was a small change in the drone of the propellers; something that, for all its slightness, is most noticeable in stable cruising flight. It did not take flight engineer Bob Anstee by surprise. He had been leaning forward already, looking intently at the propeller RPM gauges. 'Pitch lock No.4 prop.', he announces. The No.4 propeller control unit (PCU) was not doing its job in controlling the propeller RPM. It should have been keeping the RPM constant and identical to that of the other propellers, no matter that conditions changed, by minutely adjusting the angle at which the blades met the airflow. The problem the engineer had declared meant that the propeller blade angle was now stuck. That change in the note had been caused by No.4 RPM drifting away from that of 1, 2 and 3.

**Feather No.4**

There was a drill to be carried out and Bob Anstee moved the relevant switches. But the involved reversion to the propeller control standby system had no effect. There was now only one solution, the propeller would have to be feathered and the engine shut down. In this condition, with the propeller blades edge on to the air flow, the flight could be safely continued. Bob pressed the feathering button. There was no effect. Control of a propeller is essential so there was a standby system. That switch was moved to the feather position.

**Horrendous scream**

With that, there was the most horrendous scream from the propeller; its speed was completely out of control and it was rotating like a windmill in the 300+ mph 'wind' created by the aircraft's forward movement. The throttles were snatched closed to reduce speed as quickly as possible. The propeller RPM had risen so high that the needle on the gauge had snapped off inside the glass. With the speed reduced to 130 knots the scream was lowered to a howl but the RPM was still far too high and had to be reduced if the propeller was not to disintegrate. Instant recall of their studies of propeller theory led to the crew's next move, to descend. Flying at a lower level at the same *indicated* airspeed would reduce the *true* airspeed of which the propeller RPM is a function.

Eventually, with the aircraft flying at 120 knots at 1500 feet, they could tell, by the decreased noise, that the RPM had been reduced to an acceptable figure.

**Ditching inevitable**

But not much else was acceptable with the situation in which they now found themselves. They were still four hours flying away from Gan and the fuel, which had been enough at normal economical cruising height, was now, at 1500 feet, calculated as being insufficient. But there was no choice but to continue towards Gan at the lower height and, at least, get nearer to the island. A ditching seemed inevitable. There was a lot of time to contemplate this as the time ticked by.

**'Shackleton at 12 o'clock!'**

Their spirits rose as the third hour of the emergency approached and they were sighted by the Search and Rescue Shackleton aircraft based at Gan; the aircraft had been rapidly launched after their declared emergency. As the Shackleton shadowed them, the number of miles to Gan reduced and it did seem that there might now be just enough fuel to make it. Any relief was damped as the vibration from the sick propeller seemed to increase. But the lights of Gan appeared faintly on the horizon. Luckily the weather was good and they were able to position the aircraft on a straight-in approach. By now there was so little fuel left that it was insufficient to register on the gauges. But they made it, touching down smoothly on the coral island's friendly runway. So the Norman Rose crew had seen it through - engineer Bob Anstee, copilot Roy Johnson, navigator George Dobson, signaller John Beardon and air quartermaster Joe Robinson.

When the cowlings of No.4 engine were opened, a large part of the propeller reduction gear fell out.

**Deserved praise**

Two signals are worth highlighting from the welter of paper generated by this incident:

FROM: AOC-IN-C TRANSPORT COMMAND

TO: AOC-IN-C FAR EAST AIR FORCE

ON 19 DEC BRITANNIA XM519 FROM KHORMAKSAR TO GAN SUFFERED MAJOR FAILURE OF NO 4 ENGINE WITH RISK OF DISINTEGRATION AND STRONG POSSIBILITY OF DITCHING STOP AIRCRAFT HAD PASSED PNR AND WAS FOUR HOURS FROM GAN STOP SOS ACTED ON BY GAN AND FULL SAR PROCEDURE IMPLEMENTED STOP BRITANNIA INTERCEPTED 315 MILES FROM GAN STOP LAUNCH GAN DESPATCHED AND ALL SHIPS IN VICINITY WARNED STOP BRITANNIA FINALLY MADE LANDING BUT RAPID RESPONSE OF GAN INSPIRED CONFIDENCE AMONGST CREW AND PASSENGERS AND REFLECTED EFFICIENCY OF HIGHEST ORDER STOP GRATEFUL IF YOU WOULD CONVEY MY THANKS AND CONGRATULATIONS TO ALL CONCERNED FOR FIRST CLASS PERFORMANCE END

And for the crew another signal:

... THE UNNERVING EXPERIENCE OF FLT LT ROSE AND HIS CREW ... PASS ON THE DIRECTOR OF FLIGHT SAFETY'S PERSONAL CONGRATULATIONS FOR A FINE DISPLAY OF AIRMANSHIP AND CREW DISCIPLINE IN WHICH THE KNOWN RISKS WERE EFFICIENTLY AND WISELY MINIMISED AND THE AIRCRAFT SAVED BY THEIR ACTION END

For a suitable postscript a step forward is taken to June 1963. In The Queen's Birthday Honours List, Flt Lt Norman Rose was awarded a Bar to his Air Force Cross. Master Engineer Bob Anstee received the Air Force Cross to add to his Air Force Medal.

In later years, when Norman Rose secured his entry in '*The Guinness Book of Records*' as the longest serving pilot in the Royal Air Force with 47 years unbroken service, he attended a presentation ceremony. He is seen here with Norris McWhirter and Roy Castle. (*Norman Rose*)

SEPTEMBER 28th

## B.E.M. AWARD

**Presentation of the British Empire Medal to Chief Technician Oxtoby by the A.O.C.-in-C. Transport Command on the 28th August, 1962 in the V.I.P. Lounge, Air Terminal Building.**

**In attendance Mrs. Oxtoby, Miss Oxtoby, Master Oxtoby, Station Commander, Wing Commander 'A', Wing Commander Tech., S.A.M.O., Station Warrant Officer, Mr. Haywood and Gp. Capt. Bax, Bristol Aircraft Company, and a S.N.C.O.'s from the section, Britannia Servicing Flight.**

Another 1962 award - the British Empire Medal is presented to Chief Technician Oxtoby of Britannia Servicing Flight by the AOC-in-C Transport Command. (*Lyneham Globe*)

The adventures of Messrs. Ad Minn and Org at Wootton Lynstoke continue ...

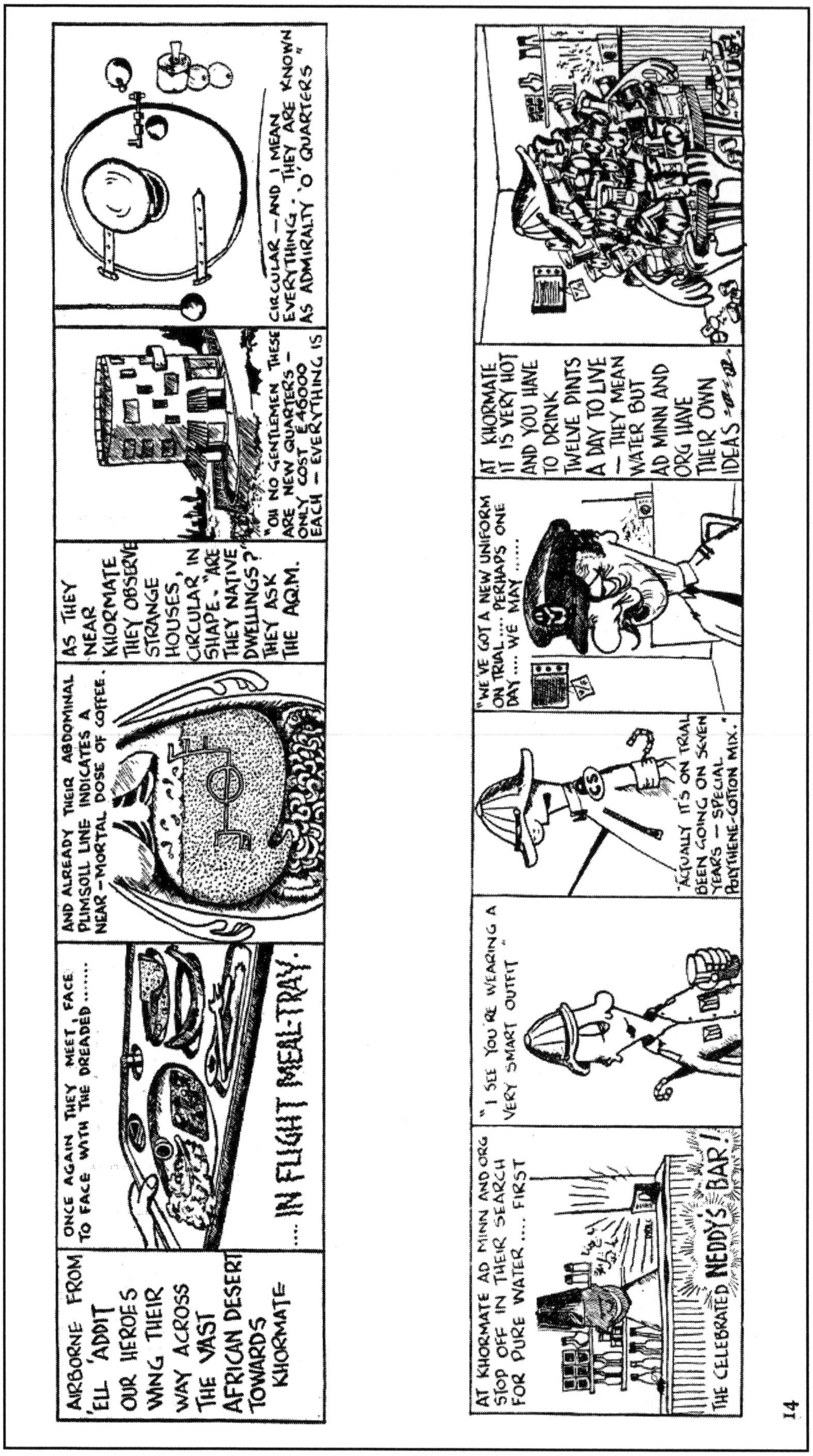
AIRBORNE FROM 'ELL 'ADDIT OUR HEROES WING THEIR WAY ACROSS THE VAST AFRICAN DESERT TOWARDS KHORMATE
ONCE AGAIN THEY MEET, FACE TO FACE WITH THE DREADED ......
.... IN FLIGHT MEAL-TRAY.
AND ALREADY THEIR ABDOMINAL PLIMSOLL LINE INDICATES A NEAR-MORTAL DOSE OF COFFEE.
AS THEY NEAR KHORMATE THEY OBSERVE STRANGE HOUSES, CIRCULAR IN SHAPE. "ARE THEY NATIVE DWELLINGS?" THEY ASK THE AQM.
"OH NO GENTLEMEN THESE ARE NEW QUARTERS - ONLY COST £46000 EACH - EVERYTHING IS
CIRCULAR - AND I MEAN EVERYTHING. THEY ARE KNOWN AS ADMIRALTY 'O' QUARTERS"
AT KHORMATE AD MINN AND ORG STOP OFF IN THEIR SEARCH FOR PURE WATER.... FIRST
THE CELEBRATED NEDDY'S BAR!
" I SEE YOU'RE WEARING A VERY SMART OUTFIT "
"ACTUALLY IT'S ON TRIAL BEEN GOING ON SEVEN YEARS — SPECIAL POLYTHENE-COTTON MIX."
"WE'VE GOT A NEW UNIFORM ON TRIAL.... PERHAPS ONE DAY.... WE MAY .....
AT KHORMATE IT IS VERY HOT AND YOU HAVE TO DRINK TWELVE PINTS A DAY TO LIVE — THEY MEAN WATER BUT AD MINN AND ORG HAVE THEIR OWN IDEAS
14

CHAPTER SIXTEEN

# 1963 - Busy Busy

Two attempts have been made to leave 1962 and move on. Here is a third. 1962 will not let go; it went out with a fury. On Boxing Day the snow started to fall. In the evening, I went outside my Lyneham married quarter to check the weather; large flakes were falling quite steadily. I secretly hoped that it would continue all night and delay my schedule departure next morning away from the family Christmas. The wish must have been quite fervent for it did indeed snow continuously and in the morning any movement looked totally impossible.

**Determination afoot**

But I had to go through the routine of getting ready which, considering the weather, included the rather ludicrous donning of my KD tropical uniform for we always flew in uniform appropriate to the destination. Our's was Aden, then Singapore. To my astonishment, the crew bus came to a slithering halt outside the house, on time. Clearly there was some considerable determination to keep going.

**Still snowing heavily**

This became evident when we finally made it to the aircraft, which was in a hangar. It had been put in there overnight so that, in spite of the snow, it could be loaded, refuelled and prepared for the departure. As the preparations continued, everyone was there, from the Station Commander down. It was still snowing heavily.

All night the snow ploughs had struggled to keep the taxyways and runway clear. Human force was now at work as snow was shovelled to clear the area around the hangar doors. Now was the time for the test. Three tractor tugs were attached to the aircraft, one in the normal way via a towing arm attached to the nose wheel. The two reinforcements were to pull on cables attached to the rear of main wheel bogies.

**Tug of war**

All was set. We, the crew, our planning complete, were in our seats on the flight deck. The major purpose of the flight was to reposition the slip crews down the route after the Christmas break. Our restive fellow aircrew were boarded. Then the tugs started the push from the front and pull from the rear. As we proceeded backwards, all was well whilst the tugs were within the hangar but as they drove on to the skating rink outside, the battle was lost. Back we came into the hangar. There was a further attempt. The elements once again won the tug of war. It appeared that the struggle was over; I would be going back home to my family.

**Full speed astern!**

'This time we'll take a run at it!' I had never before, or ever since, gone so quickly backwards in an aeroplane. We were outside. Being at the ready, the engines were started in a trice. We taxied towards the runway. The weather had definitely served, so far, its Jack, Queen and King - here came the Ace. The wind direction meant that we had to use the furthest runway, 07, and part of the taxyway to that was uphill. Before the hill we had struggled. At the hill we failed. But that determination was still at work and the hangar team came to us with their shovels.

**Up and away!**

We made it to the runway. As we lined up, it looked a sorry sight. At the edges were the banks of dirty scraped back snow; the surface was rutted, a grey sky hung overhead. The brakes were off and, after a bumpy, noisy roll down the runway we were airborne and into the cloud. Two minutes later we burst out into brilliant sunshine. We did not have another cloud all the

Snow ploughs attached to refuelling bowsers battled with frozen snow.
(*Mike Joyce*)

way to Singapore. There we spent ten days. That 1962/63 winter carries notoriety. After we left, the snow just kept on falling and the whole of the British Isles came to a standstill. In spite of desperate measures, not a single aircraft left Lyneham until 6th January. This reached Singapore on the 8th. We were back in the UK by the 9th. The snow was still there. This would go into the record books as the worst winter in Wiltshire since 1881.

**Record breaker**

From 23rd December to 7th February there was continuous frost and until the end of February there were only three occasions when the temperature rose as high as 35°F. Following the Boxing Day fall, there had been three heavy blizzards on 29th and 30th December. The highest of the drifts at Lyneham was 15 feet in the south west corner of the airfield. On the camp itself there were seven foot drifts and the most astonishing thing, perhaps, was the five foot drifts on the open runway! When this had been cleared there was an average of 4½ inches of ice on the runway and taxyways with many rolls up to 18 inches thick on the main runway.

It took some 90 hours of continuous operation with bulldozers, Drott shovels, tarmac heaters, Dinkum shovels, squeegees, sanders and sanding and scraping parties to make the airfield barely operational.

**Away snow**

Sunshine is brought back to these pages with the report that a Britannia supported No.139 V-Bomber Squadron on a visit to Mexico City. The writer of a report in '*The Lyneham Globe*' clearly had a lyrical pen:

'*The arrival of our Britannia over the Plain of Mexico was well-timed. To the east the snow capped volcanoes of Popocate and Ixtaccihuatl, rosy tinted in the dying sun. Below, the city, in the shadow of the twilight, sparkled like a many coloured jewel.*'

**Cold return**

I was not to escape snow and ice. With Graham Bayliss, the next January task was to take missiles for cold weather trials at the Royal Canadian Air Force Base at Churchill on the western shore of Hudson Bay. At Latitude 60° North it was cold - minus 52°C! We were looked after; a heated bus waited at the foot of steps and we were immediately whisked to our accommodation. Everything we required was there. Virtually all the base's buildings were linked by heated corridors.

**Cold problems**

Our aircraft, there were two, were not so lucky. They spent the night in the open. In the morning there were problems; for instance, heat had to be applied to the tyres to release the hold of the ice. It was a pair of anxious crews that started up; but all was well with us and we taxied to the runway. The Proteus was fitted with a 'Limiter' device to immediately detect a runaway turbine (a result of the investigation into the forced landing of the prototype on the banks of the River Severn). This could not be finally checked until a start had been made on take-off power being applied. It was a constant last hurdle at which many a Britannia fell. '*Arm the Limiters.*' was the call. The engineer's eyes would be directed at a small panel behind the captain's seat. With some relief we heard the report, '*All Limiters Armed.*' We could go, '*Set full power, call when stabilised.*' Brakes released, the aircraft sped down the runway as the engines responded to the intake of the bitter cold, power-giving air.

Our compatriots did not share our good fortune. Their limiters did not arm. Back they taxied for rectification. Then the cold which had been barely kept at bay, dug its teeth in. Pipe seals split and hydraulic fluid leaked to the ground. That aircraft was there for eight days. The captain, Flight Lieutenant McFarland, later reported to '*The Lyneham Globe*':

'*Sgt Quinn, Cpls Fryer, Wilson and Greeing laboured unceasingly under the most trying conditions on the open tarmac in temperatures down to minus 42 degrees Centigrade, with a wind chill factor ranging from 1800 to 2450. Throughout this bleak period, when on occasions no sensible Canadian would poke his nose outside the door, Sgt Quinn and his team persevered, improvised and finally won the battle.*'

**Corporal Fryer remembers Churchill**

Forty plus years after this Churchill event the author and the erstwhile Cpl Fryer above, with a new name, Peter de Frère, corresponded. As a result there emerged this account of that cold delay.

'*1962 and 1963 were busy years for Transport Command and this meant plenty of work for the Mobile Servicing Flight Team. The first job I remember was the ill-fated trip to Port Churchill in Canada ... When take-off time arrived in the morning, there was a problem with the isospeedic switch. This, on the Britannia, was a no-go item. It was taxied back to the dispersal where it was also discovered that there was a hydraulic leak in the braking system. Thus began a fight to get the aircraft back into the air that lasted eight days.*

'*The temperature was around minus 45°C and the Canadians kept a constant check on the wind speed to monitor the wind chill factor. When it reached the figure at which water would freeze solid in three minutes, all outside work was abandoned and all personnel were confined to the inside of the building. They even put guards on the exit doors to prevent people from going out. I have to say that, in our case, this was most unnecessary.*

A destination for a lucky crew. (*Lyneham Globe*)

*'It was in these conditions that we had to repair the isospeedic switch and isolate the leaking hydraulic pipe. The cold weather clothes we had been given before leaving the UK caused the Canadians much amusement. The Parkas were more like tents than jackets and the silly boots, known I think as mucklucks, were probably left over from an Amunsden expedition. Luckily, when they stopped laughing, the Canadians took us into their store and kitted us out properly. Regrettably, they insisted on having the clothes returned before we left.*

*'The electrician, I think it was Pinky Greening, had great difficulty working on the faulty switch. Tools could not be handled unless they had been warmed up first and it was necessary to direct warm air onto the working area and the worker's hands during any operation. We were forced to work in pairs so that we could keep a constant watch on each other for the signs of frostbite, the first indications being a sudden whitening of the skin. When you consider that all we could see of each other, through the aperture in the fur hood, were frosted eyebrows and the tip of a nose, you will understand the problem. We found that we could only work outside for ten minutes, before the extreme cold forced us back into the warmth of the hangar, and then we had to take all our equipment with us. It really was that bad.*

*'By the time we had fixed the switch and turned our attention to the hydraulic leak several days had passed. Every system in the aircraft had frozen solid and even the wheels were stuck in the ice. We were able to borrow some warm air blowers from an American detachment and, with the wheel covers in place, tried to melt the ice sufficient to free the aircraft. In the meantime, fuel was leaking from all the seals in the system and oil was running down the propeller blades where the seals were frozen solid. I can remember taking a piece of rubber from my toolbag and snapping it like a twig, it was so cold. We also had problems with the ground power unit which regularly came to a frozen halt and had to be pushed manually back into the*

The original caption read: 'Two gentlemen who seem better equipped than Peter. Sadly they have not been identified.' But Ron King came up with the information: *'The beardless one is Geordie Morpeth (Crew Chief). Nanook of the beard, was known as Mac; the full name escapes me, but if it is who I think it was, he was a Spec. NCO from the Specialist Instrument Section.'*

*hangar to thaw out. This machine drank oil by the pint and needed constant replenishment, which was impossible outside in the cold because the oil simply congealed in the spout. I have not encountered conditions like that before or since.*

*'We had excellent accommodation in a long, interconnected building that was centrally heated to 78°F. This was great until you had to dress up to go outside, then you sweated profusely as you put on your gear and walked the long corridor to the exit door. We then had to trudge through the snow to the aircraft dispersal which, in itself, was an effort. The food was excellent, as you would expect over that side of the Atlantic. Breakfasts were freshly cooked and you could have your eggs done to your taste while you waited in the queue: sunny side up, easy over, or over hard. When the cook asked one member of our Team how he would like his eggs he replied 'boiled', which almost caused a permanent rift in Anglo-Canadian relations.*

*'We did not see much of the aircrew, they were not billeted with us and liaised through Sergeant Pete Quinn, our Team Leader. It was Pete who later received an AOC's Commendation for our efforts, as was the way with the RAF.*

*Eventually we managed to isolate the burst hydraulic pipe and to free the ice from around the wheels leaving the aircraft, in our view, ready to fly ... the nettle was grasped and we flew out of Port Churchill and on to Gander where the temperature was a mere one degree below zero. We lost around a gallon of oil from each engine during the flight but little else was wrong when we checked the aircraft over in the mild climate of the Newfoundland base. The rest of the trip was uneventful.*

**Get a flavour of one of those 'good' trips**

With Britannia flying there was a lot of 'nitty gritty' much of which is reflected within these pages. But for some there were rather grand tasks. This anonymous account from '*The Lyneham Globe*' is given in full to give a feel for what those trips could be like:

*'On Easter Monday, Brit. 392 was positioned at Cranwell for a tour of the USA. with 75 senior cadets and 15 officers from the RAF College. It being holiday time, Cranwell was even more abandoned than Lyneham when the Brit. made its arrival in the most un-Easter-like weather. One ATC officer quadrupled as Approach, Local, Surveillance, Radar and Talk Down*

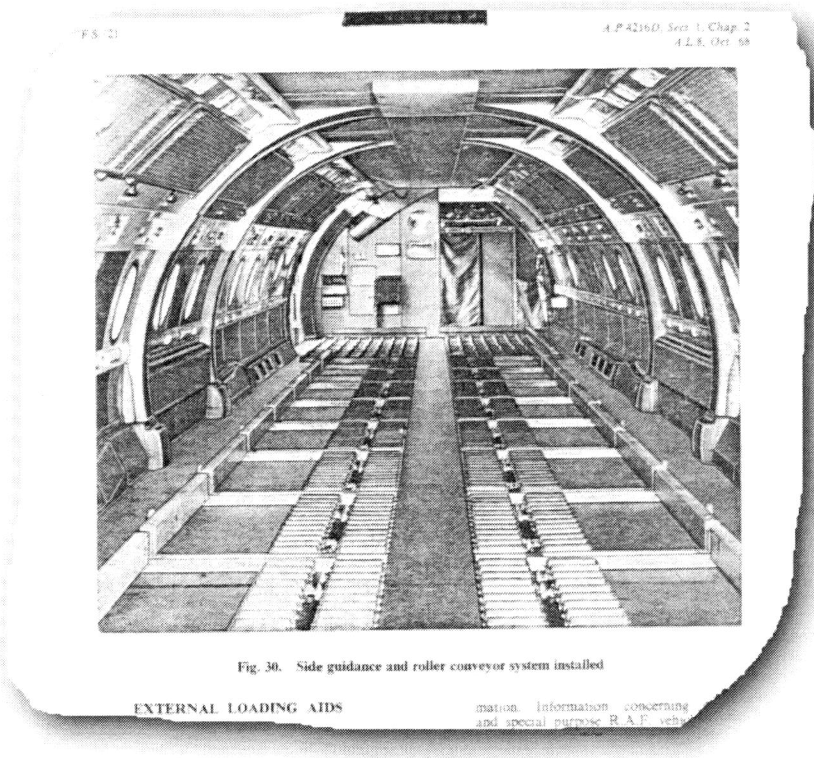


A cutting from an Air Publication item on 'Side Guidance', which is discussed overleaf. Note the rails at the side which 'guide' and the rollers on the floor which allow pallets to be easily pushed between the rails.

Photographs that illustrated the 'side guidance' system. (*Lyneham Globe*)

## MOD. M1044

### ALIAS "SIDE GUIDANCE"

THE "Beeching Report" on the future of the British Railways has led to a great deal of conjecture as to what will be done with all those miles of railway lines.

*Above:* Pallet No. 2 in position.
*Below:* Pallet No. 3 in position.

Our photographs show the system of side guidance for the loading of pre-lashed pallets. This of course, has nothing whatever to do with railway lines (I wonder what **will** happen to them?) Trials have been carried out with the system as shown. This makes provision for securing a pre-loaded and restrained pallet: these pallets are to replace the fibreglass ones already in use. The aim is to dispense with lashings and freight positioning on the aircraft thus reducing loading time. It is hoped that with this system in operation the time taken to load an aircraft will be no longer than that taken to refuel it. We hope to see it in operation quite soon.

The Caravan Missio...

SELECTING THE

*Controllers and apparently covered a considerably greater distance during the approach than the aircraft did. He was also SDO that day but was reasonably cheerful for all that.*

*'Within 30 minutes of touchdown the funereal atmosphere had vanished and expectant cadets appeared from everywhere to poke and pry into the aircraft, which was to carry them on their long awaited trip to the USA. Numerous families, all of whom were apparently anxious to help ensure that all was well for the morning departure, soon joined them. Wg. Cdr. Tech. at Lyneham had plumbed some hidden depths of manpower over the Easter Grant to see that 392 had been cleaned and would no doubt have been pleased to hear the favourable comments on the aircraft. At 0900 on 16th April we were off from Cranwell using far less of their runway than we had threatened, much to the relief of the crew and no doubt the hardy types who came to wave a fond farewell. They were all*

*ghoulishly equipped with cameras - just in case. After a flag stop at Gander, where the weather was even more depressing than in England, the party arrived at Andrews Air Force Base in Washington DC late that afternoon to begin the merry round of visits. The Washington tour started with interesting briefs on the USA in general and the USAF in particular from members of the British Embassy and Air Attaché's staff. These briefs were heard in the rotunda of the British Embassy, which is a magnificent new building apparently designed in an attempt to 'out-American' the Americans.*

*'At this stage the Air Attaché played host at a cocktail party and the Britannia played up and went u/s. The majority of the crew were thus withdrawn from sightseeing to work on the aircraft and its attendant problems. Thus they missed the arrival at the Capitol of 75 Cranwell cadets in civilian clothes sporting the most exciting display of headgear ever seen in that august building! Many of them kept the old flag flying with bowlers and rolled umbrellas, while the remainder were decked in everything from deerstalkers to Russian fur balaclavas. It looked as if the United Nations had invaded the holy of holies. Flt Lts Carter and Mortlock treated themselves to a look at Colonel Glenn's space capsule but decided that perhaps slipping was after all, the best way of getting around the world in a hurry.*

*'Nick Carter was impressed enough to try and go into orbit round the*

Aircraft were now responsible for all trooping. Here, the *Oxfordshire* is seen at at Aden on one of her last trooping voyages. (*Lyneham Globe*)

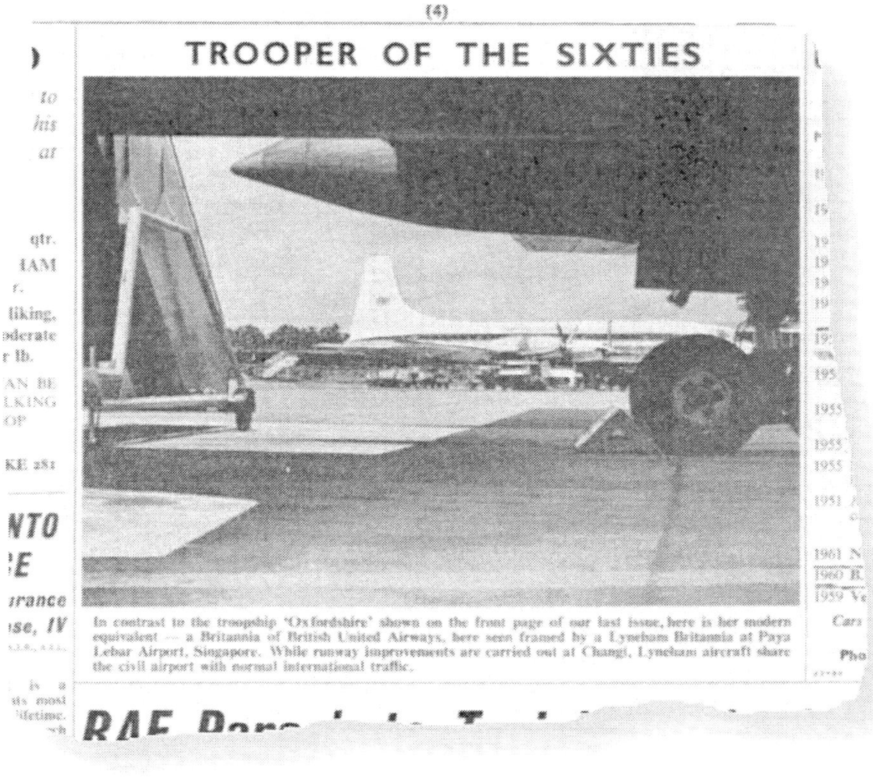


In contrast to the *Oxfordshire*, here is her modern equivalent - a Britannia of British United Airways, one of the civil charter troopers. It is framed by a Lyneham Britannia at Paya Lebar Airport, Singapore. While runway repairs were being carried out at Changi, Lyneham aircraft shared the civil airport with normal international traffic. (*Lyneham Globe*)

*peritrack in a big new American car temporarily loaned by a friendly passing major. It had buttons for everything but keeping our intrepid copilot on the correct side of the road. However, at least he got into the left-hand seat for one circuit. The next stop was at Offut for a visit to Strategic Air Command, which left our passengers in an advanced state of amazement at the wonders they were shown in the bowels of the earth. Being in Nebraska, which is described on every car licence plate as 'The Beef State', the crew decided to order a Salisbury Steak for lunch and settled back to enjoy 3 or 4 lbs. of juicy sirloin. Will all future visitors to Nebraska please note that a Salisbury Steak is second in content only to a British Railways Rissole!*

*'The main purpose of the tour was the annual exchange visit by Cranwell to the USAF Academy perched on the edge of the Rocky Mountains at Colorado Springs. We were greeted at Peterson AFB by a 116-piece band. Why is it that our overseas friends have still not learned that 'Colonel Bogie' is not the appropriate tune to play when celebrating the arrival of British guests? The Captain fought manfully with great bursts of brake dwell to overcome a whole hive of highly polished sousaphones and in spite of all their efforts managed to stop in roughly the right place. Transport Command Air Staff Instructions are to be amended limiting the number of sousaphones allowed on the tarmac at any one time. We realised that Lyneham's fame had not reached such a far-flung outpost when the Ops. Officer enquired of Sqn. Ldr. Chamberlain if he was '... the Commander of that tharr Canadian Britannica?' However, the next three days were spent in a flood of hospitality, which taxed our resources to the utmost. Sleep became secondary except when forced on us by the effects of what must be the greatest fillet steaks anywhere in the world.*

*'The captain and copilot covered themselves with blisters on a heavenly golf course; Chief Techs. Manley and Annison covered themselves with grease to get 392 serviceable again; Sgts. Mills and Holmes covered themselves in dust with sightseeing in the Rockies and Eric Mortlock covered himself with glory at the various social functions. The cadets meanwhile were covered in confusion at the bevy of beauty that had been imported from Texas and Oklahoma to make their stay a little more memorable. The confusion arose from the inability to choose one girl from what must have been the most exciting galaxy of talent outside of Hollywood.*

*'The end came all too soon on the 23rd April, when we were forced to leave this magnificent setting and head for our last stop at McGuire AFB near New York. Once again Brit. 392 developed a spot of trouble and the captain had an exciting time dashing around New York trying to coincide with some spares from the UK in time to make the scheduled take-off time. The contact was made just in time in a bar on Broadway and a number of highly suspicious York Cops eyed our wooden boxes of spares which felt more and more like a bank strong box as we struggled manfully back to the bus station with them. Sgt. Mills and C/T Annison mentioned later that they narrowly missed being involved in a double shooting on Broadway earlier that evening which explained why they viewed us with some misgivings.*

*'Despite maintaining schedule on our last departure the flight did end in disaster for the copilot. Nick Carter had carefully guarded his brief case containing the imprest throughout the flight. He even resisted some advances from the rest of the crew to vanish (with the imprest) to Las Vegas. At McGuire however, he made the mistake of putting a large bottle of whisky in his case then dropped it on the tarmac. Ever since our return, the accountant officer at Lyneham has been busy distilling dollars'*

**Operation Pedal**

So, special flights, as described above, exercises, VIPs, 'showing the flag' and the constant demands of the Changi Slip - some part or all of this was now the routine of Britannia life. But the real thing was still the 'Operation' with trouble flaring up in some part of world which needed the swift and distance-swallowing capability of our Strategic Transport Force.

Such a situation occurred in July 1963. A deterioration in security in Georgetown, British Guiana (now Guyana) on the northern coast of South America, had arisen with riots after a long general strike. Operation 'Pedal' was declared and the 2nd Battalion The Green Jackets plus supporting personnel, 500 men in all, were flown out.

**Side guidance**

An indication of how there was a continual effort to improve the efficiency of the Transport Force was the introduction of 'Side Guidance' around this time. Securing 'things' in aircraft has been a challenge ever since Orville Wright strapped himself to his wood, canvas and string device at Kitty Hawk in 1903. With all its sophistication, the Britannia came on the scene when boxes, bags, crates, equipment and awkward shaped freight were still loaded individually, piled on the floor and secured with chains, straps or lashing tape, whichever was appropriate.

'Side Guidance' was the partner of 'Palletisation'. The freight would be previously loaded on a metal pallet, virtually the width of the aircraft floor, and secured. When loading time came, the pallet was raised to the freight door, manoeuvred into the aircraft on a 'mat' of metal balls on the floor inside the door and then slid down the aircraft on rollers between rails - this was the side guidance. The ultimate function of these rails was to secure the pallets, and thus the load, using pins through the rails into the pallets. Loading and unloading time was much reduced.

**Tour of 'The Islands in the Sun'**

A feature of these years was 'nothing spared' VIP flights. Soon after midnight, 6th May 1963 Britannia Special 1076 departed Lyneham for the AOC-in-C Transport Command's tour of 'The Islands in the Sun'. No.99 operated the flight for Air Chief Marshal Sir R. Huddleston. The route flown was Lyneham - E1 Adem - Khormaksar - Gan - Cocos Islands - Mauritius - Salisbury (Southern Rhodesia) - Waterkloof and Jan Smuts (South Africa) - Ascension Island - Lagos - Sal (Cape Verde Islands) - Gibraltar - Lyneham - 23,186 miles covered at an average speed of 316 mph.

A nice touch of reports on such flights is that the team effort is acknowledged. The practice is extended here:

*'The operating crew members were Sqn. Ldr. J. G. Bourn, Flt. Lt. A. Thompson, Flt. Lt. D. Green, Flt. Lt. A. Brown, F/Sgt. K. Weatherall, Sgt. Ryder and F/Sgt. Blanchard. The ground crew, who did their usual magnificent job, was Ch. Tech. Williams, Cpl. Smith, Cpl. Fryer and Cpl. Clark. The crew would like to thank Wg. Cdr. Wood for his assistance as unpaid Escort Officer, and Sgt. Scott for his able assistance in the galley area.'*

Ex-AQM Pat Tweedie (4th from the left) remembers the last trip from Christmas Island. The 'Welcome' sign was brought back to Lyneham. (*Pat Tweedie*)

**Overflight problems**

Military, long range air transport operates in an uneasy environment. Day-to-day, the problems for some overflights exist but are predictable. Clearly flights over Warsaw Pact countries were forbidden except in very special circumstances. Countries of similar disposition would also be disinclined to allow such flights, no matter how distanced they might be, viz Cuba. A strong sense of neutrality might also be a barrier, the classical example of this being Switzerland. Sympathy with, or allegiance to, another country also produces strange bans. Finally there can be straightforward animosity and Egypt, in this era, would fit that bill.

Generally, this world situation is fairly static and can be planned around; any changes are reasonably foreseeable. This cannot be said of times of tension; just when freedom for air transport is of paramount importance. It can be that, on these occasions, unpredictable loyalties and other motives, prompt countries to ban overflights of their territory and air movement is frustrated. This was seen during the support of Kuwait in 1961.

**The Westabout route**

Contingency planners, therefore, would want to anticipate such problems and attempt to have routes established that would not be subject to the vagaries of national whim. One such route has already been mentioned, the Cable Route, a largely over the sea path with island stops. The first steps to establish another such route commenced on 10th July 1963; it was to become known as the Westabout Route. This made the not unreasonable assumption that we were likely to be supported in most of our matters by the United States of America; so a route was established, and exercised over the years, which would allow us to reach the Far East, flying westwards, and only using airfields under the jurisdiction of the USA.

**Fact finder**

On the aforementioned day, XL658 departed Lyneham, captained by Wg Cdr John Lewis, OC 511 Squadron, carrying Air Marshal Sir Patterson-Fraser on a fact-finding liaison visit along the proposed route. Britannia ground equipment was also carried for off-loading at each of the intended staging posts.

Thus the first Westabout Route was established via the 'Top of the World' USAF Base at Thule in Greenland; Elmendorf Air Force Base (AFB), near earthquake prone Anchorage, Alaska; the US Navy facility on Midway Island in the Central Pacific Ocean, the scene of the 1942 battle that was to be the turning point of the Pacific War, and then to the AFB on Guam, the southernmost island of the Mariana Islands, a series of volcanic mountain peaks and uplifted coral reefs in the Eastern Pacific which form a chain southwards from Japan. From there, the more familiar territory of Singapore could be reached. This route to the Far East, and its successors, was to be regularly exercised during the lifetime of the Britannias. It was to free us of all the chains of restricted overflight, albeit at some extra cost of time and money. It was also to provide many a ground and air crew with a bit of variety in their route activities.

**Cornflake cargo**

In addition to the stays at the proposed staging posts, this flight also took in Honolulu for a, much to the crew's chagrin, two hour only fuelling stop and Christmas Island, one of the Western Pacific Gilbert and Ellice Islands and erstwhile test area for our nuclear weapons and, at that time, still manned. It is reported that, due to some mismanagement, there was a surfeit of cornflakes on the island and Britannia 658 alleviated this by transhipping 2,500lbs to Changi!

**Weather watch**

Pictures of the Earth's weather from satellites are now 'old hat' but in 1963 they were still in their infancy and there was much research in order that the information that they provided was usefully and correctly used. A vital aspect of this work was to relate the picture from space to earth-observed weather. This could be done as a matter of routine for many parts of the globe but there were decidedly blank areas and one of these was known, almost exclusively, to crews of the Strategic Transport Force, the seas between Aden and Singapore.

As a result, Lyneham crews were invited to assist in this research and be rewarded! It was required that, using a 35mm camera, two photographs be taken of some significant cloud effects. These were to be taken at an interval of ten seconds which, with the travel of the aircraft, would provide a stereo effect. The position of the aircraft and the time was to be recorded.

The reward was quite significant in those impecunious days, US$1 per pair! The researchers were so greatly encouraged by the results that they received from Lyneham crews and, whilst wishing them to continue with their efforts, they also arranged for aircraft bound to and from Singapore to have two ciné cameras installed. These were modified to enable them to take single shots at four second intervals. On one 100 feet roll, 1,000 miles of Indian Ocean could be recorded.

**Swan Song**

A transport tradition is that one should have a 'good' last trip before leaving the squadron on posting. This could be a comparative thing! If one had spent the majority of one's tour doing Changi Slips, exercises to Barduffos, Norway, passenger flights to Gibraltar and back in a day and the like then a trip to Gander, Newfoundland might fit the bill! If, however, you have been a Flight Commander for your tour with, dare one say it, the pick of the trips, then that Swan Song has to be something pretty exotic. Or so it might seem when one reads in the *Lyneham Globe* of 99's Squadron Leader Tony Davies' last trip. In the interests of not providing too much excitement, only extracts of the account are given:

*'A Memorable Swan Song ... Squadron Leader Tony Davies and crew had a change from gun running and local war support recently when they carried the NATO Defence College on Operation 'Southern Voyage'.* (Author: Perhaps I'll have to withdraw that 'pick of the trips' remark!) *Departing Lyneham on 27th March, Paris was the first stop (night). A quick tour of the city and a few samples of the local brew and the crew were ready for their 10 hours sleep prior to take-off. At the unearthly hour of 1315 they set off for Lisbon ... Three days were spent in this delightful city touring the local beauty spots by day and local hostelries by night. And so on to Luqa, for one night stop only (thank goodness) ... Next stop the NATO base at Izmir. Only one night was spent here ... Our next port of call, Ankara, the capital of Turkey, or as one of the crew members described it, 'the Aden of this trip' and a hurried departure for Istanbul, truly a magnificent city with its ancient minarets and castles. After an excellent meal in the American Club with party to follow ... all was set for the following day's tour of the Bosphorous. A really interesting trip, the length of the river up to the entrance to the Black Sea. ... back to work and on to Athens... An extremely interesting day was spent visiting the Acropolis with a little shopping expedition to follow ... After a 'well-earned' rest, course was set for Naples where a tour of Pompeii was organised for the afternoon. The following morning saw several early birds arriving at the USS Enterprise; we were all suitably impressed by the efficiency of the United States Navy ... All too soon the gay city of Naples was left behind for the stately city of Rome. General Martino, Commandant of the NATO College, invited all the crew to lunch. This was held in the National Gallery. After an excellent lunch, a tour of Rome included a visit to St. Peter's and was thoroughly enjoyed ... The following morning was the final day of the tour. A short flight to Turin, where the College visited the Olivetti works, on to Paris and farewell to the enthusiastic passengers whom we had carried for a fortnight ... The crew certainly enjoyed the trip and it was a fitting 'Swan Song' for Sqn. Ldr. Davies ...'*

**Passenger time**

I return to my log book and an entry for 18th July - passenger Lyneham to Sondrestrom via North Pole (13 hours 15 minutes). It is not the custom to enter passenger flying in log books but I obviously thought that spending so much time 'down the back' was worthy of recording! But it is part of a story and a close shave.

**Polar flights**

The flight was one of a regular commitment for the Britannia Fleet that continued throughout its life. Each year two flights, in close succession, were carried out for the benefit of the RAF's 12 month Specialist Navigation Course (later renamed the GD Aerosystems Course). They were routed over the North Pole as, in those high latitudes, magnetic compass information becomes useless and aircraft navigation develops another challenge. The back of the

For the Spec N Course polar flights, tables with seating were located throughout the aircraft On each was a different piece of advanced navigation equipment. The students did a spell at the different stations to experience the properties of each. (*David Berry*)

aircraft was converted into a 'flying laboratory'. All manner of navigation devices were fitted for monitoring in the critical polar situation. Many manufacturers installed, for scrutiny, their latest equipment, the sophistication of which increased over the years.

**Gyro steering**

In the early days, the only method to overcome the problem of magnetic anomaly was to turn off the magnetic monitoring of the compass gyros and steer on the gyro information only. The performance of the gyros would be checked to establish the rate at which they 'drifted' and there would be allowance for this. It was something of a challenging exercise and did not always work out. John Bourn remembers:

*'Nav made a mess of it, all gyros toppled, never reached North Pole. Landed back at Lyneham 11 hours later!'*

... form covering the whole 270 parameters, in this way assessment of the serviceability of the MIDAS can be made. ... rises above a premeditated level, sinks beneath a premeditated level or rises/falls in excess of a certain rate of change.

**Gyro Pack—comprising of a Rotorace Directional Gyro, Power Supply Unit and Servo Amplifier.**

A MIDAS tradesman then examines the F700 and notes all the reported aircraft defects during the flight. The relevant parameters ... then played out, ... The actual functions and th[e] levels can be preset by the operat[or] at will, in practice the levels w[ill] be set at unservic... leve[l] ...

The CL 11 Gyro Pack.

**The CL11 Low Rate Gyro Pack**

From 1965 on this pack could be fitted to any of the Britannias when they were undertaking Polar flights or flights to extremes of latitude. This extract from the *Lyneham Globe* will give something for ex-navigators to get their teeth into:

*'Navigators, as you throw your SD cap on the hat rack of the Britannia these days have you noticed the unobtrusive mounting rails and power socket on the bulkhead. They are there to provide you with better navigation equipment for polar flying; they are the mountings for the CL11 Low Rate Gyro Pack. Although only the fixed fittings are obvious the complete packs (as shown in the illustration) are held in the, Instrument Section of the Communications/Electronics Squadron and can be fitted quickly when required.*

*'The CL11 Gyro Pack has been designed to provide extremely stable, but*

*'arbitrary' heading information. The drift rate of the system, with latitude correction applied, is less than ±1 degree per hour. The latitude correction range is from 90 degrees North to 90 degrees South with an accuracy of better then 0.5 degrees per hour.*

*'The pack comprises a Rotorace Directional Gyro, Power Supply unit and Servo Amplifier from the Directional Gyroscopic System Type CL11, and a Latitude Controller and Master Indicator from the Gyro Magnetic Mk. 7 System. These components are mounted on a tray 19 inches x 10 inches. The Directional Gyro contains an electrically driven azimuth gyro, which has freedom about a horizontal spin axis, a horizontal axis at right angles to the spin axis and a vertical axis. The unit is filled with helium and hermetically sealed. Heading information is fed into the Master Indicator via the Servo Amplifier, from a synchro assembly mounted on the outer gimbal assembly.*

*'As the gyro is affected by apparent azimuth drift, which ranges from -15 degrees per hour at the North Pole, zero at the equator, to +15 degrees per hour at the South Pole, this has to be corrected. This is done by two small electro-magnets (one for northern hemispheres, one for southern) mounted on either side of the inner gimbal bearing, which apply a torque which causes the gyro to be precessed at the same rate but opposite to the apparent drift. The supply to the two electro-magnets is from the Power Supply Unit via the latitude switch and central on the Latitude Controller.*

*'The synchronous output of the Master Indicator is used to enable CL11 heading output to be used as heading input into the Ground Position Indicator instead of normal Smith's Flight System heading, when flying over the Poles. Potential users of this navigation aid are welcome to come along to the Electronics Centre and familiarise themselves with its presentation and operation.'*

**Thule closing in**

It was practice for the aircraft to be double-crewed for these Polar flights so that maximum training could be obtained, and for the flight in July 1963, I was the copilot of the crew for the return leg. All did not go well for the outbound crew. As the hours slowly passed and they progressed towards the Pole the weather reports for the ultimate destination, Thule AFB in Greenland, became more and more gloomy. At 87 North it seemed imprudent, with the fuel remaining, to continue any further. If a landing at Thule was not to be possible then the nearest diversion airfield was Sondrestrom, some two hours flying to the south.

It did seem, at the top of the descent to the airfield, that the weather might just permit a landing; but Thule, as it could, won the day and nothing was seen from the radar approach. Things were now a little serious; whilst there was obviously enough fuel for the diversion, it was only just the right amount. This prohibited another attempt at a landing at Thule and meant

Objective achieved! The display indicates 90° North, the North Pole.

that the aircraft would have to be flown to its maximum efficiency to Sondrestrom. From the overshoot, the climb was to the optimum cruising level for its weight, above 30,000 feet.

**Not a lot to spare**

With such a long diversion flight, adverse winds can be a problem. They were. The fuel was low. It was a very tense crew that commenced the descent to Sondrestrom. There were communications difficulties so an emergency state was declared to increase awareness of their problem. All came good and they landed safely. A ground check of the fuel revealed that there was just 375 gallons left. If this seems a lot then set it against the tank capacity of 8,500 gallons and it can be seen that it was only enough really to wet the bottom of the tanks.

**Bang!!**

The foregoing has been elaborated somewhat in order to bring out the significance of the next day's events, when it was our turn to take the helm for the return flight to Lyneham. All was well on the cold but sunny Greenland day as we settled into the climb. Passing through 15,000 feet there was a bang from the rear of the aircraft. The popping of ears and the rapid rate of climb of the cabin altitude told us that pressurisation had been lost.

We did not have to surmise for long; as we started an emergency descent and return to Sondrestrom, the air quartermaster reported that the curtains over the toilet doorway were streaming rearwards, well nigh horizontal. The toilet was being well and truly flushed; we had lost the external cap that kept the toilet gate valve closed. Back on the ground at Sondrestrom we were astonished to find that they had the facility to manufacture a replacement cap, which was done and we were back in the air within a couple of hours.

The patched-up windscreen panel of the Boscombe Brit is 'Stage Right'. The author just makes it, 'Stage Left'! Story below. (*David Berry*)

**A close thing?**

So what was so significant about this series of events? It hinges around the fact that the toilet gate valve had not been touched since we left Lyneham and so this failure, for whatever reason, could have occurred at any one of our cabin repressurisations. The one prior to the failure had been on the climb out from Thule the day before. If it had happened then, it would have been disastrous. It has been related that the aircraft had to be climbed to 30,000+ feet in order to eke out the fuel - then there was only just enough. But man does not survive unpressurised at 30,000 feet without oxygen - and, for the passengers, there was none.

**Another oxygen tale**

Later, in these pages, the Boscombe Down Britannia will feature. The author was lucky to be one of the ex-Lyneham/Brize Norton people to operate this aeroplane in a unique job. A considerable and excellent aspect of its task was the amount of time one spent in the USA. An

Captain Bill Robinson receives some technical undercarriage advice from Sergeant Curly Beauchamp.
(*Bill Robinson*)

inevitable part of a Britannia flight to America is staging through Gander, Newfoundland. We were on our way home and, when we reported for the flight, Gander was throwing at us some of its particularly cold weather. On this occasion, using some 'Windscreen Heat' to try to clear the frost, one of the panes cracked. We always carried a team of the technicians from the civilian staff at Boscombe. Like their RAF crew chief compatriots, an unserviceable aircraft on route was a challenge. So, out came the 'Speed Tape' - a famously strong adhesive product - and the window was patched up. However, it was not going to be a good idea to subject this temporary repair to a large pressure differential - so we flew the Atlantic at 12,000 feet.

It was dusk as we neared Ireland and with 45 minutes or so to go for a night landing at Brize Norton - Boscombe was definitely '9 to 5' - it was a good idea, as we had been flying for six hours at the official height limit for crew's non-oxygen flight, for us to breathe some of that vital gas. I donned my oxygen mask - and some unseen hand was turning up the lights illuminating my flight instruments! It wasn't that, of course! It was a demonstration of the effect of oxygen deprivation on the senses.

It **was** a smooth landing at Brize Norton!

The end of another route trip - the approach to Runway 25 at Lyneham. (*Lyneham Globe*)

The adventures of Messrs. Ad Minn and Org at Wootton Lynstoke continue ...

THE LEG FROM GIN TO CLANGI LIES ACROSS THE INJUN OCEAN WHICH AS A GREAT POET ONCE SAID OF ITS CALMNESS
THE CREW HANDLE THE SITUATION IN THEIR CALM MANNER
... BORN OF YEARS OF EXPERIENCE.
ASTROLABE
LODESTONE CHARTS
THE NAVIGATOR WARNS THE CAPTAIN THEY ARE NEARING LAND.....
... THE LAND OF JACK ... ARTA ...
OVER WHOSE LAND FILTHY BRITISH MUST NOT FLY
THE NAV PRUDENTLY AVOIDS THE LAND OF JACK ARTA AND NAVIGATES BY THE STARS (ALSO STAYING NEAR TO THE COAST)
OLD MOORES 1963 ALMANAC
AQUARIUS LEFT HAND A BIT
PISCES A BIT AND THEN A LITTLE LEFT A BIT
ARIES A BIT BACK UP AND TAURUS
AND SO THEY FIND THEIR WAY TO SLINGAPORE
LIAISON OFF S/L THATAWAY
AD MINN & ORG ARE IN SLINGAPORE IN SEARCH OF PURE WATER..... ... BUT FIRST OF ALL THEY MUST EAT..... SO OFF THEY GO TO THE CLANGI CLEEK TLANSIT MESS – FOR THEIR FIRST AUTHENTIC CHINESE MEAL
BLOWN WINDSORS FISH & CHIPS CORNED BEEF MANCHESTER TART
"NO HAVE LUNCH TICKET NO HAVE LUNCH."
2 days pass
AND THEN WHEN THEY ARE FEELING A LITTLE BETTER THEY TRY TO FIND OUT WHAT WENT WRONG
"WE DONT THINK MUCH OF THIS FOOD"
MEMO
OIL
FLOUR
"ITS CORDON GREEN COOKING IN HERE MATE – THATS CORDON BLEU THATS GONE OFF A BIT."
"WELL MAY WE OFFER YOU THIS.... FOR YOUR OWN USE .... IT WILL PROBABLY IMPROVE THE COOKING HERE."
MEANWHILE BACK AT WOOTTON LYNESTOKE.....
21
AD MINN & ORG OFFER THEIR CONGRATULATIONS TO THE C.O., OFFICERS AND S.N.C.O.s OF No 511 SQUADRON ON THE OCCASION OF THE SQUADRON'S 21ST ANNIVERSARY NOVEMBER 1963
16

CHAPTER SEVENTEEN

# Mercy, Snakes and a Fuel Leak

If there had been an attempt to claim a Britannia record for the last chapter's flight time of 13 hours and 15 minutes, a cry would have gone up from Norman Rose:

*'On 6th May 1963, in XM517, we flew Air Marshal 'Iron Jaw' Jack Davis from Lyneham to Nairobi direct. I believe that this was the longest ever PLANNED Britannia flight, 14 hours from 'Doors Closed' to 'Doors Open'.'*

**RAF Form 540**

Every Royal Air Force squadron is obliged to record its month's activities on a Form 540. This should be a narrative

In May 1962 the AQM brevet was introduced. In the following year ten SNCOs of the WRAF received the badge and became the first WRAF members, in the history of the RAF, to be granted aircrew status. Nine of the ten are pictured here. From the left they are: Sgt Marie Wood, FS Ann Bowden, Sgts Dorothy MacKay, Margaret Wood, Joan Talbot, Jean Douglas, Maureen Glennon, Edna Devine and Hazel Mogg.

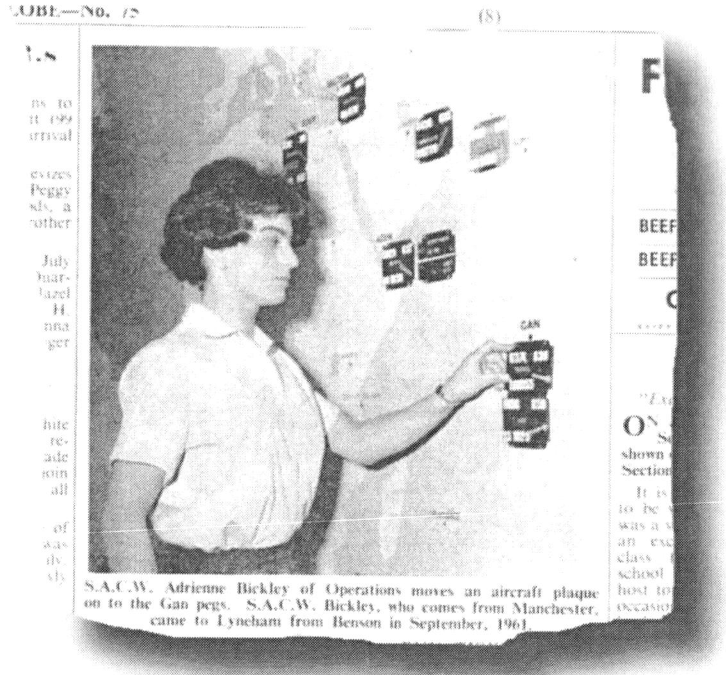
S.A.C.W. Adrienne Bickley of Operations moves an aircraft plaque on to the Gan pegs. S.A.C.W. Bickley, who comes from Manchester, came to Lyneham from Benson in September, 1961.

Lyneham Ops would have played its part in the aeromed implementation. (*Lyneham Globe*)

account of activities and the full details (aircraft number, crew names, flight particulars, time flown) of each of the month's flight. The latter part, a mechanical process, is generally well done. The former, which is largely up to the composer's imagination, can be for historians, rather bleak. An example of this occurs in the 511 Squadron record for September 1963:

*'Aeromed Honolulu/UK. RAF Officer with broken neck.'*

It can only be imagined what might have been behind those few words. Servicemen breaking their necks was not an uncommon thing. Rather ludicrously, which should not detract from the seriousness of the injury, many were caused by diving into too shallow swimming pools - or indeed ones with no water at all!

**Aeromed**

In this instance, the Principal Medical Officer at Headquarters RAF Transport Command at Upavon would have been informed, by urgent signal, and an aeromedical evacuation flight requested.

Having approved it, the machinery would swing into action. The operations staff would see if, to save time, there was an aircraft in the area that could be rerouted. Assuming that this was not possible, Lyneham would be told to immediately prepare an aircraft to be flown by the standby crew that was kept at a six hour readiness. It would be scheduled to leave that six hours from the call. A further crew could be recruited. They would travel as passengers to the half way point and there await the return of the aircraft which they would then fly to the UK.

The appropriate staff at the Princess Alexandra's RAF Hospital, Wroughton would be advised and the aeromedical team on standby alerted. This would consist of a fully flight trained nursing sister of the Princess Mary's Royal Air Force Nursing Service, an aeromedical

A silhouette of what looks like a serious undercarriage problem somewhere down the route. (*Pete Hobson*)

SNCO nurse plus two nursing orderlies. In view of the seriousness of the injury, a RAF doctor would head the team. All these personnel would have received special training in airborne medical care at the Aeromedical School at RAF Lyneham.

**Gruelling schedule**

The team would be calling for the special equipment required for this patient to supplement that held at readiness at Lyneham. The engineer planners would have manoeuvred their aircraft planning requirements board and found an aircraft. This was now being prepared. The role equipment staff convert the aircraft cabin to its hospital state.

Two hours before departure, the crew report to Operations and are given the details of the flight. Because of its urgency they find themselves with a gruelling schedule - Lyneham to Gander, Newfoundland, refuel and on to Offutt AFB, near Omaha, Nebraska. There would then be the minimum laid down 14 hours rest before another hard day to McClellan AFB, near Sacramento, California for refuel before the final leg to Hickham AFB, Honolulu.

Less than 48 hours after receiving the call from the Pacific, the aircraft would be in position. The medical team will have to be satisfied with what rest they have been able to obtain during the flight for they will be at the hospital checking on the patient and preparing him for the journey. The crew will be taking their further mandatory and welcome 14 hours rest. The crew chief may have some snags to fix as well as refuelling and routine servicing.

Four hours before take-off the move of the patient would start, all done with great smoothness and care in view of his serious injury. At the aircraft, the stretcher is transferred from the ambulance to a freight lifting platform for the rise to the Britannia freight door.

Once inside everything possible will be done to recreate for the patient the comfort and care of a hospital intensive care unit. The medical staff have briefed the crew on any special requirements. It could be that the pressure in the cabin needs to be kept at sea level. This patient is going to require as smooth a flight as possible. Turbulence is going to be painful.

opportunity to wish Mr Binns a happy and pleasant retirement.

impact on the majority of our readers.

**CASEVAC RAMP PROTOTYPE**

THE smooth-looking aircraft ramp shown in our exclusive picture was designed and built by W/O Taylor, Sgt. Herriott and their compatriots in Lyneham Station Workshops.

The casevac patient might have been protected from the weather by this specially built ramp. (*Lyneham Globe*)

Troops boarding at Lyneham for Bardufoss. (*Bill Robinson*)

The humour behind many *Lyneham Globe* entries is 'lost in the mists of time' viz this item. Why is Flt Lt Fred Lace being presented with a wooden leg by a man in a dress wearing a funny hat? (*Lyneham Globe*)

**Full speed home**

The engines start and the long flight home, along the reverse of the outbound route, commences. At Offutt, the previously positioned slip crew take over so, at each of the three stops with the aircraft receiving priority treatment, it is only on the ground for an hour. That priority extends into the air where Air Traffic Control see that the aircraft receives the most expeditious routing.

At Lyneham, a helicopter awaits. The patient is in Wroughton Hospital within an hour of the Britannia landing. From the mid-Pacific to the UK, from hospital to hospital, 30 hours!

*'Aeromed Honolulu/UK. RAF Officer with broken neck.'*

went as far as Aden from where was it recalled
e part in Operation Pedal.

South Wales, this time with another brand of cigarette. The story being that if a set of various

ALL DONE BY NUMBERS. The cancer-cultivating wooden leg being delivered to the "safe hands of" Flt. Lt. Fred "Cuddles" Lace.

SHORT BROS. & HARLAND LTD. - BELFAST

**Round the world, Eastabout**

In fact, under the above headline, it is *The Lyneham Globe* that provides the real detail of this aeromedical flight:

*'September 15th saw Fred Lace and his crew depart Lyneham on the first leg of a 30,000-mile trip, which was scheduled to include Africa, Middle East, Far East, Pacific Ocean, Alaska and Greenland. The first night stop was Sal in Cape Verde Islands and will be remembered by most of the crew and passengers as the source of a particularly nasty stomach infection which lasted through Rhodesia and Nairobi to Khormaksar where Wg Cdr Henry, SMO, brought it to a sudden halt.*

*'Passengers on this flight were a Movements team, led by WO Edwards of Lyneham Cargo Shed; their purpose was to demonstrate the Britannia side guidance loading at various points along the route. The route after Aden was to Singapore via*

*Bahrain and Gan. At Singapore, Wg Cdr Povey and Sqn Off McNair joined the aircraft after being positioned there by Comet. These two comprised the medical team, which was to care for Fg Off Northmore, a patient later picked up at Honolulu. This flight received some publicity as the first RAF casualty evacuation flight via the North Polar route from Alaska to Greenland, but unfortunately, due to adverse weather conditions in Greenland, the crew was left no alternative but to, stage through Gander. However it was no doubt the first casualty evacuation flight to come from Alaska to Lyneham with only a 55-minute refuel stop at Gander. It was a weary crew that dragged its bags through Lyneham Customs Hall on the morning of 4th October.'*

Postscript: Fg Off Northmore became a paraplegic as a result of his diving accident. Fred Lace kept in touch with him over the subsequent years.

**Exercise in India**

In October 1963, No.64(F) Squadron with their night/all weather Javelin fighters flew to give demonstrations, advice and training to the Indian air defence formation. The three weeks joint exercise went by the name of Exercise 'Shiksa', an old Sanskrit word meaning education or learning. The aircraft flew out via Cyprus and Bahrain with in-flight refuelling being provided by Valiant tankers. In support, along the route and flying the men and materials, were the Britannias.

The airfield was Kailakunda, near Calcutta. My log book records that I flew there via Nicosia and Bahrain in mid-October and again at the end of the month. I remember it well. Within the means available, the Indian Air Force had prepared for our coming; but those means were limited.

There was the usual bustle around the aircraft as we disembarked. With the responsibility for the aircraft handed over, it was time for bed. It had been a long day. Came the oft asked question, 'Where's the crew bus?' A finger points, 'On its way.' Sure enough in the distance, across the flat fields of crops could be seen the top of a coach. It was moving slowly along but did not seem to get any closer. As time went by it became clear that it was having to wend its way along the road that followed the edges of the haphazard fields. Eventually it

Not the crew bus referred to in the text but one caught by Bill Robinson's camera elsewhere? (*Bill Robinson*)

came to a noisy, smoky standstill beside our aircraft. It was apparent that the bus which normally conveyed the workers to the fields had been commandeered for our use. We climbed gingerly aboard.

**Under canvas?!**

Firing on only three cylinders, the

Flt Lt Chris Cristinacce, detachment commander at Kailakunda, boards a Britannia after flag stopping at Bahrain. His rain-soaked kit was drying on lines inside the aircraft! (*Lyneham Globe*)

Flt. Lt. Cristinacce, detachment commander at Kalaikunda, near Calcutta, boards a Britannia after flagstopping at Bahrain. His rain-soaked kit was drying on lines inside the aircraft!

Could be a load for Bardufoss going into the rear freight bay - at night!
(*Bill Robinson*)

journey seemed endless; but eventually we came to a grinding halt outside our accommodation - TENTS!! This was not our normal style! Admittedly they were erected on concrete bases and were fully furnished. From somewhere had come proper beds - and wardrobes, for the visiting British ex-colonialists. As we walked from the bus, a gnarled, white cotton clad figure stood to attention with a shaky hand permanently at the salute. It turned out that he was the 'dhobi wallah', no doubt with many a memory of our military presence in the India of the past.

**Beware - snakes!**

It certainly was a night stop with a difference. It had amused us that part of our UK departure preparation had been the issue of snake bite kits. That amusement had continued as we examined the contents en route:

*Instructions:*

*1. Identify the snake ...!!!!*

The smiles slowly faded when we learnt that one of our compatriots had to beat one of these reptiles to death in order to get back from the outdoor toilets!

**Quick flip**

Back home on 5th October, Graham and I were detailed to provide a short passenger flight for Tees-Side members of the Royal Observer Corps. In 3½ hours we flew 452!

**Another record broken**

The Britannias claimed an air transport record in November 1963, the longest military airlift ever undertaken. Seven aircraft flew the 1st Battalion, Royal Ulster Rifles the 12,000 miles from the UK to Australia to take part in an exercise with the Australian Army.

**Norway**

Bardufoss was to be a constant ingredient of Britannia operations. This airfield, situated in Northern Norway, was used as the air head for many Army air mobility exercises, its hinterland providing a very suitable environment for the Army to train in its European role. In the summer of '63, Exercise Barfrost II took place and the Britannias positioned No.43 Commando, a total of 640 personnel, 15 Land Rovers, 15 half ton trailers and 30,000lbs of freight, without hitch, to this remote airfield well within the Arctic Circle. A Lyneham Globe reporter sets the scene:

*'The crews participating in the exercise found that Bardufoss, situated in a rugged valley between snow-capped hills, reminded them of Hong Kong airfield with its difficult approach procedures. 'Kai Tak without aids' was one comment. A hill on the threshold of one runway was similar to the one at Kowloon and high ground on either side of the runway was equally discouraging to those who wished to carry out a visual circuit. However, once on the ground, crews were appreciative of the unspoilt mountain scenery and crystal clear air.'*

It has to be said that this image was atypical; but it was summer. Many crews will recall that 90% of the time they saw nothing of Bardufoss until on short radar finals and when they did go on a clear day they were horrified at what they saw around them, albeit that the high ground

Royal Marine Commandos enter their buses after deplaning from a Britannia during Exercise Barfrost II. The scene represents an often experienced Britannia off-loading location - an obscure corner of an airfield with no facilities immediately to hand. (*Lyneham Globe*)

was clearly designated on the approach chart - a case of 'pictures speaking louder than words' equivalent.

Bardufoss was a continual challenge over the years. There would be the pressures of operating in an exercise aircraft flow environment; taking and keeping one's place in the queue. Most flights returned immediately to the UK after off-loading, but took place at ghastly times of day and night. Not the least of the challenges was the winter weather of this northernmost airfield. It is a tribute to crews that an aircraft not intended as a tactical, forward field, transport did survive unscathed in this alien environment.

**An incredible ground crew tale**

Ex-Chief Technician Vic Merrill served the Britannia cause for many years. He wrote the following article for the Britannia Association's own magazine, *'The Whispering Giant'*. It is included *'in toto'* as it is an unbelievable story but also because it says so much about the dedication of the ground crews of those years:

*'I stood gazing at the dark bulk of Al Lloyd, clad in cold weather gear in the gloom of the side of the Britannia, and considered the situation. There was definitely an intermittent fuel leak somewhere in No.2 nacelle, behind the fireproof bulkhead. Succeeding shifts had painfully dried out the volume with rags and run the engine, only to find a dry area or a saturated one. The criteria seemed to be the length of run and the power applied. Location of the leak by standing on a chock, just an engine's length from a rotating propeller, with head and shoulders in the hole and a torch to see by, in the slipstream from the prop, even only in superfine, was no good. The space appeared dry and, suddenly, wet - with no indication of the source.*

*'Pleas that, 'I'll put more men on it straight away,' by the shift boss to the emissaries from the Crystal Palace, followed by a smart salute, were being met, uncharacteristically, by beetled brows. Either someone had explained to them that there was a physical limit to the number of people who could be actively engaged on the job or they were having to give an explanation to a higher authority. Pressure*

The captured atmosphere of a Britannia engine change. (*Vic Merrill*)

*to get the Brit serviceable was increasing - and we could not find the location of the leak. Repair was not considered a problem, providing the site could be pinpointed.*

*'I considered the options and decided that the answer was that, in order to identify the leak as soon as it showed itself, someone had to be inside the nacelle, out of the slipstream, while the engine was running. Because we were carrying the can, the choice lay between Al and myself and our relative sizes meant that I would have to 'volunteer'. I didn't think it was fair to ask one of the troops to do it, even though a small one could undoubtedly be found. I explained my conclusions to Al and didn't let him talk me out of it.*

*'I peeled off my cold weather coat, working blue jacket and pullover, borrowed a couple of extra torches and climbed into the hole. I wedged myself across the opening and waited for the others to close the hatch. As the Dzus fasteners half turned to lock, the space I was in suddenly became very small indeed and the inside of the hatch which now formed the floor of my world was definitely not comfortable to rest on. It was quiet out of the wind and I shone the torch around to orient myself while the rest of the crew prepared for the engine run. The stainless steel shroud of the swan neck surrounding the jet pipe was just above my stomach. Behind my head and to my left and right were the fuel heater, fuel flow transmitter, fuel pipelines and adaptor through the firewall. My feet were on the other side, in the area of the fire bottles. I twisted around and ensured that I could see the whole length of the fuel system, that there were no leaks at the moment and that the spare torches were secure, working and at hand.*

*'I heard, clearly, the booster pumps go on but no leak appeared. Inverters started up in the distance and the prop brake wound off. There was a hard clunk as the starter engaged and sharp cracks as the igniters operated. As the shafts began to rotate, the blades in the engine tinkled before centrifugal force locked them in position. I suddenly realised that I could think of innumerable, adequate reasons why I should not be in the situation that I found myself. The starter pump whirred and then was a 'Whoomph' followed by a roar as the engine lit up. I became conscious of the hot gas stream passing down the jet pipe inches from my head. Ear plugs would have been a good idea but it was too late now. There came a loud bang as the prop went into superfine and the engine vibration fell a little as Al checked the flight deck gauges at idle revs. I flashed the torch around but there were still no leaks that I could see.*

*'The prop dropped out of superfine and the power increased as Al opened up the throttle in order to induce the leak; still no indications. The noise was similar to an amplified Niagara Falls without the spray. I was beginning to think that the exercise was a foolhardy waste of time.*

Mexico Visited and Unvisited

At a reception in Mexico City members of a 99 Squadron Britannia crew are seen talking to His Excellency the British Ambassador. L. to R. are seen Master Signaller Kemp, Filght Lieutenant Coburn, His Excellency the Ambassador, Sir Peter Garrad, Sergeant Sankey, Mrs. Atkinson (wife of the First Secretary of the Embassy) and Flight Sergeant Durnan.

*"That earth has something yet to show,*

... Mexican Air Force, ... Embassy, evening

A Britannia of 99 Squadron accompanied the Victors of No.139 Squadron to Mexico City in March 1963. The photograph was taken at a reception held by His Excellency the British Ambassador, Sir Peter Garrad (centre). The crew members (L. to R.) are Master Signaller Eddy Kemp, Flight Lieutenant Bill Coburn, Sergeant John Sankey and Flight Sergeant Pat Durnan. (*Lyneham Globe*)

*'Suddenly there was an overwhelming smell of kerosene and a haze appeared around my head. Droplets of fuel, like fog on a girl's hair, covered my shirt. I squirmed around and pointed the torch at the source of the spray. It was coming from the fuel heater and as I wriggled close I could see it spurting from between the steel pipe adaptor and the aluminium casing of the heater. Presumably the casing expanded more than the adaptor as the Vernatherm wax charge contracted when cold fuel passed it, allowing hot compressor delivery air to flow and heat the fuel and the casing. We had found the leak and could safely predict a completion time for the repair!*

*'Now I became a little more attentive of my predicament; my eyes were smarting; I could taste kerosene in my mouth and feel a burning sensation in the back of my throat. I put a rag over the leak and another over my face and mouth. I tried not to think of the word 'FIRE' and began sending thought waves to Al saying, 'Stop the engine and get me out of here as soon as possible.' Al, however, decided to ensure that I had enough power and time to locate the leak and proceeded accordingly. I could feel the fuel seeping through my trousers and shirt where they touched the side of the aircraft; my hair was wet, droplets were running down my back and my eyes were now smarting like crazy. I sighed - another wrecked working blue; even with dry cleaning and pressing they were never the same after a soaking by OX38 or fuel. One adopted the permanent 'scruff' look.*

*'Eventually the engine slowed and ran down as the HP cock was closed. I lay there quite still, waiting to be released. The panel underneath moved as the fasteners were undone and I wedged myself so I was not putting any weight on it. Hands grasped my feet and guided them on to the 'A' steps. Torches flashed into my face and I realised that I must be looking worse than I felt - which wasn't all that good. I was grateful for the feel of Al's hand on my arm and I heard a voice speaking in the distance explaining where the leak was; it was mine.*

*'After picking up my clothing and tool bag, I waddled across the pan towards the office in J2. My skin was beginning to burn like bad sunburn and I had a singing in my ears. The worst bit was the rubbing of skin against my trousers between my legs as I walked. In the office there were insistent pleas for me to take my sodden, smelly self away and clean up before I contaminated their clean, warm room any more than I had already. As I left, to do just that, I wondered how I could have been so inconsiderate.'*

**Tribute for 1963**

Group Captain Alasdair Steedman sums up:

*'For most of us, Lyneham's 1963*

*has been a pretty hectic year. Starting with the worst winter of the century, the station has taken emergencies, operations, exercises and scheduled tasks in its stride and, once again, I am proud to record a 100% achievement. But let there be no doubt about it, success like that doesn't just happen. It needs high and sustained endeavour by everyone in every section of the station and you all have pulled your full weight this past year.*

*'In many ways we are lucky to have such a worthwhile job to do and it is most satisfying to be able to see clearly for ourselves the results of our labours. Yet we carry a heavy responsibility and play a vital part in the defence of freedom and national and Commonwealth interests overseas. Each of you at his work carries a part of this responsibility. You have shown it could not be in better hands.'*

Amen to Britannia year 1963.

On the pages that follow are photographs of a route flyer's scrapbook - John Grimwood, ex-99 airquartermaster:

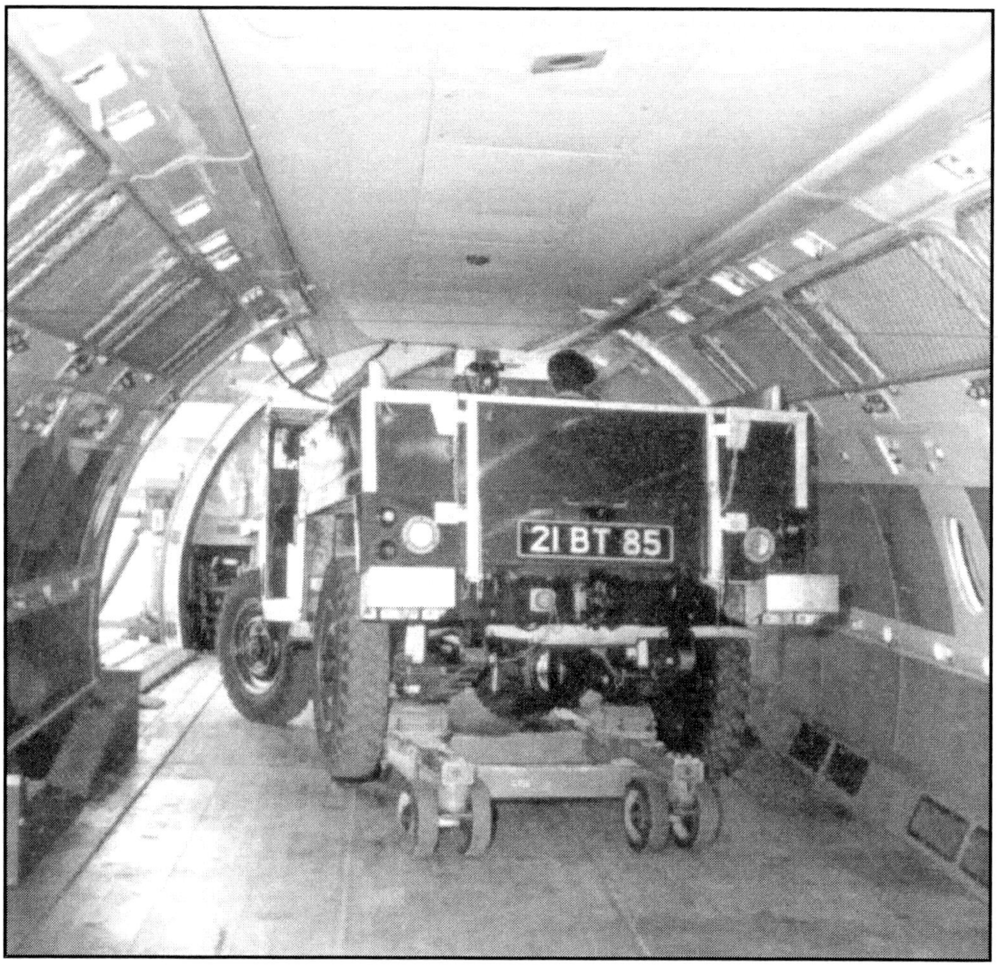


A tight squeeze!

Bombay
HERITAGE BEACH HOTEL
MONTEGO BAY JAMAICA WEST INDIES

Holiday Inn
BELIZE
CYPRUS

Katmandu 75

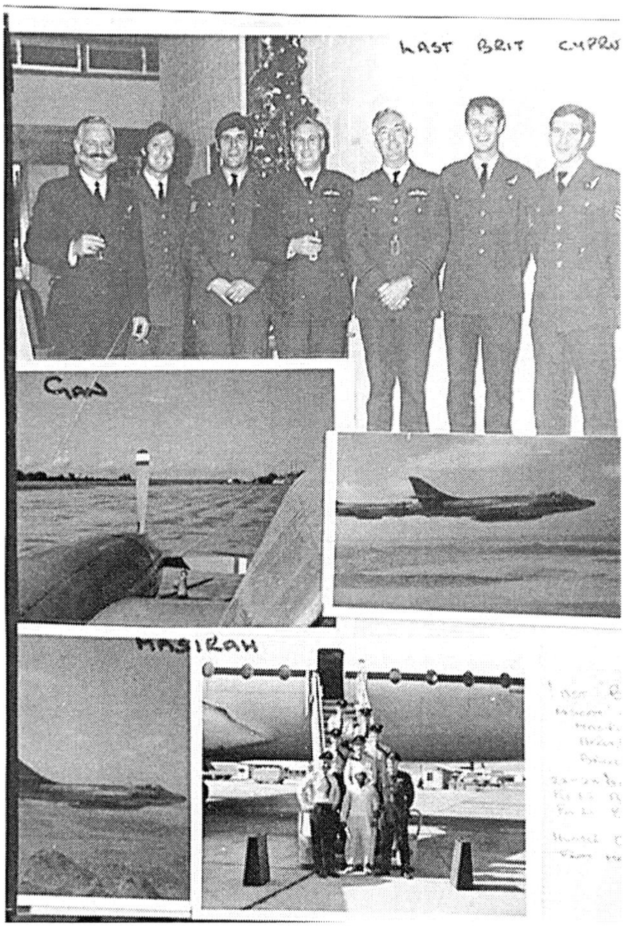
LAST BRIT
Gan
MASIRAH

HOTEL EQUATORIAL
SINGAPORE
THE SPEAKEASY
GAN

Disneyland
840
Cape Kennedy
Florida

LYNEHAM
WESTON-ON-THE-GREEN
LYNEHAM
QUOTATIONS FROM
CHAIRMAN
MAO TSE-TUNG
WELCOME TO
Offutt AFB
NEBRASKA
SAC
HOPE YOUR
STAY IS
ENJOYABLE

BOB LAU
CAMERON RESTAURANT
HOTEL
SOALTE
OBEROI
KATHMANDU, NEPAL
This is to certify that
has undergone parachute
training at No. 1 P.T.S.
and has completed
descents.
BALLOON
AIRCRAFT
FREE FALL
KNOWLEDGE DISPELS FEAR
Officer Commanding
No. 1 P.T.S.

GIBRALTAR
THE ROCK
Rosia Bay
TRAFALGAR CEMETERY

THE SPEAKEASY
OPEN FROM 10.30 AM TILL 2 AM.
ROARING TWENTIES ATMOSPHERE.
LIVE GOOD TIME MUSIC.
YOUR HOST AND PROPRIETOR — BRIAN NOLAN
" NO THICK CARPETS BUT
GREAT WALL TO WALL PEOPLE "
3C GRANVILLE CIRCUIT, KOWLOON. TEL. K-681897
(OFF GRANVILLE RD. JUST BEHIND THE PARK HOTEL)
Gemorina
WOODEN CARVING
THE SPEAKEASY
BRIAN NOLAN
3C GRANVILLE CIRCUIT, KOWLOON. TEL. K-681897
SQUADR
The Lexington
WELCOME TO McCLELLAN
AIR FORCE BASE, CALIFORNIA
Welcome to Disneyland
WALT DISNEY PRODUCTIONS
ASHOKA HOTEL
NEW DELHI

Bangladesh Biman
REFUGEES FROM
Thule Air Base, Greenland
The British Deputy High Commissioner
and Mrs John Miles
request the pleasure of the company of
Flt Sgt J L Grinwood
for a Reception
on Monday 7th October at 6.30 pm
JOCKEY CLUB OF KENYA
GENTLEMAN
MAIN ENCLOSURE
016

THULE & POLE.
ROYAL AIR FORCE COLLEGE OF AIR WARFARE
POLAR CERTIFICATE
This is to certify that on 7 AUGUST 1971
SERGEANT J L GRIMWOOD
reached the 'Top' of the World' and
circumnavigated the North Geographic Pole
D C SAUNDERS
AIR CDR
COMMANDANT.
Kathmandu
City weath
PATRICK
TAXI
773-2500
ROYAL AIR FORCE
SEA SURVIVAL TRAINING
SHAMROCK HOTEL
(SHAMROCK CO. LTD.)
223 NATHAN ROAD, KOWLOON, HONG KONG
This is to certify that
FS GRIMWOOD
has satisfactorily completed a course of training in Sea Survival and
has with fortitude undergone the rigorous requirements of this School
27 Feb 76
Flight Lieutenant

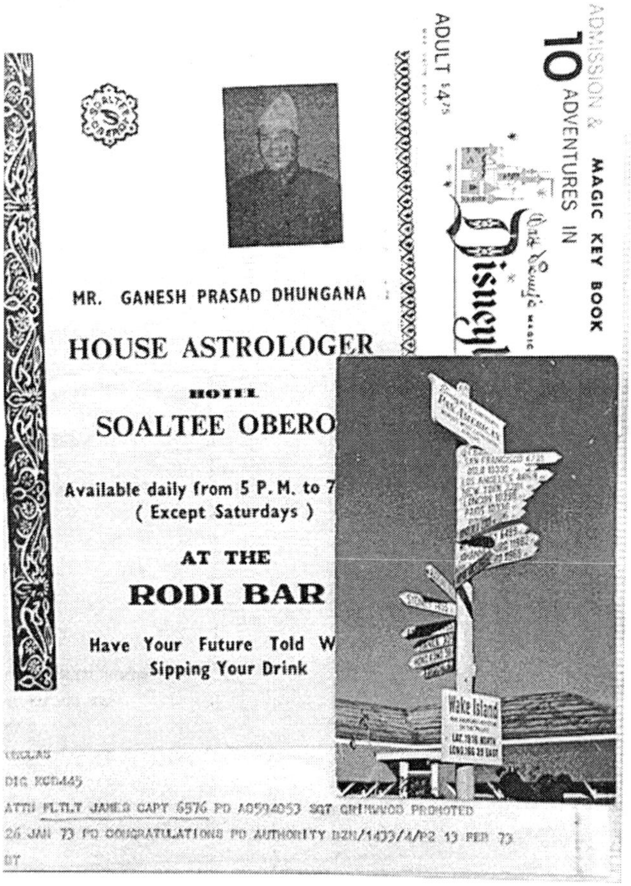


ATTN FLTLT JAMES CAPT 6576 PO A0594053 SGT GRIMWOOD PROMOTED
26 JAN 73 PO CONGRATULATIONS PO AUTHORITY DZN/1433/4/P2 13 FEB 73
BT

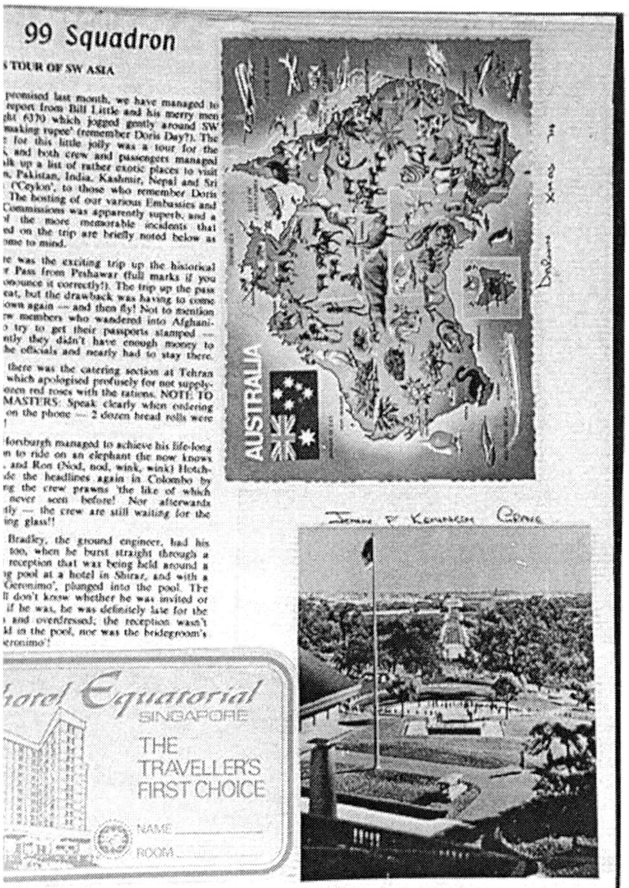

## 99 Squadron

**S TOUR OF SW ASIA**

promised last month, we have managed to report from Bill Little and his merry men ght 6370 which jogged gently around SW making rupee' (remember Doris Day?). The for this little jolly was a tour for the and both crew and passengers managed lk up a list of rather exotic places to visit n, Pakistan, India, Kashmir, Nepal and Sri ('Ceylon', to those who remember Doris The hosting of our various Embassies and Commissions was apparently superb, and a of the more memorable incidents that ed on the trip are briefly noted below as ome to mind.

e was the exciting trip up the historical r Pass from Peshawar (full marks if you onounce it correctly!). The trip up the pass eat, but the drawback was having to come own again — and then fly! Not to mention w members who wandered into Afghani- o try to get their passports stamped — ntly they didn't have enough money to he officials and nearly had to stay there.

there was the catering section at Tehran which apologised profusely for not supply- ozen red roses with the rations. NOTE TO MASTERS: Speak clearly when ordering on the phone — 2 dozen bread rolls were !

Horsburgh managed to achieve his life-long n to ride on an elephant (he now knows , and Ron (Nod, nod, wink, wink) Hotch- de the headlines again in Colombo by ng the crew prawns 'the like of which never seen before! Nor afterwards tly — the crew are still waiting for the ing glass!!

Bradley, the ground engineer, had his too, when he burst straight through a reception that was being held around a g pool at a hotel in Shiraz, and with a Geronimo', plunged into the pool. The ll don't know whether he was invited or if he was, he was definitely late for the and overdressed; the reception wasn't ld in the pool, nor was the bridegroom's eronimo'!



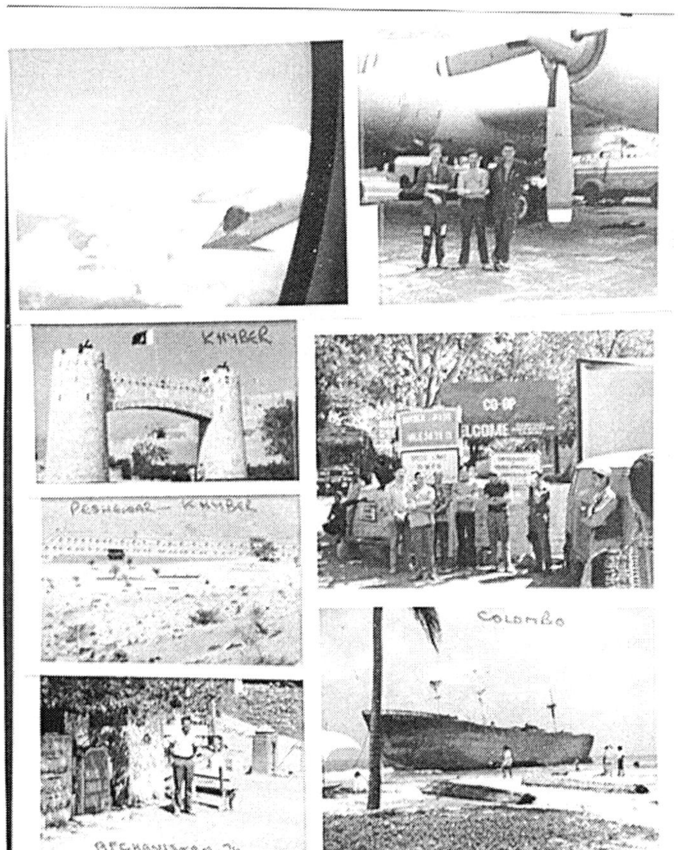

The adventures of Messrs. Ad Minn and Org at Wootton Lynstoke continue ...

Whilst Ad Minn & Org celebrate Christmas away from home the brotherhood of mankind the world over observe this festival of peace in their own traditional way ........
CYPRUS
DRAC
ADEN
KENYA
SOMALIA
EAST AFRICA
HOME
And Transport Command.......
HOME
With no pure water at Changi Ad Minn and Org decide to go down under; and ... so... to.....
AUSTRALIA
BUT THE SINGAPORE MOVERS HAVE THE FINAL SAY ....
on the way the Captain tells them...
"We have just been signalled, your kit has been sent to Copenhagen."
"But it's over there."
"And I have a trim sheet for a Japanese D.C. 8 on route from Accra to New York."
And so they arrive.....
ALICE
TO NEAREST BILLABONG
TUCKER
DRAC

CHAPTER EIGHTEEN

# 1964 - Can It Get Any Busier?

Aircrew dress was a curious topic of these times. It was decided from the start that the image of the aircraft demanded that crews should fly in uniform and not flying suits. It then had to be determined when this should be the temperate climate blue or the tropical khaki drill (KD). As has been mentioned, the rule became that you wore the correct dress for your destination. This meant that, more often than not, we wore KD.

**Dad's Army KD**

Now, the design of the RAF stores' issue KD, and of that supplied by military tailors, was circa 1930! Consequently no one wore it. The priority of every new crew member would be to get to Singapore and have some KD tailor-made in Changi Village, a well known group of traders who had set themselves up adjacent to the RAF station. There were a number of tailors to choose from so the prices were quite competitive and the service fast.

The result of this haphazard purchasing was a multifarious collection of uniforms with style differing from tailor to tailor and colour varying in every shade from a dark tan to a fetching light pinky brown! It was amazing that this was allowed to continue as there was great insistence that we should be smartly turned out, 'You are ambassadors'; and there was the injustice of it in that we were, in essence, purchasing our own flying clothing.

**Trial or trick?**

This matter did receive attention from time to time. Around the present period, there was 'The Trial of the Lightweight Blue Uniform'. This was to be put through its paces, gracing the forms of Flt Lt Alec Lindsay (511) and Fg Off Tony Gallow (99), up and down the route. There was considerable cynicism about this venture, many feeling it was just a sop to the complaining. Nothing ever did come of it.

**Headset saga**

Whilst attire is the subject, it is appropriate to move up the body and address the matter of flying headsets for radio and intercom communication. This was another curious area. The aircraft were delivered with one headset per flight deck member, a total of five. It was decided that the civilian practice of these being permanently in position and used by all was impractical. They rapidly disappeared and became the treasured possessions of the original élite.

What then were the rest of us to use? We were flying the most expensive aircraft that the Royal Air Force had ever purchased but the crew wore the cloth inner

It certainly paid the Changi Village tailors to advertise in *The Lyneham Globe*.

The multifarious KD. Rolled down sleeves and tie were dictated by regulations. Ann Culliford elegantly illustrates that the female AQMs were a little better placed, dress-wise. The colour was light blue and the material of a cotton nature. A less popular uniform replaced it; a much darker blue (with gold brevet and rank badges) it was a 'man-made' fibre and not totally suited to tropical climes.
(*Ann Bihan née Culliford*)

Copilot Alpin McGregor is the proud possessor of one of the original headsets which came with the delivered aircraft. What does the engineer have on his head?
(*Bill Robinson*)

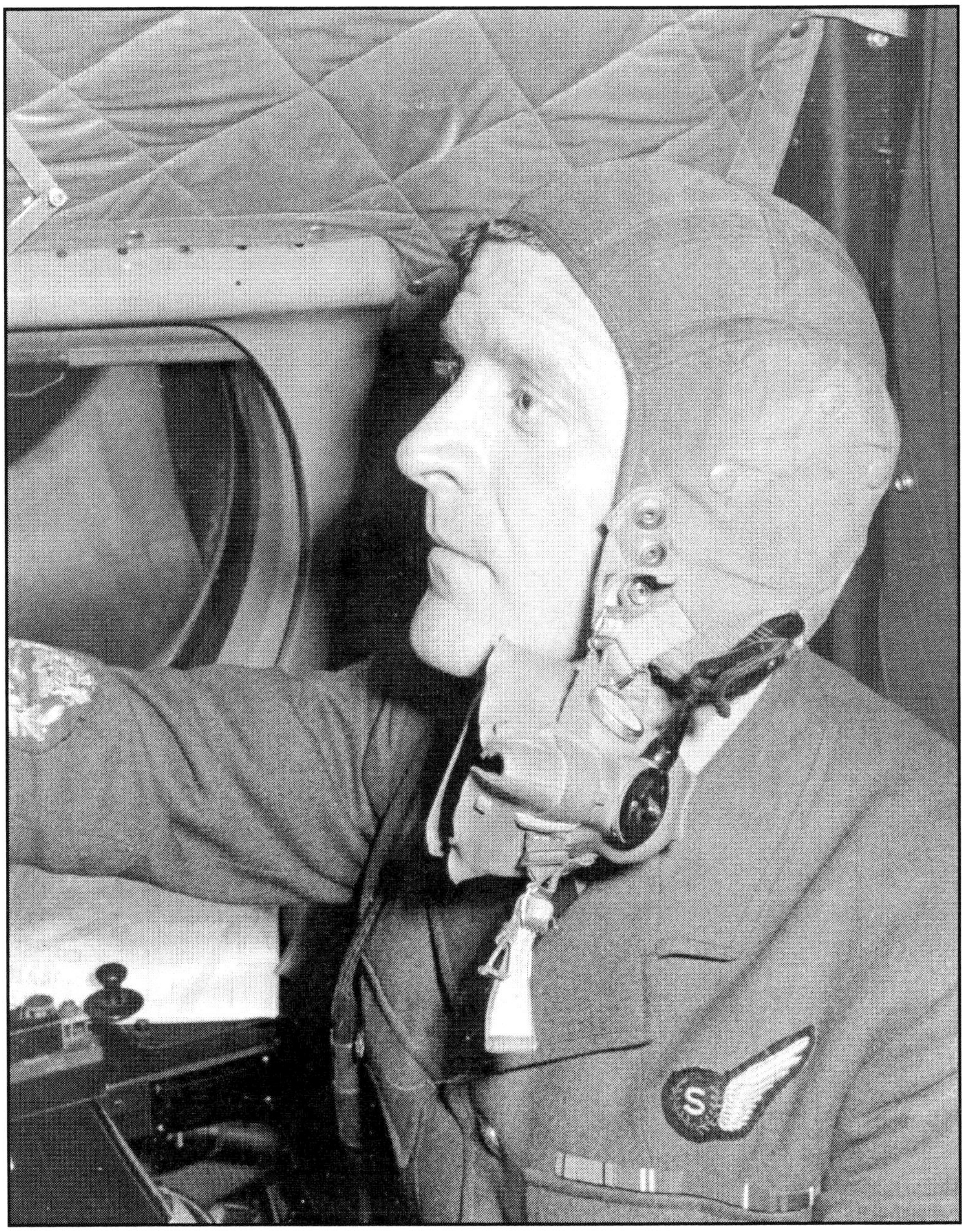

Master Signaller Bob Aindow models the 'blue bag' and oxygen mask as he adjusts his HF radio equipment. The Morse key can be seen beneath his arm. Bob is wearing 'Best Blue'. As this was an early photograph then wearing this uniform was a matter of choice (Bob was a very smart Warrant Officer). The fleet did go through a spell later where No.1 uniform was compulsory wear for route flying - an astonishing thing on reflection. (*Bill Robinson*)

helmet from the existing aircrew protective helmet (the 'Bone Dome')! This provided the earphones. The microphone was in an oxygen mask! It is unbelievable that we flew for hours and hours, all over the world, surrounded by the very latest in aeronautical technology, with a blue cloth bag on our heads and our mouths and noses covered by a ghastly rubber device. It was many years before we were issued with the more conventional airline type lightweight headset.

To return to the original coveted headpieces; those of us lesser mortals did have the occasional recompense. The cushioning of the earphones against the head was achieved with a grease inside a soft plastic shroud. These would fail occasionally and there would be a trickle of warm oil down the wearer's neck!

**Praise from 'Bing'**

The previous chapter concluded with a congratulatory message from the Lyneham Station Commander; this one continues with another, which appeared in mid-January, and this time from the Commander-in-Chief Transport Command, Air Marshal Sir Kenneth Cross KCB CBE DSO DFC:

*'We are now approaching a lull in the sustained airlift to Cyprus which, for Lyneham, has meant a continuous effort since Christmas Eve. Congratulations to all ranks on completion of tasks as planned and ordered.'*

Wing Commander Paul Barber, OC 99 Squadron, escorts the Commander-in-Chief Transport Command, Air Marshal Sir Kenneth Cross KCB CBE DSO DFC, into the squadron headquarters.

Yes, the dreaded had happened again, just as everyone was anticipating the Christmas break, there was trouble demanding the services of RAF Lyneham. Fighting had again broken out between the Greek and Turkish communities in Cyprus and six Army units and three armoured car squadrons were flown out.

**More troubles**

East Africa was another trouble spot. Towards the end of January there was a call for troops to Nairobi due to local forces' mutinies. The lift initially involved 12 aircraft and numerous slip crews and a good deal of standbys in a familiar location, the Spread Eagle Hotel just outside Nairobi. This was an old hunting lodge style place that had seen better days.

**Belfast recruits**

Things were progressing with the RAF's giant Belfast freighter at the Shorts factory at Belfast. The maiden flight was around this time. Some Britannia people were being ear-marked for the first courses on the aircraft; but this was to prove a frustration for them as there were to be many delays in its introduction into service.

**216 Rescue**

*'The 'Daily Express' reported: 'Earl Mountbatten, Chief of the Defence Staff, flew to Bahrain yesterday from*

Britannia 635 alongside a Beverley on the pan at RAF Khormaksar. (*Bill Robinson*)

This photograph of the swimming pool at The Spread Eagle Hotel, just outside Nairobi, does give rather a false picture. It was not an elegant place. (*Ian Partridge*)

*London Airport in a RAF **Comet** for a two-week visit to Delhi, Rangoon, Colombo and Aden. Contrary to normal practice, No.511 **Britannia** Squadron will not sue the National Press for libel. All crew members' wives can accept this statement as fact and that their husbands were not AWOL for 15 days.*

*'Special Flight No.1003 departed London Airport on schedule and duly arrived at Delhi on January 25th. All civilised persons, realising the importance of the date, do not need to be told that Burns' Night was duly celebrated. Taff MacEdwards, resplendent in the kilt, stabbed the imported haggis. Hooting and roaring continued to the 'weesma' hours' and tribal dancing was accompanied by the engineers' answer to Jimmy Shand. (Note for Paddy Tougher ... 'A Wild Colonial Bhoy' was not written by the BARD.)*

*'Next day - Indian Republic Day - saw a chastened crew attend the parade in near freezing temperatures and a little difficulty was encountered in convincing some members that the parading elephants were not of the pink variety. Rangoon was the next stop with the crew accommodated in luxurious surroundings. Cultural visits were made to the Shwe Dagon Pagoda (10th wonder of the world - 5,000 golden rivets) and sundry more mundane places of entertainment. Thanks to the Burmese Government for making this a most enjoyable stay.*

There are many Britannia route moments that go unrecorded - which perhaps is just as well! But here we have the kilted Taff Edwards stabbing the haggis. (*Lyneham Globe*)

*'February 1st and 'all hands to the pumps' for a quicky to Colombo. Here again the crew were living in tropical luxury whilst being entertained by members of the British community ably led by Mr. and Mrs. Alex Hogg, who incidentally extend a welcome to any visiting RAF crews. The trip ended with two days in the relaxing atmosphere of Merrifield House with all crew members taking it easy and thinking ... it must be Hell on Comets - but, nevertheless, making London Airport on scheduled time of 061430.'*

**Another faraway aeromed**

Another call came for an aeromedical flight in February and an aircraft with a double crew flew direct to Accra in Ghana, in 11¼ hours to collect a dangerously ill

This photograph is unidentified but could it be of the Britannia in support of the three Victors on their way to New Zealand for participation in RNZAF Day?

When it came time for a crew to relax, shorts and 'flip flops' (with the occasional 'desert boot') became '*de rigueur*'. (*Ann Bihan née Culliford*)

Army officer. His condition deteriorated even further on the return flight and he had to be transferred to a hospital in Malta. A more glamorous task, in the same month, was the support of three Victors to New Zealand for participation in RNZAF Day and a display at the opening of Napier Airport.

**Frustrated westabout**

In May 1964 it was planned that the Westabout Route to the Far East, surveyed the previous year, be now tested. The scenario imagined was that six Britannia loads were urgently required in the Far East and overflights of various Middle East countries had been prohibited to us. The plan was that two aircraft would position slip crews and ground crew plus equipment at Thule, Greenland; Elmendorf, Alaska; Midway and Guam islands. The lift would then start with the six aircraft leaving at two hourly intervals. Marked on a map, the staging posts looked like stepping stones to the Far East so, not inappropriately, the exercise was given the title of 'Travelling Causeway'.

All was set. The first positioning aircraft had just arrived at Thule, full of the air and ground crews, when the word came, 'Go no further, return to base!' The exercise was cancelled. Troops were required in Aden.

**A correction**

This account of the cancellation, in the first edition of this book, was challenged by Group Captain Frank Appleyard who is in a strong position to disagree ... and add extra colour ...

*'As the Flt Cdr Ops 511 Squadron tasking 'Travelling Causeway' I was deputed to set up the Westabout slip at Thule, Elmendorf, Midway and Guam - I was destined for Midway (I do not have the precise timings or dates as I deadheaded for Midway). We duly dropped two crews at Thule and, not as recorded in 'The Whispering Giant in Uniform', received a recall but continued to Elmendorf.*

*'Some four hours before departure for Midway I received a call from Base Ops - 'Contact the station commander at Lyneham soonest.' I duly got in touch with the transatlantic operator in New York (no SSB in those days), a chatty lady who asked what an Englishman was doing in Alaska. I replied that I was accompanied by ten Brit*

other attachments always excite interest and curiosity. He has, and his Vauxhall estate car is a self-contained amateur radio station, call sign G3PRR/M.

Sgt. Partridge is seen checking the loading coil on his giant car aerial; this device enables him to gain the maximum efficiency from the aerial when transmitting. Sgt. Partridge has found that "doing it himself" has helped him in his work as Air Signaller by making the connection between radio theory and practice more easily grasped.

There were a number of signallers who carried their professional activities over to the hobby zone. Here Sgt Ian Partridge, 99 Squadron, adjusts the aerial on his car which doubled as a mobile radio station. (*Lyneham Globe*)

*crews seeking to recolonise America! After a further five minute discourse on the weather et al she passed me on to a plummy London transatlantic operator who sought my destination, I replied Bradenstoke 261 (or whatever). A few moments later the call was answered and I asked for the station commander. A broad northern male voice asked what number was I seeking? I deduced that all was not well and stated that I was calling from Alaska and required a Bradenstoke number, namely Lyneham. With that he replied that I had been connected to Brackenhurst 261 in Cheshire and hollered 'Mother come quickly, I've got a chap from Alaska on the phone and he wants Lyneham, isn't that in the South?' Having assured him that I was well aware of the location of Lyneham, I managed to persuade him to replace the receiver and started anew. Eventually I raised Lyneham and asked for the station commander. Alasdair Steedman was at a drinks party in MQs and he implored me to return without delay. I explained that we were about to depart for Midway and suggested, with tongue in cheek, a return 24 hours hence. He replied that an emergency had arisen in the proximity of Neddy's bar and it was imperative that the force should return soonest; security did not permit further details over an open line.*

*'The problem that I faced was that the two Elmendorf slip crews were likely to*

MAY 8th 1964

# SWINDON HONOURS LYNEHAM

## *Borough presents us with Freedom of Entry*

TODAY a ceremony took place in Swindon that linked R.A.F. Lyneham more closely than ever to the Borough. We were presented with the Freedom of Entry to the Borough by His Worship the Mayor of Swindon.

### Defence Minister

The parade was a glittering occasion held on a windy cloudy spring day and was attended by the Minister of Defence for the Royal Air Force, the Rt. Hon. Hugh Fraser, M.P., who addressed the parade, as did His Worship the Mayor and Group Captain Steedman. The Queen's Colour Squadron of the R.A.F., and the Central Band brought the number on parade to over 700.

### March Through Town

After parading the Queen's Colour for the Royal Air Force in the United Kingdom, and the Squadron standards, our newly-granted "right, liberty, honour and distinction for all time of marching through the streets of the Borough of Swindon on all ceremonial occasions with bands playing, drums beating, bugles sounding, bayonets fixed and colours flying." was exercised.

Watched by the Rt. Hon. Hugh Fraser, M.P., Minister of Defence for the Royal Air Force, and by Air Marshal Sir Kenneth Cross, C.-in-C. Transport Command, His Worship the Mayor of Swindon, Ald. C. W. J. Streetly, presents the Freedom Scroll, in its casket, to the Station Commander. *(By courtesy of Wiltshire Newspapers Ltd.)*

Cpl. Menges is watched b...

The Lyneham Globe reports the granting of the Freedom of Swindon to RAF Lyneham. (*Lyneham Globe*)

*be savouring the delights of downtown Anchorage. I had already enjoyed a morning's round of golf and had failed to persuade a large black military gent in a punt retrieving balls to return one that I had splashed into the lake - '$1 from the Pro shop,' was the reply! I began to think that this was not my day. However the USAF MPs and the local police turned up trumps as they roamed the town with their bullhorns instructing all RAF personnel to return to base and report to their respective captains. In the event only one crew member was adrift, an AQM who it was subsequently learned had been fast asleep in his room but no one had checked; he returned by civil air. Having selected four navs for the Polar run home and alerted Thule that we would be picking up the slip crews our next problem was fuel. Together with a gaggle of our flight engineers I went to the flight line to be advised that the local fuel specific gravity was such that we required more than full tanks for the return to Thule. Despite our protestations that this could not be so, we were assured that this was the case. With no resolution in sight I elected, with the support of the two captains, for full tanks suggesting that a soft landing on arrival would be prudent and we left Elmendorf with fuel spewing on to the tarmac, On arrival at Lyneham we were met by the station commander and the respective Ops Officers, Jim Creswell for the 511 crews, and given take-off times for Aden some 16 hours hence. I was more fortunate as I received a 20-hour turnround. Having carried out a gear check of the two aircraft and checked a sample of the fuel that brought home it was established that we were in excess of 10,000 lbs overweight at Thule!'*

This author's defence was:

*'Much of TWGIU is written from personal experience with the inevitable memory failures brought about by senile*

COMMENT!—Ed.

ENJOYING swimming in Nassau, Bahamas, are (left to right) Fg. Off. Bernie Renyard of Hilsea, Portsmouth; Cpl. Tech. Tony Davis of Wootton Bassett, Wilts.; Ch. Tech. Bob Gibson of Kenilworth, Worcs., and Sgt. Edward Abbott of Bacup, Lancs. They were part of the crew of an R.A.F. Britannia which transported troops from the U.K. to Nassau.

There the troops transferred planes to continue their journey to British Honduras where they are to relieve their regiment. The Britannia crew are all from the R.A.F. station at Lyneham, Wilts.

*Caption from Frank O'Shanohun Associates Limited; photo from Bahamas News Bureau.*

**Lyneham School Fete**
*Saturday, 29th June*

The caption reads: *'Enjoying swimming in Nassau, Bahamas, are (left to right) Fg Off Bernie Renyard of Hilsea, Portsmouth; Cpl Tech Tony Davis of Wootton Bassett, Wilts; Ch Tech Bob Gibson of Kenilworth, Worcs and Sgt Edward Abbott of Bacup, Lancs. They were part of the crew of a RAF Britannia which transported troops from the UK to Nassau. There the troops transferred planes to continue their journey to British Honduras where they are to relieve a regiment ...'* (*Bahama News Bureau*)

*decay. I was at Thule when the exercise was cancelled but, clearly (now), I was a member of the two slip crews dropped off!'*

**Freedom!**

In May the Borough of Swindon acknowledged its long association with RAF Lyneham by granting the station 'Freedom of Entry'. Windy Deere remembers the occasion well:

*'Peter Ustinov once remarked that to many Americans, freedom meant being able to sit out on the front porch in one's pyjamas whilst drinking beer straight from the can. It would therefore be difficult to explain to our North American cousins that being allowed to march down the High Street with bayonets fixed and bands playing was anything other than a full scale insurrection and had little connection with the concept of freedom - except perhaps to rape and pillage. Way back in 1964 the Mayor and council of Swindon decided to take a chance on the raping and pillaging bit and offered to grant the Freedom of the Town to the Station Commander and merry men of Royal Air Force Lyneham.*

*'At that time my life was divided in roughly equal amounts between family affairs in Melksham and Squadron affairs far away from Wiltshire, and it is doubtful if I would have ever been aware of the forthcoming honour had not John Bourn informed me one morning that we were*

Photographic evidence that the flypast took place! (*Vic Merrill*)

*going to try something different. I immediately cast a wary eye upon him, but as he wasn't wearing lipstick or swinging a handbag things looked fairly safe. 'We are being given the freedom of Swindon and we've got to do a bit of formation practice,' he said. I couldn't quite grasp the connection. 'Let's do the flying and go and have a beer in the mess afterwards. I don't fancy driving all the way to Swindon,' I replied. 'No no, WE'RE not getting the bloody freedom, the Station is, and what WE'VE got to do is find some way of appearing overhead the ceremony leading a respectable formation at the exact time that 'is Worship is doffing 'is cloth cap to the Colours.'*

*'So off we took and according to my log book spent an hour in I know not what degree of peril, while one or more Britannia pilots in the accompanying aircraft brushed up on formation skills they had foolishly believed were no longer necessary. Five days later, on the 6th May the exercise was repeated, with the addition of working out a flying pattern and timing procedure that held some promise of delivering the aircraft at the right place at the right time and in the right order. The responsibility for this part of the proceedings lay heavily upon my navigation table and my shaky 'B' cat. The procedure was basically to take off, take the accompanying aircraft under our wing, so to speak, and proceed to a holding area about ten miles from Swindon. On a signal from the ground we had x minutes and y seconds to appear in all our glory at the appointed time and place.*

*'One can appreciate that success was very much dependant on exact timing, taking into account wind velocity and position in the holding pattern at the time of receiving the 'go'. We worked on that second session for two hours and forty minutes and presumably ironed out most of the problems. The signal to start the procedure was received from Lyneham ATC in response to a signal they received from an observer close to the action on the ground. This was the year 1964 and the boffins had by then developed quite efficient portable VHF equipment, so it was reasonable to assume that the time lapse between the signal being sent from Swindon and us receiving it was at the most, ten seconds, and this was allowed for in our calculations.*

*'The final practice was on the following day, in conjunction with some sort of rehearsal in Swindon. We took up our position in the holding pattern and at the signal from ATC commenced the procedure, timing the turns and routing to the parade location to the second. Everything seemed to go pretty well, for there were no complaints, and everyone appeared satisfied with the method and the result. My sleep that night was untroubled by thoughts of impending disaster on the following day, D-day.*

*'At 1515 hours on 8th May we took off in Britannia 489 and went into the act that we had been practising with such diligence, and which would demonstrate to the spectators that not only were we good at rushing Pongos to the world's trouble spots, but we could put on a pretty good demo of flying skill and superb timing when the occasion demanded. As it turned out things did work out quite well, although I think our timing was out by a few seconds.*

*So that's the little story of our flypast. Oh, just one more thing. That sophisticated VHF I was talking about. There wasn't one! The signalling system was thus: a gentleman stood close to the front of the spectators holding a white hanky. Just about within sight was a public telephone booth outside which a second gentleman stood*

It did seem that 'if a girl wanted to stay single' then the job not to have was PA to the Station Commander. We have already seen that Mike Joyce snapped up Anne Ibbotson. Now 99 navigator Robin Geach marries Joy Batterton. (*Lyneham Globe*)

NOVEMBER 6th 1964

LYNEHAM WEDDING

Flt. Lt. R. C. Geach, R.A.F. and Fg. Off. E. J. Batterton, W.R.A.F.

The wedding took place on Saturday, 17th October, at St. Michael's Church, Lyneham of Robin only son of Mrs. E. Geach, Bourne Close, Twyford, Winchester, and Joy only daughter of Major and Mrs. A. E. Batterton, Glenmore, Crieff, Perthshire, Scotland.

NEW EAST MED. MET. SYSTEM

*with two pennies clutched in his sweaty hand. At a particular stage of the parade the chap with the hanky waved it in the direction of the man by the kiosk, who then used his two pennies to phone ATC. He was presumably at the head of the queue for the telephone, for in the fullness of time we got the message. Two things come to mind; firstly, it could have come to pass that later that day three mystery aircraft flew over a deserted town square, and secondly, I just hope that the chap who worked that system out didn't get posted to an Early Warning Station.'*

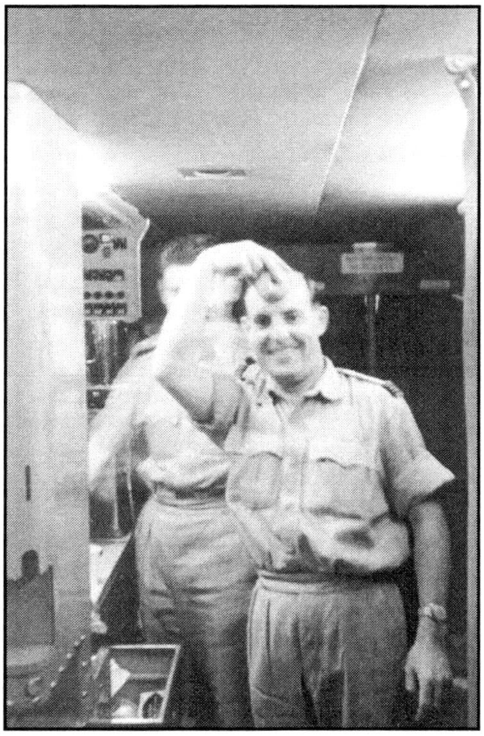

Why signaller Flt Lt John Baxter is holding up this apple is lost in those mists of time - once more. The location is a Britannia galley. (*Malcolm Fraser*)

**The other side of the coin**

With every 'flying' story there is often a 'ground' side. Ex-99 captain Guy Eddy also remembers the Swindon Freedom occasion:

*'Reading Windy Deere's account of the flypast for the 'Freedom of Swindon' caused me to recall the other side of the event.*

*'The selection of the officers who would be involved in the parade followed the usual RAF procedure.The halt and the lame were in a strong position and were not considered. Many others in positions of power convinced the powers-that-be that they could not be spared for the training period. Those of us without adequate excuse were duly required to report to the Lyneham gymnasium in our No.1 uniform to be looked over by the OC Admin. I was a fairly junior copilot on 99 Squadron at the time, not long having arrived from 'taking the cloth' at Jurby. Therefore my No.1 was still quite pristine, which was more than could be said about some of the No.1s worn by other squadron members who had also failed to find a way to escape selection.*

*'This initial selection was followed by sword drill, and for this we were spread out more than a sword and arms' length apart. A wise precaution, because it was*

This is the scene with a full load of troops on board. Some of the lack of long range definition in the photograph could be due to the amount of cigarette smoke in the air! (*Malcolm Fraser*)

The photo caption reads: *Flt Lt Peter Collins (99 Squadron) is seen above at Kuching with the Rt Hon Hugh Fraser, MP, Minister of Defence for the RAF, on a recent tour of the Middle and Far East. Flt Lt Collins flies many VIP trips ('club' subscription up-to-date) and his passengers have included the Chief of Defence Staff and the Chief of the Air Staff. His Queen's Commendation for Valuable Services in the Air was announced in the Birthday Honours List.* (*Lyneham Globe*)

It was noted that 99 Squadron 'hogged' this particular Honours List with a MBE, to add to his BEM, for Warrant Officer Maurice Flynn, Squadron Adjutant and AOC-in-C's Commendations for Flt Lt D L Hancock (Nav), M Eng Chuck Curran, MAQM George Ryder and M Sig Ernie Steele.

MINDEFRAF AND QUEENCOMMENDEE

CHURCH ... LYNEHAM
Tel. BRADENSTOKE 262

Flt. Lt. Peter Collins is seen above at Kuching with the Rt. Hon. Hugh Fraser, M.P., Minister of Defence for the R.A.F., on a recent tour of the Middle and Far East. Flt. Lt. Collins flies many V.I.P. trips ("club" subscription up-to-date), and his passengers have included the Chief of Defence Staff and the Chief of the Air Staff. His Queen's Commendation for Valuable Services in the Air was announced in the Birthday Honours List.

ARE YOU

SEND...

*pretty hazardous; there were a few Errol Flynns on show! Further selection went on over the coming weeks, during which we got to know just how many steps it took to march around the gym, with the sword at the 'Draw'. There was one final qualification for the ground force which modesty makes me hesitate to mention. We needed to be 'Steely Eyed' fighting men, so that we would impress the populace when we marched through Swindon. Practice and preparation went on for weeks and finally the allotted the day arrived.*

*'The parade was to take place in Victoria Park, Swindon. We managed to form up in good order despite having to march on grass which really is a pain because you can't hear your footsteps, and so it is difficult to keep the timing right. The Parade progressed in good order, the Band played, we presented, the Scroll was presented and accepted, and those daring young men in their flying machines flew immaculately past.*

*'Then the real object of the exercise began for us. We marched past the Mayor and High Ranks on the saluting base and out into the street. Led by the RAF Band, there were I think, three columns of airmen with rifles and fixed bayonets, each supported by officers with drawn swords. We marched along Station Road, up Regent Street and back down Commercial Road and finally back to Victoria Park again. I might have been over optimistic or just feeling tired but I felt sure the spectators*

*seemed to swell with pride as this display of defensive might marched past. All in all the parade and march through the streets took nearly two hours.*

*'At the end of the march there was one more moment of tension; when the order was given, 'Officers will replace swords'. It must be remembered that we had been marching with sword at the 'Draw' for over an hour. I was beginning to hate the thing, stuck out in front like a stick of rhubarb, elbow jammed into the side, and rigor mortis beginning to set in. It wasn't a classic drill movement but we managed it without drawing blood or doing ourselves a serious mischief.*

*'Finally it was back to Lyneham by coach and a well earned drink with those brave flying men who had endured the rigours of the fly-past. Needless to say they were doing nicely.'*

**Aden bother**

There was the continuing trouble in the Aden theatre, which was to last many years and lead to our eventual withdrawal. Rebel tribesmen in the Radfan area of the Western Aden Protectorate, encouraged and supplied by the Yemenis across the border and the Egyptians, were challenging the authority of the Federal government with the aim of enforcing the British withdrawal and the collapse of the South Arabian Federation. Continual reinforcement made RAF Khormaksar the most active and congested RAF station of the day.

This blighted spot was very familiar to Britannia crews. We have seen how it was, at this time, the standard staging post for the Far East route. There were also many supply flights specifically for the area and, on top of all this, the often called for aforementioned short notice reinforcement flights. We certainly seemed to spend an awful lot of time there.

**BG again**

British Guiana reappeared on the Britannia scene in May. During these years, civil unrest had only been kept marginally at bay with the presence of British troops. Once again reinforcements were needed as the Government was threatened. Five aircraft were required for the lift.

**'If at first ...'**

Clearly there was some determination about 'Travelling Causeway' as it was relaunched in July. All was placed in position and the six aircraft departed Lyneham at the two hourly intervals. In spite of the distances involved, the complicated organisation and the unfamiliar routes and staging posts, five of the aircraft arrived in Singapore within 15 hours of each other. The sixth had a propeller fault and was delayed on Midway.

Navigator Eric Mortlock standing guard at the British Trade Fair in Copenhagen outside one of the many Britannia Inns of this world. (*Lyneham Globe*)

I was the copilot of that lame aircraft. Ignoring the fact that it was occupied by the US Navy, but very low key, Midway was truly a Pacific island paradise. A spare propeller had to be flown to us and then fitted; so in all we spent six days there. One of the more enjoyable delays.

Frank Appleyard also had a second shot:

*'Come July, I was off yet again with Dickie Collins to Midway and I well recall the 'Gooney Birds', tiresome beasts getting in everyone's way, but the local rules did not permit giving them a boot. A sad sight was the attempt of some of the young birds trying to get airborne; the successful ones soared away if somewhat ungainly, others splashed into the lagoon. There they lay helpless as the off-shore breeze slowly drifted them over the reef where they were devoured by the waiting sharks who clearly knew that Albatross was*

*on the menu. We were well received at Andersen, Guam by the resident personnel and with a magnificent golf course - fairways like our greens, what more could one ask for on a delayed route trip?'*

**Confrontation**

So far, in 1964, the Britannia sensor of the state of world affairs had reacted to troubles in Cyprus, East Africa, Aden and British Guiana. It was now to respond to the situation in Malaysia. Indonesia opposed the formation of Malaysia with the merging, in 1963, of Sarawak and North Borneo with Malaya and Singapore. Indonesian President Sukarno declared a 'Crush Malaysia' policy which developed into 'Confrontation', a military and economic harassment. Starting with guerrilla raids of Sarawak and Sabah, there followed, in September 1964, landings of small units in Malaya. This resulted in a massive reinforcement of the British Forces which occupied almost the entire effort of the Britannia fleet.

**Instant VIP pilot**

It was thus that Flt Lt George Luckins, an experienced pilot but, then, a new Britannia captain, found himself rocketed to VIP crew status first time out of the UK. Totally caught up in the reinforcement and the crew slipping involved, he had, between 8th and 18th September, flown Lyneham, El Adem, Khormaksar, Gan, Tengah (Singapore), Butterworth (Malaya), Changi. He found himself on the 20th ...

*'... with a load of VIP Army Generals, Field Marshals and what have you ... Changi to Labuan (North Borneo), Labuan to Port Moresby (New Guinea) around the edge of an Exclusion Zone. Had a huge booze-up at the Returned Servicemen's League ... the Britannia was the biggest aircraft that they had ever had at Port Moresby at that time.'*

I note from my log book that I flew 75 hours in that September mostly oscillating between Khormaksar, Gan and Changi. It was an all-out effort.

**NATO Defence College capitals tour**

A regular commitment for the Britannia was a task for NATO:

*'On the fine sunny afternoon of 8th October last Britannia, flight No.1042 left Lyneham for Paris, Le Bourget, to position for the last of the NATO Defence College tours of the Northern Capitals of Europe. Tech Wing had run fresh out of Mk2 Britannias, but by a fine effort had produced a Mk1 roled for VIP work - an aircraft that later proved to be a most reliable steed. And to keep it good and serviceable they provided Ch Tech R J King, Sgts J F Walker and C Frith. This bright little servicing team not only kept the show on the road but also acted as guides and general advisors for everything from currency notes to nocturnal excursions. 511 Squadron provided the crew captained by Flt Lt J A Boardman; Copilot, Flt Lt G Reith; Navigator, Flt Lt G E Mortlock; Signaller, M Sig C F Manning; Engineer, F/Sgt C J Regan; Air Quartermasters, Flt Sgt J M Tweedie, Sgts B F C Mills and E Abbott.*

*'The NATO Defence College is in Paris and the Commandant, Lieutenant-General Wolf Graf Von Baudiss and his staff of deputies and Faculty advisors offer a course of some six months duration to officers of the three arms of service in all NATO countries and to some civilians who are executive administrators in NATO Governments. As the Commandant explained, each country has much to offer in its way of life and its culture. The range of economies and types of industry, the political and social problems vary so much between member countries that the lectures given at the college are best illustrated by visits such as this ... 'see and you may understand'. After a pleasant evening and following morning exploring Paris 1042 departed with its valuable cargo to Brussels for the weekend. Continental cities provide an exciting blend of the old and the starkly modern architecture. Brussels was brisk and bustling and offered a most elegant shopping centre with some fabulous window displays. Belgium was, like Britain at that time, in the throes of choosing a new Government. Citizens there are required by law to vote with dire penalties for those who fail to do so.*

*'Brussels was left to do its voting and on Sunday, 10th October, 1042 touched down at Walm airport, Cologne. There a leaking propeller blade seal curtailed a visit to Cologne and in order to meet the scheduled departure on the following day, a rapid three-engined ferry to base was made and the Monday morn saw 1042 back on the parking bay at Wahn - as if nothing had*

*happened. Tech. Wing had 'dropped everything' and had done a prop change in record time. Next stop was Hanover, a fair city. There the college and the crew were guests of the German Army at the Ratskeller in the lovely town of Celle. They were introduced to a fiery fluid called Ratsputz, which stretched the neck muscles and cured ulcers. It was a jolly evening.*

*'After two days at home, during which College members toured London, a flight was made to Renfrew, the approach to which was strongly reminiscent of the old 31 runway at Hong Kong and about as short. A bonny brace of Scottish pipers greeted the arrival of the Britannia and members went off to Holy Loch to see the submarines. 1042 was piped off to Copenhagen that afternoon. Here the copilot made friends with the 'little mermaid' and the rest of the crew went on a tour to - Elsinore, home of the mythical though immortal Prince Hamlet. Copenhagen proved to be an exhilarating place. Danny Kaye was fully justified in singing of it. The next stop was Oslo, home of the Kon-Tiki and the old Viking ships. There the kindly air force provided a vehicle for a day's tour and the sun shone its approval. Then to The Hague ... another fine shopping centre but by now the imprest was a little low and so back to Paris and a fond farewell to the passengers. A quick skip through London Airways brought us back and to reality once more.'*

Group Captain Butcher, the CO of RCAF Trenton, disembarks at Lyneham from his Yukon for a visit in 1964. (*Lyneham Globe*)

**Canadian friends**

In the 1960s there were regular liaison visits between RAF Lyneham and RCAF Trenton. The common factor was the latter's Yukon aircraft - a very close relative of the Britannia. An Internet item spells out

A visiting Yukon on the pan at Lyneham. (*David Guest*)

this relationship:

*'In January 1957 the Canadian government announced plans for a fleet of long range transports based on the Bristol Britannia. Shortly thereafter, Canadair received a contract for eight aircraft (later increased to 12). Designated the CL-44-6 by Canadair and the CC-106 Yukon by the RCAF, the new type would have Bristol Orion turboprop engines.*

*'Detailed design had already started when, on February 24, 1958, Canadair advised the RCAF that the British Ministry of Supply was unable to support the development of two new engines, the Orion and the Rolls-Royce Tyne, and had dropped its interest in the Orion. This forced a switch to the lower-powered Tyne.*

*'The Yukon design used modified Argus wing and tail surfaces and a redesigned landing gear to handle higher weights. The fuselage was similar to the Britannia 300, or 3.76 m (12 ft. 4 in.) longer than the Britannia 100. It was pressurized and had cargo doors front and rear on the left side. The Yukon could carry 134 passengers and a crew of nine. In the casualty evacuation role it could take 80*

RAF Group Captain Steedman shows RCAF Group Captain Butcher the Britannia Dock. (*Lyneham Globe*)

OCTOBER 9th 1964

WE COVER THE MED

Extension of Mediterannean Air Transport



Passengers boarding the Britannia aircraft of the first East Med. schedule captained by Wing Commander Brownlow.

ON October 2nd, the first regular flight from Lyneham to the Eastern Mediterranean left on schedule. This service is an extension of the West Med. route, operating

Passengers boarding the Britannia for the first East Med schedule captained by Wing Commander Brownlow. (*Lyneham Globe*)

*patients and a crew of 11; and in the cargo role it could carry 27,562 kg (60,763 lb.) for 5,043 km (2,723 nm).*

*'The first Yukon made its maiden flight on November 15,1959, and the first aircraft was delivered to the RCAF on June 9, 1961. In service, the Yukons performed well. In December 1961, a Yukon set a world record for its class when, on the last leg of a round-the-world flight, it flew 10,860 km (6,750 mi.) from Tokyo to Trenton, Ontario, in 17 hours three minutes, at an average speed of almost 640 km/h (400 mph). In July 1962 a Yukon remained airborne for 23 hours 51 minutes.*

*'The RCAF retired its Yukons in April 1971, selling 11 remaining aircraft and spares for $1.1 million Cdn. Canadian type approval for its use as a civil cargo transport was granted in March 1974, and several foreign operators operated them for a number of years. The sole surviving Yukon, the last of 12 Canadair delivered to the RCAF, is presently at Guayaquil, Ecquador though rumours persist that it may be returned to Canada.'*

So, to the end, the Yukon's history is very similar to the RAF Britannia's.

John Hanson unearthed an alarming Yukon/CL-44 statistic:

*'... according to the Aviation Safety Network, fully 20 of the 39 Yukon/CL-44s were destroyed in accidents between 1966 and 2002 ...'*

**Errand of Mercy**

On lst November, a Britannia flown by a 511 crew, was diverted into Ratmalana, Ceylon, to pick up a young Ceylonese boy, the son of an Inspector of Schools. The boy was ill with some rare form of cancer. After the local doctors had done all they could in the way of treatment, they contacted a specialist in London and asked for help. Owing to the unusual medical aspects of the case, the British Ministry of Health agreed to provide free treatment both for humanitarian reasons and in the interests of medical research. Transport Command was asked if they could have the boy picked up and fly him to England. A Britannia was diverted,complete with nursing sister.

**The Eastmed**

In October the Britannias took on the responsibility for the trooping flights to Cyprus and Malta. These flights were to be a continuous commitment for the rest of the Britannia years, three times per week, flying families on posting to and from the Eastern Mediterranean. For the first time in their lives, the three Mark 2 aircraft (XN392, XN398 and XN404) came into their own. These were the three airframes that had had a chequered start to their Service career. It has been seen that they arrived into the RAF via the Ministry of Supply, having been built to a civilian specification; the original intention was that they should be operated on our behalf by a civilian consortium. Now, having spent time alongside their compatriots, the fully military Mark 1s, their limitations had been fully realised. Although they were fitted with a freight door, the lack of a fully strengthened floor and the fact that some of the toilets and the galley were placed amidships, meant that their conversion to freight role was not practical. So, the lack of a general requirement, up to now, for a totally passenger Britannia meant that they had spent their time being used almost entirely for training and the occasional VIP flight. The advent of the 'East Med' commitment meant that the Mark 2s found a true role.

The schedule became a favourite one with crews, although there was an initial hurdle to overcome - an 11pm Lyneham departure!

**Mobility**

It had been the intention, with the modernisation and expansion of the air transport force, that a smaller Army should be made just as effective through it having the facility to be deployed rapidly by air. That this was being achieved had been amply demonstrated with the alerts of the year so far. It was confirmed in October and November with air mobility exercises to New Zealand and Barbados. The former was an exchange of British and New Zealand units. A slip service was set up through Winnipeg, Honolulu, Guam and Fiji for the destination, Whennapai, near Auckland. It is recorded that there were a number of unservicabilities for the return run in November.

Exercise 'Rum Jungle' saw the carriage of the 1st Battalion, The Worcester Regiment to Barbados to board Royal Navy ships for Dominica for jungle training.

**Quiet Christmas**

1964 was the hardest year yet for the Britannias; but there was a pleasing end, no major standby as Christmas approached. I note that I only just made it though - Akrotiri/Lyneham, 24th December!

**A postscript**

Two letters to amuse:

*RAF Khormaksar,*
*BFPO 69*
*26th September, 1964*

*Dear Sir,*

*On 9th September 1964, an inbound Britannia reported a possible bird strike on landing at Khormaksar. On doing the airfield inspection I found a dead seagull in the undershoot, not badly damaged, but very dead with a broken neck. It had obviously only just been killed. It was a ringed bird, which ring I sent to the Riksmuseum, Stockholm, from whence it had come. I asked if they would let me know where this bird had been ringed as we thought it unusual for a seagull to have found its way this far if ringed in Sweden.*

*Yesterday I had the reply, asking if I could give it any publicity as although they ringed thousands of birds they get very few rings returned. Details as follows: 8.011.667, Lesser Black Backed Gull (Lams fuscus?), ringed as a nestling 14-6-63 at Danaflot (5404N 1543 E) South of the island of Sturko near the town of Karlskrona, Blekinge, Sweden. Found dead 9-9-64 at Khormaksar, Arabia (1250N 4502E). This information was from the Officer in charge of bird ringing in Sweden-Naturhistoriska Riksmuseum, Vertebratavi Einingen, Stockholm 50.*

*As big a menace as bird strikes are to aircraft, this one certainly came a long way to meet his end, having travelled some 5,000 miles to hit an aircraft which came 3,500 or so miles!*

*Yours faithfully,*
*G. C. SCUTTS*
*(Local Controller,*
*RAF Khormaksar)*

... from The Times:

## No contest

*From Mr Michael Wilson*

Sir, Why is it that a heron (30mph, 8lb, resident) and a jumbo (600mph, 800,000lb, visitor) collide it is called a birdstrike ('Heathrow heron cripples Jumbo', September 9)? Also, your headline overlooks the rather serious injury caused to the first party.

Yours faithfully
MICHAEL WILSON
Lothian Cottage,
5 White Rose Lane,
Woking, Surrey GU22 7JA
September 10

No.511 Squadron in Spring 1964 - under the command of Wing Commander John Lewis

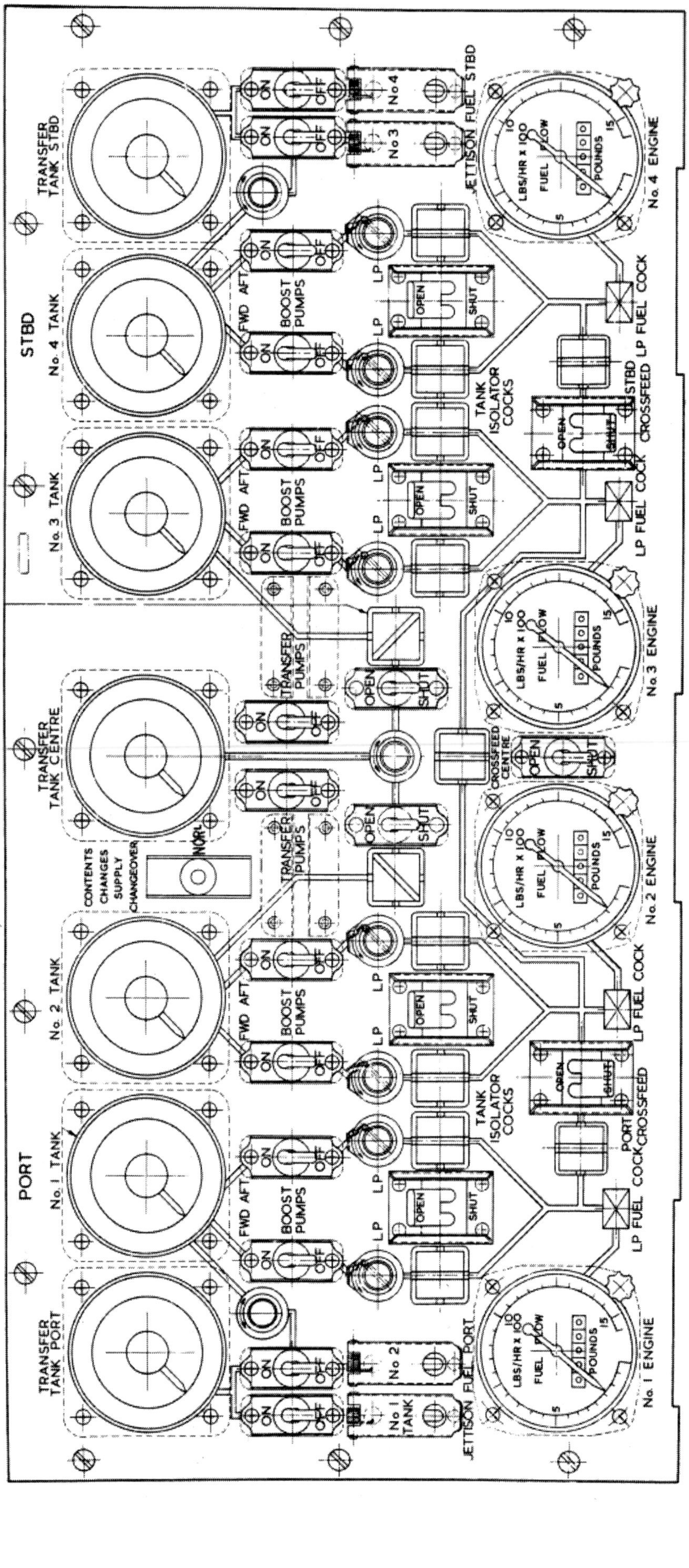


On the right arm of the copilot sat the fuel control panel - an odd situation? Not only did the engineer sit between the two pilots, sharing the engine controls, instruments and switches, but he had to manage the fuel through the remote control of the copilot's fingers!

The adventures of Messrs. Ad Minn and Org at Wootton Lynstoke continue ...

AD MINN AND ORG CONTINUE NEAR ADDLEDADE
"HI YER POMMIE!"
"THE FLYING DOCTOR I PRESUME"
"'S RIGHT BLUE —HAVE A BEER."
BUT AT.....
MADE IN BOTANY BAY
CRASH
THE BAR SHUTTERS COME DOWN.
"I ALWAYS GET A FEW FINGERS TO SET ABOUT THIS TIME."
AD MINN AND ORG FINDING NOTHING PURE IN AUSTRALIA —NOT EVEN WATER— DECIDE TO TAKE A CIVIL AIRCRAFT HOME.
"GOOD AFTERNOON —I'M THE CAPTAIN."
"HAVE A BOX OF CIGARS - EACH."
HAVANA
"LIGHT?"
"THANK YOU, WE NEVER HAD MORE THAN A DUTY FREE WOODBINE FROM THE R.A.F. CAPTAIN"
"WELL OF COURSE —UNDER HALF OUR PAY AND A TENTH OF OUR ALLOWANCES, WHAT DO YOU EXPECT!"
20

CHAPTER NINETEEN

# 1965 - Gambia, Top Cat, Sadness

The Britannia was not an easy aircraft to maintain. Many of its systems were complex and unserviceabilities obscure. By now the pool of expertise at Lyneham was well established but this had to be exported in order to maintain 'away from base' functioning. The standard routes were covered by Transport Aircraft Servicing Flights (TASF) manned in part by ex-Lyneham technicians; individual aircraft on special flights were cared for by the crew chief (ground engineer) scheme, already mentioned. In between these ends of the spectrum of flights were Operations and Exercises, possibly involving a large number of aircraft. How were these to be cared for? A Lyneham Globe contributor gives the answer:

*'Mobile Servicing Flight was formed in September 1953, consisting of four teams, each comprising one SNCO and seven men for servicing Hastings aircraft when off the normal Transport Command route. It was commanded from Transport Command Headquarters but situated at Lyneham to be available at all times. Other commitments were to assist outlying RAF Stations when their manpower was fully employed e.g. Habbaniya during the Abadan Standby when Hastings were detached there for the pending evacuation of civil personnel and Nicosia for the Suez campaign, etc.*

*'Various odd tasks were thrown to MSF e.g. damage caused to a VIP Hastings whilst flying over Turkey had to be repaired; propeller lost from a Hastings while over India causing damage; recovering engines from a crash at Khartoum, etc.*

*'The Flight operated from J3 for the first few months of its existence, using oddly enough a metal 'cage' to contain the spares, and members too, sometimes. The first change of base scene was to the old terminal outside J3 now replaced by an expanse of concrete, luckily the Flight evacuated in time to more modern accommodation, the Alloy Igloos then situated near the present site of J5.*

*'The Igloo period covered the detachments to Australia of teams to support the Montebello and Maralinga atomic epics, closely followed by the Christmas Island holiday with further bombs being dropped, this time on us, not near but with no casualties sustained. Notable among successive detachments was an exercise called Quickstep II whereby an MSF team supported a technical detachment from Abingdon to assist on Beverley aircraft flying through from Nairobi to North Africa via Entebbe, where the outfit was situated.*

*'The high point of this collaboration, which lasted nine days, was the draining completely of beer of the local European Social Club and the absolute defeat of their formerly unbeatable soccer team by our pick-up side. So great was the 'angst' in the beaten side that they hardly forbore to congratulate the victors. Their*

Sergeant Pengelly of Mobile Servicing Flight enters a route flight on his detail board. (*Lyneham Globe*)

THE LYNEHAM GLOBE—No. 145 (6)

'WE NEVER CLOSED'

A Britannia at Lyneham after the heaviest snowfall of the winter.

SPORTS REPORT Supply Squadron

The winter of 1964/65 saw some snow which must have caused some nervousness with the memory of 1962/63 still fresh in the mind. (*Lyneham Globe*)

*bitterness may have been due to the fact that all the locals were cheering the RAF and not their club!*

*'1957 saw an expansion of technical interest from the Hastings to the Beverley and Comet as major items. One or two older members had to depart during that year as working at Beverley heights induced vertigo especially after nights of alcoholic rejoicing to which many members were prone to resort to in places such as Salalah, Masirah, Sharjah and other hot spots where these aircraft operated.*

*'Until the Britannia arrived in 1957 the Flight continued in its extraordinarily varied role and met the start of Britannia operations by reducing from four teams to two. As the Britannias gradually took over main route flying from the Hastings and each Britannia going off route was accompanied by a highly trained and intelligent member of the Ground Engineers' Section (or so they would have us believe) it seemed that MSF was losing its raison d'être. But with the development of Army Air Trooping which required consistent exercising it was now evident that the Ground Engineers could not cope and so MSF came into its own once again. Exercises to El Adem, Bahrain, Kuwait, Larissa and many others proved the ever-present need for the 'Aces of the Bases'.*

*'Despite the original terms of reference for the Flight, which were mainly for overseas operations, calls for technical assistance from all over the British Isles to assist with everything from major inspections on Beverleys to assembling helicopters, were answered with immediate action and the plentiful vituperation of all, which usually comes when one is asked to fulfil an unaccustomed role.*

*'As the past has shown, Transport Command without Mobile is like beer without hops, so the members are looking forward to bigger and better things, namely VC10 and Belfast aircraft with which to continue their explorations of the more remote parts of the globe.'*

This valuable pool of technical expertise was to make its contribution to successful Britannia operations.

**MSF author**

It has been said that publicity is being given to the authors amongst the Britannia ranks. David Taylor has been mentioned already and reappears here as he spent some time with the Mobile Servicing Flight. His first book was reviewed in the Britannia

Association magazine:

*'The cover of David Taylor's book, 'A Suitcase Full of Dreams' describes it as 'An Aeronautical Journey'; the back cover tells you that David Taylor was a Boy Entrant. These are all outward signs that should tempt many ex-Britannia people to investigate further. If you do so, you will not be disappointed.*

*'It is soon evident that David is an aviation enthusiast; his keenness was initially satisfied with the Air Training Corps. It was a fairly natural progression for him to become a Boy Entrant; his trade, Instrument Mechanic (Navigation). This might seem an obscure specialisation compared with 'Engines' and 'Airframes' but it was to prove the key to the door of travel (with lots of flying) and a job for life.*

*'One charm of this book is 'What happens next?', so I will not spoil the intrigue by revealing too much here. Sufficient to say that Dave was obviously prepared to 'have a go' at whatever was available and this leads to some interesting narrative. This can be said to be highly descriptive, in parts; he is not afraid of using words to evoke a feeling for the moment: his first flight as an ATC cadet, '... the earth was down there, I was up here, up where the clouds formed, where the birds flew.'*

*'David was, for three years, an early member of Mobile Servicing Flight. Perhaps this gave him a taste for the nomadic life, for his travels thereon do not seem to have ceased and one is treated to imaginative descriptions of many parts of the world and his activities therein.*

*'The 'man in the street' would find this book an entertaining good read; ex-members of the Britannia fleet, who can relate to the author, should find it captivating.*

'*A Suitcase Full of Dreams*' by David Taylor. 345 pp, line drawings and over 60 photographs. ISBN 0 9534082 0 5. Published by Delta Tango Publications, 35 Lower Darnborough St, Clementhorpe, York YO23 1AR. Available by mail order, price £9.50 + £1.50 p&p.

**Back to work**

The previous chapter concluded by remarking on the unusual; nearly all Britannia personnel spent Christmas 1964 at home. But 1965 was not to wait long before striking. Barely 24 hours old the call came as the 'Confrontation' build-up continued and 11 flights were required to fly the Hong Kong based Gurkhas to Borneo.

**Boss change**

The New Year saw Group Captain Steedman awarded the CBE and handing over command of RAF Lyneham to Group Captain Freddy Hazlewood OBE AFC. A fitting tribute to the parting station commander is taken from a contemporaneous comment:

*'... His presence in Operations and on the apron has galvanised many crews into instant action.'*

**Freddy Hazlewood**

*The Lyneham Globe* welcomed the new Station Commander:

*'Group Captain F S Hazlewood OBE, AFC and Bar, a wartime bomber wireless operator, air gunner and coastal pilot is our new CO. Since 1962 he has been Group Captain (Operations) at Headquarters, RAF Germany. Educated at Kimbolton School, Hunts, he joined the RAF in 1939 and completed his first operational tour in Wellingtons of No.99 Squadron. In 1941 he trained as a pilot in Britain and Canada, and began a long association with Coastal Command. Joining a Wellington squadron in 1942, he flew anti-shipping and anti-U-boat strikes in the Middle East. He was commissioned in 1943 and in 1944 joined No.14 Squadron*

Someone out and about in the New Year was Master Engineer George Eastaway. '*We left Lyneham on Flight 6200 on 27th December on a routine trip to Changi. On our return we were ordered to transport a load of medical supplies to Katunayake for the relief of the Northern Province of Ceylon which had been devastated by a cyclone just before Christmas.*' (*George Eastaway*)

*(Wellingtons) in the Middle East. Soon afterwards it returned home after 24 years' unbroken service overseas and Gp Capt Hazlewood came with it, subsequently flying from RAF Chivenor, Devon, on night anti-submarine operations in Leigh Light Wellingtons.*

*'After the war he became an instructor on Lancasters and Shackletons at the Coastal Command Operational Conversion Unit, Kinloss, Morayshire. In 1951 he became Squadron Leader (Flying) at the School of Maritime Reconnaissance, RAF St. Mawgan, Cornwall. In 1954 he joined the Central Flying School Examining Wing and in 1956 took the course at the RAF Staff College, Bracknell. In 1957 Gp. Capt. Hazlewood returned to Bomber Command, flying Valiants with No.90 Squadron at Honington, Suffolk, an appointment which took him on duty to the Far East, the United States and other parts of the world. He then joined the planning staff at HQ Bomber Command. He is currently taking a conversion course on Britannias and renewing acquaintance with*

*his old squadron, No.99, which is equipped with this type.'*

Group Captain F S Hazlewood OBE AFC taking over command of RAF Lyneham from Group Captain A McK Steedman CBE DFC. (*Lyneham Globe*)

**Last African colony**

Ex-Prime Minister Harold Macmillan's 1960s 'Wind of Change' was now almost calmed. At midnight on Wednesday 17th February, the Union Jack was lowered at Bathurst in The Gambia to mark the independence of Britain's last colony in Africa. Thus Gambia, the oldest British African colony, became the 21st member of the Commonwealth. The independence ceremony was attended by the Duke and Duchess of Kent and by delegations from 32 countries. The honour of flying the Duke and Duchess to and from the ceremony fell to a 511 Squadron crew, captained by Sqn Ldr Chick Chamberlain. On arrival, they found that they were to be accommodated in the Yundum Ladies' College:

The VIP crew for the visit to Gambia by TRH The Duke and Duchess of Kent photographed on the steps of Government House. The provider of this 'treasured possession' is Master Engineer Cliff Regan who is right at the back, centre. (*Cliff Regan*)

*'This rose-coloured prospect faded, however, when it was found that the ladies had been sent on holiday!'*

**States trainers**

A mythology was to be created, and maintained over the years, that flying in the United States was difficult. Perhaps it was just a ploy to ensure the maintenance of flights with a difference, 'States Trainers'. These were a regular feature of Britannia life and the first was flown in February taking in New York and Chicago. There was a distinguished first passenger, the Chief of the Air Staff! The aircraft captain was also distinguished in his own right, Wing Commander Roy Jenkins AFC, OC 99 Squadron.

**Top Cat**

Known, with affection rather than rancour, as 'Top Cat', Wing Commander Jenkins led 99 with some style. One unusual feature for a commanding officer was that he flew constantly and in one year passed the considerable milestone of 1000 hours. Those who shared his flight deck will recall his constant aspiration to fly the Britannia as high as possible. Air quartermasters would struggle from the galley at the rear, up the steeply inclined gangway, as the aircraft hung at a high angle of attack.

Again, unusual for a CO, he held a full 'A' flying category and did his share of squadron VIP work. With any operation, exercise, detachment he would be there in the thick of it. All this perhaps gives some insight into the origin of his sobriquet!

**Distinguished flying career**

During the Second World War, Wing Commander Jenkins flew Wellingtons with Nos.8 and 621 Squadrons. From 1944 to 1947 he served with No.216 Squadron carrying out supply and glider operations in India and the Middle and Far East. Two years followed as a VIP pilot with No.24 Squadron in which time he completed over 100 flights on the Berlin Airlift. Between 1949 and 1953 Roy was the personal pilot

(5)

BRIEFING BEFORE DEPARTURE — The crew of the 511 Sqn. Britannia listen attentively to Capt. C. A. Wilson, forecaster, Det. 10, 15th Weather Sqn., McGuire AFB, N.J., as he presents them with a full picture of what they may encounter during their return journey to England. From left to right are: Flt. Lt. Fletcher, navigator; Flt. Lt. N. E. Rose, pilot; Flt. Lt. I. M. Waller, co-pilot; Flt. Lt. G. A. Salter, pilot; Capt. Wilson in foreground; and Flt. Lt. F. J. Nickson, navigator.
*Photo by courtesy of McGuire A.F.B.*

Kewnews

There was a photograph in *The Lyneham Globe* that captured the atmosphere of a Met Briefing at a USAF base during a 'States Trainer'. The caption reads:*'The crew of the 511 Squadron Britannia listen attentively to Captain C A Wilson, forecaster, Det. 10, 115th Weather Squadron, McGuire AFB, NJ, as he presents them with a full picture of what they may encounter during their return journey to England. From left to right are: Flt Lt Fletcher, navigator; Flt Lt N E Rose, pilot; Flt Lt I M Waller, copilot; Flt Lt G A Salter, pilot; Capt Wilson in foreground; and Flt Lt F J Nickson, navigator. Photo by courtesy of McGuire AFB.'*

USAF forecasters possessed the same talent as Reception Class schoolteachers - the ability to read upside down! (*Lyneham Globe*)

to the Commander-in-Chief Mediterranean Fleet. In this capacity he served for a considerable time under Earl Mountbatten of Burma and also flew HRH The Duke of Edinburgh.

Following a tour as Staff Officer to the Senior Air Staff Officer at HQ Coastal Command, he joined No.109 Squadron flying Canberra B6 aircraft. He flew the same aircraft type as Flight Commander on No.139 Squadron whose primary role was target marking. In early 1959 he flew the Chief of the Air Staff in a Canberra on a 20,000 mile tour of Near and Far East Stations.

On completion of the Andover Staff College course, he was appointed to the Operations Staff at HQ Far East Air Force. Promoted to Wing Commander in 1962, he completed the remainder of his tour in Far East Air Force Exercise Plans before taking command of No.99 Squadron in 1963.

Wing Commander Jenkins was awarded the Air Force Cross in 1949 and the Queen's Commendation for Valuable Service in the Air in 1953 and 1960. He had flown 40 types of aircraft and accumulated over 9000 hours flying. He was awarded a bar to his AFC during his command of 99. With such a record, it can be understood perhaps, why he was such a charismatic leader.

**A special VIP**

18th July 1965 saw XN404 ready for Flight 1097 to take the Chief of the Defence Staff, Earl Mountbatten of Burma, on the last official visit of his Service career. It was a little like old times as the Britannia captain was Wing Commander Jenkins. The first leg was a direct flight to Aden. Stepping from the aircraft, the CDS was greeted by a 19 gun salute, a Hunter flypast and a Guard of Honour provided by all three Services. Six hours later the VIP was being winged to the next engagement at Addis Ababa where he was to be the personal guest of His Imperial Majesty, Emperor Haile Selassie. The aircraft arrived over the airfield in an horrendous thunderstorm and it was inevitable that the 'Doors Open' time would be delayed. Later the crew were congratulated on their timing. It meant that the arrival ceremony took place during the only dry spell of the afternoon!

A very young 99 Squadron air quartermaster, Brian Jordan, remembered

**No. 511 SQUADRON**

IT'S not often we blow our own trumpet, but as a result of the efforts of 'Curly' Smith and Dickie Collins and their crews, we are justly proud of the recognition awarded us by the Ceylon Government during last month's cyclone relief operation.

A signal from the High Commissioner has been received recording his appreciation of the 'very prompt reaction' to his request for assistance. Several photographs commemorating the operation have also arrived on the Squadron. Here we show Flight Lieutenant R. M. Smith, Captain of Flt. No. 6200 with Sir Micheal Walker, K.C.M.G., and Dr. R. L. Thiruchelvam, the Director of Social Services (Ceylon).

this trip well:

*'I found myself, at a tender age, thrust into this VIP role. Being a little unsure of food presentation, I took advantage of the offer from BOAC VIP Catering to provide a cold meat plate, complete with garnishes and other frills, already laid out for serving to each person. Meal time came and I placed the BOAC creation before Lord Louis. He looked at it, turned to me and quietly said, 'You would be surprised at how many things on that plate that I do not like. Please bring me an empty one and I'll help myself.' Exit one, now much older, AQM!'*

**A troubled VIP flight**

With the reports on some VIP trips one can read between the lines and appreciate some of the anxiety that arose in trying to maintain the schedule for the passengers. 99's Flight Lieutenant Graham Bayliss and crew spent 14 days touring India and Pakistan with The First Sea Lord, Admiral of the Fleet Sir David Luce and Lady Luce on Flight No.1051. This took in Bombay, Delhi and the Taj Mahal, Karachi, Peshawar and the Khyber Pass. The next stop was Lahore where the aircraft became unserviceable and the VIPs were returned, rather ignominiously, to Karachi in a Pakistan Air Force C130. With serviceability regained, the schedule was resumed with the flight

511's correspondent wrote: *'It's not often we blow our own trumpet but, as a result of the efforts of 'Curly' Smith and Dickie Collins and their crews, we are justly proud of the recognition awarded us by the Ceylon Government during last month's cyclone relief operation. A signal from the High Commissioner has been received recording his appreciation of the 'very prompt reaction' to his request for assistance. Several photographs commemorating the operation have also arrived on the Squadron. Here we show Flight Lieutenant R M Smith, Captain of Flt. No. 6200 with Sir Michael Walker KCMG and Dr R L Thiruchelvam, the Director of Social Services (Ceylon).'* (*Lyneham Globe*)

Earl Mountbatten of Burma with the crew of XN404. Wing Commander Roy Jenkins is on the VVIP's right. Brian Jordan is on the extreme left. (*Maurice Flynn*)

from Karachi to Akrotiri and London Airport. The efforts of the flight and ground engineers, who spent many hours both at Lahore and Karachi putting the aircraft into a serviceable state, were acknowledged.

**Elevation to the peerage**

Though not of earth shattering consequence in the military aviation world, it is perhaps worthy of mention within the context of these pages that, in June, the author carried out training to convert from copilot to CAPTAIN! It was the practice, with only a few exceptions, that pilots new to the aircraft would spend between two and three years as copilots before their conversion to captain. This was sound policy. Firstly, the right hand seat had to be occupied anyway and who better to fill it than someone destined for the left hand seat. As a copilot, one was going to experience numerous places and situations and witness the operating techniques of a variety of captains and, from all this, learn a great deal.

There was an enlightened policy towards copilots in the light of this and the role that they played, in any case, in a fairly complex large aircraft. They were fully trained and tested to a standard to fly the aircraft. This statement may cause some surprise but it was not always the situation. 'Second Pilots', as they were known on previous types, were not so qualified and acted merely as the captain's assistant. Britannia copilots did their full share of the flying.

A combination of time served, proof of suitability and vacancy brought a copilot forward for conversion. He would be given three weeks of training which would adjust him to flying the aircraft from the other seat, steering and taxying (not available to the copilot in the Britannia) and additional exercises i.e. two engine approaches and landings, not practised in the right hand seat.

Having completed a sort of driving test by day and night, the fledgling returned to the squadron. There he did a route flight with an experienced captain in the right hand seat. As this would be on a route that he had undoubtedly done many times before as a copilot, it would not present many problems. The final part of the process

would be a 'Route Check' where an examiner would fly with the new captain and finally sign him up as ready to go.

My log book chronicles that I spent a short time on this latter process completing a 'screened' Lyneham to Cyprus and return flight and then being sent on a Changi Slip with the first leg as the route check to make me 'legal'. So I was now on my own. A proud moment.

**MIDAS**

The Britannia heralded a new aspect of aircraft operation - the electronic monitoring and recording of the functioning of components and systems with the aim of diagnosing and anticipating faults. The equipment went by the name of MIDAS - which is undoubtedly an acronym, the origin of which is lost in time. The November edition of the *Globe* reported that, currently, there were three Britannia aircraft flying the route with MIDAS equipment functioning and observers aboard. These aircraft were building up a library of tapes representing actual operating conditions on the aircraft and also possible patterns of failure for different components. When the aircraft landed at Lyneham, the tapes were taken to the Electronics Centre where small portions of the flight were played out in analogue form covering the whole of 270 parameters. In this way assessment of the serviceability of the MIDAS could be made.

A MIDAS tradesman then examined

By a string of coincidences associated with the first edition of this book, the author corresponded with Maureen Burbank, in Canada, who was an Assistant Air Traffic Controller at Lyneham in the 1960s. She sent the author a couple of photographs, from those days, that were taken in connection with WRAF recruiting. By what must be an incredible coincidence, Maureen spotted that one of the captain's names on the 'Inbound' movements board was 'BERRY'!
(*Maureen Burbank*)

THE LYNEHAM GLOBE—No. 150 (6)

COMMUNICATIONS ELECTRONICS SQUADRON

THE NEW MIDAS PLAY-BACK ROOM.

WITHIN the confines of the Electronics Centre and just beyond the Zantedeschia, a pair of shining swing doors, as yet unnamed, lead into the new Midas Play-back Room. Within this room you are in the realms of automation, and words like "module," transducer," "conditioning unit," etc. are the language with which chief technician talks to junior technician. From a small room in an annexe of 3.2 Midas has graduated to the air conditioned splendour of the Electronics Centre.

In October, 1964, the present records section was formed under F./S. Collins and Sgt. Adams and although the latter has ... turned to the Electrical S...

...the short space of two weeks ...were made, doors large

1,000 yards of paper and took almost a ...

The MIDAS playback equipment. (*Lyneham Globe*)

the F700 and noted all the reported aircraft defects during the flight. The relevant parameters were then played out, again in analogue form, to assess the usefulness of MIDAS in helping the diagnosis of the aircraft defects. In this way, when experience in reading the traces and recognising faults from them had been built up, the process could be reversed and the traces used to diagnose the faults. A flight to Changi took 50 hours to play out in analogue form completely and produced approximately 1,000ft.

...HOUSE IN GULF

...TEL

Also Premiums by Instalmen...

PAY AS YOU DRIVE

As you can see, the project is very ambitious, but the authorities concerned are trying to give ...

The new accommodation in Bahrain - Britannia House. (*Lyneham Globe*)

(5) MARCH 12th, 1965

DO YOU KNOW THESE MEN?

From March 8th, 1965, the advance party of Line Servicing Chiefs went into operation. Wearing orange armbands for quick recognition they advise and supervise, 24 hrs. a day, on all technical aspects of aircraft in their area. Outside their mobile office on Bay 1 are (left to right) Ch. Techs. Lowe, Hill, Horn, Bunn and Briggs.

adron

MODEL AERO CLUB

AIR TRAFFIC CONTROL

Over the years there were many experiments with technical management. This photograph marks the introduction of Line Servicing Chiefs. With their white coats and orange armbands for easy identification, they were responsible for advice and supervision of technical aspects of aircraft in their area. The names are given as Chief Technicians Lowe, Hill, Horn, Bunn and Briggs. (*Lyneham Globe*)

of paper. It was obvious that if the tape was to be run through as a quick diagnostic tool, some alternative form of presentation needed to be used. The manufacturers of MIDAS, Royston Instruments Ltd, devised such an alternative form. Briefly, the Data Processing Unit, as it was called, looked at all 270 parameters simultaneously as the tape was being played, which meant that the tape had only to be run through once (taking six minutes for a six hour flight). For each parameter there was a device called a level gate; these allowed positive outputs only if the parameter rose above a predetermined level, sank below it or rose/fell in excess of a certain rate of change.

The actual functions and the levels could be pre-set by the operator. In practice, the levels would be set at unserviceability levels dictated by previous experience. Each parameter signal was passed through its level gate and if the parameter signal had

A view from a 'Britannia House' window - the local cemetery! (*David Berry*)

Flight Lieutenant Fred Lace and crew of Britannia Flight 6225 being presented to HRH The Duke of Edinburgh by the Station Commander of RAF Changi, Group Captain B C Bennett AFC, during the Duke's visit to Singapore in February. (*Lyneham Globe*)

exceeded its unserviceability level, a code number was printed on a teleprinter. Thus the operator was presented with a piece of paper, approximately foolscap size, that told him which of the 270 parameters had exceeded their pre-set levels and the Greenwich Mean Time at which that occurred. If necessary, he could then play out the relevant parts of the tape in analogue form and from these and his experience, help with the diagnosis of the aircraft snag. The entire process from removal of the tape to the return of diagnostic information to the aircraft tradesmen could take as little as 15 minutes. These were the lines along which the MIDAS trial was progressing.

**'Britannia House'**

It will transpire that Britain will withdraw from Aden and that our presence in the Middle East be centred on RAF Muharraq, Bahrain. Perhaps, in some anticipation of this event and its use as a staging post, dedicated accommodation for transit passengers and crews was being arranged in Bahrain. 'Britannia House', as it was known, became a familiar locale for transport crews and it was opened in mid-1965. It became the 'do nothing' place. Within its confines, crews could eat, sleep (and drink) in, albeit noisy, air conditioned comfort. There was very little to attract in the heat outside.

**An apology - belated but sincere**

Ever had that situation where, with hindsight, something is blindingly obvious - but you didn't realise it at the time? Around this time in 60s, during one of the Cyprus 'spats', ex-Chief Tech Vic Merrill had that experience ...

*'I suppose almost everyone has done something, at some time, for which an apology was called for, but was not offered at the time. I comfort myself with this thought anyway. The particular incident that concerns me most occurred at Akrotiri and involves an AQM - but it wasn't my fault! This is what happened; I leave you to appreciate that I am completely innocent.*

*'It is in the 60s; the Turks and the Greeks of Cyprus are involved in another of their periodic disagreements with one another. I am sent out there with a 'turn-round' crew with the object of getting Brits refuelled, checked, loaded with evacuees and away again before the next one arrives. The passengers consist mainly of 'living out' wives and children of personnel stationed at any of the service bases on the island. Before we arrive, plans to facilitate our task are considered at Akrotiri. One of*

# "DOWN YOUR WAY" CAME L

Franklin Engelmann asking Valerie Cross for her choice of music — the B.B.C. Engineer stands at the rear.

LAST week a recording tea
the B.B.C.'s popular
programme "Down Your W
spent two days at Lyneham
paring a further edition in the

**Recorded Intervi**

Producer Richard Bur
compere Franklin Engelm
the recording engineer
station interviewing
Among those whose
pieces of musiect
heard in the Hom
don Region) inc
the West Regi
repeat today,
Commander, C
Hazelwood.

Others in t
SAC Peter Br
Air Moveme
Cross of 511
Graeme Mo
Sqn. Ldr.
Commande
216 Sqn.
on the sta

"Down
regular
17 years
Engelma
"Jingles"
called
broadca
surprise
unique
in the

The
Ter

The BBC's popular radio programme, *'Down Your Way'*, came to Lyneham in March. Here 99 Squadron ALM Val Cross is being interviewed by the compere, Franklin Engelmann. (*Lyneham Globe*)

*the ideas is to provide wireless communication between the people on the pan (us lot) with operations. This means that we don't have to race up to the offices to a phone if anything is needed; we have direct communication with God.*

*'We arrive and prepare ourselves for the first Brit to land from Lyneham. I am called to see the Officer i/c the Transit A/C Flight there who would like 'a word'. Wondering what I have done now; I go into his office. In there is the officer, of course, and one of the biggest 'Rock Apes' I have seen for years, made even larger by a large wireless-filled backpack which he carried, complete with long, whippy aerial. 'Do you mind if this corporal accompanies you out on the strip for the duration of this operation?' I couldn't see why, but, if that is what they want, why not? But the aerial?! 'I have no objection, providing he doesn't hinder me, try to talk to me when I'm working and keeps that aerial away from the aircraft,' I reply, wondering what was 'up'? 'Do you hear that, corporal?' 'Yes, Sssahh!' 'Well see that you do!' 'Is that all, Sssahh?' 'That will be all for now.' With that, we march out.*

*'Still in the dark, I dismiss conjecture and proceed with arrangements. Please note, I am NOT informed that, through the corporal, I can appraise operations of the situation at any time. The first A/C lands, is looked at, loaded and goes away, we begin to settle down to a routine. Gradually I appreciate one or two things. The corporal, who is very well trained for his task, trots around with me, evading my movements and chatting into his microphone intermittently. He becomes my shadow - there, but ignored. He doesn't impinge on any situation and never talks to me, or the groundcrew. Whenever I approach an A/C that has just stopped and the groundcrew and I look round at the fuel bowsers parked in the distance, one starts, pulls away and approaches. An aircraft lands and we wait on a pan different to that designated. It magically taxies towards us. We fail to start a ground power unit, and before we reach the 'panic' stage, a Land Rover arrives with an operating GPU and takes the old one away.*

*'Call me thick, but I just don't understand. I simply accept and resolve to sort it out later. The corporal, true to his orders, says not a word to me, or any of the crew. Now comes the bitter bit. It is dark, one Brit is taxying out, another coming in - just nice. Suddenly, the aircraft going away stops on the perimeter track. I grab my headset and run over. 'What's up?' I ask anxiously, after plugging in. 'The AQM wants to speak to you,' says the captain. 'OK,' I say, puzzled. 'I've 60 kids, 40 women and no spew bags,' wails the Q. 'I'm sorry,' say I, 'I have no bags, the phone is way over there and I haven't a clue on where to ring. Will you park while I send someone to the offices?' I gaze at the corporal who is standing three feet away, head cocked to one side, uncomprehending, with the answer to all our problems sitting on his back. 'We can't wait,' states the captain. 'Clear the aircraft.' The Brit moves away. I feel for the AQM but I'm comforted by the thought that I really can't help. That's where the apology comes in. I'm sorry, I could have helped, and I didn't. I repeat, it wasn't my fault!*

*'Later that night, another Brit stops on the way out. I rush over and contact the captain. 'Number three prop stuck on MIN.' 'OK, stop three and four and I'll try to free it if you'll maintain an OPEN selection.' I look round and spy a set of 'A' steps on the side. I drag them over, open the cowlings and look at the motor. Normally, a*

*tap with a hide-face hammer will 'free' a stuck micro-switch. I have no tools with me. Necessity, they say, is the mother of invention. It is dark, I'm alone, the aircraft must go. I reach down, take off my composite soled shoe and tap the motor with the heel. Immediately I see the shaft rotate and move the controller. I close the cowling, and contact the captain, 'It seems OK down here, is the indication off MIN up there?' 'Yes, we'll carry it to Lyneham, stand clear while we start engines.' I go in front of the aircraft and to port. The engines start. I wave OK. The captain waves. The Brit goes off.*

*'I had forgotten my shadow. Apparently, over the loudspeaker system in operations, loud and clear, comes the announcement. 'The Chief Tech has opened the cowlings. He's now beating the engine with his shoe!'*

*'Some time later, I receive some funny looks as we gather our gear and make our way to the aircraft which will take us home. It isn't till we are well on our way back that I learn the real story of our visit from the 'airmen who get all the gen', with embellishments, from the groundcrew room. The 'Rock Ape' has talked after all!'*

**Impressions of Moscow**

As the years roll by it becomes increasingly difficult to relate to how things were during the Cold War. Certainly a trip to Moscow was something of a novelty and two instances have already been quoted. Here is a fuller account from the *Globe*:

*'It rained in Moscow at midnight on July 27th. Bill Stedman and his crew can vouch for that; they were there.*

*'Task No. 1002 departed Lyneham in the early hours of 21st, loaded to the roof with a year's supply of toilet rolls and associated items for our Embassy in Moscow. A flag stop was made in Copenhagen to pick up a 'courtesy' crew of signaller and navigator, Messrs. Lukashin and Tatarinov of Aeroflot and the flight continued to Sheremetievo airfield, Moscow, where a delightful sounding girl controller talked Britanski 1002 into landing on a rough old strip of concrete called a runway.*

*'It took some time to get away to the hotel - an imposing stone and marble edifice called the 'Ukrania'. Thanks must go to John Turner, BEA's Station Officer in Moscow and Sqn Ldr Ted Williams, Assistant Air Attaché, for smoothing the path. John wears four splendid gold rings on his arm and we are sure this is the first time that we have had a four ringer helping to carry our baggage. Thank you John. A quick shower, shave and change was all there was time for before the whole crew was whisked away to Sqn Ldr Williams' flat*

...erhaps an editor for such a column could be found from within D. Mov. (RAF) staff.

Phone: BRADENSTOKE

...maksar to SAC's ...ar, Wheadon, Doncharnt, Watson and

...ED?

...orporal Brian Lewis of Med. Trooping Section was very flattered when told recently to attend for a series of publicity photographs

... ext. 204, or Cpl. Cooper, ext. 607.

**DRIVERS, AIRFRAME (W) ?**

The Bulgars (careful!) have 'em—why not us? Sgt. (W) Valerie Cross has a go at it—but safely ground-borne at Biggin Hill.

**THE INSPECTOR CALLS**

DURING the recent visit of Group Officer Felecity Hill, Inspector, Women's Royal Air Force, she met many of the 200 members of the W.R.A.F. at Lyneham.

In the photograph above Group Officer Hill is talking to Sgt. (W) Gulliford 511 Sqn., Sgt. (W) Frost 99 Sqn. and Sgt. (W) Godding 216 Sqn.



The 'girls' attract publicity! A feature of the *Globe* was its rather stilted style with names - and getting them wrong! So, somewhat uncharacteristically, we are told that, on the left we have Sgt(W) **Valerie** Cross. But to the right, meeting the WRAF Inspector, we have Sgt(W) **G**ulliford 511 Sqn and Sgt(W) Frost 99 Sqn ... they were Ann **C**ulliford and Jane Frost.
(*Lyneham Globe*)

EAST-MED'S GOOD FIRST YEAR

A passenger view of the French Alps, from a Britannia at 19,000 feet — en-route for Cyprus

A photograph of a passenger view of the French Alps from a Britannia at 19,000 feet, en route to Cyprus was used in the *Globe* to mark the first anniversary of the fleet taking over responsibilty for East Med trooping. (*Lyneham Globe*)

*for supper and drinks. We met many interesting people there and had a fine party.*

*'The next morning dawned as next mornings have a habit of doing and the quartermasters, Andy Funnell, Stu Bailey and Chris Byrnes went very early to the Embassy to prepare food for the return trip. The hotel staff had forgotten or was unaware that arrangements had been made by the Embassy to pay the crew's bills (perhaps there had been a shift change!) so they stopped the Q's from leaving until fistfuls of roubles appeared. Sqn Ldr Williams was again in great demand and with a flow of his exquisite Russian sorted out the misunderstanding. The aircraft's departure was set for 1430 hrs, local time, and this enabled those of the crew not otherwise occupied to have a motorised tour of the city. Red Square, the Kremlin and the Bolshoi Theatre figuring in the itinerary.*

*'The departure was characterised by much rushing about, advice from all sides, flight planning in kilometres per hour and metres. Engineer, crew chief and Qs working like beavers to load and lash the aircraft and prepare the trim sheet until suddenly and in good time all was ready for our VIP passenger, Sir Humphrey Trevelyan, to come on board. Lady Trevelyan and Miss Trevelyan accompanied Sir Humphrey, who was returning to the UK on completion of his tour of duty as HM Ambassador to the USSR.*

*'London, Heathrow, was surprisingly enough not being rained upon when the aircraft was parked outside the VIP Alcock and Brown suite. Only one little duty was now left for Flight Navigator Tatarinov to perform. He signed Sqn Ldr Appleyard's Cat Card in Russian for a route check from Moscow to LAP and, with a little prompting, gave him a 'B'. Does this make him a security risk?*

*'General impressions of Moscow from the crew - wide streets, massive buildings, most cars are Volgas, no dogs or cats seen, stars on everything, soldiers in big boots, little wooden buildings on the way to the airfield - one with 22 aerials, hydrofoils on the river, the gilded domes of the Kremlin - and it was fascinating to have seen it, but once is enough.'*

**VVIP aeromed**

Queen Salote of Tonga had imprinted herself on the British public when she attended the Coronation. In later years she required medical treatment in Auckland. An Argosy flew her from Tonga to Fiji.

Wing Commander R M Jenkins AFC with his men - and women. Achieving a satisfactory photograph of an air transport squadron is a considerable challenge. For this 1965 one of 99, 511 took on as much of the route flying as possible, leave was postponed, the sick, lame and weary called in! (*Maurice Flynn*)

It was alleged in the *Globe* that, on the first attempt, the photographer had forgotten to put film in the camera! Perhaps an apochryphal tale?

There the Queen was transferred to a Britannia for the flight to New Zealand. Before and after this, things did not go entirely smoothly for the Britannia as described in this report that appeared in the *Globe*:

*THE SAGA OF 1034*

*'Flight No.1034 very nearly left Lyneham with even the crew not knowing what their final destination was.*

*'However, two days before departure, the route was released, standard routing to Gan, thence via Cocos and Darwin to Fiji, from where Queen Salote of Tonga was to he taken to Auckland. On the morning of Wednesday, 27th October, Britannia XN 404, shining from nose to tail stood waiting in Bay 8. After the normal pre-flight preparation had been completed and all fond farewells made, promptly at 1000 hours, (with the Squadron Commander in the seat, it couldn't be anything else), she moved forward to start her long journey.*

*'On the descent into Bahrain the copilot realised how close he had been to being forcibly ejected through the DV window which was very badly cracked. (32,000 feet is a big drop into Tehran !) After a high level discussion between OC's 99 and 511, the Boss eventually emerged triumphant waving one starboard DV window.*

*'Sunday found 1034 setting course for Nandi. On this leg across North Australia we had a very fine view of the Japanese 'Comet' as did a BOAC 707. The following comments being passed: Speedbird - to Sydney - 'We have an excellent view of the 'Comet' up here." Comment from the flight deck of 1034: 'That's no Comet, that's the CO's Britannia.' On Thursday XN 404 stood on Bay 5 of Nandi shining again from stem to stern inside and outside. The dust of her previous travels having been disposed of; all snags rectified, all this by our three musketeers - King, Clarke and Lockyer - well done. Promptly at 1155 hours the Argosy from Tonga arrived and Her Majesty Queen Salote of Tonga was driven slowly over to XN404 escorted by Wing Commander Thomson and Flight Sister Griffiths. Flight 1034 then set course on the main stage of her mission. The door's opening time for Whenaupai was 1700 local and promptly at this time the doors were open, but alas the steps were stuck 20 yards short of the door - however the steps finally arrived at the rear door and the official welcoming party stepped aboard. Some ten minutes later Queen Salote left the aircraft and with a smile from the guard of honour formed by the crew of 1034 she left for her private residence.*

*'Our stay in New Zealand was unfortunately only too short, however, before setting course for Sydney, we did show the New Zealand Air Force how silent the 'Whispering Giant' was by flashing across the airfield at 288 knots with, of*

*course, all engines at flight idle. It was on this leg that the crew realised how lucky they were in having their own personal physician aboard. Sick parade being held every two hours on the hour. The doctor not to be out done said how lucky he was to have his own crew.*

*'On Saturday, 6th November, we left for Perth by way of Sydney Harbour Bridge, on what was to prove the most eventful stage of the journey so far, when only 90 minutes out of Perth No.1 engine had to be feathered as the oil contents gauge slowly fell towards zero. This manoeuvre brought the captain very quickly back to the flight deck with the words: 'What's happened?' Still he was able to get his three-engined airfield approach in for the month. Finally, after a number of engine runs it was clear we would require a replacement engine; so began the frantic writing of signals, which resulted in the arrival on the Monday of Flt Lt Bell, and his merry men from Changi with a spare engine. Our troubles were still not over for the one and only crane at the airport was nowhere large enough to off load this engine. After frantic telephone calls to every construction company in Perth, a larger crane was finally found, and the engine off-loaded. Our three musketeers then worked throughout the night to eventually set us on the road again. Thence, via Gan, Muharraq and Akrotiri, Flight 1034 arrived safely back at Lyneham on the evening of Thursday, 11th November, the crew somewhat weary, but happy in the knowledge of a job well done.'*

**Hastings tragedy**

The Britannias inherited the strategic transport role from the Hastings which had been a stalwart for many years. But it did not let go and continued to fly in other roles. One of these was parachute training. In the summer of 1965, an aircraft engaged in this task broke up in the air and all on board were killed. As such training was deemed necessary for air quartermasters, it was inevitable that some Lyneham AQMs were on board. An obituary names Master Air Quartermaster Joseph William Robinson (No.511 Squadron), Flight Sergeant Austin Ralph Casey (No.511 Squadron) and Sergeant Colin David Holmes (Air Training Squadron).

The Hastings were temporarily grounded. This raised a task for the Britannias as there were Hastings operating short range supply flights in the Far East. A Britannia plus two crews was detached to Changi for several months to carry out these tasks. Fg Off Bob Henderson (99) and Flt Lt Mike Joyce (511) headed the crews. The route Changi, Labuan, Kuching, Changi was flown twice per week: not an over taxing task for two crews!

**Yet another VIP trip**

*'December 8th, 1965, saw Britannia 404 'Canopus' captained by Wing Commander R M Jenkins, AFC, once more gleaming like a new pin, ready in its role as the transport for Air Chief Marshal Sir Charles Elworthy, the Chief of Air Staff, who was due to visit South America to attend the Venezuelan Air Force 10th anniversary celebrations. Because of various commitments, a last minute change of plans had removed this plum trip from the 216th, the founder members of the 'International Jet Set', and placed it in the hands of the 99th, the co-founders of that not so famous hard working sub-division the 'International Prop Jet Set'.*

*'Two frantic days of visa getting, uniform fitting, money changing, last minute whip round to cover the grog (thanks again 216) and it was 'Hey Ho' and off to South America with a pocketful of Bolivars and high hopes that Latin America was all it was cracked up to be. But first we had to work; Flight 1040 had yet to get off the ground. The Met Office had contrived to give us a 50-knot wind and driving rain for take-off from London Airport. 140-knot headwinds, which should in theory have only been 45 knots, made the doors' open time at Lajes in the Azores, subject to much speculation. Eventually the winds eased and obliging Air Traffic Controllers allowed the odd corner to be cut and 404 thankfully came to a halt right on time, no doubt as relieved as were the crew.*

*'Lajes to El Liberatador was scheduled as a 12-hour flight. Soon after take-off it became apparent that the winds which should have been, once again weren't. In fact, we wondered if we were creating a record in being the first aircraft to have crossed the Atlantic at final approach speed. The only consolation was the fact that at least we could give the CAS the same heights to fly as would have been*

*available by Comet. Eventually, all long flights must come to an end, and we gratefully made the chock time once more, ready for rapid turnaround and off across the mountains to the delights (beer and bed?) of Caracas.*

*''Twas not to be. The crew it appeared, was also to attend the parade and air display at the nearby air base of Maracay. We departed with great fortitude and eyeballs at the trail (we were assured that no one would notice, behind the dark glasses) to sit in the President's reviewing stand to see the parade, presentation. of awards and medals, the passing out of a course of new pilots, where the CAS was called upon to make one of the presentations, and finally an impressive flying display. A quick lunch and we were off on the 20-minute hop across to Caracas International Airport.*

*'Now for some sleep we thought, but 'alas' a party had been arranged, in a series of entertainments, so ably organised by Gp Capt V Rees, the Air Attaché. Should a copy of the Globe ever reach Venezuela, we can say no more than thanks for a wonderful party to Sgt and Mrs. Helson. This party set the tone for the whole of the 48-hour visit. Two days and nights of wining and dining on a scale difficult to imagine. Were there twice as many hours in the day it would have been impossible to have accepted all the invitations we had showered upon us. Somehow or other we managed to get some sightseeing in as well - mainly in transit from one party to the next. An exception was one lucky senior crew member who was driven by a charming young lady in a Ford Thunderbird, which had so many switches that he thought he was in an aeroplane and didn't bother to look outside. The copilot showed once more how much he loves his golf by adding yet another golf course to his rapidly growing list. Then it was time for off, with never to be forgotten memories of wonderful hosts, magnificent scenery and of six-lane highways which punched their way straight through the middle of mountains. Thanks once more to all who made our trip so memorable. We'd love to come again.*

*'Take-off from Bermuda for London with a foggy forecast and winds which once again set us aiming for the Britannia height record, was the prelude to a frustrated attempt at landing at London and a subsequent diversion to Manston. Even now our troubles were not over. Lyneham was also very foggy and after four attempts we had returned 'Canopus' just in time for it to set off to London Airport for another 'jolly', but that's another story.'*

**An Honest Tale**

We all know about 'Bar Talk'. One story to whizz around those environs, some time in the 1960s, was that one of our Britannias had landed at Paya Lebar in mistake for Changi ... but how many people knew the full story. Bill Oatey, ex-511 captain, does and he wrote this account for the Britannia Association magazine ...

*'I thought about writing this article some time ago when Harry Liddell told the story in which he described an incident, which had led to a bollocking from Alasdair Steedman. I actually put pen to paper following the landing on a taxiway, in mistake for the runway, at Gatwick by an Air Malta B737. But, having written my account, I put it to one side as the Editor was calling for more non-flight deck crew stories. I only rediscovered it recently in a 'rationalisation' (i.e. chucking out) of my paperwork and thought perhaps now was the time. So here is the sorry tale which led to me, too, being roasted by the Station Commander.*

*'It was mid '60s and to set the scene let me remind you that those were the days of the 19 hour duty period, i.e. two hours before scheduled departure plus 17 hours operating. The Changi Slip left Lyneham at 1000 and, because you could do two sectors in one day, you did the trip with one stopover at glorious Khormaksar where sleep was only possible after a suitable pause in Neddy's Bar. The final piece of information that you need to make sense of all this is that the regulations made provision for a significant extension to the duty period if there were rest facilities on the aircraft. I can't remember now (first sign, they tell me) if it was a doubling of the standard period, but I do recall that it allowed you to deadhead for two sectors and then operate two, so it was 30+ hours.*

*'The story starts with a signal from Ops at Khormaksar to Ops at Lyneham saying that the captain of the outbound slip crew had gone sick and would not be fit in time for the next service, so could we have a serviceable one, please. Being out of the room at the time, I was nominated and told*

Ex-navigator Trevor Perry wrote to the editor of the Britannia Association magazine: *'Originally I thought I had taken this photograph of 498 on a diversion from Thule 22/23 June 1967. This was on a 511 Trainer (Captains Don Dewhurst and Dickie Robertson) routed through Thule to pick up a RAF Expedition. Then I spotted the markings 'Transport Command' and realised it must have been an earlier date. It was taken before I joined the Britannia force whilst I was on the Specialist Navigator Course during our Polar Trainer, 18/19 July 1965. The Captain was the then OC Ops Wing, Wg Cdr Brownlow. For some inexplicable reason this and one similar are my only photographs of a Britannia. My only excuse is that the navigator had to carry too much kit to bother about packing a camera.'* (*Trevor Perry*)

*to be on the next day's departure on which the famous rest facilities would be provided, and then to take the aircraft on to Changi. To be fair, those rest facilities, which comprised a stretcher installation and a curtain round it for privacy, would have been adequate for someone tired after a hard day's something or other, but my first mistake was that I did not stay up all night before the trip. So I wasn't tired at 10am and though I may have dozed a bit, I did not sleep and ended up at Khormaksar pretty much as tired as the operating crew - and they could go to Neddy's!*

*'I am ashamed to say that another thing I can't remember is the names of most of the crew that I joined in Aden, but Dicky Tuffin was the sick captain I replaced; the nav was Ron Rowlands for whom I had a high regard and the copilot was Jim Hunter. Jim was an experienced operator who had done a tour as a Beverley captain before coming on the Britannia so I agreed with him that as it was likely that I would be slightly less comatose at the half way point, I would do the sector to Gan, and he would take the aircraft into Changi. It was a time of year when weather was not a problem, no ITCZ and all that and we had an uneventful flight to Gan and the usual 1½ hour turnround. Off we launched again on another uneventful flight. Actually it turned out to be 99% uneventful. Again, the weather was good. In fact, it was so clear that I reckon you could see Australia from the Malacca Straight - well, you know what I mean. It was the early hours of the morning and there being no other traffic around, we were told to expect a straight-in from Kong Kong, which is what we did. Jim was flying, of course, but as we turned over KK I saw a set of approach and runway lights standing out like the proverbial dog's naughty bits. I pointed these out to Jim and he set up a visual approach with the nav calling out miles to touchdown. An excellent landing, I seem to recall, but just as we were doing the superfine, brake dwell bit, I looked up and saw a rotating green light on top of a building off to the right and at last cottoned to the fact that this wasn't Changi but Paya Lebar. Surprising how untired you become with a shot of adrenalin!*

*'We switched rapidly to the Paya Lebar frequency, told them we didn't really mean it and could we go to Changi. Certainly, they said, there's no other traffic - which was fortunate since it could have been nasty had there been. Although the thought occurred subsequently that we might have been a bit more switched on had there been other traffic to stimulate our interest. Anyway, we crept into Changi shamefacedly and owned up.*

*'Fortunately, the Wg Cdr IATS was visiting Changi (another name I've now forgotten - this is getting ridiculous!) and we had a long discussion with him, as you can imagine. I explained the circumstances, said that it was my fault and suggested that, since there were no facts in dispute, it would be counter-productive to hold up the*

THE LYNEHAM GLOBE—No. 159

FLIGHT SAFETY AWARD

CPL. CLAYTON

SAC WILLIAMS

The text that accompanies these two photos reads:
*'FLIGHT SAFETY AWARD*
*On the evening of 7th June 1965, Cpl Clayton and SAC Williams were detailed to attend a crew change on Britannia XN404. On checking the No.2 propeller was free to rotate before start up, Williams notices that the propeller was only free to rotate through 180 degrees. An attempt to free the propeller was successful, but only after some pushing by Williams and some juddering by the propeller. On the recommendation of Cpl Clayton and SAC Williams the proposed flight was abandoned. Subsequent investigation revealed traces of metal in the jet pipe and the engine was changed. By their vigilance and attention to detail, Cpl Clayton and SAC Williams prevented a most probable incident occurring in the air. Neither of these tradesmen were engine fitters and this made their actions all the more commendable. For their contribution to Flight Safety, Cpl Clayton and SAC Williams have been awarded £2 by the Station Commander.'*

Hope they didn't spend it all at once!

*slip by making me and the crew non-operational. Happily, this was agreed and in due course we operated back - carefully!*

*'So, not long after, I ended up in front of Station Commander, Group Captain Alasdair Steedman, not knowing what to expect but fearing the worst. I considered that there were mitigating circumstances as I had been on the go for 30+ hours but, on the other hand, the rest of the crew were within the normal duty limit. In fact, I was knocked back from a 'B' cat to a 'C' and felt that I had got off pretty lightly. MY own sense of shame was a greater punishment. So far as I recall no action was taken against any other member of the crew.*

*'What rather upset me was when the incident was subsequently reported in the Command Flight Safety magazine in about three lines saying that a Britannia had taken off from Gan and landed in error at Paya Lebar, all under the heading of 'Bad Captaincy'. Well, that was true enough, but a bit short on explanation I felt, since I had always understood that one of the purposes of such reporting was to help others avoid the same trap. So I wrote to the Command Flight Safety Officer and said that my fatigue after 30 or so hours may not have been the direct cause of the incident but it surely was pertinent so how about putting that in the magazine. He never did, and some time later when I was stationed at Upavon in an office near his I asked him why not. He would only say that there were political factors involved which made it 'inappropriate'.*

*'As they used to say in 'Air Clues', I learned about flying from that - and about politics. Or rather, I learned about what are now called human factors, and two things remain with me from the incident. First, how restricted your span of attention is when you are really knackered, and, second, that people, tired or not, will discard conflicting evidence once they have made a decision, in this case to go for the lights we first saw. The ground on the approach to Changi and Paya Lebar from the north is broadly similar at night, but there are 'clues', and none of us read them.*

*Incidentally, the reason my cat was reduced to 'C' was my failure to follow Command instructions to use an approach aid when one is available, and the Changi radar was available that night. No reference was made to the number of hours I had been operating but, so far as I know, that extended duty period wasn't worked again. It did strike me later to question what the Changi radar operator was doing if he was in business. He must have been expecting us and had he been looking at his tube, he could have covered himself in glory. I never did follow that thought up.*

*'What had the Air Malta incident to do with all this, you may ask? Well, if you remember the incident, you may have worked out the connection - if you are not too tired, that is. We both aimed for a piece of concrete secure in the knowledge that it was the right one, and we were both wrong. In both cases nothing nasty happened as a result but, in both cases, it could have. I got involved with the Air Malta incident because at the time I was Director, Safety and Security for BAA, part of the Head Office establishment but with an office and staff based at Gatwick, and that sort of event was very much on my patch. In the subsequent liaison with the AAIB I found myself dealing with our late lamented colleague, Tony Skinner. I know you will find this hard to believe, but this seemed to involve going into various watering holes, one in particular at Farnborough, and taking on board what I have seen described as 'beverage refreshments'. We also flew the Gatwick approach at night to satisfy ourselves that there were no problems with the temporary approach facilities that were then in use. There weren't any. Captain of our company aircraft was Peter Galyer who was in the same department as me. He is, of course, ex-99 and did quite well, considering!'*

Another photo for WRAF recruiting - SACW Maureen Burbank, RAF Lyneham Assistant Air Traffic Controller. (*Maureen Burbank*)

**Quiet Christmas?**

The two squadron histories seem to go very quiet for the latter part of 1965. Perhaps there was premonition. Something *was* around the corner and, as the year progressed, Christmas approached and past records show that this was the time for the Britannia fleet to get booted and spurred.

Oil was to be the preoccupation for the next phase of Britannia life.

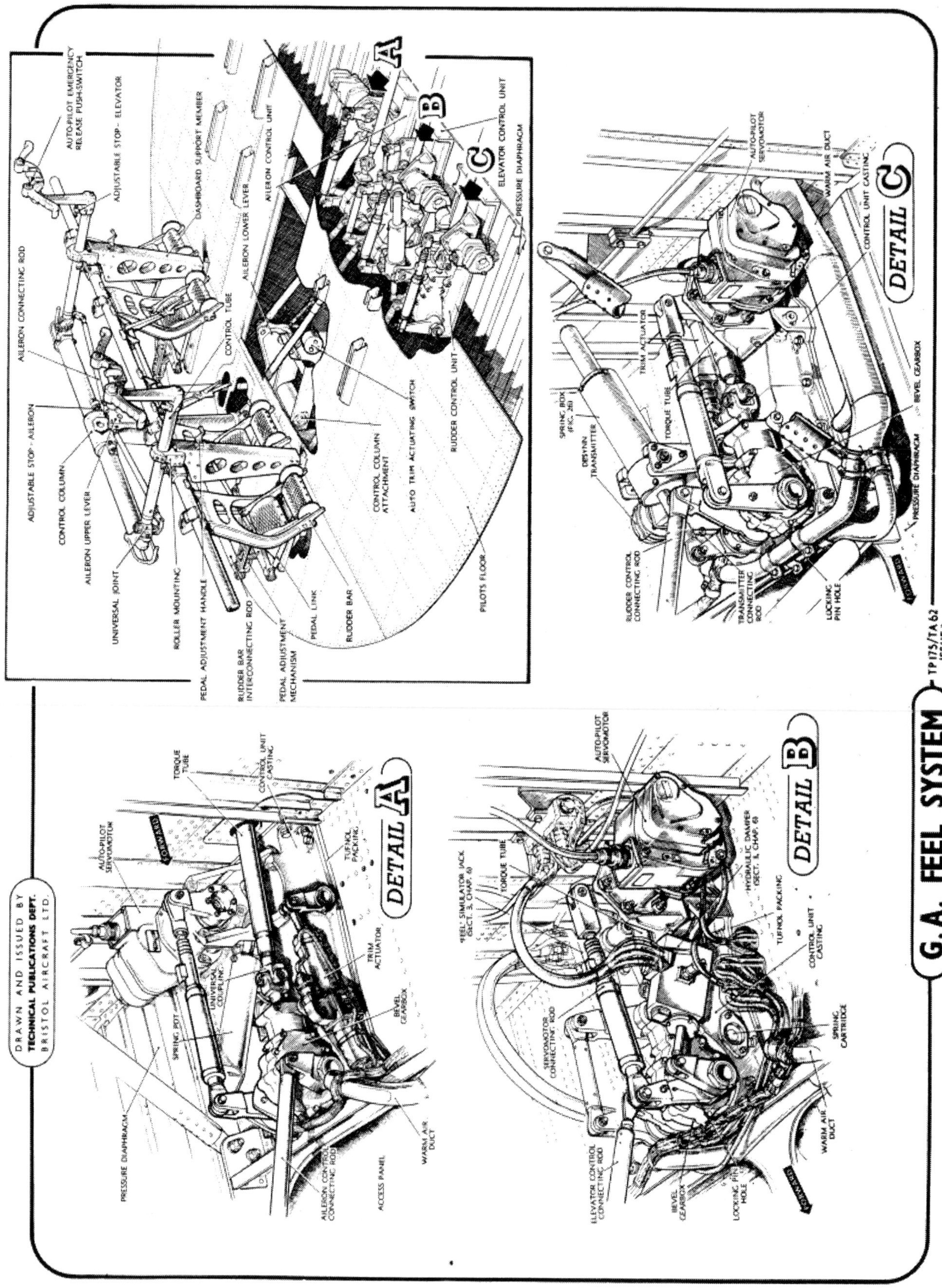


Another chance to admire the skill that went into producing these drawings.

The adventures of Messrs. Ad Minn and Org at Wootton Lynstoke continue ...

AD MINN & ORG FIND THEY ARE ONCE AGAIN ON THE FAMILIAR GROUND OF WOOTTON LYNESTOKE
now read on .....
"MUST BE A WAR THEY'RE CARRYING RIFLES."
LITTLE DO THEY KNOW IT IS A PARADE
"TELL ME DO YOU DO THIS SORT OF THING OFTEN?"
" ONLY ONCE REALLY – BUT WE HAVE 93 REHEARSALS – AND ALWAYS EARLY MORNING...
.... ACTUALLY THEY ARE GREAT THINGS, PARADES, SO ADAPTABLE. USE THEM FOR V.I.P.s, OR HANDING OUT MEDALS, OR IMPRESSING NATIVES. TURN THE RIFLES UPSIDE DOWN AND THERE YOU ARE – INSTANT FUNERAL – AND THEY ARE...
...SO GOOD FOR THE MEN."
HOOORAY
IN THE LOCAL TOWN ....
"WHAT'S ALL THIS?"
"IT IS WITH GREAT PLEASURE THAT I HAND TO YOU THIS SYMBOLIC KEY, MADE SPECIALLY IN THE SWIDNOD CARRIAGE AND WAGON WORKS (GOD BLESS DOCTOR BEECHING) GRANTING TO YOU WOOTTON LYNESTOKE
THE RIGHT OF FREEDOM OF ENTRY INTO THIS OUR ANCIENT TOWN OF – SWIDNOD"
THINKS: "I WONDER IF THEY'RE OPEN YET?"
THINKS (AGAIN) "THAT SHOULD SEE THE COUNCIL RIGHT FOR A FEW FREE DRINKS IN THE OFFICERS' MESS."
"'ERE AIN'T IT SMASHING!"
"HOW ABSOLUTELY SPLENDID"

22

CHAPTER TWENTY

# The Oil Lift

Southern Africa had been in an uneasy state for a number of years with the keeping at bay of equality for the Africans. Rhodesia (previously Southern Rhodesia) was much troubled by these demands and there had been political unrest and disturbances. After an unsuccessful federation with Northern Rhodesia (Zambia) and Nyasaland (Malawi), ending in 1963, Rhodesia was once again a colony but one demanding independence. The British Government, supported by the United Nations, was seeking a constitution, fairer to the Africans, before granting that liberty.

**Unilateral Declaration of Independence**

The white demand for independence, maintaining the existing constitution, gained strength with a favouring result from a 1964 referendum and the re-election in 1965, by an overwhelming majority, of prime minister Ian Smith on a platform of white minority rule. In October discussions between the two governments ended in a stalemate and it was now seen as inevitable that the Rhodesians would take the law into their own hands and unilaterally declare independence (UDI).

This duly happened on 11th November. The British government took their case to the United Nations, declaring that rebellion had taken place and demanding UN action in the form of economic sanctions.

This received general support and

A scene that was to dominate 1966 for Britannia people. (*Ian Berry*)

Waiting moments outside the early form of Embakasi RAF Ops. (*John Hunting*)

It wasn't all 'pain' during that Christmas away. The Britannia detachment somewhat took over the night club of the hotel. This was the very popular artiste, Terri King. A perhaps apocryphal tale is that she was subsequently invited to 'guest' at a Lyneham Officers' Mess Ball and that, on the occasion, there were a few of the members keeping a low profile! (*Lyneham Globe*)

there followed the freezing of assets in the UK, blocking of Rhodesian exports and an oil embargo.

**Oil by air**

Landlocked Zambia was badly affected by all this and one form of relief was an agreement to supply the country with oil. With no sea port and very poor road communications, other than north up through Rhodesia, the only way of accomplishing this was to be by air. Zambia also felt under some military threat and requested assistance with air defence. The latter request was satisfied by the positioning of one of the Royal Air Force Javelin squadrons at Lusaka airport. This also necessitated the provision of radar and communications and guarding provided by the RAF Regiment.

**Nairobi standby**

The Britannia concern was to become known as 'The Oil Lift'. The first hint that something was afoot came with the positioning of a number of aircraft and crews in Nairobi at the end of November 1965. They were placed on standby. I was there for 15 days, once again in the dubious surroundings of the Spread Eagle Hotel. It was not a happy time. There was tension. Our readiness state kept on being altered but nothing seemed clear. I well remember one wit remarking, 'We're just like mushrooms ... kept in the dark and fed on horse shit!' From that sprung a name that was to be attached to the Oil Lift Britannias for the greater part of 1966, Mushroom Airways. The fungus symbol is remembered to this day in the motif of the Oil Lift tie.

During this Nairobi sojourn, we did fly down to Lusaka once and introduced to its diminutive 'International' airfield. The Britannia was a large aircraft so a runway only 5000 feet long on an airfield at an elevation of 4000 feet concentrated the mind.

**Home for Christmas**

Things quietened, the immediate defence needs of Zambia had been satisfied and we were to be allowed to return to the UK - in time for Christmas. Even as we were returning the situation was changing and we were met, on our arrival, with the news that the oil embargo was on.

A plan evolved that we were to operate from, Zambia supportive, Tanzania, immediately. But ... but ... it's nearly Christmas! IMMEDIATELY!! So, on 21st December, I and 100 plus Britannia air and ground crew proceeded to Dar es Salaam to form the Oil Lift Detachment which was to last until 31st October 1966, having flown in excess of 10,000 hours.

**Oil Lift Detachment**

Six aircraft and 12 crews formed the air side; 50 technicians and air movements staff made up the balance. There were to be two delivery airfields in Zambia, Lusaka and Ndola; things were quickly established. Part of this was my crew's flight from Dar es Salaam to Lusaka and Ndola and return on the 23rd/24th. At Lusaka the Javelins were ensconced. They had discovered the sub-standard nature of the airfield; if they did not fly each day or at the least move their aircraft, they started sinking into the concrete!

Ndola was a similar airfield 180 miles to the North of Lusaka and the pattern was to be that we would fly alternate loads to each of these.

**Hotel Kilimanjaro**

We found ourselves incredibly well accommodated at Dar. It was the time for African countries to display the intended status of their new won independence by grand building. Tanzania's took the form of brand new five star hotel, the Hotel Kilimanjaro, and this is where the detachment was 'barracked'. We were the very first guests and became used to being viewed by the local people strolling through the foyer to savour their new acquisition.

**Banging drums**

The flying of the oil gathered pace; some crews flew on Christmas Day. Ex-Flight Sergeant Martin Jones, signaller, now rechristened an air electronics operator, because of the elsewhere advancing RAF technological environment, recalls:

*'Christmas Day 1965 always remains in my memory as Captain Bob Henderson and crew were detailed for a load to Lusaka. I remember tuning in The Queen's speech on the radio compass. It seemed strange to be flying fuel into Zambia to assist the blocking of Rhodesia's UDI and be speaking to Salisbury Air Traffic Control Centre as part of the flight was in Rhodesian airspace. Relations over the air were always quite cordial. Another*

Barrel loading in progress. This photograph must have been taken before a safer fork lift technique was developed. This is described later. (*Ian Partridge*)

*memory of those flights was the banging noises from the oil drums as they expanded and contracted during the climb and descent.'*

**Nairobi return**

There was obviously some nervousness on the part of the Tanzanians in being party to this oil enterprise. This was heralded by us being instructed to fly in civilian clothes and culminated in our withdrawal on 4th January to Nairobi. So it was farewell Hotel Kilimanjaro and 'Hello again' to the Spread Eagle.

Nairobi was to continue as our springboard to Zambia for the rest of the lift. The six aircraft flew two sorties a day carrying 56 x 44 gallon drums on each. The lot of the crews was to be on 'earlies' (0500 take-off) or 'lates' (land Nairobi 2200). The lot of the ground crews was to have a very drawn out day punctuated by three bursts of intense activity.

**More Hunting**

A return is made to the account of long serving Britannia radio fitter, John Hunting:

*'Towards the end of 1965, the big trip to look forward to was Exercise Triplex West; I was really looking forward to spending two weeks at Hickam Field, Honolulu. However, instead of the Hawaiian high life, I ended up spending nine months in the depths of darkest Africa! Good old Mr Smith declared UDI and the Oil Lift began. I went to Nairobi on one of the early flights. It was a little eventful in that on the approach to Bahrain, the Eng advised that there was a red light on one of the main undercarriage legs. We landed safely but, because we had an urgently required ground comms radio cabin on board, we continued on to Khormaksar with the undercarriage down - it took a long time! After a night in the delightful(!) Red Sea Hotel, it was on to Nairobi for my nine month stay.*

*'We initially lived at Eastleigh but worked at Embakasi; later we moved to the Spread Eagle Hotel. Work was very pleasant at the civil airport, meals (usually goulash) in the Terminal Building and much scrounging of ground equipment from East African Airways. I reckon that I probably set a record when I towed a Brit with a Land Rover, much to Ernie 'Fod' Dunnett's astonishment. It was not all work though, occasionally, the evenings were spent sampling the delights of the Sombrero and Hallians night clubs.*

*'I also spent a while at Lusaka where the Brits shared the apron with 29 Squadron Javelins, the occasional BUA VC10 and a Zambian Airways Viscount that mysteriously became a Rhodesian Airways Viscount by flipping over a nameplate on the fuselage. We lived in the Showground - surely one of the most unique RAF stations ever! The airmen lived in the Cattle*

An outbound load of full barrels.
(*Ian Partridge*)

'... sooner or later, one of the forks will pierce the skin ...' (*Bill Robinson*)

A Lyneham Globe photo of the upright outbound load. (*Lyneham Globe*)

'Empties' loaded horizontally make a cool seat for a 'cool chick' - Sgt(W) Val Cross. (*Lyneham Globe*)

*Exhibition Hall, the NCOs in the Poultry Hall and I think the officers were in the Menagerie! The only excitement I can remember at Lusaka was when a Brit taxied off the runway and sunk up to its axles in soft edges. It took us much digging and pulling with an agricultural tractor to extract it. Despite the shortage of oil, we managed a weekend camping trip to Kariba Dam and an 'interesting' flight in a Zambian Air Force Dakota to Livingstone and the Victoria Falls.*

*'After a short break back at Lyneham, it was back to Nairobi again followed by a spell at Ndola; this time we lived in a school. I shared a classroom with four or five others and have vivid memories of sitting outside in the sun listening to the World Service and hearing England winning the World Cup. The only interesting thing about Ndola was having to reverse the Brits on a meandering path into their parking bays and leave it to the well practised team to unload the oil drums. Back to Nairobi again and then a long trip around the Middle East as a servicing team known as Cpl Hunting + 6. Finally, it was back to Lyneham in late '66 on the last of the Oil Lift Brits. From then on, I was trained as a Transport Aircraft Servicing Specialist (TASS) completing courses on the VC10 and Belfast before being posted to Gan in September 1967.'*

**Near miss**

This maximum effort of 12 sorties per day was not made any easier by the constraint that arrivals and departures from Zambia had to be completed in daylight due to lack of night flying facilities. This meant some congestion in the air and on the ground for two periods of the day at Lusaka/Ndola. Ex-511 navigator and Flight Commander, Squadron Leader Nick Barlex recalls establishing the pattern of flights:

*'Flight Planning was as basic as the available nav aids, the airways system and destination airfields. But the need to deliver the maximum payload in the time available meant that the spacing between flights had to be reduced to the lowest acceptable. The plan made, the first wave of aircraft departed at suitable intervals.*

*'One morning the first flight to Ndola had arrived, unloaded and was airborne and on its way, outbound, back to Nairobi. The second inbound flight was now approaching Ndola trying to pick up the NDB and talk to Ndola Air Traffic. Eventually they made contact with the tower and with the outbound aircraft. Prudently*

An example, on the Oil Lift, of Parkinson's Law of Military Air Freighting: *'If space is available something will be found to fill it!'* The load here is wardrobes! (*Ian Partridge*)

*they enquired of it, 'What is your present position?' Back came the reply, 'I am climbing approaching Flight Level 180 about 50 miles out.'*

*'On the flight deck of the inbound flight the navigator was quizzed, 'How far out are we, Nav?' '50 miles!!!' was the rapid, terse reply - and the aircraft was at Flight Level 180. Suddenly 500 feet was lost as the captain thrust the control column forward. Seconds (and it seemed only split seconds) later a shiny, glowing, shimmering Britannia passed inches? feet? very close and over the starboard wing. ''Did you see us?!!', came the call from a shaken captain. 'Say again,' was the relaxed reply. Obviously not. But for good radio calls and VERY good reactions, the start of the Oil Lift could have been marred by a very nasty accident.'*

**Fork lift cunning**

With its door sill over 10 feet from the ground, loading freight on a Britannia always presented an eternal challenge and this was certainly so when the load was to be 56 barrels. The only practical way was two at a time by fork lift; but one of the 'Laws of Air Transport' is that if a fork lift is frequently manoeuvred close to an aircraft then, sooner or later, one of the forks will pierce the skin! A technique was developed to reduce the inevitability of this. The forklift was pre-positioned below the freight door. It would lower its forks to the ground and two drums rolled on. With the forks now tilted back, they would be raised to the sill; there, with a gentle tip, they would be rolled into the aircraft. The empty forks would be then lowered for the process to be repeated. For unloading the procedure was reversed. This method meant that the location of the fork lift remained unchanged and the risk of an accident was almost entirely eliminated. When unloading, the tilt as the barrels reached the ground was used to give them some impetus which was seized upon by the local labour to keep them rolling to the lorry at the perimeter.

As the aircraft taxied in, the air quartermaster would be unchaining. With all this, remarkable turn round times were

The Britannia squadron commanders and OC Ops took turns at commanding the Nairobi detachment. Here Wing Commander Jock Kennedy, OC 99 Squadron, is seen being greeted by President Kuanda on a visit to Lusaka. (*John Hunting*)

Another lorry load of drums arrives. (*Ian Partridge*)

accomplished; twenty minutes from landing to take-off was the record. The military Mk1 Britannia's reinforced freight floor was tough but not rugged enough to stand up to the ravages of oil barrels. The rims could cause considerable damage and it was part of the cost counted at the end of the day.

**Peering president**

Zambia was pleased with our efforts. President Kuanda was at the airport to welcome the first official load. Unfortunately the Britannia's arrival was somewhat inauspicious, as already mentioned by John Hunting. Turning off the runway, it cut the corner slightly and one side's main wheels sank into the inadequate taxiway edge. The next day's national paper photograph of the President, under the aircraft wing, peering sympathetically at the sunken wheels, did not quite convey the hoped for PR image of the occasion!

**Danger money**

We were not alone in this oil relief.

Group Captain F. Hazlewood, the Station Commander R.A.F. Lyneham, Wing Commander Kennedy, O.C. 99 Squadron and Wing Commander Jackson, our technical man in Nairobi, inspecting seal drums to be used on the oil lift into Zambia.

The controversial rubber drums being viewed by the senior engineering officer in Nairobi, Wing Commander Jackson, Lyneham Station Commander, Gp Capt Hazlewood and Wg Cdr Jock Kennedy. (*Lyneham Globe*)

Loading at Majunga with the Britannia Freight Lift Platform.

It is recorded that, by the end of February, 2,243,584 gallons had been air-lifted by the joint Royal Air Force, Royal Canadian Air Force and civilian contractors. The commercial operators contracted to support this air lift did become something of a thorn in the flesh of the Royal Air Force crews. It was learnt that they were being paid 'Danger Money' for flying exactly the same loads as the Service crews. It is believed that this produced some discussions in high places and as a result we received an enormous increase in our allowances. This marked a turning point in the financial aspect of route flying. Up until then it had actually cost us money to go away. This was not the inevitable expenditure resulting from having to pass time in some foreign part but the withdrawal of a 'ration allowance' that married personnel were paid at home. This was cancelled whilst we were away as we were then being fed by the Service!

**Mutiny?**

It can be imagined, from what has been described, that standard metal oil drums were a very inconvenient and impractical means of conveyance. There was an attempt to improve on this by using rubber tanks like very strong inner tubes for huge wheels with an extremely small axle. These were intended for tactical operations where they would be placed in the field for refuelling helicopters and the like. They proved very unsatisfactory. They leaked. It is alleged (a euphemism for gossip in the Nairobi bars being used by the crews) that a particular flight engineer refused to take such a load, considering it hazardous. His concern was that all the aircraft electrics lay beneath the freight floor. The story was enhanced in that he was threatened with disciplinary action if he did not carry out the duty. The difficulty escalated when the rest of the crew supported the engineer. It is all surmise from the talk at the time but they were hastily sent back to the UK under the cloud of having committed mutiny. The outcome, for the bar talkers, was that the mistake was acknowledged and no further action on the crew was taken. A fact was that the rubber tank idea was dropped.

**Country Club moves in**

So, for 1966 a fair percentage of the Britannia fleet settled into a routine of three week detachments in Nairobi punctuated with other miscellaneous activities. For my part it was obviously decided that I had

A 'Condec' at the raised freight door. (*Pete Hobson*)

overstretched myself in the early stages of the Oil Lift and that I should be engaged elsewhere during February, March and April. The truth of it was that I was a very new captain and very low in the pecking order; so whilst doing my bit over Christmas had been very acceptable to the 'Big Boys', it was now time to step aside and let them enjoy the delights of East Africa! In those months, as well as doing categorisation tests, I roamed between Cyprus, Bahrain, Gibraltar, Norway and North Africa, pretty average fare for those days. But in May I returned to Nairobi and took my place in what had now become a well oiled (!) machine. In case it might

President Kenyatta and Mr. Harold Wilson discussing the fuel airlift to Zambia at Nairobi Airport, on January 13th. Mr. Wilson is talking to Wing Commander Jackson of Lyneham, who is accompanied by Wing Commander Cadamy, Officer Commanding the R.A.F. Detachment based at Kenya Air Force Station, Eastleigh.

*(Photograph by courtesy of East African Standard (Newspapers Ltd.)*

A measure of the political nature of the Oil Lift can be judged by this photograph from a Nairobi newspaper. (*Lyneham Globe*)

The loading of barrels continues, inexorably. (*Ian Partridge*)

seem that this was a matter of the occasional flight interrupting languishment by swimming pools by day and in bars by night, it should be noted that, between 5th and 24th May, my crew and I flew to Zambia and back 14 times accumulating 95 flying hours.

**Over the top hours**

June provided a contrast for me with a flight over the North Pole amongst Malta, Germany and more flying tests. In

LUSAKA TEA PARTY

Dr. Kaunda, President of Zambia, recently entertained members of the Britannia force to tea at the State House, Lusaka. This photograph, taken in the grounds of State House, shows members of 511 Squadron and on Dr. Kaunda's left Air Commodore E. James, D.F.C., A.F.C., Task Force Commander, Wing Commander J. B. Mahoney, O.B.E., Commanding Officer 511 Squadron, and Wing Commander E. D. Jackson, Senior Technical Officer at Lusaka.

A way of saying 'thank-you'. (*Lyneham Globe*)

July it was back to the Oil Lift; the 'Big Boys' had obviously sampled enough of the East African delights or, possibly, found it too arduous for their liking. Our effort this time exceeded that of the last and indicates the commitment we had to Zambia. My crew flew 16 return trips in 17 days and, with the hours flown on the positioning flight, exceeded the laid down limit of 120 hours in one month. It does seem, from my log book, that our efforts were recognised and I had some leave in August but before the month had ended I was in Nairobi again via Aden.

**A visitor**

Viewed from the UK, the Oil Lift was a curiosity and the detachment had its share of 'fact finding' visitors. Ex-511 Flight Commander Nick Barlex recalls:

*'It was an 'informal' visit by ACM Sir Kenneth Cross, the then AOC-in-C Transport Command to Mushroom Airways, the Nairobi Oil Lift, in May 1966. As I recall the occasion, John Loveridge and Alf Musgrove, as co-captains, along with Geoff Bowles and others, were tasked with flying the new VC10 on a proving/training flight via Nairobi to the Far East. The C-in-C decided to join this trip and took the opportunity, I suspect, to find out why so many Lyneham people were so keen to visit Kenya whenever possible. As I was out there doing my stint as Detachment Commander, I was given this exciting(!) news.*

*'The shiny new VC10 duly arrived at about teatime and was planned to leave (Country Club style) after breakfast the next day. On arrival, the C-in-C briefly acknowledged the assembled 'greeters' and went off to his accommodation. Come the next day, forewarned and armed, I was 'on guard' at the detachment buildings by the crack of sparrows. Sure enough, very soon after my arrival, up rolls a staff car and out jumps 'The Boss' to inspect our enterprise. After a swift, but thorough, tour he requested an office with a desk where he could write some postcards. Naturally, I gave him the Detachment office and left him on his own. When he emerged, I noticed a slight smile on his face, but he said nothing, made his farewells and was driven to the VC10 for his flight to Gan.*

*'I returned to my office and as I sat at my desk I realised that on the adjacent wall hung copies of Detachment Orders. Part of Order No.1 on Page 1, clearly in view, stated, '... all personnel are to wear black shoes during the visit of the AOC-in-C. Desert boots can be reverted to after his departure.' Oh well, sanfairyann!!'*

**A civilian view of RAF operating**

An article that appeared in *'Aeroplane and Commercial Aviation News'* caught the eye of the editor of *The Lyneham Globe*:

*'It is always absorbing to compare operator with operator, their techniques, policy and methods. As international regulations become more standardised and contracted-out crew training more popular, the differences in both operational procedures and the atmospheres in which the flying takes place tend to get fewer. The opportunity to compare military and civilian operations comes all too infrequently. On a*

The photo caption reads: *Chief Tech K Mansell showing Master Engineer Weatherall and Flt Sgt D Penfold the 'insides' of a propeller at Embakasi Airport, Nairobi.* (*Lyneham Globe*)

To the right, a photograph to celebrate the millionth gallon carried on the Oil Lift. (*Ian Lansdowne*)

Britannia captain Alan Elsegood talking with the Superintendent of Zambia Police at Lusaka Airport. Alan was one of the many Britannia captains who migrated into Civil Aviation. Appropriately his airline was Britannia Airways. (*Lyneham Globe*)

*recent trip to Africa, a member of 'The Aeroplane' staff, Michael Lumb travelled on a RAF Transport Command Britannia. Here are some of his impressions of the similarities and differences between civilian and military Britannia operations.*

*'Some things are different, of course. For one thing the seats face the other way, and the first third of the cabin is filled with unscreened freight on pallets, with lashings that look as though they would hold a young tank at 2g. The talk in the rear galley tends to be of Changi and Gan rather than of Sydney and Tokyo. The Aircraft Quartermaster is both less glamorous and attentive than a stewardess, but more efficient. (Later in the trip it was a woman AQM who was both charming and efficient).*

*'The p.a. announcements, given by the AQM, have a firmer ring of authority about them - 'You may smoke only after take-off following an announcement over this passenger address system.' (One wonders, from the emphasis, if Transport Command has had trouble from pirate p.a. systems aboard its aircraft, giving contradictory information.)*

*'But much remains the same. The atmosphere in the passenger cabin is more relaxed and friendly from the start, rather like the one that is finally achieved after a long civil flight about an hour before landing, although the boredom and monotony tend to settle in the sooner for that. On the flight deck even the details are the same. The auto-trim is playing up again, and the co-pilot gives the trim wheel sharp little jerks, presumably hoping that something in the system might be persuaded to click into place, while the engineer looks on disapprovingly and talks of relays and condensation.*

*'The captain casts an unenvious eye at a KLM DC-8 streaking for Amsterdam and home some 20,000ft above and 150kts better off - perhaps he came off Hastings and even a Britannia has advantages. He leaves Lyneham on a two-week detachment, and has no idea of his schedule once the first day's stint is over. All his flight crew have old acquaintances on the passenger list, which makes the walk back to the rear toilets more rewarding and lengthy than for a civil crew.*

*'The flight deck layout of the Britannia 253 is nearly identical to its civilian counterpart, although the radio and navaids seem to belong to a slightly earlier generation, and a signaller works steadily away obtaining weather forecasts.*

*'A Flight Lieutenant navigator completes the five-man operating crew, and brings home one of the advantages of civil three-crew operation - that of a less crowded flight deck.*

*'The obvious questions were received with some surprise and, in one or two cases, not a little indignation, the same slightly defensive attitude often 'encountered when comparisons with civilian operators were implied. What kind of fuel reserves did Transport Command operate down to if pushed? Regulations were as strict or stricter, than civilian ones. Crew utilisation? About 700 hours a year. Aircraft serviceability? Very good. Perhaps because of a military willingness to carry more unserviceability than a civil operator?*

ROYAL AIR FORCE
GALLONS

*On the contrary, it was the crews' opinion that Transport Command replaced and repaired long before many other operators would.*

*'Under what conditions did they depart from civil-type performance requirements and use full military procedures? This question, asked during the trip of several Britannia pilots, got some very diverse replies ranging from 'permission from the AOC' to 'all the time', so perhaps it was not a fair one without a knowledge of the layout of the military Flight Manual.*

*'What kind of allowances did they get on a trip? This was the question that always rang the bell. Not only were some of their base allowances stopped when they went on detachment, but, being transit crew, they were often billeted at hotels off base, where prices of the usual necessities were mostly well above the duty-free prices in the mess. This had raised particularly strong feelings at this time, since the civilian crews on the same operation were getting an additional £6 a trip in addition to hotel bills being paid.*

*'Compared with the civilian's 16, Transport Command can operate up to 19 hours with a single crew, which can make for a long day, particularly on the first, always more tiring, sector out of the UK, which usually involves a late-evening take-off.*

*'The confidence of the Transport Command crews in their aircraft and servicing personnel is as high as that found within the Corporations, and although the routine 'scheduled' flights are conducted under less pressure than prevails in the commercial world, it makes for a more relaxed operation. This, together with the advantages of belonging to a Squadron rather than a Fleet, the sharing of the same mess and living facilities, produces a different - and possibly more pleasant atmosphere than civilian crews normally work in.'*

**That Oil Lift ground crew photo**

The photograph was used in an edition of the magazine of the Britannia Association. The editor asked, 'Who do you recognise?' Dave (Ginge) Ashenden, ex-Line Servicing Squadron, Lyneham responded to the question ...

*'Who do you recognise? Well myself actually, I'm the tall guy directly behind the #1 on 1000000 gallons logo painted on the oil drum. After all these years of receiving TWG it was a nice surprise to see myself in print.*

*'It's the first time I've seen the picture but it seems logical to assume that the photo was taken at Nairobi where I spent about two months out of the four-month detachment away from Lyneham on the Oil Lift. The picture would have been taken early in 1966 when I was doing my particular stint. I was 26 then and am now rapidly approaching 62 - God, how that picture seems to make the intervening years slip by! The memory dims, in consequence I can't put names to all the faces. However, I do recognise third from the left Pete Hogg (Airframe Technician/Ground Engineer), and is that a youthful looking Curly Beauchamp (Airframes) at the other end of the oil drum? Also I'm sure that's Mike Lewis (electrician) with his head against the No.3 engine cowling - we met unexpectedly two years ago at the funeral of a mutual friend and in our reminiscing completely forgot our time together on the Oil Lift.*

*'There have been many tales in the TWG of happenings during the Oil Lift and the effort required to keep 'Mushroom Airways' operating. So here are a few of mine, triggered by the picture.*

*'First of all, for me, a detachment to Nairobi, was no big deal as I had been based there before (Eastleigh), for nearly two and a half years (April 1962 to Sept 64). Working on Beverley Second Line in the main, but as a standby Britannia rectification specialist if the need arose at Embakasi. Hence I jumped at the chance to go down to Lusaka when volunteers were called for.*

*'At that time I was a Sergeant Propulsion Fitter and my introduction to Lusaka was as part of the second wave of volunteers to arrive from Nairobi, the first wave of course having already set up the*

*operations and domestics. Dependent on rank, we were housed in various parts of the permanent site of the annual Zambian Royal Agricultural Show. Having dropped the airmen off from the coach at their 'spot', we proceeded to the Sergeants' Mess - the Cattle Pens - resulting in much subdued laughter from the officers remaining on the coach. We learnt later that their faces were a picture when they were dropped off at the Officers' Mess - the Zoo - never mind, 'All is fair in times of War!'*

*'In the cattle pens we slept on camp beds and dined in a marquee, eating food cooked and served by RAF cooks operating a 'field kitchen' and producing, as ever, superb food, particularly for breakfast - the best meal of the day, as I recall. This state of affairs lasted for about five weeks when we were moved into the dormitory of a girls boarding school/college that had been vacated for the duration.*

*'Our day to day activity at the airport comprised seeing in Brits, turning them round and seeing them off again. Obviously refuelling didn't feature. The main problem was parking space for aircraft. The airport apron was just not big enough to deal with the traffic arising from the Oil Lift. In addition to the normal civil traffic, it now had six Javelins parked full-time plus a continual flow of our Brits down from Nairobi, the Civil Brits and Carvairs down from Dar-es-Salaam, and the Canadian C-130s in from somewhere in the Congo - all of these dedicated to the Oil Lift. It was very hectic and 'oil lifters' were the bane of the airport manager's life particularly so if an aircraft was late in arriving or departing.*

*'Hence we made it big time with the airport manager after a crew had reported 'bumps' during flight while flying through icing conditions. It was No.3 engine (on 519 I think). I did the obligatory introscope check and declared the aircraft unserviceable and requiring an engine change - most of the EGVs had disappeared or were wrecked! A three-engined ferry back to Nairobi was not an option due to operational constraints. So we were directed to move the aircraft to a last-ditch parking space with the main bogies only just on the hardstanding and the tail over some wasteland*

*'Having signalled Nairobi for a spare engine and the associated gear, I set about organising the local equipment required to carry out the engine change. My request for a forklift or mobile crane capable of lifting 3500-5000 lbs. was met with a definite 'no can do'. It transpired that there was nothing of the sort within 200 miles of Lusaka. However, 'Scotty' a very helpful and resourceful Scotsman working for the Zambian Government, but who had previously worked on the Rhodesian Railways, made further enquiries regarding the possibility of the loan of a special crane normally used to lift railway coaches on and off the rails. He advised me that, due to its size, it was not normally taken on the roads and that problems might arise regarding its handling and serviceability - his disdain for the 'new' Zambian Railways management being quite clear. However, as we were all working within the remit of a 'national emergency' if I wanted it he would arrange its delivery to the airport from its normal place of residence on the other side of the City. It was our only option, and with the agitated Airport Manager hopping from one foot to the other, I asked him to expedite its delivery forthwith.*

*'By midday the next day, our spare engine had arrived from Nairobi along with Steve Stokes another Sergeant propulsion fitter sent down to give me a hand. This was unloaded and positioned nearby 519. Meanwhile, we had disconnected the engine bulkhead pipes, the 'swan neck' and the electrical connections, and also the prop was ready for removal. But no sign of the crane; however Scotty confirmed it was on its way.*

*'Whilst partaking of a well earned beer outside 'Ops' we became aware of the horrendous noise of a very powerful engine in the distance accompanied by much crashing and grating of gears. Half an hour later this huge contraption entered the airport. We were, as they say today, 'gob-smacked'. It was a crane with a 30-40 foot jib; the operating cables and other moving parts were all massive and liberally coated in rust. All this mounted on an articulated bed and towed by a tractor of similar proportions complete with a white operator and three 'boys'. It had obviously been a hell of a task just getting this 'Rig' to the airport.*

*'The operator was of matching physical proportions. 'Hans' was a huge South African of Boer extraction whose English was delivered in the way only South*

*Africans can i.e. gutturally. This was liberally interspersed with Afrikaans (the amount being in direct proportion to the agro he was suffering at the time). I hardly understood a word he said. Nonetheless, to gain the reassurances we required prior to starting the task, I asked some basic questions.*

*' 'Hans, what is the Safe Working Load (SWL) of your crane?' A pause - 'I do not know vot zis zaf verking load is meaning,' was the reply. But he left me in no doubt that the contraption (crane) could easily handle the weight of a Proteus powerplant. 'Haf no doubt, et ez a peedling task.' I felt a heel for having asked. We were provided with a demonstration of its operation and functionality. The power to operate the various cables was provided by a large and undoubtedly adequate diesel engine and the control system, i.e. selections by the operator for UP, DOWN, LEFT & RIGHT, employed a pneumatic vacuum system powered by a small donkey engine also a diesel - both engines being mounted on board the crane.*

*'To ask whether the crane had a current test certificate was definitely a 'No No'. 'When was it last used ?' I ventured. Hans was stumped, but one of the 'Boys' advised him that it had definitely been used since last summer!*

*'So without further ado we asked Hans to position the crane in front of and aligned with No.3 Engine. This entailed driving off into the distance some 75 yards or so, carefully avoiding a visiting CAA Viscount and then reversing the (articulated) rig towards the Brit. A difficult task achieved eventually at the expense of Hans' cool and many expletives in Afrikaans of which we were obviously ignorant, but the facial expressions of the 'boys' said everything!*

*'Before I continue, picture the scene if you will. A very irritated Hans sat in his small operating cab some 30 - 40 feet away and due to the general din of the airport, the noise of the two engines aboard the crane, and aircraft engine noise randomly thrown in, he can't hear us and we can't see him - plus we are all tired, hot, and sweaty and it's getting darker by the minute. We've set up one of our guys on the ground near his cab to relay instructions. First job is to remove the prop. No problem there until we request the crane jib to be swung to its left in order for the prop to be lowered onto its dolly. Notwithstanding that we have made the correct hand signals, the jib moves smartly to the right and Steve and I hang on to it for dear life and just manage to stop the Prop tips from cutting two neat slots into the fuselage.*

*'Apart from moving the jib in the wrong direction, another clear fact was now emerging - from here on in all jib or cable movements would be either coarse, bloody coarse, or disastrous! This was clearly not the time to ask whether this might be due the poor design, lack of maintenance of the crane's servo system or Hans' handling abilities! Oh how we missed the finesse and relative intimacy provided by the Coles Cranes and our civilian operators back at Lyneham.*

*'And so for the big one, the engine. With the sling fitted and the weight taken and hanging on some 30 to 40 feet of crane cable, Steve and I slackened and removed the four engine retaining bolts. We had carefully briefed Hans beforehand that at this point the whole rig i.e. crane complete with suspended load now needed to be moved forwards between six to twelve inches to allow us, inter alia, to access and release the engine/jet pipe clamps. This required Hans to move from the operator's cab to the cab of the 'tractor' - achieved after much huffing and puffing. He engaged a forward gear and let the clutch out as if he were underway on the highway and the whole rig shot forwards! Much shouting of 'STOP' from us accompanied by horrible graunching noises from the engine bulkhead area. The only things stopping the engine from moving completely and quickly forwards and away from the bulkhead were four RAF guys holding it back and various bits of bracketry and electrical connectors that weren't designed to do that! And the swan neck in the jetpipe that was just too big to come through the hole in the bulkhead!*

*'Hans reversed the rig back a few feet to restore some equilibrium to the situation. It was at this point that the donkey engine seized/expired/gave-up the ghost whilst emitting a noise akin to a stuck pig!*

*'No donkey engine equals no pneumatics equals no servo system equals no means of controlling the crane. So with one Proteus powerplant now freed from the airframe and suspended from the crane it was over to Hans for the next move. A sharp order had the three boys hard at it, rapidly*

*dismantling the engine and throwing bits into various boxes quickly acquired for that purpose - they had obviously done this before!*

*'In the meantime we examined the aircraft bulkhead for damage and unbent various bits of bent bracketry, checked the integrity of the electrical connector blocks etc. Fortunately, there was nothing too severe - there was some damaged 'refrasil' blanket but this could be covered by a 'Fit to Fly' entry in the F700.*

*'In what seemed to be an amazingly short time we heard sounds of hand cranking but no accompanying starting and running noises - all was not well! Hans asked for the boxes to be passed to him one by one, he shook each one vigorously, suddenly something fell out of one box, followed by a loud and angry outburst in Afrikaans. One of the boys suddenly turned and legged it out of the airport gate and into the surrounding bush, we never saw him again! With the help of Hans, the remaining two boys soon fixed it and we were back in business and got the Proteus down on the ground and secured for the night - we'd had enough for one day. Hans was more than happy to leave the crane where it was - he'd had a hell of a day. We retired to the domestic site.*

*'We completed the job next day with no further problems - lessons learned and all that I guess.'*

**Time Off**

*'Of course it was not all work and no play. By diligent adjustments to shift times and rosters we all managed to get the odd weekend off. And so it was that I took five guys down to see the Kariba Dam. Assisted/abetted by the ever resourceful Scotty, I managed to get the loan of a nearly new Government owned VW Combi, some maps, together with the necessary fuel (?). We threw some sleeping bags, boxes of 'C' Rations, and some beer into the back and off we went - mostly on earth (murram) roads, as I recall for about 70 or 80 miles with no problems whatsoever - fortunately the rains were over.*

*'We set up camp on the shore of Lake Kariba, got the solid fuel stoves going, cooked a meal of sorts and enjoyed our beers - all this as the sun slowly set across the Lake - fantastic stuff - just like the adverts of today for the Caribbean in fact.*

*NB: If you get the chance to visit Kariba don't miss it! Except of course this was over 35 years ago and being RAF Transport Command we tended to take these opportunities in our stride - but most people just did not move around the World in those days as freely as they do now.*

*'During the night we were reminded of the 'state of emergency' that still existed by the noise of powerful Rhodesian patrol boats as they kept an eye on the 'border' - a 'line' drawn down the centre of the 200 mile long lake. Obviously they were treating it all very seriously, after all the hydro electric turbines at the base of the dam were under their control - albeit -as I recall - still producing electricity for both Rhodesia and Zambia.*

*'In the morning, as senior member, I reminded the others that although we were there, in civvies to see and enjoy etc. we were still on duty. The 'enemy' was on the other side of the Dam so there was to be no contact/fraternisation. I had no wish to make the 'headlines', back in Lusaka. We saw Richard Lindley the ITN news reporter and his film crew almost on a daily basis - the Oil Lift story being top level daily news item back in the UK.*

*'And so we drove around to the Dam and parked on the Zambian side. A road traverses the top of the Dam, linking the two countries and across the other side the Rhodesians were in evidence. They had set up an emplacement with two machine guns and four soldiers on duty. I don't recall anything or anyone on our side. I led the party on foot about a third of the way across the road. We stopped to take stock of our surroundings; impressive doesn't even begin to describe it. It is truly a magnificent feat of engineering. On the wet side it was full to the brim and the Lake extended as far as the eye could see. On the dry side a waist high wall with no handholds seemed to dare you to look over the parapet into the huge and now almost dry Zambesi Gorge. When I did, an attack of vertigo made me back off instantly. You found yourself looking vertically down from about 400 feet, and the structure being concave in both the vertical and horizontal planes accentuated your lofty and insecure perch.*

*'We were discussing things in general, when 'Herbie', a young LAC electrician, suddenly jumps up onto the parapet and proceeds to hare along its curved edge*

A Lyneham 'tourist' took this photo of the Kariba Dam. (*Lyneham Globe*)

THE LYNEHAM GLOBE—No. 181

**TAKEN ON DETACHMENT**

Kariba Dam wall from the Observation Post on the Rhodesian side. At the nearer end of the wall are a Landrover and pillbox belonging to the Rhodesian Light Infantry who guard the dam.

*- heading for the Rhodesian side - this evidently in reaction to a dare by his mate! I, of course, was horror stricken and potential 'headlines' and career shortening scenarios streamed before my eyes whilst bawling at him to get off. Eventually, thank God, his nerve ran out and he flopped down onto the road surface a gibbering wreck. I ran over and proceeded to give him a right rollicking whilst querying his credentials at birth.*

*'By this time we were nearly three quarters of the way across and the Rhodesian Army guys had rumbled us. So we owned up but kept our distance and for about half an hour typical service banter, jokes, and light hearted political discussion ensued. All very enjoyable in fact, until that is, they started to lay bets as to whether 'Herbie' or any of us had the 'balls' to do another run in the opposite direction! At this point I called a halt to the proceedings, bade them farewell and we went on our way. Even today I still shudder at the thought of what would have happened if that lad had lost his footing and plunged into the gorge, or someone had taken a photo of us talking to the 'enemy'.*

*'The air transport element of the Zambian Air Force operated a couple of Dakotas and was based down at Livingstone - about 200 miles away. Twice a week they flew a regular return schedule to Lusaka, twice in one day. It turned out that the pilots were seconded RAF Master Pilots, and their wives enjoyed, nay insisted on, a day shopping in Lusaka - and so training schedules were arranged accordingly of course! Very handy for them, and also for us in the circumstances. A quick word and they were very sympathetic to our cause. And so over the period of the detachment, we all managed to get a day trip down to and over the Victoria Falls. You can only really take in the majesty of it all from the air and how better than in a Dak flown by RAF guys who knew the place like the back of their hands - magic!*

*'As I have already indicated the Airport was small by today's standards, - in fact a much larger one was built a few*

*years later. Notwithstanding, it catered for international and regional services. Twice a week a BUA VC-10 would alight onto the seemingly too small a runway (width wise). It disgorged its passengers and mail, took on more, and then took off again on the first leg of its return trip to London, thereby fully validating, at least for a short period of its life span, the specification that caused the aircraft to be created in the first place. No sign of any B707s here! Also, twice daily, a Central African Airways (CAA) Viscount would do a whistle stop and depart back to Salisbury just as if the 'state of emergency' didn't exist. They did not ask for or get any fuel of course!*

*'As mentioned, the runway was rather narrow necessitating the provision of a turnaround loop at each end. Generally, on landing the RAF Brits trundled all the way down to the loop and back. However, some crews successfully performed a '3-pointer' achieved via the judicious use of reverse thrust. Inevitably, to the concern of our favourite Airport Manager one failed and got bogged down. Of course the airport was immediately inoperative. And so one day it was a case of 'all hands' out and onto the runway to dig/pull it out.*

*'Whilst we were engaged in this activity, an incoming CAA Viscount captain surveys the scene from above and insists on landing. This he does and adds to our embarrassment by ending his landing run close to the stricken Brit and performs a very neat pirouette and taxies to the apron, as if to point out that a Viscount can easily do what a Brit should not be asked to do! He had made the point and thereafter I believe that 3-point turns by Brits were banned. However, his quick turnaround was stymied as the Tower refused take-off permission until we had got the Brit off the runway, which we did eventually.*

*'As a maintenance engineer, I found the day-to-day operations an interesting experience, particularly so working with the civil operators. Shortly after the engine change saga related to above, having marshalled in a British Eagle Brit the first thing obvious to me was that the No.2 Prop had one hell of an oil leak. The engine cowlings were green with oil and oil was running down the blades of the now stationary Prop. The flight engineer came down the steps with one arm behind his back, I pointed to the offending Prop and whilst acknowledging the problem he provided the 'fix' from behind his back - two one gallon cans of oil! However, whilst giving him a hand to decant the oil into the engine tank he did concede that there was no way he would be selecting No.2 engine for cabin conditioning on the return flight - they would have all choked to death! However, they and the aircraft survived, it is now displayed at Duxford for posterity.*

*'Another occasion, with a Lloyd International Brit, I was on the flight deck behind the flight engineer. The crew had completed the pre-start-up checks - we were held waiting for some package or other. I noticed that the red throttle warning light was 'ON' on No.4 engine and that 'Standby' was selected. On RAF Brits at the time this was a definite 'No Go' scenario. When I queried it with him on a subsequent visit, the F/E advised it was OK, because after all that was what 'Standby' was for wasn't it?*

*'A Carvair freighter (highly modified DC-6) suffered a starter motor failure on its No.2 engine and had no spare. The crew was determined not to be stuck overnight. The captain advised the tower he intended to perform a 3-engined take off. The aircraft positioned at the end of the runway with No.2 prop feathered. The good engines were opened up and the aircraft accelerated slowly down the runway and after what seemed an eternity it lifted off clawing for height whilst performing a slow circuit of the airfield. At the point it passed over our heads No.2 prop was unfeathered and the engine started and they went on their way into the darkening evening sky!'*

**A story with two versions**

The acrimony of UDI rolled on through the year, On 1st December Ian Smith  boarded a Britannia to fly to the Mediterranean to meet the British Prime Minister and his Commonwealth Secretary. Their destination turned out to be Gibraltar, where they were to board the cruiser, HMS Tiger, for talks that would be conducted in the strictest secrecy.

Ex-signaller examiner Peter Jordan spotted the following reference to that flight in Prime Minister Ian Smith's autobiography:

*'In November 1966 I received a dramatic message from Harold Wilson. It was an invitation to join him for talks on board a warship off Gibraltar. This was*

*indeed a climb-down for Wilson, because he had stated on a number of occasions that he was not prepared to meet me until I had returned to 'legality'. By contrast, I had always made it clear I would meet him any place, any time.*

*'We flew out of Salisbury on December 1. The aircrew enjoyed talking to me and, on the first leg, the captain asked if I would like to take a turn at the controls and moved out of his seat (Ian Smith had flown Spitfires during the Second World War). I asked him to take out the automatic pilot so that I could get a feel of the controls. It was good to find that my instrument flying was reasonable, because this branch of flying needs the greatest amount of practice. Although I had been getting in a few hours over the past years with our airforce chaps flying me around the country, this did not involve any night flying. We talked away with the number two pilot sitting in the right-hand seat with the captain moving in and out of the flight deck.*

*'At one stage someone came in and tapped the number two on his shoulder. He moved out of his seat, put his hand on my arm, 'I'll be back in a minute,' and walked out. I was happy to have no talking for a while, as it gave me an opportunity to have a good examination of the instrument panel and all the dials before me. The thought passed through my mind: I wonder what Harold Wilson would say if he knew that Captain Ian Smith (the traitor from Rhodesia) was at the controls of his RAF Britannia, single-handed with no one else in sight.'*

**'It wasn't like that!'**

Ex-crew chief, Ron King, in his inimitable style, leaps to the defence of a captain somewhat maligned in this autobiography extract:

*'Herewith a few meanderings sponsored by Pete Jordan's contribution; he is certainly to be congratulated on extracting that pearl from Ian Smith's autobiography on his trip in a Britannia. I fear much poetic licence was exercised in its presentation and an implication made against the captain and crew which I know is not true.*

*'One identifies with, 'Where were you when Kennedy was assassinated?' I was with this captain mentioned, in Portugal, I was his crew chief on the NATO*

The captions to the two photographs to the right read:

Top:

*'Men of the Royal Artillery and a logistic support unit form up on the runway at Thessaloniki, Greece alongside the Royal Air Force Transport Command Britannia which airlifted them from Lyneham to take part in 'Summer Exercise', the largest-ever test of NATO's Allied Command Europe Mobile Force. During the period 30 August to 5 September more than 3,800 troops and 6 million pounds of freight were lifted from five NATO countries to the area where the force undertook battle exercises with units of the Greek Army. Deployment of the British contribution to the ACE Mobile Force was effected by Britannias and Beverleys of Transport Command. Following a further exercise in Turkey, 'Marmara Express', the whole force was 'lifted out' again in late September.'*

Bottom:

*'Arriving at Mikkra air base, near the ancient Macedonian city of Thessaloniki, for NATO's Mobile Force Exercise, 'Summer Express', are the crew of Britannia 638, Flt Lt 'Doc' O'Connor, RCAF (pilot) 'takes the grape' from Wg Cdr C P Merrick, RAF (AIRCENT) while Gp Capt R Abrahams (Director of Air Operations for the exercise) and Sgt Bob Dawes (AQM) enjoy the joke. Looking on (far right) is Flt Lt Keith Scott, RCAF.'*

THE LYNEHAM GLOBE—No. 185 (5)

# EXPRESS DELIVERY

Men of the Royal Artillery and a logistic support unit form up on the runway at Thessaloniki, Greece, alongside the Royal Air Force Transport Command Britannia which airlifted them from Lyneham to take part in "Summer Exercise," the largest-ever test of NATO's Allied Command Europe Mobile Force. During the period 30 August to 5 September, more than 3,800 troops and 6 million pounds of freight were lifted from five NATO countries to the area where the force undertook battle exercises with units of the Greek Army. Deployment of the British contribution to the ACE Mobile Force is effected by Britannias and Beverleys of Transport Command. Following a further exercise in Turkey, "Marmara Express," the whole force was "lifted out" again in late September.

Arriving at Mikkra air base, near the ancient Macedonian city of Thessaloniki, for NATO's Mobile Force Exercise, "Summer Express," are the crew of Britannia 638, Flight Lieutenant "Doc" O'Connor, RCAF (pilot) "takes the grape" from Wg. Cdr. C. P. Merrick, RAF (AIRCENT) while Gp. Cpt. R. Abrahams (Director of Air Operations for the exercise) and Sgt. Bob Dawes (AQM) enjoy the joke. Looking on (far right) is Flt. Lieut. Keith Scott, RCAF.

(AIRCENT PHOTO)

## 511

*Only sixty-six more shopping days to*

## WRAF HOCKEY

THE Transport Command team

*Defence College tour, then commanded by Graf Von Badhassin. I only mention this in passing as I was with this captain, again as his crew chief, on this specific trip, the infamous 'Tiger Conference', with which this incident was alleged to have been associated. May I mention I have flown on many VIP trips with this captain; it has always been a privilege and pleasure to do so. Also I know that this incident, as portrayed, was not presented in its true light. I can also state categorically that this captain would never countenance such unprofessional behaviour. The actual events were somewhat different.*

*'Ian Smith was a charming courteous gentleman, whose deportment and dedication demanded respect and it was obvious from the start that he was being used and manipulated by a few politicians who lacked his charisma. He did in fact sit in the captain's seat, and fly the aircraft without autopilot; the copilot remained in his seat; the Eng was at his station and the navigator and signaller were both on the flight deck. I know because I stood behind the engineer. The captain was behind his own seat, standing at the place much favoured by TCEU route check captains. Our VIP, Ian Smith, was invited on to the flight deck by the captain, who moved out of his seat to accommodate him. He appeared in his ex-RAF Officer's greatcoat, with black buttons. This he removed before sitting in the captain's seat. We were responsible for both journeys. After the abortive meeting, as we left Gibraltar for Ascension, Ian Smith was invited back on the flight deck to assure himself that the right steer was being applied and we were in fact not Shanghai-ing him back to UK. This whole episode really needs a story - so here goes.*

Ian Smith with Harold Wilson at No.10.

*'This event was indeed in 1966 and was in fact the infamous 'Tiger Conference', held on HMS Tiger in Gibraltar. Two Brits and two Comets were involved positioned at Gibraltar via Ascension. We were No.1 Britannia - positioned at Gib and waiting. We established our Home Base in Gib at 'Chimney Corner' with the 216 crews - yes, we were talking. We were all suffering under the extreme scrutiny and interference from the 'Snowdrops' who wanted to identify labels on our shreddies before allowing us on our own ship. We were to deal with this at a later date. We got the 'Go' and held at Ascension with all the retinue. Incidentally, the 'Yanks' at Ascension were soundly thrashed at footer by a combined Brit and Comet lashed up team. The dreaded Bushy Taylor from 216 appeared in his long shorts, with moustache flying, frightening the opposition to death. Ian Smith was collected and flown into Gibraltar. We had hit a snag and, whilst we were in Ascension, decided to fix it in our stand down time. The nosewheel steering had an hydraulic leak and the follow up cables were slack. This resulted in a surfeit of hydraulic oil on my shirt and ruined my service shoes. We had a VIP on board and I had an oily shirt and was reduced to desert boots. Now, having fixed the snag, I was faced by a 'fait accompli' so a few strings were pulled by SSB to Gib. As we taxied in to dispersal at Gib down the taxi track appeared Sheila Margaret Eames on her bike waving an urgent signal for our captain - two shirts and a pair of size 10s for me. Warrant Officer Eames had previously been posted to Gibraltar from Lyneham where she had been Our Girls' mentor, and she knew everybody, believe me. She confided in me later. 'Tiny,' she said, 'your shirts and shoes generated more paperwork than the whole of the Tiger Conference.' She and I were great mates and I still miss her. It follows that by now we had formed opinions about the main performers and our statesmen had not emerged with awards for diplomacy. The cavalier fashion in which this charming courteous Ian Smith was treated by a pipe smoking pipsqueak beggared belief.* (Author: Will lawyers please contact RK direct.) *A Killicks cabin on*

*board a warship is hardly just reward for a diplomat who held the fate of a nation in his capable hands; he was trying to establish justice through diplomacy and was treated like a pariah. It was indeed poetic justice that the architect of this attitude was to fall later by his own ineptitude and political chicanery. There certainly was a change in the atmosphere when we learned the talks had failed. As was previously stated, Ian Smith, looking very sombre, was invited up to the flight deck after take off to assure himself that we were not hi-jacking him back to UK. The exercise was not without its trauma as we had some interaction in Gibraltar as most of the ground crews were 'Gibs' and the 'Claim from Spain' was strong. 'Rock' security was tight, but we still had one incident. It was discovered by John Tasker, the eagle-eyed crew chief on No.2 Brit, that some nose wheel nuts had been loosened back to the locking collars! How or when this had happened was a mystery; this was to promote massive security re-inspections on all aircraft and our inspections were even more rigorous.*

*'Before our final departure we exacted revenge. One very zealous SIB Sergeant was enlightened to the wonders of the Golden Rivet and lured into the front freight bay to examine same! Somehow the upper latch of the front cargo hatch released, and as I was stood on the forward freight floor hatch just at that time, 'Hey Presto', one pain in the butt incarcerated. It was coincidental that at that precise time the Vernon failed. We realised that as he could hurt himself or inadvertently operate the fire extinguisher system, he was released without prejudice. It was coincidental that his persistence and plain bad manners seemed to evaporate after this incident. We returned to base and I, for one, had learnt that our Lords and Masters are far from infallible - but my faith in the aircraft we flew and our air and ground crew were just reward for belonging.'*

**French Colonial**

The oil embargo put another destination on the Britannia map, Majunga in the Republic of Malagasy (previously Madagascar). The Rhodesians attempted to overcome the embargo by shipping oil into the port of Beira, Mozambique. From there it would have to be transported overland. To plug this gap a detachment of maritime

OBE—No. 188

B.E.M.s

Air Vice Marshal D. C. McKinley, S.A.S.O., Transport Command, presented B.E.M.'s to two Lyneham S.N.C.O.'s on 8th November. *Top*: Ch. Tech. King, a Britannia Mobile Servicing engineer. *Bottom*: Chief Tech. Morrice, Base Servicing Sqn.

Air Vice Marshal D C McKinley, SASO Transport Command, presented BEMs to two Lyneham SNCOs on 8th November. One was to Ground Engineer/Crew Chief and considerable Britannia character, Chief Tech Ron King. The second was to a technician typical of the all the ground crew behind the Britannia scene, Chief Tech Morrice of Base Servicing Squadron. (*Lyneham Globe*)

Shackleton aircraft was established at Majunga to provide a patrol of the Mozambique Channel. The airfield and its location provided quite an eye opener for crews of the Britannias which flew in regular supplies for the detachment. Owing much to French colonial origins, it was different! A correspondent reported:

*'The Detachment gives crews the opportunity of taking a look at a declining colonial influence. Now an independent republic, the country's second language is still French. Amusing conversations take place when schoolboy Parisian encounters African pidgin à la Légion. Well south of the equator, the climate is fairly pleasant and the pace of life very slow, the only people who ever hurry anywhere being the detachment in their Land Rover.'*

Many a story surrounds a not too salubrious place of entertainment called 'Madam's'!

**The Beira Patrol**

This detailed account of the Shackleton activity at Majunga was written for an Internet series by David Hill and is reproduced here with his kind permission:

*'In March 1966 renewed attempts*

*were being made to stop supplies of oil reaching the rebel regime in Rhodesia. The UN sanctioned a blockade of the port of Beira in Mozambique through which, it was believed, Rhodesia was receiving tanker-loads of oil. A Royal Navy task force patrolled the Strait of Mozambique and the RAF was required to supply air surveillance to identify suspicious ships which could then be intercepted and boarded for inspection. Initially, the task fell to Nos. 37 and 38 Sqns. based at Aden and Malta, but as these squadrons disbanded, and after a stint by 42 Sqn with the Mark 3, it fell to the Mark 2 units at Ballykelly to take over.*

*'The detachments were based at Majunga, on the northwest coast of the island of Madagascar, or the Malagasy Republic as it was by then known. Initially three aircraft and crews formed the detachment, and by the time the Ballykelly squadrons arrived, a bearable if somewhat spartan camp, named Camp Britannique, had been established. The airfield was shared with the local airport and some additional concrete had been laid to accommodate the Shackletons and the weekly transport aircraft from the UK. Because the government of the Malagasy Republic didn't want the RAF's presence to be seen as permanent, the facilities were required to have a degree of non-permanence about them. As a result Camp Britannique was a collection of tents and aluminium prefabricated huts located next to the airport*

*'The senior NCO's were housed in a former maternity hospital, and the HQ offices and the admin accommodation occupied a former shop in the main street of Majunga town. Various other personnel had rented flats, bungalows wherever available. The climate was hot all the year round, half the year wet, the other dry, which was hard on both men and machines.*

*'The air operations were part of Operation Mizar. The three detached aircraft had a variety of tasks; one aircraft was tasked to undertake the surveillance flights on an irregular basis as required, usually two to three per week; another was responsible for search and rescue and any other flights that might be necessary, such as a transit up to Gan, with the third held in reserve. This aircraft soon became a source of spares to keep the other two airworthy, but at least this practice contributed to a negligible sortie failure rate, which wasn't bad considering the remoteness of the location.*

*'Ballykelly's involvement started in late April 1967, 210 Sqn. providing three crews and aircraft, with 204 and 210 generally taking it turn about to provide personnel (while 210 remained based at Ballykelly) at three monthly intervals right up until the closure of the base, apart from a six month period in mid-1968 when 205 Sqn. from Singapore took over, after which the detachment was reduced to two aircraft and crews.*

*'The normal route to Majunga was Ballykelly - Gibraltar - Malta - Djibouti - Mombasa (or latterly, Khartoum - Nairobi) - Majunga, an approximate flying time of 40 hours. A major variation to this routine, however, involved a crew of 210's second detachment, which went out in October 1967. One aircraft was being rotated back to Ballykelly and WL737/Z was being flown out as a replacement. Because of the Arab - Israeli War then taking place, it was decided to keep the aircraft well away from the Middle East and consequently it was routed Gibraltar - Cape Verde Islands - Ascension Island - Kinchasa, Belgian Congo, where a war was also taking place, and on to Nairobi where someone had the cheek to let down a mainwheel tyre, necessitating a one week stopover, and then finally on to Majunga!*

*'Rotation of air and ground crews took place by RAF Britannias, which flew the regular weekly service. The aircraft were flown back to Ballykelly during a detachment change-over if servicing was due. The surveillance sorties quickly became routine, identifying possible sanctions breakers and reporting them to the navy, and also providing the patrolling frigates with very welcome mail drops. The requirement to maintain aerial surveillance in the area after Ballykelly's closure actually contributed to prolonging 204's existence, as the task was considered too trying for the highly sophisticated Nimrod then entering service.*

*'When a squadron was involved in providing the detachment, the absence of up to half the available crews inevitably put an increased pressure on the remainder in their efforts to fulfil the squadron's normal duties, which didn't seem to diminish as a result of this prolonged, and some would say futile, commitment.'*

The scene on board the Ascension Island aeromedical aircraft. (Ted Wright)

**Meanwhile ...**

In May of 1966 an alert went out for an aeromedical flight to Ascension Island. A road accident there had resulted in 11 casualties, all British. Flt Sgt Ted Wright, 99 Squadron AQM described this flight:

*'May 19th, Ascension Day, brought an unusual coincidence when Britannia 635, flown by crews drawn from both 99 and 511 Squadrons took off on a mercy dash to the tiny island of Ascension which is in the South Atlantic, midway between South America and South Africa.*

*'A road accident had resulted in eleven civil engineer casualties, all British subjects, who were to be flown home for treatment. The aircraft was fitted out as a mobile operating theatre ready to deal with any emergency, but happily these arrangements were not needed and the flight reverted to that of a normal casevac.*

*'Ascension Island is an extinct volcano, and the cone, now full of water and covered with trees, dominates the 36 square miles of lava covered rock. The island more or less supports a total population of 2,000. There are many links with history on the Ascension; the church for instance was built by the British Navy in 1843, and fortifications on the hillside overlooking the harbour include two old cannons and also two Navy guns which were removed from HMS Hood in 1934.*

*'One of the island's attractions includes the lava beds, which are the breeding ground of the Fairy Tern. These lava beds, which look, but are not, newly produced, form fantastic beds of coke twisted into bizarre shapes and trail down to the lower slopes of the mountain and finally fall into the sea. When you visit the place the air is full of Terns, wheeling and calling*

A view of the volcano from the aircraft door. (*Ted Wright*)

*only a few feet above your head.*

*'Our stay was of short duration, and although I found it full of interest I can well understand the sentiments of our patients who all expressed a desire to be away to wash Ascension's dust from their throats. A large crowd gathered to see us off, and almost the whole of the island's vehicular population lined the parking area as we taxied out.'*

**Not uncommon**

It has already been indicated that such a call-out was not an unusual event for the Britannia but this was only one aspect of aeromedical flying. There was a routine side also. All the hospitals at the overseas bases would want to return some patients to the UK for further treatment and so there were scheduled aeromedical flights. Sergeant Mike Sims of the Medical Branch remembers the ones from Bahrain:

*'I was a Senior Aircraftsman at the RAF Hospital at Muharraq when the Britannias were the main aircraft for aeromedical evacuation of patients back to the UK via Cyprus. The flights took place every other Monday. The arrival of the medical teams was always a good chance to catch up on UK news and easy excuse for a social evening and, of course, the chance to meet the young ladies who made up part of the team.*

*'Patients were prepared some hours in advance - luggage, drugs, documents all had to be readied for the journey home. For this, volunteers had to be called in to supplement the regular hospital staff to ensure a smooth and speedy loading of the patients on the aeroplane. They were moved to the airfield in a convoy of stretcher buses and ambulances. The night temperature was high as was the humidity. The smell of aviation fuel hung in the air.*

*'The 'Condecs' (mobile freight platforms that could be raised to the door of the aircraft) were used to load the stretcher patients. They were not the most reliable piece of equipment and I recall one occasion when one was stuck half way and the*

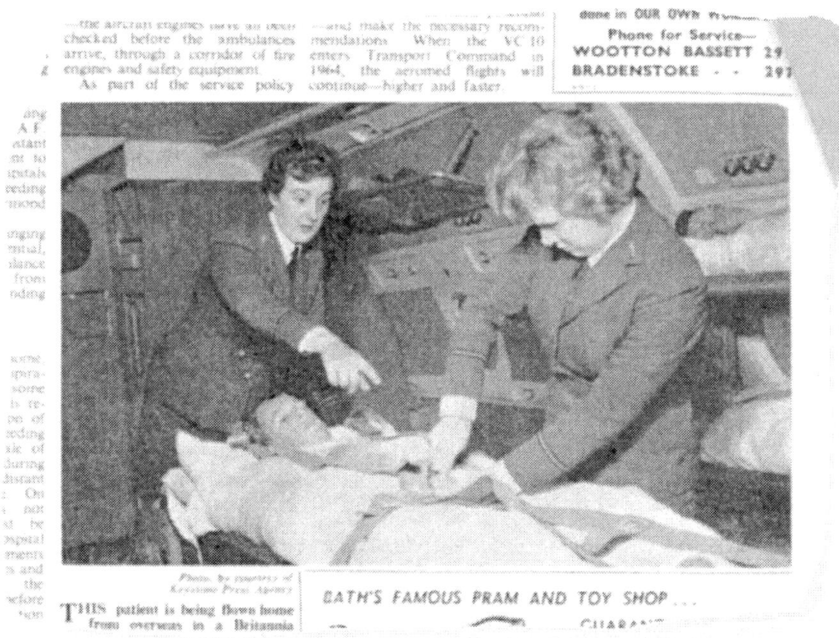


Nursing Sisters secure a patient on board a Britannia aeromedical flight. (*Lyneham Globe*)

*six stretchers had to be transferred to another Condec. That was the night that the aircraft went unserviceable and we had to take all the patients off and return them to the hospital only to bring them back a little while later.*

*'Thankfully things generally went smoother than this. The patients liked the Britannia. It was a long flight but the comfort and care they received compensated for this. After the departure of the Britannias from the Service, I felt that a large gap was left in the aeromed world and a lot of atmosphere lost that could not be found in the later aircraft used.'*

**Oil Lift ends**

*The Lyneham Globe* marked the end of the Oil Lift thus:

*'At 0815 hours local, on the 31st October 1966, the last sortie of the Oil Lift departed Lusaka for Nairobi. After many rumours the Zambian Oil Lift was officially over. For about a year, Britannia aircraft and crews of Nos.99 and 511 Squadrons had flown an average of 5½ loads of 50 full oil drums every day (*) into the Zambian airfields of N'Dola and Lusaka, some 1,200 miles from Nairobi. In addition, full logistic support was given to No.29 Javelin Fighter Squadron, RAF Regiment Units, No.1 ACC Radar Units and personnel serving with HQ Combritzam. The range and scope of this support alone was staggering.*

*'The Oil Lift operation started on the 20th December 1965, using Dar-es-Salaam as a base. On 4th January the detachment moved to Nairobi/Embakasi Airport, where they remained for the rest of the operation. The Royal Air Force Britannias operated daily and were joined for a short period by civil charter aircraft and USAF and RCAF C130s.*

*'The base at Embakasi Airport expanded from one small hut into a sizeable operations and technical site. Oil trucks rolled in day and night from Mombasa, a journey of 300 miles mostly over dirt roads, one was charged by an elephant and suffered severe damage - the truck, not the elephant. The loading and unloading of the Britannias at all airfields was carried out by the MAMS teams detached from Abingdon, Cyprus and Aden supported by locally employed labour. Using a 12,000lbs forklift, 12 x 45-gallon drums weighing approximately 375lbs each, could be swung into the aircraft each time. At Ndola and Lusaka, only 6,000lbs forklifts were available but nevertheless the teams became so expert that 50 full drums could be unloaded and 92 empty drums back-loaded in less than 25 minutes. It became indeed, a slick operation.*

*'Superimposed upon on the Oil Lift, several other tasks were undertaken by the Britannias operating at Nairobi. They included a 50-ton frozen meat lift to Aden, the withdrawal of the majority of personnel and equipment from Zambia and the positioning of Majunga detachment personnel and freight at Nairobi for onward movement to Malagasy by MR Transport aircraft. In just under one year about 3,500,000 gallons of fuel contained in 75,000 drums were lifted into Zambia. During 1,560 sorties, 10,300 flying hours were achieved on the Oil Lift alone. In addition to the fuel just under 2,000,000lbs of freight and 3,731 passengers were carried in the Oil Lift aircraft.'*

**The last flight**

Although the official end of the Oil Lift was declared as 31st October 1966, in fact the very last aircraft carrying the last detachment personnel left Nairobi on 6th November. I know, I was the captain. Because of the amount of payload required and the fuel to route via Malta, we had been authorised to operate to Military Operating Standards (MOS). Normally, in common with all the strategic transport aircraft of the day, we operated to full Performance 'A' standards. These standards are declared for civil airline use and ensure that, should there be an engine failure, in particular at the most critical stage i.e. the take-off, then control of the aircraft could be maintained. Maximum take-off weights have to be calculated, from Operation Data Manuals, to ensure this. However, every now and then, we as a military force could not afford this luxury. The job would not get done. So there was this fall back to MOS where a degree of risk existed but one considered acceptable. Part of MOS was that the maximum take-off weight was increased from 185,000lbs to 190,000lbs. This Nairobi take-off was to be at that weight. I swear we were more like 200,000lbs! It had been soaking down with rain all day as the aircraft was loaded. The sodden cargo must have weighed more than its declared

* This *Lyneham Globe* figure is disputed! There were six aircraft on the detachment and each flew two sorties per day. The load for each was 56 barrels.

weight. Furthermore, our passengers were all wily old travelling hands and under each seat and in every nook and cranny they had stowed all those things that such people transport - personal tool boxes, boxes of fruit, wood carvings, meat! Half past midnight was the time scheduled for the take-off and our passengers spent the evening celebrating the fact that they were going home. They were piped on board the aircraft by a Flying Officer signaller and sometime bagpiper, Ian Lewis. The last person to board was Squadron Leader Eric Reeves, the last Detachment Commander. He was building quite a reputation as the 'Mr Fix-It' of Britannia detachments.

**Fight for height**

We taxied out into the dark East African night. It was still raining. Nairobi has an extra long runway to cope with its high altitude, over 5000 feet amsl, and high temperatures. We needed a lot of the 12,000 feet of concrete. As we clawed our way slowly upwards into the black night, it became obvious that if we set course straight away, we were not going to have sufficient altitude to clear the high ground to the north. We would have to orbit over the airfield to gain height first. It took for ever. The use of Maximum (Take-Off) Power is restricted to five minutes. We found that the only way to make progress away from the ground was to use that power for the five minutes, rest the engines for a while and then have another five minutes worth. We eventually set course. It was the start of a long day (night). With 1½ hour refuelling stop in Malta, we landed at Lyneham over 15 hours after the Nairobi take-off - and that had been at half past midnight!

**Appreciation**

The epitaph to the Oil Lift can be provided by the message to the AOC-in-C from the then Minister for Defence (Royal Air Force):

'*Since last December, three and a half million gallons of fuel have been carried into Zambia by means of the RAF oil airlift which comes to an end today. I realise that this has been achieved in the face of considerable difficulties and has only been made possible by a great deal of hard work and sacrifice, including separation from families and dislocation of normal service activities. I should be most grateful if you would pass to all concerned my warm congratulations on a job of great importance thoroughly well done.*'

**Message from the C-in-C**

The Air Officer Commander-in-Chief wished to congratulate all concerned on a job well done. He went on to say that this operation brought to the forefront once again the excellent co-operation that can be

A final Oil Lift tribute to the loaders - and the dreaded Britannia Freight Lift Platform! (*Ian Berry*)

achieved between aircrew and groundcrews under difficult circumstances. Over 500 groundcrew of Lyneham were rotated on detachment at one time or another; all aircrews of the two Britannia squadrons did three or four tours (each of four-week duration). The percentage of on-time departures of Britannias from Nairobi was 92%; a figure that all aircrews and groundcrews can be justifiably proud.

**Another end**

Another era was also declared officially ended in 1966. 'Confrontation', the Far East Indonesian threat, was considered at an end on 11th August.

**Riding out the storm**

No flying effort would be possible without the support of the ground crew. An earlier *Lyneham Globe* photo has acknowledged that, at the end of 1966, Chief Technician Ron King, the crew chief of some note, was awarded the British Empire Medal. In later years Ron remembered one trip in particular. Those readers who know him will recognise the story telling style:

*'We were out with XN398 (Altair) on a UKB Trainer with dear old Bill Coburn as 'El Capitano'. The ATS(B) screen crew were no doubt prima donnas in their own opera but a coordinated crew they were not. Bill had to stamp his authority very early as everybody appeared to want to be captain. On leaving Changi we were down to our last Green Satin spare, the CCWR was going demi-berserk and we were off to typhoon valley - yippee! We had a good met forecast for Kai Tak, so off we went. With a rapidly deteriorating met actual, we arrived overhead Kai Tak, eventually landing - trainee captain's, but I was kind and only logged one landing in the 700. The crews went off to their various messes and I liaised with HAEC as I had a refuel, wheel change and a host of bugs to kick to death. When all was done I hauled myself down to the Sgts' Mess for a shower, change and a gallon of San Mig. I was just about to lower the first one past the Plimsoll Line when disaster struck; some misbegotten Sgt came into the bar and said I was needed on the blower - urgently.*

*'The info was that Typhoons 'Timor' and 'Estelle' were converging and were due to come through Hong Kong in about 1½ hours. They had attempted to contact the crew and were still trying. Cathay Pacific were hangaring all their aircraft, inbound aircraft were being diverted and aircraft that couldn't be hangared were being dispersed. They wanted our tow bar to move the aircraft to an engine running area - if the wind speed was forecast to exceed 80 knots then the aircraft had to be 'chock locked' and engines kept running to prevent emigration! They sent transport for me; down at the airport the wind was already 40 knots and gusting. We towed the aircraft to the running area and lashed the chocks fore and aft - nose and mains and set up radio contact with air traffic. My 'number one' in the cockpit was a Mr Yu Chee (HAEC senior supervisor) - an absolute ace. He was one of the cleverest persons it has been my privilege to meet and we have remained personal friends since that date.*

*'I was very glad that we had the ballast of a 52,000lbs fuel load. The tower*

Two intrepid 'Oil Lifters' - Flt Lts Ron Stubbs and Alan Simpson of 99 Squadron. (*Ian Partridge*)

*requested that we start engines and stabilise - the primary strike was imminent. The ground power set and the bloke on the headset were taken away as they were in danger of being blown into the props - or away. I blew superfine, went to 'Flight' and prepared to ride out the storm. The control locks obviously had to be left in but it suddenly dawned on me to trim the b****r fully nose down to help keep old Altair anchored to the deck. Now I was on my own. The headset crackled, there was an eerie glow in the cockpit, the motors roared, the aircraft was being buffeted about - all giving the impression that we were airborne and doing a Cu Nim penetration.*

*'After 1 hour 34 minutes Bill Coburn came on the headset and gave me a bollocking for swiping his aircraft when I wasn't checked out! It was great to hear his voice and he stayed with us until final shutdown, 3 hours and 16 minutes later. During that time there were some hairy moments when quite large pieces of debris were wafting about like so many feathers, striking the aircraft and some going through the props; we were indeed fortunate not to sustain major damage. On one quietish occasion, when peering through the murk, I observed that the two flags on each end of the Cathay building were flying in opposite directions. It dawned on me that we were in the eye of the storm and more was to come. It was then that I thought that being Buddhist might pay off, so I quizzed my companion as to whether I could remuster as our chap didn't seem to be having much pull in this theatre. He didn't think it would work because I wasn't Chinese!*

*'The exit came with a lurch as a final spiralling updraught hit the fin and rudder - and then it was all over. The wind slowly died away. Air traffic did a radar sweep and told us it was safe to shut down. We had burnt enough fuel to get us to Changi. With the quiet I thought, 'If some b****r drank that San Mig I left on the bar, then I hope it was off!'*

*'When we got back to Changi, the aircraft and Bill and I were commandeered for the evacuation of British Nationals during the India/Pakistan fracas (that's another story). Bill became Detachment Commander and got himself a good tramp steamer crew who all worked together like a dream - I was proud to be part of it. So, it all started as a ten day UKB Trainer but Bill and I didn't get back for six weeks and that was on our well used Brit with enough entries in the FTF Log to cancel out my POSB entries.'*

On 'Late Finals' Lusaka. (*Ian Partridge*)

In the first edition of this book there was a distinct lack of photographs of the Oil Lift. This photo is included in appreciation of Ian Partridge filling that gap. Sgt Partridge, signaller, is pictured here with his captain, Ron Stubbs. (*Ian Partridge*)

RAF Lyneham, January 1966, photographed from a Comet 2. Six of the Britannias were in Dar-es-Salam. (*Ken Guest*)

We are approaching the half way point of this Britannia journey. (*Bill Robinson*)

The adventures of Messrs. Ad Minn and Org at Wootton Lynstoke continue ...

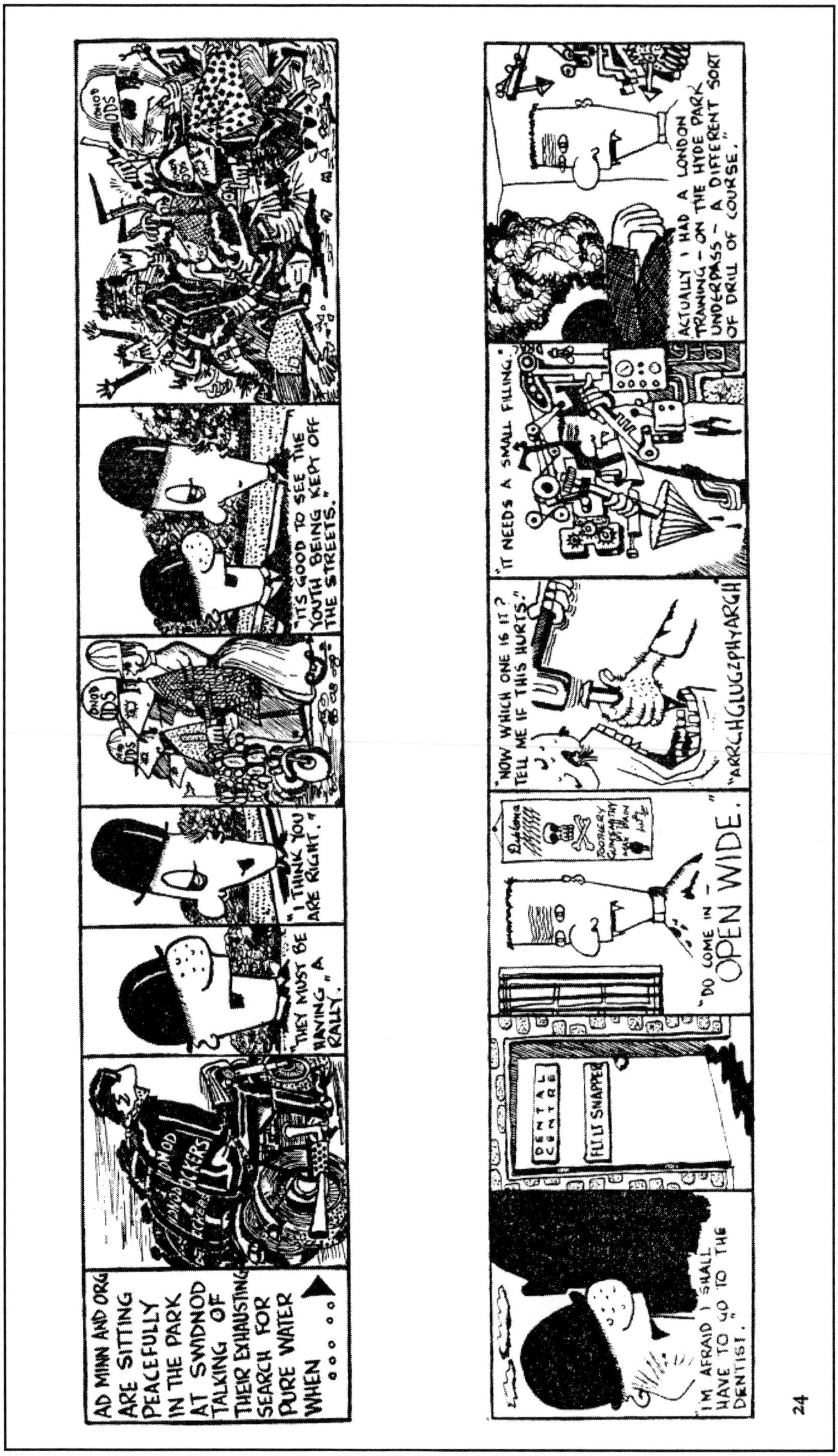
AD MINN AND ORG ARE SITTING PEACEFULLY IN THE PARK AT SWIDNOD TALKING OF THEIR EXHAUSTING SEARCH FOR PURE WATER WHEN . . . . . .
"THEY MUST BE HAVING A RALLY."
"I THINK YOU ARE RIGHT."
"IT'S GOOD TO SEE THE YOUTH BEING KEPT OFF THE STREETS."
"I'M AFRAID I SHALL HAVE TO GO TO THE DENTIST."
DENTAL CENTRE
FLIT SNAPPER
"DO COME IN - OPEN WIDE."
"NOW WHICH ONE IS IT? TELL ME IF THIS HURTS."
"ARRGHGLUGZPHYARGH"
"IT NEEDS A SMALL FILLING."
"ACTUALLY I HAD A LONDON TRAINING - ON THE HYDE PARK UNDERPASS - A DIFFERENT SORT OF DRILL OF COURSE."
24

CHAPTER TWENTY ONE

# Withdrawal from Aden

Having closed the last chapter with awards, the theme is continued as perusal of the Lyneham 1967 New Year Honours List presents some names that so well represent the people of those times. Flt Lt R C E (Bob) George, a long established 511 Squadron captain; 511 navigator, Flt Lt J R (Jack) Skrine, New Zealander by birth and now retiring from the Service and returning to his homeland, overland - a considerable character - a story was that on one route flight he woke up in a field - and could not remember which country he was in!

Flt Lt D B (Don) Walker represented the 99 captains. In the list was one of the earliest of the female AQMs, Master Air Quartermaster (W) Annie Bowden. Master Engineer Danny Brew was a stalwart in the 511 Engineers' Section. Finally, one of the 'back room boys' was acknowledged, Warrant Officer D C White, inevitably a 'Chalky', adjutant of 511 Squadron. He was the other half of one of the many happy marriages that blossomed from those days - his partner being 99 Squadron AQM, Betty Fendley.

**Fg Off Bob Henderson AFC**

Later in the year there was to be recognition of the Oil Lift effort in the Honours List with the award of the Air Force Cross to Fg Off Bob Henderson who held the record for the number of days and flying hours on the detachment.

Born in Vancouver, Bob completed a short service engagement with the Royal Canadian Air Force. In common with a number of his fellow countrymen, he then joined the Royal Air Force. Over a period of a few years there must have been up to ten Canadians serving on Britannias. Bob remained on the aircraft to its end. He then stayed very much in the strategic transport world, flying the VC10 and then TriStars. On his retirement, he must have rated as the most experienced RAF transport pilot ever, having accumulated over 18,000 flying hours.

In this era, artist Penelope Douglas travelled the route painting the transport aircraft. However, for the Belfast one, displayed in the Officers' Mess, Brize Norton, she chose the home base location. (*David Berry*)

**Route companions**

The Britannias now shared the routes with the newly acquired VC10s. The Belfasts were also establishing themselves.

A young Bob Henderson when his flying hours were around the 3000 mark. (*Bill Robinson*)

New route companions - a Belfast photographed at RAF Gan in 1968 - ... (*Ken Guest*)

216 Squadron was slowly losing its Comet 2s which it had continued to operate alongside the Comet 4s as they increased in number. The time was not far off before the deliveries of the Hercules (over 60) would commence. It could be claimed that this was the very peak of the Royal Air Force's long range air transport capability. There was also our short range brethren, the Argosys and Andovers. It was an interesting time to be part of the controlling authority for all this - or so I had to believe, for in July I was posted to the Transport Command Operations Centre at Upavon as an Ops Controller!

... and the VC10 - over some unidentified water.

A damp day at Lyneham. (*Ian Berry*)

**Waiters of the air**

In 1967, it was decided that corporal air stewards be introduced as part of the Britannia crew, primarily for flights carrying a large number of passengers. It was clearly nonsense to recruit more AQMs when, on many occasions, what was required was 'a waiter in the air'. They were drawn from the airmen and airwomen who normally staffed the Officers' and Sergeants' Messes. A *Lyneham Globe* report outlined the training:

*'January 9th saw the arrival of the first course of Air Stewards at Lyneham for two weeks training at the Air Training Squadron. With two weeks at 242 OCU Thorney Island, and one week at the School of Catering, Hereford, successfully completed, the course of 14 corporals arrived at Lyneham full of enthusiasm to complete the final two weeks of the Air Stewards' course. The five-week course starts at Thorney Island where they are taught basic air movements theory. At Hereford they are taught passenger psychology, catering and hygiene. The two weeks training at ATS consists of one week in the classrooms where they learn about aircraft emergencies and cabin airmanship to aircraft type (Britannias and Comets). The second week is mainly for air checks, including an overseas flight. It is during these overseas flights that the ATS examiner (AQM) screening the trainee steward will finally assess whether or not the trainee has attained the required standard. At the time of this report being written some of the first successful Air Stewards have returned to their parent units to await posting to one the Lyneham squadrons early February.*

*'Flying Officer A. Pritchard (ATS AQM Leader) who is in charge of Air Steward training at Lyneham reports, 'I am very pleased with the high results achieved by the first course. With the combination of good supervision of Air Stewards by the Air Quartermasters and a high standard of cabin service from the Air Stewards, this new scheme should be a big success with strategic aircraft.'*

*'The Air Steward scheme is open to volunteers from the trade of Steward (Group 19) who must be corporal or SAC qualified to corporal. The tour of duty on strategic aircraft will be for 2½ years, returning to their basic trade at the end of the tour. Successful candidates will be awarded 3/6 per day crew pay and a flying badge (not yet decided). At no time will they be allowed to fly as crew unless they are under the supervision of a fully qualified Air Quartermaster.*

The last sentence is a clue to the fact that, amongst the crews, there were some considerable reservations about how well this would work; the aircrew world *is* something of a 'closed shop'. But prejudice was broken down by the individuals recruited and they have to be congratulated on this and the standard of service which they set.

Such was their success that the scheme continues to this day.

**Champagne Charlie**

In all walks of life there are considerable characters and the air steward ranks had their share. One was known as 'Champagne Charlie'. For much of his route flying he tended to be a bit of a loner, not sticking with the crew during the off-duty time. But he obviously enjoyed himself in his way as indicated by his occasional reappearance early in the morning. Then, perhaps as a mark of a well spent night, he would insist on buying the crew champagne to have with their breakfast! It is unbelievably true that he married a belly dancer from a Cyprus cabaret. The occasion was solemnly marked, service-wise, by the attendance of his Squadron Commander, Wing Commander Jock Kennedy - of whom more will be said later.

**Tour of the Rainmakers**

A *Lyneham Globe* account of a VVIP trip that didn't enjoy a lot of sunshine:

'*Way back, around the end of January, a 511 crew departed for Changi and greater things - Britannia XN 398, superbly prepared for the VIP role by Lyneham, was on its way to collect our future Chief of Air Staff and return him from Singapore, via half the globe, to UK. The crew of twelve was captained by Sqn Ldr E E Reeves, supported by Flt Lts P J Smith and K Jenkins, M Sig P Waller and M Eng A Howden. Slaving over the stove in the galley - Flt Sgts T Reynolds and B Cluett, ably assisted by Sgts (W) Rita Bradbury and 'Liz' Robertson. Sgt 'Corky' Corfield and his henchmen, Sgts Ray Williams and Wilf Wilkins of the Mobile Servicing team completed the crew. Flt Lt I Johnson and family were to accompany the flight as far as Auckland.*

*'After an uneventful trip to Changi in a semi pax-freight role, preparations were made for the main task. Changi's special rain lashed down steadily but ceased just long enough for the farewell parade and fly-past to be performed, and Air Chief Marshal Sir John Grandy and Lady Grandy were welcomed aboard on schedule. There followed a flight through the night for a landing in appalling conditions at Darwin.*

On their arrival back at Lyneham, Air Chief Marshal Sir John and Lady Grandy are escorted into the Terminal Building by the AOC-in-C and the Station Commander. (*Lyneham Globe*)

*It seemed ironic that our fearless captain, a great gliding man, should find one of his best thermals on the Darwin ILS at 1200 feet! Leaving Darwin an hour later the calm of the flight deck was rudely disturbed by an overheating alternator necessitating the shutdown of No.2 engine, then on to Canberra where 'Corky' Corfield and Co., battled nobly with swarms of flies in the heat of the day to fit the alternator blank. The aircrew sampled the beer and 'Kiwi' Johnson shook us all by showing great domesticity - actually pouring out and drinking tea in public.*

*'We left Canberra on February 3rd with a full ceremonial send off and headed for Auckland. Sir Francis Chichester had departed in the same direction some hours earlier and despite certain cynical remarks about our schedule we are confident that we really did overtake him. Despite a first-class attempt by the copilot to ruin the navigator's timing effort our VIPs were able to meet the RNZAF Guard of Honour at Whenuapai on time, and we were all in the land of the Kiwi. After a lot of intensive telephoning by Tony Reynolds, accommodation was found in a very pleasant private hotel in Auckland. Four days were spent there, cars were hired and the local area explored. Pete Smith and Ken Jenkins had to leave one particular bar because they were not escorted by ladies. Ken's remark, when the barman raised the point, 'But we're together,' didn't help much either! From Auckland to Wellington for some more Kiwi hospitality, leaving Ian Johnson to visit friends and relatives. Here the tow-bar disintegrated but was reassembled by our intrepid servicing team, also by this time the new alternator had been fitted and it was 'all systems go'.*

*'On to Nandi, in Fiji, for a one night stay on the 9th. Here the weather set the pattern for the rest of the trip. As our Met friends say 'occasional rain' - occasionally it wasn't on us. Sir John and Lady Grandy were safely delivered to Honolulu on schedule and the crew retired to quarters in Hickam. Almost continuous rain fell and crew activity was very slight - cheeseburgers, steaks and, of course, a few beers. A full ceremonial was performed for the Honolulu departure on the 13th complete with gun salute and flower garlands. After playing ring-a-ring-a-roses with a PanAm Boeing 707, we finally headed for the US mainland and Hamilton AFB for a three-day stay.*

*'San Francisco was visited and the usual tourist activities indulged in - including a visit by some of the crew to a famous topless nightspot (Mums have been informed). Believe it or not they stayed for only half an hour, apparently they found the whole thing pointless! Just prior to departure for Peterson on the 16th, 398 was found to have a damaged ground power connecting socket. It appeared that a power unit had been towed away while still connected. The unfortunate offender had certainly picked the wrong aircraft as the USAF police really went to town on the job, at one stage they wanted the aircraft as Exhibit 'A'.*

*'Peterson AFB, near Colorado Springs, greeted us with clear spring-like weather, but spoilt it all on the last of our three days there by snowing, heavily. Most of the crew availed themselves of a tour of the USAF Academy, most ably conducted by a RAF member of the staff, Squadron Leader Jim Ridout. We were all impressed by what we saw, perhaps less impressed by what we heard. If technical equipment alone counted, the Academy would be producing supermen. Returning from the Academy tour, light relief was provided by the captain and radio expert inadvertently entering a ladies beauty salon - they thought it was a coffee house - they said. We were all relieved to see them seconds later, re-emerge, flushed of cheek but as loveable and as ugly as ever.*

*'On the 21st to Carswell - home of the F111 - in Texas, where we were greeted most hospitably in southern style. While Sir John flashed across the sky in a F111 some of us took a brief look at the assembly plant and firing trials of our nation's most recent purchase. Most impressive. Just prior to take-off, Corky and team became plumbers when a number of water pipes burst (it had been drained). At first we thought it was just another heavy shower. McDill, Florida, on the 21st greeted us with low cloud and steady rain, and kept it up for the duration of our stay of just over a day before we escaped north to Washington DC and more snow. Thanks to some very efficient work by Lyneham, a new ground power socket awaited us. This was speedily fitted and 398 was once more fully serviceable. A full ceremonial take-off on the 24th was marred by*

*the cold freezing the band instruments and we departed to the sound of drums alone - hope the Guard of Honour, etc., have thawed out by now.*

*'We looked forward to three days sun and sand in Bermuda at long last. We got more rain and gales. Even the normal refuge - the bar - was largely denied us, gold lined wallets being rather scarce on the crew, however visible sore heads indicated that the odd party developed in the late hours. Bermuda is a delightful spot and is thoroughly recommended to those who plan to win the pools. The officers spent a most enjoyable Sunday evening as guests of Sir John and Lady Grandy, before Monday evening saw the start of the last lap home. It only remains to express our thanks to all who contributed to the success of our marathon, not least to our VIPs themselves; throughout they were the perfect passengers.'*

**Withdrawal from Aden**

Royal Air Force Khormaksar, Aden had featured large in the Britannia years so far. It had been the staging post for the route to Singapore for five years before that role was transferred to RAF Muharraq, Bahrain. This still left an ongoing need for the trooping and supply services of the Britannia and these were satisfied with shuttles to and from Muharraq.

It had always been an area of unrest, which the British had attempted to police, as tribal factions fought. In latter years this increased as they battled to determine who would be in power when our now signalled departure came about. Sadly, to make the point that this day should be hastened, many British people were victims of terrorist acts. There had, therefore, been many occasions when the Britannias had responded to the call for reinforcements in the area.

Ken Marriott's enthusiasm, before his untimely death, was restoring a Sentinel tractor.
(*Ken Marriott*)

**W-Day**

It had been decided, in 1966, that independence should be granted by 1968. Perhaps there was some anxiety to expedite this for the target date became 1st *January* 1968. Was there then some soft-hearted thinking, in high places, about Christmas? For whatever reason, W for Withdrawal Day became, after several minor changes, 29th November 1967. Much had to be done for this mammoth pull-out from this huge overseas garrison. Families had to repatriated, stocks run-down, men and equipment transferred to the new hub of our Middle East representation, the Persian Gulf. Finally, there was a need to maintain a secure base to the end so that there could be a safe evacuation of the last elements.

**Tense times**

There was considerable nervousness about this. Plans were made for us, if necessary, to come out fighting. An early sign of this apprehension was the families' evacuation planned for May to July. Over 6,000 people needed moving and their vulnerability was thought to be such that there was a scheme to ferry them to the safe haven of nearby Djibouti in Argosys and Beverleys for assembly for the flight to the UK. In the event this was not considered necessary and the Britannias, VC10s and Comets flew into Khormaksar to collect their precious loads of women and children. They left at a rate of 200 passengers a day. To cut down on ground time, whilst loading, the Britannias kept Nos. 3 and 4 engines running. The anxiety over the move was not unjustified. Tension was mounting and there was some relief when the operation was completed ten days before the target deadline of the end of July.

Attention now turned to the movement of units. Some were to be disbanded, some amalgamated, some to relocate at Muharraq and Sharjah. The Britannias were there for all this - and throughout it all, terrorist activity continued, making a fighting withdrawal a real possibility.

**Last days**

The final withdrawal approached. Fourteen Britannias were involved at this

The scene at RAF Muharraq, Bahrain at the time of the Aden withdrawal. *(Ken Marriott)*

The Ops Cell at Muharraq. Sqn Ldr Eric Reeves is in the centre background.

stage. It was the first test for the new Hercules fleet. Such was the slickness of the operation that an Army unit could be on armed duty in an area of Aden, backing out from it as they handed over to the local military, to board an aircraft and be in the UK within 24 hours. One of the secrets of success was the devolvement of operational control of the airlift to a very local level. Our man on the spot was that Mr Fix-It again, Squadron Leader Eric Reeves.

Thus, what rated as the biggest air lift since Berlin, was successfully completed. It might be construed that the evident planning, efficiency and massive resources used in its execution were perhaps a deterrent to the evil forces that threatened a bloodbath.

**Bullion Britannia**

Contact with large sums of money creates interest and excitement - and is remembered! Ex-99 signaller Bob Shergold recalls a trip at the time of the evacuation:

*'Going back through my log books, I found an interesting task which was captained by Sqn Ldr Sharpe. The Aden withdrawal was under way, and we took out the freshly printed money for the new Republic, and then brought the backing for the currency, the bullion, to the UK. A number of quite extraordinary alternates were looked at by the crew including Tabriz, Elazig, and Beirut. The only trouble was the courier, who looked a cross between James Bond and Arnie Schwarzenegger sat on one of the crates the whole time. So we handed over to the slip crew at Akrotiri with the load intact.*

*'The flights to Khormaksar during this period carried a Quartermistress and another WRAF member because the passenger loads consisted mainly of families. When we arrived in Aden, and parked in the revetment, an Eagle Airways Britannia followed us in. Movements were very surprised as they actually had no passengers to send back to the UK, all the families had gone.*

*'Now, if my memory serves me right, the engineer on our crew was my old mate Brian Phelps. Picture the scene in Merrifield House that evening. Sitting there with the first 'Slops' of the night, and in walk our two girls and three air hostesses from the Eagle crew. Not an Officer in sight. We quickly bought the first round ... chatted, as you do. Dreamt a little, as you do. Then I was called aside by our Q. Delicate question. Would you believe it, all five girls indisposed and the NAAFI was closed. Could Brian and I go down to Steamer Point and buy the necessary? Now they didn't flash adverts all over the Telly in those days and I certainly could not claim to be an expert so we were given a shopping list. So young, so gallant, we downed our beer and set off for the main gate and the taxi rank ... well a stretch of*

Evacuation aircraft - Belfast, Britannia and civil Dakota.

*oily sand. One was allowed out, but it was not encouraged. We picked the best looking Merc, explained that we wanted the chemist's shop in The Crescent at the Point and off we went. Mhaala Straight was deserted as was the shopping area at the Point, but the shops were open. We told the driver to wait, and with the shopping list darted across the pavement and into the chemists. Being girls, they couldn't all have the same, but the shopkeeper was delighted to see us and we were soon back in the taxi and heading back. Piece of cake. Hang on though. Do you remember that at the end of the Straight there was a roundabout where you turned left to go down past the Red Sea, a house and Goat Market and so to Khormaksar, or there was a short cut down through the Shanty Town. That's the way our driver took us and when about halfway down he stopped, muttered something like, 'Won't be a minute' or 'Death to the Infidels' (my Arabic was never good), got out of the taxi and disappeared down an alley. A crowd began to gather round the vehicle and I began to think some worried thoughts. We locked the doors in quick time and decided that one of us would climb in to the front seats, release the handbrake and let the car roll down the slope and onto the main road at the bottom where we would meet an Army patrol. However, before the plan went into operation the driver reappeared, packet of sandwiches or whatever in his hand, jumped in and off we went. He certainly did not get a tip. Back at the Aircrew Hilton we found that the girls had all gone to their rooms, so we delivered the shopping to one of the rooms and repaired to the bar. In all my Service career I have never been so scared as I was that night. That's all from the Memory Bank.'*

One cannot help but let one's mind drift into thinking what the headlines in the tabloids would have been if Bob and Brian had come to grief - clutching their 'shopping'!

**Bullion Guard**

Ken Marriott BEM, an ex-MT man, also recalls a Britannia with a valuable load:

*'One day, whilst I was on routine guard duty during the evacuation from Aden, a Britannia landed at Muharraq which we were told would need an armed guard throughout its stay on the ground. As this was an extra duty it was most unwelcome - more time out in the sun in the heat of the day.*

*'I was detailed to take first turn on guard and dutifully walked out to the aircraft on its arrival. I was told to stand at the bottom of the aircraft steps and allow nobody on board. About an hour later the Brit was ready to go and, with the removal of the steps, I thankfully returned to the guard tower. The aircraft reached the end of the runway, stayed there for few minutes then taxied back to the dispersal - u/s. The guard again deployed whilst repairs were made.*

*'Off went the aircraft only to return again - same problem. The repairs took a little longer but this time it got airborne. After its departure we were told that the aircraft was carrying the gold and money reserves from Aden back to UK and that some poor Treasury official had had to*

The stricken 638 photographed the next day. The undercarriage collapsed; the nose wheel was forced up through the freight floor behind the navigator. He was lucky as this narrowed the gap between his table and the seat back and he could only just squeeze out. AQM Jimmy Kane-Smith opened the forward door and was astonished to see the propeller, with its bent blades still being driven round and round, digging itself a hole in the muddy bottom. (*Des Taylor*)

*stay on board all the time. At the time it was a pain and we, the hot and sticky guard, were glad to see the back of it.'*

**Britannia major accident**

There was a sad cost of the evacuation of Aden to the Britannia fleet. On 12th October 1967 at 11.00 pm local time, Britannia XL638 ran off the end of the runway at Khormaksar when landing. It came to a halt in shallow muddy water.

**'Greaser'**

It was a typical Aden night, not a breath of wind, the heat not intense like the day but nevertheless the temperature, along with the humidity, very high. The lights of the airfield and the surrounding area were shimmering in the hot rising air. Khormaksar's runway surface was a dense black and incredibly level. If a smooth Britannia landing (not a regular event as will be discussed later) was to be done anywhere, then Aden was the place. It happened that night. For all its beauty in flight, the Britannia became ungainly near the ground. But not this night - it was 'greased on'. There was a cheer on the flight deck. The next part of the routine (an appropriate word, for it happened at the conclusion of every flight with rarely any difficulty) was to select reverse power to start slowing the aircraft.

**Brake dwell**

The first action was to bring a lever, on the left hand side of the throttle quadrant, to the rear. This did two things; firstly it lifted a flap at the rear base of the throttles. This had prevented them being moved too far back, and into the reverse power range of movement, in the air. The second result of the rearward movement of the lever was that it entered a detent which activated a microswitch which, in turn, armed the reversing circuits of the propellers.

The next action, by the flight engineer, was to lift the throttles over a gate and move them rearwards a small amount to a position known as 'Brake Dwell'. This gave the first couple of degrees of reverse pitch. It was essential, at this stage, to 'dwell' (pause) and check that there were green reverse lights illuminated for each propeller confirming that the propellers blades were indeed in the 'brake' mode i.e. in reverse negative pitch; otherwise, even though the throttles were being retracted, forward thrust would be applied, given by the still positive blade angle of the propeller.

**Into the water**

It is believed that, in this Khormaksar incident, for some reason the reverse lever was not properly located; the reversing circuits were not armed and each time the engineer selected the first stage of reverse, to try and get the green 'armed' lights, forward power was being applied. The attempts were abandoned too late and the aircraft ran on to the concrete-hard sand of the overshoot area and then into the water.

The copilot, John Hanson, reported the entry in his logbook:

*'1967, October 12th, Britannia XL638, Brown, Self, Bahrain - Khormaksar, Cat 5 - full stop.' 'I remember putting the crash switches to 'Normal' just before the start of the expensive noises.'*

**The day remembered**

Jock Manson was known to many Britannia people, being on Belfasts in the Brize Norton days. He wrote to the Editor of the Britannia Association magazine:

*'I met the crew in the Flight Planning section at Muharraq in the middle of the night. I had just come up from Khormaksar via Masirah and was asked for my advice about the latest situation in Aden (since we were locals - 105 Sqn). By this late stage in the proceedings, the Army had lost control of (or had retreated from) Sheik Othman town and therefore no longer had control of the causeway. This meant that everyone had to land on 26 and take off on 08 (regardless of the wind). There was also a general strike in progress at the time and fuel was unobtainable. We had to get there with round trip fuel, or, at the very worse, at least enough to get to Djibouti to pick up more. We suggested that, if they were able to tank enough fuel to get back to Bahrain, it would be a very good idea. I believe they decided to do just this.*

*'You can imagine how I felt the following morning when I heard that they had gone off the end! I kept wondering if the last straw was the extra fuel that I suggested they take. The one good thing to come out of that prang was that the Judge Advocate General was on the jump seat and the 8 Squadron pilot's court-martial had to be cancelled.'*

**Demolition**

This accident reduced the fleet to 22. It would have been likely that it would have remained at 23 through all the years had it not been that the evacuation of Aden was in full swing. The Britannia was noteworthy for its very high tail; that of the beleaguered aircraft constituted a runway obstruction and it had to be blown off with explosives to allow the withdrawal flights to continue without delay. Undoubtedly, in a more relaxed situation, salvage would have been possible.

As the finishing touches to this book were being completed, there was a communication from Donald Davies: 'I served at RAF Khormaksar as a SAC Fireman from April to November 1967 and was on night duty on Thursday 12th October. When XL638 landed I was doing my two-hour stint on guard duty at the gate of the Fire Section compound. After seeing and hearing many a Britannia land, I was waiting to hear the sound of the reverse pitch coming in. It didn't. I then heard the crash alarm going off and ran to the vehicle I was manning that shift. We made our way to the scene of the crash at the Causeway end of the runway. On arrival we found the barbed wire perimeter fence intact and (luckily) the tide was out. Using ladders we scaled the fence and made our way to the aircraft. It was difficult to walk/run through the clinging mud. The crew had evacuated the aircraft. On entering we were astonished to see that the nosewheel had come through the floor. Obviously, our first concern was if anyone was still on board. We then looked for the correct switches to stop the propeller which was still turning slowly. I can remember our joy at being successful. We were then ordered to leave the aircraft.'

(*Continued on page 347*)

The lever to raise the safety flap and arm the reverse system is on the left. Here, the four throttles (bottom centre) have been lifted and pulled back to a detent, the 'Brake Dwell' position. If all is well, four lights (green) should then be illuminated indicating that it is safe to continue retracting the throttles, applying reverse power. (*Des Taylor*)

The damaged nose area is seen from this view. (*Des Taylor*)

**Sadness**

The loss of the aircraft was deeply felt by all, not the least the ground crew back at Lyneham. Dave Ashenden was a Sergeant engine fitter there at the time:

*'I was particularly saddened when I learnt of the reason for the accident. Only a few months before, whilst checking reverse thrust during a ground test of another aircraft, I suddenly realised that we were in forward thrust and sure enough the green reverse arming light was out. A check of the arming lever showed that it had jumped out of its detent and had edged forward enough to release the arming microswitch.*

*'Subsequent investigation revealed that, although by design, the lever was held*

The bent and broken propeller blades - and mud everywhere. The copilot, John Hanson recalls that he escaped through one of the emergency windows over the wing and started to swim: '*... and I wound up going out to sea for a while! We had a Judge Advocate on board that night. He was travelling for a court martial of an 8 Squadron Flying Officer which had to be delayed 24 hours whilst the Judge Advocate had his scalp repaired. I met the luckless Flying Officer in the bar that evening and advised him not to mention he was aircrew. The Judge was off that sort for a while!'* (*Des Taylor*)

A helicopter view over Aden Harbour on demolition day. (*Des Taylor*)

*into its detent by the spring side force of the lever, 12 years or so of use had reduced the side spring force due to wear on the layshaft bearing, coupled with wear of the gate itself. The result was that under conditions of severe vibration (e.g.landing and ground testing) the lever could jump out of the detent. A quick check of the other aircraft then at Lyneham revealed that there was a fleet problem.*

*'Discussions with other propulsion technicians confirmed the tendency for the lever to jump out during ground testing. We laid these facts on the table of our hierarchy. Due note was made of our advice but no action was taken - I believe it was thought that we were overstating the case. However, after the demise of 638, urgent remedial action was taken.*

*'A measure of the ground crews' feeling for the Britannia showed itself at that time. All the technical staff that I encountered, particularly the older hands, were saddened by the loss of the aircraft. The Britannias were well maintained, probably over serviced, in fact, and to lose one after all that 'tender loving care' for such a trivial technical problem seemed to knock a hole in everyone's morale.'*

**Hindsight**

On the aircrew side there was much wisdom after the event. It emerged that the situation had occurred before but to experienced engineers and/or captains. The two concerned at Aden were both new to their roles. This was a combination that was generally avoided.

Also, one could judge the little attention that had been given to this particular malfunction by the amount it now received. Not a simulator sortie would go by or ground examination be held without reference to this fault and its correct remedy. Finally, an amendment appeared for the aircrew 'bible', the Britannia Pilots' Notes, with much stronger wording on the subject.

(*Donald Davies account continued from page 345*): 'Cannot remember really what happened then except that we made our way back to 'dry land' where all sorts were assembled - ambulance, police, duty officers etc. I can remember discussing access to the aircraft and suggesting pallets to make a walkway. I think that most of us who had been out to the aircraft then returned to the Fire Section to clean up.'

**Blame**

But the aircrew world is very much one that takes account of 'where the buck stops'. The captain and engineer were held to blame. As they left the squadron, there were many of us who thought to ourselves, 'There, but for the Grace of God, go I.'

**Queen of the Sky - an alternative view**

After that 'doom and gloom' here is a bit of light relief. Windy Deere spotted this 'gem' in his copy of '*Retired Air Line Pilots of Canada*' magazine. The author, Captain Michael Higgs, kindly gave permission for it to be reproduced.

*'Nothing is so surprising to a man as the arrival of old age. In Canada, as some of us already know, old age reaches you in both the country's official languages when a plastic card arrives in the mail. From the vantage-point of maturity, you can then look back with a new perspective at the excitements of youth, and you can begin to re-arrange your memories so that they will be a comfort to you in old age.*

*'Some things can never be forgotten, and among my own recollections many of these relate to my term of service on the Bristol Britannia. This aircraft, which in 1960 was still one of the largest propeller-driven transports in the world, had a number of engaging peculiarities. The ground school, which lasted for eight weeks of classroom time and a suspiciously variable number of hours in the simulator, was quite an eye-opener for those pilots who did not speak academic English. This put me in an unfortunate position, because although I had spent my own childhood in England, indeed in Bristol, I too could not translate or explain many of the expressions in the Flight Manual. For example, the outlets for the air conditioning system generally known as 'eyeballs', were referred to aboard the Britannia as 'punkah-louvres'. This was not the only vocabulary left over from Imperial steamship lines. But I had been three years on the DC6B and (I thought) I had a general background in working 4-engined transports on long-range operations. I was 27 years old, and therefore knew everything. It should not be forgotten that, in those days, Trans-Pacific and even (in winter) Trans-Atlantic flights were considerable undertakings. From the comfort of today, it is not easy to imagine droning along among the cold fronts at 17,000 feet and 220 knots, for 15 or 17 hours, to get to Europe. The Britannia represented a brave attempt to improve on this, and I was happy to be a second officer aboard such exotic equipment. The alternative, anyway, would have been a lay-off.*

*'The trade of 'second officer' was essentially that of Flight Engineer and was fairly new in aviation. It had come into being only with the introduction of aircraft, which could stay in the air longer than the average pilot could stay awake. Each airline had its own opinion and policy in this matter. The railway-minded management of Canadian Pacific, of course, considered that flight-crew were like diesel locomotives: once started, they would run until switched off. Canadian Pacific Airlines were against second officers on principle, and the word 'feather-bedding' was sometimes heard in the classroom.*

*'As a schoolboy in England, I had often seen the prototype Britannia in flight near Bristol. As an air cadet, I sometimes flew as a lucky passenger in one of the Tiger Moths operated by the local RAF Reserve Squadron at Filton. Filton was also the factory airfield of the Bristol Aeroplane Company, or BAC, the builder of the Britannia. I had even seen the legendary Bill Pegg, their chief test pilot, in the canteen there. He was having coffee (I suppose) after performing a light-hearted but grotesquely dangerous slow-roll over the roof in the company Bristol Fighter. This was a spluttering biplane, which had somehow survived the First World War and was kept as a sort of factory mascot. These recollections were far from my mind when I encountered the Britannia again in a serious ground school. The first thing established here was that the word 'airplane' should never be used, as it was American. 'Aircraft' had the right sound, but to the disappointment of our instructor, it soon became evident that there was no way to prevent students saying 'Brit' rather than Britannia. It was quite possible to fail ground courses in those pre-computer days, because your answers were on paper and could not easily be amended. I knew very little about electricity, and was dismayed to find that the aircraft was very electrical indeed. In a sort of mad scientist show of overkill, it had the conventional high-voltage and low-voltage systems found on most aircraft, but then it*

There were a fair number of 'doll's eyes' on the inverter panel.

*had a medium-voltage system as well. These were all interconnected, which required more transformers, converters and inverters than you can imagine. I realised that it must have been designed by the sort of high-school physics teacher who likes to tell you about Wheatstone's Bridge. A few people (I was not one of them) understood that Wheatstone's Bridge, invented by him in 1843, had four arms and could measure inductance, capacitance, resistance and frequency by comparing current flowing in combinations of them. I did know that Wheatstone had also invented the concertina, a sort of small accordion or squeeze-box useful in tavern singsongs, but this was not much help.*

*'The details of the Britannia's 3-voltage electrical system need not concern us here, as the operation of it was displayed in flight on a large panel showing a schematic diagram in clear white lines. The opening and closing of various relays was shown by a neat little indicator called a 'doll's-eye'. These were small circular windows, behind which a line on a moving card was aligned to show a relay open or closed. If the power failed, the eye closed. The panel contained 20 gauges, 20 doll's-eyes, 15 switches and 12 warning lights, and the whole thing was cunningly mounted behind the First Officer's seat in such a way that neither of the front-seat pilots could see it.*

*'The power-plant was the Proteus. It was probably named after the Proteus of Greek mythology, a 'prophetic old man of the sea and shepherd of flocks of seals. He knew all things, and could assume whatever shape he pleased'. The name Proteus also occurs in microbiology. where it means a 'genus of rod-shaped bacteria usually found on decaying matter in the human intestine', but that was probably not what they had in mind. In another triumph of design, the incoming airflow, having been turned through 180° in the intake duct, entered the back of the engine. There the compressor forced it forward to the turbine, which was immediately aft of the propeller. The exhaust was then again turned through 180° into the tailpipe. The general layout was much like that of a trombone in a jazz band. In certain conditions of temperature and humidity, this arrangement led to a rapid build-up of ice at the corners, and it was quite normal for this ice to break away in heavy chunks, which were swallowed by the engine. The engine would then suffer an immediate flame-out and make a strange noise. The cure was 'continuous ignition', provided by what in a diesel would be glow-plugs. The resulting automatic re-start always produced a muffled bang, which alerted the passengers, and was described in the hand-book as 'bumping'. If all four engines were bumping, as I discovered on one of my first flights across the Gulf of Mexico in a tropical storm (we were tracking along a moist thundery front, of course) this bumping produced a sound like a competition among drummers. The in-flight crew rest positions were a stack of three bunks just aft of the cockpit door. They were separated from the rows of passenger seats by a heavy leather, or perhaps canvas, curtain. This kept them quite dark inside, although the chatter and cigarette smoke of the passengers always seemed to get in. By some ancient tradition, navigators always had the top bunk and the cabin crew, to avoid climbing the ladder in their skirts, used the bottom one. The first officer, on the occasion of all this noise and bumping, was taking his crew rest in the middle bunk. It was a dark and stormy night, about 3 o'clock in the morning. He was a large man, and was in the habit of removing his false teeth before sleep, keeping them under his pillow. After a hearty series of bangs, all four engines flamed out at the same*

*moment. There was a loud silence as we eased the aircraft into a glide, but before we could begin the relight sequence, the door flew open with a crash and the bug-eyed, frantic figure of the resting pilot burst into the cockpit. He had been woken from a deep slumber by the sudden end of the engine sound, and had of course left his teeth under the pillow. His face could be seen only in the blue flickering of St. Elmo's Fire, which was running densely over all eight panels of the windshield. 'Mwhat the mwhuck are yoob gibe dooint' he shrieked. In the yellow glare now reflected from the cloud as fountains of fire belched from the tailpipes, there was no time to explain.*

*'This sort of thing was (in theory) to be prevented by the use of what were called 'B-Skin Jets'. In the labyrinth of the engine, a system of air-bleeds at the elbows was intended to prevent ice formation. The structure was reinforced by additional layers of metal, or skins. These had been originally designated by the designers as No. 1-Skin, 2-Skin, 3-Skin, and another skin. But to prevent giggling in the office the names were changed to A-Skin, B-Skin, etc. Each throttle carried a knob, to help when lifting it to get into the reverse thrust range on the ground. For some reason known only to designers, numbers one and two were coloured a bright yellow, while three and four were green. During a discussion of this in class, a voice from the back shouted 'It's for yellow captains and green first officers!', which left the speaker's own rank in doubt for a few days.*

*'The propellers of the Britannia were huge, square-tipped, four-bladed windmills, which could be reversed rapidly on landing, to provide impressively short roll-outs and good control on the ground. I remember a landing at Sondrestrom in which one of them failed to reverse and also failed to indicate this, so that reverse power produced a troublesome wiggle as we attempted to stop. Our skilful captain sorted this out, but there was no time for me to write anything in the logbook. On reaching the ramp I explained matters to the ground engineer (there was only one) who said 'I can fix the problem, just write it up after departure'. After refuelling, we started engines, checked that the propeller controls now worked normally, and took off into the black night. When I looked at the book, I saw that the engineer had written, in the 'Action Taken' column, 'Part 43/H6-0174 replaced'. In the 'Defect Column' I was able to write, 'Prop malfunction on landing. Suspect part 43/H6-0174.'*

*'On another occasion at Sondrestrom on a calm summer morning, the engineer stopped talking on the nosewheel interphone during refuelling. The aircraft, although now very heavy with fuel, began an unaccountable rocking movement. I could only imagine an earthquake, but a look at the nearby mountainside revealed no trace of avalanche or disturbance. The voice of the engineer suddenly came over the VHF. He said, 'You are being attacked by a musk-ox. This is the breeding season. He has just walked in off the tundra, and he is having an unusual relationship with the nosewheel.' At least, that was the gist of what he said. The furious creature was soon driven away by horn-blowing jeeps, and I wrote in the log 'Attacked by musk-ox while parked. Check nose-leg for musk.' I never saw the reply to this.*

*'Another oddity about the Britannia was that, about a quarter-century before the introduction of fly-by-wire controls on fighter aircraft, its control surfaces were not connected in any way to the so-called control column in the cockpit. There was no control wheel as such, but each pilot had a set of what appeared to be motorcycle handlebars. Push-pull was normal, but roll control was obtained by pushing one side down; there was no sense of rolling the wheel to get bank angle. Instead of control cables, a vast spidery system of push-rods, bellcranks and 'suitable linkages' extended to the trim tabs of each surface. The tabs would, in principle, move the controls and in turn these influenced the flight of the aircraft, but an airspeed of at least 80 knots was needed. The system meant that at the start of every take-off, both ailerons and the elevators hung down at full deflection, while the rudder just streamlined itself in whatever crosswind happened to be blowing. We soon became used to startled remarks from other aeroplanes when this was noticed. In his autobiography, Test Pilot Bill Pegg describes in detail the problems he experienced, on the Britannias first flight, with elevator overbalance, weak feel, and strange feedback. I remember one attention-getting example of this when (for*

*the one and only time ever) I initiated a go-around from the centre seat. We were landing at Callao, the seaside airport of Lima, after a long, long flight down the Peruvian coast. The rising sun was just showing over the Andes, the weather was reported as patchy fog, drifting over the runway in a little seabreeze of about four knots. We had made two approaches, only to be foiled at the last moment by a patch of fog over the threshold. Fuel was short and our captain, determined to land next time, made an abbreviated sort of pattern for the next approach. We could now see the threshold nicely between the slow moving white patches. Both front seat pilots were engrossed by this, secure in the knowledge that all pre-landing checks were complete, and were nursing the aircraft towards a slowly moving touch-down zone. I became aware of these circumstances:*

*(i) We were at $V_{ref}$ +5 knots*

*(ii) Full flap was extended*

*(iii) The engines were at idle power*

*(iv) We were already below limits, though still in the sunshine*

*(v) We were indicating a vertical speed of 900 fpm down.*

*'At that moment the world vanished as we sank into the top of a solid undercast. I applied maximum emergency power with an instantaneous shove of my hand, and the engines howled up to a seldom seen torque. Under the influence of such a slipstream against its huge flaps, the Britannia reared up like a mad whale and wallowed out on top of the fog. The first officer, whinnying in terror, was trying to push his handlebars through the instruments. He said later that 'it felt funny'. The captain also continued to fly, but after the exchange of a few abrupt words about the application of nose-down trim, all ended well. We had blown the fog away, and landed normally from the next approach.*

*'The public relations name of the Britannia, invented perhaps by a sales team from the factory, was 'The Whispering Giant'. It was certainly much quieter than today's jets, but towards of the end of its service with CPA it became known as 'The Whimpering Heap'. I recall one of its last flights, which was a charter from Toronto to Santa Maria to pick up a group of Portuguese immigrants. There were no passengers on board, and the destination weather was not good. Our captain, a man of vast experience, squeezed every last ounce of fuel aboard, and perhaps thinking to justify this in case it should be questioned by the bean counters of the CPR, filed Gander as the alternate, rather than a more conventional place in Europe. On arrival at Santa Maria we found the weather below limits and getting worse. We made an approach to prove this, then pulled up and returned to Gander. I reflected that it is not often that someone will designate an alternate on the other side of the Atlantic, and then actually go there. There were other considerations here though, the aircraft was needed for charters in North America that same week and hence there was an operational reason for taking it home. The in-flight time was 14 hours and 52 minutes, which gave me plenty of time to admire the venetian blinds, or perhaps roller blinds, fitted inside the cockpit windows to keep out troublesome sunshine. These could be pulled down by a little string with a loop on the end, and would not have looked out of place in the washroom of a transcontinental train.*

*'Another aid to cockpit comfort was the fuse-tester. There were about 600 fuses accessible to the second officer, which could be removed and tested, but the fuse-tester itself was protected by a fuse. There was no explanation as to how this could be checked, and testing fuses in flight could be very tedious. Propeller synchronisation was another problem. The basic signal was derived from a group of tuning forks, of exactly the kind used by a piano-tuner. They were electrically stimulated (of course) and sang in sweet harmony in a control box behind the bulkhead where the navigators sat. Occasionally a propeller would drift out of synchronization with the others and an annoying slow rumble would be felt; when this happened the navigator would punch the upholstery over the offending box with his fist. Some hardy individuals could produce the required result by nodding their head sharply backwards against the wall, which became almost a Pavlovian reflex. You could see them do this even when sitting back in a passenger seat during rest periods.*

*'Before we say goodbye to this wonderful old aeroplane, I must mention the cockpit telephone. This was stowed in the ceiling of the flight deck immediately over the centre seat, and by the obvious applica-*

*tion of Murphy's Law, would fall on your head at moments of stress, as in turbulence or during a heavy landing. It would then swing about in a wide arc on about five feet of curly black cable, distracting the front-seat pilots and posing great danger to your teeth. Like the fact the emergency (manual) hydraulic pump was under the captain's seat, there was no explanation for this design feature, but as The Whispering Giant drones quietly away into the sunset with doll's-eyes winking, punkah-louvres blowing, tuning forks humming, and engines bumping, while the navigator pounds the wall, we have to agree that it was very, very interesting.*

Captain Michael Higgs retired from Canadian Airlines International in 1991. Towards the end of his Canadian flying career, he flew DC-10s and B-747s. He currently lives in Vancouver with his wife Rosemary. Michael's interests are travelling, writing and sailing.

This photograph is the sad postscript to this chapter - XL638, 'Sirius', lies in the Aden mud. (*Stompy Stableford via Jock Manson*)

The photograph that accompanied Donald Davies' account - pages 345 and 347. (*Donald Davies*)

The adventures of Messrs. Ad Minn and Org at Wootton Lynstoke continue ...

"...YES BUT WHAT ABOUT MY GIRLS...."
GIRLS
LATER
STATION PENPUSHER SQN.
"OH YES, HERE AT WOOTTON LYNESTOKE WE HAVE A FINE SELECTION OF THE R.A.F. (W) FINE GIRLS..."
"....IN ALL SHAPES AND SIZES AND IN EVERY SECTION..."
"NOT ONLY DO THEY DO A JOB OF WORK - THEY TAKE PART IN EVERY ACTIVITY."
"AN ACCIDENT?"
"NO MATE, JUST ONE OF THE GIRLS - A NASTY CASE OF SUNBURN ON THE TOPLESS."
"YOU KNOW I THINK IT'S TIME WE HAD A HOLIDAY"
"TRUE - IT'S BEEN ALL GO THIS YEAR"
AUTHORITY FOR LEAVE IS GIVEN BY THEIR MASTERS (WHO HAVE NOW CHANGED THEIR NAME TO MODWATSIT)
"HOW ABOUT A ROUND OF GOLF?"
"YOU'RE ON"
AT NEARBY SOURENCHESTER
"HAVEN'T WE MET YOU AT WOOTTON LYNESTOKE?"
"YOU ENJOY THE GAME?"
"WELL - GOOD AFTERNOON SIR - NOT REALLY, BUT IT HAS ITS - GOOD AFTERNOON SIR - ADVANTAGES - NICE DAY SIR - JUST THINK OF - HELLO SIR -"
"THE FRESH AIR AND - GOOD AFTERNOON SIR - EXERCISE, SO GOOD FOR ONE - HELLO SIR - AND ONE DOES GET TO MEET PEOPLE - GOOD AFT..."
26

CHAPTER TWENTY TWO

# Farewell Transport Command

At 7.30 pm on 31st July 1967, I climbed the stairs of the Headquarters building at RAF Upavon to start my night-shift of duty in the *Transport* Command Operations Centre. Right on midnight the green phone rang - our direct link with the Air Force Operations Room (AFOR) in the Ministry of Defence. Luckily, I must have had some premonition that this might happen for I replied, 'Hello AFOR, this is *Air Support* Command Operations Centre.'

**New role, new name**

After 24 years, Transport Command was no more. It had been decided that the title no longer matched the role of the Command that was now evolving; one to coordinate all manner of air support required, in particular by the Army. In this, traditional 'Transport Command' support was represented by the strategic transport force, the Britannias, VC10s, Belfasts and Comets. But now taking shape was the enormous fleet of Hercules aircraft that would bridge both strategic and tactical support.

Short range tactical support was represented by the Argosys and the Andovers. And then there were the helicopters. Offensive support was to be added

RAF Changi was a bustling place in the 60s and 70s. Note the livery name - Royal Air Force Air Support Command. (*Mike Joyce*)

... worldwide control now existed ... (*Bill Robinson*)

with the introduction of the Harrier and Phantom. One command structure was required to control this force and coordinate its use with the Army.

Clearly, it could no longer be called Transport Command and so Air Support Command was born.

**Proper control**

The 'scruff of the neck' of command and control was being 'grabbed' at this time. There had not been progress in this field to match the pace of the modernisation of the transport fleet. Certainly in the first few years of Britannia life, the legacy of the Hastings era was the basis of communications to and from aircraft in all parts of the world. But now the new aircraft, VC10s, Belfasts and Hercules, were supplied fitted with powerful, pilot operated, voice, single side band (SSB) HF radio. The Britannias were being modified to this SSB standard. This gave the facility to break away from the past where route communications, i.e. the 'business' or 'company' messages, were the poor relations of the air traffic communications systems. Information on loads, passengers, spares, new schedules, crew dispositions and so on was now being given its own network. For air to ground communications RAF SSB HF stations were established at Upavon, Cyprus, Bahrain, Gan and Singapore. Thus aircraft proceeding along the trunk route to Singapore could directly pass messages to the staging posts. A routine was established where aircraft 'checked in' with the station in whose area they were flying. The staging posts operations rooms were also all linked to each other and to Upavon by their own teleprinter network, on line 24 hours a day. With all this, it could be truly said that operational control was being exercised by the Command Operations Centre at Upavon. Displayed on the walls was the itinerary of each aircraft flying a route. With the information coming in on the teleprinters, clerks kept this display up-dated with the latest position of the aircraft.

'The Flow Computer' built by the author. Five days were represented on five boards, butting together. When a day was complete its board was 'unloaded' and slid out of the right and placed in the left. It was then 'loaded' with lengths of wood representing the itineraries for particular flights. White was airborne time and black time on the ground. A glance up and down the lines would reveal any turnround clashes. When an aircraft was delayed its lengths of wood could be slid along to the new timings and the check for conflictions carried out.

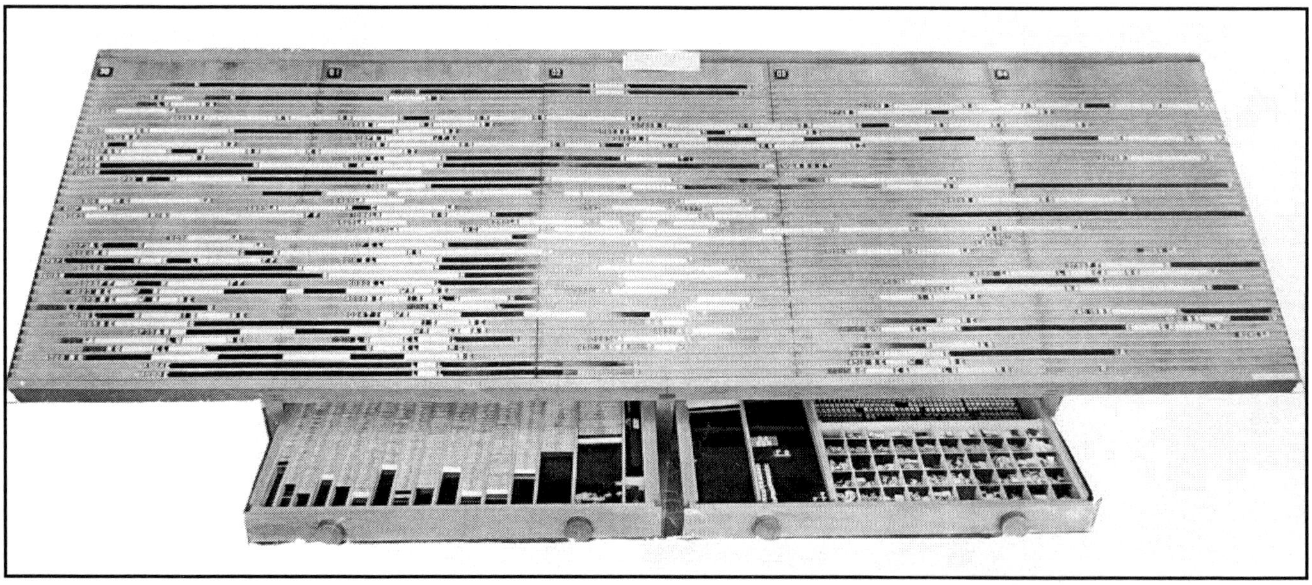

One of the author's fellow 99 captains and Ops Controllers at Upavon was Flt Lt John Le Gras. He was an artist and this is one of his Britannia paintings entitled 'Gander Flagstop'. (*John Le Gras*)

**Flight Watch**

This system covered flying in the Mediterranean and the Middle and Far East but, increasingly, the fleet was operating in other areas, in particular North America. The civil airlines had been similarly tackling company communications and had established a commercial network. So, Air Support Command was contracted into this and used it just like an airline. Upavon was the company headquarters, the 'airline' was given the callsign ASCOT and the signal's designator RR. So worldwide control now existed. The system was given the title Flight Watch. It is a compliment to its major architect, the then Wing Commander Ops at Upavon, a communications enthusiast, Wing Commander Basil D'Oliveira, that Flight Watch is still used to this day, largely unchanged from the original concept.

**The Flow Cell**

So, from Upavon would come direct instructions to staging posts and crews on the timetables for the aircraft and which crews were to operate them. When unserviceability was encountered the network could be used for requesting spares. Upavon could adjust another aircraft's itinerary, if necessary, for the expeditious supply. When the aircraft was serviceable, the new timetable would be issued. Some care was needed here. In the original plan, staggering of the aircraft along the routes had been engineered. This was essential; a Britannia arriving at Gan, say, at the same time as a passenger laden VC10 would present an impossible task for the staging post. So, if the plan had to be adjusted because of unserviceability or whatever, that separation had to be maintained.

This became a well nigh impossible task for the one operations controller on duty at Upavon, so a 'Flow Cell', with its own controller, was established. The original itinerary plan for all aircraft had been devised, some six weeks previously, at a controlled pace, with graph paper and pencil. In the Ops Centre, speed was the essence; an aircraft was now serviceable and required a new itinerary. A wooden device, which was essentially an analogue computer, was designed and built by the author to cope with this problem. It remained in use until the demise of trunk route flying.

**A coincidence**

In the late 1960s, in the Ops Centre at Upavon, one of those strange coincidences occurred . The Senior Ops Controller was Sqn Ldr Tony Cullum ... the name of the Duty Ops Controller was placarded ... Flt Lt J M Le Gras. Today was a little different for Tony. He was entertaining his father, retired Wg Cdr W A Cullum OBE, who had the distinction of being one

'The Famous Five' of the 'coincidence' story. Front row, L to R: Cpl J P Ridge, Cpl T W J Nash, LAC W A Cullum. Back: LAC Jeffrey Royston Williams Reuben Earle Sladden, AC1 John Edmund William Le Gras
(*Tony Cullum*)

of the five members of the first NCO pilots course at RAF Duxford from 1921 to 1922. It was one of the Trenchard experiments which successfully heralded the era of the NCO pilot. Wg Cdr Cullum is taken to the Ops Room floor and espies John Le Gras' name. 'Your father was on the NCO pilots' course with me!' Sadly there could be no reunion as Sqn Ldr John Edmund William Le Gras died in 1963. As a result of the meeting an old photograph of 'The Famous Five' was dug out. Son John did try to obtain some more information with a story in the RAF News but with no luck. He visited the Duxford Air Museum and in a room dedicated to the Duxford of the past he came across another picture of the five u/t pilots. It was obviously taken at the same time as the other but in this one the '5' were wearing helmets, masks and goggles. John wrote to the curator to tell him of Tony's photo. Many years later he again went to Duxford and to his disgust the display had been dismantled. But on peering through a window he could see the photo and was disappointed to note that there had been no reaction to his information.

**Other jobs**

The evacuation of Aden did not completely eclipse all Britannia activity in 1967. There was still capacity for the smaller things in life. The Mayor and Corporation of Swindon were flown in a Britannia captained by the Station Commander, Group Captain Freddy Hazlewood OBE AFC. On a flight to Thule, Greenland an RAF Expedition Team was carried. They planned to make the first crossing on foot of North Ellesmere Island. 15th August 1967 marked 99 Squadron's 50 years of service which was duly celebrated. Many past commanding officers attended. The Far East was not neglected and, in October, there was another Westabout reinforcement exercise, 'Sunshine Express'. A landmark was removed from the air transport map with our withdrawal from Nicosia although, with the Akrotiri facility, our activity at the mid-island airfield had been minor for a number of years.

Very large NATO exercises were becoming a regular part of the Britannia's lot. For the second year running, Mikkra air base near the ancient Macedonian city of Thessaloniki was the air head for the test of NATO's Allied Command Europe Mobile Force.

**At long last**

1967 marked a beginning of an end. Earlier in this chapter was the sentence, 'The Britannias were being modified to this SSB standard.' Modification No.1336 was in full swing. Firstly, it provided the aircraft with VORs. As previously reported, way back in the pre-delivery days it had been said that this piece of navigational equipment was essential. Ten years later it almost amounted to criminality that we were flying around the world without it; but such are the ways with much defence spending - or lack of it.

**Getting from A to B**

Much navigation of airliners is along airways, corridors in the sky in which aircraft fly and are controlled by Air Traffic to ensure safe separation. These 'corridors' are orientated on beacons which determine their start and finish, change of direction or junction with another.

The old beacons, which were now well and truly being phased out, were known as NDBs (Non-Directional Beacons). In simple terms they operated on the same principle of obtaining the strongest signal with a portable radio by turning it. The beacon emitted a signal on a particular frequency, aerials in the aircraft were turned, remotely, to determine the direction. Like all radio signals, there were limitations on range, interference by weather, other transmissions and so on. It was out-dated.

In their place, VOR (Voice Omni-Rotating) beacons were being installed. The essential difference, simplified, was that they transmitted very high frequency directional signals which told the receiver where the beacon lay in relation to it. It was not subject to the shortcomings of the NDB. The world was rapidly changing to this system; we flew the world; it was time we had it.

The second purpose of Mod 1336 was to remove the old HF sets and their Morse keys and fit Single Side Band (SSB) radios. As described, these were extremely powerful by comparison, less prone to interference and carried very clear voice transmissions.

**Trial**

On a sunny June morning in 1967, XM519, fitted out with these modifications departed on a round the world trip to test them out. All went well and the modification of the aircraft proceeded.

**Goodbye**

There was a sad element to this. With the installation of SSB, communications no longer became a specialist task. Pilots could accomplish it; so it was farewell to the signallers. We were sorry to see them go. It meant the loss of many characters and they had established quite a reputation of being very willing to step outside their specialisation and help out in all manner of ways along a route.

So gone forever was the oft heard flight deck call, 'OK Siggy, tell them ...'

**Holes Holes Holes Holes**

Ex-Chief Technician Vic Merrill, who enjoys telling a tale, takes us back again to the ground crew scene and remembers a time when holes were a preoccupation:

One of those stalwarts from the signallers' section - Master Signaller Ken Heseltine outside a Gander, Newfoundland hotel. (*Ted Wright*)

*'We were walking back from the Brit, in front of the Crystal Palace, in the early hours of the morning. It was misty but not cold. There were no aircraft engines running but the inevitable power sets were, with their exhausts glowing red hot.*

*''Is that you, Vic?' came a shout from the gloom. 'Yes, what's the matter?' 'They've found one of the Brits with the holes.'*

*'We hurried along to J2 to 'Rects' to find the room virtually empty. No need to ask, everyone who could would be out trying to see the holes. I hurriedly cleared the cards for the work just completed, dropped my tool bag off in the crew room*

*and headed for THE Brit on Bay 16. By this time everyone seemed to be on their way back to J2 and from the snatches of conversation floating in the air, it was obvious that it really was a 'Brit with THE holes' and Geordie Lawson had an 'idea'. Fresh clues. I wondered and pressed on.*

*'I neared the Brit to be greeted by Master Engineer Taff Edwards. 'Have you seen them yet, Vic?' 'I'm just going up, what do you think, Taff?' 'Beats me, boyo, see you back at the hangar.' And he disappears towards J2, flat hat towards the back of his head, tilted to one side, Blue jacket belt unbuckled and swinging, top button undone.*

*'How did Taff know when there was something up? Time and time again he would appear from nowhere, at all times of the day or night, at Lyneham or down the route, with his quizzical look and 'I brought 518 in with ... I thought it was ... what have you found ... how will you fix it?' Followed by, 'Any interesting snags lately?'*

*'Sometimes I thought Taff never slept. But he wasn't bad to have around. He was one of those people to whom you could explain what you were doing and be understood!*

*'Not only that, but he could make sensible suggestions and he appreciated that, even with the best will in the world, work took time and diagnosis often longer.*

*'I went up the Giraffe steps and into the aircraft. The 'carpet' was pulled back and there, in the light of my torch, behind the captain's seat, I could see them. They were nothing like I had imagined from the descriptions given. For one thing, they were not ALL holes in the metal in the literal sense, more indentations, half moons and semispherical depressions all with a diameter about the same as a 2BA bolt. There were only seven or eight of them, although there were more holes in the floor covering as though further unsuccessful attempts had been made to penetrate the floor.*

*'I concentrated on the metal of the floor, there was no apparent pattern in the whole or part. I pictured rugger boot stud marks in my mind; they were similar, bigger, but not the same. At least there were 'sets' with rugger boots but here there was no symmetry at all. I gave up and went back to the crew room where theories and suggestions from the sublime to the gorblimey were being hurled back and forth. Rectification of the holes was tedious, not clever or satisfying and could be 'carried' until the aircraft went into the 'Dock' but, what was the cause?*

*'Some ideas were:*

*- a demented Engineer using the floor as an anvil to crack cob nuts.*
*- mice!*
*- Bristols getting rid of sub-standard sheet.*
*- ball lightning!*
*- metal fatigue.*
*- aircrew playing cricket.*
*- somebody sucking the ceiling in the freight bay!*

*'Gradually, in the following weeks,*

A step back to November 1965 and a unique occasion preserved in a photograph from Cliff Regan, *'I was the flight engineer and the captain was Jim Cresswell. I know it was out of Khormaksar in November 1965. I think the VVIP was the Chief of the Air Staff.'* In fact, those *Lyneham Globes* now reveal that it was Task 1031 bringing home the C-in-C Middle East. (*Cliff Regan*)

Although 'Air Support Command' is plain to see, the date and place of this rather grand occasion is not known.

*the stir subsided as no theory fitted all the facts. But then, much later, I did hear that a certain Captain did like his coffee delivered by someone wearing VERY high heels and that a pair of non-regulation high heeled shoes had been spotted in a bag carried by someone getting on to a crew bus - but that idea seemed as dizzy as the rest.*

*'I suppose it would have been appropriate to have used the 'Erichsen (cupping) Test' or Mohr's Theory but at the time I calculated a stress typical for aluminium, the diameter of the 'implement' as an 'eighth', took into account probable impact forces and arrived at an indication of a mass of 100 to 120lbs.*

*'For some time my hangdog expression on meeting aircrew was caused by footwear examination and estimation of weight. I never did form a firm conclusion, but there was that young navigator ...!'*

**Ex-Brat remembers for other ex-Brats**

Ex-Halton Apprentice Colin Rowlinson - ex 99 Squadron flight engineer - came to Britannias via aircrew training, a very full Bomber Ops tour on Lancasters, post-war Lincolns, RAF B-29s and Shackletons. It therefore was a very experienced flight engineer who was chosen to be amongst the first of the Britannia ones. He wrote his reminiscences for an ex-Brats magazine. This is part of the Britannia memories:

*'Early in May 1959 my 'mole' in SHQ told me of a letter from MOD calling for volunteers from Shack squadrons to train for Britannia aircraft who would be interviewed at Transport Command Headquarters, Upavon. My application was filled in and ready by the time my squadron CO received the letter. Events continued in a forward direction and on 21st June 1959 I handed in my flippers, completed clearance chit and said goodbye to RAF Coastal Command. My feelings reminded me of those two old Gents in The Muppet Show who used to sit in a box and at the end of*

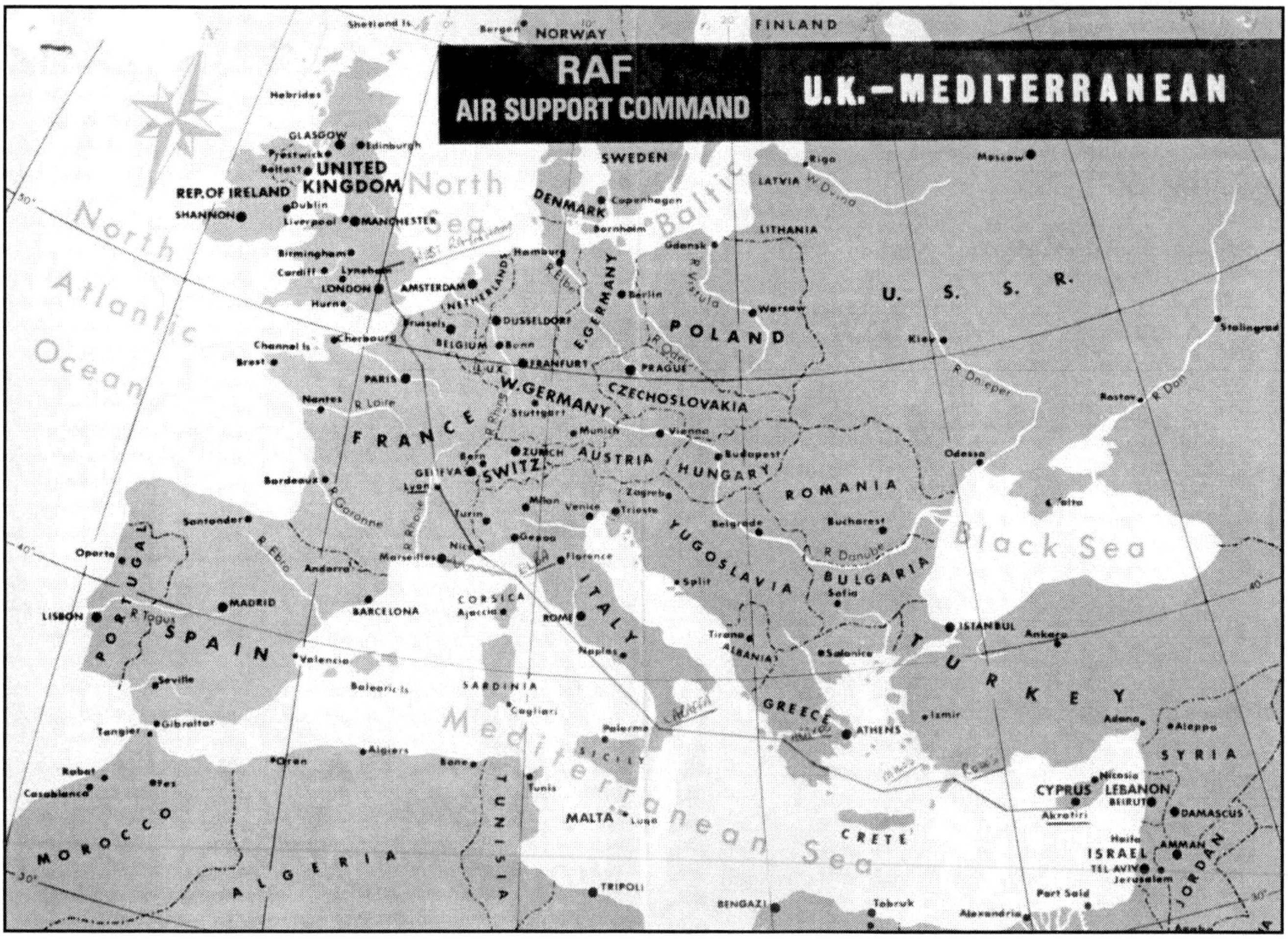


A tradition of those RAF transport flying days was the 'Passenger Map'. This was dutifully completed each hour by the navigator and passed amongst the passengers.

*the show would pass their opinion. I remember one such conversation that went something like this: 'Do you believe in life after death, Henry?' 'Yep - every time I leave this theatre!' That just about sums up my feelings when I said goodbye to Coastal. Thank heavens I only had to leave it once.*

*'On 21st June 1959 I arrived at RAF Lyneham and checked in. The Britannia training boss mapped out the next 12 months that lay ahead of us, starting with three months at RAF Melksham learning (?) the theory of electricity and the ins and outs of instruments. We later discovered that the whole course was a bit of an overkill as we only had to put switches 'on' and 'off' - and things worked or they didn't. After a suitable break, we (there were 12 of us) started at Bristol's Filton factory and for the next six months built the Britannia, rivet by rivet - another slight overkill. The rest of the crew members, pilots, navs and signallers, were coming off their respective assembly lines and the day came, back at Lyneham, when we met up and having been crewed up we settled down to three weeks of pre-simulator classroom bashing. This was all to do with the operation side of things, so it was in our own interests to sit up and take notice. The other side of the coin was that if you didn't take notice you got slung off - simple remedy. Three crews at a time were in the simulator (not all at once) so it meant hanging about again until the time came for one's own crew to start - which was on 22nd September 1960 - remember, I left Coastal on 21st June 1959 - a lot of chalk went on blackboards in that 15 months ...*

*'Britannia training progressed and on the 5th November 1960 we were airborne for the first time in a, then, very modern aeroplane - look no parachutes. What with simulator training, flying training and poring over books and diagrams at home, after having put the children to bed, life was never dull. By the end of November we had completed the 'local' flying, both under tuition and solo and the time had come for what was called the 'route trainer'. This was an introduction to flying the Transport Command routes all over the world, although only some were covered on our*

In 1967 99 Squadron celebrated its 50th Anniversary. The then CO, Wing Commander Freddy Yetman, does the necessary to the birthday cake. (*John LeGras*)

*particular programme. The aircraft complement consisted of three instructors one of each trade i.e. pilot, nav, and 'siggy' plus student crews; the classroom attitude was still there, with instructors taking down copious notes and at the end of each leg a full de-brief was given on each student's performance. It will be appreciated with all that number of people on board there was administration chaos from the word 'go'. It was to become so much easier later on when we were let loose on our own, one has to learn the hard way doesn't one? The route taken for my batch of crews was Lyneham - El Adem - Khormaksar - Gan - Changi - Gan - Karachi - Nairobi - El Adem - Nicosia - Idris (C.Benito) - Lyneham. We departed on the 30th November 1960 and arrived back at base on the 10th December. After a few days off to recover and four more hours local flying - still under the eagle eye of instructors - we were finally allowed out of the country with an aircraft on our own. This was called the 'route solo'. It was a freight-only trip to Nicosia and back. The freight arrived safely at both destinations and so I suppose our 'Lords of the Air' assumed that future passengers would be equally safe. Training now complete and on the 23rd December we presented ourselves to the CO of 99 Squadron. For my part I looked forward to the future and the different parts of the world to be visited. As the man said, 'Be sure to get what you like, or you might have to like what you get.' How true. It makes one helluva difference to life.*

*'Squadron life was good; the world was our oyster, so to speak. There were routine trips to Germany - Cyprus - Germany (Canberra squadron detachment changeover). The Singapore schedules were eagerly sought after by all the crews as it provided a base for good shopping at good prices. The island of Gan hadn't long been opened up as a staging post and this was a very pleasant station, the RAF's 'Jewel in the Indian Ocean'. Air Ministry countered that with the hellhole of RAF Masirah, off the Arabian coast, they think of everything. It was about this time that 'Indulgence Travel' came to my notice. It was 'seat availability' travel for families of the three*

The web site of ex-Cpl Air Movements, Jim Aitken, provides a reminder for Colin of Idris. (*Jim Aitken*)

*Services. As we had very good friends from St. Eval days out in Changi, my wife and I thought it would be a good idea to put this scheme to the test. I filled in the application forms for my wife plus four children for the Lyneham - Singapore flight. The squadron CO duly signed giving his approval and they were sent off to Movements at Air Ministry. Not long after, we were notified that five seats had been allocated on Comet Flight No. so-and-so to Singapore. We still have the receipts from the Lyneham Movements Check-in Desk. 'Amount received £3.12/- .' When the time came to return to UK, seats were available on a Britannia and the receipt from the Changi movements said 'Amount received £3.18/-.' so I suppose that made the Brit 6/- better than the Comet. This travel scheme was used quite a lot by the families.*

*'Once or twice a year the Britannia squadrons had a mobility exercise, the idea being to position crews at selected airfields around the globe and wait for troops to be flown out from Lyneham and transported to the 'bush fire', wherever it was. (That was in the days when Britain was prefixed with Great and there was a lot of red colouring around the world.) This gave the aircraft continuity of movement, i.e. first stop - one crew off another on, refuel and on your way. That vaguely was the idea. One such exercise (sans troops) took us from Lyneham to Thule (Greenland), up to Elmendorf (Alaska), down the other side to Honolulu, on to Wake Island, Midway, Guam, Singapore, where the well- flogged route back to Lyneham was regained. My crew was fortunate to be off-loaded at Midway Island to await our aeroplane. Because of a technical hiccups somewhere along the way, we were forced to spend three days on the island. There wasn't a lot to do; we had a bed, a bar and a beach all within a 50-yard area - bliss. We also had for company a great many Goony Birds. The mother would plant her egg anywhere, and fly off in search of squid to bring back to her chick, which by the time she returned should have hatched out with a little help from dad. It was fascinating to see them 'arrive' in the world, and later on, when they had grown a bit, hilarious to see them try and synchronise legs and wings in a 'take off' run to get airborne. This took several attempts and once having got their act together and got airborne the next thing was getting down. After many attempts, ending up base over apex, they eventually got it right, 'legs down, wings out and the stall coming at 1mm above the sand' - perfect. A few years later the BBC produced a documentary for TV on this very subject. It was on Midway months later that there happened to be a Britannia staging though that had a lot of room for freight. The Americans offered the crew a shuffleboard - a long table with a smooth surface where different coloured 'weights' were 'pushed' down and some sort of conclusion arrived at as to who had won. You may gather that I'm not well up on the shuffleboard game or its terminology. However the offer was accepted and was duly loaded aboard. It arrived at Changi where it was off-loaded to make way for priority freight. The table was left outside the freight shed and subjected to the tender mercy of the afternoon monsoon; this warped the playing surface and made it rather undulating, however it was eventually transported to Lyneham and positioned in the Sgts' Mess, where restoring enthusiasts got to work and made an excellent job of the playing surface, but it was still slightly 'out of true' and the lead weights didn't run exactly to line, which made the game more enjoyable, rather like sizing up the 18th green for a 12 feet putt.*

*'Whilst enjoying life on the Britannias, a cloud appeared on the horizon in the shape of a rumour drifting in from the Irish Sea referring to a large 'sea' flying boat, or was it a 'land' flying boat? The mists cleared and it became concrete that Short Bros had a rather large Sunderland on the drawing board, but this time it would*

A Belfast photographed during the Oil Lift. The ground equipment obscuring a clear view is interesting in its own right. It illustrates how much was required for a long and intensive detachment - ground power sets, Land Rover, servicing steps and crane are in view.

*have an undercarriage that went up and down. Ho! Ho! Ho! said us, never work, said us (remembering the Stirling) looking at each other nervously, knowing full well that if it did work, they - the RAF - would be looking for people to man it, and we knew the pool of wisdom from whence they would come - us. Also on the horizon was the VC10 which wasn't exactly setting the tills ringing with export dollars, and as the RAF was in need of another transport aircraft to take troops to imagined 'bush fires', and certain ladies to Washington (they now have the TriStar) here was an opportunity for the RAF's global mobility capability to go 'up market' hence the lack of enthusiasm for the Shorts product; stuff the props, lets have the pure jet, was the attitude. I often wonder what would have happened to Transport Command if the Comet, Britannia and VC10 had all been a commercial success.*

*'Its funny how it is that when a person isn't 'on the scene' to say 'Why me?', as it were, he gets 'volunteered' for something, although I can't really blame that way of thinking on the events that were to govern my future 'career' - (same world, same routes, different aeroplane), it would have happened anyway even if I had been there. It happened thusly. My crew was on our way homebound from Singapore and our arrival at Bahrain coincided with the arrival of another Brit that was outbound UK - Singapore. The flight engineer on that crew, whom I didn't much like, couldn't wait to splutter through his false teeth, 'You are posted on to Belfasts.' (The trendy name given to the Shorts product). So the little cloud on the horizon had become a reality and HQTC were getting their crews together. I had much earlier volunteered for VC10s, along with everyone else, wanting to shake off the propeller image. Looking back I suppose I should have thought logically, RAF-wise, and volunteered for Belfasts.*

*'By the 12th August 1965, the clearance chittys were completed and 'au revoir' said to the Brit. The 'selected' 12 engineers sallied forth to the non-flying haven of RAF Brize Norton, which was under 'Care and Maintenance' following the departure of USAF B47s and B52s. The RAF hadn't yet arrived in force; there was a lot of 'flexible' thinking going on at MOD and TCHQ. The planned Belfast course was definitely 'planned' but the dates were a little bit vague, to say the least. Things sorted themselves out eventually and off we went. Three weeks at Smiths (Cheltenham) on the Flight Systems, Auto Pilot and Auto Land. Three weeks at Rolls Royce (Derby) on the Tyne engine and 16 weeks at Shorts (Belfast) on the aircraft proper. More chalk dust off blackboards to contend with. It wasn't until mid-June 1966 that these courses were behind us and we returned to the tranquillity of Brize Norton - still with no aircraft but more occasional blackboard work (must keep the aeroplane fresh in the minds of the chaps!).*

*'Everything comes to he who waits and sure enough on 16th August 1966 (we left Lyneham 12th August 1965) we were*

It has been seen that RAF Lyneham was granted the Freedom of Swindon during the Britannia years. Each subsequent year the right to carry arms through the town is exercised. This is the colour party of 99 Squadron. The Standard Bearer is Flt Lt Tony Marshall, Colour Party Warrant Officer, Master Signaller Brian Thatcher and Colour Escorts, Flt Sgts John Grimwood and Keith Govey.

Sharp eyes may be able to discern that this postcard is of a 'Royal Air Force Air Support Command' aircraft. Note the covered ramp at the rear door of the aircraft. This was used for disembarking aeromedical patients. (*Joy McArthur*)

*airborne in the Belfast for the first time. A look back at comparative flight times of Britannia/Belfast and the Belfast took up to two hours longer than the Brit for the same trip. Should have been called the 'Belslow'. The Belfast had a very big flat loading ramp, which caused a large amount of drag. The aircraft were later to have the 'flatness' of the ramp rounded out and speeds improved - this was the GT version. One of the requirements of a Belfast crew was patience; the landing destination would be reached eventually. It meant that the can of beer you always looked forward to at the end of a flight was coming towards you at a slower speed. The Belfast had six bunk beds fitted with bedding and toilet facilities; also it had a galley on the top deck so hot meals could be served. It also had an in-flight refuelling system. Put all these pieces together and you could have a 'double crew' operation of 35 hours flying. The two crews would be knackered after that, so said the Aviation Medics. To my knowledge it was never carried out - thank the Lord.*

*'Here I pause for a little technical chat. The aircraft had an instrument for every possible thing to let you know what was going on in the various systems, EXCEPT one to indicate the oil tank contents! Now every A/A U/T F/E will know that oil is the lifeblood of an engine. The only indication we had if there was a loss of oil was the frantic wavering of the oil pressure-indicating pointer. The engine was very prone to an oil leak around the fuel heater and the best way to find it (on the ground of course) was to open up the cowlings and start the engine, place a tall ladder behind the whirling prop and climb up it and check for said leak - ask Steve Jones, 41st 'A' Sqdn. This was a little task that came his way when I arrived at Akrotiri on three engines.'*

Colin Rowlinson was to return to Britannias and his story will be continued.

**One of the Canadians**

It has been reported that there were quite a number of recruits to the Britannia from the Royal Canadian Air Force. Amongst them was Flt Lt Tony Gallow - but his background wasn't straight 'Canadian', as is revealed in this press cutting from the RAF News on the occasion of his departure, in 1967, for an exchange tour with the USAF:

*'Flying with four air forces in an aviation career of 13 years - this is the probably unique record of Flt Lt A. F. A. Gallow who is just starting a three-year exchange posting with the United States Air Force.*

*'Tony Gallow, born at Bloemfontein, joined the South African Air Force in 1953 and after training went to a Harvard squadron. In 1956 he transferred to the Royal Canadian Air Force for five years, flying B25s at a navigation school*

The Gallow family ready for the 'off' to the USA. (*RAF News*)

*and later joining No.404 Squadron which flew Neptunes, then Argosys in the maritime reconnaissance role. In 1961 he joined the RAF and has flown Britannias on No.99 Squadron at Lyneham ever since. To date he has logged about 6,000 flying hours.*

*'During his exchange tour with the USAF Flt Lt Gallow will fly C-141 four-jet Starlifters of Military Airlift Command from Travis Air Force Base, San Francisco. He will be accompanied at Travis by his Canadian wife, Alicia, and their three children. In our picture the Gallow family are seen with their bags packed once again and - it seems - junior in charge.'*

Tony was sent a copy of this photo. He responded:

*'Thanks for sending the photo of our young family. It was taken just before we set sail for the USA and the commencement of my exchange tour with the USAF. It was such a long time ago, but the memories of those three years are still very strong. I often say that those three years were the best that I spent in the RAF. The flying was superb on a recently introduced aircraft ... the Starlifter, more commonly known as the C-141. As I had never flown a pure jet before it was arranged that I would do a famil course on the Comet 2 and Comet 4. I managed to get about 40 hours on the Comets before leaving. Travis AFB was ideally located for quick visits to either San Francisco or Lake Tahoe. The children loved every minute of it.'*

**A hot time in Limmasol**

Chris Harwood was a copilot on 99 Squadron. He was about to convert to captain when ill health struck. As a consequence he moved into the Air Traffic world and eventually became a senior member of it. Like so many ex-Britannia people, he remembers his days. Here he recalls an

There was a reward for the construction of the 'Flow Board' featured at the start of this chapter. This Ministry of Defence letter, from the Chairman of the Suggestions Committee, brought the news:

*SUGGESTIONS SCHEME*
*The Suggestions Committee has studied your suggestion for an aircraft flow control board with considerable interest. The Committee has no doubt that this control board, devised and manufactured by you as a voluntary task has greatly improved the method of control of RAF aircraft along trunk routes. I am pleased to tell you that the Committee therefore decided to make you an award of £75 (Seventy Five Pounds) ... I should like to add my personal congratulations for an excellent effort and I hope that if you have any further constructive ideas you will put them forward.*

The photograph shows the C-in-C Air Support Command, Air Chief Marshal Sir Lewis Hodges, presenting the cheque to the author. There was a further subsequent 'reward' - the AOC-in-C's Commendation for meritorious service. Whew!

alarming route occasion:

*'It wasn't just the Eastmed schedules that took us to Akrotiri; virtually everything that started at odds + 500 out of Lyneham seemed to pass through there, particularly after Colonel Gaddafi fell out with everybody and denied us the dubious privilege of operating through El Adem. This little episode happened in 1967.*

*'On this particular occasion - and it must have been in the summer, because it was particularly hot - we had arrived at Akrotiri from wherever and consumed the odd bevvy before leaving for Limassol. We were accommodated at the Astir, which I seem to recall was used predominantly on Eastmeds, which this wasn't. I was no great fan of the Astir anyway, but it did have its funny side. In a rare and casual junior moment, I recall glancing through a copy of the hotel brochure, though God knows why. It declared itself to be '...conveniently situated opposite the Municipal Offices (for what crazy purpose, I found myself wondering) and immaculately appointed, suitable for the most fartidious visitor.' Somehow, that penultimate Stanley Unwinism of a word rang true, often quite literally, with an RAF crew in residence.*

*'Anyway, on with the yarn. After a swift shower, we all met in the dining room in time for dinner and followed what was appearing to be a time-honoured practice of trading the soup course for a further bottle of Keo apiece. I never did have soup there - although I didn't rate Keo much either, so the soup was probably horrendous, despite the trade-in apparently to the advantage of the hotel. A few more beers later, we toddled off on the short trip to the Square. I don't think any of us would have bothered to go there at all had it not been out of bounds. On the other hand, in those days there was not much else on offer anywhere in Cyprus. Three years earlier I'd finished a tour as a Hastings captain on LXX Sqn at Nicosia, and things had scarcely moved on from the fairly staid entertainment opportunities in the capital.*

*'We called in at two or three bars/clubs, and strolled back in the intense humidity round about one o'clock. I think that the eight hours from throttle to bottle rule was being strictly complied with, not that this had any effect whatsoever on the story. As a copilot not entitled to a solo room, I was sharing with Harry Bray, an*

*amiable navigator if ever there was one. Once installed in our dimly lit air-conditioned accommodation, we prepared for bed.*

*'In those days I had sufficient hair to cover my scalp and justify the investment in a comb. I kept the comb in my back pocket, but it slipped from my hand as I tried to place it on the bedside table and it bounced on the uncarpeted parquet flooring, and shot under the bed. The light levels were so dim that I couldn't see it in its new home, but in those days I was also a smoker and I used my Ronson Varaflame lighter to illuminate and locate my beauty aid.*

*I then headed to the bathroom, but was pulled up short by a shout from Harry, 'Oy, your bloody bed's on fire'. Of course, he was perfectly correct. You tend not to say silly things like that in the early hours, even if completely sober. The underside of my single bed ( I emphasise this - the single bed - in case anyone thinks that my relationship with Harry was anything other than proper, decent and naturally heterosexual) was covered in some sort of hessian, and the flame from my lighter had obviously caught one of the looser strands hanging down. It was blazing quite fiercely, and was obviously bone dry in an air-conditioned room. Harry next said, 'Where are you going?' since I continued to head for the bathroom. 'To get some water to put it out,' was my reply. Having run the bath on two bath towels, I returned with two tooth tumblers full of water. Harry had managed to turn the bed over and it then took us quite a while with water, wet towels and some physical violence to extinguish it completely. In the meantime the room had filled with smoke and heat, so we had to open the windows. This progressively let the smoke out, but inevitably the heat and humidity of the Limassol night charged back in and made the weedy air conditioning largely defunct.*

*'Turning the bed back the right way up, we found that although all the bottom of the base had burned off, and the base itself was quite badly charred, only a little of one corner of the mattress was burnt. It was essentially sleepable, and the chances either of finding a new room or a new bed at that time of night was probably nil, so that is where I managed to grab a couple of hours sleep. Harry didn't get much sleep either, but he was very good about it and even more so later that morning. The room still stank of smoke, and we had to leave the windows open after the smoke had gone in a vain attempt to diminish the smell. It had achieved very little other than to let the sticky night in and when we finally got up to shower, towels were in short supply. At this point we decided not to ask for more towels to avoid lengthy explanations.*

*'I decided to come clean (no pun intended) as we checked out, so after breakfast I asked the receptionist if I could speak to the manager, without saying why. He would perhaps have pitched up a little earlier had I done so, because on being told about the unfortunate incident he rather lost his cool and said that I could not leave without paying for the damage I had incurred. I drew breath to make clear my response to such an unappreciative reaction when Harry, who by this time was beginning to run short of good humour, burst forth with a considered and positive response on my behalf. Making it clear that the manager or owner could not possibly be running a hotel, particularly one used to accommodate RAF transit crews, without proper fire insurance, then that was obviously the way forward, rather than an attempt to offer a sort of blackmail to a man who had decently told the truth about an accident, which was not an act of vandalism. Furthermore, for how much longer did he anticipate that he would retain what was obviously a lucrative contract if he were to continue threatening in that vein? Finally,*

A presentation ceremony in November 1967. Flt Lt A R Wood of 99 Squadron receives his 'Mention in Despatches' from the Station Commander, Group Captain N E Hoad AFC. Flt Lt Wood's award was in recognition of his services in Sarawak. Gp Capt Hoad was previously OC 216 Squadron. It is to him that the author is indebted for the pen and ink drawings that feature in this book. (*Lyneham Globe*)

*why on earth did he not have serviceable smoke alarms in operation? ( A good one, this, because I don't think that this was yet a legal requirement in the UK in 1967.)*

*'The manager then clammed up, having agreed that of course what Harry said was right, and that he had forgotten that of course he was insured. On the crew coach back to Akrotiri, with two of us smelling strongly of badly burnt toast, I reiterated my thanks to Harry for his intervention, while wishing I could have got in first. Harry, back to his usual Bray way was professional to the last. 'I don't like being spoken to like that, and anyway we've got a schedule to keep and he was threatening to delay us.'*

*'Some people are just better than others!'*

**More memories**

Mike Joyce was stirred to remember his Britannia days:

*'I started flying with the RCAF in 1955 learning to fly on Harvards. I then taught people how to fly them for the next 5 years. During this time I met my first Britannia. I was landing on Rwy 36 at Winnipeg in a T33 SILVER STAR jet on a still air day. About 500 feet up I found myself tossed 90 degrees. Recovering and enquiring I was told that I had flown into the propwash of the CP AIR Brit landing just ahead! The T33 had an AUW of 16000 lbs. This was 1959.*

*'Like many other RCAF pilots (Bob Henderson for example) I transferred to the RAF in 1961. After a refresher course at Strubby on Meteors, including my first single seater, a Mk 8, I was sent to Little Rissington to learn how to be an RAF instructor! I considered I had done enough of this and after 30 hours on the Jet Provost, I went to the course director one Thursday and requested to do something else. He asked what and I suggested Transport Command. The next Tuesday he told me to report to Lyneham the following Thursday for Britannia Course number 25. So I packed up and drove my Thunderbird to Lyneham. My instructor was the renowned Jack McWicker who, on the route trainer into Hong Kong, May 1962, reminded me to watch the ILS instead of the scenery!*

*'During my flying time on Brits, I had the rank of Flying Officer and was not promoted to Flight Lieutenant until working in Ops in FEAF. Here are some of the reminiscences from my log book with 511 Squadron over the next five years. These anecdotes may spark similar memories:*

*Misjudging the round out at St Mawgan because of the width of the runway!*

*The solid arrival when doing a flapless 'touch and go' and taking the inboard power off too early!*

*The use of full reverse on the first landing at Lusaka as the runway looked so small!*

*The interminable roll for take-off at Nairobi on the last flight out at MOPS weight!*

*Never really understanding the soccer ball electrical diagram!*

*Taking over at least a month to really begin to understand the Smiths Flight System!*

*Using the north south runway at Lyneham. This may have been because of a bogged Britannia on runway 25 after an aborted practice three-engine take off!*

*Taking a poll of both the 16 passengers and crew regarding where they would like to spend New Year's Eve after an engine shut down between Athens and the toe of Italy! We decided on Malta.*

*Being asked by various people, mostly in the USA, if the aircraft was under control as the flying surfaces were pointing in strange directions.*

*Being sent by Ops to the Calne strip parking area for an MCT detail to find the aircraft allocated was a true three-engined Britannia as one propeller was missing.*

*Marking the nose wheel with the crew's initials so that, at the final destination, whoever's initials were at the bottom bought the first round!*

*'Some highlights or otherwise of some of my flights:*

*As copilot to Fred Lace on a medivac from Kuwait to Heathrow with a Kuwaiti Royal taking 11 hours. This was after flying in from Aden, adding another five hours.*

*As copilot to Wing Commander Lewis on a flight from Sharjah to Nicosia, waking up after my 1½ hours off, approaching Tabriz to find everyone else snoozing.*

*As copilot to Don Dewhurst with a*

*double crew (Keith Cloyd) for a medivac pick-up in Accra. Flying time Lyneham to Accra - 11 hours 15 minutes.*

*My first flight as a fully qualified captain on the 2nd February 1965. This was followed by a flight on the 5th February as a single crew to Australia and back.*

*Being the lowest paid Britannia crew with a Flying Officer copilot, two Flight Sergeants, a Master Signaller and a Corporal AQM.*

*Being allocated a Battle of Britain flypast in September 1966.*

*Returning from my last flight from Lusaka to Nairobi and flying around the top of Mount Kilimanjaro for photos and then proceeding about 500 feet AGL to Nairobi, November 1966.*

*Taking the C-in-C of Training Command, Sir John Davies, on a Westabout to Travis (his daughter's wedding) and being asked by the USAF Ops. Officer: 'How come a bum Lootenant is flying a General around?!!' (He had mistakenly assumed a Flight Lieutenant crew member was the captain.)*

*On the same flight, at Guam, Anderson Field, using the parallel taxiway for take-off, to maintain the schedule, as the main runway was closed because of a crashed aircraft. According to the book, which proved correct, if I backed up and had all four water injections working, it would be just long enough. It was! We left a large dust cloud over the construction equipment at the departure end where they were lengthening the taxiway. Base Ops allowed me to do this, taking no responsibility for my action, but at least they removed the construction crew.*

*A landing in Naples at the NATO base with a full complement of armed soldiers on a flight to Cyprus after one of them had collapsed. The ground marshaller, a USN officer, was amazed when he lost his hat as we backed up through 90 degrees into a parking spot. I never knew how the Diplomatic people straightened things out or what happened to the sick soldier left behind at the base hospital.*

*An alternator overheat after take-off from Bahrain at night with the copilot reminding me that, 'maybe we should dump some fuel before returning to land.'*

*My final flight from Gander to Lyneham on July 21 1967 before posting to FEAF.'*

**A journalist's view**

In March 1967 the '*Weekly Scotsman*' ran a two-part feature on a 99 Squadron trip from Hong Kong to Lyneham. It is possibly not entirely a coincidence that the captain and two of the airquartermasters were Scots. It has been reproduced here in its entirety as an interesting insight as to how reporters interpret events. It has to be said that, for a non-flyer and allowing for journalistic licence, Roderick Grant does very well.

*(Apologies for quality but the resource was a photocopy of the articles kindly provided by the daughter of Jimmy Lee, the flight engineer. Sadly he died in a train accident whilst serving on 99.)*

# The Globetrotter ...

THERE he goes again, briefcase in hand, up the gangway of his R.A.F. Britannia on the start of another trip round the world. His name is Alistair Graham, a Cupar-born Globetrotter, member of a select group of ever-ready air crew, prepared to fly anywhere at any time. The exotic life of the Globetrotters sounded so fascinating to Weekly Scotsman writer Roderick Grant that he decided to see for himself - in Cyprus, Bahrain, Gan, Singapore and Hong Kong, aboard a "Whispering Giant" commanded by a Scots captain, with two other Scots in his flying team. Roderick Grant's reports ...

"Mike Papa November Uniform Golf you are now five miles from touch down. Prepare to lose height and begin your descent. Maintain your present heading and do not acknowledge any further instructions unless necessary."

The radio crackled and the voice of the Air Traffic Controller at Hong Kong's Kai Tak airport went off the air. Royal Air Force Transport Command's Bristol Britannia 635 obeyed the instructions. The captain, her lord and master, saw to that.

Fit. Lt. John Hall, co-captain on Flight 6417, called for a reduction in power. "Torque 250".

"Torque 250," came the instant reply from flight engineer, Flt. Lt. Jim Lee. Seated slightly behind and between the two pilots, poised over a bank of levers and switches, he leaned forward and with a delicate touch adjusted the throttles.

The flight deck was dark save for the reflection from several bulbs on the control panels and the lights above the radio operator's and navigator's desks. Outside winds buffeted against the 124-foot fuselage.

Far below, to the right, through the gathering storm clouds, I could see the colour of Hong Kong and Kowloon spread out like the lights of some gigantic fairground.

**Darkness**

Through the windscreen the red warning light on top of a radio beacon appeared dead centre with the nose and some distance below.

The intercom came to life once again.

"Final approach checks, navigator," requested Flt. Lt. Hall, The navigator, Flt. Lt. Hugh Westell, stopped work on his charts, reached across his desk and began to read from the prepared checklist.

"De-icing."

Both the engineer and the

*Wing Commander T.L. Kennedy, A.F.C. (38), captain; a native of Hawick and commanding officer of No.99 Squadron. Married with three of a family, he joined the Royal Air Force as an airman fitter in 1946. "I love flying and I think the tremendous thing about this job is this squadron spirit - the idea that as a team we rely on each other so much."*

aircraft's senior captain, Wing Commander Thomas L. Kennedy, commanding officer of No.99 Squadron, sitting in the co-pilot's seat (the right-hand seat) checked the lights and replied simultaneously: "Wing and engine de-icing off,"

Navigator: "Auto-Pilot."

Co-pilot: "Master switch off."

The checks continued and the aircraft flew on through the darkness.

Master Signaller Frank Burke, the radio operator, in constant touch with the ground, listened intently for any instruction, which the captain wished to have passed on. The headsets were filled with the sound of voices. British voices. Voices on the ground and in the air.

Voices from aircraft above and to the left and right of us. All had a message to be passed on - all waited instructions from the ground.

A few miles in front the lights on Victoria Peak began to show. Kai Tak airport is one of the world's most difficult airports at which to land. There is only one runway. An aircraft captain has only two choices. The first - to land from the sea through a gap in the mountains. The second- to come in low over the city towards the mountain peak, then execute a sharp turn to starboard when only a short distance from a huge painted and illuminated sign set on the mountainside. This brings the aircraft to within a few hundred feet above the tallest building and almost at the touchdown point on the runway. We followed the latter course.

The "chequer-board" as the painted sign is called began to assume alarming proportions as the "Whispering Giant" flew towards it. The two pilots sat erect in their seats, judging every foot and watching their instruments. It was now possible to see cars and people on the streets below and pick out restaurants and nightclubs from the coloured signs on their rooftops.

The chequer-board seemed to fill the entire windscreen. At last - the crisp order to change course. Flt. Lt. Hall moved the controls over and the mighty

*Flt. Lt. John M. Hall (34), co-captain; married with one child. Joined R.A.F in 1949 and has flown Vampires, Hunters and Lightnings. " Flying the Britannias is the most satisfying flying job I have done. Flying a Comet, they say, is like driving a Jaguar. Flying a Britannia is like driving a Rolls-Royce."*

*Flt.Lt. Hugh Westell (34), navigator; married with two of a family. He joined the R.A.F. as a National Service officer in 1951. After a spell as personal navigator to the Air Officer Commanding No.21 Group, he decided to make the service his career. "I love this job - to me navigation is a real challenge. Every take-off and every flight is different in some respect."*

aircraft responded at once. We swung over to starboard in a tight turn and the runway lay stretched out before us.

Blocks of flats and offices swept past under the wings.

The engine power was reduced once more and the Britannia began to drop towards the touchdown area. The lights ran far out to sea and from 250 feet the runway seemed extremely narrow.

Down we went - the captain forcing the machine earthwards with all the power he could muster. Crosswinds plucked at the nose sending the aircraft veering to the right.

Flt. Lt. Hall brought her back on course again.

One hundred feet to go and the runway's centre line lay in line with the aircraft's nose. Another gust, even fiercer this time, tried to haul the Britannia's nose skywards. The captain held her down.

The propellers were idled - 50 feet to go. The white-crossed lines at the start of the runway disappeared. A slight shudder

*Led by the captain, Wing Commander Kennedy, the crew climb aboard. At the back are the two Scots airquartermasters - Sgt. Bob Brown from Windygates, Fife (second from the left) and Sgt. John Jenkins from Lanark (third from the right).*

was felt on the flight deck when the touchdown came and the ten wheels connected with the mass of concrete.

The brakes were applied. There was no visible reduction in speed and the aircraft thundered along the runway towards the sea.

The captain's quiet voice asked for "Reverse thrust," The engineer acted. The four propellers were brought under power again - this time to be sent spinning in the opposite direction. With a roar from the four Bristol Proteus turbo-prop engines, the aircraft began to slow down - the great force throwing the crew against their safety belts. In several seconds it was all over and the Britannia was brought to a halt. The navigator began his after-landing checks and the pilots brought the aircraft round to taxi back along the runway to the dispersal area in front of the airport buildings.

Four hours and fifty minutes had elapsed since we left Singapore and in the passenger compartment at the rear or the aircraft, behind the 23,000lbs of freight, the 22 passengers unfastened their safety belts.

The two airquartermasters, Sergeants Bob Brown and John Jenkins, finished the paperwork, while ground engineer, Sergeant John Tasker, entered the flight deck to consult with the flight engineer on what servicing was required for the aircraft while it was parked at Kai Tak.

**Baggage**

Steps were placed against the door beside the flight deck and the door opened A blast of cool air swept inside.

The crew finished the last of their checks and each man began the hunt for his personal baggage. A small coach arrived and one by one we lugged our bags, suits and other belongings down the steps and on to the coach. With a loud rasping of the gears, the Chinese driver hurtled us forward over the concrete towards the airport buildings.

While the flight deck crew visited the flight dispersal offices, the two air quartermasters gave a list of their requirements, for both crew and passengers, for the return journey, to the catering section.

Within ten minutes we were back aboard the coach again and with another ear shattering gear change our Chinaman swept us out of the airport and into the hustle and bustle of Hong Kong. It was a 20-minute drive to the hotel and in these 20 minutes we encountered more danger than we were to experience during the entire flight of almost 19,000 miles.

In and out of the traffic, between buses packed with cheerful Chinese (it was Chinese New Year and everyone was on holiday), across pedestrian crossings, pedestrians scattering in all directions, our driver maintained breakneck speed in order to reach the hotel. Every other driver seemed to be in a desperate hurry as well. Horns honked loudly and angrily, old Chinese women shook gnarled fists behind us and firecrackers, set off to celebrate the coming of the New Year, were thrown into the streets from all directions, to explode with extreme violence. With the noise of the bursting crackers in our ears and the furious speed at which we were being driven, it was like running the gauntlet of a fierce terrorist attack.

I remarked that everyone seemed to have gone crazy. From behind a pile of suitcases an unknown voice remarked philosophically: "They're all mad." A quick broadside, a screaming "U" turn and the driver trod on the brakes in front of the glass doors of the Shamrock Hotel. We staggered out, muttering undiplomatic remarks about the Chinese race in general and our driver in particular.

Rooms were allocated and the Wing Commander told his crew that early calls would be given at 6.30 a.m. on the Saturday morning. A coach would pick us up at 7 a.m.

**Nightlife**

A shower and a change of clothing and we were ready for a look at Hong Kong's nightlife.

Transport Command crews, and in particular the crews of

*Master Signaller Frank Burke (48); radio operator; married with four of a family, he signed on in 1940. Has spent 21 years in Transport Command. While dropping supplies to a British Greenland Expedition was involved a Hastings crash. For ten days along with the rest of the crew, he waited for rescue on the Greenland ice cap. "It's much safer flying in long-range transport aircraft compared with the civvies, They don't carry a radio operator. Because we do, a higher safety factor is involved."*

No.99 Squadron's Britannias are well used to this routine by now. Take any one of them and ask him of the places he has visited and the names roll easily off his tongue: San Francisco, Bahrain, New York, Chicago, Singapore, Tokyo, Cyprus, the Bahamas.

Apart from Britannias on regular scheduled flights to Singapore, Cyprus and Aden several times a week, they are called upon to fly aircraft to other parts of the world for a variety of reasons.

In 1966 Transport Command aircraft flew 34 million miles and carried 136,700 passengers. Royal Air Force crews get more opportunities of building a strong team spirit amongst themselves than do crews of the civilian airliners. In some airlines, for example, when the aircraft arrives at its destination the captain is taken by car to a hotel, where he lives on his own. He is not expected to mingle with his crew. In the R.A.F., crews stay at the same hotels, irrespective of rank. Apartheid of this sort is not practised.

**Procedures**

On civilian airliners the crew arrives at the airport, prior to departure, to find all flight planning work has been done for them. Take-off speeds, landing speeds and other necessary calculations have been made. R.A.F. crews do their own calculations. From information gleaned from the Meteorological Office, the operations room and flight planning, the navigator calculates the speed at which the aircraft will lift off the ground.

He has many different circumstances to take into account - temperature, wind, aircraft weight, etc. Although this would seem to be an extra chore, which the R.A.F. crews have to endure, they do not regard it as such. They want it no other way. By doing their own planning and calculations and discussing procedures amongst themselves, where each man's view is taken note of by the captain, who makes the ultimate decision, they can be absolutely satisfied. It is this satisfaction in knowing that they have been able to check and double-check not only their own calculations but those of their companions as well that makes them crews of the highest order.

*Flt. Lt. James R. Lee (41), flight engineer, married with two of a family, he joined the R.A.F in 1939. His first aircraft was a Manchester bomber. "The Britannia is a good aircraft - it has no vices."*

The safety record of R.A.F. long-range transport aircraft is second to none.

## The Globe Trotters - Part Two

THE stormy weather had cleared and sun shone brightly when Britannia 635, otherwise known as 'Bellatrix', made her way along the taxiway to Runway 13 at Hong Kong prior to departing for Singapore. Over the R/T came the voice of a Cathay Pacific pilot requesting permission to land. A DC-8 took-off in front of us, bound for Saigon.

We reached the end of the taxiway and the final checks were in progress as the aircraft moved on to the runway.

"Royal Air Force Flight 6417 you are clear to take-off on Runway 13," announced the controller.

The windows on both the captain's and co-captain sides, open to assist their vision when the aircraft was taxiing, were closed and the Wing Commander gave the thumbs-up sign.

"We're off"' he said.

At 400 ft. the flaps were drawn in and we went through the gap in the mountains at the entrance to the harbour. With the after take-off checks in progress, Sgt. Jenkins appeared with coffee for the crew. Hot steaming coffee - just right for a Saturday morning at 9 a.m.

We were soon at our cruising altitude of 16,000 ft. and the autopilot was switched on. Brilliant sunlight flooded the flight deck reflecting a harsh, white glare from the cumulonimbus clouds, which appear in alarming sizes over Southeast Asia.

**Information**

Royal Air Force airliners fly through civilian airways (areas of airspace designated for use by aircraft controlled by radio beacons and ground operators. This took us over South Vietnam

*Sgt. John Tasker (28), ground engineer; married, he joined the R.A.F. in 1954. Specialises on Britannias. He is required to look after the maintenance of the aircraft on the ground when it flies 'off-route' - to such places as America, across the Pacific, Australia and Hong Kong. He has been round the world six times as well as working on a Royal flight. "This job is fascinating."*

for 20 minutes. Visibility was excellent and it was possible, although we were at 16,000 ft. to pick out roads, villages and even lorries on the ground. We were about 40 miles to the east of Saigon and the headsets constantly picked up the voices of American pilots and ground control passing information back and fore.

A large number of fires were burning in an area of about ten miles radius and as we passed over Da Lat thick smoke spiralled upwards from a massive fire on the outskirts of the village. Several aircraft were in the near vicinity but were not visible.

Ten minutes ahead of schedule, thanks to a helpful tailwind, we touched down at R.A.F. Changi in Singapore. When the doors were opened there was a marked contrast in the temperature compared to Hong Kong. Wave upon wave of hot still air poured into the fuselage. Within minutes the sweat began to run.

Never has beer tasted so good as the glasses of 'Tiger' (a local brew) that were handed round when we reached the Changi Creek Hotel in Changi village.

The passengers aboard the Britannia were Ministry of Defence officials carrying out research into facilities for handling R.A.F. transport aircraft at staging posts between Britain and Hong Kong. They needed nearly three days to complete their job in Singapore. Take-off was planned for 9 a.m. (local time) on the Tuesday.

For the next few days we relaxed in the splendid tropical climate. Visits were made to shops and market places in search of bargains thrust eagerly at us by grinning Indians and hopeful Chinese. Electric razors of the highest quality for £5; watches, worth £25, for £5 or £6; Cameras, radios, blankets, sheets, shirts, socks and ties - all for prices which bordered on the ridiculous.

When the door was shut and the crew baggage sorted out behind the flight deck on the Tuesday morning, the pile of possessions had grown considerably.

**Altitude**

When the cruising altitude was reached the captain informed the passengers that the 2050-mile flight to Gan would take 6 hours 45 minutes. Over the Straits of Malacca, round the tip of Indonesia - then forward across the wide expanse of the Indian Ocean.

Because of the flying distance over the sea on this stage of the journey, the navigator has no radio beacons to aid him in keeping the aircraft on course. Using a sextant Flt.Lt.Westell took readings from the sun's position and calculated the aircraft's position from the information he gained. This was carried out every half-hour. After the second check on position it was found that the Britannia was burning too much fuel we began a further climb to 20,000 ft. The greater the altitude the less fuel is burned up.

Just before 1 p.m. (local time) we saw the tiny island of Gan far below us set in a sea of emerald green. Scattered around it were the neighbouring islands in the Maldive Group - all small and looking exactly like

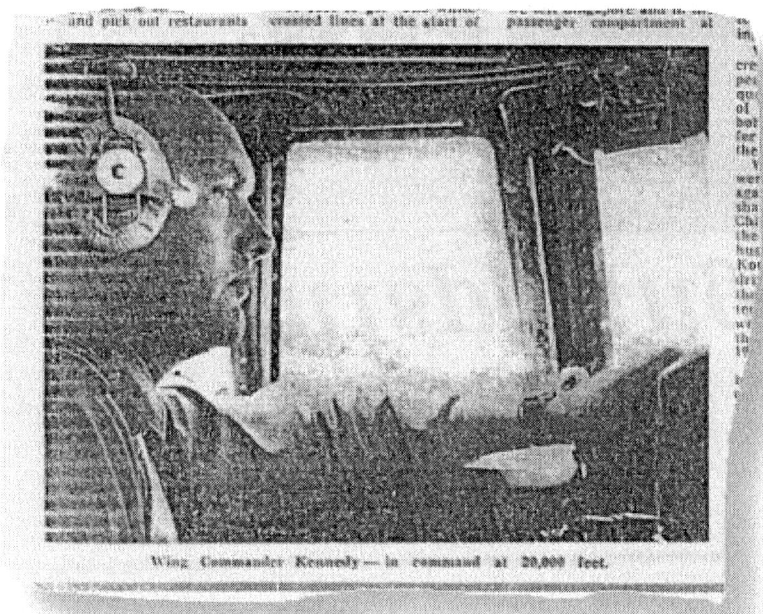

*Wing Commander Kennedy - in command at 20,000 feet.*

the desert islands displayed in the best of travel advertisements. The captain made a visual approach on to the island's single runway and touched down exactly on schedule.

**Electric**

Two hours later we were swimming in the warmth of the Indian Ocean between great coral reefs reflecting a variety of colours and sporting razor-sharp edges,

Crews enjoy their stays in Gan. The entire island is one huge R.A.F. station and in this part of the world beer, spirits and cigarettes are at rock-bottom prices. Whisky at 14s 6d per bottle; the finest brands of cigarettes at 10s 6d for 200 - who could ask for anything more?

Three hours out from Gan on the 2090-mile leg to Bahrain, in the Persian Gulf, the passengers tucked into their main meal. Meals for both passengers and crews are prepared on the ground and kept hot by electric heaters on board the aircraft. Cold meals and snacks are kept in refrigerated compartments until served by the two air quarter-masters.

Passengers are served from a practical and sensible list of menus - both hot and cold - and the crew members can order up their own individual requirements. In both cases the standard is high.

At 16,500 feet the 22 passengers got down to roast chicken, roast and boiled potatoes, garden peas, peaches and cream, followed by cheese and biscuits and coffee. Prior to this they had received a cold drink immediately after take-off plus coffee or tea and before landing at Bahrain there was assorted canapés and coffee.

At 3.30 a.m. (local time) two days later we landed at R.A.F. Akrotiri, in Cyprus, in a howling gale and blinding rain. Time and again the runway lights were blotted out as the rain was driven across the windscreen. Once on the ground it took the combined efforts of both pilots to hold the "Whispering Giant" as she protested at the state of the waterlogged runway.

Amidst the whine of the electric motors and the throaty roar of the engines the captain told his crew: "It's a seaplane we should be using in conditions like these."

The rain was still lashing down when we reached the Curium Palace Hotel, in Limassol, as the cold grey dawn began to break over the Troodos Mountains. Thanks to the wintry weather we saw little of the sunny Cyprus we see on the pages of every travel agent's brochure.

Shortly before midnight the following day the air traffic controller at R.A.F. Lyneham, in Wiltshire instructed Wing Commander Kennedy: "Turn 250 degrees and descend to 1500 feet."

**Midnight**

We were ten miles from touchdown. The pre-landing checks were in progress. The comforting thump of the undercarriage going down was heard and as proof the three green lights that signify that all is well, shone out from the centre of the control panel.

"You are now half a mile from touch-down. Take over visually."

The Wing Commander brought his charge down towards the lights of home, On either side of the runway they shone out in welcome. There was only 100 feet to go.

"Torque 200 . . . Idle."

The flight engineer obeyed.

Any moment now.

"Superfine."

The engineer made a further adjustment.

The wheels kissed the tarmac.

"Reverse thrust."

After 18,840 miles a final ear-shattering roar from the four engines cut through the frosty midnight air. It announced triumphantly that Flight 6417 had returned.

One of the 'bibles' of Britannia route flying, originally known as the Sector Fuel Payload Tables. For numerous routes, it outlined the diversion, 70% wind component, probable take-off temperature, fuel required, payload, maximum take-off weight, cruise mode and time. Its major use was at the pre-planning stage. On the actual day calculations were made based on the pertaining conditions.

The adventures of Messrs. Ad Minn and Org at Wootton Lynstoke continue ...

LEAVING THE HAIRDRESSER AD MINN & ORG MEET A STRANGE PROCESSION .....
"AND WHO ARE YOU?"
"WE'RE THE BESNOS BOYS — A POLITICO ECONOMIC GROUP — WITH
THE ELECTION NEAR THERE MUST BE NO HINT OF OVER-EXPENDITURE. THUS ON THE PREMISE THAT IF SOMEONE CAN FLY HE SHOULD BE ABLE TO CLEAN A FLOOR WHEREAS THE CLEANERS CANNOT NECESSARILY FLY: THE PILOTS HAVE BEEN GIVEN BROOMS!"
PER ABLUTIO AD ASTRA
AS WE CLEAN AS WE FLY!!
— AND AT NO EXTRA COST!"
WHILST AD MINN AND ORG HAVE BEEN ABOUT THEIR WORK THE GREAT BRITISH PEOPLE HAVE BEEN CHOOSING A GREAT LEADER FROM AMONGST THOSE GREAT PARTY-POLITICAL TELEVISION ENTERTAINERS.
"CLICHÉ... SIX PLATITUDES... ONE FEEBLE WITTICISM ... DEAR LADIES ... APPEAL TO T.U.C.... MUMBLE .... THREE PROVERBS .... ECONOMIC PROSPERITY.... NUCLEAR ARMS.... CLICHÉ..."
HEAR HEAR
... SIR YORRICK DOUGLAS GNOME ....
AND OF COURSE
"...THREE MISQUOTATIONS.... TWO PROVERBS .... A LITTLE NONSENSE... BAN THE BOMB.... CLICHÉ .... GREAT WORK OF UNIONS.... TECHNOLOGICAL ADVANCES... ECONOMIC CRISIS..."
'ERE 'ERE
.... MR HARRIED WINSOME ....
NOT FORGETTING
"WHERE? WHERE?"
.... MR GRIM JOMOND.
"THE SOVIETS HAVE THE BEST IDEA ON CHANGE OF REGIME — NO NONSENSE — OVERNIGHT INSTANT MINISTER!"
28

CHAPTER TWENTY THREE

# Steady Years - and People

After headline years with the Oil Lift and the Aden evacuation, 1968 and 1969 might be considered a more routine period for the Britannia fleet. They might also be regarded as the years during which the death knell for the Britannia was first sounded. Economic crisis brought the first swingeing defence cuts in 1968 and the decision to speed up our withdrawal from the Far East and the Persian Gulf.

**Fearless talks**

Rhodesian UDI had continued to hold out despite international disfavour and economic sanctions. In the Autumn of 1968 talks were arranged to try and settle the matter. The neutral 'ground' of HMS Fearless off Gibraltar was chosen and a succession of Britannia flights were the vehicle for Mr Ian Smith and his party from Salisbury via Ascension Island.

Events were reported by a 99 Squadron correspondent in the *Lyneham Globe:*

*'From Our Man in Gib*

*'For the meeting of Mr. Wilson and Mr. Smith the 99 Squadron Ops Officer was whisked away from his graphs and boards and deposited in Gibraltar kicking and screaming as Detachment Commander. During the lunch hour of Saturday, 6th October, a Britannia touched down at Gibraltar en route for Ascension Island. Only one passenger, our man in Gib disembarked, and was met by the Station Commander Group Captain G. H. Burgess, and the OC Flying Sqn Ldr G. B. Bell. Gibraltar was all out at that time to receive its AOC-in-C for the annual inspection on Monday. A tremendous amount of speculation surrounded the mysterious Britannia movement which was dispelled to a certain extent by the cover story of a long range USA trainer via Ascension, (would you believe!).*

*'During the morning of Monday the 8th the AOC-in-C Coastal Command arrived, followed shortly by the announcement of the proposed meeting of Mr. Wilson and Mr. Smith on the 9th. A week of intensive activity for Gibraltar began with the arrival late on the 8th of Mr. Wilson's Comet plus a reserve aircraft, followed shortly by Wing Commander Yetman with a reserve Britannia full of the London Press Corps. The Rhodesian Prime Minister arrived by Britannia at teatime on the 9th. For the crews came a period of stand-by for the return flights, while our man in Gib ran in small circles endeavouring to ensure that all was prepared for a quick smooth get away of the aircraft, at short notice if necessary.'*

**The Britannia crew**

The original standard Britannia

Mr Ian Smith embarking at Ascension Island in October 1968 (by steps specially positioned from Lyneham?) (*Curly Richards*)

crew consisted of a captain, copilot, navigator, flight engineer, signaller and at least one air quartermaster, possibly more depending on the number of passengers. The captain would be 'experienced'. The lowest level that this reached was in the latter days of the aircraft's service when pilots came straight from training to be copilots. Some of these, after their three year tour, became captains. Generally captains had completed two or three tours previous to their copilot tour on the aircraft (very few people went straight into the left hand seat) followed by a captaincy. This had been the tradition. It has to be said that when it was broken by the first tour copilots, they did extremely well.

The navigator also usually had experience of other aircraft as did the engineer. But again, recruits came straight from training as the awe of the aircraft, which was so strong in its early days, gradually eroded.

Up to 1969, the fourth member of the crew was the signaller. They started to disappear that year with the SSB modification having been carried out on most of the aircraft.

Finally there were those vital members 'down the back', the air quartermasters. Later, to better describe their role, the trade was renamed airloadmaster. Finally the Britannia witnessed a progression in passenger care with the introduction of the previously reported air stewards.

**The constituted crew**

The 'constituted crew' had been a tradition in large aircraft since their earliest days. It was considered a good idea that the same people flew together; they would mould into a team. This was tried in the early Britannia days and abandoned. That 'team' could become very sloppy and non-standard. It was difficult to administer - for instance, all the crew had to take leave at the same time. Also there was the inevitability of some people 'not getting on' and, the extreme case of this, an individual who nobody 'got on with'! If he were a captain, it was very difficult.

The true tale is told (I was there) of an attempt to reintroduce the constituted crew system on 99 Squadron. A large piece of paper was pinned on the board with the squadron captains' names along the top. Crew members were invited to put their names below the name of the captain with whom they wished to fly. The list had to be taken down after a few days when captains X, X and X had no names below theirs.

So, the system of each aircrew trade section (pilots', navigators', engineers', signallers', airquartermasters' and stewards') allocating individuals for each flight remained the norm for the whole of the RAF Britannia's life.

**Two engines shut down**

This year's annual Westabout exercise was named 'Villain'. The villain of the piece for Flt Lt Jack May and crew was XL640. The story is available from a ground crew viewpoint. Ex-Sergeant Dave Ashenden is the narrator:

*'I was, at that time, an engine fitter and had been at Andersen AFB, Guam for ten days or so, working shifts, servicing the Britannias through to Singapore and then back again. The exercise was complete and it was time to jump on the 'sweeper' aircraft XM517 returning back to the UK. First stop was Wake Island. On landing in the afternoon we were told that 640, ahead of us and en route Wake to Honolulu, had turned back - with TWO engines shut down! As the only propulsion man with rectification experience, I was detailed to stay and await 640's return. Everyone else was pleased to get on with refuelling 517 - Christmas was approaching.*

*'More news came through on 640; it was Nos.1 & 2 engines that had been shut down. The Wake USAF/FAA rescue immediately launched the Grumman Goose and all emergency services were on alert. Evidently their experience of successful landings of USAF four engined transports with two out was not good, particularly when both engines were on the same side!'*

**Great stuff!**

*'Night fell and at last 640's lights appeared overhead, it was good weather. We all watched as it circled and eventually crossed the runway threshold for a perfect landing. It taxied in and stopped smack on the white spot. Great stuff! The Yanks were amazed and the captain (a Canadian gentleman, as I recall) treated the whole thing as an everyday occurrence.'*

**Prop surge**

*'My problems now began. I*

*managed to get the captain and engineer to one side for a debrief and ascertained that No.2 prop had surged (a known problem usually associated with an intermittent fault in the propeller tacho generator) and the engine was shut down and prop feathered. However, for some reason unknown to the aircrew, whilst confirming the feather on No.2 prop, No.1 suddenly feathered itself!!'*

**Finger trouble?**

*'This particular phenomena was well known to Britannia propulsion technicians. I had 'done it' during ground testing. It was a 'finger problem' associated with the poor design of the standby propeller control selector switch. I have no doubt that ex-Britannia people are already ahead of me.'*

Training detail complete. Captain Bill Robinson descends the utility version of aircraft steps with his crew. (*Bill Robinson*)

Captain and nav - Flt Lts John Caskie and Dave Smith. The name 'Regulus', of latter day significance, stands out. It was the last Britannia to fly.

**Bad design**

No sides are being taken! What is being implied is that whilst the correct propeller was feathered on the normal system, when it came to the second part of the drill, which involved confirming that feathering by doing it again, using the standby system, then the wrong propeller had been selected i.e. No.1 instead of No.2.

The switch *was* indeed badly designed. It was a rotary one with a stop for each propeller, 1, 2, 3, 4. But there were two positions before this, LOCK and OFF. The trap is to think that lock is off, next click No.1, next No.2 - run the standby feathering system and you are in for a surprise. Without making judgements, it did subsequently become the drill that, when operating the switch, it was turned fully clockwise and the clicks counted *back* to the required propeller - 4, 3, 2!

**Welcome home!**

Sergeant Dave Ashenden's account continues with many days of rectification followed by air tests. Eventually the aircraft was declared serviceable and proceeded homebound. They taxied in at Lyneham very late on Christmas Eve to a champagne welcome from the Station Commander!

**Regain generation handle**

1968 contained another interesting technical saga for a crew. It has been said that the Britannia broke new aeronautical engineering ground with its dependence on electricity which operated actuators activated by switches rather than the solid levers etc. of old. It may have been some flight crew wariness of this, at the design stage, which resulted in the installation of a device known as the Regain Generation Handle. It was located centrally and prominently, above the pilots' instrument panel coaming.

The electrical system was incredibly clever with all sorts of automatic control and protection systems but the feeling obviously was that, if all else failed, there should be a way to eliminate all the sophistication, reset the alternators and have a very basic system with which an emergency return could be accomplished.

**Stowaway fly**

It was a last resort device which is how it came to have the informal title of the OMC handle. OMC? 'Oh! My Christ!' There were tales of early civil airline crews using it in a panic but it was never used in anger during its military service. But it was operated.

On a flight out of Lyneham to Cyprus in June of this year, a fly, deciding that it would like a bit of Mediterranean sunshine, had settled itself on the flight deck. The crew did not approve. The captain lashed out; his hand caught the OMC handle! Electrical chaos reigned. All the things that should have happened, did - and more! It was a subdued crew that brought the aircraft back to Lyneham.

**Operation Banner**

Ever since the re-establishment of the Army as an attempted peace keeper in Northern Ireland in the early 60s, the Britannias had the task of unit changeovers, aeromedical evacuation and resupply. With most of the troops coming from Germany, 'Banner' runs between Gutersloh and

In later years Ann Culliford used to show this photograph to her young son to prove that she used to fly, but it was not Spitfires or Hurricanes! Taken in January 1965, (L to R), Chris Burns, Jill Witt, Ann and Rita Bradbury. (*Ann Bihan née Culliford*)

A ceremony to mark 'Mac' MacLeod's 5,000 Britannia hours. The caption did not contain details of the occasion. (*Lyneham Globe*)

Aldergrove became a regular Britannia activity. In 1969, the violence had much increased and many flights were required, some at short notice.

**An eye for a story**

Two personalities emerge from the records for the year. Flt Lt Barney Lydiate, 99 Squadron captain, having previously suffered an eye injury, had his medical flying category restored. This does not seem a remarkable news item. But it was a first. Barney was an aeromodelling enthusiast. He had been adjusting a running engine when the screwdriver caught the propeller and a piece flew into his eye. As a result he lost the sight in that eye. But a battle was fought for him as it was seen that he could still perfectly safely fly transport aircraft. He thus became the first one-eyed RAF pilot and successfully continued his flying career through to retirement some 20 years later.

**5000 hours first**

The second news item was that Flt Lt Torquil MacLeod became the first Royal Air Force pilot to log 5000 hours on the Britannia. 'Mac' spent six years on 99, two as a copilot, four as captain. He then went to the Air Training Squadron (Britannia) as an instructor/examiner and reached the 5000 milestone. Even then his Britannia days were not over as he was to move on to the Air Support Command Examining Unit as the aircraft's representative.

**Posting policy rethink**

Torquil's career portrayed the new attitude to aircrew postings. The traditional Service tour of duty had always been 2½ years. It was certainly a feature of my early flying days. It did seem that one struggled most of the way up one ladder only to be kicked off and to the bottom of another. Enlightened thinking of retaining experience on the Britannia did not come immediately and it was a strange feature that the initial recruits, who were mainly very experienced Transport Command people, were posted after their 2½ years.

It was only with the second wave of which Torquil, and myself, were typical members, without that previous experience, that the posting policy became a little more flexible and many crew members remained on the aircraft for many, many years - 11 at Lyneham and Brize Norton in my case!

**New York! New York!**

So many Britannia reminiscences are of that 'good trip' that came people's way, now and again. Forgotten are the less magical occasions. Here, ex-511 navigator and Flight Commander Harry Marshall, who also enjoys telling a story, comes on stage to remember a 1969 flight and captures perfectly how things were - mostly:

*'Frank Sinatra says it's a wonderful town. Well he probably knows it better than I do. But in the course of 37 years in the Service, I did get to spend one night in New York, to be precise, on 28th November 1969, courtesy of a 511 Squadron Britannia.*

*'There were several strange things about this. First, it was not a trainer; we actually had a payload each way. I forget who or what we took to New York but I do recall that we picked up the Air Warfare Course, fresh from a fortnight's holiday in the States and Canada, at Gander for return to Lyneham. Second, I did not pen my own name to the schedule. When the month's task came in I was somewhere between Changi and Lyneham, so, I had no say in the matter. I did ask Stu Robeson how my name got there and, as I recall it now, he said something to the effect that he thought I would like a trip to New York. I couldn't argue with that, could I? Third, when I*

*dropped into the pilots' section to see who the captain was, it turned out to be Red Sankey. Had to be a plum trip, hadn't it?*

*'A couple of days later I checked into Station Ops to look at the schedule and plan the route. Good start time I noticed: 9.00am departure. Then the bad news; New York via Gander - 15 hours ground time - same route back - arrive Lyneham 3.00am, Day 2. Not a lot of time to see New York, I thought. I caught up with Red Sankey, 'Not too good a schedule,' I said. 'Worse than you think,' he replied, 'When we have dropped off the passengers at New York, we have to start up again and park the aircraft the other side of the field.' Then, with that smile that people adopt when they have extra bad news to impart, 'And that comes out of the 15 hours on the ground!' It turned out that he too had been away when the task came in. I don't know how the rest of the crew found their way on to this 'goodie'.*

*'Come the day and we got off to a bad start; the Doppler wasn't working. The '10 minute' box change took the usual hour and we set off looking at an even shorter stop in New York. Yes, you've guessed it, the adverse winds to Gander were more adverse than forecast; the scheduled seven hours became eight. Naturally, we fared no better on the run down to New York and by the time we had parked the aircraft and got into two taxis for Downtown New York it was 6.00pm their time and already dark. God knows what time it was in the UK: this I refused to contemplate. It was raining now and the freeways into the city were full. We followed the same car, at about three feet distance, all the way into the centre and all I could see was the sticker on the back window saying 'What are our boys doing in Vietnam?' I wondered what our boys (and girls) were doing in New York.*

*'We checked in at the hotel, a rather old fashioned but noisy and cheerful place. More a pub than a hotel I thought; nothing like the usual motel. By now, standing at reception, we looked what we were, a grubby motley lot in need of a shower and change of clothes. Red and I agreed to meet in the bar. I got there first and had a bourbon and something. The bar was busy and before long a pleasant American introduced himself and asked if he could buy me a drink. I have always been impressed with how kind Americans are to strangers but right now I did not feel up to making small talk with someone I did not know. 'Sorry,' I said, 'I'm waiting for a friend.'*

*'Red arrived and after the second drink we both felt a bit better. I began to take note of our surrounds. The bar was full, music came from somewhere, there was plenty of noise. But odd: something was missing. What was it? The penny dropped like a bomb; not a girl in sight. We were in a gay bar. And what had I said to my American would-be host, 'Sorry, I'm waiting for a friend!'*

*'By now our 15 hours was down to something like eight. A quick bite and bed (with the door locked!) were the order of the day.*

*'The radio alarm came on seemingly just after I had got to sleep. Breakfast in the hotel; a taxi drive to JFK (still in the dark, of course); airborne on time, as the*

The rapport between captain and engineer needed to be strong. Here Bill Robinson examines the under belly hydraulic bay with his engineer. (*Bill Robinson*)

From the Norman Rose photo album: *'XM637 - nosewheel change in the trees - result of a heavy landing by copilot at RAF Laarbruch.'* (*Norman Rose*)

*sun came up. We arrived also on time at Gander, much to the chagrin of the Air Warfare Course who had been studying our schedule for some days and fully expected a happy last night stop at Gander.*

*'We departed on time and, satisfyingly, arrived on the advertised time, to the minute, at Lyneham. I believe that Red had to taxy quite slowly to achieve the last minute or so; but he was quite adept at that. We wound everything down and did the long crew coach tour of Lyneham and its surrounds as we dropped individuals off. Red and I were the last two on board as we reached the OMQs. Aware that there would be no warm reception for either of us at 4.00am, we sat in the bus for a few minutes and shared our thoughts on Upavon planning staffs.*

*'Later in the day, unable of course to sleep now that I had the chance, I drifted down to the squadron. The nav office was deserted, as usual, apart from Stu - as usual, standing by the planning board with chinagraph in one hand and cloth in the other, happily re-arranging someone's next month. 'Good trip?', he enquired nonchalantly. 'Fine,' I replied, equally nonchalantly. 'Do the same for you some day', I added. And I did, but that's another story.'*

**An Electrician Remembers**

Many aircrew became quite blasé about their travels. It perhaps takes the memories of an infrequent traveller to open eyes. David Hamshire writes ...

*'Following a longish spell on Beverleys at Abingdon, my posting to Lyneham in October 1964 was to be the commencement of a chapter that was to take me through to the end of my service career - nine years later. One unit I did not wish to be posted to was the Electrical Bay. Where did they send me? Yes, the Electrical Bay - a relatively new and smart building, which had become a role model for the Royal Air Force. Anyone of importance who visited Lyneham would be taken to the combined servicing unit where all things technical and electrical were taken apart and put back together. As a result of the status of this showpiece of industrious activity, it was decided that it must always be 'sparkling'. Friday afternoon was clean-up time and regularly we washed and scrubbed items that didn't move or couldn't be moved. Here is a tale of what not to do when it comes to water and electrics!*

*'The floor of this palace was pale green and could be polished until you were blinded by the reflection. Service shoes were made of black rubber! On Fridays out came buckets and brushes to restore the floor to its original glory. Unfortunately, as was to be proved later, there were gaps in the floor surface as a result of removable boards for access to trunking routes for the many cables that supplied the workstations. Water disappeared!*

*'Most of those involved in the*

*approved regular cleaning methods wondered about the wisdom of the procedure and expressed some concern to the ones that mattered but, sadly, to no avail. After a few months I managed to get a move to Red Team in J I hanger and a chance to get my hands on the Whispering Giant. A few months later - was it about Christmas 1965 or 1966 - I returned from a few days leave to witness the sad remains of the electrical unit. To keep the Brits flying, component hours had to be extended as so much equipment had been lost in the inferno that followed our various and numerous warnings. Maybe we were viewed as coming up with reasons for not wanting to wash and polish but by now I was working elsewhere and counting my blessings that I was not the poor airman that was on duty that fateful night when the great fire of Lyneham broke out. What seemed the most ironic of all was a report that the Fire Brigade, having got the fire under control, then requested an increase in water pressure. This resulted in a fractured main and soon no water at all was available and the fire consumed the rest of both building and stock!*

*'Five years on the 'Dock' may seem to some that I had done something dreadful. Perhaps my contribution to the fire may have been the reason? In truth, however, I enjoyed the work and became very familiar with all the nooks and crannies of this wonderful machine known for its electrical complexity. Wiring up - or the other way round - the two timing devices for the tailplane de-icing systems which were located under the toilet floor was always a challenge needing patience. The Britannia was generally known as the electrician's ultimate challenge. And, it wasn't a fly-by-wire aeroplane!*

*'After four years (and others had the same idea), it was time, I considered, to see the world. We were unhappy that in some sections of our military airport that some of our contemporaries were always jetting or propping off to far away places*

The RAF Britannia was always in demand for air displays. Here is a slow flypast at the Rolls Royce Open Day at Filton. (*Rolls Royce Heritage Trust (Bristol Branch)*)

One of the stalwarts of the engineers, Master Engineer Reg Pearson. It is remarked how fortunate the fleet was not to suffer tragedy in view of the exposure of its members to world-wide hazards of various sorts. Such good luck did not follow Reg into his civilian flying career. On one trip he contracted malaria so badly that he died. His ashes were scattered from one of his company's, Redcoat, aircraft over the Atlantic. That flight too was to be ill-fated, as described in Appendix 1.

*tropical. Finally our protestations seemed to bear fruit. Two electricians would be allowed to go on trips and after that no more grumbling! Names went into a hat. Whose would come out? Mine was first and Brian Watling's followed. Wow! Where was it to be? Brian's was a route trip to Singapore and on to Hong Kong before turning round for the return home. What awaited me was rather special.*

*'The new Vice Chief of the Air Staff, Air Chief Marshal Sir Peter Fletcher, was to make a series of visits to places various and needed a reliable mode of transport. I was told he could have had a VC10 or Comet but preferred the Britannia. So it was that XL635 was prepared both inside and out and, on the day, 18th of November 1968, crew and VIP party walked out to what was to be home for the next four weeks. In an effort to make her look her best the tips of the four large fans had been painted yellow, red, white and red. When spinning round they looked great.*

*'My notes and recollections do not cover everyone on board but I do have the names of those up front - in the left hand seat was Flt Lt Hall, the right seat was occupied by Flt Lt Ford (who also kept the money!), Navigator was Master Navigator Cave, Signaller, Master AEOP Partington, Engineer Flt Sgt Burton. At the rear doing their bit were AQM Hamer, Air Stewards Cpls Hall and Rounsfull. Sorry but I do not have first names. Yes, I would like to know where they are now. If any of the above are members of the Association, please get in contact.*

*'Departure was at 09:10 on Monday the 18th and the direction flown took us over the Alps and down to Nicosia, reached at 16:45 local time.*

*'Accommodation on this trip was going to be 'No expenses spared!' The Ledra Palace was very comfortable. The next morning required a trip to the airport to ensure 635 would be ready and willing for departure on Wednesday and the rest of the day was free. Cyprus before partition was really quite a nice place with freedom*

*to roam, which I did.*

*'Wednesday dawned clear and sunny and departure was timed for nine o'clock local. Wheels were leaving the ground by 09:05 and the next leg of our journey took us north to Turkey, over the Tauras mountains and all the way round to Bahrain. Was that really Mount Ararat in the distance? It seemed it was. For all who flew this route the sight of oil wells in the desert will not have been forgotten as surplus gas was burnt off. I later had a spell at Sharjah and Bahrain with 84 Squadron on Andovers and covered this route quite a few times during returns to the UK.*

*'For the crew it was fortunate that Sir Peter had much work to do once we had delivered him to his destination. For us, and especially when on a RAF base, others looked after our lady of the skies. Strange, looking back, but I wonder how I managed to sit an exam in the afternoon of Thursday the 21st at Muharraq. It must have been something to do with promotion but for the life of me I cannot remember what or why. Nevertheless, I did take an exam and, I trust, passed!*

*'You may have guessed it but departure the next day was again at 09:00. This time we were heading east and looking for a little island in the Indian Ocean. I had not been to the Far East before and Gan was a wonderful introduction. Perhaps for those stationed there it may have soon lost something of its magic but for me it was glorious. Sadly, such places were abandoned long ago. We arrived at 17:25 and I was getting used to a working day spent in the air, getting paid extra for it and asking others to refuel and fix any snags by the next morning! The extras were by now building up and I was looking forward to the next stop, Singapore and three days of shopping!*

*'Gan was only a night stop but postcards were dispatched to wife and family before departure. I had been married for less than two years! Saturday was to be a killer. We had to leave by 08:00! I believe the early departure was because of the duration of the trip, as Singapore was not reached until 17:20 local. I had heard of the importance of Singapore as a shipping terminal but to see so many ships either loading or unloading as we gradually lost height was quite something. The clouds were an awesome sight too as Flt Lt Hall tried to avoid some of the larger ones, which at the time were dumping copious quantities of water on the poor wretches below. Changi was the airfield we aimed for and again friendly RAF types promised to care for our charge. It was now the 23rd November and Changi Creek Hotel was base as we had three days of leisure. I could get used to this way of life!*

*'Whoever chose our route must be congratulated. Wednesday the 27th dawned bright and clear and a nine o'clock departure was again scheduled. I think it must have been 09:00 off chocks because it was 09:05 that we became airborne, heading now for Australia. Perth, to be precise, which was reached at 17:15 local. This time*

658 departing from RAF Lyneham in 1965. (*Ken Guest*)

RAF carpenter Ken Guest also had a route trip in 1965. He took this photograph of Gan from a Shackleton: '*I managed to scrounge a flight on one of the occasions that it flew to warn shipping in the vicinity that a weather balloon was being launched from Gan and that the rocket may fall in their area.*' (*Ken Guest*)

*we found ourselves in the Rhodes Hotel but only for one night. Departure the following day was timed for the afternoon and a morning spent in Perth yielded more goodies to stow in the rear freight compartment - which by now was getting rather full! A full sized Lancaster bomber on a pole at Perth airport warranted a photo. I wonder if it is still there? Departure was at 13:50 and soon large bush fires were seen raging out of control with the resulting smoke drifting to the horizon.*

*'Canberra in 1968 seemed unusual for such an important city. Laid out like a collection of villages, land was obviously not a problem and the wide-open spaces meant walking to places of interest was impossible. Then, I suppose, the Australians did have plenty of land so why not use it! The Canberra Rex Hotel was our accommodation and the standard of care had moved up a further phase. Four full days of sightseeing meant wheels would be useful. By now I could afford to hire a car and it was off to see the sights. I went to the local Baptist Church on Sunday and was befriended by Mr and Mrs Parsons from Buxton Street. Invitations to a Bar-B-Q and to their home for a meal demonstrated a kindness, which I sincerely appreciated. I was, after all, a stranger. True Christian charity.*

498 on a Lyneham parking bay, 1965. A Hastings is back left. (*Ken Guest*)

*'There must have been a delay for some reason on Tuesday, December 3rd. It was 09:10 before the wheels became unstuck and we were setting course for Wellington, North Island, and New Zealand. Flying time was only 4 hours 15 minutes and once again we were looking forward to new sights and places. A train ride to Johnsonville enabled me to see a little bit of 'England' in the Southern Hemisphere. If I thought Wellington looked like England then Christchurch was to be a step nearer. Sir Peter had, I understand, relatives in the South Island and so we had to go there! A sensible departure time of 15:05 on Thursday the 5th for a short hop to Christchurch found us arriving one hour later. The New Zealand Air Force brigade did wonders for the crew, arranging a bus tour of the district around Christchurch including Port Lyttelton and Governors Bay.*

*'Now some additional fun started. Sunday was special. It was the 8th December 1968 and I had reached my 23rd birthday. Departure from Christchurch was timed for 09:00 and destination this time was Nandi, Fiji Islands. We stayed the night and the next day - Monday the 9th - saw us leaving at 09:10. Shortly after departure we flew over a thin black line in the sea and, behold, it was the 8th again! I was to have my second birthday in two days. I have only once crossed the date line and I had absolutely nothing to do with our schedule! After Fiji we stopped for fuel at Pago Pago in Samoa and then pushed on to Hawaii. Hickham U.S. Air Force Base was our destination but it was a late arrival at 23:15 local time. What day was it? We had left on the Monday but it was now Sunday again. We had gained a day! I shall always remember Hickham for its size and the huge number of aircraft based there. It seemed to be one gigantic piece of concrete.*

*'Globemasters and Cargomasters were everywhere. The beach at Waikiki was a not-to-be-missed attraction and there was plenty of time to spare. By now, however, one of Bellatrix's fans was playing up. I believe it was number one and it was in need of some TLC ('Tender Loving Care' for those not familiar with the term). Whatever the cause of the problem, the engine fitter was chiefly involved and I only had to lend a hand. We must have had some success because access panels were replaced and our charge was deemed to be serviceable.*

*'A long haul over the Pacific to the American mainland was next and so a slightly earlier departure of 08:30 on Wednesday the 11th saw us heading for the West Coast of America. Now that I have been there, I can visualise the B-17s flying into Hickham, as the Japanese attacked Pearl Harbour and Hickham on December 7th, 1941. 'Tora, Tora' is the film to watch if you haven't seen Hickham, before - and it is available on video. We had arrived on December 8th!*

*'Our destination was McClellan U.S Air Force Base, outside Sacramento and only a few miles inland from San Francisco. No. 1 prop was still playing up but having got so far we hoped it would do the decent thing and last the distance. We had, so why not the many parts mechanical and electrical that had proved reliable - so far! It was only a night stop at McClellan and the next day it was off to places somewhat cooler. Ottawa, to be precise, and now for a real change in temperature. I believe it was 25 degrees below zero. No longer the tropical uniforms we had worn since leaving Lyneham but into blue and as many extra layers as could be fitted.*

*'Things mechanical now looked worse and despite hours of coaxing the prop finally won the day. An urgent message went off to the UK for a replacement and nothing to do but wait. We managed to find a nice warm hanger for our charge but the future was uncertain. Finally, our replacement propeller arrived but so did the decisions. Sir Peter was not to be kept waiting for the prop to be changed and ground tested; it was remove the VIP fit from 635 and fit it to the replacement Brit that had brought the new propeller. From here I seem to have lost interest. I do not have details of which aircraft rescued us but I believe it was one of the Mark 2s. There were only a few of them but which one it was I cannot remember.*

*'The trip was completed on schedule with an arrival back at Lyneham on 14th December. It was a pity we had not managed to keep 635 going the distance but these things happen. Imagine if we had needed a new prop in Christchurch? Some in Whitehall would no doubt have said it was because Sir Peter's relatives had influence!*

*'My once in a lifetime round-the-world working trip will always be remembered. I have the photos to prove it. But, seriously, how many get the chance to do something like this and get paid extra for the privilege. I very much enjoyed flying in the Britannia and went aloft whenever possible - mainly on test flights after major servicing. It was with some nostalgia that a few months ago I visited Kemble and witnessed the fans turning on 496. Long may she be preserved for those of us who kept the Whispering Giant in the air as well as those who crewed our 'Lady' to places exotic.'*

**Mobile Air Movements Squadron**

Known simply as 'MAMS teams', these were the people who made the Britannia's job meaningful - a transport aircraft without a load is like a pub without beer!

Warrant Officer Ian Berry has written copiously on the topic of MAMS. This is the part of his history relevant to the Britannia years:

*'UKMAMS was officially established on 1st May 1966, forming at RAF Abingdon with six six-man teams. Each team consisted of a Flt Lt/Fg Off, Flt Sgt, Sgt, Cpl and two SACs. The first OC was Sqn Ldr Bill Jacobs. On the same date FEAF MAMS was also formed at RAF Changi with two to four teams, NEAF MAMS was formed at RAF Akrotiri with two teams and AFME MAMS at RAF Khormaksar with two teams. When Aden closed in Nov 1967 AFME MAMS became GULF MAMS and moved up the Gulf to RAF Muharraq. Their final demise came with the Gulf drawdown in the early 70s. FEAF MAMS also became casualties in 1970 (approx) with the closure of Changi and Seletar. NEAF MAMS soldiered on until 1975 when they too were disbanded.*

*'UKMAMS at Abingdon grew from six teams up to 12 teams by 1970, replacing the teams lost overseas. In February 1974 the 12 teams were transferred to RAF Lyneham and the Air Movements Squadron there took on the title of UKMAMS. With the move to Lyneham the OC UKMAMS became a Wing Commander and the DSAMO a Sqn Ldr. There are no civilians employed on mobile duties but the officers are from the Supply Branch and complete what used to be a three year tour.*

*'How are they controlled? Well, UKMAMS is still considered to be a lodger unit at RAF Lyneham. The teams are tasked by what is now HQ 2 Group, which used to be 38 Group, which used to be 46 Group ...*

*'The criteria for UKMAMS was*

Warrant Officer Ian Berry wrote: *'The 'Men in Black' are Blue Team, NEAF MAMS at Akrotiri, 1972'.* (*Ian Berry*)

The difficulties experienced by Movements staff when it came to loading the Britannia are encapsulated in these photographs of a loading trial.
(*Ian Berry*)

*and still is:*
*a) Providing Movements assistance to RAF Air Transport aircraft anywhere in the world where established RAF Movements Organisations do not exist.*
*b) The initial setting up of a Movements Organisation at any airhead/location on a temporary basis until relieved by permanent staff.*
*c) The reforce of existing Movements Squadrons when so tasked.*

**Strategic Line Servicing Squadron**
The *Lyneham Globe* ran a series entitled '*Know Your Station*'. This was the article on Strat LSS:

*'Line Servicing Squadron is an unpretentious squadron, which seldom comes to the general notice of the Station. Yet its importance at the 'sharp end' is undisputed. Its contribution demands a high order of expertise, a sense of urgency and a dedication without which the efforts of the rest of the Station would not see fruition.*

*'The Squadron task for the last 11 years has been to ensure that Britannia and Comet fleets are maintained at a high standard of serviceability so that aircraft can be produced 'hot to trot' at the scheduled times to meet the Station Tasking. Naturally, when dealing with complex aircraft, things don't always go according to plan, and there is the occasional 'cough' when an outbound aircraft decides it doesn't want to go.*

*'The consequent cliff-hanging act of trying to predict new serviceability times with hot breath from all directions misting the scene is not an unfamiliar part of Squadron life. On these occasions the ceilings at LSS control get bruised (the Engineer Officers' heads don't seem to suffer), finger nails progress elbow-wards, and it is said that the thermals generated over the terminal building make soaring a popular pastime for seagulls!*

*'The Officer Commanding Strat. LSS is Sqn. Ldr. Doug Samuel, in between daily crises, he apparently takes an active*

*part in RAF rugby circles, but since joining Strat. LSS in October 1969, he finds he has tussles enough. Right-hand man to OC Strat. LSS is Flt. Lt. Pete Nutt, who has apparently been directed to a recuperation tour on Gan following his stint in the hot seat as OC Administration Co-ordination and Support Flight. The hardware of the Squadron consists of four aircraft preparation and rectification flights, A, B, C and D, commanded by Flt. Lts. Spud Murphy Ray Weeks, Ned Purdue and Tom Jenkins respectively.*

*'Each flight has a strength of about 60 men, ranging from LAC to Chief Technician as producers, under the direction and control of a Flying Officer Duty Shift Officer, with a Flight Sergeant in support. Every man is highly trained, from the mechanics to the latest recruits - the aircraft technicians and their expertise cover the electronic, electrical, propulsion and airframe trades. A shift system is employed to give 24-hour cover. This means that shift personnel spend two-thirds of their working time outside normal station duty hours and get little chance of coming into contact with the rest of the station. Every tradesman is aware of the importance of his job, and the part it plays in the overall servicing and flying task.*

*'Pride of achievement is an inherent characteristic of Strat. LSS personnel, and morale is maintained at a remarkably high level considering the pressures of urgency and the difficult and arduous working conditions which they often experience. Most first line servicing is carried out in the open, and in winter conditions (most of the year at Lyneham) it's no picnic. The effort of each shift is controlled and co-ordinated from control room where the trade job controllers organise and allocate their workloads to tradesmen. Priorities are indicated by the Preparation and Rectification Co-ordinators display board, which also indicates the requirements and progresses the preparation of scheduled aircraft. The debriefing of complete aircrews takes place here, and the co-operation of crew members in answering the job controllers' incessant questions when they have obviously 'had enough,' is greatly appreciated and plays an important part in the rapid diagnosis of defects and recovery of aircraft ready for the next task.*

With all their engineering expertise, marshalling and like jobs had to done. (*Maurice Blencowe*)

*'Admin, Co-ord and Support Flight is made up of three distinct sections, each being under the overall control of a Warrant Officer. The Administration Section, with Warrant Officer Jock (the quiet one!) Murdoch in charge has done a fine job in coping with the never-ending bumph explosion. Sometimes, even in the Orderly Room, the inevitable pressures of Line Servicing are felt, and on the odd occasion when things get too much, a familiar Irish accent is noted in the comment that ' ... this bl**dy place is getting like Odham's Press.'*

*'Under the control of Warrant Officer 'Taff' Atkinson is the Mobile Engineering Section. This section consists of the Air Support Command Mobile Servicing Flight and the Ground Engineers' Section. The 'Mobiles' are essentially a team of highly trained men of varying specialisations with the overall task of supporting, anywhere in the world and at any time, the various types of Air Support Command aircraft, when engaged on exercises or special flights.*

*'The Ground Engineers, both for the Comet and Britannia aircraft, are largely employed on off-route flights and as such are often the only engineering personnel accompanying the aircraft. They are all SNCOs, trained and experienced in every aircraft engineering aspect. Although on the surface the day-to-day activities of this section are orderly, panics do occur. On these occasions even our 'Taff' has been heard to swear.*

*'The third section, under Warrant Officer John Doherty, is the Preparation and Rectification Support Section. This is made up of the two Britannia Flying Training Servicing Teams, the Squadron Stores - which incidentally is considered by those in the know, to be the best in the Command - and of course, the four Trade Managers. It is this section which has the responsibility of ensuring co-ordination between the four P. & R. Flights, investigating aircraft defects, incident reports, the 'now famous' ADDER (aircraft departure, delay and early return) sheets and in general terms, assisting the P. & R. Flights in any way possible.*

*'In many ways the achievements of this Section have been due to each individual's efforts. Quality control of all the Squadron's activities comes under their scrutiny and we like to think this cross-check has resulted in aircraft being better prepared for route. It would, however, be remiss to forget how much the success of the Trade Managers has depended on the goodwill of other sections, both in the flying and support squadrons. This help has been invaluable and has been greatly appreciated.*

*'This account of the Squadron organisation and activities is in the nature of a swan song, as it is soon to depart with the Britannia fleet to Brize Norton. The Squadron will have many regrets at leaving Lyneham in June. There has been a fine spirit and fellowship prevailing throughout Engineering Wing, and indeed throughout the Station; we are leaving behind some sincere good friends and colleagues. At the same time we look forward to continuing our rewarding task in a new environment at Brize Norton. There will be many problems but if the same high order of co-operation is forthcoming from supporting Squadrons and Sections as has been enjoyed at*

Did the Britannia years see the birth of Political Correctness? We did have 'Pilots' Notes', but they were the last - they became 'Aircrew Manuals' ... but our 'Check Lists' were 'Flight Reference Cards'!

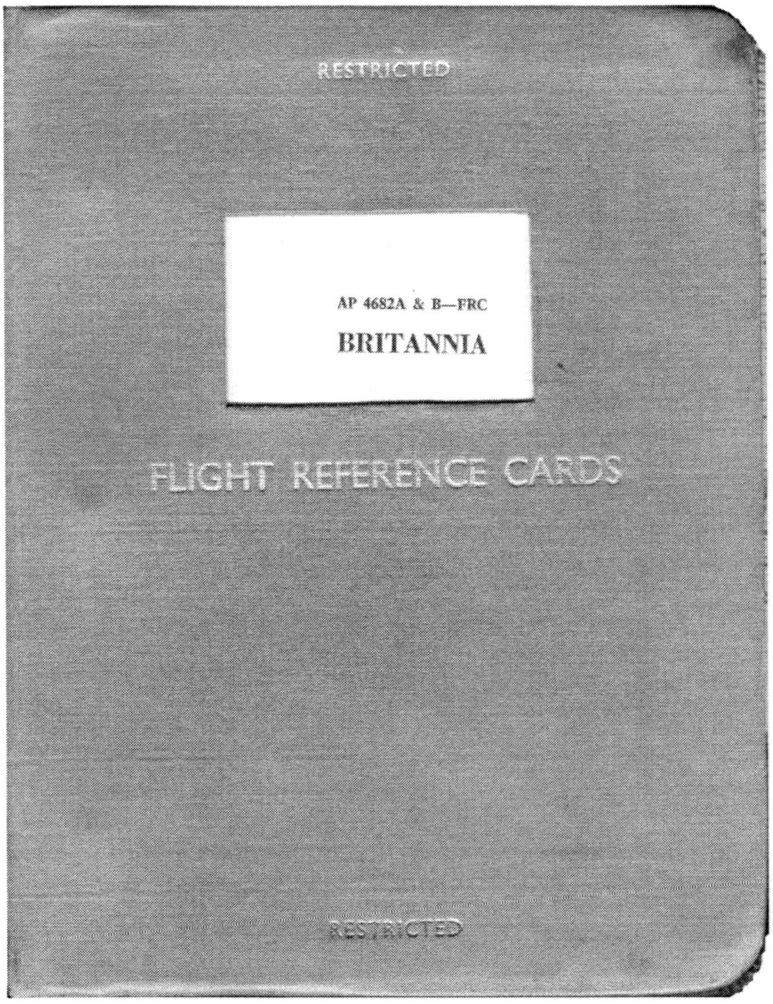

A smart Land Rover in a smart aeroplane. This is a good impression of the RAF Britannia's strengthened floor - and of the stowed passenger hand baggage racks - which stood up incredibly well to constant stowing and 'unstowing'!

*Lyneham, then the end of one very successful era will be the start of an equally rewarding one at Brize Norton.'*

**Record year**

The chapter opened with the comment that 1968 and 1969 might be considered a more routine period for the Britannia fleet. But it is chronicled that 1969 was 'another record year for Air Support Command'. Wing Commander Geoff Bowles writes:

*'Almost all movements to and from the United Kingdom were carried by air. More than 75% of the scheduled passenger movements in terms of air miles flown were made in ASC aircraft.*

*'Over 430,000 passengers were carried, of which a half were families of servicemen or government officials and nearly 2,300 were aeromedical patients. The Commands aircraft flew an estimated 56 million miles ...*

*'The growth of Brize Norton was illustrated by the movement of 130,000 passengers and 8,400 tons of cargo through the station compared with Lyneham's 155,000 passengers and 17,000 tons of cargo.*

*'An appreciation of the scope of the Command's activities can be gained by the fact that it supported Army units in at least 26 overseas countries including Belgium, British Honduras, The Caribbean, Canada, Cyprus, Denmark, Ethiopia, Fiji, France, Germany, Gibraltar, Hong Kong, Iceland, Italy, Malaysia, Malta, New Zealand, Netherlands, Norway, Persian Gulf, Solomon Islands and the United States.'*

**Back on flying!**

The Britannia played its part in all this. But was it the peak before the start of the descent into the trough? Whatever, my assistance was again at hand; at the end of the year I was posted back to 99 Squadron!

CHAPTER TWENTY FOUR

# A Moving Time

Royal Air Force Lyneham had been the home of 99 Squadron ever since 1947. 1970 was to see the end of this long run. It had been decided that Lyneham should be the Hercules base and that 99 and 511 Squadrons along with their technician compatriots should move their Britannias to RAF Brize Norton alongside

Station Commander, Group Captain Croucher marks the occasion of the last Lyneham route departure with a bottle of 'bubbly' for the crew. Captain Jimmy James accepts the bottle. To his right are copilot John Caskie and navigator Tony Bennett - a considerable contributor to this book. Just a part of flight engineer Mike Hobbs is to be seen. Sadly, in spite of research, the ground crew cannot be identified. (*Tony Bennett*)

99 Squadron's Colour was flown into RAF Brize Norton. On the left is the CO of the time, Wing Commander (later Air Commodore) William C Milne. (*John Smith*)

the other long range strategic transport aircraft, the VC10s and Belfasts and leave Lyneham as the dedicated Hercules base. There were some misgivings about this. Lyneham fitted comfortably, rather like an old shoe. Purpose built accommodation had been provided for the Britannia Squadrons. At Brize Norton, squadron members felt a little like poor relations reflected in the much inferior squadron buildings which were located on the non-domestic side of the airfield. But resilience is an aircrew characteristic and before long the squadrons were comfortably settled in.

The move had been carefully planned and route flying continued almost unabated. Over the period of the relocation, aircraft would depart on route from Lyneham and return to Brize Norton. The last route aircraft departed Lyneham on 15th June 1970.

It was impossible to move two elements of the Britannia scene at Lyneham. The 'Dry Dock', which had been cleverly devised for major servicings of the aircraft, was dismantled. Such servicings were now to be carried out under contract at Filton. The Britannia simulator remained behind. It was considered too difficult and risky to move.

**Brize Norton's past**

The 1930s saw an upsurge in the strength and capabilities of the RAF. A number of new airfields were built to accommodate new units. Brize Norton was one such airfield. Construction began in 1935 and layout of the airfield had to be approved by the Society for the Preservation of Rural England and meet the requirements of the Ribbon Development Act. The design of the hangars and messes was approved by the Royal Fine Arts Commission. This included the Lutjens-style, three-storey Officers' Mess. The first occupant, in August 1937, was No.2 Flying Training School. The task was to give advanced flying training to newly qualified pilots using Hawker Hart, Fury and Hector biplanes. An element of the new station was storage and maintenance and No.6 MU was established in October 1938 and had a 13-year life dealing with many thousands of aircraft. Airspeed Oxfords and Harvards were added to the FTS fleet in 1938. Concentration on training with the Oxfords followed in 1940 and the pace of this training required a relief landing ground at Akeman Street. The Luftwaffe attacked in August 1940 causing considerable damage with the destruction of two hangars and their contents of 46 aircraft. In 1942 the station's role changed to glider pilot training, in particular the conversion of Hotspur pilots to larger troop carrying Horsas. This was a huge operation involving a fleet of 34 Whitley bombers for the towing of 56 gliders. Training gave way to operations in 1944 when glider force units, assembling for the invasion of Europe, moved in. Albemarles towed the Horsas. With the MU handling more than 1000 Horsa gliders from 1942 onwards, this made Brize Norton a busy and vital air base, making a huge contribution to the airborne assault of Europe.

With the end of the War, the last gliders left at the end of 1945 and the station became part of Transport Command with the establishment of the Transport Command Development Unit. This unit carried out loading trials and the like with Dakotas, Liberators, Yorks and Stirlings. Later there were Hastings and Valettas. The first true air transport role of Brize was the carriage of overseas freight by a transport version of the Halifax flown by No.297 Squadron. But the station returned to flying training in 1949 with Harvards and Mosquitoes flown by the Central Flying School and No.204 Advanced Flying School. This was relatively short lived with Brize Norton being one of 40 airfields in the UK to be handed over to United States Air Force. This led to the closure of the MU. The runway was extended to accommodate the operation of B29, B36, B47, B50, B58 and KC135 aircraft for the 13 years of USAF occupancy.

The Americans relinquished the airfield in 1965 and Transport Command once again became the user. This was the start of the era of the VC10 and Belfast to be joined by the Britannias on their move from Lyneham.

**Pipe band to Chile**

1970 was a busy year. It started with some pomp when an aircraft of 99 Squadron conveyed the band of the Royal Scots Greys to celebrations in Chile. The navigator was of some eminence. He was the CO of the Squadron, Wing Commander William C Milne. He remembers that particular route flight well:

'*We took the pipe band to Chile to commemorate the Battle of Valdivia 125*

A Brize Norton photograph that captured the zenith of the Royal Air Force's strategic transport fleet. It came from the collection of Curly Beauchamp who, in his time, was the Warrant Officer i/c the Brize Norton Base Hangar, which is the backdrop for this picture.

Turnround time at Gibraltar. (*David Berry*)

*years earlier. This battle featured - as undoubtedly readers will know! - a renegade British admiral of Scots descent, Cochrane, who is still a folk hero in Chile. 'The trip was not without incident. We lost an engine and had to wait in Recife in North East Brazil until a spare found its way to us. As usual, although we were carrying a pile of spare bits and pieces, we did not have an engine driven fuel pump, the offending item.*

*'Thanks to some inspired fiddling by my co-navigator - he sneaked the broken pump into the packing case in place of the new serviceable one so that protracted arguments with the Brazilian customs did not delay the installation work - we managed to reach Valdivia with six hours to spare.*

*'We were generously hosted by the Chilean Air Force who attached a liaison officer to us for the whole of our time in their beautiful country. All in all, therefore, it was a memorable trip.'*

**Farewell El Adem**

Withdrawal was a continuing feature and, without a great deal of regret, El Adem, the long standing staging post and exercise airfield in North Africa, was evacuated. Westabout reinforcement of the Far East was exercised. The routing for this was Gander, Newfoundland; Offutt AFB, Nebraska; McClellan AFB, Sacramento; Hickham AFB, Honolulu; Nandi, Fiji; Guam then the final destination, Changi.

**Bersatu Padu**

Further attention was paid to the Far East. The intended withdrawal from the region was approaching and reassurance was being given that the area was not being totally abandoned. Treaties would be honoured. A demonstration of how effectively and quickly support could be rendered was provided by Exercise Bersatu Padu from April to August; five nations participated.

The Britannias played their part in the massive positioning and recovery required and, in between, the necessary resupply. Training was carried out in the theatre in conditions likely to be met in contingency reinforcement after withdrawal.

Feathered at Recife.

**Polish tribute**

For most of its Britannia years, 99 Squadron had a distinguished Polish pilot as one of its captains. Flight Lieutenant 'Wed' Wedrychowski had survived more challenges by the time he was 21, during his escape to this country, than most people experience in a life time. An appropriate task arose for him in May 1970. The Polish wartime leader, General Anders, famed for the Monte Casino epic, had died in London. A Britannia of 99, captained by 'Wed', flew the coffin and mourners from Gatwick to Rome so that he could be buried with his fallen comrades at Monte Casino.

**Rescues**

Many times in its history, the Britannias had rescued British Nationals from sticky situations throughout the world. One such event took place in June. An aircraft was re-routed from Cyprus to Beirut to pick up refugees from Amman. Amongst the passengers was Sqn Ldr P R O'Connor DFC RAF (retd) who had been CO of 99 Squadron from May to September 1944!

The next month there was another rescue, following a coup in Muscat and Oman in which he had been shot, His Highness Sultan Said bin Taimur, Sultan of Muscat and Oman was flown on a special aeromedical flight from Cyprus to Brize Norton. A further mission of mercy was flying medical supplies and blankets to Lima, Peru which had been struck by an earthquake.

1970 concluded with yet another Far East exercise - 'Sunflower'.

**Britannia aircrew life**

Past Royal Air Force fliers might muse on the different life style, to their's, of Britannia aircrew. Whilst the way of life might have seemed glamorous to many, especially with the publicity that would surround the more exotic flights, there was much hard routine work. One constant demand on men and machines has been described, the 'Changi Slip'. Up to September 1971, when our rundown of forces in Singapore had reached a level not to require it, an aircraft left daily for Changi, slipping crews in Aden (later the Persian Gulf) and Singapore. This meant that the aircraft was out and back in three days. For the crews it meant a planned ten days away but, because of delays, this could stretch up to three weeks. The average

The mourners at General Anders' funeral. 'Wed' is the second RAF officer from the right. (*John Westaway*)

Groundcrew and passengers join the crew for a photograph of the last route departure from RAF Lyneham 15 June 1970. Crew: Les Swift (steward), Pat Horne (ALM), Mick Hobbs (engineer), Tony Bennett (navigator), John Caskie (copilot) and Jimmie James (captain).
(*Tony Bennett*)

squadron member would complete one of these most months. In the year under review, 1970, I did three between April and July.

Then there were shorter times away, the Mediterranean trooping flights, movement of BAOR units, Norway exercises - Gibraltar, Sardinia. Exercises could range the world. Flights in North America became more common place as the years passed. So the month's line against each name would be fairly full with route flights.

**Periodic Refresher Training**

Then there was training. Britannia equipped 99 and 511 Squadrons had inherited what was the traditional training pattern of transport squadrons. Monthly continuation training, in the air and the simulator, was carried out at squadron level. Then each squadron member would, at an interval dependent on the 'Category' he held, present himself to the examiners for a 'recat'. For pilots this consisted of a day and night flying test, simulator check and ground examination. There was also a check during a route flight. The instant pass/failure nature of this was replaced, in later years, with a Periodic Refresher Training scheme. A squadron crew would spend a fortnight together, under OCU instructors, being retrained and their ability, to determine their new category, was assessed at the end of the period. This was a much more satisfactory use of training resources but it took brave men to change a system that had been running, apparently successfully, if accident figures are a measure, for so many years. The training branch at Upavon at the time of the changes was headed by Wing Commander Paddy Mahoney, a recently previous CO of 511 Squadron.

**A tribute to Paddy**

The news of the death, in 1997, of Wing Commander Mahoney prompted Harry Liddell, who himself was a considerable contributor to the training world, to write on Paddy's influence on pilot training procedures of RAF Transport Command:

*'There have been three significant watersheds in the training of RAF transport crews: the first comprehensive scheme drawn up under the then C-in-C, Sir Ralph Cochrane, in 1946, the tenure of Wing Commander Tubby Rixon as OC TCEU during the period 1958-60 and Paddy's occupancy of the post of Wing Commander Training at Upavon in the late 1960s.*

*'Immediately after the war, Transport Command was facing a near-crisis; many of its most experienced crews were on their way out to civilian life, and of those that remained a good number wished to follow as soon as possible. A deterioration in standards of aircraft maintenance due to a similar loss of trained technicians, aggravated by a spares shortage consequent on the termination of Lend-Lease compounded the situation, the net effect being a serious rise in the accident rate. After passing out from OCU, crews at this time received little or nothing in the way of continuation training; indeed, from the writer's own experience exercises such as asymmetric flight were regarded as highly dangerous and so hardly practised at all. Clearly something had to be done, and so the concept of regular monthly continuation training was introduced, backed up by a rigorous regime of frequent assessment and examination - the dreaded Categorisation System.*

*'This served its purpose for many years, but was both cumbersome and inflexible; it also perpetuated many older methods of training that were sanctified by antiquity rather than merit. Thus pilots were examined on their ability to perform peculiar timed gyrations on instruments, while aircraft designed for the transport role were frequently subjected to near-aerobatic manoeuvres like steep turns (and on primary instruments at that!). During conversion courses, heads were stuffed full of useless detail such as the finer points of airframe construction or the arcane behaviour of AC electricity (remember the Filton course on the Britannia electrics, apparently designed for would-be boffins?); nobody dared consider anything so radical as ditching all this useless garbage, and concentrating on the concept of need to know.*

*'On this fossilised scene burst the charismatic figure of Tubby Rixon, who hit the Command like a whirlwind after assuming control of TCEU in 1958. At this time the air transport world was largely piston-engined, but he foresaw that the new generation of aircraft looming on the horizon - Britannia, Comet 4, Argosy et al - demanded*

When 99 Squadron celebrated its 50th anniversary in 1967, a number of past COs attended. Jock Kennedy is 4th from the left. Other COs of the Britannia era are the host, Wg Cdr Freddie Yetman (7th left), Paul Barber (8th left in the rear row). Forward and to the right is Wg Cdr Roy Jenkins. (*Ted Wright*)

Wing Commander Paddy Mahoney and his wife Nell being ceremonially towed away from 511 Squadron on the occasion of his posting in July 1966. (*Lyneham Globe*)

*fresh thinking and new methods. To the horror of the die-hards, out went steep turns, patterns A & B and other antediluvian rubbish, while ground training was likewise subjected to a radical rethink. He also gave some thought to the faults of the continuation training system, but was unable to do much about it during his time in office; besides, he was well aware of the risk of causing a backlash from the 'reactionaries' if too much was attempted too soon.*

*'Unfortunately he was succeeded by a man who, although one of the most delightful and good-natured people it was possible to know, was probably the most 'reactionary' of the lot; as, a result, the early 1960s were a period of ossification. Of all things that cried out for a change, the continuation training system stood head and shoulders above the rest, its rigid inflexibilities a monument to Service backwardness; for continuation training was unsupervised, and furthermore the monthly task took no cognisance whatever of how much route flying had been achieved during the preceding weeks.*

*'In retrospect it really is amazing how long it took for these idiocies to be identified, for the hazards of one and the wastefulness of the other were indeed gross. Not only were exercises such as asymmetric flight potentially dangerous if carried out solo, any errors went uncorrected until such distant time as the next categorisation test fell due; while as for the rigidity of MCT, most of us have memories of intensive and largely wasteful training details crammed into the last few days of the month (often at weekends) following weeks of intensive 'real' flying down the route. The cost to the Exchequer was enormous, and any supposed benefit largely negative; furthermore, emphasis was mainly on airborne training, little provision being made for classroom work.*

*'Paddy was arguably the first of many occupants of his Upavon chair to take a long, hard look at a set-up sanctified by time, its rules virtually carved on tablets of stone. Supervised training at regular intervals had long been the rule in the civilian world, and under his direction the new Periodic Refresher Training largely replaced monthly continuation training for all RAF transport crews from late 1969 onwards; to whispers of 'Quis custodiet ipsos custes'?, only the training captains themselves were to continue with a limited ration of MCT.*

*'So, in lieu of the much-disliked regulated self-training task, crews were now to be withdrawn from the line every six or twelve months (depending on category) for a fixed two-week period of 100% supervised classroom and flight training. The change was also popular in itself, aircrew now being free of the dreaded shadow of MCT and knowing far ahead when their PRT was due. Morale was also much improved, since the sure promise of an unbroken two weeks at base was a considerable contribution to domestic harmony!*

*'The scheme lives on, a worthy monument to the man responsible for its inception, any extra expenditure on increased training staffs more than offset by savings in aircraft hours. In early days sometimes known as 'The Mahoney Scheme', Paddy himself intensely disliked this appellation and insisted on its correct title; but those of us who were around at the beginning and assisted in getting it off the ground, will always tend to regard PRT as a worthy memorial to a highly respected and much liked man.'*

**Duty crews**

So, training would fill part of that row by each name. Then there were duty crews. Reaction was an essential ingredient of this modern and effective transport force so two crews were always available at six hours notice. Other standbys would be

A photograph taken when RAF Lyneham was very firmly established as the Hercules base - 1990! It was taken from the open rear door of a Hercules by Ex-RAF Lyneham carpenter Ken Guest, who has contributed to this book. The pilot of the aircraft was his younger brother, Wing Commander David Guest, the then CO of 30 Squadron. (*Ken Guest*)

instituted as circumstance demanded. There was also a Duty Working Crew which carried out air tests and other odd jobs.

Add all this together - route flights, monthly training, duty crews - then there were station duties, leave, courses - even the odd bit of sickness - and each month was pretty full.

**Those perspex boards**

Harry Marshall mused on all this in later years and how our lives were controlled - and revealed - by the perspex boards with their chinagraph pencil marks which were a feature of each aircrew section office:

*'All the planning was done on huge and heavy perspex boards which filled all and every office wall space that was available and whose purpose was to depict, in multi-coloured chinagraph markings, where we and our aircraft were supposed to be at any given time (and that not often together) now and in the immediate future.*

*'The most impressive, without any doubt, were those monster boards which monopolised the joint 99/511 operations room and which projected all Britannia aircraft movements in a welter of V-like symbols some two or three feet high. These I never began to understand and on reflection I realise that this was meant to be the case or why else would they have attracted their own high priests, known in lay terms as operations officers, who alone were allowed to install the initial plot and then, still alone, adjust it as expediency demanded by the appropriate application of duster and fresh chinagraph.*

*'But by way of insurance I always made a practice of pausing to admire the art work and to speak politely to the board custodians whenever I happened to be passing by. All to little avail when my next posting found me at Upavon as a contingency planner and I had to draw hundreds, if not thousands, of the damn things: still without fully understanding them. Fortunately we planners never got the contingency plan more than approximately right so in consequence our flow charts were never more than approximately challenged.*

*'But I digress. I did not intend to dwell on aircraft flow charts. It is the 'people' charts that will forever come to my mind.*

*'I suppose there were some variations in how things were portrayed in the various sections that comprised the squadron: pilot (x2), navigators, engineers, ALMs, air stewards (no signallers in my day, they were already redundant). But from what I saw the essentials were the same. Each office housed the same heavy boards attached firmly to the walls. The horizontal axis portrayed exactly two months of the crew member's life, identified by columns of individual days. The vertical axis listed everyone's name, naturally enough in alphabetical order from the top down.*

From the Norman Rose photo album: *'VIP flight - Chief of the Defence Staff, Admiral of the Fleet Lord Hill-Norton and Lady Hill-Norton. Singapore to Gatwick 25 - 28 May 1970. XL658*

*M. Eng Jock Allan, Cpl Wood steward, Flt Lt Geoff Bradford copilot, C/T Blakely ground eng, Lord and Lady Hill-Norton, Sqn Ldr Norman Rose captain, Sgt(W) Hazel Bingham ALM, F S Paddy Harper ALM, Master Nav George Davies nav.'* (Norman Rose)

*'The message portrayed was just what each individual was programmed to do for the next two months and could not have been simpler or clearer: colour coded horizontal lines indicating all activities by name and date. And the beauty of it all was that it was there permanently, well nearly permanently, for one and all to see. Not only could you tell at a glance, whenever you came in from wherever you had been, just what you were going to do for the next month, or sometimes two months, but you could also see what everyone else was going to do, or not going to do, across the same time span. Nothing could be fairer than that, could it?*

*'I can still, in my mind's eye, see the navigators' board in the 511 navigation section across all the years that have since gone by. The Changi Slip still dominated all else. That blue line, for blue was the colour for route, was the first to be allocated and if you drew a Changi Blue that was the month largely catered for. Sure you could expect to pick up a run to any of our Mediterranean or European destinations and back but that would be a much smaller blue line. Add the red stand-down appendages to each flight (three days for Changi, one for most of the rest) and there weren't too many days left to fill. The stand-by crew (green I think) was a joy that you could do without; particularly if the section played it straight and it was not negotiable. But wouldn't it be nice to acquire one of those yellow 'Day Offs', written in such minuscule lettering as to be only just visible. Must have a word with the leader to see how you get one of those. Then there was the brown colour for never going anywhere - training. Yuk!*

*'What else was there to see? Time to have a look at the task as a whole; for that's what the board portrayed, crises and specials apart. Was it a busy month or not? Where were the 'jollies'? Time you had one of those. A quick look at who was doing the States Trainer and that Nairobi run. No surprises there.*

*'It was all there, for one and all to see. Where else could you stand, alone, unharassed, take your time, see what was going on, and in the final analysis assess how you in turn were being assessed by your fellows? And how was it all done?*

*'Perhaps I was a slower learner than most or perhaps no one let me into the secret early. Perhaps it was a simple matter of time and standing on the squadron but I must have been halfway through my short two year tour before the penny dropped.*

*'Normally the squadron offices were all deserted. And properly so. Sitting around in the crew room just to be counted was a thing of the past. The routine was planned and catered for in advance. All that was necessary, back at the ranch, so to speak, was someone able to trigger any response to the short notice and unexpected task. Individuals would pop in and out of the section of course but they wouldn't stay for long. Most days, that is. But mid-month,*

*say a little earlier, about the 11th, if memory serves me correctly, there would be a noticeable increase in numbers. Still mainly in the mornings of course, just to do a little admin, put in a leave pass (funny leave must have had a chinagraph colour too but I can't remember it), even amend a publication or two.*

*'Perhaps it took me a while to learn about these gatherings because, oddly enough, I never seemed to be at base at this time. Activity would continue and if anything increase, individuals still dropping in casually, looking obliquely at the board, speaking quietly with the leader, drifting away. Until, suddenly and magically, a veritable frenzy of the old hands would congregate together. Never were there so many willing Indians. Never was the leader so supported by his team. Never was there so much liaison with other sections. Next month's task had arrived. And they would all help to carve it up. Perhaps so-and-so should not go there. Allocate the Changis first, the Majungas, and the rest would fall into place. Now it would be time for reflection and more balanced, helpful suggestions, 'Those weekend Akrotiris are a bit of a bind boss, but I'll do one if you like. Just to help out.' 'Gander and back. Well I know it's not everyone's cup of tea, but if you need someone ...'*

*'And, in no time, it was all done. Everyone happy. The office back to its normal tranquil self. Just the telephone minder and the boards. Wonder how we would do it now with today's technology?'*

**Hot loads!**

Over the years it occasionally fell to the Britannia to carry loads of a nuclear nature. Not unnaturally, these were shrouded in some secrecy and careful attention was danced upon them. One person who seemed to have more than his share of such freight was 99 ALM Richard Ling. Appropriately, he came to aircrew training from being an armourer on 14 Squadron with their Canberra B(1)8s at Wildenrath, equipped the US Mk7 weapons and previous to that on V-Bombers. All this was preparation for a civilian career as Sales Manager in the Atomic Weapons Establishment. In subsequent years he visited the ex-RAF Britannia stored at Kemble - XM496:

*'In a way I wish the airframe had been that of 497, the aircraft I flew on which delivered to Nellis AFB, Nevada, a new nuclear weapon fusing device. Little did I know at the time that this was something I would learn to handle with some care a few years later at Cape Canaveral when I was responsible, for four years, for the safety of the assembling and launching of 12 Polaris ICBMs.'*

In the Britannia Association magazine Richard appealed for anyone who had flown 'hot loads'. The above stirred a memory for the Editor - your Author - one that has troubled his conscience for all these years. Publication may be some form of expiation:

*'I can recall a Britannia nuclear flight. I believe the load was intended for Japan. It goes without saying that I was concerned with the more mundane aspect i.e. Akrotiri to Muharraq - slip. The flight number was 6423 on 11 December 1970. My only way of identifying it in my logbook is to look for the engineer's name - Bernie Burton - and the fact that, in spite of the aircraft being part of the Changi Slip, we took it on to Gan the next day. The reason follows but first our Muharraq arrival. We were heavily engaged in our wind-down beers when there was a panic call to get back to the aircraft. The team monitoring the load reported readings way over the top. By the time we arrived the problem had been sorted out; Bloggs had his meter set on the wrong range!*

*'There was considerable pressure to keep this load moving so, when we emerged from our sleep, we discovered consternation - the aircraft was still at Muharraq - the crew taking it on had had a prop snag. Later, when I had retired to bed once more, there was a knock at the door. It was Bernie; 'I'd take the aircraft on, with that snag!' Not really weighing up all the consequences (you'll remember that to keep moving was the big aim when on the Changi Slip) I contacted Ops and told them of our willingness - which they leapt at. So we took the aircraft on to Gan.*

*'There were congratulations and recriminations on our move. Jock Kennedy happened to be down the route in his capacity of Gp Capt Ops at Upavon - he was in the picture and said, 'Splendid!' This was not the reaction of the slip crew from whom we had stolen the aircraft! When I look back, it really wasn't a 'done thing'!*

*So, after all these years, I hope that Eric Denham and crew will forgive me - and Bernie Burton!'*

This stirred the memory of ex-99 captain, Guy Eddy:

*'My 'nuclear' flight was on 28 February 1971 in 491 and was all a little bit of 'cloak and dagger' stuff. I had to read and sign signals at Changi Ops to the effect that I would limit any communication to US Air Traffic to a minimum and on no account mention what we were carrying. Also, if a diversion became necessary, we were not to use a US base in any circumstances, which on a Changi to Tokyo flight made things a little difficult. Another stipulation was that we were not allowed to land at Tokyo before 2am local time.*

*'We must have left Changi at around 4pm, because my log book says that we did two hours day flying, and landed at Tokyo 10 hours and 10 minutes later. I understand that the load we were carrying was nuclear fuel rods for the reactor of a power station that had just been completed in Japan. They looked more like a Greek artefact than anything else. Because of its weight, it was chained on big spreaders and was accompanied by the required man in a bowler hat. He had travelled all the way from the UK with the load and every hour took radiation readings of his parcel of goodies. We were warned against sitting on it - bad for the piles, I think! Anyway, it quietly sat where it was chained and behaved itself throughout the trip.*

*'We duly arrived at Tokyo, Haneda at about 1.50am and couldn't believe it when we were told to join the holding pattern across the bay. After 10 hours flying that was just what we needed. There was no other traffic and the airfield was, in effect, shut. At 2am lights came on and we were allowed to land. We were escorted to a parking bay with police and troops all over the place, waving guns about. Crew and myself were kept shut on the flight deck whilst the load was taken off. This was achieved in about a quarter of an hour. Then the convoy was away and gone, like thieves in the night. The escort had earlier said that they had to be out of the Tokyo area before daylight. It seemed that within 20 minutes there were only the crew plus handlers and Customs left at the airport.*

*'We had 24 hours in Tokyo from 3am to 3am - not quite what you'd pick, given a choice. As we crept away in the dark, Tokyo hardly knew that it had been graced with a visit from the RAF'*

This story illustrates the oft-quoted phrase on Britannia operations - 'Been everywhere - seen nothing!'

**'Your posting is No.53 Britannia Course starting in August.'**

Tony Bennett recalls his early Britannia days - and those that followed ...

*'Nos.24 and 36 Squadron Hastings were winding down in late 1967 to be replaced by Hercules and, towards the end of a foreshortened first tour, I found myself on the remaining seven crews on 24 Squadron. The two years spent at Colerne had introduced me to the gentle pleasures of travelling the world at a leisurely 180 knots (not to mention Salisbury Plain, PTS Abingdon, SEAC, Roller Conveyor, and bean bags); I could only but wonder whether fate, in the hands of the 'Posters', would decree that three Caribbean Trainers in nine months would be punished by a posting far removed from the erstwhile delights of Transport Command.*

*'So it was on returning to Colerne from a 'Med' run in November 1967 that I was met by one of my fellow squadron first tourist navs, who, through clenched teeth, told me that the 'Posters' wanted one navigator for Britannia fleet, and that I had been the chosen one, much to the chagrin of the other six 24 Squadron Navs. Keeping my back to the wall, and watching my every step, I awaited confirmation from on high. There was no confirmation, and no news was definitely not good news, particularly as the Squadron Commander had twice pursued the matter on my behalf.*

*'The death throws of the Hastings were short and sad. After a farewell parade and flypast, my last two flights were to ferry aircraft to Lindholme (29 Jan 68) and Shawbury (5 Feb 68) - a strange and eerie sensation as the engines on the stripped and bare aircraft were shut down for the very last time, and the crew boarded a coach for the journey home.*

*'Then, in February, the posting notice arrived - 'Detached to 36 Squadron Lyneham to hold for No.13 Hercules Course at Thorney Island in July 1968'. Working on 36 Squadron Ops desk was an interesting and enjoyable experience, as indeed was the 'perk' of a Changi Slip as*

*Supernumerary Crew in June! Then it was two weeks leave prior to setting off for Thorney and the well-known delights of Hayling Island in the summer. I had even sent my bike ahead. Five days before I was due to arrive at Thorney I had a phone call asking me to work on 36 Squadron Ops for the next two weeks. Patiently I explained that I would be at Thorney on No.13 Course and would therefore be unable to oblige. 'Don't you know?' was the reply 'Your posting is No.53 Britannia Course starting in August.' I went straight to the pub for a prolonged celebration. On return to Lyneham the following week I naturally made a few enquiries. My posting notice to Britannias was dated May 1968 and had been sent to both Colerne (stationed unit) and Lyneham (detached unit). Neither Station passed the information to me, each leaving it to the other - a severe case of left hand/right hand.*

*'After my foreshortened Hastings Tour on No.24 Squadron I was 26 years-old and had the vast total of 1130 flying hours, 827 of them on Hastings. As I walked into Air Training Squadron at Lyneham that lovely summer's day in August I pinched myself for I had always believed that you had to be 35+ and have at least 5000 hours to be a navigator on the 'Shiny Fleet'. Of course, with the introduction of the VC10 into service the previous year perhaps the Britannia became No.2 on the 'shiny list'! Anyhow, times were a changing, for there were three of us young bloods on 53 course - Dick Parsley, Dave Crawshaw and me. The ground school course was hard work but enjoyable.*

*'Perhaps the most demanding aspect was Aircraft Performance, coming after the Performance X of the Hastings! However I very slowly came to grips with it - and even to enjoy the subject (?). We also learned to avoid Harry James by taking evasive action in the ATS building, for Harry had a tendency to ask tricky academic questions as an epilogue to passing the time of day. Time was rushing by, and with our minds crammed with information we were considered fit to fly. The great day for me came on 21st October 1968 - copilot conversion under the eagle eye of Fred Lace in 498. Three hours and the first three of many NDB procedures. Over the next month Captains McCleod and Whiteight raised the number of NDB's to 2l!*

*'The highlight of the course had to be the Global Trainer and to me it was a dream come true as we set off on 23 November 1968 in 660 with my mentor, Harry Bray, to keep me on the straight and narrow. Nicosia, Bahrain, Gan, Perth, Canberra, Darwin, Changi, Hong Kong, Guam, Wake, Hickam, McClellan, Offutt, Bermuda. Oh what memories the names evoke, too numerous to list, but every Britannia aircrew and groundcrew member*

An undated photograph from 99 Squadron's archive. Note the scaffolding. (*Maurice Flynn*)

636 on 'Finals' at Brize Norton, April 1973. It would appear that No.4 engine is shut down. (*Ken Guest*)

*will have their own fond recollections of a voyage that seemed to come from a travel brochure. After 12 days intensive flying we were deemed to be in need of a rest which was taken as a weekend in McClellan. I was lucky enough to spend the time in a flat with four girls in San Francisco who showed me the sights of the city including those (Golden Gates) that could only be seen through the mist and fog which seemed to have arrived for the weekend as well. The girls had laid on a big party for us all, but regrettably only a few of the crew could make it, which was rather a shame, cos it really was a good thrash! We arrived back on 11 December with 18 days dirty washing, and then, after The Lord Mayor's Show came the 'Ground Cats' before the Christmas parties began. So it was thus that I proudly joined No.99 Squadron on lst January 1969 with 70 hours on type and a shiny 'D' Cat, looking forward to six happy years flying Britannias.*

*'Less than two weeks after arriving on 99 Squadron I was winging my way Eastwards on my first Changi Slip. Winging very slowly, for it was 18 days after leaving UK that we started inbound from Changi, eventually arriving back at Lyneham 25 days after departure. Three days each in Akrotiri, Muharraq, and Gan gave ample time to sample their respective attractions, from Louca's Bar to the 'Cassbar' to the 'Blue Spitoon'. By the time we arrived in Changi the sideburns and moustache-growing competition was well under way and comfortably led by my mentor, Chris Clarke. Stu Reid had by this time taught me that it was necessary to carry a box of King Edward cigars at all times on route!*

*'A week in the 'Changi Creek' and we began to bear resemblance to a bunch of pirates as the skin darkened and the facial hair continued to thrive. The shopkeepers began to recognise us and by the end of four days of 'free' refreshment I was a sucker for the hi fi, and ended up with a complete set. (Still all working today). The return journey was relatively uneventful, and we all began to look for the finishing line. Akrotiri saw the judging of the facial hair competition, which CC won by a mile and then we were back in Blighty in the middle of winter with a deep tan and loads of dhobi.*

*'I remember thinking 'I could get*

*to enjoy this'. As long as they are not all 25 days! We had returned just in time for a Squadron Games Night, which was a lively occasion to say the least. I was removed from the line up for the Schooner Race team by Wg Cdr Yetman who did not recognise me as one of his boys. Regrettably, due to an admin oversight and my prolonged absence since joining 99 Squadron, an arrival interview with the CO had not been arranged. All was dealt with and I rejoined the team. Then I was off again, this time on holiday in Stockholm for a week staying with Maylie Anderson (whom I had met in Sidmouth) and her family. Two weeks earlier I had been lying on the beach in equatorial Gan, and now I flew BEA into the depths of a Swedish winter in temperatures of below -10°C, snow everywhere, and no cold weather clothing. However, it was great fun and I saw most of the sights, without getting frostbite including a visit to Uppsala Cathedral and its beautifully carved altar. Regrettably I didn't learn much Swedish in spite of trying.*

*'My second Changi slip in April was more business like - nine days - and included an engine shut down at top of climb out of Changi, subsequently jettisoning a considerable amount of 'Go Juice' in the vicinity of Sinjon. There must be a happy medium between 9 and 25 days, I thought. However I was not to find out for the rest of the year, for ahead lay the 'Med' routes, and the 'Cento' route to Bahrain.*

*'In the spring of 1969, the striking US dockers were causing havoc with freight movements on the Eastern seaboard. Thus it was that I found myself three times in six weeks operating into New York. The arrival at night was something I could have hardly imagined. A myriad of lights and the non-stop, flat, almost incomprehensible instructions from Air Traffic Control. Miss instructions in the air or on the ground at your peril. On one occasion we had on the flight deck Sqn Ldrs Williams and Lecky-Thompson who were to fly the RAF Harriers in the London - New York Air Race in May. They, like us, were almost speechless at the sight and sound. No doubt on the day they had a frequency to themselves.*

*'In the pay rise awarded in 1969 it was announced that single officers would receive the same pay as married officers. This had always been a bone of contention, and the announcement was wonderful news, for increasingly 'singlies' were looking for more freedom in their lives, and this award effectively gave it to them. In theory we still had to live in the Mess, and pay for food, but with the extra money we could afford to look for somewhere outside Service environments. In my case four of us rented a flat in Castlefields, Calne, and had a marvellous time (one of the four married the girl upstairs!). However it was cold and bleak in the winter and an effort to light the coal fire each time, but worth it.*

*'In August Northern Ireland became a high priority with the start of Operation Motorman and rotational flights were to become a large part of the Britannias workload for the remainder of their service. For instance in three days in November 69 I flew 11 sectors. It is truly amazing how some memories are etched on one's mind, and so vividly recalled. Thus my logbook shows ten days in November 1969 when in 658, under the command of Wg Cdr Eric Reeves, we flew to Madeira, Ascension, Lusaka, Nairobi, Mauritius, Gan*

FAREWELL LOTTIE

WHEN No. 99 Squadron prepared to leave RAF Lyneham for their new location at Brize Norton it was realised, with regret, that the services of Mrs. Bryant were to be lost.

Many people contributed to the Britannia effort, however remotely. Mrs Lottie Bryant, who came to Lyneham in 1944, kept the headquarters of 99 Squadron at Lyneham spick and span. Her services were lost with the squadron move to Brize Norton. A presentation was made to mark the squadron's gratitude for her services. Wg Cdr Wm C Milne does the honours. In support are four 99 captains - Dave Lloyd, Bob George, Jimmy James and Bill Coburn. (*Lyneham Globe*) *and inbound to UK.*

*'This was a happy, most enjoyable trip, typified by John Hanson in his striped blazer almost singing 'The Desert Song'. It was also the first (and not the last) time that I had seen such abject poverty and squalor in the world, this time in the environs of Lusaka. I felt humbled. Also, for the first time, I realised how small the world had really become. The Americans operated a satellite tracking station from the highest part of Ascension Island. Whilst we were visiting our guide took what we believed from its clarity was a local call. 'The spare you just requested will be with you in the morning'. From the bottom of the mountain? No - from the next flight from Houston, Texas. And a casual meeting with an American in the Horseshoe Bar in Ascension. Four days later same American, same hotel in Mauritius. Uncanny.*

*'So, at the end of my first year on Britannias, the world was at my feet so to speak. Exactly two years ago I did not know what the 'Posters' had in store for me. Now I had visited continents and countries that I had only seen in an Atlas or in a travel brochure, places that I would not otherwise been able to visit. And there was more to come!*

*'New Year 1970 was a surprise package. Late on 30 December I learnt that I was off to Malta the following day for a week of Captain Conversion training for Flt Lt Dick Felix. So it was a shock to arrive at the Officers' Mess on New Years' Eve to find a Fancy Dress Party about to wind up. We were invited to join the fun, but dress was a problem at short notice. Dick showed his initiative and we all found something to wear. There were a lot of Roman togas. And we flew on 1 Jan, a little jaded I recall. By now I had learnt that all departures to Changi left Lyneham at midnight (something to do with Changi opening hours!) and that sunglasses should be donned before the morning sun burned your eyeballs out in the left turn overhead Nice en route Akrotiri. Inbound you could expect to operate Changi - Gan - Muharraq - Akrotiri- - Lyneham without a glimpse of the currant bun. I was glad to have bought a watch that told me the day and date as well as the time. The main problem was waking up in the half-light at 6 o'clock - was it 0600 or 1800? Only time would tell (I knew I should have bought a 24-hour watch).*

*'Another trip mainly at night was down to Majunga. I thought it was a*

A flashback to the start of this chapter - the scene at Lyneham prior to the move of the Britannias to Brize Norton. (*Keith Marriott*)

*splendid task, with a night stop in the Roche Rouge 'Hotel'. This had definitely seen better days, and these were sometime ago. The laced wrought iron balconies around the inner quadrangle conjured up the French colonial atmosphere of its heyday. Now however, decay had set in and the food left something to be desired. A good insecticide was needed too to see off the mozzies and cockroaches before retiring. It was as well to check that your roommate was not duplicating the spraying, cos come bedtime it was somewhat difficult to breathe air rather than DDT.*

*'Before then a good time could be had at the permanent detachment followed by a cultural evening at Madams 'Night Club' with a few overpriced beers. The Gozzome checks should make sure that you are all together and no one had been enticed off into the night for late entertainment that would be regretted in the morning and the cause of anxiety for the foreseeable future. I could now see why grown aircrew went ashen at the mention of Majunga, and would quickly look for some excuse not to go, if tasked. Thus the morning after the night before found flight planning a none too easy task in surroundings comparable to a Graham Green novel of a decaying French colony, a wooden slatted building with a veranda, and a squeaky rotating ceiling fan and limited facilities. The captain's KD had acquired an L shaped tear at the knee and some dust stains on a misjudged exit from the back of a Landrover, and the copilot had misplaced one of the lenses of his sunglasses at some time that morning. I was intact, but found it difficult to do the many hundreds of calculations required for such a trip. It was an uneventful flight for after one acknowledged call to East African Flight Watch all went quiet for the next six or so hours. No one wanted to talk to us as we cruised along at FL 200. It was also very quiet on the flight deck with a flurry of activity every half-hour, especially the use of the sextant on what was a good leg for a navigator. Approaching Masirah we established contact with Bahrain Flight Watch and requested climb from FL 200 to FL 210 from Masirah to Bahrain.*

*'Twice Bahrain queried this, and it dawned on us more or less together that we had just operated for six hours at the incorrect Flight Level (FL 210 instead of FL 220). We quickly set things straight, continued and landed at Bahrain with no problems. At the debrief in the copilot's room we opened the beers and burnt the incriminating flight logs in a waste paper bin and hoped that would be the end of the matter. 1970 saw the beginning of the end of our presence in Changi, and the Ascots were winging their way to and fro even more during the withdrawal. I flew nine Changi slips during the 18 months to June 71 with sufficient time off to explore Singapore well. On the third of these slips we departed Lyneham on 15 June in 520. As we left the Terminal Building for the aircraft we were met with a bottle of champagne and a photographer for a crew photo. Unknown to us until then was that we were also the end of an era for Lyneham. We were operating the last route Britannia to depart from Lyneham before the fleet moved to Brize Norton, and we returned to Brize on 1 July.*

*'Accommodation at Brize was in short supply for 'Singlie' pending the completion of the Officers' Mess extension in January 1971. There were, however, about ten three-bedroomed wooden bungalows available, which had previously been occupied by American families. These were fully fitted and furnished and we eagerly took them. I shared with Rod Cassady and Peter Headley. Suffice to say we had a ball. All the advantages of living out, living in, and at reduced cost because they were substandard!*

*'There were some who found the Changi Slips tedious. Whilst understanding their point of view, I enjoyed all of them. The staging posts were so different to each other. At Akrotiri, whether staying in the Transit accommodation or downtown Limmasol, there was usually some entertainment. But, personally, I did not care for Bahrain. Even the enlightened regime of Brit House under Cass Binns, with films and Persian/Welsh barmen and access to the Malcolm Club palled after (say) four days.*

*'Gan was different. A tropical paradise where, as a break from sitting in the sun on the white sands lapped, in almost total silence, by the clear blue waters, one could retire to 'The Blue Lagoon' for a gin and tonic and a read of last week's Telegraph. All this for free. Now a package tour for around £1000+? Changi was full of opportunities. To tour the city, water ski in the Straits, or sit in Raffles Hotel with a*

Nick Symes writes:
*This photo taken when we were descending through the Straits of Gibraltar. We were asked if we were agreeable to being intercepted and escorted for a short while by two Hunters that were on their regular permanent detachment defending the Rock and flying the Flag. I was subsequently sent this photograph as a thankyou.*
(*Nick Symes*)

Note: It is interesting to notice how the propellers have been 'frozen' in this photograph. Must have been a high speed film and fast shutter speed.

*drink. Not to mention Bugis Street late at night watching the 'Shims' work the street. The LOAs were enough to buy a couple of beers at most of the staging points, unless, that is you were 'Single' in the days before equal pay. If your Slip did not include two nights in Changi, then it was not worth claiming your allowances otherwise you 'owed' the Queen for going on route. An anomalous situation!*

*'Going West to the New World was more desirable. Hotels and allowances made the difference, having some money to spend in the cities. This gave rise to 'The Country Club', and could have been the reason that I only went East in the first nine months of 1970. In November I flew on a Green Flag exercise to Namao (Edmonton). The schedule gave us three days in Namao. This was great, and I had arranged to stay a couple of nights in Calgary (100 miles from Namao) with two girls in their flat. That all turned to worms when we had to divert to Calgary - good news - and had a 16-hour ground time - bad news.*

*'The next month I found myself on a 'States' Trainer commanded by one David Berry. This got off to a bad start, having to shut down No.2 engine (and RTB for a 24-hour delay) even before we reached 20 West. One of my abiding memories of this very enjoyable, relaxed trip* (Author: Many people who flew with me talk of being 'relaxed' - I wonder what they mean?) *was being asked by ATC Chicago to break off our approach and fly a visual left-hand circuit at 1000 feet and then make a visual approach to land. The visibility was not good, and most of what could be seen was acres of concrete. A laconic voice enquired 'Confirm you are on 31 Left?' With a rapid, slight adjustment, to the left, we soon were! That Chicago O'Hare was the biggest airfield in the world was brought home to us on departure the following morning. After an inordinate time creeping slowly forward to the holding point behind a diminishing queue it was our turn. At the holding point I counted 47 aircraft behind us. Checks on*

*the roll and we were off.* (Author: Sorry to interfere, again, but I can still remember the kick I used to get from that ultimate test of Britannia crew cooperation - the successful completion of all the drills and then checks, intended to be done at a standstill on the runway, as we kept moving around the corner onto that runway - and then being able to apply full power, as we lined up - please continue Tony!) *I hope the ones behind us made it! I was a passenger on the leg from McClellan to Charleston and for the first time appreciated how vast the continent of North America really was. Three hours over the Rockies, Three hours over the Mississippi Basin, one hour over the Appalachians, crossing 11 States from California to the Carolinas. Forty times the size of UK!*

*'The final route of 1970 was a Changi Slip, but included a one-off extension to Tokyo, a unique trip, and not one that I would like to repeat. We had already clocked up over 25 hours in positioning at Changi to pick up our aircraft on 14 December (including a 'no notice' route check from Gan to Changi on the 12th by Ted Drake of ASCEU). The load was nuclear fuel rods encased in concrete positioned on a pallet by the forward freight door. The route was almost a straight line routing up the South China Sea, abeam Manila and Taiwan. Full tanks placed us at Maximum Take Off Weight and such was the nature of the trip that we were not allowed to use any diversions en route, and had to arrive at Tokyo International after the airfield had closed for normal traffic at midnight local. The trip took 10 hours and was uneventful, at least until we landed. We were all colours, safety services, nuclear services, you name it. The crew were standing clear of the aircraft and the forklift (!) had just moved the load when it slipped. At that we left not wishing to see what happened next.*

*'We had 24 hours in Tokyo, to again depart after midnight with a similar load (spent I would imagine). Twenty-four hours is the worst time for a stopover, as ideally you need two sleep periods. This is difficult to achieve. The alternative is one, but when? At the beginning, end or middle of the ground time. Often sleep is difficult and one ends up without. In this case our ground time was foreshortened and with some stress. I had cleared through immigration, but found that I had left my passport on the aircraft. The bureaucrats would not let me in without a passport, and not let me out through immigration either! We arrived at the hotel about 2am and had about eight hours sleep. Andy Mills from Sidmouth worked for Barclays International and met us at lunchtime, where we discovered the phenomenal cost of living! After three to four hours sightseeing of this amazing city it was time to eat and go to bed again. Unfortunately I could not sleep and was thus tired before we even started the return leg. The weather was poor and most of the way we flew at 200kts in icing conditions, with my eyeballs working flat out on the CCWR. The return took 11 hours arriving early afternoon. I couldn't sleep. I have never been so tired, and couldn't think rationally. We had flown 46 hours in 10 days, 21 of them in the last 45 hours.*

*'The following day we flew to Gan, and then climbed in the back home to Brize, another 33 hours in the aircraft. The phrase 'punched, bored or countersunk' comes to mind. 650 hours in 1970, doubled my hours on type!'*

Tony Bennett's account of his Britannia days, before he eventually became a Queen's Flight navigator, will be continued.

**Jock Kennedy**

This chapter opened with the news that the Britannia fleet was moving to Brize Norton. When there was a ceremony in June for the formal arrival of the Squadrons from Lyneham, the 99 Squadron Standard was greeted by Brize Norton's Station Commander, Air Commodore T L Kennedy AFC. This restored contact with the Britannia which he had had since 1965. In that year he had taken over command of 99 Squadron.

On completion of that tour he was posted to HQ Air Support Command as Group Captain Strategic Operations. In this time, his appearances along the route were not an unusual sight. Promotion came again at the end of this tour. It was at a time when it was considered desirable that the station commanders of Lyneham and Brize Norton should not be Group Captains but Air Commodores. Air Commodore Kennedy assumed control of Brize Norton. This was at the beginning of 1970 so it was not long before Britannias were part of his scene again. Some allege that perhaps that was

Air Chief Marshal Sir Thomas Kennedy unveiling a plaque at RAF Brize Norton in 1994 to commemorate the Britannia years there. Britannia Association Fred Lace applauds. A similar plaque, provided by the Association, was installed at RAF Lyneham. (*David Berry*)

behind the decision that there should be the move from Lyneham!

Jock Kennedy, a Scot through and through, joined the Royal Air Force from his native town of Hawick in 1946. I was told the story of his joining by the ex-Adjutant of the Royal Air Force College, Cranwell. One day an airman sought the Adjutant out in the College building and told him that there was a young man in the entrance hall who wanted to join the RAF. Jock had decided to by-pass recruiting offices and the like! It worked and he became a member of the first post-war entry of the College.

On graduation he started on his long association with transport flying and trained as one of the first copilots on Hastings. Captaincy followed and in his Hastings' years he served on 24, 297 and 511 Squadrons. In 1953 he went on an exchange tour with the Royal Australian Air Force. Dakota flying took him all over Australia and to Japan and Korea during the war. Return to the UK put him on the first rung of what was going to be a very tall promotion ladder. As a Squadron Leader he went to 27 Squadron as a Flight Commander flying Canberras. Another flying executive tour followed when Jock took command of the jet squadron at the Ministry of Supply Radar Establishment at Pershore. Five years of 'career' ground jobs followed before he returned to the transport fold with the command of 99.

After Upavon and Brize Norton there followed 15 years of acceleration through the Air ranks and it was Air Chief Marshal Sir Thomas Kennedy GCB AFC who retired in 1986. His last three posts were Deputy C-in-C Strike Command, AOC-in-C RAF Germany and, finally, Air Member for Personnel.

For all this eminence, Sir Thomas retained the common touch. It is said that he wished to be knighted as Sir Jock but this could not be allowed! Nevertheless, that is the title he cheerfully answers to now. If you had ever served under Sir Jock, as was my privilege for the best part of six years, then you were never forgotten. Britannia people feel very proud that he was once one of us.

# CHAPTER TWENTY FIVE

# Royal Connections

The year 1971 was a Royal one for Brize Norton. Her Majesty The Queen visited the station on 12th March. A crew from 99 and 511 Squadron were presented to Her Majesty: I had the honour of leading the 99 crew. By way of a topic of conversation and to demonstrate the worldwide nature of our job, the Station Commander, Air Commodore Kennedy, advised Her Majesty that I had had my appendix removed in Jamaica!

**I left my ...**

This unique route activity had indeed taken place the September before. We had flown Royal Navy personnel out to Kingston via Newfoundland and Bermuda. Arriving in Jamaica at the very sociable hour of 5.00 pm, we repaired to our booked hotel. A night of modest revelry - not an unusual occurrence - followed. In bed I suffered an attack of remorse as well as every kind of stomach and bowel upset known to man. 'You certainly overdid the rum and cokes last night, Dave!' But, in the morning, as I clung to the washbasin trying to shave, I realised I was really ill. By midday I was on the operating table! Three weeks later I returned home courtesy of Air Jamaica to New York and RAF VC10 to Brize Norton. Some sing, 'I left my heart in San Francisco' ... I have a variation ...

An example of the Britannia rescuing British Nationals occurred in March when aircraft went to Dacca in East Pakistan and evacuated 100 people. The disturbances in this area were to lead to another major task for the fleet in 1973/74.

The Westabout exercise this year, 'Sunflower 71', had a difference. The destination was Darwin and the route was Gander, USA, Honolulu and Guam.

**New Year's Eve at Goose Bay?**

Harry Marshall remembers a New Year's Eve - that wasn't New Year's Eve!?

*'Memory has always told me that I spent the New Year's Eve of 1971 in Goose Bay, Newfoundland. I have told the tale many a time amongst friends far and wide when discussions of past New Years have triggered the memory: usually after dinner and a drink or two and late at night. So much so that it seems to sit naturally as a complement to my night in New York,*

Subsequent to HM The Queen's visit to Brize Norton, the author made this display cabinet for the Visitors' Book containing Her Majesty's signature. (*David Berry*)

A not totally unfamiliar route scene - No.4 engine feathered. Note the experts are there - the aircrew, ready for some subsequent socialising in their civilian long-sleeved shirts, ties and slacks.

*previously retailed within the pages of the Britannia Association magazine. There was much similar about the two flights: just a quick dash across the Atlantic and back, itself not our usual route, a wonder as to how I and not someone else had picked up the schedule, weather that I could have done without, a minimum ground stopover, the strangest of nights and a sense when it was all over of unreality. The very opposite of déjà vu, the question of did that actually happen? There is even a similar sound about the two to jog the memory - New York - New Year.*

*'It came therefore as a rude shock when I turned to my log book to verify the details and discovered that it was actually on the 2nd January, 1971 that our Britannia departed Brize Norton and 3rd January that we set out from Goose Bay on the return journey. Why then, if the New Year had come and gone had it seemed that we were so isolated on this particular flight with the Atlantic virtually to ourselves each way? A look at an old diary revealed the truth, January 2nd was a Saturday, January 3rd a Sunday. The Western world and the world's airlines had tagged the weekend on to the New Year's Day and the holiday, normally a two day event had stretched to four days. I will use the correct dates of the flight for this chronicle but I fear that my anecdotal recall in years to come will inevitably lapse and I will begin as I always have begun with, 'Did I tell you about the New Year's Eve that I spent in Goose Bay?' And like the Ancient Mariner, not waiting for any reply, proceed to do just that.*

*'As was the case with my New York trip, this flight was not considered a particular gem by the squadron. Looking back to see how it came my way I note that I spent from December 10 to December 20 on the Changi Slip. Enough said. The month's task for January came 'in' when I was 'out'. This time the pilots' section was equal to the task, they ducked the flight completely by offering it to the OCU. What could be more proper? After all it was designated as a 'training' as opposed to a 'route' schedule. The OCU, equally adept at musical chairs and grateful for the odd route crumb came up with just one captain and offered to do a route check on a squadron captain (complete with a*

A nosewheel at Lyneham - but is it a Britannia? (*Bill Robinson*)

Another occasion when wives were being carried - with some loss of dignity?! The location is unknown as is what is being shouted by the officer on the left. The indications are that it wasn't something very gentlemanly! Perhaps an interesting social comment is the look he is getting from two of the 'Locals'!

*squadron crew, of course) in return. Game, set and match to the pilots' section who, after due consideration, found that they had no captains available for this particular time but could come up with a copilot to be checked, if necessary. As a sort of parenthesis, it never ceased to amaze me that route checks were usually carried out in conditions inversely proportional to the pilot's ability and experience. The best of the best, the 'A' category captains, of undoubted skill and many years of experience, were checked from Lyneham or Brize Norton to Akrotiri - a 'bread and butter' run. The newest of copilots found himself operating a sector he had never seen before. But I did not set out on this story to ride any hobby horses. As I have already hinted, the purpose of the flight was itself unusual. Route training flights were very rare birds indeed and usually meant that the payload had to be protected - protected, that is, from other bidders with a higher priority. It came as no surprise then that our payload was for the return flight from Goose Bay to Brize Norton only. We went totally empty from Brize Norton to Goose. Another, earlier training flight must have taken the payload there in the first instance. And this, of course, was the case - a case to which no*

Refuelling at Akrotiri. (*David Berry*)

*one, in his right mind, could object.*

*'We, Royal Air Force Strike Command to be specific, operated then a permanent detachment of RAF personnel at the Royal Canadian Air Force Base of Goose Bay from which our V-Force aircraft, Victors and Vulcans, gained radar and route experience over the Canadian wilderness to the north of Goose which was said to be similar to the Russian Steppes over which their war task would take them. The tour for these RAF detachment personnel was of 13 months duration - and unaccompanied. Over Christmas and New Year this 'unaccompaniment' was lightened and alleviated by a wives' visit courtesy of two Britannia training flights. Ours was the less cheerful of the two - the return journey.*

*'One of the joys of flying west from Brize Norton by Britannia was that we usually started at a sensible time. This flight was no exception. We were airborne on time at 0900 hours on the Saturday morning. By five minutes past nine it was clear to me that we were facing our first problem: the Doppler was not working. If I recollect properly, and if I am wrong there will be many to tell me so, an unserviceable doppler navigation system was a 'No Go' item on the Atlantic route. A spot of consultation with the captain was called for.*

*'I remember this particular morning well. When I broke the news at a convenient time, the captain and engineer joined me at my table for a mini-conference, our copilot in charge of the aircraft. We agreed that, without the Doppler, we might drift off track a little, or even more than a little, but that even so, we were unlikely to face any collision risk. At our particular level, 20 something thousand feet, the route skies were, on this one day, ours alone. A look at each other, a shrug of the shoulders and we continued on our westerly heading. We were right: we never heard another aircraft on our radios but instead we began to hear, over Flight Watch, that we had another problem. Goose Bay's weather wasn't any too good. To be precise, it had been snowing there for quite a while now, it was still snowing and it was going to continue snowing. The snow was accompanied, naturally enough, by very low cloud, medium and high cloud.*

*'After some 6½ hours, on time and on track, I was modestly pleased to note, we were able to talk to Goose direct on VHF. 'Not nice,' they said, 'fully overcast, cloud base about 200 feet, visibility a quarter of a mile.' The snowploughs (all 14 of them) were working flat out. If we cared to make an approach, they would haul them off the runway at the last minute. The good news was that the runway, or most of it, was clear of snow and dry, as can happen with that dry Canadian snow. The captain tried for more reassuring news, 'Have you any recent arrival reports from other aircraft?' 'We've had no take-offs or landings for the last two days,' was the reply. I, with little to contribute to this part of the flight, was left with nothing but admiration for the snowplough drivers literally hoeing their lonely furrows, day in day out, with so little visible reward.*

*'The approach and landing was not without tension but, fortunately, without drama. The route check was forgotten. The copilot resumed his copilot duties. Everything was as predicted. We broke cloud at our 200 feet limit, we saw the runway in time to land, the snowploughs had done their job, the runway was clear. Taxying in was more difficult than landing but eventually we reached the RAF detachment hangar. Only three-quarters of the Britannia would go in; we left the tail outside in the snow.*

*'There was no official movements staff as such at Goose Bay but the Ops detachment set up to look after the V-aircraft had no difficulty handling a Britannia. They noted our fuel requirements and said that they would clear the snow off the Britannia tail just before start up the following morning. In next to no time we were*

*off in our efficient, snow-not-a -problem, Canadian service transport to our different messes; this the usual drawback in operating from a military airfield in the 60s and 70s. There were just the six of us on the crew. Three officers, three senior NCOs. No girls, no corporal stewards either. We had foreseen this sort of problem. Even so the officers went one way, the sergeants another. What we had not expected was that the Canadian Air Force still operated, as did the Royal Air Force, the 'permanent' and 'temporary' accommodation system. Why this nonsensical differentiation was perpetuated for so many years I shall never know. Even at RAF Gan, which only ever existed for transit aircraft to stage through, the permanent staff, those stationed there, had their separate messes and air conditioned single room accommodation whilst the transit aircrew, with just the one notable exception, lived in more spartan accommodation and shared a common, far from luxurious, all ranks mess hall with one and all, passengers, women and children included.*

*'But at Goose Bay, on New Year's Eve (well nearly) and on a mercy mission? The transport dropped us as near to the temporary accommodation, inevitably Nissen Hut like, as it could. There had been no attempt at snow clearance of the surrounds. We reached our rooms by walking through waist-high snow with our bags held above our heads. Great fun after a seven hour flight. The rooms themselves were unglamorous but functional, well heated and one per man. There was no drink or food in sight. We glumly showered, changed (jacket and tie of course) and set off on another route march in single file to the 'Transit' Officers' Mess. Not surprisingly we were the only visitors. At some stage of the evening a meal was provided and served. At 6pm, not a minute earlier or a minute later, the bar was opened.*

*'There was, of course, no other form of entertainment. Not even a TV as far as I can recall. We found an old fashioned record player and persuaded it to work and we played the two (single) records available over and over again. I was reminded of Kuala Lumpur Mess many years ago. There too we had two records one by Doris Day, the haunting 'Only a Shanty in Old Shanty Town', the other by Marlene Dietrich whose title I never remembered. At Goose Bay, nearly 20 years later it was as if time had stood still. Over a beer or two, things improved; the barman proved friendly; we alternated our drinks and our records. Again, strangely and singularly I only remember the one: Nancy Sinatra singing 'These Boots Were Made for Walking'. The song could not have been more fitting. As the mess closed up for the night we walked back through the snow to our distant solitary rooms.*

*'Came the morning and we couldn't wait to get away through the snow again, on to the on-time and efficient transport, to the aircraft. The tail section of' the Britannia had accumulated three or four feet of snow by now. As we entered the hangar the aircraft looked a strange and sad sort of bird, the front three-quarters absolutely normal. There was of course nowhere to flight plan, just the counter top of some sort of Ops set-up around which everyone milled. Our passengers were already waiting for us in the same hangar, the majority dressed in fur coats and not looking very happy. 'You won't be able to go today,' our RAF contact said happily. 'Brize is out - zero visibility - black ice.' We disabused him of this illusion, pointing out that Prestwick and St Mawgan were wide open and asked for the snow to be removed from the tail of the aircraft.*

*'We left on time, the snowploughs pausing in their task again just to allow us to get airborne. En route we listened every hour to the Brize Norton actuals. No change, sky obscured, black ice, zero visibility. We diverted to St Mawgan where the weather was spring-like and disgorged our passengers who set off happily by rail for home. We progressed to the inevitable temporary accommodation for another exotic night stop. Next day, on advice from OC Ops Brize Norton, we set off for Brize at about mid-day. The fog would have lifted by then; the ice would be gone. Over Brize Norton at 200ft on the approach we were still in thick cloud; one pass was enough; we returned to St Mawgan and our temporary accommodation. The following day we got home OK. Two days later my planned programme caught up with me rather earlier than I had expected. This time I didn't mind. Nairobi via Akrotiri and Bahrain had a better ring to it.*

*'Sitting around the pool at the Nairobi hotel three days later, life didn't seem too bad. No snow, to the contrary the*

There is an affinity between the sea and the air. Consequently, there was quite a liaison between Britannia slip crews and the members of the Marine Craft Unit at Gan. A trip on an MTB - and a bit of a 'drive' - was a pleasant way to pass some time.
(*David Berry*)

*temperature in the mid-20s; no temporary accommodation in a variety of messes, all the crew together in the one location. Goose Bay seemed a lifetime away. I wondered, idly, if it was still snowing there.'*

**Lost oil**

Rolls Royce, which had long ago engulfed the makers of the Britannia's Proteus engines, Bristol Siddeley, was having a tricky time and the supply of replacement engines became critical; some resourcefulness from the engineering staff was needed. Ingenuity was always a requirement when dealing with Britannia servicing. An example is a particular fault of that time. Flt Lt Bas Appleyard was a victim:

*'... the oil consumption was recorded at three pints per hour. This rose to four and the engine was shut down. On landing no external oil leaks were found. The engine was ground run and after one hour the lost oil reappeared.'*

Northern Ireland affairs took a further turn for the worse with the introduction of emergency internment powers and many Britannia sorties were required for troop reinforcement - and, sadly, aeromedical flights.

**Goodbye Changi**

Summer saw the Far East withdrawal in full flow with passengers and freight being flown to the UK. Royal Air Force Changi had been like a Mecca for transport crews for all the post-war years. It was the terminus; the place to take a deep breath and ready oneself for the return journey. It had atmosphere. This was heightened for the aircrew in that the transit accommodation was located on the water's edge - Changi Creek Hotel, which has previously been described. On 28th November 1971 RAF Changi officially closed. The remaining transport movements required were conducted from RAF Tengah on the western side of Singapore Island.

***Sergeant* Hunting**

The Britannia associated career of John Hunting has been followed at various stages in this narrative:

*'After my year on Gan I returned to the Line at Lyneham in '68. In June '70 we all moved to Brize Norton. Life on the 'Line' there was very much the same although having Curly Beauchamp as the boss made things somewhat easier. In 1972*

658 at RAF Tengah in company with the aircraft that was to inherit the 'routes', a RAF Lockheed Hercules.
(*Ron King*)

*I was promoted to Sergeant, got married and ended up posted to Tengah; there I spent three years as TASS fitter on all the transport and other types of aircraft. I stayed in Singapore until the end of the RAF presence and was the last of my trade to leave the island. The end of 1975 thus saw my return to the UK and with it the end of my involvement with transport aircraft, and in particular the Britannia, that had lasted virtually unbroken since 1960.'*

**... and Bahrain**

As well as the Singapore rundown, 1971 saw our withdrawal from Bahrain. RAF Muharraq had been the staging post in the Persian Gulf for many years. As previously reported, it even sported dedicated transit accommodation for transport crews, Britannia House. We now moved to less salubrious quarters at RAF Masirah on the island of that name, off the north east coast of Muscat and Oman.

**One up on 216**

Part of RAF life is inter-squadron rivalry. Even though they worked so closely together, 99 and 511 were always prepared to have a go at each other. But, perhaps, the prime joint target was their old Lyneham compatriots, 216 with their Comet 4s. They had remained at Lyneham and were now a dedicated VIP flying squadron. There was a lot of 99 delight when, in September, there was a callout for an aircraft to go to Thessalonika to transport the C-in-C, Air Support Command to Naples, thence to the UK, when his Comet went unserviceable!

**Old soldiers**

Uneventful hours of flying from one point to another produce many boredom breaking crew activities. One such event took place on a Gutersloh flight in October when the captain, copilot, navigator and engineer calculated that the total of their RAF service was 112 years! There is a point here for readers of the wartime and immediate post-war period when it seemed that the belief was that if you flew beyond the age of 40 you would crash! Fifty five was now the Specialist Air Crew retirement age and most flew up to this point.

**Another farewell**

Yet another withdrawal area was Malta. Led by Prime Minister Dom Mintoff, the mood was for the British to go. Talks took place throughout the year with Lord Carrington, the Minister of Defence, over the future of the island's military bases and the Britannia was on constant call as the VIP transport. Lesser mortals were also conveyed as the evacuation of military dependents was accelerated.

There was a further Royal connection for 99 in March. HM The Queen visited Mauritius and a Britannia conveyed the Royal Mauritius Standard and members of the press.

99 Squadron's Form 540 mentions what had been for many years a route diversion with a difference for squadron members. Every three months an aircraft on the 'Changi Slip' would be extended to Osan, Korea. This was to exchange the Honour Guard of the UN Peace Keeping Force, a long left over legacy of the Korean War and the disputed 38th Parallel.

**NATO emphasis**

The UK's declared greater involvement in NATO, with a decreasing global role, was tested in the September 'Strong Express' huge European exercise.

**Christmas rescue**

Britannias raised the spirits of No.40 Royal Marine Commando in December. HMS Albion had been steaming homebound with them on board when the troubles between India and Pakistan signalled that a Royal Navy presence in the area might be required. Albion called into Gan and offloaded the commandos. Britannias played their part in getting them home for Christmas.

**Special Sub-Lieutenant**

The chapter started on a Royal note; it concludes in the same vein. In November, 511 Squadron flew HRH Prince Charles to Gibraltar. It perhaps should be more accurately reported that, to join their ship, a party of junior Royal Navy officers, including Sub-Lieutenant HRH The Prince of Wales RN, were amongst the passengers on a Britannia flight to Gibraltar. Master ALM John Browne remembers:

*'A message was passed from on high, 'Under no circumstance was the young Prince to be given any special treatment.' The crew had other ideas!*

*'At the mega crew briefing,*

His Royal Highness is **SECOND** down the steps!
(*John Browne*)

*Captain Fred Lace was informed of the Royal Haute Cuisine. Yes, the notorious pink tray, complete with sticking lid, containing a chicken salad! Fred, being a connoisseur of all things culinary, was not amused. The back end team convinced him that some married quarter crockery and cutlery would enhance such basic fare. The problem would be how to serve HRH without his pals becoming jealous. Some cunning was required.*

*'The scheduled flight was designated VIP - Flight Number 1054. The Prince had just qualified as a pilot so, once airborne, he readily accepted an invitation to visit the flight deck. Whilst he was getting to grips with XL658, we fed the lesser fry and later placed before HRH the contents of the pink tray lovingly transferred on to bone china. It would have needed greater miracles of transformation than this to appeal to a Royal palate and the meal was politely left to one side. John Saunders, the crew chief, seemed determined to add to his family album. Standing discretely behind 'The Seat', he aimed his Box Brownie mere inches*

*from the Royal ear. The subject, no doubt sensing the hot breath, turned his head. 'Boots' did not charge for the consequent blurred result.*

*'As we taxied in after a superb cross-wind landing, I suggested to my lovely female compatriot ALM, Sgt (W) Muriel Hardy, that she should alight into the afternoon sun carrying the ship's papers and HRH's ceremonial sword. Against protocol, she leapt down the steps ahead of the VIP. I stayed well hidden sensing that this would be my first and last VIP flight!*

*'Many years later I had the opportunity of asking His Royal Highness if he had any memories of his Britannia flight. His only recollection, but apparently a vivid one, was of the ghastly antique gents urinal!*

A rather pensive looking Prince walks away from his RAF Britannia flight. Could his mind have been on that chicken salad? (*John Browne*)

FLAPS 15°

MAXIMUM TAKE-OFF WEIGHT FOR ALTITUDE AND TEMPERATURE

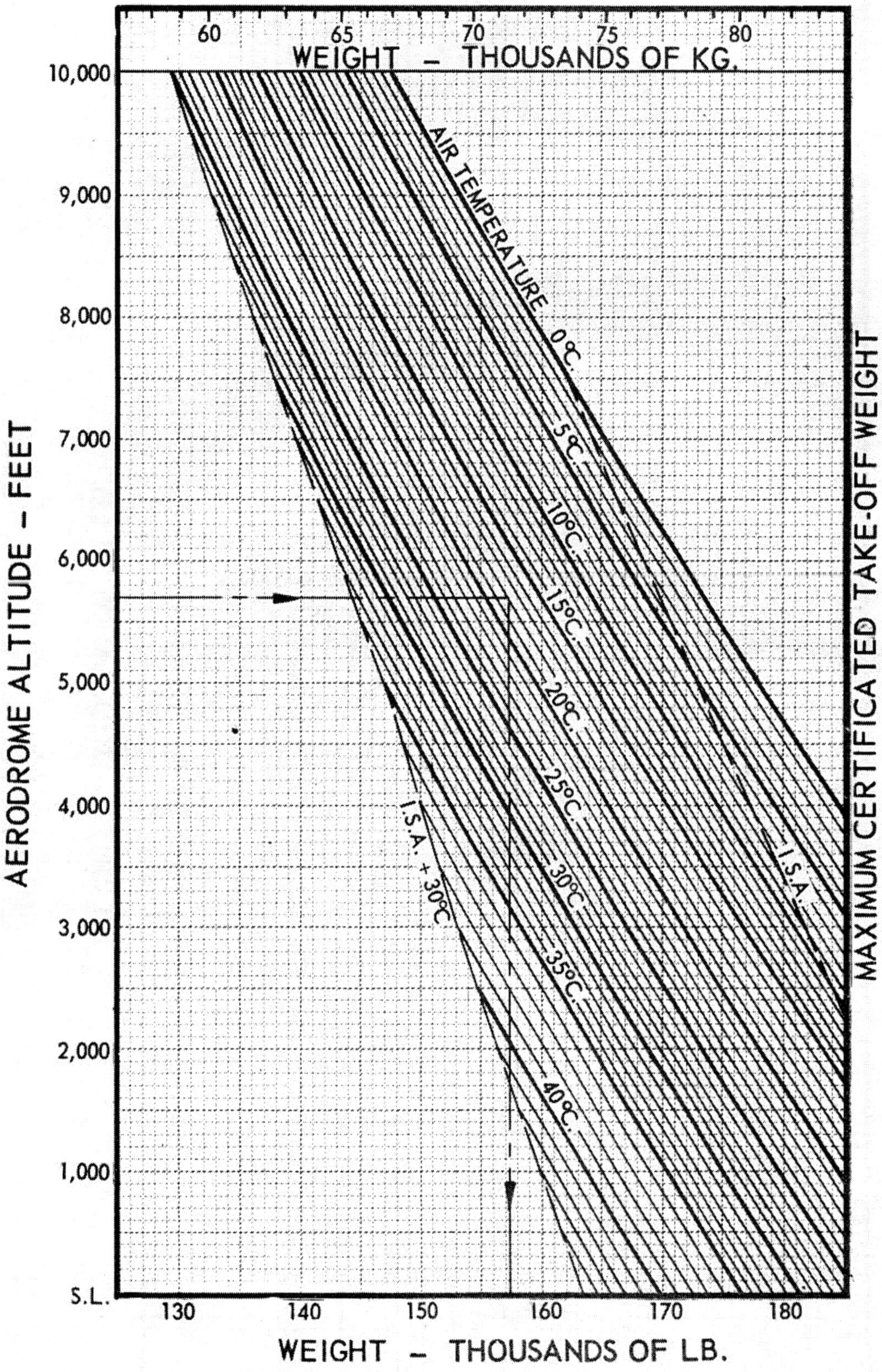


The RAF Britannia was very much operated to the same performance standards as civilian airliners. Basically this meant restricting the weight, in relation to prevailing weather conditions, runway length and airfield elevation, so that an engine failure at any stage of the flight (including the most critical one of take-off) did not precipitate a further emergency. This is one of the graphs from the Performance Manual. Very rarely, for vital operations, the performance standards were ignored.

CHAPTER TWENTY SIX

# Brush Strokes

The range of experience (and age) on the Britannia fleet was now very wide. A correspondent of '*The Gateway Gazette*', the Brize Norton station magazine, admitted to having just over 800 flying hours in his report on Master Navigator George Davies clocking up his 10,000th hour flying on a Cyprus to Brize Norton trip. On landing, he was greeted by his wife Connie and daughter Maureen and his 511 CO, Wing Commander Rod Hutchings.

Master Navigator George Davies DFM - plus bottle of Tiger! (*Mike Joyce*)

**Master Navigator George Davies DFM**

George enlisted in the RAF at the age of 18 and trained in South Africa as an observer; he was awarded his flying badge in 1943. After various Bomber OCUs, he joined 630 Squadron flying Lancasters and completed a tour of Operations in the costly winter of 1943/44. At the end of this tour he was awarded the Distinguished Flying Medal. He spent the rest of the war imparting his knowledge on Wellington OCUs.

Back on the squadrons after the war, George flew Lancasters, Lincolns and Washingtons with 12, 149 and 44 Squadrons. This took him up to March 1953 when he joined Coastal Command and flew

Not a photograph taken at the time of the 'hot' story overleaf, but it looks as if it could be pretty warm here as well.

What is this? Answer later.

Sunderlands at Calshot, Pembroke Dock and Singapore. In this time he visited Gan before anyone had thought of building a big runway and on one occasion 'sailed' a Sunderland home after an emergency landing on the sea out from Singapore.

When the Sunderland units disbanded in 1957/58, Master Navigator Davies joined the transport world. He flew Hastings on 48 Squadron and with FEAF Communications Squadron as a VIP navigator. After a tour at HQ Transport Command he joined the Britannias in 1965. One third of his 10,000 hours was on the Britannia between 1965 and 1971.

**Hot stuff**

An unknown correspondent reported on a 'States Trainer' of the period:

*'We left El Toro, California for Yuma Marine Corps Air Station in Arizona where we were to collect a tank trial team. Our scheduled ground time was only 1½ hours and we were picking up 6½ tons of freight and a team of 20 marines. On arrival we waited ten minutes before anyone came to the aircraft. It was then explained that it was not 'shift change' but Labor Day! The temperature, which had been a pleasant 85°F when we landed, was gradually rising. Eventually our load arrived on a lorry with a fork lift. There were 30 boxes, the lightest being just over 300lbs, the heaviest 1300lbs. These boxes were raised to the door by the fork lift and then had to be man-handled down the aircraft as no ball and roller had been fitted.*

*'The temperature had now risen to 115°F. To add to our discomfort, when lashing the cargo, there was the occasional large black spider or scorpion. That quick 1½ hour turnround ended up nearly a four hour one - and then it was a seven hour flight to Washington.*

*'I really cannot end this account without praise for the two girl ALMs who sweated it out alongside us. A quick shower and change and they appeared at the top of the steps looking immaculate to greet the passengers with a cheery smile and an apology for the delay.'*

**An engineering difficulty**

The move from Lyneham had presented many difficulties for the engineering staff. With the move came a name change from Strategic Line Servicing Squadron to Britannia Line Squadron (BLS). At the time it was commanded by Squadron Leader Doug Samuels. Under him were nine officers and 300 SNCOs and airmen. Their greatest difficulty at Brize Norton was that the aircraft parking, offices and facilities were all on the southern side of the runway and all the route departures and arrivals took place on the northern side. This meant that the aircraft had to be towed to and fro. A trouble shooting party, consisting of an engineering officer and one fitter for each trade, was sent across one hour before departure. This was expensive in man hours but effective in curing last minute unserviceabilities thus reducing delays. A team was also required to meet arriving aircraft to be debriefed on faults.

**Gruelling schedule**

BLS operated 24 hours a day, manned by four shift teams commanded by a Flight Lieutenant with a Flying Officer, Flight Sergeant and 70 men. They operated a controversial 12 hour shift system introduced at Lyneham just before the move. Each team completed three 12 hour days (0800 - 2000) followed by three nights (2000 - 0800). This earned them six days stand-down. This gruelling schedule met with early opposition but came to be ardently supported. Its advantages were that there were less shift changes than with an eight hour system and the handovers were mostly between the same shifts. All this was managed from a control room with a Duty Shift Officer and a SNCO job controller for each trade.

**Another Vic Merrill tale**

To close, for a moment, the topic of ground crew, it is appropriate for Vic to tell another story:

*'Are you Chief Tech Merrill?' I turn and look at the airman behind me. He is 'too young'; by that I mean he is fresh, eager, unbowed by responsibility or being messed about, the stars still in his eyes. As smart as a person in clean overalls who had never been near an aircraft could be; desperate to be old, dirty, experienced and working on the Britannia. I had glimpsed him now and then in the preceding couple of nights, hovering round, trying to be part of the scene. Unfortunately we were a little 'pushed' and it is easier, and quicker, to do the jobs ourselves than to spend time initiating newcomers into the art.*

*''Yes, what's the problem?' He shuffles and hangs his head. Having made the big step, he had become tongue-tied. I wonder what stories he had heard about me and how I could live up to my reputation if I didn't know which one he had heard. I decide that he thought that I was a big, bad Chief so I growled. 'Come on, I haven't got all night.' 'Please, I want to go on a pressurisation run.' Shades of Oliver Twist, where do they get them, I wonder? 'Have*

Strategic Line Servicing Squadron at RAF Lyneham. Sitting at their hatches on the left are the trade managers. (*John Hunting*)

An anxious crew, in their civilian rig, await the verdict on an unserviceable engine.

*you got a chit from Sick Quarters?', I ask. He shook his head. 'OK, go to Sick Quarters and tell the MO that you want a chit to do pressure runs and I'll take you if, and when, you get one.' 'Will you? I'll get one, thanks.' He turned and ran. That's that I thought.*

*'The Britannia was 'pressurised' so that passengers could still breathe air nearer to the pressure they were used to at ground level while in flight. This is above the pressure outside an aircraft flying at a high altitude. When it became necessary to change a window, a door or a seal, for example, the integrity of the airframe sealing had to be checked afterwards. This entailed building up the pressure inside the aircraft, while it was on the ground, above the outside pressure. The difference in pressure between the two could be up to eight pounds per square inch. The effect on those inside is basically the same as diving to a depth of 18-19ft (about 5.5m to the initiated) in water, and staying there.*

*'On the following night I receive a pressure run to do, down on the 'Calne Road', after a freight door seal change. 'Calne Road' was just about as far from J3 as it was possible to get. As we started out on the long trog down to the aircraft, the youngster came rushing up waving a slip of paper at me. 'I've got it!'. I felt nonplussed, the nut had gone sick straight after night-shift that morning, waited in the inevitable queue, and got his chit, before sleeping. 'Did you see the MO?' 'Yes, he wanted to know if I had a cold. Then he signed the chit.' 'OK, come on then.', and off we went. Arriving at the aircraft we heave a ground power unit from the next one on to ours and prepared for the run. Four of us clamber up 'A' steps into the forward freight bay and then in to the main cabin, closing the freight bay door after us.*

*'We have one man outside on the headset which was plugged into a socket in the nose wheel bay. Inside. the airframe men hover round the pressurisation panel, each attempting to see it, around the copilot's seat. I occupy the captain's seat and the 'new boy' was hanging around the entrance to the flight deck. He seemed to be enjoying his first run 'inside' the Britannia, I hoped he wasn't going to be disappointed.*

*'After digging around in my pocket, I find and blow up my balloon. It amuses me to see it gradually shrink to a limp skin as we approach maximum differential and then regain its swollen glory as we depressurise.*

*'Everything is OK inside, so I check with the 'headset man' outside. He has no problems but suggests that we get this job over with so that he won't be late for breakfast, again! 'Breakfast' was a meal in the middle of the night, usually starting at 3am.*

*'I have another look round and then start all four engines. When they were warmed up and settled down, I open them*

*up a little and tell the airframe men that they can start pressurising. JPT is monitored to ensure a rise as the pressurising valves are opened but there are no problems. The air begins whispering into the flight deck and pressurisation commences. One airframe man goes off down the main cabin and listens and feels for air leaks around the doors.*

*'Our visitor is momentarily forgotten but I needn't have worried. He is busy trying to see what I was doing, what the airframe people were up to, what was outside, inside and everywhere else, simultaneously. I check the instruments and contact the headset man, nothing wrong, everything going as it should. I remind the airframe man not to increase pressure too quickly in view of our first-timer and we settle down as the pressure builds up.*

*'Just as the relief valve 'blew,' at maximum pressure, I feel, rather than hear, a 'Thump' behind me as the 'new boy' passes out cold. So much for his chit and 'Thankyou, Sick Quarters.' We check him as far as we can, gently, but can see nothing apparently wrong. He is pale, unconscious, but breathing, he has a pulse and doesn't appear to be over-heated. We pick him up and lay him on coats on the cabin floor in the 'recovery position' and cover him with more clothing to keep him warm. Luckily it is a 'freighter', the seats had been removed, except for the usual few at the back of the cabin. Meanwhile, the aircraft has settled down at maximum differential. Immediate, fast, aircraft depressurisation could do our airman more harm than good; I need advice asap.*

*'I get through to the 'headset man', bring him up to date with the story as we know it and ask him to slope off to a phone in the Crystal Palace. He is to inform the Shift Boss of the situation. For the moment we are stymied; I suggest to the airframe people that they finish off their checks on the seals. My balloon lies limp, wrinkled and lifeless, but still looks fitter than our visitor. Meanwhile, with the door checks finished, we begin to depressurise, very slowly. One airframe man watching the patient to see that he does not appear adversely affected.*

*'Soon after I estimate the time of the call for help from the Crystal Palace was made, I see umpteen Landrovers and an ambulance converging on to the aircraft. They throw their shadows first forward, then back, as they pass the light masts and go through the tendrils of fog coming up from the Calne Road proper. They park in a semicircle around the front of the aircraft. It would help if they turn off their headlights, I can't see out.*

A photo for nostalgic eyes - a boat chugs down Changi Creek. (*David Berry*)

*'The engines are still running, the aircraft still pressurised. None of the throng now milling about outside could contact us, as there isn't a headset between them. Our 'headset man', having run all the way to deliver his message had, in his mind, relieved himself of all responsibility and succumbed to the warmth and comfort of the Crystal Palace. There he relaxed, caught his breath and rested a while, his headset tilted to one side so that he could hear.*

*'Various silhouetted figures appear in front of the aircraft, some waving torches, some their arms and obviously shouting. There they are, anxious to impart knowledge derived from training, experience and rank, but stuck outside. I am more than willing to hand over responsibility but marooned inside and in no position to help them. We continue to slowly equalise pressure but I am reluctant to increase the rate, in case it affected our patient: stalemate.*

*'There had been enough fuel on board for a normal pressurisation run but it is getting a little thin by now. I stop No.1 and ensure that we can maintain our present depressurisation rate without increasing the revs on the other three. I then stop No.2 and open the fuel crossfeeds. The*

*people outside can now get the steps from another aircraft in position. The trouble seems to be that there are not enough 'Troops' to do the actual manhandling. They finally decide who tells who to do what and the steps are trundled into position. I feel the steps touch the aircraft and someone trying to open the door.*

*'Suddenly my headset crackles as the 'headset man' arrives back from the Crystal Palace, I ask him to give the headset to the MO who I assume is with the ambulance. Someone comes on who identifies himself as an 'Officer' and demands that I open the door into the aircraft. The door can't be opened yet I state, thinking it's the MO, and begin to explain the symptoms of the patient as far as I could.*

*'There is another crackle on the headset and a different voice says he is Squadron Leader XXX and he wants an explanation. My spiel is begun once more but he interrupts and tells me to stop the engines, immediately. More crackling, now it's a Wing Commander; I wonder vaguely where they find one at this time of night. I ask if he is a Medical Officer, he says no, but that he would get one: silence.*

*'Lights flash outside, people wander about; someone bounces up the steps and tries the handle on the door again. Engines drone on, the pressure still dropped slowly. I wish I felt brave enough to increase the rate, but our patient is still 'out' and I don't know what to do for the best. The airframe men think the whole thing hilarious, I'm more than a little worried.*

*'The headset comes to life and someone says he is an MO. I explain what had happened, the situation at the moment and that at the present rate we wouldn't be able to open the doors for another 15 to 20 minutes. He tells me to hold depressurisation at the present level until he gets through again, to watch the patient, keep him warm and report any change. The Brit drones on as the airframe people watch our patient. I monitor the gauges and listen to the 'headset man' describe the to-ings and fro-ings outside and moan about the lack of breakfast.*

*'Finally the MO comes back on, 'Resume depressurisation at a normal rate, providing the patient doesn't react. I want him out and into Sick Quarters as soon as possible.'*

*'Depressurisation doesn't take us long and the airframe men are able, at last, to get the door open. Sounds of footsteps on the main cabin floor make me turn to see a multitude of people standing around, still and silent, gazing at our prostrate airman. Relieved at no longer being near the centre of people's thoughts, I carry on with the task at hand. The engines are stopped, the aircraft switched to ground, everything turned off except the lights, and my balloon deflated. The patient goes off, on the stretcher, into the ambulance and away. Quietly, and as if by magic, all the people and vehicles disappear; it is as if nothing had happened and eerily quiet. The ticking from the engines as they cool and contract seems louder than ever before. As we isolate all the systems, I idly wonder where everyone had come from and where they have gone.*

*'We push the steps from the aircraft and secure it, blank the engines pick up our gear and retrace our steps wearily towards J3. The job cards are cleared and we go off to see if we can get anything to eat in Transit. When we return, we are told that the patient is 'satisfactory', which can mean anything. Also, someone in Operations in the Crystal Palace wants an explanation from me on why I had been running a Britannia with no one outside on the headset!'*

The tail of 658 sports an anti-collision light. This was a modification (like the VORs) to the RAF fleet which lagged woefully behind civil airline practice and seemed only to be done when it became imminent that there would be a ban on the RAF Britannias using civilian controlled airspace. (*Pete Hobson*)

**The nose cone**

It has been mentioned that a difficulty was presented to the training world by the move to Brize Norton; the simulator could not be moved from Lyneham; so crews had to journey for their simulator training. Apart from this inconvenience, a valuable training aid for the OCU Ground School had been put out of convenient reach. All crew training was now the responsibility of No.241 Operational Conversion Unit, Bristol's school having been disbanded with the declining use of the civil Britannia by major airlines.

Brize Norton had acquired the Britannia nose cone that had been located at Filton for instructional use. This was now placed alongside the OCU building and could be conveniently reached from the classrooms. With the loss of the handy simulator facility, steps were taken to try and make the nose cone more 'RAF-like' and with components that responded to switching. Various items that had been salvaged from the demolished Khormaksar aircraft were used in this project. There was much electrical ingenuity with variable success the main enemy being rising damp through the foundations on which it stood!

GATEWAY GAZETTE THREE

241 OCU ANNOUNCE THE OPENING OF THE BRITANNIA SYSTEMS TRAINER

| | | |
|---|---|---|
| Technical Advisers | | M Eng 'Taff' Edwards<br>Flt Lt Potter |
| Nuts and Bolts | by | Mechanical Engineering Squadron |
| Internal Fittings | by | Aircraft Trim Section |
| Seats | by | Station Photographic Section |
| Photographs | by | Station Workshops |
| Carpentry | by | Aircraft Components Bay |
| Illumination | by | Britannia Line Servicing |
| Structure | by | Department of Environment |

OC 241 OCU wishes to thank all concerned for their co-operation and valuable assistance in the renovation and completion of the Systems Trainer.

A newspaper cutting reporting the champagne launch for the new systems trainer. Wing Commander Eric Reeves now commanded No.241 OCU. Amongst his staff was Flt Lt Gillie Potter and M Eng Taff Edwards. (*Gateway Gazette*)

**The story of a nose**

That nose cone had a history. It was from the second Britannia prototype G-ALRX which force landed on the banks of the River Severn on 4th February 1954. The aircraft had only flown for 51 hours and, as Sir Archibald Russell has already related, this was a considerable setback to the development programme. The flight could have ended in tragedy but for the skilful handling of the Chief Test Pilot of Bristol's, Captain A J (Bill) Pegg. When climbing through 10,000 feet there was a failure of the reduction gear of the starboard inner engine. With the free turbine design of the Proteus, this left the propeller turbine unloaded. In this condition it rapidly oversped and exploded causing considerable damage and an oil fire so intense that it could not be extinguished. An immediate return was initiated to Filton, speeded by the sight of the fire glowing in the starboard wing. As if this were not enough, two of the other engines shut themselves down and immediate disaster was only averted by the rapid work of the two flight engineers who managed to restart them.

Making it to Filton had been marginal and this added problem made a forced landing inevitable. Captain Pegg decided to use the muddy banks of the low tide River Severn and executed the landing with such skill that the Britannia was relatively undamaged allowing everyone to escape without injury. Survival was aided by the extinguishing of the wing fire by the mud. A race against time then took place to attempt to pull the aircraft out of the water but this was not achieved for 48 hours and, in that time, the scouring of the sea water had taken its toll and the aircraft was a write-off.

However, and most importantly, the rogue engine was recovered for examination and the failure of the reduction gear determined. As a result the gearing was changed on subsequent Proteus engines and a protection device evolved to detect a 'runaway turbine' and automatically shut the engine down before any damage could result. These were the aforementioned 'Limiters' that had to be 'Armed' before each take-off.

But this was not the end of

The nose cone at Boscombe Down prior to it being erected on stilts. (*David Berry*)

G-ALRX; much of the main fuselage, landing gear, flaps etc were sectioned for instructional purposes and the aft end used for torsional and fatigue tests. The front part became 'THE Nose Cone', the flight deck trainer for Bristol's Air Service School for training customer airlines' crews, including Royal Air Force aircrew. When this training ceased it was given to No.241 OCU. With the eventual demise of the RAF Britannias, the 'Nose Cone' was to live on. It found its way to the Aeroplane and Armament Experimental Establishment (A & AEE) at Boscombe Down, where a Britannia was still being operated, and was used there as a crew trainer. When that Britannia was sold in 1984, the nose cone was not going to give up! A potential use was seen for it by A & AEE's Aeromedical and Safety Training School (ASTS) as a passenger escape chute trainer. It stood there for many years, raised on stilts, as if it were a memorial to those splendid route flying days of 'The Whispering Giant'.

**Good Show**

It is inescapable that this book is centred around the aircraft and, in the main, the tasks accomplished by it. But there are background stories. One was reported in '*The Gateway Gazette*', the Brize Norton station magazine:

*GOOD SHOW, LAC BRIAN GREEN, BRITANNIA LINE SERVICING SQUADRON*

*Whilst on night shift on 26th August 1971, LAC Green observed, in the early hours of the morning, a light flashing at a fuel hydrant near to the squadron buildings. He approached the hydrant to find a civilian crouched over a fuel valve and, before Green could give chase, he was thrown to the ground by further intruders and severely beaten about the face and chest. Although in great pain and extremely dazed, Green made his way back to the squadron buildings to raise the alarm. The attackers were thought to have been copper thieves and, although not apprehended, his action prevented the theft of valuable metal and damage to expensive equipment. With complete disregard for personal safety, Green displayed commendable courage and devotion to duty in challenging an intruder who might have been a saboteur. He has been awarded a sum of £10 from the CO's Amenity Fund as an expression of the Station's gratitude.*

**An icy story**

Constant reference has been made to the engine icing problem of the Britannia. This was an internal engine problem - but ex-511 captain Chris Jackson experienced a variation on the theme:

*'Our dear old Britannia was always a challenge providing a series of ever changing problems for each member of the crew to solve, individually and as a team. She scared the s**** out of me on more than a few occasions but one that springs to mind and one which, I am ashamed to say, was not well reported at the time, occurred on a States Trainer. On the leg from Miami to McClellan I felt the need to go down the back and find somewhere comfortable to have forty winks. We had spent the previous night in Bermuda and if I mention that the two flight engineers were Jan George and Dave Allen you might understand why I was feeling somewhat jaded. As I was trying to nod off, we went into some thin cloud which produced slight turbulence; the loadmaster moved to his seat and put his headset on. It seemed that I had only dozed off for seconds before he was shaking my shoulder, "All is not well up front - I don't know what's the matter." When I reached the flight deck I found that my fellow captain (who was supposed to be keeping an eye on things) was leaning on the fuse panel, without a headset on and apparently unaware of any problem.*

*'The second navigator was in my seat and showing some interest in the activities of the flustered engineer, Dave Allen, who wasn't looking too happy at all. A glance at the engine instruments showed the compressor rpm at their limit, the torque gauges reading between 100 and 150 and the JPTs pretty high. What was going on? I looked out of the signaller's window at the engines for inspiration and saw that there was so much ice on the front cowl that there did not appear to be any gap between it and the spinner!*

*''We've been there,' I hear some say! Well, yes. Except that we were at 20,000 feet over The Rockies (and that was also the minimum safe height) and the outside air temperature was about minus 20. Now the speed was reducing at a fairly alarming rate and we were still in cloud. I got the navigator out of my seat and told him to produce a topo. I asked the controller if he could give us any radar assistance as we have to start a descent below MSA but he replied that this was not possible so we just had to start down, maintaining about 150 knots and full chat. It was about that time that crafty old Dave Allen came up with an idea which I don't think had been tried before. He suggested disabling the cowl heat on a pair of engines and, in spite of the temperature being way below the cowl heat range, turning it on the other two to see what happened, 'The worst thing that can happen,' he reassured me, 'is that those two engines will stop - and, right now, that won't make much of a difference!' Fate, luck - or maybe Him up there - stepped in before we could try this; we descended into the clear after only 500 feet or so and the ice vanished all by itself. The view of the mountains was breathtaking! The old Brit could always give you a surprise.'*

**An Autumn in Edmonton**

Harry Marshall recalls an occasion when a slip crew did very little slippng ...

*'I have written earlier, on two separate occasions, about a night-stop in New York and a New Year's Eve in Goose Bay. Just when I thought that I was, so to speak, written out about my Britannia experiences it came to my mind, after I must admit some prompting from the author, that I might just have a story to tell about 'An Autumn in Edmonton'; thereby completing a North American trilogy. And in case anyone says, 'Didn't he ever go Eastwards?' the answer is, 'Yes, and twice as often.,' but that's all been said before.*

*'Where would we be without our log books? Particularly when trying to recall events of 30 years ago. There it all was ... well nearly all. Four brief entries: 29th October 1970, Brize Norton to Gander, 30th October, Gander to Edmonton, 3rd November, Edmonton and back, 50 minutes, 5th November, Edmonton to Gander; Captain Flt Lt Luckins. When I say nearly all there, that's about right but there are a few interesting omissions. Sadly we navigators only recorded the aircraft captain in our flight details and for the life of me I cannot recall the rest of the crew members. A pity, particularly in the case of the flight engineer, who had an interesting part to play in this little saga. Then again there is no mention of the nearly flight on 4th November when we got a fair way down the Edmonton runway before George thought the better of it. Thirdly, the observant amongst you will have already noted that rather like British European Airways, when they were known as the Flat Earth Society, we too seem to have run off the end*

A view from a cabin window.
(*Bill Robinson*)

*of the world when we reached Gander on the way back. And lastly, there is no mention of the strange events going on in the Marshall household back at Brize Norton when we did eventually get home. Perhaps as well. Not everything should be recorded in log books.*

*'A little background first. You will recall that in 1970 we, the West that is, were at the height of The Cold War with the Soviet Union. Canada had a large part to play in this for the RAF and the British Army. On the East Coast, and based at Goose Bay, the RAF kept a permanent detachment from which the V-bombers pottered around, to the desolate North, over territory which was said to be similar to the Russian Steppes. Further west, Suffield I think was the name of the place, the British Army were similarly based, or rather their tanks and heavy armour were pre-positioned, and battalion sized troops were periodically rotated from Germany or the UK to Edmonton and back to carry out their war-like exercises in similarly wide open spaces representative of cold and inhospitable Russian mainland, which could not be simulated elsewhere. My trip with George and the rest of his crew was part of one of these battalion rotations. And this was most definitely a rotation. Each aircraft involved was absolutely full each way. This too was significant to my story.*

*'I have no recollection at all of the first day's flight to Gander which suggests that there was nothing unusual about it. Although, again looking at my log book I see that I have recorded 7:25 night flying. Perhaps I got that in the wrong column. Perhaps not. In any event it is not relevant. Day 2 does however stand out in my memory as one of the most interesting and most pleasant Britannia flights I ever made. This was definitely all day and covered territory that I had never expected to see. We took the scenic Northern Great Circle route (*) in the most brilliant of weather. Another 7½ hours with little for any of us to do except look out and enjoy the sort of geography lesson I personally could well have done with 20 years earlier when first trying to get an appreciation of that strange country. We were off airways, but always within TACAN range, so my task was easy. There appeared to be no other traffic anywhere. The visibility was unlimited. I, unusually, spent much of the time standing up and peering out as far as I could in the Britannia purely for pleasure, particularly when we crossed the Southern Great Lakes which really were Great.*

*'George and the copilot spent their time talking to controllers who sounded just like radio hams, eager for a chat with 'Ascot who?' and with none of the precision, impersonality and urgency of our normal watchers. The copilot reported that there was talk of snow (in October?) at our destination but it never materialised and we landed, again 7½ hours from take-off, in perfect, albeit extremely cold, weather. We were the first of the passenger carrying slip and were met and looked after efficiently as ever by our own detachment headed by none other than 511 Squadron Canadian detachment commander, Al Thomas. We retired to our hotel in downtown Edmonton, from where we ventured only briefly (it was very cold) before turning in. Our hotel departure for Gander was scheduled for mid-day the following day.*

*'I think most of you will agree that a mid-day start is better than a midnight start: but not a lot better. The morning, when most of us are at our brightest and best, is scarcely fulfilled by breakfast and packing and a hotel bedroom is a hotel bedroom anywhere in the world. A look outside revealed a strange, to me at least, weather picture. Where I had been prepared for either extreme of snow or unlimited visibility there was neither. The sky was overcast and if I hadn't known better I would have thought we were in some kind of dense bygone English fog. If I remember*

* A subsequent magazine correspondent, who shall remain nameless, had an eye for detail and challenged the description of the route:

*'HM's piece was amusing and enjoyable, as his writings always are, but I must query the description of his Gander - Edmonton sector as being Great Circle - sounds more like a rhumb line to me if they saw the Great Lakes; had he really been on a G/C track they would surely have crossed the southern part of Hudson Bay.'*

Well, it was said, 'an eye for detail'!

*the condition aright across the years, we were suffering from a fog occasioned by ice crystals. That's what the locals told us anyway, prefaced to dispel our ignorance by the superior remark, 'Too cold to snow.' Right or wrong, I was prepared to believe them. It was very very cold and I couldn't see very far. Neither could the pilots of our incoming Britannia at Edmonton. One pass at 200 feet was enough and off they went to Calgary of stampede fame and our alternate, some considerable distance away. We hung around for a while until we were told we were not required. I think the decision was that it would be easier for the incoming crew to take 12 hours off and stay with the aircraft rather than get us to Calgary. In any event we and the detachment were clearly superfluous to immediate requirements. We would be called again in 24 hours time.*

*'Another exciting hotel stop was followed by a repeat performance on the next day. Same long drawn out morning, same drive in the same weather, similar approach by Britannia, similar overshoot, similar landing at Calgary, same non-requirement for Luckins and crew. The only change in the situation was Al Thomas's decision to re-locate himself at Calgary with most, if not all, of his detachment leaving George and the rest of us as the RAF's sole and by now near permanent detachment at Edmonton, continuing our troglodyte like existence in the hotel. Back at the ranch at Upavon it must have been a close run thing as to whether to re-designate Calgary as the terminal and Edmonton as the alternate but the Army still preferred the latter. Finally, to our great relief the weather cleared and on the 3rd November the last aircraft on the slip proper made it into Edmonton and George and crew plus a complete complement of soldiers were set fair for return to Gander and thence Brize. Well nearly.*

*'In the event we only managed 20 minutes into the flight before George and the flight engineer decided there was something wrong with one of the engines, or perhaps it was one of the propellers, and we returned once again to Edmonton. Some two or three hours later after much pilot, flight engineer, ground engineer discussions, we re-embarked, passengers and all, to try again. One of the joys of being a navigator is that you do not have to listen to such discussions but I did enjoy the captain's take-off briefing. Whilst it was not exactly what I would describe as formalised, I clearly remember the bit about, 'If the fault's still there we'll recognise it before we get to 30 knots,' and the flight engineer's confident response that that would give him plenty of time to resolve it ('Get it sorted out,' were the exact words) before we had to worry about V1.*

*'That did interest me. Unlike all the other aircraft of which I have been a crew member, including the VC10, only on the Britannia did I have the responsibility of calculating and 'calling' V1. The subsequent*

RAF Lyneham from a Britannia, February 1970. (*Ken Guest*)

*attempt at take-off went as predicted (time for another 'well nearly'). The propeller fault had not gone away, George and the flight engineer both recognising this early in the take-off run. The flight engineer confidently undertook his rectification: trimming, fine tuning, whatever. The dialogue between captain and flight engineer began. The Britannia in that oh-so-slow acceleration mode continued to gather pace. I watched the airspeed building up with increasing interest. George finally called it a day before I had to make my intervention; comfortably in time but not quite so comfortably as I had expected, the flight engineer still protesting that he was 'nearly there.'*

*'I was not privy to the whole of the subsequent pilot, flight engineer, ground engineer de-brief but gathered that George was not best pleased when 'tomorrow' crept into the conversation. 'What do you mean tomorrow? We've still got 14 hours crew duty time left.' I thought that was stretching it a bit but the point was well made.*

*'In the end (well nearly) it was another two days before we got airborne for Gander after a spare part of some kind had been sent from Brize. Now we were definitely the last aircraft of the slip and our plan, we had long since lost any thought that anyone else least of all the Squadron might have some other sort of plan, was to deliver our aircraft at Gander, jump into the back, and get back to sanity and some decent Autumn weather before the English winter struck. The first problem was that we were a bit short of seats in the back. The second problem came for me via a signal waiting for George, when we landed at Gander. Purporting to come from OC 511 Sqn, (on a Saturday?) it identified the seat problem on our aircraft and instructed the vital return of another 511 Squadron navigator from yet another slip crew located at Gander for the sweepers instead of myself (both spelled out by name) 'So as not to disrupt next week's programme.'*

*'I can still recall George handing me the signal. 'You're not going to like this,' he said. Having digested the message I paused awhile before replying. 'I'll fix the seats,' he said, 'I take it you'll deal with the other matter.' He did and I did and 6½ hours later, I having had a comfortable ride on the soldiers' baggage, we were back at Brize. I thought my reception from Carole was little strange when I got off the crew coach and opened the door of our married quarter. She and Dick and Jill Parsley were innocently having a cup of coffee. It was Saturday morning about 10.00 am.*

*''But you're not due back until Tuesday,' she said. I thought that I understood her confusion. After all, whoever heard of a Britannia and crew returning early at all, let alone four days early. I explained. We chatted a while. No one left. It had been a long day. I said I thought I would just have a little nap. I forget what, but I had forgotten something, and pottered downstairs a minute or two later to find the three of them enveloped in smoke trying to put out the fire that had developed in Carole's sewing box where she had thrown her lighted cigarette when I unexpectedly returned. You see, Carole and I both gave up smoking a year before I joined 511 Squadron.'*

**Aborted take-off**

1971 closed with a strange incident at Mombasa which was to cast doubt on the current standard of aircraft performance of the now well used RAF Britannia fleet. It was nearing the end of December when a take-off was commenced at the coastal Kenyan airport. The temperature was high, the wind light, the runway short - the aircraft heavy.

However, all the necessary calculations had shown that the weight was within limits. As the aircraft rolled down the runway, it did seem to the crew that the acceleration was slow; this reached the point where the captain considered that there was something wrong and that there was insufficient runway remaining to get airborne. He abandoned the take-off. Back on the airport apron, three possibilities had to be considered:

- there had been a miscalculation of the performance figures and the aircraft was too heavy for the length of the runway and the prevailing wind and temperature conditions.
- that the aircraft was heavier than had been calculated.
- there was something wrong with the aircraft to affect its acceleration.

These were all considered. The

performance data was rechecked: all correct. The aircraft was unloaded and all the items reweighed: no discrepancy. It became the turn of the aircraft. One obvious problem, binding brakes, was eliminated. This left under-powered engines. Engine runs were carried out and the results were unbelievable; each one was down on the figures obtained and recorded at regular intervals by monitoring tests back at base. No immediate reason for this could be determined and after many days of more checking and anguish, a crew captained by OC 511, safely flew the aircraft, devoid of its freight and returned with it to the UK. Tests there showed the engines to be serviceable and delivering the correct power!

From all this arose doubts about either the thrust the engines were developing in the tropics or the integrity of engine ground running techniques in hot and humid conditions. It also raised the broader issue of whether the oldish Britannias were now performing to an acceptable standard as dictated by the original Operating Data Manual.

The ultimate investigation of all this was to lead to a story in 1973.

AP 4682A & B—FRC | Card 12 (AL 1)

**TOP OF DESCENT CHECKS**

| | | |
|---|---|---|
| Fuel panel . . . . . | C | Contents and configuration. Booster pumps all ON |
| Humidifier . . . . . | C | OFF |
| Pressurisation . . . . | C | Set for destination |
| Sidescreen demisters . . | P/C/E | ON and NORMAL |
| CRPM governors . . . | E | OFF and HIGH |
| Flaps . . . . . . | C | Selector UP, switch NORMAL |
| Seats and harness . . . | All | Secure |
| Compasses . . . . . | C | Compared. RMI checked and beam compasses set for let-down |
| Steering switch . . . . | P | ON |
| Altimeters . . . . . | P/C/N | Set and compared. QNH logged. Transition level checked |
| Overspeed limiters . . . | E | ARM at 10,000 feet |
| Reversing lights . . . . | E | Tested |

**FIELD APPROACH CHECKS**

| | | |
|---|---|---|
| Passenger sign . . . . | E | ON |
| Hydraulics . . . . . | E | ON-LOAD. Pressures and lights checked |
| Sidescreen demisters . . | P/C | ISOLATE |
| Altimeters . . . . . | P/C | Set and compared |
| Reverse briefing . . . | P | As directed by Captain |
| JPT limitations . . . . | E | Noted, cursors set |
| AQM's report . . . . | Q | All secure |

LANDING

RESTRICTED

This book is getting towards ...

... the shut-down checks!

**PRE-LANDING CHECKS**

| | | |
|---|---|---|
| Undercarriage . . . . | P | DOWN. Three greens |
| Brakes . . . . . . | P or C | Parking brake off. Pressures checked, exhausted. Lights out |
| Altimeters . . . . . | P/C | Set for landing |
| Propellers . . . . . | E | PRPM set. Synchronisation OFF |
| Pressurisation . . . . | C | Set for landing, PRV opening |
| Fuel . . . . . . | C | Checked for landing |
| Flaps . . . . . . | C | 15° and checked |
| Inverters . . . . . | E | All ON |
| Oil coolers . . . . . | E | Open |
| Search radar . . . . | N | STANDBY |

" Complete to finals "

**FINAL APPROACH CHECKS**

| | | |
|---|---|---|
| Shut-off valves . . . . | C | SHUT |
| De-icing . . . . . | E/C | Wing and engine de-icing off |
| Auto-pilot . . . . . | C | Master switch OFF, channels out |
| Threshold speed . . . . | N | .........knots |

" Landing checks complete "

RESTRICTED

CHAPTER TWENTY SEVEN

# Treasure - and Gurkha Flying

At the beginning of 1972 the Britannia fleet provided material for a 1978 main front page story of the '*News of the World*'! Fortunately, this was not sleazy copy but an example of sensationalism. The topic was the air transport of the solid gold death mask of the Egyptian boy Pharaoh, Tutankhamen, and other priceless tomb relics, from Cairo to Brize Norton for exhibition at the British Museum. The load was uninsurable so military transport was used to provide the necessary security. The 99 Squadron crew, captained by Flight Lieutenant Rick Laurie, flew to Akrotiri on 24th January and then to Cairo the next day. The half dozen packing cases, with their precious contents, were easily loaded within the two hour turnround and the aircraft was then on its way back to Brize Norton. Navigator Flight Lieutenant Jim Webb contrasted the scenes at each end of the journey:

*'As we taxied in at Cairo there was one sleepy Egyptian guard, in his galabeah, lounging on top of the crates on a trolley, his rifle cradled in his arms. We were deliberately scheduled to arrive at Brize Norton in the dark and, judging by the flashing blue lights, every police car in Oxfordshire seemed to be there. The crew were not allowed off the flight deck until the aircraft had been unloaded.'*

**The load sheet**

The airloadmaster, Sergeant(W) Pat Horne, kept a copy of the load sheet, part of which reads:

| Case | Height | Width | Depth | Weight |
|---|---|---|---|---|
| No.19 | 15" | 29" | 29" | 250lbs |

Contents:
Item 14: Scarab.
Item 16: Pectoral with winged scarab holding boat.
Item 19: Gold bracelet with lapis scarab.
Item 40: Kherep Sceptre beaten gold.
Item 48: Sheet gold collar.

The contents of another case simply reads: 'Item 21: Mask'.

From April there was a constant queue of people formed outside the British Museum waiting their turn to view the 50 items on display. Such was the popularity of the exhibition that it was extended from September to December. The Britannia crew was invited to attend the museum for a special viewing.

**Curse of the Pharaohs**

What of the '*News of the World*'? It would not be a wish to be bracketed with

The front page of 24th September 1978. (*Pat Horne*)

NEWS OF THE WORLD

THE 12p ONE

Beware of the sexy dreams machine

The end is nigh Sez Les

Death shall come to him who toucheth the tomb

EXCLUSIVE: KING TUT CURSE HITS THE RAF

HOW DISASTER STRUCK THE BRITANNIA CREW
- The pilot dies
- The engineer dies
- The steward has two heart attacks
- The WRAF girl has a serious head operation
- The navigator's home is destroyed

WRECKED

SHOCK

that publication by repeating the allegations here. Sufficient to say that they made capital out of the so called 'Curse of the Pharaohs' and the sadly premature (early 40s) deaths, some time later, of the captain, Rick Laurie and the engineer, Ken Parkinson. These they embroidered with details of the 'bad luck' of other crew members, some true, some false. Jim Webb, who was obviously not going along with this nonsense, is quoted by them:

*'... I don't believe in it at all. As far as I'm concerned, it's all coincidence ... if you take any group of people you are quite likely to find tragic coincidences ...'*

The story will probably never die. In 1997 TV personality Michael Aspel had a series entitled 'Strange But True' and this myth was featured.

**An interesting exercise**

It had now been decided to withdraw all of our Armed Services from Malta and Operation 'Wean' was launched under the command of Air Chief Marshal Sir Christopher Foxley-Norris, Chief of Personnel and Logistics, MOD. He described it as, '... an interesting exercise - a page of history is being quietly turned ...' The plan was to evacuate, in February, over 5,500 service dependents in a seven day period. This was mainly carried out by the VC10s but the Britannias were there in support. In particular two aircraft were fitted out in the aeromedical role. One of these grabbed the banner headlines of the newspapers - 'STORK SPECIAL!', it having a gynaecology team on board. The load was 21 pregnant ladies. There was some speculation that the 'Persons on Board' figure for the landing might be higher than that for the take-off! The Maltese situation provided other tasks. As an example, in March Prime Minister Dom Mintoff was flown by 99 Squadron on three separate occasions in as many weeks.

**OCU instructor/examiner**

1972 was the year of my elevation. I was posted from 99 Squadron to the OCU in the dual role of flying instructor and operating examiner. The former task involved instructing pilots new to the aircraft and copilots converting to captain. Also, as has been seen, there was now an instructional element in the categorisation process. Crews now spent a fortnight with an instructor, such as myself, on refresher training. There was also an examining element to this as it was up to the instructor, at the end of the fortnight's training, to assess the ability of the pilots and award an appropriate category.

Another element of the instructing/examining was 'route checking'. At the same interval as the refresher training, an instructor would accompany the candidate pilot on a route flight in which he was engaged. At its conclusion, helpful advice would be given and a route flying category awarded. From this and the category from the refresher training and a Squadron Commander assessment, the pilot's ultimate operating standard would be determined. 'A' was Exceptional, 'B' Above Average and 'C' Average. 'D' was inexperienced, whilst 'E' was, basically, a fail: 'In need of further training'. This classification might seem rather cumbersome but it was a system that had stood the test of time and was all part of transport life. It gave useful guidance to squadron executives when deciding the suitability of a particular individual for a task. But, not the least benefit was the 'pride factor'; it gave people something to strive for and, in so doing, they achieved a higher standard.

**Circuits and bumps**

A desire to teach and be helpful, qualities not possessed by all, particularly in days gone by, were useful attributes for the OCU job. Patience helped too, as much of it could be tedious; hours and hours of instrument flying patterns and circuits and landings. Going on route as an observer was not quite the same thing as doing it yourself. How rewarding it all was depended on one's philosophy. But there were material rewards. We did have our own route flights when there was an attempt to offer us something a little different; but the biggest bonus was the 'Global Trainers'.

**Round the world classroom**

For each instructor the turn came, twice a year, to lead the student crews new to the aircraft on their route training flight. Appropriate to the flying they might have to do, this was a circumnavigation of the world. With our own aircraft, an instructor for each aircrew trade and two student crews we set off eastwards. Fifteen days later we would return from the west. Our standard route was Cyprus, Persian Gulf, Gan, Singapore, Hong Kong. Here we would have a three day break, carrying out some local flying on one of the days to introduce the newcomers to the idiosyncrasies of that airfield and its approaches. Then it was off to the Pacific islands of Guam, Wake and Honolulu. North American landfall was California and the USAF air base by Sacramento, then to one in Nebraska, Offutt. The last port of call was familiar Gander, Newfoundland. The North Atlantic was the final challenge. In all honesty, it was too much for the students but there was considerable resistance to giving up such a fantastic routine - and there was the 'Baptism by Fire' element.

**A student's view**

Many, many years later a student reflected on his global trainer. We have met Squadron Leader Harry Marshall. Here he reflects on his preparation to be a navigator Flight Commander on 511 Squadron:

*'Looking back, at some distance now, over a varied and reasonably long flying career as a navigator, I find that nearly all of my flying fell into categories that can only be described as routine or repetitive and as such, many individual flights have tended to merge into one or to be expunged completely from my (diminishing?) memory. I suppose this is true for all of us to a greater or lesser extent. On the other hand, the near disasters and the unusual flights remain as vivid now as when they happened ...*

*'I remember vividly the Britannia, round the world, trainer that I was lucky enough to be on in 1969 ... it certainly figures high on my list of 'unusual' flights.*

*'The concept of a round the world trainer was a bold one and those responsible for running it past our financial masters of the Ministry of Defence must have been excellent advocates. To purloin one, sometimes two, Britannias from a hard working fleet every few months for use by the Air Training Squadron, without passengers or freight, solely for the benefit of some ten student pilots, navigators, air engineers and air quartermasters, with of course a matching number of instructors, and then to dispatch the aircraft on a leisurely, Eastabout, 16 day schedule with two days on the ground at Changi, a 'spare' day at Hong Kong and two more days off at Sacramento, was a feat of no mean skill.*

*'This was all achieved by the simple central argument that, as the Britannia was tasked world wide, its 'new to Squadron' members must be experienced in world wide operations prior to joining their Squadrons.*

*'Whatever the pros and cons of this argument and what battles had been fought to win the day were of little or no concern to me and my fellow students of that particular course that assembled at the Air Training Squadron in early 1969. We soon learned of our good fortune in partaking of this particular experience and in fullness of time I was one of the students in the first of these two trainers in June. Prior to this we had carried out a ground school devoted almost exclusively to Britannia 'performance' and this had been followed by the necessary circuit work for the pilots and air engineers to learn how to handle the aircraft. The crew briefing prior to departure also stays in my memory. It appeared that there would be some 20 of us 'crew only' on board. I noted that the aircraft captain, or more correctly the aircraft commander as there were two other captains travelling, was not impressed with a crew of this size. The logistics of getting us all together at pick-up time prior to departure featured large in his briefing and I can still recall the stricture that anyone not there at pick-up time would be left behind, wherever 'behind' happened to be. We were also briefed that the first thing that we all must do on arrival at Changi was to purchase the proper uniform of the day. We might not be better crew members then (this mournfully) but at least we would look the part. One other aspect of the briefing that comes to mind is that for the first time in my life two of my fellow crew members were girls.*

'... as the Britannia was tasked world wide ...' (*Bill Robinson*)

*'I have always noted that the best flights begin with an on-time departure. Conversely, a long delay promotes, at the very least, a sense of irritation and frustration. Our departure fell between these two extremes. We were just an hour or two late; not because of unserviceability and we had all managed to turn up on time. Strangely, Akrotiri would not accept us for an overnight stay as planned. It appeared that they had an exercise on and had no accommodation for a crew our size; this from the biggest RAF station in the world, at the time. We went instead to El Adem. I was pleased that I was beginning with a 'day off'; my fellow student navigator could do whatever replanning was necessary.*

*'If Akrotiri was the biggest (and best?) RAF station, then El Adem was the smallest and, without doubt, the worst. The base was in the final stages of rundown prior to handover to the Libyans and sadly its condition was a fore-runner of much that we were to see down the route in forthcoming years. There was just a handful of Service personnel left and most of the usual facilities and services had been withdrawn. Anything of remote value that could be moved had long since departed to the UK. We still maintained the mess/rank structure and, almost unbelievably, the 'transit' accommodation for temps like ourselves. We dined in the former in mausoleum-like unease and slept in the latter in prison-like gloom: bunk beds, three to a very small room, no air conditioning of course, mosquito nets. I hadn't seen a mosquito net since a Kuching night stop back in 1953. We left El Adem to the Libyans with no regrets on the following day and made our way pensively to Bahrain.*

*'This was my first turn at navigating the Britannia. It should have been easy: beacon to beacon, watch the fuel flow, begin the descent at the proper time. Somehow it wasn't. The aircraft went a lot faster than I did and got to Bahrain without any notable assistance from me. I would have been totally depressed were it not that the copilot and air engineer seemed to be doing just as badly, if not worse, judging by the chat on the intercom. The Bahrain 'Hilton' wasn't too bad after all we had heard about it beforehand. Compared with El Adem it was 5-Star. Perhaps things were going to pick up.*

*'By now most of us had had one 'go' at operating the aircraft and, equally, the staff had had one look at us. On the ground it was time for breaking into socially smaller groups and this initially, and I suppose naturally, took the shape of students sitting together at one side of the room and staff at the other, each group I suspect following the traditional pastime of pondering on the inadequacies of the other. As most of the student pilots and navigators on our particular trainer were ex-V-Force and the air engineers and air quartermasters were without previous experience, there was more than the usual number of inadequacies to ponder.*

*'The next day showed the benefit of previous up-to-date route experience. We were scheduled for an afternoon departure from Bahrain. Not, as I thought at the time, to demonstrate how suited the long sleeved KD shirt and black service tie were to Bahrain at midday in June, but so that we navigators could relearn how to do Astro on the way to Changi.*

*'I was up bright and early in the morning joined by some of the other trainees to go downtown Bahrain before the sun got too hot. Back to the 'Hilton' for coffee, followed later by lunch and then to pack. It was a nice relaxing morning. There were no members of the staff crew in sight; strangely they did not surface until midday. We ran the gauntlet of the afternoon sun and took off on the first leg to Gan. Shortly after take-off, I found myself stifling a yawn and, good heavens, I was to do the second leg to Changi. Perhaps that early morning walk had been a bit premature. The seven and a half hour flight to Gan seemed endless. Oddly, the next six hours to Changi sped by. There was no weather that night and the stars, as always, were where they should be. I was ready for the rush at BP but once again failed to keep pace with the Britannia. She was proving a hard mistress. The aspiring copilot fared no better. We landed, taxied in, disembarked somewhere just before dawn: students easily recognisable by their multi-hued KD and haggard expressions; staff still reasonably smart and awake. A wind-down beer was never more called for. As I reached out gratefully for my first a friendly mentor had the last word, 'Don't forget to have your KD fitting before you go to bed.' I recalled there was also the little matter of the domestic shopping list. What was it that Fred Trueman said after a*

The entrance to the transit accommodation at RAF Changi - the Changi Creek Hotel. Old transport hands would assume that the photograph dated from the 60s or 70s. In fact it was taken in 1994 when the building had become the Changi Country Club! (*Keith Govey*)

*winter tour of the Caribbean? 'I had to prove t' wife that I'd been somewhere.'*

*'Changi then was at its best and I have always considered it the best station that the RAF ever had. Sadly we all knew that we were to leave forever in 1971 and we transporters were soon to see and participate in a run-down on a much bigger scale and of far greater impact than we had just glimpsed at El Adem. But for those two days in 1969 our thoughts were happily insular and life was fine again. If not halfway on our trainer we felt that we had at least more than just begun.*

*'Refreshed, and peacock-like in our new uniforms, we set off for Hong Kong; truly the last outpost of the Raj. I have no recollection of the flight, being a passenger once again, but looked forward eagerly to seeing the colony once again on our spare day, after a gap of some 14 years. I never did fully understand the mechanics of the 'spare day'. It was noted in the schedule as time for continuation training. But this was difficult to fit in at Kai Tak. In any event, it was no surprise when the 'spare day' became a 'day off' ...*

*'... So far our Britannia had behaved like a proper lady. On the remainder of the flight across the Pacific she was to show us her vices.*

*'To date we had seen nothing of the engine icing problem for which she was truly famous. This was scarcely surprising as, with an empty aircraft (always a trainer's weakness), we had been able to file a flight plan for the mid-20s flight levels and climb above the problems. We planned to do the same coming out of Hong Kong for the Phillipines but in the event air traffic would have nothing to do with it. Instead we found ourselves held at about 180 in thick, wet cloud.*

*'From a distance of 24 years I cannot remember how long we were there but it was long enough. As the navigator, I was appalled how our ground speed had dropped off; 80 or so knots less than planned and the ETA, the navigator's holy grail, was running away from me. But no one up front seemed remotely interested in the ETA, or come to that the navigation.*

*'The flight deck was suddenly full of interested bystanders looking at the engine instruments. Even my ever constant companion, the screen navigator, was peering forward and not sideways. I couldn't see the engineer and I knew he was only two or three feet away. There was a distinctly unhappy feeling about and I gathered it was because all the engines were not working all the time at the efficiency expected of them. Eventually, after 30 minutes, or was it an hour, we were cleared to climb and normal operations resumed. But my ETA was gone forever.*

*'Guam came and went. So did Wake. The only thing I recollect about*

*Wake was a pre-flight snippet from one or other of the staff that no aircraft went unserviceable there. I was pleased that we did not break the record.*

*'The leg into Honolulu was my route check, much of it at night again. The stars remained friendly and I was determined this time I would not be late for top of descent. Naturally, I over corrected and we spent more time at the bottom of descent than at the top. But no one was over critical. We were looking forward to our Honolulu night stop and then to Sacramento, surely the high spot of the flight. But our fickle Britannia had one more trick to play. When the gear was selected down one of our main wheels failed to register a green. We read all the check lists and did all the right things but all to no avail. We flew low over the tower and a friendly American controller said that the gear looked OK to him but then added, thoughtfully, that we shouldn't rely on him as he had never seen a Britannia before. We circled and circled and circled the bay. Finally the inevitable decision was made. The aircraft commander assumed the left hand seat, the students were banished to the back of the aircraft. The landing was made. All wheels were down and locked.*

*'The students and most of the staff crew departed for the hotel. Very pleasant accommodation but I kept well clear of the outdoor patio. I have always had an inclination to vertigo and the 17th floor was a bit high for my liking. I wondered what Honolulu would be like for our enforced stay whilst the undercarriage was fixed. But surprisingly wonders were worked as we, at least some of us, slept and we departed on time for Sacramento where we acquired an additional day off whilst running repairs that had been made on the undercarriage were fully remedied with a part that had been despatched from the UK.*

*'Sacramento was all that the pre-trip hype had suggested it would be. A balmy, idyllic climate, a modern motel where we could take breakfast outdoors and enjoy the afternoon by the pool (common enough these days but a rare treat for the average Brit in 1969), excellent restaurants downtown. It was almost a pity to draw pay and had El Adem really figured on the same flight? We left all too soon, but thus fortified the rest of the trip was all downhill. A long but very easy day via Offutt to Gander in the undemanding American environment and with the Britannia on her best behaviour again; an unusually heavy weight take-off from Gander due to the sudden accumulation of frozen salmon and crates of Lowenbrau; an uneventful flight across the Atlantic, an ocean much more suited to the Britannia's whims than the Pacific; and we were back at Lyneham on schedule. Oh yes, for the mathematically minded, by the simple expedient of missing out Bermuda from our planned schedule.*

*'And was it all worth it? Well, on the credit side the trainer had achieved its purposes. We students, most of us, had been adjudged fit to join our squadrons. We had seen how the Britannia performed in all manner of conditions. We had observed at first hand a variety of 'ground' conditions. We had learned how big a factor sleep, or lack of it, would play in our new lives. We had bought our new uniforms without dwelling unduly why we and not the Service were paying for them. On the minus side the flight had been an odd mix of start and stop,*

It looks as if this 'down the route' undercarriage snag was a bit more serious!
(*Pete Hobson*)

*of rush then dawdle, and there had been too much wasted time sitting in the back twiddling our thumbs. I agree we were to see a lot of that on the squadron too, but surely it was unnecessary on a trainer. And the crew was certainly far too large. We never did become one big happy family. In retrospect, a long retrospect, I wouldn't have missed the experience but at the time, on our return to Lyneham, I and my fellow students (let alone the staff) were not so sure. I remain today unconvinced that 'round the world' was in fact the best way to go. But it was 'unusual'.*

*'For me there was a neat little postscript to the trainer when I joined 511 Squadron a few days later. the navigation leader welcomed me and in due course showed me his planned introduction to squadron flying. 'We've got the annual polar trainer for the Spec N course next week. Thought you might like to have a crack at that. It's a bit different to the routine.' 'Thanks, but no thanks,' I replied. We settled for a run to Luqa and back instead.'*

**Endorsement**

Harry Marshall contributed the above account to the Britannia Association magazine. This prompted the following response from training guru Harry Liddell:

*'Harry Marshall's excellent feature on Global Trainers prompts this letter for he has put into words some of the doubts about their worth that bothered me at the time. Indeed it is significant that although tried for a brief period with the VC10 they were soon dropped, despite being organised on arguably better principles; these included carriage of cargo wherever possible, faster schedules and fewer trainees per aircraft. I think the objections to the travelling circus type trainer might be summarised as follows:*

*Administrative difficulties with such a size of crew at best unwieldy and often almost unmanageable.*

*The relatively small amount of actual work undertaken by each trainee.*

*Consequent on the above, much of the space normally available for payload was occupied by 'idle' crew.*

*Global operation meant that for a large part, payload was not offered (Trans-Pacific especially).*

*'Due to the above factors, the bean counters naturally viewed global trainers with a very jaundiced eye indeed, and with some justification.*

*'Above all I think the concept of such trainers was flawed, in that they were based on the theory that it was necessary to actually conduct trainees along a particular route before they could be considered competent to operate it. This has always been pure hogwash as, once qualified, any average crew member should be able to operate pretty well anywhere in the world without further ado, and so a modicum of supervised training along almost any route should be all that is required. The only exceptions to this are possibly the occasional busy/difficult airport, such as Hong Kong or (arguably) JFK, plus certain facets of US route operation, which could be covered by good briefing anyway. The absurd and unnecessary restrictions imposed by Command ASIs on carriage of*

One of the Britannia traditions - a crew wind-down beer! (*Pete Hobson*)

*passengers during training flights served to further degrade their dismal financial showing, much to the joy of said bean counters ...'*

**This instructor's final word**

Whilst acknowledging what has been said above, for me the 'Globals' were my most satisfying Britannia days: being the 'Headmaster' captain of a global flying school with 25 instructors and students on board.

**Impounded**

South America featured large to the delight of some lucky crews. 511 navigator, Flight Lieutenant David Court-Smith remembers one of the flights:

*'The Falklands were, in 1972, quite forgotten by most people. A small detachment of Royal Marines carried the banner in the islands and they had to be relieved every so often. At the beginning of Easter week we departed from Brize Norton carrying the 'new guard'; after night stops in Newfoundland, Jamaica and Peru we arrived at Punta Arenas, on the Chilean side of the Straits of Magellan. The next day the Marines set off for Port Stanley, on the Falklands, in the Antarctic survey ship, HMS Discovery. The troops they took over from were eventually taken to Montevideo in Uraguay where another Britannia would whisk them home. Our own journey back to the UK was enlivened by a temporary impounding of the aircraft during a refuelling stop at Buenos Aires - someone hadn't told Customs we were coming!'*

**Equator ceremony**

Yet another South American task for 99 was to collect a Victor squadron from Peru. There were indulgence passengers on board, the wives of the crew of the Royal Fleet Auxiliary, 'Sir Percivale' which was due to arrive in Lima on the same day as the aircraft. It is perhaps as well not to let the imagination dwell too long on the picture behind the report that, '... during the flight a 'crossing the line' ceremony was arranged by an ingenious ALM'!

**South America again**

In April a 99 Squadron crew 'went south' to collect the replaced Royal Marine Falkland Detachment disembarked from 'Discovery' at Montevideo. The Britannia route, both ways, was Sal, Cape Verde Islands; Recife, Brazil then Montevideo. To speed the return journey, a slip crew was left at Sal on the outbound journey. Their lot was not an enviable one. This island was visited from time to time by the Britannia; in particular it was part of one of the 'Cable Routes'. It was an inhospitable place; volcanic and rocky, devoid of vegetation because of deforestation by early settlers and the introduction of goats. Perhaps its unwelcoming atmosphere was also due, in some part, to the ghost of its past as an assembly point for the slave trade. Flight Lieutenant Clive Osborne was the copilot and takes up the tale:

*'Spent a very unpleasant evening in a primitive and disgusting hotel and departed the next day leaving behind a very demoralised slip crew with the prospect of three days in this hell hole.*

*'En route to Recife we had booster pump problems and on landing the aircraft was declared unserviceable. We found we had a language problem but I managed to find 'Consulado Britannica' in the telephone directory ... an hour went by at the airport when we were challenged by a large man of military bearing, in a white suit, panama hat and black rolled umbrella, 'Are you the RAFF lot?!' So our acquaintance with Sydney Bannerman, Proconsulate, began ...'*

**Bad news**

Clive's story continues with details of the great social suffering they endured for four days whilst waiting for the spare parts. With the new pump fitted they were airborne for Montevideo - and the fault reoccurred! So a similar routine was reenacted in Uruguay - except, this time, the Embassy staff were there to meet them; bad news obviously travels fast in diplomatic circles. The outcome of all this was that the return journey was started 11 days late - that poor slip crew on Sal!

**Loyal toasting**

Dave Court-Smith has another memory of 1972:

*'The month of May provided a divertissement from run of the mill activities - an 18 day romp around Europe with the NATO Staff College based in Rome. The flight had VIP status, which meant an on-*

*board bar for the passengers. My major task as navigator was to announce the crossing of each international boundary so that representatives of the new country could propose a loyal toast!'*

**Sgt ALM to Wg Cdr Supply**

511 ALM Jon Mayo left the Britannia fleet in January 1974 for OCTU and a subsequent career in the Supply Branch, reaching the rank of Wing Commander. In spite of the bulk of his career being away from flying, he obviously still has the fondest memories of his Britannia days. Moving house unearthed a photograph and sent him to his log book:

*'The photograph was taken on a trip on which I was ALM together with 'Smiley' Donnelly. 519, Ascot 6962, departed Brize for a night stop at Binbrook on 27 October 1972. The captain was Chris Jackson and the copilot Nick Symes - the nav Stu Pierce. Our mission was to take the GD Aero Systems Course around the USA and Canada for three weeks. Our itinerary took us to Gander, Andrews, Friendship, Warminster, Eglin, Ellington, Dallas, Nellis, El Toro, Winnipeg, Wright Patterson, L G Hanscom, Ottawa and then back to Binbrook It was an excellent trip for the crew in that when the pax had disembarked, we were hosted most royally by some interesting people. Perhaps readers can identify the other crew members. I am the tall, in those days young, bespectacled one standing next to Chris Jackson.'*

Jon Mayo's photograph of the crew of Ascot 6962. What building is the backdrop for this picture? Ground Engineer John Insley provided the answer. (*Jon Mayo*)

**Also remembered**

Ground engineer John Insley's memory was stirred by the sight of this photograph:

*'On browsing thorough a copy of 'The Whispering Giant', my attention was immediately caught by a particular photo. On reading the accompanying letter, more memories gradually surfaced and a trip to the loft to dig out my Ground Engineer's log book was called for.*

*'All was revealed - Ascot 6962 was designated as 'Exercise New World' and, as Jon Mayo said, left on 27 October 1972 and returned on 17 November. The photo in question, if my memory serves me correctly, was taken on the steps of a government building - possibly the State legislature - during our stay over on the East Coast. We were being hosted by the two gentlemen on the left of the group who had just shown us around the magnificent building where, in one chamber, members were in the process of taking a vote on penal reforms for women's prisons. This, however, did not stop the Speaker of the House from interrupting the proceedings to acknowledge and welcome 'Visitors from Her British Majesty's Air Force'. Not in the least overawed, Chris Jackson replied with a most eloquent and gracious 'off the cuff' thank you which, I must say, impressed me no end.*

*'Later we were given a whistle stop tour of the American Naval Academy at Annapolis and were hosted to a splendid meal at a rooftop restaurant overlooking the harbour.*

*'Many pleasant memories of that trip come to mind, particularly as it was*

*only my second as a u/t Ground Eng. More notable ones were going to a party at 'Bacon's by the Beach' with Jon Mayo whilst we were staying at Fort Walton Beach - possibly the less said about that the better!*

*'Another story revolves around one of the more enterprising members of the crew who accepted an invitation from a dubiously gendered ex-pat to visit his dancing academy on our way through Los Angeles. There being safety in numbers, we all trooped off to the appointed hotel where - credit where credit is due - we were dined royally and were offered seats in what was considered to be the prime position in the ballroom. The evening promised to be interesting as we had been told, over our meal, that it was 'PWP Night'. What was PWP? 'Why, Parents Without Partners!' we were assured. During the course of the evening, the penny dropped - our prime seating was placed in such a way as to draw the customers into the ballroom because 'PWP Night' turned out to be a senior citizens' evening outing and we were the bait! After a number of us had been pounced upon and dragged on to the dance floor, we took it in turns to hide in the toilet until it became too cluttered with Zimmer frames and the ablution activities of the elderly drove us back to our table. I seem to remember Smiley scoring a point, having been laid siege to by an ageing, grey haired, lantern-jawed, Buzz Lightyear look-alike, who insisted he was a 707 captain. The chase lost impetus when Smiley asked him if the numbers referred to his age! Parents Without Partners was quickly dubbed Pensioners Without Principles!*

*'Another incident concerning Smiley, and this time Jon Mayo and myself, centred around the odious task of re-arranging the passengers' baggage and cargo before each flight. Earlier in the trip a number of bottles of spirits had been acquired from various sources and, during the flight, a bottle of 100% proof vodka had become cracked and started to leak. Rather than pour it away, the contents were decanted into a '7-Up' bottle and stashed away with the rest of the imprest goodies and promptly forgotten about. Some days later, baggage humping was again in progress; the task complete, three sweating bodies are slouched on the aircraft steps,*

XL658 bearing the livery 'Royal Air Force'. This photograph was taken on the occasion of the last Britannia flight into Decimomannu, Sardinia, 3rd December 1975. Musing on the smart appearance of this aircraft it is interesting to note that within six weeks it was 'scrapped'. (*Maurice Blencowe*)

*trying to catch a breeze. Smiley disappears into the depths of the galley and returns with a large bottle of soda just as the coachload of passengers arrives. Just time for a quick swig - ladies first of course - the rest is up to your imagination. You might picture one, red-faced, hoarse voiced, AQM serving coffee and biscuits to the VIPs!*

*'Well, enough lamp swinging; things that happen on detachment should stay on detachment. But then, surely, the Squadron Official Secrets Act should be void after 25 years!*

*'Now to the real point of putting pen to paper. The names to go with that photograph were:*
*Captain: Chris Jackson, Copilot: Nick Symes, Nav: Stu Pierce, Engineer: Brian Bardon, AQM: Smiley Donnelly, AQM: Jon Mayo, GE: Bill 'Snake Eyes' Akehurst u/t GE: John Insley.*

**Another name change**

The UK's declared greater involvement in NATO, with a decreasing global role, was tested in the September 'Strong Express', a huge European exercise. Also in September there was yet another Command structure change which reflected the shift in our defence philosophy. The title 'Transport Command' had disappeared in 1967 when it was recognised that one Command should embrace all elements of 'Air Support'. Under the one commander there was not only the strategic and tactical transport aircraft but also the offensive support which

Groundcrew at Calcutta. (*Richard Ling*)

now included Harriers and Phantoms. This smoothed the control of all these elements in their cooperation with the Army. The necessity for this was no less in 1972 but it was decided to have a single operational Command within the Royal Air Force and Air Support Command was absorbed into Strike Command. The aircraft painters had to set to work again; the Britannias now bore the simple legend - 'Royal Air Force'.

**The Gurkha lift**

The story and traditions of the Gurkhas are familiar. One feature was the enlistment with days of walking to the recruiting centres. Then followed a demanding land and sea journey for the enlisted lucky few and their dependents. This had been partly alleviated in the years prior to 1972 with the provision of a trooping flight, by Air India 707, between Calcutta, Hong Kong and return. This still left a train journey from and to Nepal. It was long and hazardous in itself but the war between India and Pakistan had made it dangerous. There

Gurkha embarkation at Kathmandu. (*David Court-Smith*)

A passenger's view of the approach to Kathmandu. (*Richard Ling*)

were stories of passengers being left for days in trains in sidings without food or water: Gurkha children had died. It was decided that this should be allayed with the provision of an airlift for the whole journey between Nepal and Hong Kong. From 1972 the Britannia ground and air crew manned a detachment in Hong Kong dedicated to this task.

**Making sure**

An element was that, on the way to Kathmandu, Nepal, the aircraft had to refuel at Calcutta. The Indians were incredibly sensitive about such flights with military overtones and insisted on them being

The photo that caused the aggravation! (*Richard Ling*)

operated to a very tight schedule in order to stay within the diplomatic clearance given. For this reason, on the three mornings that the aircraft were scheduled to depart Hong Kong, two aircraft would be prepared and ready to go in case the first became unserviceable on start up.

**Indian difficulties overcome**

There were many other difficulties of operating in this area, both natural and man-made. Clive Osborne remembers:

*'The flight to Kathmandu from Hong Kong was very interesting. A very early start was made to take advantage of the cool morning temperatures. The 7½ hour route to Calcutta took us over Saigon, Phnom Penn, Bangkok and Rangoon. We had received advice on avoiding getting entangled in the Vietnam War. Overflying Vietnam, the USAF bomber streams returning south could be seen and it was quite a spectacle to see the airfields of South Vietnam absolutely covered in warplanes.*

*'A most frustrating but, because of the poverty, highly moving part of the trip was the flag stop at Calcutta. The Gurkha passengers were under strict instructions*

En route to Kathmandu there was a view of Mount Everest. (*Richard Ling*)

*not to leave the aircraft. Photography was completely banned by the Indian Air Force authorities. This was not to be treated lightly. On one occasion a loadmaster took a picture of an IAF heavy jet taxying out. He was arrested. The aircraft was carrying the Indian President!*

*'One of the challenges at Calcutta was negotiating an 'Air Defence Number' to enable us to overfly India. One had to deal with an Indian Army corporal who, in turn, spoke with a bloke in New Delhi. The voice level was such that it almost made a telephone unnecessary. The long process of getting this number was usually left to the copilot whilst the rest of the crew did battle with Indian Customs. After one or two of these sessions, I tested the effect of a bottle of whisky. The required number appeared immediately!*

**Unforgettable**

*'The first approach from the south into Kathmandu is unforgettable. A range of mountains skirts the airfield, west to east to the south of the airfield, at heights up to 7 to 8,000 feet. The tops are usually in cloud but as you came over the ridge, the cloud would clear to reveal the most beautiful green bowl nestling at the foot of the Himalayas. After descent there followed a most interesting visual circuit, in and out of temples on the high ground. A tight turn on to the final approach seemed to be only 100 feet above the mountain tops and, to finish off, the approach end of the runway was preceded by a sheer cliff. All the first timers into Kathmandu landed well down the runway and then it was full reverse. This must have amused the Thailand Airlines DC8 pilots who regularly placed their much larger aircraft neatly on the very end of the 7500 feet long, 5000 feet high runway.*

*'The whole detachment was very much enjoyed by all concerned. The ground crew and all the support services worked particularly hard to ensure that all went smoothly.'*

**Go to the top**

There were difficulties at Kathmandu with its limited local facilities having to cope with this sizeable and regular

John Grimwood, an un-named steward and local inhabitant just get into the picture dominated by a curious background. (*Richard Ling*)

*One of the number of ex-RCAF pilots to serve on the Britannia fleet for many years was Bud Bird. With these photographs, sent to the Britannia Association magazine, he wrote: 'Here are a couple of photos for your perusal that I thought you might find interesting. I haven't the slightest idea where I got the negative for the first one, but it turned up in the waste basket, when throwing out a bunch of 'useless' items. When I saw it, I figured it might be worth printing, and this is what turned out. Judging from the hills and the low stone wall in the background, it must be Kathmandu, but the story behind it is a mystery to me. (Author: Looks like a full Gurkha load for Hong Kong.) The 496 on the tail, I reckon, makes it of particular interest. The other one is easier to explain. Also in Kathmandu, it shows a rather rowdy 511 crew preparing to return to Hong Kong. From the left: ALM Jim Armstrong, copilot Mike McCartney, steward John ? , nav Dougie Graham, eng Glen Church, me, and a padre that I only barely remember.'* (Bud Bird)

operation. Flight Sergeant John Grimwood, airloadmaster, remembers the proving flight in September:

*'We arrived to find that nothing had been organised, fuel, catering, accommodation. Phone calls to the British Embassy reached the Military Attaché who promised to speak to the Minister of Food. Meanwhile we sorted out a hotel. We had all settled in the captain's room for a beer or two when the phone rang. It was the Attaché, 'I have had a word with the Minister of Food and he is going to speak to the King in the morning.'*

*'Nothing like taking your problems to the top!'*

**Namaste**

Ex-511navigator David Court-Smith is something of a 'Wordsmith'. His experience of two detachments in Hong Kong on this Gurkha Lift led him to this contribution to the Britannia Association magazine:

*'The orange November sun struggles to free itself from the pall of pollution, which mantles the colony of Hong Kong. Its flame fingered rays pick out the dew drops*

*on the lawn of the Officers' Mess, RAF Kai Tak - an emerald set in a concrete clasp; reflect brassily from the rush hour traffic on the K' Tong road; and highlight the blue, grey and white livery of the Britannia sitting out on the apron.*

*'XL640 - named Antares, the great celestial beacon lying in the constellation of the Scorpion - is being readied for departure. Surrounded by catering vans, luggage trolleys, fuel bowsers and other accoutrements of the aviation services, she is the hub of the universe for those who support and fly her. Eventually the throng thins out and the aircraft's raison d'etre becomes manifest ... the passengers arrive. Men, women and children; a planeload of smartly-dressed Nepalese. These Gurkha soldiers and their dependants going home, some on leave, others at the end of their posting or service. The RAF has the trooping contract and will fly them to Kathmandu. The return flight tomorrow will carry families refreshed from their leave in the hills of Sherpa-land, and new personnel for Hong Kong and Brunei; there could also he a handful of wide-eyed remits for the training battalion at Sek Kong.*

*'Today there is a VIP on board - a VIP by virtue not of his rank but his courage; a Warrant Officer holder of the Victoria Cross. On 21st November 1965, in Borneo, Lance Corporal (as he then was) Rambahadur Limbu, of the 10th Gurkha Rifles performed such feats of valour when rescuing wounded colleagues under enemy fire that he was awarded the Commonwealth's highest military honour with its prestigious purple ribbon. In a nation famed for its martial prowess, bravery is taken for granted but extreme bravery commands respect. The Warrant Officer is pleased with his reception.*

*'Up on the flight deck it's time for some action. 'Hong Kong Ground, Ascot 6846 requests start clearance, IFR to Calcutta.' The Indian government requires the trooping aircraft to land at Dum-Dum Airport, where it will be given a quick turnround. Nobody will leave the aircraft other than for supervisory duties; the necessary scrutinies and form-filling will be performed on the spot by representatives of the Customs and Immigration Service and the myriad servants of BOAC (India) Ltd.*

*'Antares departs to the south-east, climbing through the Lei Yue Mun Gap and following the prescribed path with a little help from the electronic pharos sitting atop Mount Kellett. The route will follow airways running over the capital cities of four Asian countries - Viet Nam, Cambodia, Thailand and Burma - before entering the sub-continent via the Bay of Bengal. Soon the aircraft settles down at 12,000 feet, an initial cruising level dictated by the need to avoid the possibility of encountering moisture within the engine icing temperature range. There's nary a cloud to be seen at the moment but by midmorning the land masses ahead will provide the potential for cumulonimbus build-ups.*

*'At this height there's plenty of power from the engines and as the needle of the air speed indicator approaches Vno the engineer delicately adjusts the power so as not to exceed the magic figure of 258 knots. The VOR needles begin to waver, the TACAN range counters are playing fruit machines, and the navigator is on his own. The captain strolls back into the cabin to see how the passengers are faring. Some are dozing, including the valourous Warrant Officer; his features have not softened in repose, and he emanates an aura of restrained aggression - noli me tangere!*

*'Down below, just breaking the rippled surface of the South China Sea, is the North Reef; a tiny atoll, it is of no significance to anyone except mariners and aviators. This is the junction for Viet Nam.*

*'The RAF Planning Document*

From the Norman Rose photo album: *'Kathmandu 1974 Ghurka airlift. UKMAMS officer (Fg Off Brian Hunt) and his Sergeant with our 'Staff' at Britannia House. They were known as No.1 and No.2 and performed all the duties - cook, waiter, cleaning, barmen etc. Brit crews brought rations and beer from Hong Kong and shared with MAMS. Nos 1 & 2 are displaying the 99 and 511 crests.'* (*Norman Rose*)

*suggests that 7500 feet above ground level is the lowest safe height to traverse this war-torn country - safe from the small arms fire maybe, but what about surface-to-air missiles? In fact, the difficult areas are mainly north of the point where we cross the coast and there's rarely any re-routing necessary. Da Lat and Saigon come and go and ahead the Cambodian capital of Phnom Penh sprawls about the mighty Mekong river. The duty cunims are starting to build and the aircraft is just about ready to climb another 10,000 feet, right through the icing range and up into the colder regions aloft. Air Traffic Control is provided by the USAF but they don't seem to trust their radar in this sector and although it's quiet on the radio there's a lot of military traffic around; the climb will have to wait until Antares comes within Bangkok's purview.*

*' 'Good morning, Ascot. Radar identified. How's the old Britannica today?' Bangkok ATC is run by American FAA civilian controllers seconded to the Thai government and they are first-class (as always). 'Good morning, Bangkok. Actually, it's called a Britannia and it's ready for flight level 220.' 'Allrighty. Bangkok clears Ascot 6847 to climb and maintain level 220. Have a nice day.'*

*'Down below the klongs are thronged with 'hangyao' boats - skiffs with very long drive-shafts on their motors; tourists flock to gaze with awe on the Emerald Buddha; and Phatphong Street slumbers after its all-night exertions. The radios are busy this morning over the Piccadilly Circus of southeast Asian aviation, and some of the callsigns add a touch of style to a matter-of-fact procedure. DYNASTY - China Airlines - conjures up the pomp and power of the ancient emperors. Canadian Pacific's EMPRESS is nearer home, as the hotels in CP's chain are all called that in honour of Queen Victoria. CLIPPER is redolent of the fabulous PanAm flying boats, which ranged the Pacific Ocean between the wars. And GARUDA, the airline of Indonesia, is the name of the mythical winged creature who was the mount of the Hindu god Vishnu (it also stands for Good And Reliable Under Dutch Administration!). Come to think of it, ASCOT has a certain je ne sais quoi about it, just a hint, maybe, of a race of thoroughbreds.*

*'The next national boundary to cross is that of Burma; it is also their ADIZ and they are very touchy about it. A call on the HF gives them details in plenty of time but later on, on VHF, an unfortunate pilot is giving his excuse for transgressing the rules; 'Rangoon, Air India is very sorry not to have contacted you earlier but my HF is not enjoying any current.' What a delightful phrase.*

*'Down below the gold-sheathed Shwe Dagon pagoda glints in the late morning sunlight, like 'a sudden hope in the dark night of the soul' as Somerset Maugham once wrote; Burma could certainly do with a few more Shwe Dagons in the current political climate. Out now across the Bay of Bengal, all shimmering sea and not a cyclone in sight! And suddenly it's top of the drop. Calcutta, the original capital of British India, is a vast, sprawling metropolis and the airport lies to the northeast in an industrial area called Dum-Dum. Here is the arsenal where the expanding bullets were first produced, but today the biggest threat to life and limb is the Black Kite; dozens of these large, highly successful birds of prey patrol the aerodrome and its environs, and a sharp lookout is in order. Seven hours after leaving Hong Kong, Antares touches down safely on the strip of corrugated concrete, which passes for a runway, and taxies to the apron. The turn-round commences.*

*'The contract does not allow for fuel uplift at Kathmandu, so the onload here has to ensure sufficient for the Calcutta-Kathmandu-Calcutta stages plus diversions (from either destinations) to Varanesi - the ancient and holy city of Benares. The landing weight at Kathmandu has to be kept within Performance A parameters - and for a runway 4400 feet AMSL, and only 6000 feet long that can be tricky. Luckily the rules are surprisingly tensile and the pencils extremely blunt. The weather at destination is the other problem; Kathmandu is a VFR-only airport! The city lies in a bowl in the foothills of the Himalayas and amounts of cloud can be variable - forecasts are necessarily vague and conditions can change rapidly. It's all a matter of 'suck it and see'.*

*It is worth noting here that the contract only operates outside the monsoon period!*

*'Antares departs to the north-west, over Dhanbad - India's coal capital - and then turns towards the rice fields of Patna, on the sacred river Ganges. Behind the floodplain march the foothills of Nepal, capped with cloud and heavy with jungle. As the Britannia approaches the trusty NDB at Simra, gateway to the Kathmandu Valley, the vista opens out and the horizon becomes wall-to-wall mountains ... but at a distance of some 80 miles the visual impact is very disappointing. The effect is of a slightly irregular row of snow-covered peaks all merging into one another, not at all the spectacle conjured up by thoughts of the mighty Himalayas with eight of the world's highest, peaks. Closer views are, of course, more impressive as far as the immediate scan is concerned but the panoramic sweep has been lost.*

*'However, the crew's thoughts turn to the immediate problem of finding a suitable hole in the apparently 8/8ths cloud cover. The ATC wallah is optimistic: he says he can see blue sky overhead! And indeed, as the aircraft homes to the airfield beacon the runways are revealed below and the captain takes Antares through a series of manoeuvres which would do credit to the Red Arrows. Once below the stratocumulus the fairy tale magic of the situation becomes apparent.*

*'The valley floor is a mosaic of green and brown cultivation, which climbs far into the surrounding hills in the form of innumerable little terraces disappearing into the now dissolving clouds. Farm settlements punctuate this agricultural tapestry, some coalescing into hamlets, others nestling up to urban sprawl of the city. The whole prospect is enriched by two great religious edifices - Swayambhunath temple and the Bodhanath stupa.*

*'The stupa - one of the largest in the world - sits a mile or so to the north of the airfield and is close to the approach path on runway 20. On top of an enormous squat dome sits a tall pagoda-like structure seemingly supported by incredibly long, prayer flag-laden guy lines; on its square base are painted four huge pairs of eyes, surveying the cardinal points of the compass. As Antares turns onto finals the southern pair of eyes watch with Interest; to undershoot the runway would mean hitting a bluff above the Bagmati River.*

*'With a welcome roar superfine, brake dwell and full reverse resound across Tribhuyan airfield and 640 taxies slowly to the unloading area; it is just after 3 o'clock in the afternoon Kathmandu time, and the sun is already getting close to the western mountain. First to board the aircraft are the RAF Movements team, based here to support the contract, but just behind is one of the enigmatic but indispensable characters who seem to attach themselves to military enterprises the world over. 'Namaste,' he beams, palms together in the traditional salute. 'Welcome to Nepal.'*

*'His name is Padambahadur Limbu, but he normally answers to 'Number One'. Organiser and supervisor par excellence of all those little tasks which can drag on interminably if left to the whim of the average local, he is thoroughly enjoying himself. Whilst not seeming to be officially*

'I am the Windhorse!
I am thought at its clearest,
Emotion at its noblest,
Energy at its most abundant.
I am Reverence.
I am Friendliness.
I am Joy.
Plunging or soaring,
I leave behind me
A rainbow track.'

*From 'Song of the Windhorse' by the Venerable Sangharakshita*

From the Norman Rose photo album: *'Britannia House - Kathmandu 1974. Rented house instead of staying in hotels. Captain had the 'VIP Suite' at the top - crew had a room each as did the resident MAMS team. Bar, games and comfortable lounge and dining room.'* (*Norman Rose*)

*employed by anyone, he appears to find remuneration in one form or another, and his efforts are greatly appreciated by the crew, who are anxious to get to the hotel as soon as possible. Daylight disappears rapidly as the afternoon wears on, the rim of mountains surrounding the city cutting out the sun's rays; sight-seeing and photography become quite difficult but well worth the effort.*

*'Kathmandu is probably one of Asia's dirtiest capitals, but the fantastic three-tiered temples, the widely used and beautifully carved wooden decoration with sacred and profane subjects cheek by jowl, and the gaudily painted and flower-bedecked shrines present a mediaeval image that is almost enhanced by the debris and the rubbish. Everywhere there is the bustle of street commerce - sellers of vegetables, pedlars of souvenirs, dealers in gems and purveyors of ice cream (a major brand is named after the Monal, or Impeyan Pheasant, national bird of Nepal) mingle with the throng of pedestrians, cows, cyclists and the occasional car. A multitude of more permanent emporia line the lane and squares, advertising their wares with beguiling and often amusing use of the English language; pride of place must go to the proprietor of the Eden Hashish Centre, who proclaims his establishment to be 'Your old and favourite joint!'*

*'The crew's hotel is currently the Soaltee Oberoi, situated in the western suburbs with the temple of Swayambhunath as a backdrop, but rumour has it that a Muharraq-style, 'Brit House' may he opened soon, hopefully not next to the cemetery. The hotel's restaurant is adequate but uninspiring, and there are other places to eat safely; 'Yak and Yeti' belonging to a larger-than-life Russian émigré called Boris, and Aunt Mary's run by an American lady and much frequented by the more affluent hippies.*

*'The night air is sharp, the stars shine like crystals. The itinerants - of all races - have bedded down around Durbar, the central square. Somewhere the haunting strains of a sitar mingle with the wood smoke from a hundred hearths as the bakers prepare for the morrow. From the moon drenched mountains of ice and snow comes a frigid breeze: ten thousand prayer flags rustle at its passage, and from them ten thousand windhorses launch out into the celestial dome, carrying wisdom and blessings of the prayer flag texts to all beings in the world.'*

**Thankyou**

In December the Gurkha Brigade Major presented a plaque to the Hong Kong Britannia Detachment to mark this successful beginning of the Gurkha Airlift and Direct Air Trooping. He praised the work done by the detachment and thanked them on behalf of the Brigade of Gurkhas. Apart from the breaks enforced by the monsoon season, the BritDet continued its task right through to the end of 1975.

**The Rowlinson Gurkha Lift**

Colin Rowlinson's reminiscences for his fellow ex-Brats is continued with an account of his Hong Kong to Kathmandu time - and life in Civvy Street:

*'My general application for a return to Britannias had borne fruit and I said 'Goodbye' to the Belfast and 'Hello' again to the Brit. After going through the chalk dust, flight simulator and the 'circuit & bumps' routine, I rejoined No.99 Squadron all bright eyed and bushy tailed. The routes around the world were the same but somehow seemed a little better. 'How young the captains looked,' thought I. One of the Britannias' tasks was a seven week detachment to Kai Tak, the object being to take the resident Gurkha battalion - or whatever the Army called it - back to Kathmandu and bring a fresh lot back to Hong Kong; this involved a refuelling stop at Calcutta. On one such occasion the aeroplane went sick and we went to an hotel for the night while it was fixed. Driving or rather being driven through the streets of Calcutta made me wonder if Mother Teresa knew the size of the task she had taken on; I couldn't believe the squalor these people were living in. The hotel still had a touch of the British raj about it, most of the boys (cleaners) were still wearing ex-RAF/Army KD complete with (some) red eagle shoulder flashes, if you please. On arrival at Kathmandu airport our kit was off-loaded and we were on our way to Brit.House, on the outskirts of the capital, our own place of residence, to stay the night. It had been a private house with several rooms and it accommodated visiting crews nicely.*

*'We brought our own food and drink with us and the cooking was done by anyone of the crew who fancied his hand at being 'Floyd' for the night. Life was very serene, supping a beer in the cool of the evening, gazing out at Mount Everest in the distance AND getting paid to do it. We took a closer look at Everest on the way back to Calcutta. This detachment offered the 'Seat Availability' scheme to be put into use again and my wife joined me at HK and we stayed at the China Fleet Club (HMS Amar).*

*'Because of the cut back in the defence budget, the writing was on the wall for the Brits and Belfasts. Rumours were rife (as usual) about the future, but the routine flying carried on as usual. I managed another trip up to HK, this time to replace an aircraft on the Kathmandu run that was running out of hours before it was due for inspection .*

Photographic proof that Colin Rowlinson was on that parade. He is on the extreme right. The Reviewing Officer, ACM Sir Denis Smallwood is talking to fellow flight engineer Pete Hobson. The then CO of 99 Squadron, Wg Cdr Geoff Bowles looks on.

*'The future of the aircraft and not least, the aircrew, was becoming a hard and fast fact. The aircraft would be given an extensive air test to bring them up to Certificate of Airworthiness standards for the British Register. They would then be flown to RAF Kemble, parked on a disused runway and 'put to bed' i.e.. chocked, covers and blanks, etc. Bring in the auctioneers. Of the ten Belfasts, I think 'HeavyLift' bought five, one went to Cosford museum, the remaining four were put to the electric saw - I think, not too sure on that point.*

*'As for the aircrew, our CO got us together one day and read out the details of the redundancy scheme received from MoD. It didn't include long in the tooth people like myself so I had to look around at the options. All the aircraft had gone and on the 6th January 1976 the Disbanding Parade was held in the big hangar at Brize Norton before dignitaries and families, supported by the Band of the RAF. Quite a misty eyed moment for the more ancient among us when the Squadron Standards were paraded for the last time; a large chunk of our service lives went with them. It then struck home that the party was indeed over, AMEN. I still have the programme recording the event.*

*'The option I found was Boscombe Down. The only Britannia still operating was there, so I stated my case and in February 1976 I said, 'Goodbye Brize Norton - Hello Boscombe Down.' Time passed quietly there, no high blood pressure*

*or heart attacks, but I had the feeling that time in the RAF was running out. I always believed that long term decisions will make themselves when the time comes. That time came for me at Christmas 1976 and early in the New Year I went up to Adastral House, London, to the posting/release section and saw the Sqn Ldr in charge (whom I knew from 99 days) and posed the question, 'How soon can I get out?' He replied, 'Four months from now; when you get back to base submit release forms from this date and in the meantime I will look around for your replacement.' Nice chap. Forms were submitted and in due course my release date came through, 15 May 1977. In the weeks preceding that date I thought it might be a good idea if I went up to the Civil Aviation Exam Centre at Redhill and took a couple of exams for a civvy licence (just in case), although I had no intention of flying again. Release date came and after completing my clearance chit and giving my Identity back to the RAF, I said 'Farewell'. I left 18 months sooner than I need have done so they didn't have to drag me out through the squadron gates kicking and screaming 'I don't want to go.' FIN ... that was my song. Je ne regret rien.'*

The civilian part of Colin's story continues in Appendix 1.

**The Banana**

A strange anomaly of Britannia life was that the butt of flight deck jokes, the low form of life known as copilot, would one day be treated with respect - it did pay to give one's captain all the help one could! IMC remembers a copilot who was being given a hard time ...

*'With modern technology, we are used to accident investigators sifting through an unpromising pile of debris from a disaster and telling us exactly what went wrong; the failure of the 'O' ring seals on the Shuttle Challenger solid booster rocket for instance. However, in the early 70s, I was almost a participant in a disaster, the cause of which would undoubtedly have remained a mystery.*

*'One's first few months in any new job can be quite a challenge, especially if it is your first real one after four years of training. So it was for the copilot and navigator me, as we set off on an early squadron trip to Hong Kong. With experience you learn to listen to all the things coming into your headset and mentally filter and sort them out. To the novice it can be quite baffling. The key, of course, is anticipation. You know the agency is going to say 'Flight level'. It may sound like 'Fight', 'Fright' or something, but where the novice is distracted by this anomaly, the old hand has moved on and copied the rest of the message.*

*'So our new copilot started to have problems when we left the Queen's English of London Control and joined the mangled vowels and distorted consonants of the world's ATC. Having read back total garbage to Athens on our way to Akrotiri, he received the benefit of the captain's wisdom that we would be better off with a monkey on the radio. A slightly odd thing to say perhaps, but something that lodged in the mind of the flight engineer. As we embarked for the leg to Bahrain, the engineer took with him on the cockpit a large stalk of bunches of Cypriot bananas. I never saw much in them myself. They were very small, normally green and steadfastly refused to ripen when taken home. Perhaps the engineer was on a new diet.*

*'As we called Ankara, the copilot managed to confuse himself and the controller as to our desired flight level for the cruise. At this juncture the engineer said: 'Time to feed the monkey.' He then tossed the copilot one of the small bananas. Each time he made a mistake, the lad received another one. By the time we got to Singapore, the copilot had decided that the joke was wearing thin and had started to lash out with rulers etc at any banana throwers. However, human nature being what it is, and the stalk having an apparently inexhaustible supply of inedible fruit, it seemed a shame to stop.*

*'The crunch came on the flight to Hong Kong, just after passing the ghostly forms of 'Prince of Wales' and 'Repulse'. The copilot got very serious after an inbound offering, and announced that he was giving the engineer a direct order not to throw any more fruit. Further to that, he would charge him if he did. Was this to be the end of the fun? It appeared so.*

*'However, never dismiss the lateral thinking ability of the human mind. As we embarked for the flight from Hong Kong back to Singapore, the copilot was down the back sorting out the imprest while we waited for some errant baggage. The engineer*

*showed us his handiwork on the flight deck. Ex-Britannia people will recall that the cockpit had an 'eyebrow' window either side at the rear above the other windows. These were sometimes a source of unwanted sunlight and were normally covered by a small blind. Behind this blind the engineer had placed a banana. He had rigged up some twine so that he could release the blind from his seat. We tried it out. Excellent! The banana fell on to the copilot's seat as if by magic. And, of course, nobody would have thrown it!*

*'We awaited the next lapse on the radio by the copilot with eager anticipation. Getting in and out of Kai Tak was always interesting. The locals were quite cavalier at times, with a Cathay Convair 880 doing a visual circuit inside the harbour with a small fuel load on an air test. But then the 'Smokey Joe's' pilots were in a world of their own. However, our crews always seemed to treat the area with the respect it deserved. Today it was the copilot's take off, and the captain said, before the copilot came back to the flight deck, 'No bananas till top of climb!' It was a lovely day as we rolled down the runway. Just as I called 'V2', ATC, in a voice of urgency, came up with a classic one of those badly timed and irrelevant transmissions. 'Ascot 6251, Speedbird 451 is inbound.' Just as we started to climb away, the copilot was wrestling with the significance of the transmission. His peripheral vision caught a glimpse of the silhouette of the 747 behind the eyebrow window blind. Collision was imminent. So at 200 feet he applied lots of left bank and pushed the nose down. The captain's reflexes and survival instinct cut it. He caught it a few feet above the water and the aircraft and its 100 occupants climbed safely en-route. Meanwhile, Speedbird was calling Chung Chow inbound, some miles away. It all went rather quiet for while, then the captain said: 'I think we all learned something there.' We certainly had.*

*'There were no more bananas, and by the time we got home, we were all good friends and the copilot's RT had perked up no end. What if the captain's reflexes hadn't been so quick??* '... the investigators could find nothing unusual in the wreckage, save for the body of the engineer which was found to have a banana inserted in ...'

**Standard for 511**

Back at base, ceremony ruled the life of 511 for a number of weeks of 1972. On 5th May they were presented with their

The Squadron Colours on parade on a later occasion: 511 on the left, 99 to the right. (*John Smith*)

This is not necessarily the Luckins formation - but a similar occasion. (*Dan Gurney*)

Standard by Air Chief Marshal Sir Denis Spotswood. Flight Lieutenant George Luckins notes that practice for the flypast started on 28th April and went on every day for two hours until 3rd May. This was all in vain:

*'On the day of the presentation the cloud base was 300 feet. I hurt my back during this formation practice and have suffered with a slipped disc ever since.'*

**Britannia enthusiast**

What makes a Britannia enthusiast? There are the obvious 'types' but this would not include a doctor in Switzerland, who ordered a copy of 'The Whispering Giant in Uniform' (TWGIU). It also would not include a South Wales Roman Catholic parish priest.

The Reverend Tony Furlong responded, many years ago, to an offer made to the general public that they could become subscribers to the Britannia Association magazine. A copy was regularly despatched to him at Ratcliffe College, Syston, where he was the chaplain. After a number of years, contact was lost but this was re-established with the publication of TWGIU. The author's curiosity was aroused and the question was asked, 'How come an RC priest is a Britannia enthusiast?'

*'I instantly became an aeroplane nut-case following my first flight (in an Aer Lingus Viscount) at age five! My local airport in those days was Speke and a small band of us spent many a happy Saturday and school holiday through the 1960s spotting and snapping anything that moved. Although the basic airliner movement at that time tended to be a Viscount, DC3 or Ambassador, British Eagle Britannias would appear on periodic maintenance and trooping flights (usually for the TA) would produce the occasional RAF Britannia - perhaps with your good self on the flight deck! Even not much older than ten, I saw in the Britannia an aircraft that looked so right to quote the opening words of TWGIU. This conviction has stayed with me to adulthood. I was an air cadet through my teen years in a Liverpool squadron and later studied in Loughborough, gaining a degree in Transport Management and working, briefly, with BAA at Heathrow, before my childhood Catholic faith matured into a force which changed my life's direction. Such is my unremarkable story - Parish Priest and Britannia fan - now you know which came first!'*

**Changi - end of an era - life without the Slip**

The Reverend Tony Furlong, with a group from his college, on a visit to Brize Norton in August 1972. The Escort Officer is Fg Off Mark Simich. Mark was a member of that distinguished band of first tour copilots.They were remarkable for their ability. The majority of them confirmed this in later life realising senior positions. Mark returned to New Zealand to become a senior captain with Air New Zealand.

Tony Bennett continues the perusal of his log book and nav logs and shares his memories with you ...

*'On returning from the Tokyo trip I was lucky enough to have three days stand down (those were the days) which ran into Christmas Grant. Since October I had hardly spent any time in 'Splinter Village', as the old bungalows were known. Returning after Christmas I found that the Officers' Mess extensions were to be completed by February, and that strenuous efforts were being made to 'evict' the tenants of the village (removing kitchen equipment, furnishings, and, ultimately, the electricity). Thus it was on arriving back at Brize from a 10 day Changi that I found the village empty. I had kept my key and managed to last a few more days before eviction to one of the 'cells' of the New North Wing. I resolved to get out, and as luck would have it, a cottage came up to rent in Milton under Wychwood. A month later Rod Cassady and I moved in.*

*'I moved straight out again on a 14-day trip to Majunga, so it wasn't until the middle of March that I really took up residence. Life was good. Her Majesty The Queen paid a visit to Brize in March. Cast in my memory is the picture, as we departed the Officers' Mess in a crew coach, of a dozen or so airmen with sawn off fork handles creating an instant flower bed of cut daffodils. After the visit the daffs were removed.*

*'We quickly settled in Milton and were accepted into the social scene by a group of locals of our age, so it was something of a shock to set off on a 20-day Changi slip on 11 April, which included five days in Bahrain outbound.*

*'Sitting in Bahrain waiting for the slip aircraft to arrive from UK could become tedious after a few days. Read the papers, meet other crews as they came through in the build-up to leaving Singapore, watch the VC10 loadmistresses play darts, see a different film each day, and of course learn a little Persian/Welsh from the barmen. At least it wasn't too hot, and there was a swimming pool at the Malcolm Club, not to mention remarkably flexible bar hours at Britannia House. Life could be pleasant apart from the wailing calls to prayers.*

*'639 arrived on 20th April 1971 and after a normal turnround departed about 2200 local. As we approached TOC, I decided to calculate a couple of astro shots in advance and opened the drawer for the Air Almanac and the AP 3270s. Empty! Absolutely empty. Someone had not checked departing Brize. It was not disastrous, for we could fly by dead reckoning, use the powerful NDB at Gan, or (shame) ask the C130 ahead to work out the astro shots for us. The real problem was that we knew that on crew change at Gan the nav was being attended by an ASCEU route checker who wouldn't take too kindly to yours truly not carrying out his pre-flight checks.*

*'After a discussion privately with the captain providence intervened, and we lost an engine necessitating a return to Bahrain. The duty flight planning clerk was summoned from his bed and we drew a set of said documents to carry on the aircraft for the duration of the task. The rest of the trip was uneventful, but I had learnt a lesson. Just suppose it had been the Atlantic. From then on the first check I made was 'Navigator's Drawer'.*

*'We returned from the Changi slip on 1st May, and for some reason I did not fly again in May. Possibly I had a sinus wash which would have kept me grounded for a couple of weeks. Certainly I had a social life, which had not happened for some time, and was most welcome. I even played a couple of cricket matches. Sport had declined since I joined Britannias, and I always seemed to be en route when the hockey and cricket matches were played so much so that I was no longer asked. Fortunately home town Sidmouth always seemed to be short of players and I could almost guarantee a game by turning up. This went on from 1963 until I went to Finningley in 1975, when I didn't get home much.*

*'The beginning of June was back to reality and another Changi Slip with the withdrawal in full flow. These slips had brought to light the anomaly with regards to Local Overseas Allowances (LOA). Basically, if you were married a 15-day slip would be worth £15 in LOA. If one was single messing charges on RAF bases were payable. Only in hotels in Singapore were allowances the same. Even then LOA for one night in S'Pore did not cover the Singly's payments down the route. It therefore cost the Singly to go on the Slip unless there were two (or more) nights in S'Pore. The only way round it was not to claim allowances on F6663. (That caused a wobbly among the Accounts Section!) The problem soon disappeared as Changi closed on 28 November, joining El Adem, Malta and Muharrraq as marking the end of an era and soon to mark the savage cuts in the Transport fleet.*

*'The captain on this occasion was the same as almost a year previous to Majunga. Trouble seemed to lurk around every corner, and so it was in Gan. After a leisurely evening in the Blue Spitoon the captain retired early. When we retired later there was no sign of him in the accommoda-*

# Family affair lifts off

HIGH-FLYING brothers Mark and Nick Simich made airline history yesterday when they took to the skies together at the controls of a jet liner.

And joining the jet-setting brothers for the 767 flight from Auckland to Perth was proud mother Mary Simich, 67.

It was the first time two brothers have worked together as captain and co-pilot on any Air New Zealand flight.

"There are about 70 pilots in the 767 fleet so the chances of us flying together were fairly slim," said Mark, (above left) eldest of the two.

## Pick-me-up

And when they discovered they had been rostered together, they decided to treat their mother to a ride to mark the occasion.

"It's been my ambition for years to fly with one of the boys and getting the two is a double bonus," said the Pakuranga grandmother as she checked in.

Mrs Simich has recently been unwell and the trip was also intended as a special pick-me-up.

"I'm very excited and looking forward to it, although a little apprehensive too," she said before their departure.

She was given a VIP tour of the flight deck before take-off — but was adamant it was the last she would see of her sons during the 7½ hour flight.

"I doubt whether I shall bother them. They will be far too busy. They have a job to do," she said.

And there was no brotherly rivalry up-front either for both agreed that Mark as captain was the legitimate boss.

"It's just another flight as far as Nick and I are concerned, although it is a privilege to have mum along," he said.

Britannia Association members are kept up-to-date with news of past members coming from different sources. The Association magazine's editor was sent this New Zealand newspaper cutting which is an up-date on Mark Simich. The story with the photograph is that, for the first time Captain Mark and his First Officer brother Nick shared the controls of an Air New Zealand flight. It was arranged for their mother to be among the passengers.

*tion area. Surmising that he might be in the Sergeants' Mess we commandeered a S & R bike conveniently parked outside the Block and set of in search, the copilot driving and me navigating from the front basket in total darkness.*

*'Without warning the skies opened and a crosswind hit us - instant IMC! Soaked through we found the Sergeants' Mess and the rest of the crew. Settling down in the bar to see out the storm we received a telephone call suggesting that there might be some serious bother if the bike wasn't returned ASAP. The journey back took twice as long and we were absolutely sodden. At least the rain in Gan is warm.*

*'And so to Changi, where we lost the captain in Bugis Street. He did, however have the remarkable ability to find home-base even if without recall. Should have been a navigator!*

*'Eight weeks later I was back in Gan with one of the most charming captains you could wish to meet. He saved me from myself by suggesting that as my Bacardi bottle was empty I put it down and go find my bed. I did both but when I got my act together I realised that in my alcoholic state I had avoided all the storm drains en route to my basher. Some were not so lucky when sober.*

*'On return from this trip at the end of August there was time to catch the breath, and realise that (apart from May) I had spent half of each month away since the beginning of March. It had meant an irregular social life, meetings with girl friends, home and away. However it transpired that I was to spend little time away until the end of December. This did not cause me the hassle that I imagined, and I became quite used to life in Milton under Wychwood.*

*'It was about August 1971 that it slowly dawned on me that my Tourex date was rapidly approaching, hard as it was to believe that three years had literally flown by. So I was delighted when I was re-toured, little realising what might follow.*

*'It was only recently when looking at my log book entries for 1970 and 1971 did I realise how similar those two years were. Four Changi slips (January, April, June and August; three Muharraqs (March, May and August and a Majunga in March). What could we expect in 1972 without the slip?*

*'After the New Year we discovered that heating the cottage in Milton was difficult, expensive, and not as effective as we would have hoped. Some weeks later in a particularly cold spell we found that there were some tiles missing in the roof, and that we were literally heating the streets. Power cuts during the 'Winter of Discontent' led to gatherings in the local pubs, home or away depending on the area affected.*

*'This didn't last too long, and for me was broken by Exercise Travelling Causeway - reinforcement of the Far East by the Westabout route via McClellan and Hickam. We positioned by VC10 at McClellan during which the exercise was cancelled due to troubles in Central America. Awaiting recall instructions I spent hours making flight plans for all contingencies and routes. Our aircraft, which had turned around in Hickam, was to route McClellan to Bermuda. This was one of the routes I had planned - hoorah! The nav on the crew behind (Bill Marsden) borrowed the Flight Plan to photocopy as they were routing the same way. After about 15 minutes Bill appeared ashen faced clutching the remnants of the flight plan which had caught fire. After a coffee and cigarette all was sorted. Just another day!*

*'Spring rapidly put in its appearance and social life was renewed over a wider area. There were 'singlies' in rented accommodation in every direction roughly within a ten-mile radius of Brize. One of the requirements for approval for one or more single servicemen to live out was to have a telephone. This was not a requirement for a married couple living up to an hour away. As far as I know no one missed a flight or call-out - although I came close on one occasion (something to do with clock changes).*

*'Although the main withdrawal from the Far East was complete February found us in Hong Kong and Tengah, which was open normal hours only, and caused a few flow problems, not least with Akrotiri which fielded almost everything thrown at them through 1970 and 71, although we perhaps did not appreciate it at the time. I have no doubt that everyone involved with the Britannia Fleet could write a book on Akrotiri and Cyprus from the bête noir of accommodation (on base or downtown Limmasol) to the Ladies Mile beach to the brandy sours at Loucas Bar etc. Now Akrotiri introduced restricted hours which*

*effectively reduced us to a 'window' and certainly gave us some anti-social departures from Brize. Not all bad news because a pre-dawn landing and a 15 minute walk to the south-eastern cliffs, gave the most unforgettable sunrise in completely calm conditions.*

*'The number of flying hours remained high in 1972 (perhaps with increase in Northern Ireland rotational flights, and the use of Decimomannu). My log book records 196 hours in three calendar months - June July and August, with 80 on an Australian task, including Gan to Perth (Hands up all those who have heard about the navigator who nearly missed Australia!) and onwards across the appropriately named GAFA to Townsville via the reconstructed Darwin. This task gave us two clear days in Townsville whilst the aircraft continued on its task to Fiji. Unfortunately Townsville appeared closed and evacuated other than a Police Car out of Cagney & Lacey whose officers seemed convinced that looking for a restaurant or pub after 9pm was an indictable offence. We returned to Brize via Tengah and the old route on 30 August.*

*'There followed, with hindsight, the most eventful period of my life to date. Before being positioned in Hong Kong on detachment to operate the Gurkha trooping flights there were several additions to planning not least spending two weeks PRT on 242 OCU. This was with Flt Lt Berry who had recently joined the staff. Thus it was on 21 September I found myself tightly strapped in my seat lined up on RW 26 looking at the aforesaid David Berry in awe, wonder, and amazement, that anyone should want to do a three-engine take off 'for real' unless absolutely necessary, Performance 'A' notwithstanding.*

*'This was followed five days later by an Ops call-out to Bardufoss with a night landing. The take off from Bardufoss also tested ones careful calculations of the limits imposed by the terrain. It was probably just as well that the take off should have been in daylight when we could see, just like Hong Kong without so many lights.*

*'Much has been written about the transportation from Cairo to Brize of the treasures of King Tutankhamen in January 1972 but little about the return journey in December. For one brief moment in time I saw my name on the crew list, but not for long. Consolation prize two months in Hong Kong.*

*'Before leaving UK for Hong Kong I had to move out of the cottage in Milton, which was sad because we had enjoyed our stay and had been made most welcome by the local community, something I have never forgotten.*

*'Fortunately I had been offered a place in The Round House at Lechlade. The Round House was one of five built in 1790 as watchmens' houses on the Thames Severn Canal at the lock linking the Canal with the Thames at its highest navigable point. The cottage was originally a ware-*

Air Traffic Control, Tribhuvan Airport, Kathmandu. (*Richard Ling*)

*house, which had been converted into three bedroom accommodation. It has to be one of the best places to live in the area even if it needed some attention to the water supply and drains! (For aficionados 'The Thames and Severn Canal' by Humphrey Household tells it all.)*

*'When Fairford was reactivated in about 1967 I believe that it was occupied by 'singlies' from Lyneham. When I moved in during the first week of October it was to join Mike Newell and Fred Moffitt. Almost immediately I was off to Hong Kong for two months to operate the Gurkha Rotation Flights to/from Kathmandu, returning to Brize on 21st December just in time for Christmas.*

*'Much has been written about the Gurkha Airlift, and more has been discussed wherever and whenever two or more ex-Britannia crew have met in the 30 plus years since the airlift began. I apologise to no one about the content of these memoirs, but would merely say that I have belatedly put pen to paper before my memory disappears, so that my grandchildren will know that I had been involved in the airlift - one of the most amazing experiences of my life.*

*'I had always wanted to see Nepal and its mountains since it was announced on Coronation Day 1953 that Hillary and Tenzing had climbed Everest. Now that the Britannia fleet had been tasked to 'rotate' the Gurkhas between Hong Kong and Nepal, thus alleviating some of the hardships experienced walking for days from the recruiting centres and continuing by train and sea, I had the chance. My captain was Bob Howell and we had a fine crew once it was established that I could navigate even though I had a hole in my bottom.*

*'So, having positioned at Hong Kong, acclimatised to the time change and to the cacophony of noise from the high rise tenements within yards of the Officers' Mess at Kai Tak and flown some HK familiarisation flights, we were ready to go.*

*'On 27th October we set off very early from Kai Tak for Calcutta, seven hours away. With due deference to the Vietnam War, routing was over the sea until Bangkok then uneventfully to Calcutta. The turnround was reasonable in steamy heat notwithstanding the bureaucracy inherited and refined since Clive came to India.*

*'We were incredibly lucky as we approached descent for Kathmandu. The*

'... and beneath us the ever increasing number of irrigated terraces maximising the use of the land ...' (*Photo Richard Ling*)

*mountains were breathtaking, the visibility so good, air so clean and distances so deceptive. The lush green valley of Kathmandu in the near distance and beneath us the ever increasing number of irrigated terraces maximising the use of the land.*

*'Then just as it seemed that we had left it too late to turn on to finals for the southern runway, there we were. Animals were crossing the runway, having the right of way, but just cleared in time for us to land half way down it, then using full reverse to come to a rapid halt.*

*'The passengers disembarked and in their Samtani shiny western suits with their radios, tape recorders and other signs of Western living, set off on the journeys back into the hills from whence they came. The aircraft was serviced and prepped for the return flight next day and a few sweeties and chocolates given to the dozens of children who appeared to see 'The Big White Bird'. When they had cleared Customs and Immigration the crew went by elderly bus to the hotel Solti Oberoi leaving the flight engineer to tidy up and lock up which he did some 30 minutes later. Both vehicles took a little longer than expected to drive through Kathmandu, as it was rush hour. The cows held the right of way and the few drivers were playing havoc in the streets driving anywhere on the road with dust and dung everywhere.*

*'The hotel was palatial by Nepalese standards, and apparently the only licensed casino in the sub-continent. Dinner cost £7 in the hotel, which was put in perspective by the poverty, we were later to see around Kathmandu where we ate well in a local cafe for 50p for a choice of roast yak, boiled yak etc*

*'The following morning our flight engineer set off for the airport ahead of the rest of the crew to prep the aircraft. We arrived to be met by the engineer and an*

*animated group of Nepalese officials who explained that the engineer could not leave Kathmandu as, according to his unmarked passport, he had not entered the country in the first place, a 'Catch 22' situation, which was resolved ultimately by some high level diplomacy for which the British were renowned, with generous assistance from Scotland and another bag of sweets for the children. What we didn't know was that the airfield closed at 1700 and everybody went home. So much for security!*

*'It was touching to see the children scrabble for the sweets, particularly those who recognised individuals on the detachment and who seemed to make sure their siblings were looked after first. I am reminded of a five-year old boy (Gordi) totally protecting his sister aged about two. Our outbound Gurkhas were young fit and eager to board the aircraft after three or so days coming from the mountains. If they were in awe at the sight of The Whispering Giant, it was as nothing to what the future held.*

*'The return flights themselves were uneventful through Calcutta and on to HK where we prepared for a night arrival. The view and arrival were breathtaking with a myriad of lights from a distance culminating in the landing on a narrow strip of land that constituted the runway. The Gurkhas sat impassively taking in the change in their lives that the future held for the next two years - as did I.*

*'During this first stage of the detachment we operated seven sorties, the first on 27th October, and the last returning HK on 14 December. On the fourth task we had a day free in Kathmandu which enabled us to do the tourist bit and truly appreciate the country, the city, the villages, the architecture, the numerous temples, the total cultural experience, the poverty, the vivid colours. My Sidmouth house is named Patan after a small village outside the city, which I will remember forever, with views of marvellous temples and carvings, not all with sexual connotations.*

*'It would have been a wonderful experience to have taken a flight around Everest, which was operated by Air Nepal on a daily basis, weather permitting, for about £20. Sod's Law struck and the only chance I had was thwarted by fog, which did not clear all day.*

*'After back to back sorties we had time off which was put to good use with some sightseeing. Steve Coyle (511) and I took a leisurely ferry to Cheung Chau exploring the island, alleys, the graveyard where the occupants are buried vertically for a limit of seven years because of a land shortage. We wondered at the numbers of pigs which I understand came from China. After a glorious warm day, we returned in time for the Happy Hour in the Mess followed by a party.*

*'Numbers were small for both events for there were only five living-in members. An invitation was usually sent to QARNC nurses at the British Military Hospital, who tended not to go because of the lack of males. This time four or so accepted the invitation. Not much attention was paid during Happy Hour except for one girl who was attracting the men like moths to a flame - including me! As we were all jostling to accompany the one girl to the food another challenged me with words to the effect, 'What's the matter with me?' For the next four or so weeks we spent most of our free time together exploring as much of HK as possible. Little did I realise as we departed HK for home on 16th December that my days as a bachelor were numbered - although not for a while.*

*'One of the ongoing problems of the CCWR was the failure of the radar, particularly operating in high temperatures, causing overheating. Thus it was of considerable concern on the detachment and with spares running low a keen ground crew going though the system with a fine toothcomb and the servicing manual discovered that a cooling unit had not been checked and cleaned since the year dot. The tube apparently was clogged with years of nicotine build up and this was causing overheating. No more smoking King Edwards on the flight deck - or pipes!*

*'The result of this was that up to an hour could be saved on the leg Calcutta to Hong Kong at night by routing across Vietnam with the use of a reliable radar, which we duly did. This turned round and bit us on the very last sector when, with a VIP (AVM Sir Brian Burnett) an hour delayed out of Kathmandu, we cut the corner routing over Vietnam and smack in the icing range. We didn't need the CCWR there were so many CBs going off it was like daylight on the flight deck. After a lengthy period performing relights in no particular order we eventually coasted out at Da Nang and amazingly re-established radio contact as we left the storms behind us eventually landing at our original scheduled time. Great stuff.'*

CHAPTER TWENTY EIGHT

# Operating the Britannia

With all that precedes, it might be time to satisfy any curiosity on the subject of operating the Britannia. There have been allusions to engine icing problems, loading difficulties, miscellaneous unserviceabilities and the like but no direct reference to the actual handling of the aircraft.

**Beauty or beast**

It is natural, if somewhat chauvinistic, to start with the view of the pilots. For them the Britannia really was the 'Beauty and the Beast'. There were times when it was a dream to fly, effort being rewarded with accurate and smooth results. Other times, try as one might, the return was not there. The perfect example of this was the landing, the smoothness of which was more in the 'Lap of the Gods' than the hands of the pilot. All sorts of theories were postulated on how to achieve a 'greaser', the proposer having had a good run using his method. Then would come his downfall - a 'crash' would appear out of the blue, even though the same technique had been employed. This was the pattern for everyone. My own theory on this unpredictable situation centres around the 'free floating' flying controls.

**Free floating**

With a large aircraft some assistance is needed for the pilot to move the control surfaces - aileron, elevator and rudder. Various methods have been used over

The wolf in sheep's clothing? 496 landing at Gan. It is interesting to note that the main wheel bogies do trail - but not very much, compared with some aircraft. Only on the, rarely achieved, smoothest landings was one aware that the rear wheels had touched first. From this shot it might seem difficult to believe that it was possible to touch down nose wheel first. This was quite smooth until the main wheels crashed to the runway with the selection of reverse! *(David Guest)*

A relaxed captain - Squadron Leader Alec Wickes. (*Malcolm Fraser*)

the years evolving, these days, into the common use of hydraulic assistance. But at the Britannia design stage such sophistication was not available. With the 'free floating' system , the flight deck controls were not connected to the main control surfaces but to smaller surfaces on those main controls, servo tabs. Taking the elevator as an example, when the pilot moved the control column forward to lower the aircraft nose he would be moving the small control surface on the trailing edge of the elevator up. The forces from the airflow on this moved the elevator down, the effect with normal flying controls when the control column was moved forward. So, the nose was lowered.

To return to the landing problem, obviously the effectiveness of the servo tabs varied with the airflow and it could be that this became very sensitive at the lower speeds of the landing phase. Whatever the reason, pilots certainly had a cross to bear when it came to touchdown.

For knowledgeable onlookers at take-off, the Britannia's free floating controls could produce an alarming sight. As the aircraft was taxied on to the runway, the controls were unlocked. With no airflow, at this stage, to 'stream' them, it was possible for one elevator to be up and the other down.

**Handful sometimes**

The control column to servo tab link was gearboxes, torque tubes, screw jacks and push-pull rods and levers. It is not surprising, therefore, that there was some 'lost motion'. However, one did get used to this and the aircraft could be flown quite smoothly although it could become something of a handful when trying to counter the effects of turbulence at the lower levels of circuit and approach flying.

A somewhat strange postscript is added to the subject of the Britannia's free floating controls; they received a mention in the Royal Air Force's own church of St Clement Danes, The Strand in 1992 in an address by Air Chief Marshal Sir John Aitken, KCB. He was paying tribute to Air Chief Marshal Sir Alasdair Steedman, who had died that year. Acknowledging his Lyneham years, he mentioned that the Britannia was one of Sir Alasdair's abiding passions and how, at an only recent social occasion, he was heard expounding the virtues and vices of the aircraft's 'free floating controls'!

**Flight system**

The Smiths SEP 2 autopilot, used for most of the climb, cruise and descent, was unsophisticated but adequate. Its facilities included a height or speed lock and heading following. It was possible to do an Instrument Landing System (ILS) approach entirely on the autopilot. The allied Smiths Flight System (SFS) was one of the first flight director systems. Apart from giving the conventional pitch, roll and heading information, the essence of such a system is to tell the pilot where the aircraft is in relation to a navigation aid and to give assistance in placing it in another relationship to that, or another, aid. Pilot recruits from aircraft more basically equipped, instrument-wise, initially found the SFS something of a challenge. The facility to have the aircraft flying down the compass was a particular confusion.

**Harry Liddell remarks ...**

... *The comments on certain aspects of Britannia handling provoke reflections. Yes the Britannia did tend to hard arrivals, and the floating controls no doubt had something to do with it; their operation at low speeds must have been subject to inputs other than pilot-induced ones, such as eddies or gusts. Another factor to my mind was that in the landing attitude the bogies lay more or less parallel to the ground, and it is (I think) a fact of life that the greater the angle of dangle, the softer the arrival is likely to be; logical if you think about it, as the aircraft's weight is absorbed more gradually by the undercarriage legs as the bogies are slowly 'rotated' to the parallel position (watch film clips of, say, 747 arrivals for verification). The VC10 is a good example, its dangling bogies giving even firm arrivals a degree of softness; indeed Pilot Officer Prune himself would have little difficulty in achieving a relative 'smoothie'.*

*'The SFS, although an advance on the G4B or suchlike, was in my view unnecessarily complex, and its ability to fly apparently in reverse served no very useful purpose. The Elliot-Bendix system fitted to the VC10, although technically backward in comparison, was preferred by myself and many other ex-Britannia people (though not all, I admit); it had been a BOAC spec and as there was not enough money (even in those days) to fit a development of the SFS or similar to the RAF version, we had to make do.'*

**Navigator's challenge**

Much has already been made of the problems facing crews with engine icing. This needed careful choice, at the planning stage, of height to fly and some ingenuity, when flying, to avoid the critical levels. The problem was at its most critical

An early flight deck scene - one of a number of photographs taken by Harry Liddell on a Far Eastern Route Trainer, August 1959. The aircraft was a Mk2 - XN404. Note those headsets! (*Harry Liddell*)

The navigator's station with navigator Pete Squirrel at the controls. (*David Court-Smith*)

in the Indian Ocean region. The control of all this required considerable skill from the navigator in his extraction and application of information from the performance manuals.

This was not the navigators only challenge in the Indian Ocean. He had to find the island of Gan. Squadron Leader David Court-Smith writes of the navigator's lot in Britannia life:

'*The basic navigation equipment was an analogue computer called the Ground Position Indicator (GPI) Mk4 married to a doppler radar known as Green Satin; the doppler fed drift and ground speed into the GPI which also received a heading input from the compasses. Before take-off, you set the total distance for the route into the GPI, using the figures from your flight log, and as you progressed the counters ran down to read zero at your destination. The track angle of each leg had to be fed in at the beginning of the leg and the GPI would show whether you were left or right of - or, occasionally, on - track. The position was corrected from time to time using a fix, i. e. overhead a beacon, range and bearing from a ground feature identified on the radar or from TACAN or - if none of these was available - one or more position lines from a heavenly body, using the sextant.*'

**Position uncertain**

'*In order to avoid the potentially dangerous effects of severe turbulence and icing, the build-ups of towering cumulus and cumulonimbus had to be circumnavigated wherever possible. This was carried out using a combination of the Cloud Collision Warning Radar (CCWR) and the Mk1 Eyeball and could result in the aircraft being a long way off track before a clear path through could be established. Unfortunately, the across-track readout of the GPI was restricted mechanically to 89 nautical miles left or right - if you deviated further than that, the instrument did not register, so your actual position was uncertain and would remain so until some means of getting a fix was found.*

'*Another 'gotcher' was the tendency for the Green Satin to unlock over calm water; in theory the instrument should automatically freeze the figures at their last correct value but this often failed to happen and if the drift needle hit the stops at maximum deflection it could cause the GPI to go into a condition known as 'continuous rotation', thereby causing navigational chaos. You had to keep a constant scan of instruments whilst flying in the tropics.*'

**Unusual praise**

Breaking from the traditional pseudo-antagonism between pilots and navigators, I have to say that I feel that the navigator had the most taxing job on the Britannia flight deck. The rest of us had our moments but there was a constant pressure on the navigator. Perhaps a feel for their standard of accuracy can be given by reporting that, on those Indian Ocean legs, it was not at all unusual to see one of our compatriots flying in the other direction, indicating highly accurate track keeping.

**... V1 ... V2!**

The navigator had a role during the take-off run; he was required to monitor his air speed indicator and call out the two vital speeds - V1, beyond which the take-off *must* continue and V2, the speed at which the aircraft is lifted off the runway. We return to David Court-Smith for a story of a take-off he well remembers:

*'During my OCU I had managed to get in some extra route flying - the staff had been given an East Med and Peter Pipe had taken me along to do the work; the result was that when I passed out, I had enough route hours to be awarded a full C category. I arrived in Harry Marshall's office to find a state of near-panic: crews were in desperately short supply because the sweeper from an exercise in Calgary was delayed by fog, and re-rostering those available back at Brize was becoming a considerable problem. My paperwork caused people to scratch their heads - technically I was quite legal to navigate on my own, the time-honoured squadron acceptance check being convention rather than command - but eventually the bosses decided that I would have to be used. When they briefed me on the trip I was to have, I couldn't believe it.*

*'My captain was John Duff and the copilot Frank Allen: the itinerary was pax to Gander, then pick up Flt 6692 to Bergstrom AFB just outside Austin, Texas - weekend off, return to Gander, home in the back! This was, I expect, the least demanding of the flights on offer but it was like a red rag to a bull as far as some of the older squadron navs were concerned; I well remember hiding myself in a corner of the flight planning room when I was preparing my logs, and Gordon Pearce coming over to introduce himself and having an apoplectic fit when he saw where I was going. John Duff was obviously very wary about having me on the crew, but to Uncle Frank it was no problem - I was to discover during my time on 511 that he didn't know the meaning of the word! Anyway, we got to Gander courtesy of 99, and picked up the aircraft - which was the last part of Exercise Gobi Desert; we were taking American soldiers home after an exchange in the UK, and our return load would be British troops who had been exercising in the States. We had no problems getting to Bergstrom and were delighted to find that the USAF had provided the crew with two official cars, driven by a pair of young airmen, for the whole of the weekend. We all had an entertaining time!*

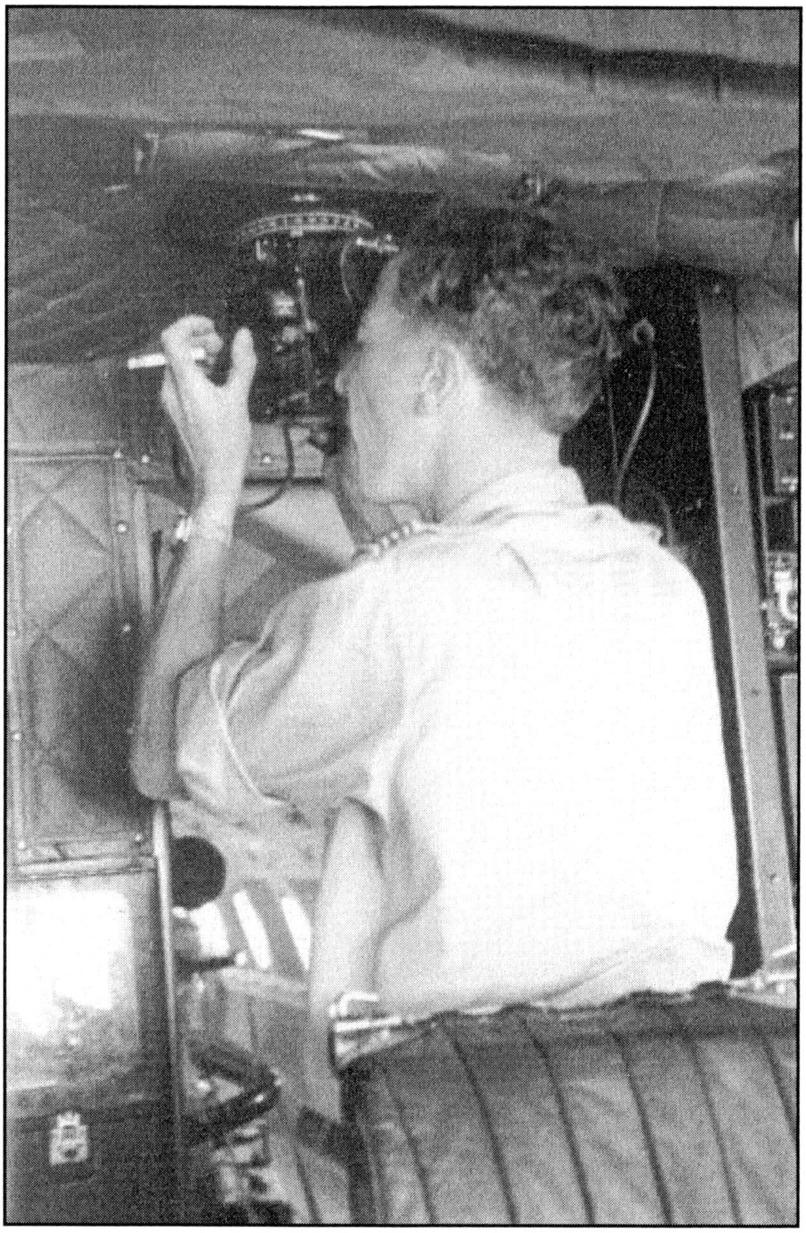

Navigator Pat Patterson at the Britannia's sextant - with the ubiquitous cigarette of the 1960s. (*Malcolm Fraser*)

*'Come Monday morning, everything seemed in order (except - surprise, surprise - for the Gander weather) and we were off chocks on time. It was a bit warm but the 12,000 foot runway was more than adequate - just as well, as I shall now relate. You probably remember that the navigator called out the take-off speeds, although the operating pilot had them written on a plastic whatnot provided by the nav. My ASI had been operating normally up to about 90 knots, and then I got the impression that the needle was slowing down; it took me a few seconds to accept the fact and blurt out, 'My ASI's packed*

Flight Planning at Lyneham. (*Lyneham Globe*)

*up!' The captain immediately aborted take-off, and we cleared the runway and shut down. I'm sure that we hadn't exceeded V1 (or not by very much) - or else the conscientious copilot would have called it, but it was obviously a very awkward time for yours truly. Investigation of the pitot heads revealed that some grotty Texan insect had infiltrated the system, and after several hours delay, we were on our way.*

*'The Gander weather broadcast churned out the same dismal story every hour: 'Indefinite ceiling, vertical visibility zero, sky obscured, horizontal visibility zero, fog' - the dreaded WOXOF! Suffice it to say that we saw the lights at about 201 feet agl, landed safely, and climbed into the back for the flight back to Brize. That was the end of my first squadron trip. And a very educational one it had been. I got my acceptance check on an East Med shortly after and settled down to an uneventful five years on 511 - but John Duff never flew with me again!'*

**Finally**

We will allow signaller Flying Officer Ian Lewis to add a postscript on the subject of navigators:

*'There was an occasion between Aden and Gan when the captain's request for a position was met by a curt 'Standby' from the nav. Forty minutes later the repeated request evoked the response, 'If you must know, and I really can't think it's any business of yours, we are exactly 6,373 miles on 097 radial from the Public Bar of the Red Lion, Calne.' Temperamental these artistic types.'*

Experts will be able to identify that this is the navigator's station on a Mk2 aircraft. (*Harry Liddell*)

**The flight engineers**

The Britannia flight engineers were an extremely knowledgeable band. It has been said that the aircraft systems were complex and advanced for their day. The engineers took great pride in understanding these technicalities and were a great comfort should a problem arise.

It has been previously recorded that it was mistakenly thought, at the design stage, that the Britannia could be operated without a flight engineer. For this reason, there was no dedicated engineer position with its own panels and controls. They were all placed where the pilots, so say, could see and reach them. When it was decided that an engineer was essential, a seat was provided for him between the two pilots. As a result of this late addition, his situation was ergonomically unsound; 'Britannia Engineer's Back' was a common complaint. Some panels and controls he could not reach; for instance, the copilot controlled the fuel and pressurisation. The layout brought about another strange Britannia phenomena in that the pilots never touched the throttles. Perhaps this tradition was

A snag down the route and the flight engineer, Len Shout*, is at the aircraft when one of the crew, in civilian clothes, calls to see 'how it's going'. The fault was obviously not a standard one as evidenced by the presence of the photographers. (*Bill Robinson*)

*But was it Len Shout? See text below.

established as some compensation to the engineer for being ignominiously perched between the two pilots, instead of having his own corner. The pilots called for the power they required which was then set by the engineer; a system that required some getting used to.

It is strange how one did come to accept this and it was only when flying subsequent aircraft that one realised what a penalty it was always having to call for various power settings. This was most noticeable, of course, on the final approach. Just a little more (or less) was required but a change of 50lbs of torque on each engine had to be called. Dealing through a second party also meant that some anticipation was required. Some approaches were quite illuminating, the power change requests coming at ever increasing intervals with the pitch of the voice rising with each call. If things were bad and you were really high then a resort was to call for minimum power on the outboard engines, 'Flight idle the outers'. I once heard anxiety convert this to, 'Idle the flighters'!

***Was it Len Shout?**

The photograph was published in the magazine of the Britannia Association with a request for details of who, where, when? Ron King thought he had the answer to those questions ... which led him on to remembering ...

'*Your picture puzzles me. I do not think it is Len Shout. I think it is a Mobile Team working on XL658 (Adhara) having gone duff at Khormaksar. This was en route to Changi for the MoD icing trials. They were changing a prop parking brake actuator.*

Long time instructor engineer, Taff Edwards, checks out the nose-wheel bay during his outside check. (*Malcolm Fraser*)

One of the crosses that the flight engineer sometimes had to bear - completing his pre-flight outside check of the aircraft in the pouring rain! Master Engineer 'Smudge' Smith at Thessalonika, 1967.

*This snag was eventually tracked back to a cannon plug on the bulkhead. I know because I was dragged out of 'Neddy's Bar' to find it and Titus drank my cold 'slops'. The team was FS 'Bogus' Travers (Elect), Pete Clarke (PB Fitter), Cpl Jock Ewan (Engines), Pinky Greening (Elect) with the avometer. If this is so* (Author: Which it's not - but keep going, Ron, I'm sure there's a tale or two coming up!) *Sqn Ldr John Owen was the trials captain, Titus Oates the engineer. I was the crew chief. On that saga, we went through three engines, four props (burnt out anti-icer mats), two Napier spray mats (tail plane) and one fin Napier mat (U/S in continuous). I flew on all the sorties and did that frigging thing give me a hard time.*

*'We finally came back with the starboard tail mat blocked up with 12lbs of stopper (bought in Changi Village), two props on cyclic, faith in the Met man and God in the fog locker. We had to get back for the final evaluation of the warren-ducted cowl. From the calculations emerged the accepted anti-icing figures. Pity no one thought about the adiabatic complication and calculated its adverse effect; if engaged in the wrong precipitate conditions, the warren ducting turned into a super Kelvinator - we lost many engines due to this phenomenon. The temperature band was quite wide and relied on deft operation of the EGVs and skilled calculation of precipitate ingestion. The end result was that the system was an expensive flop; but we were stuck with it because MoD would not spend any more money. There were many good alternatives. If we had had the Orion instead of the Proteus we would have experienced 'No Problems'. Hey, Ho, they were still bloody good days, though.*

The query was whether it was Len Shout (photo, previous page) as he, in his modest way, had not confirmed it. Later he came clean, 'It's me - but I can't remember what the snag was!'

No matter how well the aircraft might be operated on the flight deck, it was the load-master's attitude towards his or her passengers which left a lasting impression. This photograph of Sgt Sandy Bain 'doing his stuff' was taken under the particularly trying conditions of Operation Lucan, which is described in the next chapter. (*Ralph Dexter*)

**The signallers**

It has been seen that the Britannia's High Frequency (HF) radios were modified during its lifetime in line with developing technology. Certainly, up until this time, the signaller was a vital crew member when long range communications were required using morse. This would be, in the main, on the long sea legs and over remote land areas. The rest of the time, short range Very and Ultra High Frequency (VHF and UHF) was available and the pilots could have operated the radios. Woe betide the one that did! Rather like the engineers and the throttles, the signallers guarded their corner and insisted on making every transmission from the aircraft. It was understandable; they took pride in it and had to be on board so they could not be expected just to sit there doing nothing. Surprisingly, as a pilot, you did get used to the strange exercise of saying on intercom, instead of transmitting yourself, 'Sig, tell them we're downwind to land.' There was some sitting up straight in the pilots' seats when the signallers disappeared with the installation of voice Single Side Band (SSB) HF sets.

Ian Lewis, once again, adds a touch of humour:

*'One of my ambitions was to be a signaller on Andovers. This was so that, on*

Sergeant(W) Judy Holcombe, ALM 511 Squadron.

*approaching the south Kent coast and being told by London to QSY to Paris, I could say, 'Paris this MPTWA - an Andover on 'andover over Dover, over.' For a time, I did adopt the rather unhealthy habit of addressing the foreign FIRs, over which we flew, in their own language. This was one method of getting a response from the French; the other being to leave out half your callsign so that they didn't know you were British military. I recall, having reported, 'Roma questo Ascot Sie-Uno-Due-Tre - positione Amber Uno Alpha ore cinque-cinque levale due quatro zero arrivo sopro Ponza uno-cinque Malta,' being amazed at the response of, 'Roger, old man - got your position, thankyou - call Ponza."*

**Down the back**

Last but not least was the airloadmaster. Contrary to civilian practice, where there is a considerable gulf between the flight deck crew and the 'Cabin Staff', we considered the airloadmaster, possibly assisted by an air steward, very much part of the Britannia crew. This reflects his, or her, greater responsibilities in the military environment. On one flight they might only be engaged in the essential but perhaps slightly demeaning task of supplying food and drink to the passengers and crew. Equally they could find themselves, on the next leg, at some remote location, totally responsible for the correct loading of an awkward, heavy, hazardous cargo with the minimum of facilities and time always an element.

With their ancestors being volunteers who joined the crew to 'give a hand', they inherited a cheerful willingness to do all they could to help things along.

**Team effort**

It would have been natural to have headed this chapter 'Flying the Britannia' but it was a team effort and we were indeed fortunate with the individuals that we had who worked so well together to successfully OPERATE the Britannia.

On the occasion of one of the visits to Lyneham of the RCAF Yukon crews, Annie Bowden (2nd left) and Betty Fendley (right), both of 99 Squadron, greet the female members of the Canadian team. (*Lyneham Globe*)

**An air steward's story**

Jimmy Hunter was one of the first air stewards and subsequently an AQM. He recalls his training and Britannia days:

*'I have read stories from pilots, navs, engs, sigs, ALMs but no air stewards. It was only after a further avid read of 'The Whispering Giant in Uniform' (Author: 1st Edition!) and the enjoyment I got from 'Tales from the Crewroom' that I thought it may bring back some good memories of what life was like for an 'Ultra-Keen' and 'Shining-New' task force - The Air Steward. Perhaps I'd better offer my apologies in advance for any aspects of misinformation, mix up of names, wrong flight numbers and wrong captains to crew scenarios that no doubt will occur throughout this article. Memory being what memory is and the time that seems to have flown past is my excuse - and I'm sticking to it! So, for all the lads and lassies that I may get confused with, I blame the misting of years and the clouding of memory. So I think it a good idea to start where all things start - 'In the beginning ...*

*'It was no great surprise to me that my boss at RAF Uxbridge, the Station Catering Officer, suggested that it was time*

No.1 Air Stewards Course

Back row L to R:
Cpl Hall
Cpl Hunter
Cpl Rosbotham
Cpl McGowan
Cpl Clark
Cpl Morrison
Cpl Cook
Front row:
Cpl Edge
Cpl Grieves
Cpl James
Cpl Smythe
Cpl Rounsfull
Cpl Flannigan
Cpl Hodkinson

*for Corporal James C Hunter to pack his bags and disappear asap. One of those 'erk' and WRAF officer liaisons, perhaps. So, with hindsight, it is that officer that I have to thank for nudging me into what turned out to be a new career and a very different direction that changed my whole life.*

*'To simplify and shorten the story, I found myself being selected and posted to RAF Thorney Island on No.1 Air Steward Course. The first thing that came to light was that it was clearly evident that our instructors, MAQMs George Davidson and Paddy Tweedie, (there was another instructor, he had a huge, long, bushy moustache - George ..?) had to sort out what an air steward should know about the workings of the 'back end' of a Britannia! After much ado, corrections, deletions, additions, changes, etc. we were finally informed that our 'Terms of Reference' would consist of ensuring that the crew and passengers were fed and watered with the correct amount of liquids and at correct timed intervals between, along with a full knowledge of all emergency procedures. Imagine - the cream of the RAF Catering Group - we were all corporals on the first course - being sent to RAF Hereford to 'learn' to make sandwiches! Most, if not all, had had the experience of running messes and were well experienced to cope with members of the Royal Family and all the highest ranks in all three services as well as all the foreign heads of state.*

*'So, as you could understand, it was with some confusion, apprehension but great excitement that we were finally posted to our 'Operational Units' via 241 OCU at RAF Lyneham on 12 December 1966. This was originally to be for a 2½ year stint, but later extended. The first operational AQM who was given the unenviable job of getting us trained up in emergency procedures, catering, and all aspects of 'aircrew' behaviour and decorum was FS Jimmy Kane-Smith. He, incidentally, was the ALM, with Air Steward Dave Edge, in the write-off in Aden of XL638. As 216 Squadron was still operational at Lyneham, we did have the occasional visit from one of their VIP qualified Quartermasters - one John Hardy. I think this would be a good time to mention that by becoming air stewards we unwittingly lost all chances of ground promotions. If we only could have been at normal promotional trade levels I'm sure that we would have many very experienced Sgt air stewards flying today!!*

*'Although there were 14 of us on the first course, 216 Squadron only wanted two stewards. Now I had to decide ... was it a 'good move' to go to 216, or would I be better off to stick with the rest of the guys, (it was all males then), and join either 99 or 511? Anyway, lots were cast and Bob Morrison and Tony Cook were dispatched to the 'Smoothy Comet'! The rest of us were split up 50-50 and I finally found myself a member of 511 Squadron which turned out not only a lucky move but also a decision that was to change my whole life.*

*'As with the AQM instructors, the squadron AQMs didn't quite know what to do with us. Of course we were in the same situation. It was a very different set up from working in a fully equipped mess to finding*

No.171 Basic AQM Course

Back row L to R:
Sgt Lindsay
Sgt Wood
Sgt Fellows
Sgt Mayo

Front row:
Sgt Cooper
Sgt Fuller
Sgt Hunter
Sgt Payne

*yourself trying to produce a 'gourmet delight' at 21,000 feet, surrounded by ghastly plastic trays and unmanageable, very breakable, knives and forks! There we were, travelling through the sky at 250 knots in this 'aluminium tube', and we were expected to do it quickly and efficiently and look happy at the same time which, of course, we soon were able to do. It was at about this time that I thought that - at last - Hunter had made the right move to the right place at the right time but, most importantly, with the right people. Yes, I was going to enjoy my tour with this 'moving catering machine'!*

*'One of the first points I became aware of was the rivalry, first between the Comet and Britannia crews, and then between the two Britannia squadrons. This led to some trickery and scheming master plots - although , I always think that competition will bring out the best of any trade but more specially within the RAF! I would like to think that the introduction of airborne stewards improved the catering standard and the life styles of all the crew members during the exceptionally long hours that we spent in the air. But we, as a group, being very new to this type of work were bound, as any other 'targets' would be, to be the subjects of much mirth and merriment! We would have to learn to 'take it' but soon got into the swing of the lifestyle and plotted our own revenge tactics.*

*'Don't forget that we had no official training in either the art of flying or the mechanical intricacies of the technology therefore, 99% of airborne terminology was pure 'gobbledygook' to us! As a matter of fact it was to most of the new AQMs as well. Terms like superfine and brake dwell (to name but two), used on a daily basis, meant absolutely nothing to an air steward.*

*'A later story revolves around Terry Flannigan. Because young Terry was a very conscientious and efficient air steward, some of 'us' more understanding AQMs - as a little bonus - used to permit his like to 'sit, head set on' but with strict instructions not to utter a word. The flight deck crews - knowing that Terry was devouring their every word - would take full advantage of his untrained ear to this terminology and laid their dastardly plans accordingly. Hence Terry would hear 'Margarine.... Ache Twelve' as he listened on headset. Of course, the insertion of this new terminology went straight over his head . When this was fully discussed over a 'wind down' beer, everybody was very much amused. But, after a discussion between the air steward and the 'well known' AQM - perhaps revenge was on this air steward's mind - it was decided that the contents of the next 'Honkers Stew' would remain a galley secret - oh God! Just thinking about the addition to the menu of a much favoured - or shall I say flavoured! - gastropod mollusc brings back the memory of the knowledgeable smile exchanged between the air steward and AQM; a common reaction whenever the 'margarine' story was retold by the flight deck crew.*

*'A fact that most other aircrew trades didn't seem to understand was the vast amount of time that the air stewards spent on their feet! No time for half an hour shut-eye on a flight deck seat for us and on one of those awful long legs - remember, it took us over nine hours flying time from Gan to Majunga! Looking back I often wonder how any of us actually not only survived, but were expected to make up trays of sandwiches and flasks of tea for supper at what was loosely called our hotel! Perhaps the apt word was 'loosely' if we had to rely on the cuisine that the locals had prepared for us!! God! What a place! Remember how we had to operate a DDT canister before we could enter the accommodation 'cells'? And cockroaches the size of officer's hats!*

*'But we did get to visit some lovely places; Gan was my favourite rest stop although Changi and Kai-Tak had their good points as well. The Westabouts were a different kettle of fish altogether though. The air steward could really come into his own, using his imagination wandering round the supermarkets of the USAF bases. Keith Floyd had nothing on the fresh salmon and lobster salads that could be created with a little imagination - aided of course by a generous copilot distributing the goodies from the imprest.*

*'I suppose I'd better stay within the laws of QRs and not say too much of the antics that occurred - pity really - but I suppose most of the readers are married men with families now and I would like to keep it that way. One little snippet I must tell you about is the time the crew had to have a 'whip-round' to raise the 'bail-cash', or was it a bribe?, to free their captain from a cell in Gander. Strangely enough I saw and*

A tasty breakfast for someone! This galley scene may puzzle some AQMs and air stewards. Firstly it looks so immaculate - secondly, the layout may not immediately ring a bell. The reason for both is that this was a fairly new (1959) Mk2. (*Harry Liddell*)

*chatted to him at a reunion. I was tempted to mention the occasion - but common sense prevailed and a smile was sufficient to know that he remembered the incident well; one of the best kept secrets in the halls of Mystery and Imagination that is the History of the RAF Britannia's' lifestyle, never to see the light of day - I hope!! Then to see the guitar-touting DB arriving - well, say no more! That's another story! As long as the evening at 'Brit House' ended with an 'Early Breakfast Chitty', one could go to sleep happy. Although smoking in bed was soon to be banned!? And then the story of the time we had to wear name tags. Mine was 'J Hunter'. Spare a thought for young Alan Nutt!*

*'From a very personal point of view there are one or two officers that I owe a great deal to and I would like to take this opportunity to thank them. One was Squadron Leader R (Dicky) Robertson. It was he who interviewed me to ascertain what the 'Rules and Regulations' said about the qualifications that one required to remuster to become an AQM. This information was not only given fully but also accompanied by a recommendation from him, to the powers that be, that I may - if fully qualified - attend the Officer and Aircrew Selection Board at RAF Biggin Hill. That being learned, I found out that I only needed one more qualification - The RAF Education Test Part II, of which I only needed one more subject - geography. Here I come to thanking the second officer - Flt Lt Pat Hobbs. He was the captain of Flight No. 6061 on 27 June 1967. He found out that, because we were behind schedule, (Yes! U/S in Gan!), I would miss an examination that had been organised for me to take at Tengah. But Pat, being Pat, contacted the Station Education Officer in Singapore and I was permitted to take the test five hours after everyone else in the RAF! Although we had been 'on the go' for 16 hours, we landed at Tengah and I took and passed this exam. Immediately after, I completed the relevant paperwork and applied to Biggin Hill to take the aircrew examinations.*

*'The conclusion of my tale must be to tell the reader that I was then posted on to 99 Squadron, a point that I found quite strange - after all, they used to be 'the other lot'! Anyway, thoroughly enjoying the life, the job, the people until the sad ending of the Britannia in 1975. Posted first to Puma Helicopters at RAF Odiham, then concluding my service as MALM, (the youngest in the RAF?), with many thanks due to the loveliest girl to wear an AQM brevet - Pat Magill née Howard, finally at 10 Squadron back at RAF Brize Norton, where I received a medical discharge on 31 August 1978, aged only 36 years!!*

*The Britannia whispered in,*
*Did its duty quietly.*
*Made lifelong friends of crews*
*And went to sleep, 'A' category.*

The sad postscript, to this addition to the Britannia story, is that this lively contributor to 'life', Jimmy Hunter, died at a premature age.

**Tricks!**

A lot of power lay in the hands of those who, in addition to sorting out the technical side of their work, also provided 'creature comforts' - such as food and drink. Roy Castle commented on the fact that crew chief Ron King was assisting in the maintenance cum restoration of 496 - of which more concludes this book:

*'Chief Technician Ron King and I flew together on many occasions. If Ron has*

*anything to do with the old girl's restoration you'll get a first class job done because he would look after them like a mother. Ron's forthright attitude to bumbledom would open many doors. Get him to tell you about his minor altercation with US Customs and Immigration in Denver, Colorado some time! Not all our Chiefies were as obliging. I continually faulted the cracked plastic trim in the galley of one Brit in the F700 but one crew chief would drill two holes at either end of the cracks, date it in felt pen and mark it FTF (fit to fly). OK it was not structural but this galley was unsightly and unhygienic and the holes and scribbles may not have inspired confidence in some of our passengers. Anyway, even an AQM has his pride.*

*'One day I had the good fortune to carry this Chief on that very aircraft so offered him the spare AQM seat next to the deformed galley, asked him for his preferred brew, drew a crack on a paper cup and punched two holes in it and dated it FTF. Keeping two fingers over the holes I served him his NATO standard and watched that ghastly concoction dribble over his lap. The old bird got a refurbished galley but I will not be flying over for any reunions in case he may be there and recognise me! I have not met any ex-Britannia people in my 30 years in Australia ... I had to retire from air traffic due to ill health ...*

*'One day while on the console trying to steer aircraft into each other at the Melbourne air traffic operations centre I was shaken by the shoulder by my colleagues and asked to look out of the window. 'Look, Mick, there's one of your old tubs!' They had never seen a Britannia but had heard enough of my boring anecdotes about them to be able to recognise one. It was an Indonesian registered tramp freighter and a CL44, obviously on its last legs, and was not allowed to land in Australia again. But it was good to see that enormous tail taxying along the perimeter track once again.'*

**The Crew Chief theme continues**

Tom Lowe feels that the lot of our Ground Engineers has been neglected ...

*'Much has been written both in this magazine and the book, 'The Whispering Giant in Uniform', about the people who flew the Britannia and serviced the Britannia squadrons of 511 and 99, but very little has been written about the Crew Chiefs (Ground Engineers) recently, apart from, sadly, an article by the late Jimmy Hunter, extolling the virtues and expertise of the air steward, and quite rightly so. So I thought it time the crew chief deserved a mention, so here goes.*

*'Who were they? How many were there? What was precisely their work? When did they come into being?*

*'The term crew chief was adopted from the USAF. The RAF preferred the term ground engineer, the emphasis being that they were not aircrew as such. They were introduced by the RAF, firstly on the Victor, Valiant and Vulcan bomber force and shortly after that by Transport Command. Their role was to accompany the aircraft when the aircraft was going 'Off Route', that is to say the aircraft would be flying to destinations where there was no ground support.*

*'Who were these ground engineers? I'll try to name those that I knew, that supported the Britannia, forgive me if I have left anybody out for the memory is fading somewhat in my advancing years. They were all SNCOs taken from the aircraft trades:*

*Chief Technicians:*

| | |
|---|---|
| *Akehurst (Bill)* | *Dunnett (Fod)* |
| *Holton (George)* | *Felstead (Bob)* |
| *Lowe (Tom)* | *Loan (Ted)* |
| *Sharpe (Ted)* | *Blakely (George)* |
| *Brookes (Ken)* | *Jose (Bob)* |
| *King (Ron)* | *Lansdowne (Ian)* |
| *Lister (Ted)* | *Saunders (John)* |
| *Simmonds (Tim)* | *Tasker (Johnny)* |
| *Willingate (Les)* | *McKay (Black Mac)* |
| *Marley (Ben)* | *Hunt (Leigh)* |
| *Insley (John)* | *Akehurst (Bill)* |
| *Lewis* | *Morpeth (Geordie)* |
| *Hargreaves* | |

*Apologies once again to anybody I have left out - and the absence of first names. (It's not the memory really, it's the gin).*

*'All the crew chiefs cross-trained into other trades, other than their own airframe, propulsion, electrical, instrument, avionics etc. They were all highly skilled and for all this they received no extra money; flying pay and crew pay was not awarded, so why did they do it, you may ask?*

*'I think I can speak for the majori-*

*ty when I say they did it, because it was considered the top job of the ground staff and if you were lucky enough to become one, you went to practically the four corners of the world. When I said that the crew chiefs did not receive any extra pay, that is not strictly true. They all, of course, when outside of the UK received the Local Overseas Allowance, but unlike the air crew and flight stewards, the crew chiefs did not receive any flying or crew duty pay. Unlike their American brothers, the crew chief was not subjected to the amount of hours he had been on duty (crew duty time) and it was for this very reason that crew chiefs were taken wherever the aircraft went, where there was no ground support. After all you couldn't expect the flight engineers to start working on the ground after just completing, a stage say of seven hours, plus the time spent on duty prior to take off. So, on landing, that was when the crew chief came into his own.*

*'Firstly, he had to fix and rectify any defects that were not 'Fit to Fly'; to accomplish this often resulted in working many hours. He also had to replenish the fuel, LOX, water and service the toilets. So let's just spare a thought for the crew chief, called several hours prior to take off, a long flight, and we all know how difficult it is to sleep on an aircraft and then having to get the a/c serviceable and refuelled ready for the next stage; at times not even grabbing a few hours in the hotel, but sometimes not having enough time to leave the aircraft. But we all loved it, every single minute, and would not have left the job willingly.*

*'I along with the majority did some years as a crew chief before a posting on to Harriers (20 Squadron) in RAF Germany. I look back over those years and feel I was privileged to be part of the Britannia scene. People often say, 'What was it that made the Britannia so special?' I would say in a word the 'People'. The aircraft and ground engineers were really very special and that is why the Britannia Association enjoys such a strong membership. Most aviation purists would readily agree that the Britannia was a very complicated but forgiving aircraft, so the people that flew it had to be special, likewise the crew chiefs, away from base on his own with some very tough decisions to make in most cases, came through. That is why, compared with their contemporaries on the ground, they regarded themselves, dare I say it, as elitists.*

*'Most, after leaving the RAF service, secured good jobs like myself, although I did burn the midnight oil to get my licence which I took at Redhill (CAA). I had stints with Air Faisal, Invicta, Monarch and Afrek, all these companies operating the Britannia.*

*'All in all, my time involved with the Britannia lasted 19 years and I do not regret or would not change a single minute of those precious years.'*

A Kathmandu scene. Note the position of the props - and that of the sun's shadow, bottom right. Compare these with the photo to the right.
(*Richard Ling*)

**Things that go bump in the ...**

Keith Manktelow wrote to the editor of the Britannia Association magazine. He remembers a very long flight from Gan to Tengah ...

*'I feel a little guilty at writing as my attendance at the annual 'bash' is woefully poor, in fact I have only made it once. However, as a life member I still look forward to receiving 'The Whispering Giant'. Reading a recent copy, with all the wonderful articles, forced me to put pen to paper in an attempt to assist in the production of such an interesting magazine. I am truly amazed how your correspondents can remember all the names of the crew members that they had flown with, all those years ago. I got to thinking of what, if anything, had happened to me whilst serving in the Queen of the Skies.*

*'And so it was that I went to the bookshelf to retrieve my Royal Air Force log book, blow off the dust, (not that we have a lot of dust in the Isle of Man, it's just that it has been there for 22 years now) and*

*look for the names of the crew who were aiding and abetting me on one of my early flights to the Far East on which I can recall a strange occurrence. To my dismay the log book only recorded the name of the accompanying pilot and not the other crew members, but I'm sure that those involved will remember the trip. The copilot was Clive Osborne and we departed Gan, on our way to Tengah, on a dark and fairly turbulent night. The weather was such that we were doing the usual low/high profile, trying to avoid the cowl heat range and were still at FL110 dodging around the lower levels near the base of the cumulonimbus clouds.*

*'On one particular jolt, I was sure that I heard a loud noise above the sound of the auto relights and I pointed it out to my trusty engineer. We now all sat in silence for a while waiting for the noise to re-occur. Sure enough, as we got to the next bit of bouncing around, in the base of the clouds (in spite of the navigator's efforts to avoid them), the strange noise happened again. We listened some more and we heard it again and again. It seemed to get louder - or was it just imagination? After about a quarter of an hour listening to this peculiar sound, the Eng decided that he couldn't stand it any longer and that he had to go to investigate just where it was coming from.*

*'He left the flight deck and headed back into the cabin for what seemed like an age, leaving us up front wondering if the faithful 491 was just about to fall apart and drop us into the Indian Ocean. On his return he told us of his journey down into the underfloor hold via the front hatch and how he had squeezed all the way to the back of the forward hold tracking down the noise. He then declared that the loud knocking was coming from the area of the wing-box and it happened every time the aircraft received a jolt in turbulence. This naturally caused a lot of concern amongst the crew because, by now, we were nearly half way between Gan and Tengah and this weather was forecast to be similar for the rest of the route.*

*'However it fell to me to decide what to do next; did I want a pint of Tiger after landing or would I prefer a tin of Amstel at Gan? Then there was the likelihood of a plate of sausages in Gan but there would be none at Tengah, as we were staying in the Mess. It is times like that when command is so difficult! So I took the Tiger route on the basis that the weather was forecast to be marginally less turbulent going on to Tengah than it would be turning back to Gan.*

*'We pressed on listening to every bump and bang with growing concern and it seemed the longest flight I have ever had in a Britannia even though we kept on reassuring ourselves that the British made the strongest planes in the world! On reaching Tengah we recorded our findings in the Form 700, much to the disbelief of the resident engineering officer and proceeded to the mess bar for the usual ritual of trying to get the copilot to buy a beer. Having succeeded, plus several more, I decided it was time to find out what, if anything, the engineers had discovered was wrong with 491.*

*'You can probably imagine my surprise when, after several calls (because they*

The substantial wing root of the Britannia. (*David Berry*)

A Kathmandu scene. - continued. The sun is lower - and the propellers are lined up. The crew chief has been at work. (*Richard Ling*)

*were a bit unsure to begin with) that they told me we would not be going anywhere the following day because the whole fleet had been grounded temporarily whilst they established the seriousness of what they had found. It seems that where the wings are joined to the fuselage in the wingbox area there are several bolts that pass through angled pieces of meal attached to the wings and fuselage. Apparently what had happened was that, over the years of bouncing up and down in turbulence, the bolts had managed to make the round holes in the brackets into oval holes. This now meant that we had round bolts in oval holes and this was the cause of the bang or rattling sound that we heard, suitably amplified by the acoustic properties of the big fuselage.*

*'Armed with the news, the crew looked forward to several days of useful shopping and sunning ourselves at Her Majesty's expense. The pundits (in the bar of course) told us that this would be a major dockyard job to repair and we should start thinking about taking out Singapore citizenship. I was therefore quite surprised to receive an early morning call a couple of days later to be told that the aircraft was now fit to fly back to Brize Norton via Gan, Masirah, Seeb and Akrotiri with me at the helm. I was curious as to the rectification which had taken place since the 'dockyard job' had been completed in apparently record time. I managed to track down a fairly senior engineering officer prior to our leaving Tengah and made the enquiries of him. He was not too sure but promised to find out for me. True to his word he returned with a slightly puzzled look on his face and declared that the problem had been easily solved by the manufacture of a few oval shaped bolts!! However the fix would be only temporary as the plane would require some serious maintenance when it got home. As history shows we made it safely.'*

A trial with a new Land Rover using the Britannia Freight Lift Platform.

CHAPTER TWENTY NINE

# The Cod War and Operation Lucan

The story so far tells how the Britannias of 99 and 511 Squadrons were called upon to support a great variety of tasks throughout the world. One of the strangest of these occurred in 1973. Britain was in dispute with Iceland over territorial waters and the associated fishing rights. This resulted in many skirmishes between British fishing vessels and Icelandic gunboats; the Royal Navy attempted to police the area. Airborne surveillance provided vital intelligence and the maritime Nimrod aircraft were hard pressed to keep up the constant watch. This reached a point in July when it was decided that the Britannias could ease the situation by flying some of the patrols.

**Sea patrol**

Aircraft were detached to Kinloss. The normal Britannia crew was supplemented by a Nimrod captain and navigator and four observers. Flight Lieutenant Derek Oldham, then one of a new Britannia breed, a first tour copilot, remembers:

*'Both our flights took 10¼ hours and included one hour of night flying which was no mean feat at that time of year in North Scotland. We flew up to Iceland at high level, let down off the coast and flew anti-clockwise around Iceland at 1000 feet, returning to Kinloss at high level. The plan was to note any British fishing boats approaching the disputed waters and call in the Royal Navy to warn them off before they were intercepted by one of the Icelandic gunboats.'*

It was said that the results obtained were far better than expected. The task continued into August resulting in a very busy month. 2,517 hours were flown.

**Tony Bennett's 1973 memories**

*'Apart from the increase in 'rotational flights' to and from Aldergrove, other names began to appear more frequently; for instance, I acquired three Gibraltar trips within a month at the beginning of the year. One of these flights required a landing in very marginal conditions with strong gusty southerly winds, touching down halfway along the runway and coming to a halt mighty close to the end of the concrete. My memory is that there were three tyre changes before eventually taking off in equally adverse conditions.*

*'I moved into The Round House in October before going to Hong Kong. It seemed like a good idea to take the Officers' 'C' promotion exam in the spring as tasking seemed lighter, and my days away on route likely to be very low - eventually twelve in four months. So I planned the six-month self-study course into three months. And while on exams it also seemed a good idea to take the CAA Flight Navigators' Licence as exemptions were given to Royal Air Force 'B' Category transport navigators, leaving Performance 'A' and Air Law as the only exams to be taken. These were relatively easy and on production of some recent logs and charts as proof of route experience and a Medical by Doc Cassidy, I became the proud owner of a brand new Flight Navigators' Licence, which generates considerable nostalgia, every time I see it!*

*'I had to learn to live with the Concorde, which was based at Fairford. Living three miles finals wasn't exactly heaven when she was flying circuits; the light fittings shook, the windows rattled as the aircraft rolled on R/W 26. But a wonderful place to live and see such a marvellous machine. A unique experience.*

*'Having taken the Promotion Exam I felt ready for a relaxing route trip, and that is what I got. We positioned at Gan in time to operate a double shuttle from Gan to Tengah, which gave us five days in Gan.*

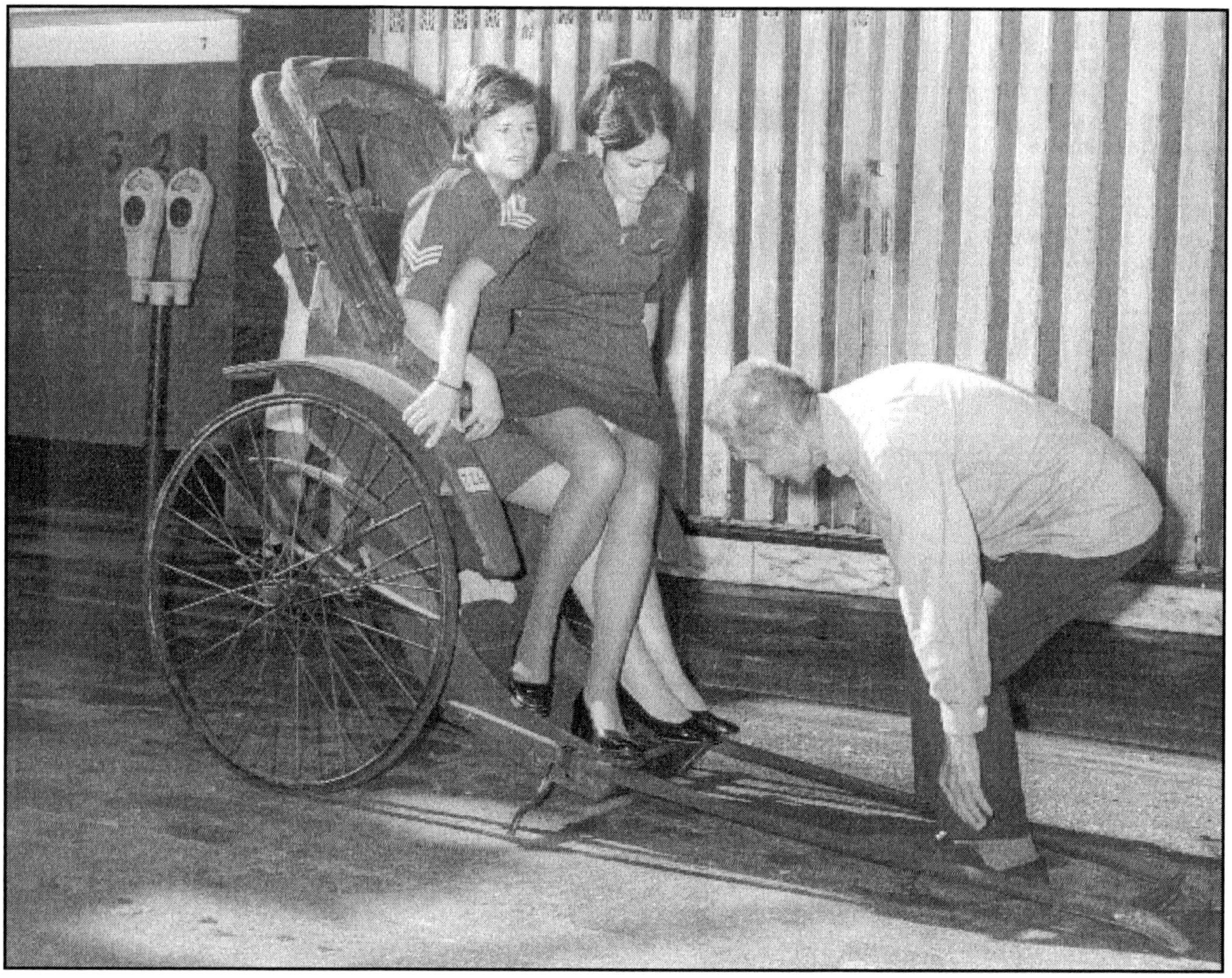

As a good looking aircraft that seemingly roamed the world, the Britannia naturally attracted publicity; add to this female crew members and you have a newspaper article. A Daily Express reporter travelled on a 'global' with a crew in 1973 to write on the life of 'the girls'. The rickshaw riders are Jan Robinson and Sheila Batchelor; the name of the driver is not known! (*Ralph Dexter*)

*What better than a lie-in, late breakfast, one hour in the morning sun. Repeat in the afternoon. Complete the Telegraph crossword after dinner. Belated thanks RC for your company and teaching me how to do the Telegraph crossword. I see that nowadays such a Maldivian sojourn would cost around £1,000, and that's before the G&Ts. With Far East slips no longer required most tasks were six days or less except for some operations. Nevertheless there were some interesting routes for the next six months, the first of which was a six-day 'slow' to Jamaica uneventful except for the torrential rain which ruined our stopover and also the last leg from Bermuda to Brize on 21 June with a diversion to Prestwick.*

*'My log book for July shows a series of flights from Germany to Decimomannu in Sardinia, (a NATO weapons training base) interrupted only by two annual air tests, in four days, both of which required recovery to Brize, asymmetric. Bad news happens in threes. Sure enough the list of those who had passed the 'C' Promotion exam appeared in the Officers' Mess and my name was not on it. Having worked diligently I found it hard to believe, but there it was, failed by five marks out of 250!*

*'At the end of August both squadrons were involved in what was one of the more unusual tasks ever undertaken, and became known as 'The Cod War'. This lead to skirmishes between seaborne forces with airborne surveillance provided by Nimrod aircraft. Some of these tasks were to be undertaken by the ubiquitous Britannias based at Kinloss, with each crew increased by a Nimrod captain and navigator. We also carried an extra Britannia navigator. The idea was to transit high level to and from Iceland letting down to patrol at 500ft, weather permitting, to track, identify, and report the movements of British and Icelandic vessels, particularly the gunboats.*

*'Fuel planning, to give the optimum time on patrol and an appropriate*

Loading to far-away places with strange sounding names ... and being paid for it
By Peggie Robinson HONGKONG Friday
Popular Pinafore ...
and Raggedy Again—35
Dorothy Ward Ltd.

The article in the Daily Express of 17th November 1973 that featured Janette Robinson and Sheila Batchelor on a Global route trip.

*position to return, was the first consideration and whilst on patrol an accurate update of position was necessary. The nature of the task gave rise for some improvisation by the two Britannia navs and we discovered that, in our case, one nav would operate as normal and the other would be a nav radar. The only 'comfortable' position to operate the CCWR was to perch on the cylindrical life jacket container. Not very satisfactory, but successful, changing roles every 1½ hours or so. On my radar watch I picked up a very strong return as we flew anti-clockwise on the north side of Iceland at a range of 120 miles. One of the strongest returns I can recall. It was large, slow moving and on our track.*

*'For the next 100 miles we speculated, and decided that it was on the surface. At 20 miles it was as strong as ever, but nothing was seen with five pairs of eyes, and a pair of maritime binoculars - until about five miles away, there it was - a huge whale lying on the surface. After that I certainly had a greater respect for the CCWR but the rest of the patrol was an anticlimax!*

*'The most rewarding of the three sorties we flew, was ironically in the worst weather. Just as we levelled off at 1500 feet after descent to commence our patrol, right beneath us through a hole in the cloud was the Icelandic Gunboat THOR in pretty rough seas. This was particularly pleasing as she had not been seen for two to three days. And then for us a remarkable week was over. Three sorties in seven days each of 10 hours 15 minutes, operating in a totally different environment. What next?*

*'Three days later we were on our way to Nairobi via Masirah carrying some units of the army on exercise. It was pleasant to have a night stop there with a sojourn under the Thorn Tree, particularly for those involved in the Oil Lift. This was before my time regrettably. On my last visit to Nairobi in 1988, on the VC10, the Thorn Tree with a concrete patio and plastic covered tables no longer reflected the ambience of those bygone days.*

**From the Daily Express ...**

**Loading to far-away places with strange sounding names ... and being paid for it**
By Peggie Robinson HONGKONG Friday

*'Bring your bedroom slippers, said the man from the Ministry. I gave him an old-fashioned look. Hurriedly he explained that they were because my feet would swell in the aircraft. In the nicest way he was trying to say that it would be 'all go' joining 22-year-old Janette Robinson on a glamour trip around the world.*

*'Jan has just become the RAF equivalent of an airhostess - a loadmaster - and would be paid £34 a week for the 'chore'. She was up before dawn preparing for the flight called Polaris at Brize Norton, Oxfordshire. With her was Sheila Batchelor, also age 22, making her last 'global' before leaving to get married.*

*'First there was all the baggage to be checked. She is also responsible for ordering all the food needed on the trip, for checking the trim of the aircraft by stowing everything on board. And, having been dumped in the sea in a dinghy and been through a survival course in the mountains, she knows just what to do if the aircraft has to ditch.*

*'The captain, tall, rangy Flt Lt Bill Lowe, 32, and his crew climb aboard and we are off for a quick flip to RAF Scampton in Lincolnshire to pick up a cargo of V-bomber crews of 44 Squadron off on an exercise. Before Land's End is behind us,*

*Jan and Sheila are handing out snacks to their charges. Soon we run into a headwind that is cutting our speed by 100 miles per hour. We are going to be late getting into Gander, Newfoundland. We push our watches back by three and half hours as we land at Gander. A quick shower and the girls change into pretty dresses. All the crew set off together to see the town where beer is 25p a glass and the chips are called 'Wedges'.*

*'Back into the slim-fitting blue dresses the RAF provides for Loadmasters, Sheila and Jan shepherd us aboard for another flight, this time to California. It is going to be a long day. When we touch down at Sacramento, in California, we are eight hours behind England. The hotel is good. A night out follows, then up at 7.30 to take off for the millionaires' paradise, Honolulu. Put back watches by two more hours and we sweep down on the island paradise. Honolulu is just what we expect after following TV's Hawaiian Eye series - big, brash and expensive; but enjoyable all the same.*

*'We take off for Wake Island, a tiny horseshoe-shaped coral atoll in the middle of the Pacific. On the way, the copilot announces via loud hailer: 'We are crossing the International Dateline. It is now tomorrow.' I can only hope that I don't lose a day's pay over this dateline business. Just minutes among the dazzling white coral, then off to Guam, a much bigger island. We are now ten hours behind England. Most confusing. We are also feeling tired. A swim in the hotel pool helps. But all the time changing seems to be catching up on me.*

*'Hot sunshine as we take off for Darwin on the northern tip of Australia. Down into the tropical heat of Darwin and we say farewell to our V-bomber friends. There are coconut palms and mango trees round the hotel where the crew are to spend the full day off from flying which regulations specify. We have flown 12,692 miles. Jan and Sheila pull on swimming suits and plunge into the swimming pool to escape from the heat. The rest of the crew follows them.*

*'Now on to Brunei, a little Sultanate on the top of what used to be Borneo. We are told that 90 Gurkha soldiers are waiting to be picked up. There is consternation when they turn out to be men of the Royal Malayan Regiment. For ham sandwiches have been ordered for them - and as Muslims they do not eat ham. Jan and Sheila have to rush around finding other food for them.*

*'Rickshaws are gliding through the streets in pleasant sunshine when we touched down in Hongkong. 'It is fabulous,' says Jan. And Sheila, the veteran globe-circler, agrees. We are now well over half way round the world - with thousands of exciting miles still to be savoured. Lovely life these girls lead. Come to think of it, mine's very rosy at the moment.'*

**Concorde aid**

1973 started with some style for a 511 crew under the command of Flight Lieutenant Bud Abbott with a special flight to Johannesburg in support of Concorde hot weather trials. The aircraft was XM496 which was to become an historic Britannia, being the last one to fly. With its preservation at Kemble, which is covered later, there has been research into its history. Strangely, the only momentous flight recorded for it is this Concorde support.

**Tutankhamen returns**

511 also went to Cairo in April to return the Tutankhamen treasures.

**Log book reflections**

Dave Court-Smith's reminiscences from the 1973 pages of his log book give a flavour of squadron life of the time:

*'Early in the year I was rostered for a couple of runs down to Decimomannu in Southern Sardinia. This schedule positioned at Wildenrath for a night stop, then went down to Deci and back to Wildenrath the next day, recovering to the UK in the evening. The object of the flight was to give HQ staff in Germany the chance of a quick visit to the detachment of fighters at the newly commissioned NATO weapons practice camp and to change over air and ground crews. Arriving at Deci was quite a cosmopolitan business with Italians controlling the middle airspace, Germans the radar and Brits the visual traffic.*

*'Several flypasts at various Open Days took place during the summer, one of the more unusual being at Sywell (Northants). The occasion was Aviation Womens' Day (or some such title) and as we flew around the display area our*

A flypast at the Rolls Royce Families' Day at Filton, September 1974. The nose down attitude indicates that 'The Whispering Giant' act was being performed. Whilst the Britannia was famed for its quietness under normal operation, the effect used to be heightened for air show audiences by diving on to the airfield at the maximum normal operating speed (258 knots) and then pulling the power off as the aircraft sailed past the crowd. (*Rolls Royce plc, Bristol*)

*loadmistress gave a little pep-talk about women in the RAF which was patched through the VHF radio into the display's loudspeaker system.*

*'Units of the British Army, particularly infantrymen and engineers, obtained valuable military training and provided much needed practical assistance whilst on exercise in various Commonwealth countries. In April we flew soldiers out to Sharjah, in what was then the Trucial Oman, for desert training and took some resident troops over to Nairobi. Later in the year I was involved in flights between UK and Kingston when British and Jamaican soldiers enjoyed exchange visits.'*

**Surprised airman**

*'Exercise Shabaz in May involved the countries of CENTO so the CENTO Deputies, headed by Air Chief Marshal Sir Peter le Cheminant, flew around the area in a Britannia. Of interest to the military historians in the party was the fact that the airways system in that part of the world follows closely the route taken by Alexander the Great on his Asian conquests. From Ankara we went to Diyabakir where a disastrous piece of Turkish Air Force marshalling provoked the Turkish General on board to rush from the aircraft and strike the hapless airman to the ground; our arrivals at Teheran and Karachi were less sensational.*

*'A very different venture was the annual flight over the North Geographic Pole, when staff and students from the Specialist Navigator's Course at the RAF College of Air Warfare, plus a number of research scientists and company representatives, filled the aircraft with the latest 'gizmos' and trundled off to spend the night (rather a misnomer as the sun doesn't set up there in mid-summer) at Thule, Greenland. The following day saw us heading up to 90 North and eventually the master Inertial Navigation System in the cabin assured us we were on top of the world; most of the other instruments agreed to differ! As the aircraft's own compasses were useless at high latitudes, we had a Sperry CL11 low drift gyro fixed up to feed into the Ground Position Indicator and employed the gyro-grid system of navigation. Once I got used to the rather odd readings on the compass, I found it worked quite well. Incidentally, the flight from Thule to Brize Norton was 10 hours 40 minutes, the longest that I ever did in a Britannia.*

*'In September a party of MPs from NATO countries went on a fact finding tour around Northern Europe and Scandinavia during the autumn exercises. At one Norwegian base we taxied for over five minutes through a forest before reaching*

*'... filled the aircraft with the latest 'gizmos' ...'*

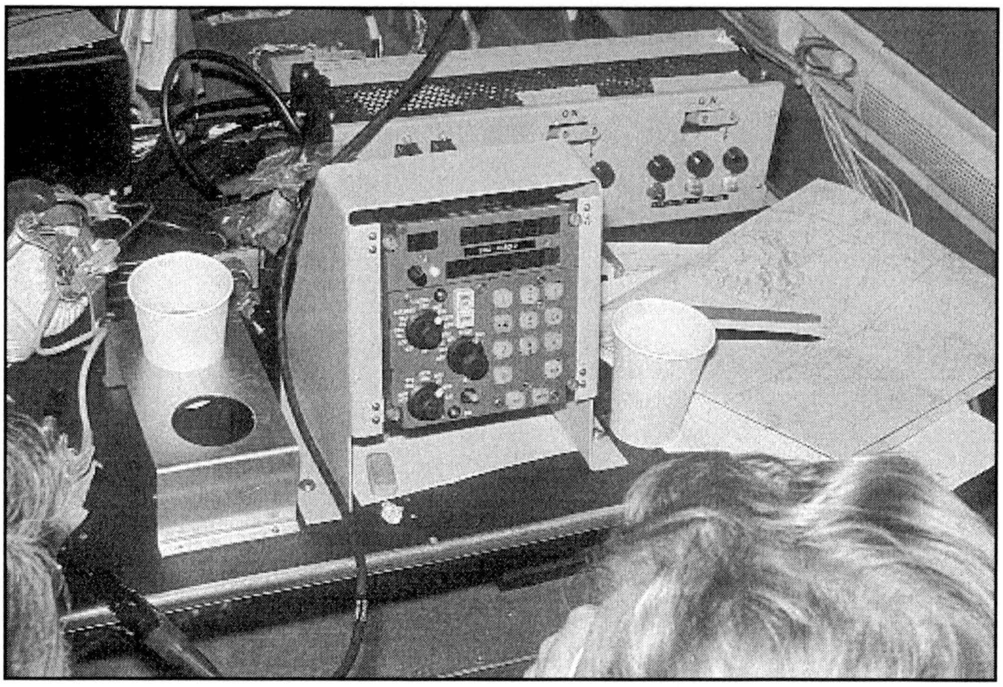

*the extremely well hidden command bunker. 1973 was nicely rounded off for me with another Hong Kong detachment.'*

**10,000 hours**

Many RAF aircrew will have participated in this milestone ceremony - or indeed were the centre of it. Wing Commander Frank Appleyard, the then CO of 99 Squadron, reveals some subterfuge behind one of these ...

'*Drew Shaw was my Pilot Leader on 99 Sqn, guarding the 'plum trip book' most zealously - no one, but no one was permitted to allocate 'plums' but himself. In the Spring of 1973 he confided that the year was to be a momentous one for the Shaw family; he and Ina would, celebrate their Silver Wedding Anniversary, he would have been a Flt Lt for 25 years and he would achieve his 10,000 hours. As I had no control of the first two achievements I resolved to be in at the last event. A careful check of his log book indicated that June would see*

Champagne for 10,000 hours - Wing Commander Frank Appleyard, an unnamed Army major and Flight Lieutenant Drew Shaw.

*his 10,000 hours target met. During the May tasking for June he had elected to pick up a slow Hong Kong PCF (more F than P as it turned out). This suited my purpose and the prospect of two weeks away with diverse night stops was even more attractive. We departed on 31 May, routing via Luqa for Akrotiri where we picked up 491 for the rest of the trip. I had established that, unless other forces were brought to bear, he would achieve the requisite hours on arrival at Tengah, inbound from Kai Tak. As we would be staying at a plush hotel in Orchard Road I had no wish to cough up for an expensive bottle of Champagne (£15) in Singapore and I was also aware that Drew, as a good Scot, was most unlikely to treat the crew, I had already contacted the Stn Cdr at Gan, an old chum, to lay on the silver tray plus photographer for our run inbound.*

*'Prior to departure from Brize I had alerted the Eng, name escapes me, not to query the lapse times as I wished to time the arrival at Gan with the 10,000 hours. I duly slashed 10 mins off the Akrotiri to Masirah leg with a modest observation from Captain Shaw, but after a night stop and filling him with malt in the Mess, he was content. Further adjustments were made on the run to Gan and Tengah accompanied by more grunts from the left hand seat; the Eng however confirmed my timings. Potential disaster appeared at Tengah as we were re-routed via Brunei inbound and outbound to Kai Tak. I managed to persuade Drew that the weather was such that a low level high speed cruise was in order - to this day I do not know how he bought it! With the swiftest passage to Hong Kong, plus night stop and hurried return to Tengah again via Brunei, Drew announced on arrival. 'Well, Boss, despite you, I've done it!' I had to disabuse him saying I am sorry Drew but you are five minutes short of the target - again verified by the Eng. After a further night stop in Singapore, with a very disenchanted captain, we left Tengah the next morning and as soon as we were airborne the entire crew congratulated 'himself'. On approaching Gan, and taking the opportunity when Drew had retired aft, I enquired if all the necessary arrangements were in place. I was assured that they were, in addition they had a VIP to greet Drew. An Army Major who had spent some 18 months, on his own living in a tent on the island, surveying it for a potential military potential as described in 'The Whispering Giant in Uniform'. On arrival, a Mess waiter with silver tray complete with bubbly, plus Major and photographer were there to greet us as the accompanying picture shows. A further night stop completed, my participation in the exercise was over and normal lapse times applied. I suspect that 491 is at least one hour short of its F700 record.*

*'I am pleased to report that Drew was subsequently promoted to Squadron Leader (Spec Aircrew - no mean feat).'*

**Get out of that!**

Tony Bennett has reason to remember 1973. He went back to his collection of 'more interesting' navigation logs ...

*'Having opened the folder marked 'Ones to Keep' and blown the dust away, I am looking at a log and chart dated 21 June 1973. Why does this warrant a place in the archives? Let me try and remember.*

*'Sqn Ldr Pete Hay and his crew had operated slow to Kingston, Jamaica via Gander to pick up an inbound exercise aircraft and slip at Bermuda - in turn picking up XM518 on the slip, 48 hours later. It was in this 48 hours that the crew, which included Ron Hendrick, John Browne and Jimmy Hunter, took the name of 'Hay's Angels'. We had hired mopeds and drove, in loose formation, across the beautiful island, discovering some of its many delights. We were scheduled to depart Bermuda at 1500 GMT. On arrival from Kingston, 518 was re-roled to operate as Ascot 6423 direct to Brize Norton with a full passenger load. Computer winds were not available at flight planning, so the time taken for the re-role was well spent in dusting off and using the navigator's template - a rare event. The total fuel required was 66,000lbs with minimum diversion fuel - Britannia operators will recall that, at certain SGs, 66,000 was full tanks! The forecasts for the UK airfields were good with a large high pressure system sitting over northern Europe. We eventually took off from Bermuda at 1730 GMT. The delay in departure was to be crucial, as subsequent events will show.*

*'The first four hours of the flight were uneventful. But we had slowly been losing time for no obvious reason and the fuel was running steadily below the 'Howgozit' line. The hourly cheeks at 2200,*

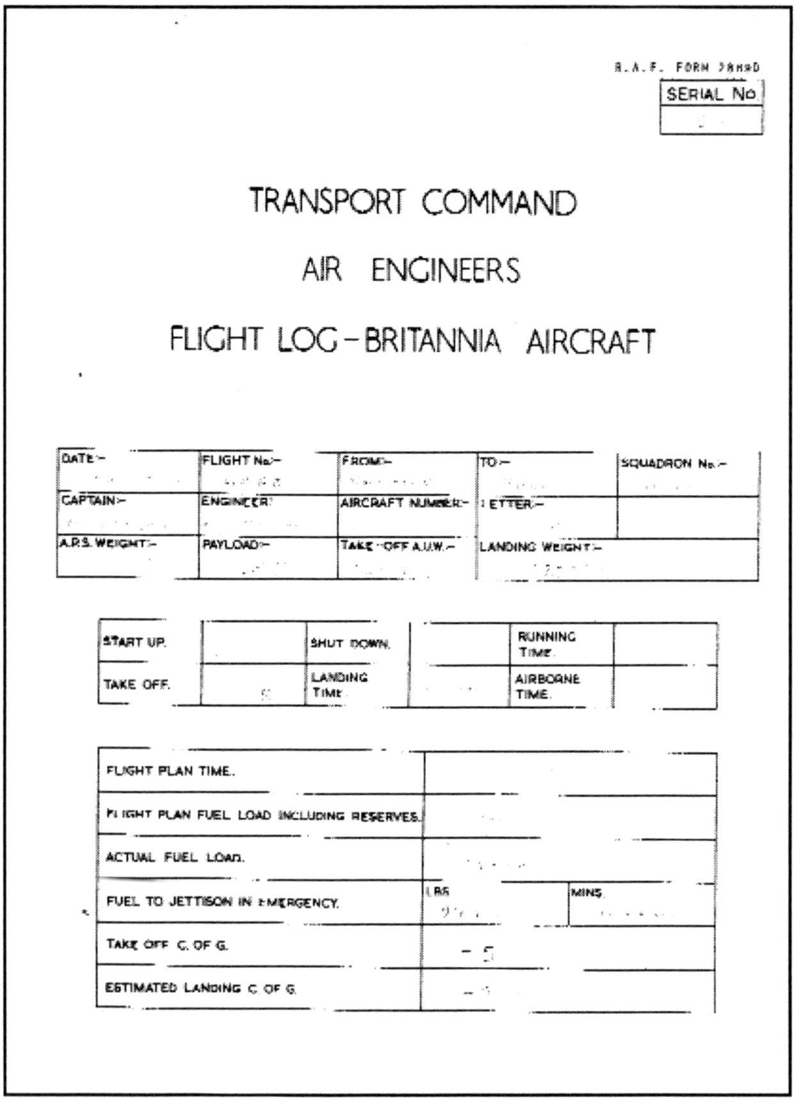
R.A.F. FORM [illegible]

SERIAL No

TRANSPORT COMMAND

AIR ENGINEERS

FLIGHT LOG - BRITANNIA AIRCRAFT

| | | | | |
|---|---|---|---|---|
| DATE:- | FLIGHT No:- | FROM:- | TO:- | SQUADRON No.:- |
| CAPTAIN:- | ENGINEER: | AIRCRAFT NUMBER:- | LETTER:- | |
| A.P.S. WEIGHT:- | PAYLOAD:- | TAKE-OFF A.U.W.:- | LANDING WEIGHT:- | |

| | | | | | |
|---|---|---|---|---|---|
| START UP. | | SHUT DOWN. | | RUNNING TIME. | |
| TAKE OFF. | | LANDING TIME. | | AIRBORNE TIME. | |

| | | | | |
|---|---|---|---|---|
| FLIGHT PLAN TIME. | | | | |
| FLIGHT PLAN FUEL LOAD INCLUDING RESERVES. | | | | |
| ACTUAL FUEL LOAD. | | | | |
| FUEL TO JETTISON IN EMERGENCY. | LBS | | MINS. | |
| TAKE OFF C. OF G. | | | | |
| ESTIMATED LANDING C. OF G. | | | | |

A vital document for the 'fuel critical' flight, described by Tony Bennett, would have been the Engineer's Log. Numerous readings were recorded once per hour. The majority of engineers took great pride in the neatness and accuracy of this log.

*just after sunset, showed that the expected tail wind had not materialised - indeed there was a headwind! We were now 30 minutes late on ETA Brize with the associated fuel used - and, to boot, the Green Satin now started to misbehave. We passed critical point, Bermuda/Brize at 2242 and at 2300 there was moderate clear air turbulence as the wind began to change. Here comes the tail wind - better late than never! We passed the point of no return Bermuda at 2312 and noted that the Brize forecast was OK, as indeed were most of the UK airfields. They had been good for the past six hours even if the temperatures had been slowly dropping towards the dew points - and there wasn't a lot of surface wind to talk about ...*

*'Then it started to happen. With about 900 miles to run and an ETA at Brize of 0300, the UK airfields started to go out in fog, one by one, as the temperatures fell to the dew point. At 0030 the Brize forecast was poor and Prestwick was nominated as diversion. Even the airfields in northern France were going into fog. At this stage we climbed to flight level 250. It was apparent that we didn't have enough fuel to route to Brize and then divert to Prestwick and when the 0100 Brize actual was received with cloud as 8/100 feet, the decision was made to divert to Prestwick, which, along with Glasgow, was OK.*

*'We discussed climbing towards the top of the flight envelope, considered closing one engine down (three engine stabilising height was FL240) and a few other things, not least the route to avoid Irish airspace as we did not have diplomatic clearance for overflight. Prestwick began deteriorating - Glasgow was also going out - and we were running short of go juice with nowhere else available. After planning all we could and being given priority by radar units to route Brecon to Wallasey to Pole Hill, we were cleared for descent at 0332 for a straight-in radar on runway 31 with a break-off height of 580 feet. Prestwick was now: 'Wind calm, 2,000 yards visibility, temperature +9' - adrenalin rising!*

*'At 0344, the runway visual range for 31 was 1100 metres and for runway 13 'poor'. The captain's brief was to continue the approach to 31, if we have to overshoot, to fly a teardrop for runway 13 and if that was unsuccessful we would land off our last approach on 31.*

*'The radar approach seemed interminably long and in the last few seconds I stood up to add my eyes to those that were searching for the runway lights. Suddenly there were the lights and at 0358 we landed at Prestwick, wind calm, RVIZ less than 1,000 metres, fuel remaining 4,000lbs.*

*'On the landing run, in reverse thrust, all four LP lights were flashing ... the fates were good to Hay's Angels that night!'*

**A conflict of opinion**

In spite of the sophistication now of the control of strategic transport operations, there was still a respect for the decisions and actions of the captain and his crew - they being the people 'on the spot'. But there were occasions when questions were asked. Tony Bennett continues with his memories which include one such challenge:

*'As trips go it was to be a leisurely two weeks. Position at Brunei to operate an empty aircraft to Sydney to pick up 75 Gurkhas who had been on exercise in Australia; return to Brunei, where we would slip and await to operate the next exercise aircraft to Hong Kong, 48 hours later, before recovering to UK.*

*'Flight planning the task at Brize Norton beforehand the captain, Flt Lt Stan Ford, and I realised that the taskers in their wisdom had planned the aircraft to operate Brunei to Sydney direct. The answer to our query was that the third edition of the Sector Fuel Payload Tables showed that, in October, a Britannia could operate from Changi to Edinburgh, a distance of 3150nms, with a 70% fuel load of 64000lbs in 10 hours 15 minutes, with a Long Range Cruise. So, therefore, it could operate Brunei to Sydney - also a distance of 3150nms. We pointed out that Long Range Cruise would be impractical if we were to encounter any cloud or precipitation in the early part of the flight and that we would not have enough fuel to carry out a stepped climb. There were other considerations, such as lack of Customs Health or Immigration facilities at the listed diversion Richmond, which was not a designated Port of Entry. We suggested that it would be preferable, indeed advisable, to flag Darwin which would only add one hour to the total time. This was rejected. Our parting shot was a request that, with a full seat fit, the payload not be offered to Changi.*

*'So, after an uneventful few days we found ourselves booking into Ang's Hotel to await our aircraft. For some reason communications with Brunei were, shall we say, limited and the old maxim 'No news is good news' made us feel a little uneasy when after 48 hours we were still unaware of our bird's location, and signals we sent were unanswered. (It later transpired that our aircraft was mega sick in Akrotiri, so we were in fact waiting for the next one in the slip).*

*'Playing things very much by ear, the captain and I were having a leisurely breakfast on the fourth day, after a lengthy discussion the previous evening with a Hercules crew on the relative merits of San Miguel and the local beer. The hotel receptionist came to our table and advised us that our crew transport was outside. Can he be serious? Out of the blue, no signals?*

*'Rounding up the crew, packing the bags, paying the bill etc took us about an hour, and we set off hotfoot for the airport. On arrival we were amazed to see 54 New Zealand indulgees put on by movements at Changi. This was embarrassing if for no other reason than we hadn't catered for them! The fuel we had booked for Ascot 6405 was full tanks and XM491 had topped out at 66000lbs when we arrived. Off to Met. First problem, no forecast available for Sydney. Second problem, no forecasts available for diversions. Third problem, 5/8th AC/AS 14000-18000 feet for the first three hours, right in the icing range. The flight plan fuel, including diversion fuel for Brisbane (Port of Entry) was 69000lbs. At this point, the decision was made to flag Darwin. The fuel for Darwin was 30000lbs, which would put us 4000lbs overweight for landing. Rather than attempt to de-fuel this was accepted.*

*'So we eventually took off at 1630 local time on 11 October 1973, glad to be airborne. Sure enough, the forecast cloud was there and we levelled off at 13500 feet to remain clear of the cloud. The rest of the leg was uneventful, and the extra fuel burnt at 13500 feet put us just over max landing weight. For reasons I cannot recall we spent two hours on the ground at Darwin, eventually getting airborne at 2300 local. The flight passed quietly during the night, not a lot happening in the GAFFA. We were rudely surprised by a call from air traffic with about two hours to go, and approaching PNR, to be given the Sydney forecast and told that due to severe and extreme weather in New South Wales our diversions were Melbourne and Brisbane.*

*'It was at this point that we were thankful to say the least that we were not on a direct flight from Brunei, running low on fuel and scratching for somewhere to go. We eventually landed at 0700 local at Sydney with 4/8ths at 600 feet, visibility 3000yds in heavy rain. It rained continuously for the 24 hours we were in Sydney, and apart from getting wet in King's Cross, I had to make do with the view of the Harbour Bridge and the Opera House from my window in the Gazebo Hotel, a view I was not to see again for 27 years.*

*'The return to Brunei was uneventful, and we then had three days to wait to operate the next aircraft to Hong Kong. What had been an enjoyable trip to date*

*then turned sour with some unpleasant signals from Command winging their way to Brunei questioning the professional integrity of the crew in operating from Brunei to Sydney. Suffice to say these signals were somewhat aggressive one ending 'Pray, what is the problem?' We were told that on return to UK the captain was to present himself to Command and that my logs and charts for the leg were to be submitted for analysis. The three days in Brunei were not the most pleasant that I have spent on route, a considerable amount of time spent responding to the signals and writing a report on the flight. The captain was drained, and it showed.*

*'I remember arriving back at Brize and returning to the Squadron to be met by the Flight Commander with the news that the captain was to phone Command immediately. The first few minutes were spent with the phone at arm's length as the vitriol of the signal traffic was continued. In one of the pauses the captain asked if the caller would like to hear part of the report over the phone prior to its submission. Thirty minutes later we emerged from behind closed doors and the incident was over. My logs and charts were no longer required, and were placed in a folder as 'one to keep', and remained there for 22 years until I rediscovered them recently!*

*'Whatever caused the wrath of Command is now part of history. Turning the page in my logbook I see that within four weeks I was with Keith Manktelow in Karachi for two weeks as part of the UN relief operation - but that's another story!'*

Flight Lieutenant Guy Eddy remembers that there was considerable anxiety amongst the refugees about flying in a military aircraft: '*... so the United Nations logo was painted on the side in an effort to reassure them. Because there was a backlog of refugees at the Karachi end, we were cleared to put small children two to a seat. On 12th November we had POB (People On Board) figure of 150.'* (*Guy Eddy*)

**Lucan exchange**

October brought the start of a Britannia involvement in the sad business of moving people as a result of war and political and religious difference. East Pakistan had fought for its independence from West Pakistan for a number of years and now, with it established as Bangladesh, there were 160,000 POWs and refugees in the 'wrong' country. Thousands of Bengalis in Pakistan wanted to be in Bangladesh. Equally non-Bengalis in Bangladesh felt they should be in Pakistan. The UK had agreed to assist in the UN repatriation scheme and Operation Lucan was launched. Four crews and two aircraft were established at Karachi to fly two round trips per day to Dacca. Later the collection point was Chittagong. Some of passengers were in an appaling state and many crew members were badly affected by their plight. The detachment ceased in February 1974 and in its time it moved over 16,000 people from Pakistan to Bangladesh and nearly 14,000 in the opposite direction.

**Struck down**

Norman Rose also remembers the perils for the crews:

*'Few of us escaped 'Karachi Gut' The worst case was my poor old Nav, Pete Wrighton. On one of our trips to Dacca he complained of feeling unwell and he just got worse and worse. He stuck it till we got on the final approach but then he passed out. During the turnround we did what we could for him and he pleaded with us not to take him to hospital in Dacca. I must say the thought filled us with dread too. We threw the book out of the window and decided to get him back to the hospital at Karachi. Poor Pete drifted in and out of consciousness and was very ill indeed.*

*'Once airborne, Pete Magill, the Co, shot back to the nav's position and my flight engineer, Tug Wilson moved over to the copilot's seat. We had a rough ride with India throwing up its most active Cbs at us. Pete just made it but he was dangerously dehydrated and we lost him for quite a while.'*

**The smell**

*'It amazed us flight deck crews on Operation 'Lucan' how our long suffering ALMs and stewards stuck it down the back. The conditions were absolutely appaling.*

Norman Rose amongst his passengers. (*Norman Rose*)

*The fuselage bulged with more passengers than seats and some of the poor creatures had never seen an aeroplane before, let alone sit inside one in rough weather. Most were terrified; no one could speak English. They were sick all over the floor and seats and went to the toilet wherever they happened to be. The smell was indescribable. The back was hosed down and disinfected after each flight but it never got rid of the stench.'*

**Kiss of life**

*'Even in those foul conditions our cabin crew managed a little humour. Coming out of Dacca one day with a particularly unwashed looking lot down the back, Sgt Barry Young and Cpl Barry Penny beat urgently on the flight deck door (it was always kept firmly shut) and announced that an 80 year old crone needed mouth to mouth resuscitation. Quick as a flash Tug Wilson declared we had an emergency on the flight deck. Only the grin on Sgt Young's face gave the game away - but, on reflection, the image put us off our coffee which came up shortly after!!'*

**Tony Bennett has Lucan memories**

*'Our crew, led by Captain Manktelow, was to position Karachi from Brize to operate the second phase to Dacca. The aircraft due to take us and a 511 crew went unserviceable before we could board and remained so until departure was rescheduled for the following day. It seemed a*

'Lucan' passengers prepare to board. A lucky few take advantage of the shade from the tailplane! (*Guy Eddy*)

Ghastly Operation Lucan - but humour can shine through in the saddest of situations. (*John Grimwood*)

*good excuse for a delay party at The Round House. At this we agreed arrangements for the transport the following day which was that we would be dropped outside 'The Crown' in Lechlade and picked up by one of our compatriots of the other crew who also lived in Lechlade. It soon became obvious that something had gone wrong, confirmed by a phone call that our lift had left his home. The nearest taxi was busy and we calculated that time was rapidly running out to meet the check in time. We even tried to hitch hike from outside the pub. Then in an extraordinary gesture the landlord of 'The Crown' closed the pub and drove us to Brize in time for departure. Saved a few red faces.*

*'On arrival Karachi accommodation was in the Speedbird Hotel Annex, like a motel with chalet rooms around a courtyard. Across what seemed to resemble the Trans Karachi racing circuit was the hotel and restaurant but little else I can recall apart from the swimming pool. One thing rapidly became clear - there was no beer! . No panic, the duty frees were on their way, but, since the start of Lucan, temporarily held in Islamabad by the Customs. Meanwhile limited beer was available in the restaurant at an exorbitant price.*

*'By the time we had finished our first sortie, a couple of beers were definitely needed but not available. Tension was mounting and signals sent to Brize requesting that F1t Lt Tom Caxton* (* An 'In' joke of the time - 'Tom Caxton' was a popular home brew beer kit of that era!) *be detached to Karachi ASAP. The first sortie to Dacca went well the route taking us parallel to the Himalayas and about 300 miles south of them. Little traffic, and not a lot happening. Eventually reaching Dacca we landed avoiding the holes in the runway caused by bombing. There were a lot of military around the pan one of whom bore a close resemblance both in size and uniform to Idi Amin, and carried a big stick. Out of the brush surrounding the apron lots of children*

Three photographs that convey Operation Lucan's sadness - people being shifted because of differences in religion and politics.

*appeared running to the rear steps fighting for the clear plastic aircraft rubbish bags as they were off-loaded and ripping them apart foraging for food. The Amin figure seemed to enjoy beating them off with his stick. To file a Flight Plan, obtain weather, visit Air Traffic, discuss departures etc we had to negotiate crowds around the Terminal, carrying the appropriate pieces of paper to different floors, each being rubber stamped for the next bureaucratic process. Then we had to renegotiate the open stairs avoiding the discarded betel nuts. This was as nothing to what was to come starting with the Take Off Performance, avoiding the holes in the damaged runway as the aircraft increased speed in the roll.*

*'When we arrived back at the aircraft, the passengers were queuing to board under the supervision of the loadmasters and officials of the Red Cross. Poverty stricken, virtually without possessions, bewildered but fed and watered by the Red Cross for the five hour journey, which was probably the first meal of substance for several days. At times there were two children to a seat giving us about 140 passengers on 110 seats. The food and drink passed straight through and caused terrible problems. Most did not speak English, and those who did were co-opted by the loadmasters as 'bog wallahs' in an attempt to control the use of toilets. Conditions deteriorated as time passed, vomiting and going involuntarily to the toilet wherever they were. The smell was appaling. I left the flight deck once, spoke with a few passengers, but had to retreat to the silence of the flight deck and contemplate life.*

*'If ever a beer was needed it was on return to Karachi, but Tom Caxton had still not arrived and negotiations with Islamabad were still taking place. So it was a bottle in the restaurant to accompany the curry in the evening. The menu was varied mainly in the type of curry. The difficulty in choosing was helped by the letters and numbers and A 49 seemed like a good one with a name something like Murgh Palach - can't remember everything after 30 years!. Another beer whilst waiting. When the food eventually arrived the plates were cold and the rice only warm. Our intrepid captain summoned the head waiter and complained mainly in gestures that it needed to be hotter. Whilst waiting we became aware of faces appearing around various corners looking in amazement and anticipation. The food arrived and we started to eat. Two mouthfuls and it was agony and after a drink of beer we were incapacitated much to the hilarity of the staff. Should you ever have an A 49 be careful of using the gesture for hot and look out for secondaries!*

*'After about a week the duty free*

From the Norman Rose photo album: *'Dacca Dec 73. United Nations High Commission for Refugees airlift. Rear: Cpl Penny, M Eng Tug Wilson. Middle: Sgt Barry Young, Flt Lt Wrighton, Cpl Medic. Front: Flt Lt Tomlins, C/T Murphy, Sqn Ldr Norman Rose. Extreme right Flt Lt Pete Magill.'* (*Norman Rose*)

*finally arrived from Islamabad, some of it was believed to have evaporated in transit. Flt Lt Caxton had also arrived and joined the detachment just in time for a party given by the detachment at which we entertained some British Airways crew, who had a nightstop, and Donaldson who were also involved in the task. Now we had a surplus of duty free, several weeks' supply and about a week before we left for home. The flying itself was fairly straightforward and became routine except for some questionable Air Traffic Control in the Dacca area which involved Calcutta particularly when we were the first aircraft to extend the evacuation via Chittagong. The round trip was about nine hours.*

*'After the first phase of the task, the aircraft were changed over in a sorry state back to UK. Latterly the aircraft were recovered empty, infested with cockroaches and other undesirable creatures. We flew seven round trips in twelve days and were recovered to Brize on 5th December in need of several good scrub downs and some clean clothes.*

*'I called at the Crown in Lechlade a few days later to thank the Landlord for rescuing us some two weeks earlier. We gave him some whisky and cigarettes, also a copy of the Britannia print, for which he was most pleased. Not quite the end of 1973 - after Christmas I joined John Caskie and the rest of his crew on 27th December for the annual air test on 517. Regrettably this was cut short due to a double prop malfunction (it says in my log book without any further details) and we returned to Brize. I then see we re-tested it again on 30th and that while we were Duty Crew for good measure we air tested 635.'*

**Final Lucan thought**

Ex-Britannia people remember many of the flights they completed during their time on the aircraft. Those who were engaged on Operation 'Lucan' would prefer to forget that unhappy interlude.

**MALM 'Ben' Bendelow**

Aircrew are recruited from many 'walks of life'. Many of this era's loadmasters, because of the way they were recruited, had varied pasts. MALM 'Ben' Bendelow was one such. Sadly, he died in April 1973 whilst still serving on 99 Squadron. An obituary appeared in the Brize Norton station magazine:

*'MALM 'Ben' Bendelow died in Halton Hospital on 4 April 1973 after two months of illness. He was buried with full military honours at Black Bourton Churchyard after a funeral service in the Station Church. A fly past by a No.99 Squadron Britannia took place during the committal service.*

*'Ben had a long and active service career starting with the Merchant Navy during World War II. The ship in which he served was torpedoed and Ben was captured and became a POW. He managed to escape twice but on each occasion was recaptured. After repatriation at the end of the war Ben enlisted in the RAF as a Physical Training Instructor and served as a Staff Instructor at the School of Physical Training. Later he qualified as a PJI and*

The queue of refugees boarding the aircraft. (*Norman Rose*)

A happier 'Lucan' photo.

*served on the Staff of No.1 PTS. Ben remustered, in 1957, to the GD Branch and served as a squadron adjutant in Germany during which time he organised holiday flights to the UK and back for Servicemen and their families. He was so successful that PSI took over the organisation.*

*'Ben later qualified as an AQM and served in Aden as a local examiner on the Argosy aircraft. On his return to the UK he served with No.242 OCU at Thorney Island. On completion of his Argosy tour he was posted to No.99 Squadron and remained with us until his untimely death.'*

*'Plans had been made by Ben to leave the Service and start an even more demanding role as a 'white fish' fisherman. He had paid his deposit on a trawler fishing boat and the keel should have been laid in May. It shows the strength of Ben's character that he should tackle such an arduous job so late in life when most of us would be content to put our feet up. He had completed his pre-release course, a coxswain's course at Mountbatten, days before being taken ill,*

*'Ben was a true character, kind, friendly, helpful and knowledgeable, a 'father' to many of the younger squadron members, full of good advice to those who asked for it. The sympathies and condolences of all squadron members go out to his widow and children in their time of bereavement.'*

**Mombasa remembered**

At the close of 1971 there had been that mysterious incident at Mombasa when a take-off had been abandoned because the captain considered that there was insufficient runway remaining. Subsequently it was found that the engines, when tested in the hot and humid Kenyan coast conditions, were all below par when compared with the figures that had been obtained in the UK. Obviously, this gave cause for concern and the matter had been investigated and debated for over a year. It was decided that, whilst the two matters seemed to be related, there were in fact separate issues. Had the performance of the Britannia deteriorated over the years to the point where the data in the manuals was dangerously over-optimistic? Was the information for adjusting engine ground testing figures for temperature and humidity correct? Out of these questions came the decision to mount a special flight to obtain data to answer them. I was appointed to captain this task.

**The second segment climb**

The trial was to be conducted on a flight from Brize Norton to Singapore and return with extra days at Gan to gather additional data. The plan was to record power figures for each take-off and then carry out a 'second segment climb' and measure the height increment. At each stop the engines would be ground tested. The 'second segment climb' was chosen as a way of measuring the aircraft performance as it is a defined configuration for which height gain figures are available in the aircraft's performance manual. As was described at the start of this account, it had been decided that the modern Royal Air Force transport fleet should, unless it was operationally impossible, conform to civilian operating safety standards. Part of that decrees that the aircraft should be at such a weight for take-off that, should an engine fail at any stage, then either the take-off can be abandoned or safely continued. To continue, it is obviously necessary to be able to check that the aircraft, with only three engines operating, can reach flying speed within the runway remaining. It is also a vital requirement that it is determined that there is sufficient performance to clear obstacles in the immediate climb out path.

**Gradient of climb**

To check this, a graph is provided in the Operating Data Manual (ODM) which gives the gradient of climb that can be expected, at the planned take-off weight, in the prevailing conditions of temperature, atmospheric pressure and wind. For our purpose, from that gradient we could obtain the height we should achieve in the ground distance covered.

**Engine shut down**

The graph had been constructed for the configuration that the aircraft would be in immediately after take-off so, for the trial to be valid, our aircraft would have to be flown in that condition. It was not a commonly adopted one. Firstly one engine would be shut down and its propeller feathered. The graph assumes that the most critical one has failed; for the Britannia this was the starboard outer, No.4. The flaps are at the 15° position and the speed kept just three knots above the take-off speed. Full power would be maintained on the three live engines. There was a five minute limitation on running the engines at this setting so it was intended to maintain the climb for that length of time to get the best figures.

**Long five minutes**

On 19th May 1973 we departed Brize Norton in XL657. The first of the climbs was carried out on our departure from Akrotiri the next day. Five minutes seemed an awful long time. Our refuelling stop from there was Seeb International in the Oman which was being used, temporarily, in place of Masirah. In spite of the fact that it was night, the temperature was 30°C. Whilst carrying out the five minute climb after take-off, we experienced overheating of the alternators on all three of the running engines. This was a serious fault, in fact the emergency drill for such an overheat called for the engine to be shut down. Each alternator was permanently connected to its engine so the only way of reducing its speed, and the fire risk, was to stop that engine. Clearly, with warnings on all three we were poorly placed.

**Speedy Paddy**

The flight engineer, Paddy Tranter, rapidly restarted the shut down No.4 engine allowing the power on the others to be reduced. With that, two of the warning lights extinguished. The engine associated with the remaining light was shut down and a safe landing was made at Masirah.

**Trial resumed**

Much investigation at Masirah, and soul searching back in the UK, followed this incident. The immediate result was that the flamestats associated with the warnings were found to be badly calibrated and, in fact, there was no damage to the alternators. With this determined we were allowed to proceed but without carrying out any more climbs. By the time we reached Singapore, sufficient investigation had been carried out to reassure people that it was safe to resume the trial and we did so on our return journey to the UK.

**The results**

Worthwhile data was gathered from the ground runs carried out and from it amendments made to the graphs and techniques which would eliminate the anomaly experienced at Mombasa. The climb figures too proved useful. From them it was determined that, whilst the Britannia's performance had deteriorated, it had not done so to the point of doubting the information in the ODM. However, it was recommended that the situation be monitored with an annual check.

The trial, therefore, had satisfactorily answered the questions posed but had raised another one. What was the integrity state of the alternator overheat warning system? It was decided to test this with a further trial. I was once again the appointed captain.

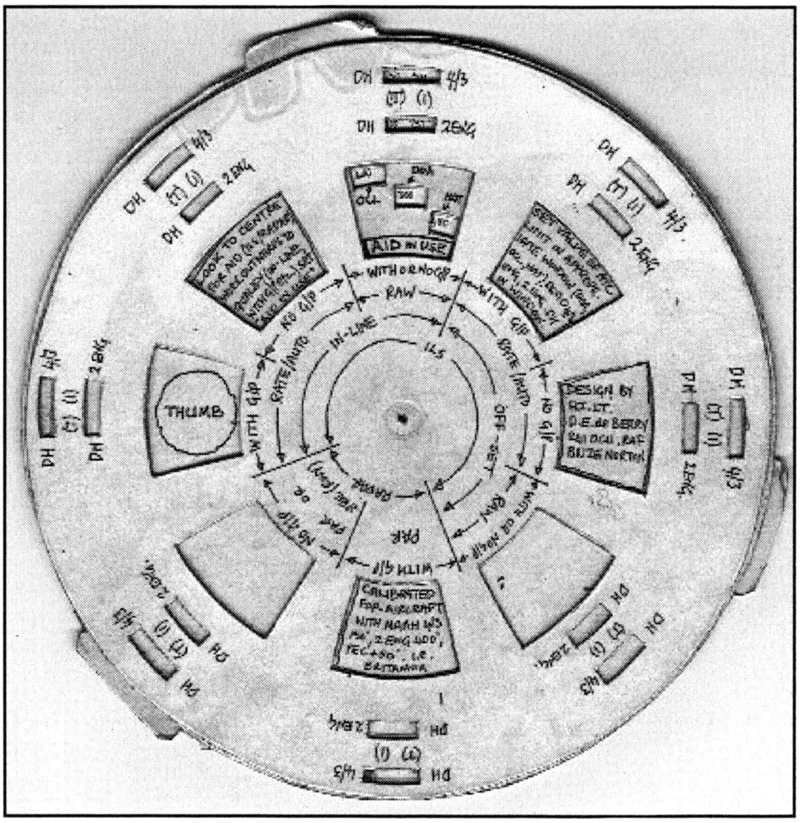


**Off again**

The alternator air cooling ducts of XL635 were fitted with heat sensing devices and on 13th July we set off for Singapore once more. The schedule was not totally dedicated to the trial. We carried freight for various destinations. In fact it was a hectic itinerary; between 13th and 19th we flew Brize Norton, Akrotiri, Masirah, Karachi, Gan, Colombo, Tengah, Colombo, Gan, Karachi, Masirah. On most of these legs the 'Second Segment Climbs' (SSC) were carried out and duct temperature information gathered.

**More trouble**

Departing Masirah on 20th July, preparations were being made for the SSC. With No.4 engine shut down and flap set, full power was just being applied when surging was experienced on No.1 engine. The climb was abandoned, No.4 engine restarted and No.1 shut down. We would have to return to Masirah. During the approach and landing surging was experienced on all three running engines and it did seem that total failure was imminent.

**Three engine change**

So, again I found myself at Masirah with a serious fault being investigated. It was decided that all three engines should be changed.

To compound our problems, a casting in the port undercarriage leg failed whilst the aircraft was being manoeuvred by the ground crew, necessitating a whole leg change. These mammoth tasks involved a Belfast flying in with the engines and spare leg and a VC10 with the necessary ground crew. Nine days later the jobs were completed and we departed, without incident, for the UK.

**The cause**

What had been the problem? For the take-off on the fateful day, water injection had been used for the take-off. Extra power could be obtained by adding water to the fuel/air mixture entering the engine. The water had to be pure. It was not unusual for us to carry 45 gallon drums of this distilled water on some flights for subsequent use. At Masirah the injection water was obtained from the sea water distillation plant which provided the domestic water for the station. It was discovered that, on this day, the water was contaminated and had seized up critical 'blow-off' valves in the engines.

I will always remember 1973.

Whilst the author was instructing on the OCU, an amazingly complex system was introduced for calculating the lowest height to which a pilot could fly when making an instrument approach to a runway/airfield in conditions of low cloud and/or poor visibility. A device was designed to help with the calculation. The words of the AOC, Air Marshal Neil Cameron, sum up the outcome: *'Although it rather looks as though production costs and possible future modification to the overall concept will preclude the adoption of your idea, nonetheless, I would like to congratulate you on your initiative and thank you for the painstaking effort which I know went into the design of your calculator.'*

Oh well ... back to obscurity!

*(David Berry)*

AP 4682A & B—FRC **Card 13** (AL 2)

## CHECKS AFTER LANDING

| | | |
|---|---|---|
| Reverse pitch . . . | E | Reverse cancelled. Lever at ARM. Superfine ON. Propellers to MIN and OFF |
| Pressure-head heaters . . | E | OFF |
| Controls . . . . . | C | Locked |
| Windscreen heat . . . | P | OFF |
| DV windows . . . . | P/C | Released |
| Shut-off valves . . . | C | Nos 2 and 3 opening |
| IFF . . . . . . | C | Off |
| Landing lamps . . . | P | TAXY / RETRACT and TAXY |
| Leading edge lights (night) . | E | ON |
| Flaps . . . . . . | C | 15° or Up and OFF |
| Inverters . . . . . | E | Set for taxying |
| De-icers . . . . . | E | All OFF |
| Sidescreen demisters . . | E | OFF and ISOLATE |
| Radio, and radar . . . | P/N/C | All off except one VHF or UHF |
| Brakes . . . . . . | P | Checked |
| Trimmers . . . . . | C | Reset for take-off |

**Shut-down checks** (*overleaf*)

**LANDING**
(*continued*)

RESTRICTED

CHAPTER THIRTY

# The End in Sight

Operation 'Lucan' continued its sad progress into 1974 coming to an end in February. Air loadmaster Flight Sergeant John Grimwood sums it all up with a story:

*'One of the local baggage unloaders was emptying the belly hold of the few possessions of the refugees when the door came off its catch. The damper mechanism was U/S and the door came crashing down on his fingers cutting them clean off. I rushed to find the UN man who employed the local labour. 'One of your locals has cut off his fingers,' I panted. 'Don't worry,' he*

Squadron Leader Iain Brotherton, 'Lucan' detachment commander, with some members of his team. (*Iain Brotherton*)

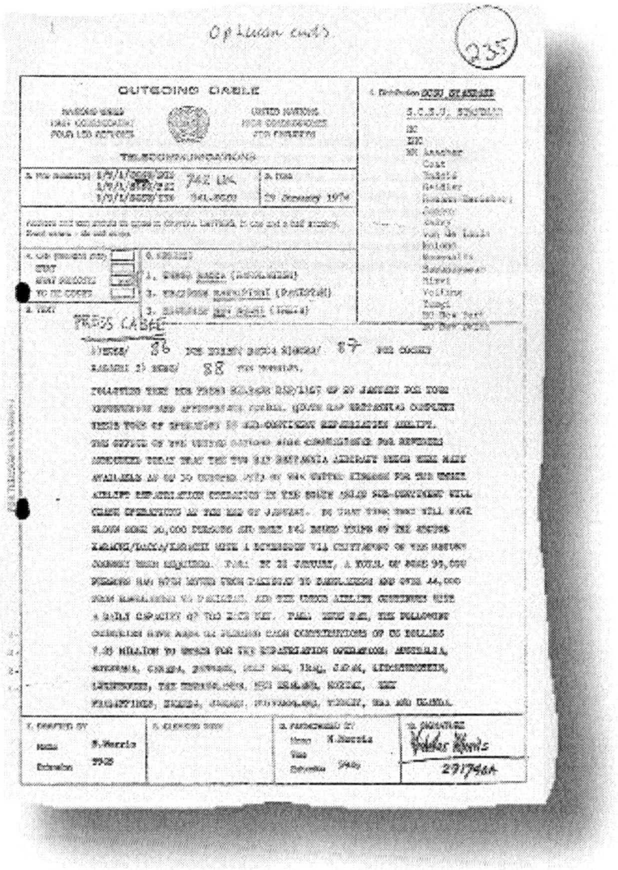

OUTGOING CABLE

PRESS CABLE

The Office of the United Nations High Commissioner for Refugees (UNCCR) press release on the cessation of RAF participation in Operation Lucan. (*Richard Ling*)

*replied, 'I will get you another one straight away.' The injured loader was wheeled away on a trolley, screaming, and another took his place. How cheap life is in that part of the world.'*

**United Nations press release**

Richard Ling's thirst for things historical took him to the United Nation's Archives, firstly New York and then Geneva. They came up with a Britannia related press release issued by UNHCR and sent out on the cessation of Operation Lucan. The text reads:

'*RAF Britannias complete their tour of operations in sub-continent repatriation airlift.The Office of the United Nations High Commissioner for Refugees announced today that the two RAF Britannia aircraft which were made available as of 30 October 1973 by the United Kingdom for the UNHCR airlift repatriation operation in the South Asian Sub-Continent will cease operations at the end of January. By that time they will have flown some 30,000 persons and made 148 round trips on the sector Karachi-Dacca-Karachi with a diversion via Chittagong on the return journey when required. By 28 January, a total of some 90,000 had been moved from Pakistan to Bangladesh and over 44,000 from Bangladesh to Pakistan, and the airlift continues with a daily capacity of 700 each way. Thus far, the following countries have made or pledged cash contributions of US$7.25 million to UNHCR for the repatriation operation ...*'

The press release continues with a list of the donating countries and outlines that three chartered aircraft will continue the airlift from 1 February. Many Association members will well remember Operation Lucan.

(*Author: The arithmetic of the above is somewhat puzzling - but that's what the cable says!*)

**The axe is raised**

There was disbelief, with the continuing effort, particularly of July and August, that the end of the Britannias was a real possibility. Was there hope of a reprieve?

**Inside MOD**

I now know that such a dream was naive. Squadron Leader Harry Marshall has already been introduced as a navigator Flight Commander on 511 Squadron 1969/71; a tour followed at Upavon as Sqn Ldr Contingency Plans. There he soon discovered that Britannia life was not all it seemed to those at the 'coal face':

'*... contrary to what you and I thought when we flew the route to Changi, it was the 'contingency' or 'war role' that kept the Britannia and the rest of the Air Transport Force in being. And the primary war role in those days was to move 3 Div and 38 Group (masquerading as the United Kingdom Mobile Force UKMF), with their weapons, from the UK to Germany if a European crisis occurred. To do this in ten days or so took all the VC10s, Belfasts, Britannias and Hercules working flat out.*'

Being closer to the 'action' he saw how the need for economy was taking its grip:

'*Towards the end of 1973 the Air Force (and the Navy and Army) were feeling the pinch. Equipment costs were soaring and the accountants told us we were spending too much on 'people' and not enough on 'things' ... we, the Air Force, set out on a series of 10% cuts. By now the finger was beginning to point at the Britannia.'*

The action for, now promoted, Wing Commander Marshall moved to MOD in February 1974, where he joined Air Plans:

*'This was the time when the Ted Heath government was in conflict with the miners. Most of the country was working a three-day week and there was no heating or electricity at specified times. ... Things could not get worse but of course they did. Ted Heath went to the polls and Harold Wilson defeated him. ... We got the lights back and a Defence Review - the infamous 1974 Defence Review. As one of the small Air Plans team, I expected to be in the thick of it. Labour's directive to us (the three Services) was simple. At that time defence spending was running at about 6% of GDP. We were to produce an option for Force Levels at roughly 4½% of GDP for implementation in 1975. We (Navy, Army and Air Force) could sort out the agreed answer anyway we liked, but an answer there had to be. If we didn't produce one for implementation in 1975, they would. And their cuts would be arbitrary.*

*'Not a bad proposition. With the sting in the tail we clearly had no choice but to get on with it. But, how on earth were we three Services to come up with a best case, jointly agreed solution that would effectively reduce the expenditure on each of our budgets by some 25%? We had already been through the teeth and the tail bit and found to our amazement that the two were connected. (Writing now in 1994, I see that nothing changes as the French would always insist. For the Defence Minister to call his post-Cold War Defence Review of 1993 'Front Line First' it looks as if he has lopped the tail off completely. I hope he doesn't live to regret it.) It would have been much simpler had each Service been able to formulate its proposals for reductions in isolation. The pain would not have gone away but we could at least have decided unilaterally what we most needed to keep and shed what least concerned us. But in overall Defence terms what was expedient to our Service was not always acceptable to the other two and nowhere was this more apparent than with the Air Transport Force.*

*'Once the new Labour Government had given its Defence directive there had naturally to be early high level Service discussions to establish the ground rules to which we planners could work. As far as the RAF was concerned, given the magnitude of the cuts demanded, it was clear that the Air Transport Force could not survive unscathed. The only question was how deep the cuts would be. One argument freely circulated suggested in its simplest form that an aircraft which was not equipped to fire guns or drop bombs was at risk.'*

We continue to stalk these 'corridors of power' to learn of that fateful decision:

*'For a week or two it was rather like a phoney war for the planners of all three Services. No use getting excited until the guidelines filtered down from on high. Then one Friday afternoon (it's always Friday for these occasions) the buzz was about that the higher level decisions had been taken. My fellow planners and I were, in MOD jargon, on call. To my surprise I, the transporter, was the first to be let into the secret. The surprise did not last very long. 'Harry,' said my superior, 'we know*

Apart from the trooping flights, Gurkha units were often transported by the Britannia. Here men of the 1st Battalion, 2nd King Edward VII's Own Gurkha Rifles board at RAF Changi on their way to Brunei.

From the Norman Rose photo album: *'Karachi 20 Aug 74 - Special UK to Singapore - night stop Karachi. Rear: Al Sealy screen eng, Mike Wilsmer copilot, John Smith nav. Front: Norman Rose captain, local storekeeper, Jan Robinson ALM, ? Brown ALM, Jim Crowe flt eng. Foreground: Sgt Tooke.'* (*Norman Rose*)

Somewhere - some time - some improvisation in the aircraft towing department. (*John Hunting*)

*where we are going now. You're the transporter.' I began to get the drift. Even so the follow-on question left me a little numb. 'How do we get rid of the Air Transport Force?' 'All of it?', I asked. 'Yes. All of it.' he replied. 'Give it some thought over the weekend. We have to get cracking first thing on Monday morning.'*

*'Of course, it didn't quite work like that. The Army wouldn't have worn it anyway and second thoughts prevailed. But with that one question on a sunny afternoon in May of 1974 I realised then that, whatever else we saved, the bell had finally tolled for the Britannias.'*

Harry's story continues with much frank detail which is not for these pages but, perhaps, will be told elsewhere at an appropriate time. Sufficient to say that the Britannia was doomed and any hopes at Brize Norton were ingenuous.

It is strange to reflect that, with this 'Sword of Damocles' hanging over it, the fleet carried on its activities at the same, if not increasing, pace. For example, the Hong Kong Gurkha lift continued out of the monsoon season. When it closed at the end of its 73/74 session over 7,000 passengers

All the ingredients of a detachment - its Land Rover towing the ground power set, the KD clad ground crew, local labour. The seats are waiting to go on board after the load. (*John Hunting*)

and nearly 400,000lbs of freight had been carried on 66 tasks. Not one of these had failed to make the one hour deadline imposed by the Indian diplomatic clearance limitation. But what of July and August that had raised hopes?

**Another Britannia author**

The contributor of the above insight into MoD, Group Captain Harry Marshall OBE DFC, is one of that band of ex-Britannia fleet authors. His book, entitled '*A Truckie's Tale*', was reviewed in the magazine of the Britannia Association:

*'If you want inspiration to write a book about your flying experiences then here it is. Harry Marshall, erstwhile navigator Flight Commander on 511, has made a number of contributions to this magazine. He has also gathered remembrances of his transport aircraft career in this charming book. Perhaps the most appealing section is the first where he describes his tour on Valettas, as a brand new navigator, in the Far East. Many of you will be able to relate to the agonies of those early days. Section 2 moves on to our own ground, his Britannia days. He next describes a 'transport' tour but one behind a MoD desk. Harry was the Air Transport man in Air Plans when the axe was raised for defence cuts of 1974. When it fell, the Britannia fleet was no more. Many of us at the 'coal face' had a naive impression of what was going on 'up there'. Read Harry's account for a real insight as to how such things are decided. The final Marshall 'truckie' tour was as OC Ops at Brize Norton where he kept himself in flying trim with the VC10.*

*'This is a book to which you can relate 100% and Group Captain Marshall is to be congratulated on his perceptive view of how things were and presenting them in such a readable form.'*

The book, a softback with 135 pages, is mail order available at a special offer price of £13.45 inc UK p&p from: J & KH Publishing, PO Box 13, Hailsham BN27 3XQ.

'Tent City', RAF Fairford - the temporary home of the Britannia technicians during the Brize Norton runway resurfacing. (*Brian Prosser*)

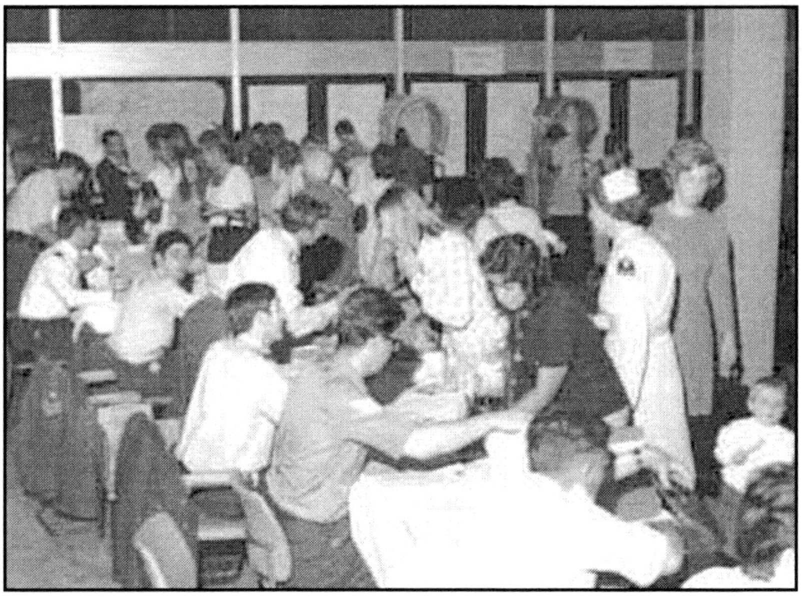

Passengers for the Cyprus evacuation flights being 'checked in'. (*Norman Rose*)

**Invasion!**

On 20th July Turkey invaded Northern Cyprus and it soon became clear that a major airlift was required to evacuate from the island tourists, dependents, British Nationals, in fact people of all nationalities and walks of life, caught up in the conflict. The Britannias joined the VC10s, Comets, Belfasts and Hercules in a huge emergency evacuation set to rival the Aden withdrawal as the biggest airlift since Berlin.

**All out**

It meant an all out effort. To ease planning crews remained as originally constituted. Some did the round trip, UK - Cyprus - UK, with only an hour on the ground at Akrotiri. Those that stayed had the minimum rest of 14 hours in a room shared by three. They took their own bed linen - and toilet paper!

Emergency sleeping arrangements in the No.2 Officers' Mess, Akrotiri. (*Norman Rose*)

**A first hand account**

Once again, Squadron Leader Norman Rose was in the thick of it:

*'I was 'slipping' at Akrotiri with Messrs Flt Lt Cater, Blackwell and Timber, ME Robbins, MALM O'Reilly and Sgt Tooke. Early on the morning of 20 July 1974, we taxied out en route to Masirah. This took us out over Nicosia and north into Southern Turkey. Our request for take-off was met with a 'hold'. After about ten minutes we began to fret but then we were given a 'line up and hold'. 'Stops and props' completed, XL659 began to stoke up inside but still the tower held us because they could not obtain our clearance from Nicosia Centre. Remember the Brit's inefficient air conditioning on the ground? We were hot, perspiring and frustrated by the time we were told to return to dispersal because 'Paratroops are descending on Nicosia'! I shudder to think what might have happened if we had gone off over Northern Cyprus and Southern Turkey that morning. We heard later that from 5am, Turkish jets had been bombing and strafing with troops pouring ashore in landing craft from nine Turkish warships standing off Kyrenia with their guns bristling.*

*'We all spent the day wondering what was going to happen, listening intently to the Forces Broadcasting Service; they did a really magnificent job keeping everyone appraised of events, minute by minute. CFBS gave families detailed instructions on what to do and where to assemble for the rescue convoys. The reassuring and unruffled announcers undoubtedly kept those families calm and avoided panic. At one point I well remember an astonishing and dramatic announcement to families in Famagusta, 'Keep your heads down and stay away from windows; Turkish jets are running in from the sea and strafing.'! Akrotiri was a hive of industry and a tower of strength that day, coping with such an extraordinary and unexpected emergency.*

*'The full impact of what was happening slowly became apparent. Helicopters of all three Services were dashing in and snatching stranded tourists from the beaches along the northern coastline and airlifting them to rescue coordination centres. They made some dramatic rescues, ably assisted by the Royal Navy. RAF families were evacuated from Limassol and were hosted by the residents of the base married*

*quarters. No.2 Officers' Mess was opened up to accommodate rescued tourists, most of them with only what they stood up in. They were given drinks, food and blankets to sleep on the floor. Every available person helped out; my crew and I tended those in No.2 Mess till late that night.*

*'By the morning of the 21st, the good old Brit fleet began trickling in to start a mass evacuation. My crew and I manned Ascot 6030 with XL659 for the UK with 23 French, 2 Belgian and 60 British tourists, mostly women and children, some still in bikinis! MALM O'Reilly, Sgt Tooke and my Corporal steward (name unknown, I regret) chivalrously dispensed whatever clothing we could find; copilot Cater turned up the cabin temperature as high as he could.*

*'No sooner had we contacted France Control than they wanted to know if we had any French Nationals on board so I let one or two have a little chat. Immediately we were cleared 'direct Abbeville, no position reporting required.' The controllers were profuse with their thanks to the RAF.*

*'Towards the end of the flight, one of the French tourists appeared at the flight deck door with a sheet of paper which had signed and addressed testimonials from each of his fellow countrymen. I still have that piece of paper pasted in my log book and I quote:*

*'RAF Forces are the model of organisation and amiability ...'*

*'We never forget this special trip. Thankyou for your softly assistance.'*

*'I never thought the RAF could do such things. All my best wishes for you and your families in the next years.'*

*'Thankyou for your kind assistance. Also everybody at Akrotiri. We shall tell our sons what the RAF is.'*

*'Thankyou to this crew for taking care of us so kindly. We shall remember the RAF.'*

*'We all had the opportunity to notice the ability and kindness of the RAF especially to the crew of this flight.'*

*... and many more. Vive le RAF et l'entente cordiale!!*

*'Brize runway was being resurfaced so we landed at Fairford. Brize Norton were efficiently geared up for the airlift of a full Britannia every three hours.*

As the end of the Britannia is contemplated it is interesting to reflect on this picture of the strategic transport fleet at its peak. (*Cliff Regan*)

*The logistics and organisation required to receive, document, feed, clothe, accommodate and finally repatriate the thousands rescued from Cyprus was mind boggling; but they did it! As for us, we had our 15 hours and were ready to return to Cyprus for another load.*

*'Just another story of what the good old Brit Fleet could do when called upon.'*

**A close thing!**

Tony Bennett has cause to remember this particular phase of Britannia operations:

*'Following the Turkish invasion of Northern Cyprus during the summer of 1974 the skies were alive with the sound of Ascot callsigns shuttling between Brize Norton and Akrotiri at all hours of the day and night to recover service families and civilians from Cyprus. Thus it was that on 7th August 1974, within ten weeks of the end of my six years on Britannias, the most frightening incident of my flying career occurred.*

*'We left Brize in XM518 around 2000 BST and spent several uneventful hours following the well worn grooves in the airways. It certainly was most unusual not to have the sun burning our eyeballs as we turned over Nice, indeed we could almost see the throbbing nightlife beneath us. Meanwhile the flow of information between the Ascots on company frequency with the Britannias coming the other way helped to pass the time, along with an early breakfast.*

*'Leaving Rodos for West Point at Flight Level 210 contact was eventually made with Gata Radar who were providing service instead of Nicosia. As usual descent for Akrotiri was to be two minutes after West Point and we advised Gata accordingly. At West Point we were told to maintain FL 210 due to opposite traffic. It was a beautifully clear night and about 0330 Local Time, and there was no other traffic on frequency. The copilot was flying the aircraft, the captain was looking visually for the opposite traffic and I was looking for him on the CCWR. We all could see the aircraft converging from about 30 miles, below, slightly left and climbing, tracking to pass marginally to our right. We were closing at 13 miles a minute.*

*'Suddenly the captain called 'I have control' and banked the aircraft to the left. As he did so, I heard the noise of jet engines over our four Proteus and, looking out of the Navigator's 'porthole', saw a blur of lights as the traffic passed. The captain told Gata that an aircraft had just climbed through our level. Gata responded that the traffic - a Boeing 707 operating for the United Nations - had been told to maintain FL190 until clear of us. Gata called the 707 and asked for his altitude. Passing FL220 was the reply, and no he hadn't copied the instruction to maintain FL 190, and no he had not seen any opposite traffic!!*

*'Having established that all was well down the back (fortunately) the captain requested descent for Akrotiri and the latest weather. Just to prove that one problem follows another, back came the reply that Akrotiri was 2500 metres in fog. Normally this would not have been a problem and we could have held off until it dispersed at dawn - not far away.*

*'However Sod's Law prevailed in that Cairo was our Diversion Airfield, and we didn't have the fuel to hold at Akrotiri and divert to Cairo if the fog persisted! As if the adrenalin wasn't already flowing. The last twenty minutes or so seemed to pass in slow motion as we completed the approach and landed safely on Runway 29 in misty conditions. After shutting down the aircraft it didn't take long to track down a crate of beer. Thirty minutes and two cans of beer later I was legless. I wasn't the only one.'*

**Pet special**

The lift continued to the end of August; refugees one way, reinforcements and supplies the other. It was decided in the end that Service dependents living outside the Sovereign Base Areas should be flown home. A 'Pet Special' was required. The unsettled East Mediterranean situation continued to affect aircraft routings through the year. After a long standing ban, overflight of Egypt was negotiated in order to overcome some of the difficulty.

With all this demand on Britannia services it is easy to imagine the hopefulness, at Brize Norton, that there would be a change of heart in the corridors of power.

**Still some 'Jollies'**

Bread and butter tasks continued, Northern Ireland trooping was a constant demand, exercises abounded. NATO proved its ability to reinforce with 'Bold Guard'. But scattered amongst this were 'tasty morsels' for some. Clive Osborne found himself on the island of Diego Garcia in the Indian Ocean:

*'We took the Governor of Seychelles on a fact finding visit. We set off from Masirah for the Seychelles on 3rd July and after the worst landing of my life (the approach there is like Gibraltar out of wind limits) we spent a very pleasant night stop on the island.*

*'The next day we embarked the Governor and his staff for the 3½ hour flight to Diego. We landed there in the middle of the 4th of July celebrations - great! We were shown all over the island - a beautiful horse shoe shape lagoon. On 5th July, a little the worse for wear, we departed back to the Seychelles and I recovered a little of my lost reputation with the Governor and a very anxious looking Group Captain, who had been with us all along, on the flight deck. Even the controller in Seychelles Tower said, 'That's much better!' A fascinating and enjoyable trip.'*

**Mickey Mouse visited**

Dave Court-Smith had his share of 'goodies':

*'During August I got my one and only look at Australia when we ended up at RAAF Townsville, on the coast of Queensland, to pick up some naval personnel. The return flight to Singapore went through Darwin, so my experience of the Antipodes was limited to two rather primitive outposts!*

*'Somewhat more salubrious were two States trips - a trainer which included one day off at El Toro MCAS (change here for Disneyland) and a tour by the Specialist Navigator's Course which included three days off at El Toro!'*

**An Historical Flight**

We continue with David Court-Smith - but has he not been taking his tablets? Or perhaps he has taken too many!

*'In my little story about the 'grotty Texan insect' infiltrating the air speed indicator system, I said that, after an interesting initiation with No.511, I settled down to an uneventful five years on the squadron. That statement is not strictly correct - Harry Marshall's nostalgic article, 'Perspex and Chinagraph', about the movement boards around which the life of the unit revolved (I think leave was black!) reminded me that I had quite a finger in the pie as far as the nav's board was concerned, having become deputy nav leader to dear old George Ogden.*

*'Of course that meant I didn't have any good trips myself (if you believe that you'll believe anything!), but one month I arrived back at Brize from a delayed States Trainer to learn that the programme for the following month had been completed; so it was with considerable interest that I went to the Squadron (on my stand-down) to see what the fickle finger of fate had lumbered me with. There, almost hidden amongst the Aldergroves, the Duty Ops and the odd East Med, was a five day Ascension.*

*'Wondering just what sort of disaster my mates had arranged for me, I went along to the combined Ops Room to see what more information Eric had on the flight. Pax to Gib on the Friday, a 99 crew bringing the aircraft in from Pisa/San Giusto (west coast of northern Italy) first thing Monday morning for us to flag Sal (in the Cape Verde Islands) and arrive at Ascension late evening. The information on the load was non-committal - a couple of tons of freight and a handful of passengers; plenty of room for fuel on the Sal-Ascension leg!*

*'The weekend on the Rock was very pleasant and come Monday morning we were keen to get off into the Wide Blue Yonder; en route weather and terminal forecasts were good and the aircraft arrived on time with a serviceable Green Satin - with over 3,000 miles of sea to traverse, the old Doppler was absolutely essential!*

*'Once at cruising height, the captain went off for a long discussion with the loadie; when he returned to the flight deck we asked about the passengers. He was reticent in the extreme and when I eventually went down the back for a leak I saw that the cabin was partitioned off like a VIP fit but with curtains all around and just a walkway down the side of the fuselage. There was absolutely no one to be seen. The loadmaster and steward chose to be busy with no time to answer questions - so I went back to work and got out my Air Almanac!*

*'Sal is a barren and inhospitable place - the Portugese equivalent of Masirah; I had a night stop there once with*

*George Luckins and to say he was unimpressed is an understatement. We refuelled without disembarking our invisible load; airborne again, we headed south, ahead of schedule - there's not much fat when you have two six hour legs in a 16 hour crew duty day.*

*'I sent back the passenger map - just in case someone was awake - and wound up the sextant. HF comms with Wideawake (the voice callsign of Ascension) were good and it was with considerable relief that we learned that the weather was fine and the wind right down the runway which runs between two large hills and is very prone to nasty gusts if there's any sort of cross wind. The captain was doing the chatting on the radio and it was obvious that some sort of code was being used - mysteriouser and mysteriouser!*

*'Well, to cut a long story short, we found the island, landed and were parked somewhere out in the sticks; a covered gangway was wheeled to the rear door and whoever they were that had been in the aircraft were whisked away. As the copilot and I were tidying up the flight deck, the loadmaster came up, smiling. 'I bet you were wondering what all that was about!', he said, 'Well, apparently they were brought from Elba to Pisa by boat, with a load of luggage - I gather there's a frigate in Georgetown harbour which is taking them on to St Helena. By the way - the senior passenger asked me to give you this.' It was the map I had sent back a few times and on the back was written:*

> Merci beaucoup pour un trajet historique.
>
> Bonaparte

**A reporter's view**

'*Airframe*' is the newspaper of the BAC factories of Filton etc. In February 1974 it published an article by Dagmar Heller who flew on a 511 flight to Luqa:

*'In these days of jets, super-jets and supersonic jets, it is not difficult to forget the turboprops of the Fifties. Yet the Bristol Britannia is still very much in evidence with the Royal Air Force today. Their fleet of 22 Britannias, (19 Mk1s and three Mk.2s) which form part of No.46 Group's long range strategic transport force, are, according to Wing Commander W. H. Croydon, Commanding Officer of No.511 Squadron at Brize Norton, probably doing more work at the present time than they have ever done before.*

*'No.511 Squadron, who share the operation of these Britannias with 99 Squadron took delivery of its first in 1959. Now, 14 years later they may well have only reached the halfway mark, as there is no question of a replacement for a long time to come.*

*''For the crew', it says in the booklet handed out to every passenger who flies with the RAF, 'the flight began some hours before take-off'. We all know this to be true, of course, but how many get an opportunity actually to put it to the test?*

*'It was quite an experience for me, therefore, when I flew recently as staff/crew member on Britannia Flight 6162 to Malta. Up before the lark at 0230 for a 0500 hours take-off, followed by a drive round a pitch-dark, practically deserted aerodrome collecting other members of the crew, we arrived at the air terminal building At about 0330 where the flight for me was about to begin.*

*'I had arrived at Brize Norton the afternoon before expecting to fly out as a passenger in the normal way. But 511 Squadron, it seems, had other ideas. 'If she wants to know what, it's like to fly in a Britannia, we'll show her,' were the words (more or less) of their C.O. And so they did!*

*'I had not been talking long to Squadron Leader Bill Oatey, in charge of training, who made me welcome, before my geography was being put severely to the test. By the time I had been shown round their headquarters, attending the briefing of the crew I was flying with the following day, and later spent a pleasant evening with Wg Cdr. Croydon, Sqn. Ldr. Oatey, Flight Lieutenant David Court-Smith the navigation leader, and Flying Officer Ralph Dexter who is in charge of the Air Loadmasters, I had come to the conclusion that the 24 or so crews in each of the two Britannia squadrons ranked amongst the most widely-travelled people I have met.*

*'Their scheduled passenger routes which form only a part of their operations - West Germany, Gibraltar, Sardinia, Malta, Cyprus, Masirah on the Arabian Coast, Gan in the middle of the Indian Ocean,*

AFTER arrival at Luqa, Malta. Left to right: Corporal C. Pike (steward), Sergeant A. Plummer (air loadmaster), Sergeant Pam Harker (air loadmaster), M/Eng. G. A. Vials (flight engineer), Flight Lieutenant H. A. Timbers (navigator), Dagmar Heller (BAC press officer), Flight Lieutenants I. C. Molyneaux (co-pilot) and F. G. Allen (captain).

The crew line up with Dagmar Heller after the flight. Is the article evidence of what a lot of information can be extracted by a pretty face or was she just paying a lot of attention?
Left to right: Cpl C Pike (steward), Sgt A. Plummer (air loadmaster), Sgt Pam Harker (air loadmaster), M Eng G A Vials (flight engineer), Flt Lt H A Timbers (navigator), Dagmar Heller (BAC press officer), Flt Lt I C Molyneaux (copilot), Flt Lt F G Allen (captain).

*Singapore and Hong Kong - were dismissed as a routine affair. In their role as back up for the Army in NATO, the Britannias are flying all round the world.*

*''We change over the guards in South Korea', someone said. I must have looked blank. 'You know, the United Nations Truce Guards at Osan' . . . What else? 'Oh, Kinloss to Norway to exchange troops, NATO troops on exercises from West Germany to Canada, big exercises in Turkey, flying troops to Norway and other Scandinavian countries' I was scribbling furiously ... and once a year we fly as far north as possible and also as far south.' Where, why? 'Over the North Pole to test out the latest equipment from the College of Air Warfare and to Punta Arenas. Where's that and how do you spell it?*

*''The Straits of Magellan and PUNTAARENAS'. What for? 'To change over the Royal Marines on the Falkland Islands and Punta Arenas is the nearest airport.'*

*'Help, I thought, I wonder how many they get like me? But that was not all. 'Last month a Britannia flew the Royal College of Defence Studies round the Indian continent. The aircraft kept on schedule right round the 32 days ... and in the monsoon period ... and of course you know that a Britannia and Hercules went as support aircraft for Concorde during its hot and high trials in South Africa.' This was more like home ground, but not for long ...*

*'We also station two Britannias in Hong Kong to fly Gurkhas to Kathmandu. This is out of the monsoon period and the crews normally remain out there for eight weeks.'*

*'One could go on indefinitely. Prince Charles flew to Gibraltar in a Britannia, they helped in the flood disaster in Ceylon in 1964 ... it really means that when VIPs are on the move or whenever one reads that the RAF's transport aircraft are involved in flying troops to any part of the globe, are going to anyone's aid or being called upon to carry out any exercise at a moment's notice, the Britannias will be carrying out their share of the work.*

*'It was still dark outside when we walked out to our Britannia Mk2 XN392, 'Acrux' which stood looking rather lonely in a solitary pool of light. All the RAF Britannias are named after stars, except one, XL 636 Argo which, inexplicably is a constellation. I have this on the best author-*

*ity, from Flt. Lt Court-Smith, who as navigation leader, ought to know.*

*'Our first call at the Air Terminal had been to pick up the task diary for the flight (each flight has its own task diary in which everything relating to the flight is logged), then on to Operations, Met and Flight Briefing. 'Some fog', said the Met man, and diversions would be Military: Manston and Valley; Civil: Prestwick, because Gatwick and Manchester were closed due to night flying restrictions. The weather charts showed the usual highs and lows, warm and cold fronts (not to mention occluded) which normally throw me into a panic, but our captain, Flt Lt F. G. Allen looked pretty relaxed.*

*'Flight planning on scheduled runs is considerably simplified by the use of the squadron's own standard Navigation and Flight Plan Log sheets which give a reducing distance for the whole journey, and for each sector the safe altitude, distance and standard flying time between each reporting point, magnetic track and ground speed. Radio Flight Logs give equivalent information in the form of frequencies, navigational aids, position reports, and so on, for the copilot.*

*'Our copilot, Flt Lt. I. C. Molyneaux, and navigator Flt Lt H. A. Timbers, has this all under control and Notams, danger areas, aircraft weight, take-off distance, V1 and V2 were checked as a matter of routine. On board the two Air Loadmasters, Sgt. A. Plummer and Sgt. Pam Harker together with Steward Cpl. C. Pike were busy getting everything ready for the boarding of the passengers.*

*'Having settled myself into the fifth, normally vacant, crew seat, I put on my headset, spread out my charts and did my best to hear everything that was being said ... pre-flight checks, last minute weather, temperature and wind.*

*'The passengers boarded at 0445 and when the captain had been assured that the chocks were under the wheels and all props free, the engines in turn burst into life. First starboard No.3, followed by No.4; then after the doors had both been shut, No.2 and finally No.1. All that remained was for the loadmaster to advise the captain that the emergency drill had been carried out and all passengers were strapped in. This done, I heard the captain's words 'Ground - clear to go'. It seems a long time since my day had started and we were still on the ground!*

*'Once airborne we settled down in a gentle climb for Woodley and at Midhurst had reached our cruising altitude of 21,000 ft. To increase the fatigue life of the Britannia, the cabin pressure is not allowed above 6 psi and the aircraft cannot therefore cruise much higher than 20,000 ft. Our climb out took about 25 minutes, but what the Britannia lacks in speed it makes up for in comfort. The flight deck is roomy and the noise level extremely low. The passengers, too, sit in more comfort than in some modern jets.*

*'We crossed the British coast at Worthing and from then on our route took us via Rambouillet, Nevers, Clermont Ferrand, Montelimar and Nice. By this time it was broad daylight and we could see the Alps and the countryside below. Then over the sea to Elba and on to Sicily - Ponsa and Palermo being the reporting points there. We reached Gozo at 0855 and after all the foreign accents en route it was refreshing to hear the crisp, clear voice of the air traffic controller at Luqa giving final instructions for landing.*

*''6162 you are dead on centre-line, 5 miles out ... 4 miles out ...' and so on until we touched safely down at 0907, coming in from the south over the sea. Smoothly, easily and efficiently ... thanks to the RAF and its evergreen Bristol Britannia.'*

**Tony Bennett's last year**

*'Britain was suffering the effects of the oil crisis, a three day working week, and a national coal strike. Also the noises coming from the top were not hopeful for the Forces, particularly the RAF transport fleet.*

*'However, first up in 1974 was a seven day Far East in 44 hrs with night stops at Gan and Tengah 'out' and 'in', with turn rounds in Masirah and Colombo (both of which were my first visit and in Colombo my last as well), trying to buy some 'precious stones' in the latter as well as coping with another no notice route check.*

*'For the next six weeks little happened which meant that I did spend some time at home when spring was around the corner. Two major events occurred. Firstly I was posted to Cranwell for the Staff Nav Course (snc) in October. I was not happy*

*about this and didn't take it well. With hindsight it was the best thing that could have happened to me. I missed the sudden announcement of the forthcoming decimation of the transport fleet and some of the more unattractive postings. I passed the snc and was posted to Finningley in March 1975 from where I would be in a reasonable position to make Specialist Aircrew. Secondly my girl friend was posted to Germany from the end of May.*

*'Meanwhile life went on even if Arthur Scargill continued to make it difficult. Price rises were in a vicious spiral and in a well known drinking establishment we frequented beer went up from 19p to 20p a pint which encouraged some gentle baiting. The landlord responded that if I didn't like it I could **** off!*

*'The clock was beginning to run, but there were some memorable times to come including a second visit to Masirah this time for four nights in March. Transit accommodation was somewhat limited, namely Seco Huts accommodating two crews.*

*'Stopovers are always what the crews make of them, and this was no exception. Walking on the beach, gathering shells, sampling a wide range of whiskies and playing golf (not necessarily in that order). The course had a few hazards, mainly the terrain which could deflect the ball in any direction except of course the one you wanted, and a badly planned last hole where the 'Brown' (sand mixed with oil to make a putting surface) was directly in front of the Transit accommodation. Any over club and the ball landed on the corrugated roof like a shell, causing considerable disturbance to any crew who might be asleep on their turn round.*

*'After this I had day trips to Cyprus, Malta and Gibraltar in March, so it was a pleasant surprise to see that I had been allocated a trip to USA in April. This would be my first sight of USA for over two years and it looked as if the country club was alive and well. An interesting task being a Special to Nellis (Las Vegas), via Goose Bay, converting to a Trainer. It was a long flog to Nellis - 9½ hours plus 1½ hour refuel at Cleveland and minimum ground time at Nellis to depart at 0730 for Los Angeles to New Orleans to Washington (Andrews) and night stop.*

*'None of these places had I been to before nor would I likely see again, so I determined to make the most of it. After a couple of statutory beers in 'the crew room' I went off to see the Strip in Las Vegas, and took in a show (name escapes me) on the free servicemen's ticket given by the hotel we stayed in. By midnight the early call at 0430 wasn't too far away. As I hadn't touched a drop since 2300 1 decided to stay up just for the atmosphere and ambience of this unique place which I couldn't begin to describe. I took just an hour sleep, but is was so worth it.*

*'It goes without saying that New Orleans is also something special and that Bourbon Street is THE place, but most of all I wanted to see Washington as I probably would never otherwise get the chance, and there was so much to see.*

*'Again after a couple of post-flight beers I decided that the only way to see anything in such a short time would be by taxi - so hang the cost. Making my way to phone a taxi I met the co pilot who was about to do the same thing. Bonus!!.*

*'A tired, elderly taxi arrived and we told the driver that we just wanted to see as much as we could in three hours. No problem he said, he had his girl friend with him. If we wanted to stop and see anything just say. We saw everything I can now think of - and some more. On the way back to Andrews we stopped for a beer. When he dropped us and we settled up I seem to recall it cost 16 dollars! ! The rest of the crew were where we left them.*

*'Brize tasks operated from Fairford in June and July while the runway was resurfaced. A difficult time for both units, but little memorable flying except on 16 June when Mike Newell captained 658 on a ferry flight from Fairford to Brize. I was the navigator. It was a sunny Sunday and we were in the garden of The Round House until it was time to go to Fairford. Start up and taxi, Take off, RW 08 straight over The Round House, land Brize, back home for G&T's and lunch. Flight time 10 minutes - just!*

*'So my swan song approached. Perhaps coincidentally it was a Far East task, as was my first on 99 Sqn. The difference was 23 days for the first, a mere eight days for the last. Some things change, some things change forever. Singapore reclaimed and redeveloped before my eyes over the six years that I had known it. Of course some*

*things never change. Gan will always be the same in my eyes.*

*'Suddenly it was over. My last trip was a double Aldergrove shuttle; shut down checks; walk away with one last look at 496 which was also the airframe in which I flew my first 99 Squadron leg some 3250 hours and six years almost to the day.*

*'At least I would miss the trauma of the briefing of 3rd January 1975 outlining the cut backs in the transport fleet over the next twelve months and the sadness at the demise of the Britannia.'*

**Yet another author!**

At the end of 2004 '*No Time on the Ground*' was published. It was reviewed by the Editor in the Britannia Association magazine thus:

*'The Britannia ranks contain several writers: David Taylor, Windy Deere, Harry Marshall, Nick Carter and yours truly. There is a new recruit to that number. With my lifetime of aviation, I am aware that some pilots were a lot more enthusiastic than I about the actual flying. If they couldn't fly then it was like cutting off their right arm. Many of you will remember Graham Bayliss - and he comes to mind in this category. Also I have come to realise that a number of my compatriots took a greater interest in the areas we were flying over and our destinations - David Court-Smith has, from time to time, proved that point in this magazine. Then, as illustrated by the list above, there are those with an inclination to pen their recollections.*

*'The new recruit qualifies for each of the three categories listed above. Ex-511 captain Ken FitzRoy has written a book aptly entitled 'No Time on the Ground'. This covers his 50 years of continuous flying in the Royal Air Force and in civil aviation. His was not a straightforward start in the pilot world - he had to work at it - and that effort and enthusiasm continued through his flying lifetime. It would be inappropriate to give details of this here - it would spoil the surprises in the book - but sufficient to say that he sampled practically as many types of flying as exist - and did a tremendous amount of it. Qualifying for the second category above is demonstrated with quite vivid descriptions of the routes he flew and the locations he stayed. It really is a kaleidoscope of aviation.*

*'Ken makes an early statement in the book that this is not an account of his personal life but there are glimpses and they are most poignant.*

*'His book is a good read and is highly recommended. Read it to put into perspective your own flying - and to show that you must have spent a lot of time flying around with your eyes shut!'*

A paperback with over 100 photos, '*No Time on the Ground*' by Ken FitzRoy is priced at £15, plus £1.50 post and packing, and is obtainable from:
Woodfield Publishing, Woodfield House, Babsham Lane, Bognor Regis PO21 5EL
Tel: 01243 821234
e-mail: info@woodfieldpublishing.com.

If you wish to order from a bookshop then the ISBN is 1-903953-71-5.

**1974 over**

So, the Britannia's penultimate year was complete. What the future held for many was to be in the melting pot of 1975.

CHAPTER THIRTY ONE

# The Boscombe Brit

The end of the RAF Britannias was nigh; but the Ministry of Defence was to continue operating one of the type at the Aeroplane and Armament Experimental Establishment (A & AEE) at Boscombe Down. It perhaps should be explained why this statement does not read, 'all but one of the RAF Britannias was to be scrapped'.

**Boscombe's role**

The past tense is used for what follows as some aspects have changed over the years. The role of A & AEE was to test aircraft, and associated equipment, about to enter service to see that they were up to specification and to establish operating envelopes for Service use. It can be seen, therefore, that A & AEE stood between the makers and the users: the aircraft companies etc. and the Armed Services. The role had to be an impartial one so it was appropriate that A & AEE should not have been part of the Royal Air Force. It was controlled by the Ministry of Defence Procurement Executive, MOD(PE).

**Hastings replacement**

The Establishment's task necessitated much test flying in a variety of conditions, some of it overseas. Over the years A & AEE had established its own air transport facility. In parallel with the RAF, the Hastings had been the mainstay for the post-war years then, as the 70s approached, it became apparent that a replacement was due. After much deliberation it was decided to gain from RAF experience and buy a Britannia. These were now available on the used aircraft market as they were definitely past the first flush of youth. The major airlines had replacements and the Britannias were now being operated by the smaller charter companies.

**XX367 acquired**

In September 1971, financial approval was given to purchase a Britannia and by November the military registration number XX367 was being painted on the side of a 300 Series aircraft. This model was the ultimate stretched version of the aircraft which put it at the same size as the RAF's 200 Series but, initially, without a heavy duty freight floor and forward freight door.

**Well used model**

This Bristol Britannia 312 was built at Filton as one of a batch of 18 aircraft ordered in August 1955 by the British Overseas Airways Corporation (BOAC) and was registered with the company as G-AOVM on 21st May 1957. The aircraft first flew at Filton on 29th April 1958, was granted a Certificate of Airworthiness on 13th May

The Boscombe Brit served with British Eagle for some years with the name 'Team Spirit'. A 'sister ship', British Eagle's 'New Frontier, G-ANCF, was photographed at Lyneham in 1966 whilst working on a MoD contract. Charlie Fox now lies in pieces at Kemble with the hope of some restoration. (*Ken Guest*)

1958 and delivered to BOAC on 10th June 1958. It was used initially on the Trans-Atlantic and Los Angeles routes but was later transferred to the New York - West Indies service. Following BOAC's purchase of Comet aircraft, G-AOVM was leased in March 1964 to British Eagle. It was repainted in their livery and named 'Team Spirit'. The aircraft was used for UK and European flights as well as occasional trooping flights to the Far East for the Ministry of Defence. In 1967 the aircraft ran off the runway at Istanbul. Temporary work was carried out for it to be flown to Speke (Liverpool) for permanent repair and the fitting of a freight door. It was rolled out

XX367 overflying Boscombe Down. The hangar behind the nose was its 'home'. It housed 'B' Squadron and was known as the Weighbridge Hangar.

From the Norman Rose photo album: *'Boscombe Brit 1978/79 - Akrotiri 26th Oct 79: Sqn Ldr Dave Bridger,Sqn Ldr Norman Rose, Sqn Ldr Steve Yarrow, Sqn Ldr Ken Newman, MALM Dally, FS Dunne, MAEOp Bob Shergold(?).'* (*Norman Rose*)

at Speke in the livery of Southern Cross International but was never flown by that company and a further repaint restored the British Eagle colours. The company suffered an economic collapse in November 1968 and G-AOVM flew the last scheduled flight, a cargo of oranges from Israel to Heathrow. The aircraft was then sold by BOAC to Air Spain who commissioned Marshall's of Cambridge to overhaul and repaint the newly registered EC-WSY for delivery to Palma in November 1969. It was then re-registered EC-BSY and used by Air Spain mainly on European routes but occasionally for charter flights through East Africa.

**Delivery**

The next re-painter was MOD. It was flown to Lasham via Gatwick on

Saying farewell to one of the last Boscombe Brit captains. A & AEE Commandant, Air Commodore Reggie Spiers, presents a Basset photo to Dave Bridger to mark his undying love for the aircraft! Moving up the steps there is his fellow captain of the time, the author. Then Al Bowen (nav), Mick Bowden (ALM), Roy Lockert (ALM), the real Bob Shergold (AEOp) and Lenny Edwards (Eng).

11th November 1971 and delivered to Boscombe Down on 3rd May 1972. The first flight with A & AEE took place in August 1972 and the first route trip was to Nicosia in the September.

**Crewing**

The obvious recruits to fly the Boscombe Down Britannia were ex-RAF Britannia people. I was fortunate to be one of that band. Indeed, I was the last.

**The Britannia's role**

XX367's job at Boscombe Down was as the bus and lorry of the Establishment. When an overseas trial had to be carried out, as they frequently were in the 70s and early 80s, then trial and engineering support equipment was required as well as the supporting personnel. All would be loaded into the Britannia. Destinations were literally world-wide. Hot weather trial requirements took the aircraft to Arizona, Singapore and California; cold weather to Canada and Norway. Torpedo trials used a facility in the Bahamas and the Britannia went. Indeed, it held a record in its time for the largest aircraft to land on 4000 feet coral strip on the island of nearby Andros. Australia featured through A & AEE weapon trial use of the ranges there.

**Other jobs**

Its use extended outside MOD(PE). The occasional general air transport task was carried out for the RAF. Examples were European tours for various Service staff and defence colleges and VIP flights with parliamentary representatives and government ministers. Lord Louis Mountbatten was flown on one occasion. With the demise of the RAF Britannia fleet, the 'Boscombe Brit' assumed responsibility for the two flights a year by the Specialist Navigator's Course (now renamed the GD Aerosystems Course) over the North Pole. During the Falklands War assistance was given to the Air Transport Force by flying some of the essential, out of theatre, routes. One of these took the aircraft to Kathmandu.

The shortness of the Andros runway (4000 feet) for a Britannia is not totally conveyed by this photograph.

**Polar flights**

It has been recorded that a regular commitment of the RAF Britannias was those polar flights for the GD Aerosystems Course. Preserved is a booklet prepared for the 1981 flights undertaken by the Boscombe Brit. For navigation aficionados, an extract gives an insight to the complexities of these flights:

*EXERCISE FAR NORTH*
*'ARIES 81'*
*NO 14 GD AEROSYSTEMS COURSE*
*POLAR TRAINING FLIGHTS*

*INTRODUCTION*

*1. The GD Aerosystems Course (GD ASC) includes a flight trials training (FTT) element. This FTT element is divided into 2 phases, the first phase comprising 7 flight trials in which the navigational equipments of the Dominie T Mk 1 aircraft are evaluated. In the second phase modern heading reference systems, inertial navigational systems and long range navigational aids are operated and assessed at high latitudes in 2 flights to the North Geographical Pole. The aircraft used for these flights is a Britannia aircraft operated by the Aeroplane and Armament Experimental Establishment (A&AEE.), Boscombe Down. The Britannia aircraft is specially fitted out with a variety of avionic equipments provided by both Industry and the Service. The polar flights are designated Exercise Far North and represent the culmination of the FTT syllabus.*

*2. The first polar training flight was made in 1945; the aircraft used on this flight was known as 'Aries V'. In keeping with the Aries tradition, Exercise Far North 1981 will also be known as 'Aries 81'. The 'Aries 81' flights will take place during the period*

The Britannia was operated by Air Transport Flight, 'B' Squadron. The contrasting and lesser role was also to fly the dreaded Bassetts. Pictured with one are: Ted Hilton, Clive Osborne, Ken Newman, the author, Eric Heaton and Mick Bowden.

*9-17 Sep 81. The flights will be mounted from Brize Norton in the MOD (PE) Britannia; the aircraft will be operated by an A&AEE crew.*
*3. This document briefly outlines the equipment which will be carried on the Aries 81 polar training flights, describes the duties to be conducted by the trials crew, and details the administrative arrangements for the Exercise.*

*AIM OF EXERCISE FAR NORTH*
*4. The aim of Exercise Far North is to provide GD Aerosystems Course students with experience in the use and evaluation of heading reference systems, inertial navigation systems (INS) and long range navigation aids at high latitudes. Specific objectives within this overall aim are:*
*a. Recognise the limitations of IN as a navigational aid on long endurance flights.*
*b. Recognise and understand the capabilities and limitations of all navigation aids and systems at high latitudes and remote areas.*
*c. Recognise the problems of acquiring accurate datum information in remote and Polar regions.*
*d. Recognise the limitations of gyromagnetic and inertial systems at high latitudes.*
*e. Recognise the problems inherent in the evaluation of prototype equipment by airborne study of breadboard designs and in-flight discussion with representatives from Research Establishments and Industry.*
*f. In conjunction and consolidation of TS and AST syllabus, understand and be familiar with the ground EW systems used by NATO/NORAD.*

*SPECIAL EQUIPMENT FIT FOR 1981*
*5. The following items of equipment will be installed in the passenger compartment of Britannia XX367:*
*a. Inertial Navigation Systems (INS)*
*(1) Litton LTN-76 INS .*
*(2) Litton LTN-72 INS .*
*(3) Ferranti FIN 1012.*
*b. OMEGA System*
*(1) Litton LTN-211 OMEGA .*
*c. LORAN Equipment*
*(1) Decca ADL 81.*
*(2) Decca ADL 21.*
*(3) T19900 Automatic LORAN C Navigator*
*(4) Decca 1028 Marine receiver adapted for airborne use.*
*d. Integrated Navigation Systems. Three integrated Navigation Systems will be carried. The first is a Sperry-Decca Navigation System (SDNS) and consists of the following elements:*
*(1) Decca 9447 TANS .*
*(2) Decca Doppler 72.*
*(3) Sperry SOP 500 Twin Gyro Platform (TGP).*
*In the second system the SGP 500 TGP will be replaced by the Louis Newmark 6000 Attitude Heading Reference System (AHRS) feeding heading information into a second 9447G TANS. The third system is a*

*pre-production model of the Decca R-NAV system and consists of a Navigation Computer Unit and a Control/ Display Unit.*
*e. Gyroscopes*
*(1) Sperry CL 11 Gyroscope.*
*(2) Sperry MRG2 TGP.*
*f. Navstar 3 Set..*
*g. Computers and Calculators*
*(1) Hewlett Packard HP 85 Desk Top Computer.*
*(2) A variety of Hewlett Packard hand-held calculators, will be carried.*
*(3) Texas Instruments Desk Top Computer and a variety of hand-held calculators will be carried.*

**A personal account**

After those rather indigestible facts, the following comes as a pleasant relief! It is a well written account of that Polar Flight by Mr Len Vass. Something of a Boscombe Down personality, Len was the Senior Air Traffic Control Officer. He wrote the following article for '*Airway*', the staff newspaper of Britain's Civil Aviation Authority:

'*Part of the Aerosystems Course of the RAF's Department of Air Warfare at Cranwell, the 1981 flight was undertaken for the College's special polar navigation Exercise Far North, using the only remaining Britannia in RAF service, XX367. The Navstar equipment had earlier been fitted into the aircraft at A&AEE, along with numerous other systems, including four separate INS platforms, three Loran systems, among them an Auto-Loran C, and a Sperry twin-gyro platform, used to supply heading information to Aerosystems students on board.*

'*For crew navigation purposes, a Smiths' flight system in gyro mode was utilised, the aircraft's own Loran C being used only to permit the writer to familiarise with the browns and greens of a Loran lattice in high latitudes. All 'imported' systems were to be used in cross reference to and checks against Navstar performance. Computers and calculators were fitted to assist Aerosystems personnel.*

'*Squadron Leader Dave Bridger captained the Britannia, with Flt Lt Dave Berry as copilot; Navigators were Flt Lts Dave Boden and Jim Webb with whom I was slotted and seated with for most of the flight. Signaller, Bob Shergold and Engineer, Joe Major made up the remainder of the flight deck crew, with Master Air Load Masters Roy Jones and Chas Fellows.*

'*We left Boscombe on 8 September to position overnight at Brize Norton and departed early the following morning for the 9-hour leg to the USAF base at Thule on the Baffin Bay coast of NW Greenland. Routing was via Stornoway, south of Iceland to Sob Story (a USAF communications post in SE Greenland on the ice cap) - abeam Sondrestrom - Upernarvik to destination.*

'*Thule is generally bleak, certainly remote but with magnificent scenery around and en route - if, that is, you, like your scenery in Arctic colours! It made a change from Salisbury Plain, but I would not personally rush to emigrate ... for an ATCO it is unique, if only to learn that BMDH values*

The author's annotated copy of the instruction's map.

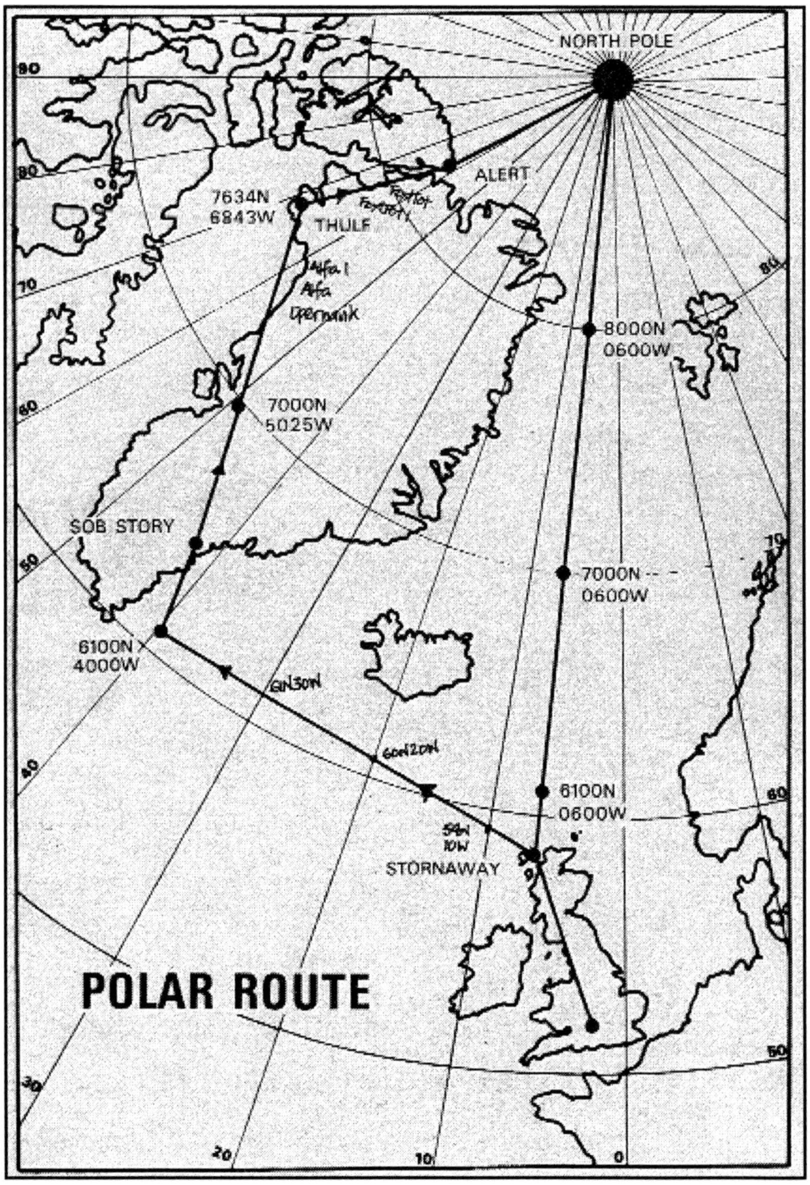

*given to aircraft are dependent on the varying height of icebergs on the final approach to runway 16! And there are plenty.*

*'On 10 September I met Capt Larry Wood, USAF Chief Controller at Thule and some of his staff. They are normally only there for a year - probably quite long enough. Thule weather has its vicious side, as we were later to experience. All visitors must abide by the rules of its weather alert system in various phases, as it can be difficult as well as dangerous to attempt to remain vertical in some conditions.*

*'The USAF later arranged for some of us to visit the giant 'Guardian of North America', the Ballistic Missile Early Warning Station - BMEWS - some 12 miles from Thule astride a mountain plateau at the edge of the ice cap itself. It was a most impressive, albeit somewhat awesome visit for an ATCO with relatively straight-forward ATC radar interest.*

*'It was during the BMEWS visit that the cold but increasing breeze turned quite nasty with sudden 100 mph gusts coming off the ice cap, as an apparently typical September katabatic - a wind caused by the downward motion of air due to convection - flow set in, delaying our return to Thule due to severe white-out conditions. This also resulted in a 24-hour delay for our ongoing flight to the North Pole, 800 miles away. The next day was only slightly better but the forecast for 12 September came good enough to allow departure in light wet snow at 1957 GMT. With a right turn off RW 34, we gyro-headed north.*

*'We passed over Alert, a CAF outpost on Canada's most northerly territory, Resolution Island, just over an hour later at FL190. As an aside, it is interesting to note that immediately after the Canadian Parliament acceded to pressures to introduce greater equality in the women's branches of the Armed Forces, 40 CAF ladies were duly posted to Alert which, perhaps, was not quite what they had in mind! However, the CAF chaps probably did not object ...*

*'Just north of Alert, the little remaining open water that could be seen from the cockpit came abruptly against the solid wall of the polar ice cap. We had called Alert on R/T but got no reply from this, the most northerly inhabited settlement in the world. Perhaps Dave Bridger summed it up, 'I reckon that at 2115 on a Saturday night, if they are doing what they ought to be doing, they won't exactly rush to answer a call from a Brit up here in the cold!' ... Playing cards, no doubt ... !*

*'We climbed to FL210 for the run to overhead the North Pole. A bright but low sun still shone on a pink-hued floss below. It was difficult to differentiate between cloud and the white nothingness -*

A rather anonymous looking crew featured in the photograph to accompany the polar flight article.

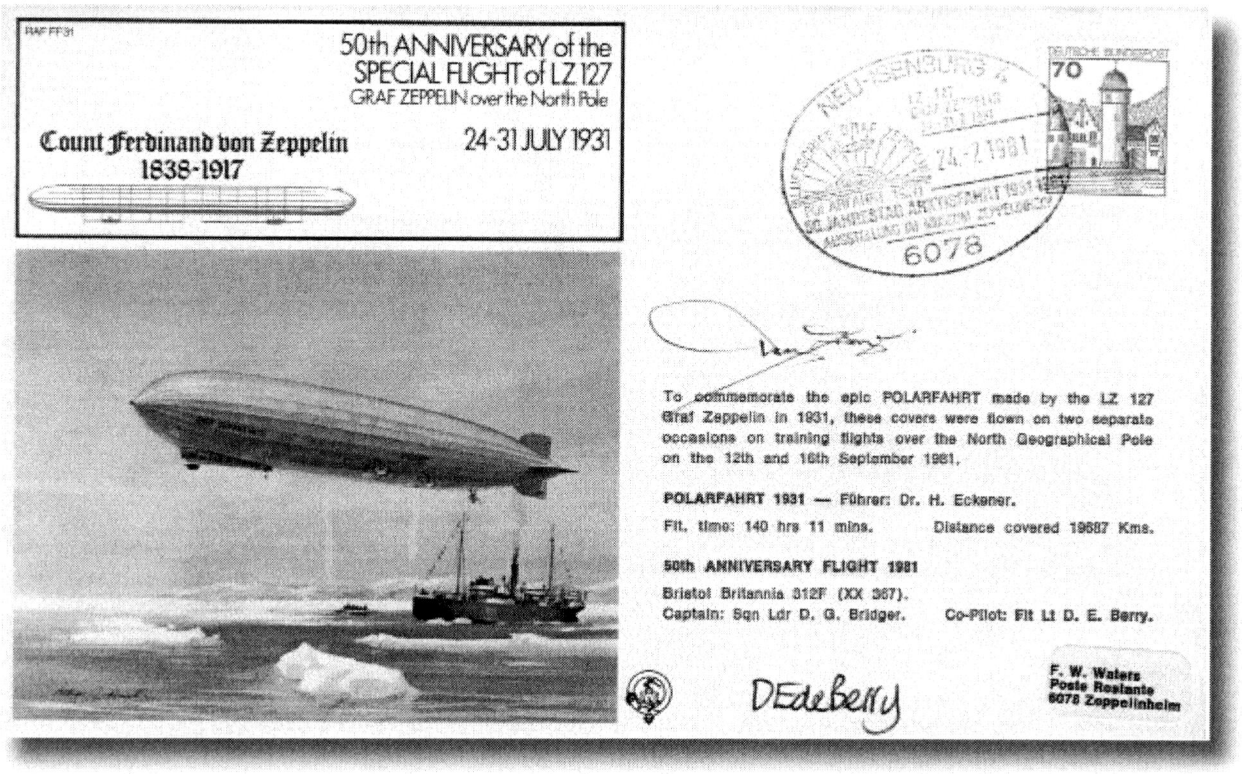


Historic note: The 1981 flight also happened to be chosen to commemorate the 50th anniversary of the 1931 polar expedition flight led by Dr Hugo Eckner at the controls of a Graf Zeppelin airship. Accordingly, a consignment of philatelic cover envelopes was duly stowed in the freight hold of XX367 for carriage over the Pole. The covers were sponsored by and sold through the RAF Museum, Hendon.

*one ruminated that Peary and Nansen were welcome to what they thought they might find down there. Normal Doppler and INS fixing back up used by the navigator was augmented for the final run-in using Navstar as Jim Webb transferred with a long lead to that particular black box. With increasing 'feel of moment' and what amounted to a countdown, Navstar twinkled its digital read-out on 90N right on the 2234Z ETA. And so we came to the top of the world on a Saturday night in September. An orbit took us momentarily into Sunday, quickly round the world and back again to Saturday as we passed 180W (or was it east?)*

*'GPS Navstar will interrogate any four from up to 18 satellites which might be available in orbit (there were eight at this time). These are chosen to suit the selected aircraft track. It maintains constant reference to and phase comparisons with these satellites, converting highly complicated data and equations to provide a phenomenally accurate geographical position and actual height of the aircraft. It can do so even when one or more selected satellites fall below the aircraft horizon, as one did on this flight.*

*'Average Navstar accuracy, after comparison with other systems, was to within 7 metres - give or take a centimetre! Ours was a Magnavox system, the other current contender for the market being developed by Rockwell Industries. It is very much an example of the by-product of space technology. An ex-RAF Navigator ATCO brought up the hard way on dead reckoning cannot help thinking how much it has all changed.*

*'From the North Pole, we settled on to the long haul back southwards to Stornoway, nearly 2004 miles distant, climbing progressively through the long Arctic twilight to FL260 and eventual darkness of night in lower latitudes. Though actually warm enough, the cockpit and crew compartment seemed to get colder but that was probably due to the creeping fatigue we all felt. It had, after all, been quite a week!*

*'Descending to warmer UK altitudes, 4mm of rime ice encrusting all exposed metal parts of the cockpit interior melted, producing quite a rainstorm on to all crew members, the writer included. Indeed, the captain later asked for his raincoat as a prerequisite for descent below 10,000 feet! He had been dripped on before,*

The 'Wind Trial' in progress.

*of course. When Dave Berry greased us onto RW 26 at Brize at 0636 on 13 September, we had taken over 10½ hours to route from Thule - but not by the pretty route.*

*'Although I have to emphasise that this can only be an observation of a non-expert, GPS Navstar performance was, to me, impressive. One feels that it is destined to revolutionise global navigation techniques so long as satellites are allowed to roam in space under controlled conditions. Development costs have of course, largely been absorbed in that satellites are already there, hence purchase and installation costs for Navstar are expected to be comparatively low. However, it also follows that the future of Navstar will only be as good as the peace we all hope and trust will prevail for future years.'*

**Wind machine**

Its latter days were marked by two strange occurrences. The first was a direct involvement in trials work, albeit a rather ignominious one. It was the time of the Falklands War. In the South Atlantic, weather was a particular problem of which a strong wind was a constant feature. A need arose to improve the covers to put over the Phantom aircraft to provide some element of protection.

Having been designed and manufactured, the question arose as to their practicality in the Falkland situation; could they be fitted to the aircraft in a strong wind? How was this to be tested other than waiting for a UK windy day? The Britannia provided the solution. It was used as a wind generator. With engines running and the Phantom parked astern, the trials team battled with the covers. Not one of the Britannia's most glorious moments.

**Killer wake?**

The other strange occurrence during its twilight days took place on a clear summer's day. Crew training was being carried out using the airfield at Bedford. The Britannia shared the circuit with a Hawk. After a roller landing the crew were advised that the Hawk had crashed on the runway. It had been following the Britannia on finals, became caught in its wake and control lost. It ended up sliding down the runway inverted; the two man crew survived but the protective helmet of the rear seat occupant was worn through by the friction with the concrete. Bedford was another arm of MOD(PE) and was equipped with a HS125 capable of assessing the turbulence generated behind an aircraft. With no doubt an element of self interest, it was decided to assess the Britannia's wake. Very late in its life, it was found to be extremely strong so perhaps it was fortuitous that there were no such incidents during its service when

XX367 being 'author landed' at Filton on 29th April 1983. This was the 25th anniversary of its maiden flight. There was great enthusiasm at Filton for the occasion and all, bar one, of the original test crew were gathered for the event. (*British Aerospace*)

Filton enthusiasm is evident from this photograph outside the Brabazon Hangar. (*Roger Carvell*)

The Boscombe crew meet the 'maiden flight' crew. The author/captain is on the extreme right. Above the civilian crew is MALM Mick Bowden. Sloping up, L to R, Master AEOp Bob Shergold, Sqn Ldr Ken Newman and Sqn Ldr Clive Osborne. At the top is Master Engineer Al Kidson. (*Roger Carvell*)

awareness of wake turbulence was not of the latter day degree.

**25th Anniversary**

Although XX367 was living in 'the shadow of death', there was still cause for celebration. 29th April 1983 was the 25th anniversary of its maiden flight. This occasion was marked with a flight to Filton. The Editor of '*Propliner*' magazine reported on the visit:

*'April 29 - it wasn't supposed to be a particularly big or important press day for British Aerospace at Filton, Bristol. A small number of mainly non-aviation press had been invited to Filton on this day to see Britain's (and indeed Europe's) last operational Bristol Britannia return to the airfield from where she first flew a quarter of a century ago. Britannia 312F XX367 'Team Spirit' (formerly G-AOVM and EC-BSY) was celebrating her 25th anniversary. But Filton got slightly more than it had bargained for.*

*'Operating for the Aeroplane and Armament Experimental Establishment (A & AEE) at Boscombe Down in rural Wiltshire since 1972, XX367 was crewed on this moving day by members of the Air Transport Flight, 'B' Squadron, headed by Flt Lt David Berry and Sqn Ldr Ken Newman, Commanding Officer of the Air Transport Flight. Mention must be made of flight engineer Alan Kidson, a devoted Britannia crew member. Initially flying Hastings, Hercules and Britannias in the RAF, he later joined the A & AEE and has been flying XX367 for five years. Signaller Shergold was posted to the Britannia Flight at Boscombe Down in 1979 and became the only (and is now the last) radio operator still flying with the Royal Air Force. Almost 20,000 combined flying hours have been accumulated by the 6-man crew.*

*'Hoards of sightseers, most of which had tuned into the local radio stations early that morning, turned out in force to watch the lonely Britannia arrive, The fact that a radio station had incorrectly broadcast the aeroplane's 12.15 arrival time as 11.45 just meant that everyone arrived well in time to see the Britannia circuiting the airfield at a few thousand feet. En route from base at Boscombe Down XX367 beat up former RAF Britannia bases at Lyneham and Brize Norton, with Kemble thrown in for good measure,*

*'Close to schedule the Britannia crossed Filton's perimeter road, a sight captured so many times in the past by Bristol photographers, and continued to perform a low, slow fly-by overhead assembled crowds with 'every thing hanging down'. Banking to the right sharply old XX367 circled the airfield for a second pass. But this time the press who were fortunate enough to be close to the runway were afforded the most magnificent sight (and sound) of the Britannia executing a very fast, clean pass directly overhead at*

The advert that marked the military end of Britannias.

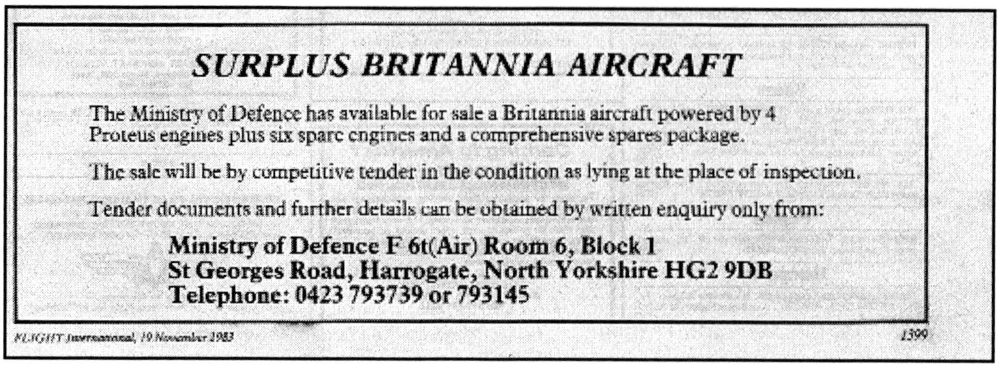

**SURPLUS BRITANNIA AIRCRAFT**

The Ministry of Defence has available for sale a Britannia aircraft powered by 4 Proteus engines plus six spare engines and a comprehensive spares package.

The sale will be by competitive tender in the condition as lying at the place of inspection.

Tender documents and further details can be obtained by written enquiry only from:

**Ministry of Defence F 6t(Air) Room 6, Block 1**
**St Georges Road, Harrogate, North Yorkshire HG2 9DB**
**Telephone: 0423 793739 or 793145**

FLIGHT International, 19 November 1983 1399

*what could conservatively be called 'low level'. Flight members later assured Propliner that this manoeuvre was a standard overshoot. Certainly Propliner's Roger Carvell got what has to be the most remarkable recording ever made of a 'Whispering Giant' in action.*

*''Team Spirit' was available for inspection after landing, and while her 6-man crew were being dined with some of the original Bristol Aeroplane Company aircrew that had originally flown the same aircraft 25 years earlier, she was towed in front of the old Brabazon hangar, from where the majority of the 85 Britannias built emerged during the 1950s. As if that wasn't enough for the misty-eyed romantics, the Britannia was later towed to a position on the West side of the airfield where she nestled between an RAF VC10 tanker and a late production Concorde, the future of which is uncertain.*

*'As the clouds darkened, the afternoon rain hit Bristol. Three hours after the dramatic arrival, the Britannia crew boarded their aircraft for the short return flight to Wiltshire. Her departure was equally impressive. Streaming propeller vortices, the lightly laden XX367 climbed away at a sprightly rate and passed overhead the hangar in which she was constructed.*

*'The Boscombe Britannia is due for a major overhaul in September, and while approval for this costly exercise has already been given, her crew was not entirely sure whether the aeroplane would continue in service. Initially it looked certain that XX367 would undergo an overhaul, Monarch Aircraft Engineering at Luton being a likely candidate for the task. But during the Greenham Common Air Tattoo in late July, at which the Britannia was present, her crew believed that the aeroplane would not fly past September, and would then be put up for disposal, not to be replaced. With the demise of AFREK in February this year, just six other Britannias remain in regular use. Five of these have the miserable consolation of spending their last days in darkest Zaire. However, without Zaire's present demand for Britannias only two would remain active.'*

**It had to go**

Economy was now the Defence Budget by-word and having this large aircraft dedicated to only occasional use was seen as an unaffordable luxury. In any case, the number of overseas trials was decreasing and there was an increasing move towards joint trials with the manufacturers. Civil charter would suffice for this lesser requirement. So, on 30th September 1983 we taxied the aircraft from its home at Boscombe's Weighbridge Hangar to an unused dispersal on the south side of the airfield. Its sale was advertised in the aeronautical press.

**Sold!**

The eventual buyer was Katale Aero Transport of Ostende, already operating a number of ex-RAF Britannias in Zaire. The sad day came on 14th February 1984 when we flew the aircraft to Cranfield where it was handed over to Katale.

**Last military Britannia flight**

It had not been anticipated that we would fly the aircraft again; it had been assumed that the purchaser would collect it. However, the aircraft needed an avionics fit to fly out of the UK and it was considered inappropriate for this to be carried out by a civilian contractor at Boscombe Down. So it came about that a very rusty RAF crew was to fly the aircraft to Cranfield.

Suitable weather was awaited for the flight as, in its sale condition, all the

avionics, bar one VHF/UHF set, had been removed. Fortunately, considering the time of year, such conditions presented themselves on the second possible day. Fate was not tempted, the undercarriage remained down and locked for the ferry flight. We landed at Cranfield at 1455 hours on 24th February 1984. The first RAF Britannia landed at Lyneham at 1752 hours on 19th March 1959; not quite the 25 years.

**Bargain!**

It is alleged that the selling price was £180,000 and that amount of money was earned with the freight load on its flight from Ostende to Zaire.

On the last flight the Britannia rendezvoused with a light aircraft carrying Britannia enthusiast, journalist and *'Flight'* photographer, Stephen Piercey. Sadly, very shortly after this event, Stephen was killed in a mid-air collision whilst engaged in air-to-air photography at the Hannover Air Show. (*Stephen Piercey*)

Boscombe Down life went on for the author after the scrapping of the Britannia. He continued as a staff pilot on 'B' Squadron flying the Hercules, Andover and Comet and acting as copilot on trials aircraft. This Hercules flight deck photograph was taken at El Centro, California during parachuting trials. Mrs Berry had joined the detachment! (*David Berry*)

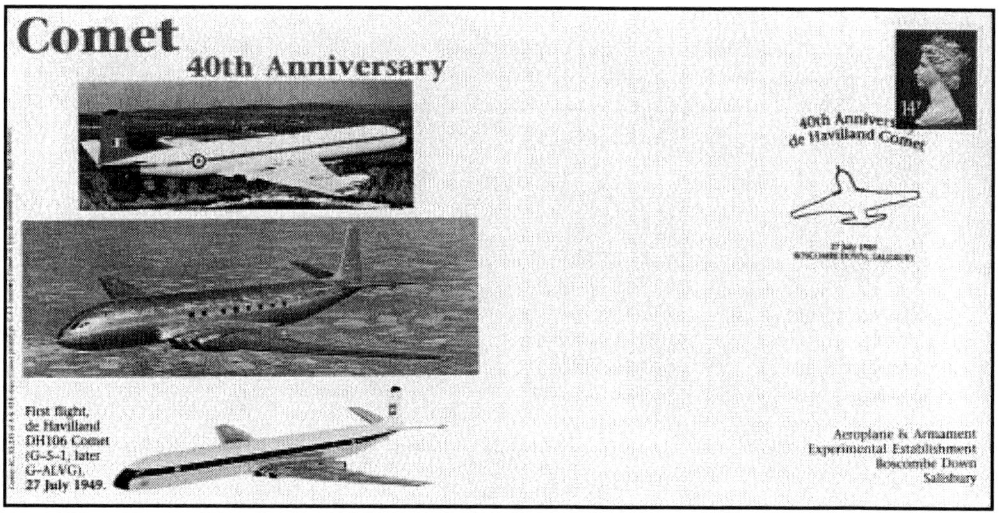


A compatriot of the Britannia at Boscombe Down was a Comet 4c - the 'flying laboratory' used for the flight testing of navigation and avionics equipment. This First Day Cover, to celebrate the 40th anniversary of the Comet, featured the Boscombe aircraft.

The Boscombe Britannia was a much photographed aeroplane. Here it flies across, close to Boscombe Down, Salisbury Plain.

XX367 undergoing major servicing in the Weighbridge Hangar, Boscombe Down. It is interesting to note the companions which illustrate the range of A & AEE work - and the versatile skills of the servicing craftsmen. The 'weighbridge' element of the floor can be detected between the Britannia and the other two aircraft. (*Al Kidson*)

The author's Argosy flying was curtailed by this incident at West Freugh - the undercarriage would not lock down. At the controls was Flt Lt Dudley Jackson. (*Dudley Jackson*)

Life at Boscombe Down was never dull!

CHAPTER THIRTY TWO

# The Final Year

If there was doubt in anyone's mind that this really was going to be the last year of the Britannia then that uncertainty should have been completely removed on 3rd January 1975. The Air Officer Commander-in-Chief Strike Command Air Chief Marshal Sir Denis Smallwood GBE KCB DSO DFC visited 99 and 511 Squadrons to give brief details of the effects of the defence cuts. The Britannias were to be run down, starting April. All hope was gone. Training of new crew members had ceased so those who had been posted had not been replaced. The remaining band wondered about their future.

**Crews threatened**

It might seem the case that, with this intention, there would be little for the squadrons to do in 1975. This was not so. Cyprus still loomed large in the tasks. The troubles directly affected crews. A coach, bringing one into Akrotiri for their flight, was attacked by a local mob. Stones were thrown, breaking windows. On another occasion, a hostile crowd gathered outside the main gates and the RAF Regiment had to escort the crew. In yet another situation it was thought prudent to fly a crew out of their hotel in nearby Limassol, to the base, by helicopter.

It is strange to reflect that these incidents are worthy of comment because they were exceptional. It is surprising that, with all the operations that took place in so many hostile situations, there were no such direct confrontations. Similarly, it is amazing that there was not a single road accident casualty considering the amount of travel there was in coaches and taxis in parts of the world not renowned for their road safety record.

Anthony Hastilow contributed this photo, from his memorabilia, taken on a turnround at Decimomanu in 1974. He identifies the ground team: 2nd left, Anthony; just the head of Jock Barry; Wg Cdr (Ops) Betts; 'Tricky Dicky' Kent (Movements Officer); Master Aircrew Phil Mann (Ops Officer). Crouching is Jim Marchant (UKMAMS) and at the rear, 'Thumbs Up' Taylor. There are well known faces amongst the air crew. (*Anthony Hastilow*)

Ex-511 captain Nick Symes wrote: '*This was taken on the 7 July 1975 - the copilot was Phil Grant. We were descending through the Straits of Gibraltar when we were asked if we were agreeable to being intercepted and escorted for a short while by two Hunters which were on their regular permanent detachment defending the Rock and flying the Flag. I was subsequently sent the photograph as a thank you.*' (*Nick Symes*)

**Tasks continue**

Closing down such a large fleet of aircraft was obviously a considerable task signalled by another visit to Brize Norton by the AOC-in-C in February.

The Hong Kong Detachment soldiered on with its admired work, airlifting the Gurkhas and their families between Nepal and Hong Kong. In May the detachment had to evacuate its aircraft to RAF Tengah on Singapore Island because of a hurricane approaching Hong Kong. The weather was also difficult at Kathmandu and the Vietnam War was not helping. Because of a threatening situation, new routes had to be flown.

**Cold and hot**

Gander in Newfoundland had been very much a Britannia airfield, its gateway

A 1975 champagne and cake ceremony to mark Squadron Leader Norman Rose's 10,000th hour. (*Norman Rose*)

to North America. Flight Lieutenant Lawry Green remembers a February trip:

*'We arrived on the day that Gander experienced a record low, -15°F. Hercules and Belfasts were all having trouble but we handed our aircraft over to a slip crew and they were away in an hour and a half. For our two day stop the weather remained just as cold and with a 30 to 40 knot wind. God knows what the chill factor was! But we took our aircraft out on time to the sunshine of Nassau and Belize.'*

Lawry was also involved in an aeromedical flight at short notice. On a flight to Masirah the call came to go to Gan. A nursing team was being flown there from the UK in a VC10. A Royal Navy ship had put into Gan with a very seriously ill sailor. The plan had been to flag stop Mauritius for Masirah but the patient's condition worsened and the aircraft stayed the night. The next day, with the use of slip crews, the UK was reached. The patient recovered.

**Gan's last year**

In 1956 the Maldivian island of Gan epitomised the burgeoning of the RAF's long transport force. To take over an entire island and purpose build a transit airfield clearly illustrated the intended size and capability of that force. Now, if that was to go, then Gan was no longer required and the end of 1975 saw the last transport aircraft stage through and the winding up of the base commence.

This was planned to be complete by 1st April 1976. It was a task of some delicacy; we had taken over a native island, those local people had worked cheerfully and willingly beside us for some 20 years. There would be a generation who had not known the island without the Royal Air Force. And now we were leaving.

Formal visits of farewell were made by the Station Commander, Group Captain W Edwards to government officials in the capital, Male. Part of the local goodbyes included gifts to the local people, a set of garden furniture, a barometer from the Met Office and a complete set of the Encyclopaedia Britannica. A civilian doctor and his nurse wife, working for the Ministry

From the Norman Rose photo album: *'Colombo 11/12th April 75. Diverted from Gan due to flooding and bad weather. Rear: Nigel Berresford copilot, Steve Smith nav2, Dave White steward, Don McKay ground eng, Mike Russell nav1. Front: Dave Bromley ALM, Norman Rose captain, Rich Williams engineer.'* (*Norman Rose*)

As near as can be determined, the last Britannia flight through Gan was on 21st December 1975. This marked the start of the rundown with the despatch of air and sea freight and the handing over of installations to representatives of the Maldivian government A final parade, with the Ensign being lowered, was held on 29th March 1976. (*Sgt R Harcourt*)

of Overseas Development, arrived to take over the caring that had been provided by the RAF's Medical Centre. The Station Commander comments,

*'This was a particular cause of satisfaction as the withdrawal of medical facilities would have been a grievous blow to the local people.'*

On 29th March 1976 the RFA Sir Percivale, with the last of the servicemen on board, sailed out of the lagoon to close a chapter of RAF history.

**To the market place**

As forecast, the dreaded disposal flights started. The aircraft were to be positioned at nearby RAF Kemble, by Cirencester and at RAF St Athan, South Wales. Here they could be viewed by prospective purchasers. Lawry Green notes that, with Squadron Leader Dru Shaw, he flew XM520 to St Athan on 13th May. Many years later, Lawry discovered that he had recorded most of those last flights:

| Date | Captain | Aircraft | To |
|---|---|---|---|
| 13 May | S/L Shaw | XM520 | St Athan |
| 09 Jun | F/L Williams | XL635 | St Athan |
| 09 Jun | F/L Williams | XM491 | St Athan |
| 18 Jul | F/L Davidson | XN404 | St Athan |
| 18 Jul | F/L Davidson | XN392 | St Athan |
| 13 Aug | F/L Caskie | XM490 | St Athan |
| 13 Aug | F/L Caskie | XL657 | St Athan |
| 03 Sep | F/L Oldham | XM489 | Kemble |
| 03 Sep | F/L Oldham | XL640 | Kemble |
| 23 Oct | F/L Cotton | XL639 | Kemble |
| 27 Oct | F/L Crowther | XM496 | Kemble |
| 24 Nov | F/L Adams | XM518 | Kemble |
| 24 Nov | F/L Adams | XM519 | Kemble |
| 19 Dec | F/L Cater | XL636 | Kemble |
| 19 Dec | F/L Adams | XM497 | Kemble |
| 30 Dec | F/L Bird | XM498 | Kemble |
| 30 Dec | F/L Brennan | XM637 | Kemble |
| 12 Jan | F/L Bird | XL658 | Kemble |
| 12 Jan | W/C Robertson | XL660 | Kemble |

**Spared the gloom**

Dave Court-Smith returns to his log book:

*'I learned that my tour would end before the demise of the fleet as I was to be posted to Wake Island in the Pacific in July. My 'Swan Song' was a run down to Aruba in the Netherlands Antilles, north of the coast of Venezuela; HMS Hermes was in harbour and we took a number of her commandos back to the Canadian military training area near Fredericton in New Brunswick.*

*'And so I was spared the gloom and despondency which would undoubtedly attend the final days of this splendid aircraft.*

*'Navigating around the world was not a straightforward affair - you always had to be aware of the limitations of the aeroplane and its equipment, and sometimes you got that funny feeling in the pit of your stomach, but how reassuring it was to look out of the window and see two great propellers spinning around (with, hopefully, two more on the other side) and know that eventually you would end up at your destination with a great sense of achievement and enjoyment.'*

**Hong Kong farewell**

If there was 'gloom and despondency' then it would have been hanging heavy in the air at Hong Kong on 21st December. A correspondent of the station magazine '*Gau Lung*' was moved to write these words:

*'The last Gurkha Lift completed, the aircraft was departing for the UK with the detachment personnel on board. A solitary Gurkha played the bagpipes as the passengers boarded the aircraft. Air Commodore B G Frow, the Commander Royal Air Force Hong Kong, was there to bid the crew farewell. Cameras clicked as the aircraft taxied away towards Lion Rock, turned through the green gates and past HAEC for the Kai Tak runway. The inland direction was in use so the spectators were rewarded with a final view of XL660 climbing away against the background of Hong Kong Island then towards the hills behind Kowloon to turn and disappear to the west.'*

This aircraft, and others operating in the Mediterranean, returned to RAF Brize Norton. The official date of the last Britannia route flight was 22nd December.

**Sweet words**

Many tributes were being paid to the Britannia and to the air and ground crews that operated it. One of the most eloquent eulogies came in a signal from Major General R W L McAlister:

'FROM MAJOR GENERAL BRIGADE OF GURKHAS AND ALL RANKS BRIGADE OF GURKHAS:

Wing Commander Geoff Bowles and Air Chief Marshal Sir Denis Smallwood GBE KCB DSO DFC salute the Squadron Colours on the final parade. (*Dougie Graham*)

It is almost as if the compatriot VC10 could not bear to watch this sad occasion. (*Dougie Graham*)

Major T G Blackford (right), representing the Brigade of Guards and Air Commodore B G Frow, Commander Royal Air Force Hong Kong bid farewell to the last Britannia crew to fly out of Kai Tak. Photograph from '*Gau Lung*', the magazine of RAF Kai Tak. (*Joan Edwards née Hisbent*)

west and finally disappeared into the distance.

*The photograph shows (right to left) — Major T G Blackford, representing the Brigade of Gurkhas, and Air Commodore BG Frow, Commander Royal Air Force Hong Kong, talking to the crew of the last RAF Britannia to fly out of Kai Tak.*

TIME AND TIDE WAIT FOR NEITHER MAN NOR FINE OLD AIRCRAFT AND WE ARE ALL SAD THAT THE THREE YEAR GURKHA CONNECTION WITH 99/511 SQUADRONS AND THE BRITANNIAS IS NOW AT AN END. LITERALLY THOUSANDS OF GURKHA SERVICEMEN AND THEIR FAMILIES HAVE HAPPILY, SAFELY AND COMFORTABLY SPANNED THE AIR SPACE BETWEEN HONG KONG, BRUNEI AND KATHMANDU DURING THIS TIME. ONE OUTWARD AND VISIBLE SIGN THAT YOUR AIRCREWS GOT SATISFACTION FROM THIS CHALLENGING OPERATION WAS THE FACT THAT, BEFORE ARRIVAL IN KATHMANDU, THEY WOULD WHEN CHANGING INTO PLAIN CLOTHES PUT ON THOSE KUKRI TIEPINS WHICH BECAME, WE BELIEVE, THEIR SPECIAL PRIDE. WE WOULD LIKE YOU TO KNOW THAT THIS SMALL TOUCH AND ITS UNDERLYING THOUGHT WAS NOT MISSED BY A SINGLE ONE OF YOUR PASSENGERS TO WHOSE RESPECT FOR YOUR AIRCREWS WAS THEREBY ADDED AN UNSPOKEN BUT HEARTFELT BOND OF COMRADESHIP. THANK YOU ALL.'

**Aircrew pool**

31st December 1975 marked the official disbandment of the squadrons. As the number of members had decreased they had been brought together as an aircrew pool under the command of Wing Commander Geoff Bowles, the last CO of 99 Squadron. Evidence that he was the man for the job in those difficult days comes from an ex-member of that pool:

*'... exceptionally pleasant and cheering type of boss, firm when needed but never a bull*******. I found myself as a sort of 'Assistant Adj' on 99, Oct to Dec, and remember the tremendous amount of work he put in to try and secure reasonable postings for the remaining Britannia aircrew.'*

**Final parade**

January 1976 was a mixture of practicality and ceremony. Two aircraft remained for delivery to Kemble. On 6th January a joint disbandment ceremony was held. The parade was reviewed by the AOC-in-C, ACM Sir Denis Smallwood. The two squadron colours were paraded for the last time borne by Flight Lieutenants Steve Fowler and John Smith. Relaxation followed in the evening with a party attended by 400 past and present squadron members.

**Colours laid up**

In Service tradition, the two colours now had to be 'laid up'. 99's was flown, in one of the last two Britannias, to the Royal Air Force College Cranwell, to hang in its church, and 511's to Lyneham. There it was accepted by the Chaplain-in-Chief RAF in the Lyneham Parish Church.

**The last two**

On 12th XL658 and XL660 were flown to Kemble. 658's flight engineer, Pete Hobson, meticulous with pen and brain, recorded the crew names: Captain, Flight Lieutenant Bud Bird, one of the splendid Canadian recruits to the fleet. Copilot, Flight Lieutenant Dick King, member of that excellent breed, a first tour copilot. Navigator, Flying Officer Pat Smith, again a sharp member of that younger band. Loadmaster, Sgt Barry Young, a worthy representative of the 'workers down the back'. Crew chief, Chief Technician Bob Felstead, a totally dedicated craftsman.

660's crew was no less worthy - and a little older in the tooth.

The aircraft routed via the headquarters of Strike Command at High Wycombe and Lyneham. The Group Headquarters at Upavon had to miss out because of low cloud.

Thus an era ended.

COMBINED BRITANNIA CREW DETAIL

RAF BRIZE NORTON

DECEMBER 1975

| T NO | CAPTAIN | CREW IDENT | SQN | ETA Z | ITINERARY | ETD Z | REMARKS |
|---|---|---|---|---|---|---|---|
| 6586 | SQN LDR TUCKEY | B36 | 99 | | BZN NOV | 240225 | BRITANDET |
| | FLT LT TAYLOR | B35 | 99 | 240915 | AKROTIRI | 241045 | AIRFRAME ROTATION |
| | " | B35 | 99 | 241800 | MASIRAH | 241900 | B36 REC AKT-BZN 2087 |
| | KING | B37 | 99 | 250025 | GAN | 250155 | B35 REC GAN-BZZ 2027 |
| | " | B37 | 99 | 250835 | TENGAH | 260200 | |
| | " | B37 | 99 | 260730 | HONG KONG | 280300 | |
| | " | " | " | 280805 | TENGAH | 290225 | |
| | " | " | " | 290845 | GAN | 300220 | |
| | " | " | " | 300740 | MASIRAH | 010550 | DEC |
| | " | " | " | 011330 | AKROTIRI | 020430 | |
| | | | | 021155 | BZN | | |
| 6566 | SQN LDR TUCKEY | | 99 | | BZN | 030525 | EX LEADING DRIVE |
| | | | | 030900 | DECIMOMANNU | 031100 | |
| | | | | 031445 | GUTERSLOH | 031645 | |
| | | | | 031840 | BZN | | |
| 6567 | REMLINGER | B38 | 99 | | BZN | 041620 | EX JOWAR |
| | ADAMS | B39 | 99 | 042310 | AKROTIRI (SLIP) | 050100 | B39 POSN AKT? |
| | ADAMS | B39 | 99 | 050550 | KHARTOUM | 050750 | |
| | REMLINGER | B38 | 99 | 051235 | AKROTIRI (SLIP) | 051405 | B39 REC AKT-BZZ? |
| | | | | 052140 | BZN | | |
| 6568 | BRENNAN | | 99 | | BZN | 120830 | EX RJUKAN |
| | | | | 121115 | GARDERMOEN | 121345 | |
| | | | | 121445 | LEUCHARS | 121615 | |
| | | | | 121750 | BZN | | |
| 6569 | BIRD | | 511 | | BZN | 151015 | EX DECIPHER |
| | | | | 151230 | TOULOUSE | 151400 | |
| 6570 | BIRD | | 511 | 151620 | BZN | 161200 | |
| | | | | 161415 | TOULOUSE | 161545 | |
| | | | | 161805 | BZN | | |
| 6563 | | B44 | | | HONG KONG | 180800 | HK REC |
| | | B44 | | 181305 | TENGAH | 181440 | B44 REC GAN-BZZ 6563? |
| | BRIDGER | B40 | 99 | 182100 | GAN (S) | 182300 | B40 POS GAN |
| | TAYLOR | B42 | 99 | 190430 | MASIRAH (S) | 190630 | B42 POS MAS |
| | TUCKEY | B43 | 99 | 191420 | AKROTIRI (S) | 191550 | B43 POS AKT |
| | | | | 192325 | BZN (S) | | |

1

Page 1 of the very last 'Combined Britannia Crew Detail' for December 1975.

511 Squadron's colour arriving at RAF Lyneham borne by Flt Lt John Smith.

The 511 Squadron Colour at Lyneham Church. With Flt Lt John Smith are Master Engineer Mel Tinton, the colour party Warrant Officer and the two escorts, Flt Sgts Keith Mursell and Chas Fellows.

on a concrete base outside the base's Gateway Hotel as a permanent reminder of its service with the RAF.

After a chequered civil career it was bought by Katale Aero Transport to operate in Zaire tranporting coffee and other commodities.

it was used to transport herds of goats.

He also worked with Afrec in Athens for

The Secretary, Britannia Association, Cottage, 112 Oxford Road, Calne, Wiltshir SN11 8AH.

Manual towing honours for the last Britannia to pass through RAF Brize Norton servicing flight. The fleet was disbanded in January 1976

A 'manual tow' for the last Britannia to be serviced in the Base Hangar, Brize Norton. (*Swindon Gazette via Tom Lowe*)

658 and 660 were the last two aircraft to be delivered to RAF Kemble. 660's crew was (L to R): Copilot, Flight Lieutenant Ken Stanley, a maturer copilot - and trumpet player extra ordinaire; captain, Wing Commander Dicky Robertson, the last CO of 511 Squadron; the Wg Cdr CO of RAF Kemble; navigator, the much respected Wing Commander Geoff Bowles; flight engineer, Flight Lieutenant Harry Vye, a 'solid citizen' and appropriate representa-tive of the commis-sioned leaders of that band of conscientious flight engineers; loadmaster, Flight Lieutenant Alan Roberts, again an excellent leader of a great team.

# Conclusion

And so we close this chapter of aviation history. There are flying tales that are more spine chilling - RAF Britannia experiences in no way compare with those of war. Nevertheless, for all its civilian image, this was a military aircraft and it was operated in a time of finely balanced peace and played its part in sustaining that fragile situation. It also represented our country on the world stage. The Royal Air Force Britannia's demise can be seen as an indicator of a declining national role.

To do all this so successfully required a continuous and relentless effort - it did seem as though there were no quiet Britannia times. Its services were always in demand. Those of us who served with this fine aircraft can feel proud of the effort that we were required to make - and made. The Whispering Giant wore its uniform with pride.

# Appendices:

1. Life Goes On
2. 496 - ‘Regulus’
3. The Britannia Association
4. Glossary
5. Aircraft Histories
6. Index

APPENDIX ONE

# Life Goes On

Royal Air Force life may have ended for the Britannias but, evidently, they were a marketable product judging by the steady stream of business men who viewed the aircraft stored at RAF St Athan and RAF Kemble. The mid-70s was obviously a time of entrepreneurial activity in the lower echelons of civil air transport. At this level, having the latest sophisticated model is not important (or affordable). What is needed is as 'young' an aircraft as possible at the right price. The RAF Britannias were not 'old' by aircraft standards where the flying hours completed are more of a measure than the chronological age. Information is not available on the prices asked but these must have been acceptable as every single aircraft was sold. The first five went in the September and then an average of two a month were sold through to May; by the 26th all 22 had gone. It is alleged that one buyer went into the MOD office in Carlisle dealing with the sale and placed on the desk of the civil servant concerned a suitcase containing cash for the aircraft he wished to purchase.

**Biggest buyer**

The largest purchaser was Young Cargo, a new airline in Belgium, who

This photograph of the sales line-up at Kemble was taken by aviation enthusiast Graham Salt from the lay-by on the A429. These would have been the final batch of aircraft to be put up for sale as 658 was one of the last two flown to Kemble on 12th January 1976. (*Graham Salt*)

Geminair retained much of the old RAF livery. (*Peter Rentzsch*)

bought, or had bought on their behalf, eight of the aircraft to be registered in the block OO-YCA to OO-YCH. But the Britannia in civil life was going to have to feed on itself; in time, four of these aircraft were broken up for spares. Two did not have their Royal Air Force uniform removed before the breakers moved in at Gosselies, Belgium. Others had a minimal reincarnation with just the RAF markings obliterated, the white top, grey under-belly and blue cheat line retained and the company name added. This minor adaptation was carried out by A.M.A.Z. That and the registration number were all that appeared. They were saving up for the paint for their full title, Agence et Messageries du Zaire. At the other end of the livery scale was Eurafric whose 'roll-out' appearance was described as 'stunning'.

**Other buyers**

Other customer names give an indication of the market to which they went: Liberian World Airways, EuroWorld, Aer Turas, Guinness Peat Airlines, Shackleton Aviation, Intercontinental Meat Co, Air Faisal, Afrek Ltd, Eddie le Jeune and GeminAir Transport. Subsequent changes of ownership throws light on the life they led; Domaine de Katale, U M Patel and M I Raj, Katale AeroTransport, Transair Cargo, InterEuropean Airways, Redcoat Air Cargo, J Coggins/City Airways, Eurafric, Hubert van Overberghe, Zaire Aero Services, Centre Air Afrique, TransGulf, Air Works India, Gaylan Air Cargo, Captain John de Bry and Dnain Egly Lukim.

**Some clues**

The next insight is in extracts from the histories: '... inscription on the aircraft, 'In cooperation with Liberia World Airlines.'', 'Purchased by Domaine de Katale for spares after liquidation of Young Cargo.', 'Due to high cost and long delay, ferry flown back to Ostend.', '... flown to Gosselies for spares.', '... for cattle flights to Dubai and Seeb and meat to Kuwait.', 'Leased to Cyprus Airways 9 Sep 76 for 12 months wearing Aer Turas colour scheme and Cyprus Airways titles. Leased to GeminAir still as EI-BBH.', '... operating mainly cattle and horse flights', '... painted with a rhinoceros (known as Rhino One).', '... with coffee bean symbol on one side of tail. Operation mainly Goma to Mombasa with coffee.' and lastly, 'During Zaire invasion by Angola, May 78, used to supply Zaire Army in Kinshasa with fresh vegetables from Goma.'

**The deaths**

Finally, the various 'ends': 'Cannibalised and left derelict until broken up in 1981.', '... in 1980. Broken up at Ostend the same year.', 'Still at Goma derelict.', '... flown to Gosselies for spares on 10 Feb 76 and broken up there in 1977.', 'Sold 1979 to Airline Engineering Luton and broken up the same year at Luton.', 'Broken up May 76.', '... derelict at Kinshasa being robbed for spares and storage of U/S engines.', 'Used for spares for Air Faisal and scrapped Luton Nov 76.', 'All spares removed and aircraft broken up.', 'Aircraft lifted over fence and towed to the Fire School practice ground. Burnt during 1981.' and again those words of finality, '... broken up in 1978.'

**Britannia Café?**

Some of the aircraft suffered ignominious ends. XL657, having once during its life, flying between Belgium and Zaire, tipped on its tail whilst it was being loaded, eventually ended up at Kinshasa having been grounded by the authorities for not having a valid Certificate of Maintenance and repairs not carried out. The aircraft was stripped for spares and the engines removed. Later, as it lay in this sorry state it suffered the further indignity of having its wings and tail cut off in order that it could be transported and, allegedly, converted into a restaurant. There was a positive sighting of the flight deck section of XM520; it was installed in the 'Transit Bar' at Kinshasa!

**Engine tester**

XM517 was also the victim of the oxy-acetylene torch. Its wings were cut off outboard of the inboard engines and the fuselage aft of the mainplane trailing edge. The openings were sealed to make it into an engine test bed for Airline Engineering Ltd at Luton in cooperation with Rolls Royce.

**On 'The Box'**

XL640 became a TV star. Redcoat Air Cargo, who had acquired the aircraft, cooperated with the making of a TV series called 'Buccaneer'; a story not unrelated to the contents of this chapter, being episodes in the life of a company, 'Redair', operating on the fringe of the air transport business.

Ex-RAF Britannia crew chief Tom Lowe on the flight deck of his civilian charge - an Afrek ex-RAF Britannia. (*Swindon Gazette via Tom Lowe*)

**Drug runner**

Some notoriety surrounded the civil career of XL660. It was being operated between Bombay and the Gulf carrying meat and goats. It was returned to the UK in April 1978 for an inspection. On landing at Manston, HM Customs found 78 boxes containing cannabis resin. The aircraft was impounded and later sold by the Customs authorities and returned to the air.

**Colin Rowlinson - Civilian**

*'When I left the RAF it was with a*

The effect, at Shannon, of reverse thrust on one engine at 300 feet. (*Colin Atkins*)

*very Micawberish outlook, 'Something will turn up'. Turn up it did, by the way of the 'hopvine' not the 'grape' one. It happened thusly. I was in the 4-ale bar of the local pub, along with two ex-loadmasters, one of them mentioned a Greek civil construction company based in Athens that had purchased two ex-RAF Brits* (Author: to become Afrek)*; they would fly their own people and equipment to places where they had contracts - Libya - Nigeria and the West Coast of Africa. My ears pricked up when he said they were looking for a flight engineer. With no more ado, contact was made with said firm and, after a couple of interviews, I once again packed my suitcase*

A Redcoat Britannia. Note the rudder deflection. (*Redcoat*)

*and headed for Athens via Gatwick. Two days later I was on the flight deck of one of my ex-RAF friends, a touch of the déjà vu, I hear you warble.The next six years passed quite nicely, living in an apartment 10km outside Athens on the coast, very 'touristied'. All good things come to an end and the end came in February 1983. The firm wrapped up, the aircraft wrapped up and the aircrew wrapped up. My wife and I stayed on until June 1983 'doing' the islands and having purchased a second hand car, loaded a 2-person tent plus camping chattels and headed for 'Old Blighty Shores', via Patras - Brindisi and a few camping sites en route Dunkirk. Having re-established myself with Inland Revenue and DHSS, I settled down to becoming a 'real' civilian.*

*'To conclude, I quote from the book 'Cheshire VC'. He writes, 'Those who went more or less straight from school into the war have been brought up on the highest and most impelling motive that life can offer. Now they must be content with one that is far inferior.' How true!'*

**Crash!**

XL658 suffered two indignities; the first minor. It was named 'Diedre'. The second was of a more major nature; it crashed on the final approach into Shannon on 30 September 1977, fortunately with no loss of life. Previous to this a fire had broken out in No.3 nacelle behind the bulkhead. There then followed a long history of No.3 propeller going into reverse on the ground. When this happened whilst taxying at Shannon, for a first flight after an inspection, it was decided that this was enough and the aircraft was unloaded and three engine ferried to Luton for rectification. On the return flight to Shannon ex-99 Squadron captain, Tommy Atkins recalls a problem:

*'... suffice to say, the result of No.3 propeller going into reverse at some 300 feet on finals, with absolutely no indication on the flight deck, was somewhat traumatic.'*

The aircraft crashed and was a write-off.

**Old comrades die**

Many ex-RAF Britannia people left the Service with the scrapping of the aircraft and joined the civil flying world. Some were aided in this by a concession introduced by the Civil Aviation Authority that RAF pilots holding full transport flying categories would be exempted certain parts of the civil pilots' licence examination requirements. Not unnaturally, many found jobs with the companies that had purchased the RAF Britannias. This, sadly, led to the deaths of two of them.

**Very experienced crew**

Redcoat Air Cargo Ltd operated, at one time or another, four ex-RAF Britannias. One of the contracts they won was for the weekly re-supply flight from Lyneham to our garrison in Belize, British Honduras. XL639, now registered as G-BRAC, was returning from Central America via Boston.

Danger...ice, but no one told the plane's crew

by RALPH BARKER

NEXT WEEK: The brothers

The trees that reach for the sky

A dummy for ever in danger

Tyres save water

THE DIAMOND KEY ACCOUNT NOW WITH EXTRA INTEREST AND EASIER ACCESS.

7·75% NET

28 DAYS' NOTICE

DIAMOND KEY ACCOUNT

7·75% = 11·07%

7·97% = 11·39%

When you want a better investment

YORKSHIRE Building Society Has the key

The tragic accident was given some heartless press treatment in later years.

A magazine photograph of old RAF Britannia XM498 unceremoniously decaying at Kinshasa. (*Tony de Bruyn*)

The captain was ex-Squadron Leader Bill Coburn who had a distinguished RAF Britannia career. A holder of an 'Exceptional' flying category, he served on 99 Squadron, then as an instructor and examiner on the OCU and the Examining Unit. He left the Service from Boscombe Down where he had flown the A & AEE Britannia.

The first officer was another very experienced, above average RAF pilot with many Britannia hours. Ex-Squadron Leader Jack Jones had also served on 99 Squadron and been an instructor on the OCU. The navigator was also once one of the RAF Britannia team, ex-Flight Lieutenant Tony Beckett.

**Snow and ice**

They had arrived at Logan International Airport, Boston at 3.00 pm for a night stop; in the night there was heavy snow. The next day, at 11.00 am, the crew reported to the airport for their flight to Shannon. Whilst the pilots and navigator went to the Weather Office and filed a flight plan, the flight and ground engineer battled with snow and ice at the aircraft. There was such a build-up of snow that it had to be swept off before the de-icing fluid could be applied.

One can imagine the difficulties the crew faced. As the engines were started the snow was still falling; as they taxied the runway was changed causing hold-ups whilst Air Traffic sorted out conflicting aircraft on the taxyways. The ground was slippery and reverse power had to be used to control the aircraft.

The crew knew that they were only just below the maximum take-off weight of 185,000lbs. What they did not know, through a combination of circumstances, was that there was an area warning of:

'*... frequent moderate to occasionally severe icing ...*'

**Climb! Climb!**

As they released the brakes for take-off, almost an hour had elapsed since the aircraft had been de-iced. On the roll down the runway it hit patches of snow which smashed up on to the underside of the aircraft. Outwardly, and as preserved on the cockpit voice recorder, the crew proceeded normally with the after take-off routine, this in spite of being very severely shaken by turbulence.

Their progress was being monitored on radar and, two minutes after the take-off, the controller became concerned with their height in relation to position and followed the procedure for such a situation; 'Romeo Yankee one-oh-three low-altitude alert, check your altitude, climb and maintain niner thousand.' This was acknowledged from the aircraft with the statement that they were passing 1200 feet. The aircraft was in cloud and still experiencing severe turbulence.

After just over a minute, the radar controller again warned of their low altitude. Three minutes later Britannia G-BRAC crashed into a wooded area. Seven of the eight occupants were killed instantly; miraculously the flight engineer survived.

**Verdict**

A meticulous investigation of the accident was carried out by the American authorities. The conclusion was that:

*'... the probable cause of the accident was degraded aerodynamic performance beyond the flight capabilities of the aircraft resulting from an accumulation of ice and snow on the airframe before take-off and a further accumulation of ice when the aircraft (flew) into moderate to severe icing conditions following take-off. Contributing to the cause of the accident were encounters with wind shear, downdrafts and turbulence during the climb ...'*

Bill Coburn, Jack Jones and Tony Beckett were mourned by their old RAF colleagues whose thoughts were that a Britannia crew had never had the odds so stacked against them.

**Simulator found**

The Britannia simulator only just managed to hold out for the lifetime of the RAF aircraft. This was something of a wonder as the technology was obviously extremely dated and the upkeep of the components needed considerable ingenuity by the technicians. When the axe came the simulator was up for disposal at Lyneham (it had not been moved to Brize Norton because of its parlous technical state). Initially it went to the RAF Museum at Hendon but, much to the surprise of Squadron Leader Peter Jordan who came upon it, it eventually found its way to 'The Muckleburgh Collection' at Weybourne on the north Norfolk coast near Sheringham - a 'Tank Museum'! The author visited the museum some years later and the simulator had disappeared. The staff remembered that it had fallen off the lorry when being moved!

**Last operator?**

The Zaire aircraft register featured many of the ex-RAF Britannias. In fact, the Central African state and Cuba were to be in competition as to which was going to operate the last one. It was thought for a long time that the very last Britannia flight was that of the Boscombe's old XX367 in Zaire.

This was chronicled by Tony de Bruyn, a Belgian with an unquenchable enthusiasm for the Britannia. He was on board for that last flight on 4th July 1991 when multiple oil consumption problems were experienced. In a very comprehensive account he relates:

*'Very early in his life, this 'Propliner' correspondent developed a passion for Bristol's mighty Britannia aircraft. Apart from collecting information and pictures of this classic early turboprop transport, there was a desire to discover the mystery surrounding the activities of the world's last Britannia operators. Hence, during 1988, a trip was planned to visit the AeroCaribbean operation in Cuba. Unfortunately the ultimate experience of actually flying in a Britannia was not achieved during that trip and a later letter from Havana confirmed the operation of the last Cuban Britannia flight on 21st March 1990. On that fateful day, CU-T120 (ex-XM496) landed in an emergency, with a failed No.4 engine, at Guayaguil in Ecuador whilst operating a Peru to Havana flight. Later she made a three engine ferry flight to Havana and has never flown again.*(Author: We now know that 496 was to fly again - much to everyone's surprise - see later.)

*'Thus with the long career of the Britannia in Cuba drawing to an end, there was only one other place in the world that offered the chance of seeing an operational Britannia - the rarely visited country of Zaire. Being well aware of the inhospitable nature of this country, particularly in respect of aviation enthusiasts, I realised that this could be a rather frustrating mission. This proved to be so on my first visit as my contact in the latest company to operate the Britannia, Business Cash Flow, proved to be in the UK! Once home, and with my appetite whetted, further contacts were developed with the intention of visiting Zaire again.*

Grandad Jordan's photograph of the simulator -and his two grandsons! (*Peter Jordan*)

Business Cash Flow Aviation was the proud owner of the old Boscombe Down Britannia, a Series 312F registered as 9Q-CHY. It is photographed at N'Djili Airport, Kinshasa in July 1991 by Tony de Bruyn during his visit. (*Tony de Bruyn.*)

*'Business Cash Flow Aviation was founded six years ago by Dr Mayani, a Zairean/Belgian entrepreneur. The company's business was centred around the transport of bread and other perishable foodstuffs to cities located within the massive rain forests of Zaire and thus difficult to access via road or rail. Transport of goods by air is the only reliable and secure way of ensuring that cargo arrives at its intended destination in Zaire and Dr Mayani utilised space aboard aircraft flown by a variety of operators including Katale Air Transport. By 1985 Katale was operating the largest fleet of Britannias flying anywhere in the world with four aircraft - three Series 253F 9Q-CDT (ex-XM498), 9Q-CGP (ex-XL660) and 9Q-CHU (ex-XL640) together with a Series 312F, 9Q-CHY (ex-Boscombe Down Brit). Initially BCF paid for freight space per kilo but business was so successful that entire aircraft were chartered from Katale.*

*'Eventually Dr Mayani decided to establish his own airline. Negotiations started with Katale for the purchase of the Britannias and a price of US$250,000 was agreed for the two airframes, CDT and CHY, together with all the remaining spares. However, by the time of this sale CDT had already performed her final flight so the centrepiece of the deal was CHY. This was the former Boscombe Down aircraft which had been acquired by Katale early in 1984 and came with an impressive package of spares which included no less than seven spare Proteus engines and a warehouse crammed with other parts, most of these were still in their original factory wrapping. Except for the engines, most of these spares existed at the time of the deal between Katale and BCF. With this handsome package, BCF Aviation was looking forward to a successful Britannia operation.*

*'Having arrived in Kinshasa on the evening of July 2 1991 aboard one of Swissair's high-technology MD-11s, I was greeted by John Byrne, BCF Aviation's Technical Director and Britannia flight engineer. He provided me with a brief tour of 9Q-CHY, which had just returned from a flight to Mbuji-Mayi, we left the airport for a much-needed rest. Early on the following morning we met Captain Ray Lyons, an Aer Turas 'veteran' who had clocked up many hours flying their DC-4 EI-ARS in addition to their Britannias EI-BAA and EI-BBH. On the way to the airport we also collected the first officer, Jean-Claude Clinkemaille. We arrived at N'Djili Airport to find that the Britannia was already loaded and ready to start engines. With everyone in position, clearance was obtained for start-up, and soon all four Bristol Proteus engines were running smoothly.*

*'ATC directed us to back-track to the end of runway 06 for departure. Once lined up and with everything functioning normally Captain Lyons opened the throttles and the Whispering Giant began her 45-second long take-off run. Suddenly, Zairean skies were playing host to this magnificent lady again, and we commenced a sedate but impeccably graceful climb to our*

*cruising level. We were bound for Mbuji-Mayi with a full load of cargo consisting of cane sugar, hurricane lamps, saucepans, foam mattresses, and one very excited 'Propliner' correspondent.*

*'In order to carry passengers, 17 seats have been installed at the rear of the cabin, and they are attended to by a very pleasant stewardess named Mary Ngoma, who has been nick-named 'Number One' by the crew. On this morning's flight, she only had to provide comfort for four passengers. The one-way fare from Kinshasa to Mbuji-Mayi, a distance of 1,200 kilometres, is 1,000,000 Zaire (approximately $100). For those preferring jet travel the fare is a little higher at $120, but as the jet equipment is usually in the form of Caravelle VIs or Boeing 707 series 400s the age of the aircraft is little different from the Britannia! Taking into account that the average monthly wage for Zaireans is 150,000 Zaire, one can appreciate that air travel is open to only a very few.*

*'After one hour and fifteen minutes at our cruising level of 15,000 feet, the Proteus note changed as we commenced our descent through the haze layers into Mbuji-Mayi. From May until September there is a dry season in Zaire, with a rainy season extending through the remainder. My visit took place during the former, and this generates humid conditions with a great deal of dust in the air leading to poor visibility. Given that on occasions there are no navigation aids whatsoever, while at other times aids may be unreliable, crews are often forced to return to Kinshasa when unable to locate a particular airfield. As aircraft always uplift sufficient fuel at Kinshasa for both the outward and return journeys as few outlying airfields possess any refuelling facilities, there is never a problem with aircraft having to divert all the way back to Kinshasa.*

*'Fortunately today's crew find Mbuji-Mayi with no problem, and after a flight of exactly two hours the Britannia touches down on the 2,000-metre runway. The heavily laden aircraft slows to a halt thanks to the use of reverse pitch and once parked we are greeted by a bunch of loaders keen to empty the Britannia's large freight hold. The crew make their way to the terminal building for some rest and refreshment. I endeavour to obtain permission from the airport director to shoot some photographs of the Britannia, but two hours later a disappointed photographer joins the crew for the return flight to Kinshasa.*

*'For our return journey, the Britannia is completely empty, and after take-off we climb rapidly to our cruising level of 18,000 feet. Once level, the crew kindly offered me the seat vacated by the first officer, and with the autopilot disengaged a delighted correspondent takes his first Britannia flying lesson. With previous 'hands-on' experience being limited to a few hours on gliders, this was quite a memorable experience indeed. After a little instruction I found that I managed to maintain altitude ... well, more or less at least! After finally bringing 9Q-CHY back on to the correct heading, the task of flying the aircraft was wisely transferred to the auto-pilot.*

*'Another exhilarating moment was still to come, as without warning, some one hour and fifteen minutes into the flight, the number one engine suddenly shut itself down with no apparent cause. Several attempts by the crew at a restart were unsuccessful, thereby necessitating a three-engined landing at Kinshasa. The subsequent approach and landing were no problem for the Britannia's experienced crew, in the words of Captain Lyons, 'It's just easier with four (working) engines'. Kinshasa was reached after a flight of one hour 45 minutes, and due to the unforeseen problems with the No.1 Proteus, the aircraft was grounded for the next day for the engine snag to be resolved.*

*Bearing in mind that this is the last Britannia flying anywhere in the world* (Author: 496 had not appeared on the scene when this article was written), *and that the conditions in Zaire are far from easy so far as engineering is concerned, it is of great credit to the company's staff that the Britannia has remained in service so long. Indeed, the engine/airframe combination is unique, and with the spare parts stock of Proteus engines now dwindling rapidly it is remarkable how the type has survived in service.*

*'July 4 was spent with the aircraft grounded at Kinshasa for repair and this provided the 'Propliner' correspondent with the opportunity of visiting the BCF Aviation spares warehouse - a true Aladdin's cave which, apart from some empty beer crates,*

RAF Britannia people went in many directions. Ex-99 and Boscombe Down Britannia signaller Bob Shergold, as a retired Warrant Officer, became a member of the Body Guard of the Yeomen of the Guard. (*Bob Shergold*)

*is stacked high with Britannia spare parts. Many of Boscombe Down's extensive range of spare parts are here, while the stock has been augmented with numerous parts from other aircraft broken up in Zaire in recent years. Thankfully there are still many Proteus engine spares in stock, and the sight of the shelves crammed with items of every shape and size would suggest that there is sufficient here to keep a Britannia serviceable for many years to come.*

*'Following a series of engine runs late in the evening of July 4, 9Q-CHY was declared serviceable once again, and we arrived at Kinshasa Airport at eight o'clock on the following morning to prepare for another service to Mbuji-Mayi. Although the aircraft was fully loaded with cargo, refuelling had not taken place as N'Djili's single fuel bowser had been busy replenishing the tanks of some international flights, and it took quite a time before our turn in the queue came. Refuelling was eventually completed by ten o'clock, and we were airborne at 1024 commencing a gentle climb to our cruising altitude.*

*'On this flight I took the opportunity to inspect the Britannia's fascinating logbook. This revealed that the aircraft had flown regularly until July 12 1990 when she was withdrawn for a maintenance check, which saw her grounded until November. At the end of this work she was painted in the full BCF Aviation livery first adopted by the company's Boeing 707. Previously she had retained the brown/beige livery sported during her service with Katale together with her old British Eagle name of 'Team Spirit'. Sadly not only did her Katale livery disappear, but her old Eagle name gave way to the name 'Mwenye Mikebwe' - Dr Mayani's grandmother. She returned to service on December 1 with a flight from Kinshasa to Mbuji-Mayi, and undertook similar trips on December 2, 3, 5, 7, 9, 12 and 17. On December 6 she operated a flight to Gbadolite, the hometown of Zaire's President, which is a particularly profitable operation for the company. Crew training at Kinshasa took place on December 19, and on December 20 another flight was completed to Mbuji-Mayi. The last flight of 1990 was a half-hour test flight from Kinshasa on Christmas Day. After this flight, the crew returned to Europe for leave and the aircraft remained idle at Kinshasa.*

*'The crew returned to Zaire on May 24 1991, and thanks to the expertise of John Byrne were able to get the Britannia back into the air for a trip to Mbuji -Mayi on May 26. Daily services to Mbuji-Mayi then followed for the remainder of the month (with the exception of May 29), and twelve further trips to the same destination were made between June 1 and 22. Flights to Kananga were conducted on June 6, 9 and 12, while on June 20 the Britannia flew*

*to Mbandaka. Trips to Coma (a three hour 45 minute sector) were made on June 8 and 15; while on the return leg of another flight to Coma on June 24 No.2 engine had failed in flight, necessitating the grounding of the aircraft for an engine change. However, she was airborne again on June 29 for another flight to Mbuji-Mayi, followed by similar flights on June 30 and July 2.*

*Having brought myself up-to-date with the aircraft's logbook my attention was drawn to the flight-deck. Some twenty minutes into the flight it had become clear that No.3 engine was losing oil rapidly. The crew decided that an immediate return to Kinshasa was in order, and the aircraft was turned back and a successful landing made at N'Djili Airport at 1110. On the ground the oil leak was traced to a faulty oil pump and the snag rectified that afternoon.*

*'On the following day, July 6, we were expecting to make an early departure for Mbuji-Mayi as the aircraft was still loaded from the previous day's abortive mission. However, a fuel company representative declared that problems had arisen with the supply of fuel to BCF Aviation, and he was unwilling to replenish the aircraft's tanks until the dispute had been settled. As patience is a much-valued virtue in Zaire, there was nothing else to do but wait until BCF Aviation had sorted out their differences with the fuel company. The issue was finally settled around noon, and by one o'clock HY's four Proteus engines were purring again as the aircraft taxied out for take-off. She began her take-off run at 1304, and initiated a climb to 15,000 feet with an Indicated Air Speed (IAS) of 220 knots.*

*'Some 33 minutes after take-off we reached our cruising level, and although the oil loss on No.3 engine appeared to have been rectified, it now became apparent that we were losing an excessive amount of oil from No.1 Proteus. The crew, not wishing to risk a three-engined landing with a fully loaded aircraft, elected to shut down No.1 engine at 1417 with the oil quantity gauge by then reading close to minimum. By shutting down one engine, our cruising speed fell from 220 knots (IAS) to only 190 knots. We began our descent into Mbuji-Mayi at 1449, and upon reaching 4,000 feet Captain Lyons restarted No.1 engine prior to making a perfect four-engined landing at 1508 after a flight time of two hours and three minutes.*

*'During the turn round at Mbuji-Mayi, the oil reservoir for No.1 engine was filled to the maximum (8 imperial gallons), while the other engines' reservoirs were maintained at the normal 6-gallon level. Take-off for the return journey was made at 1652, with the lightly loaded Britannia soon reaching her cruising altitude of 22,000 feet.*

*'However, as the flight progressed it became clear that all four engines were now consuming oil at an alarming rate, thus making it likely that a poor quality batch of oil was at the root of this problem. With all four oil gauges now showing low levels, a descent to Kinshasa was begun some 83 miles from the airfield. What followed was a dramatic night-time approach into N'Djili Airport, with the needles on all four oil gauges settling on the permissible operational minimum. Needless to say, there was great relief all round on the flight deck when 9Q-CHY executed a safe touchdown on runway 24 at 1827 local time. Four minutes later, all four Proteus engines were shut down on completion of a rather eventful flight.*

*'Following the events of this flight, not surprisingly it was decided to ground the Britannia for an analysis of the oil and for No.1 engine to be changed. This information was passed on to BCF Aviation's head office and on Sunday July 7 the engineers prepared to undertake the engine*

Two 511 navigators, Windy Deere and Joe Edwards, left 99 Squadron and the RAF to join Air Canada. Come the time that navigators were no longer required, they retrained as pilots. The photograph was taken on the occasion of Joe's subsequent ordination into the Anglican Church of Canada. Windy Deere has become familiar to readers of these pages. His humour continues with the message that accompanied this picture: *'The Reverend Joe is the one in the smart frock.'* (*Wyndham Deere*)

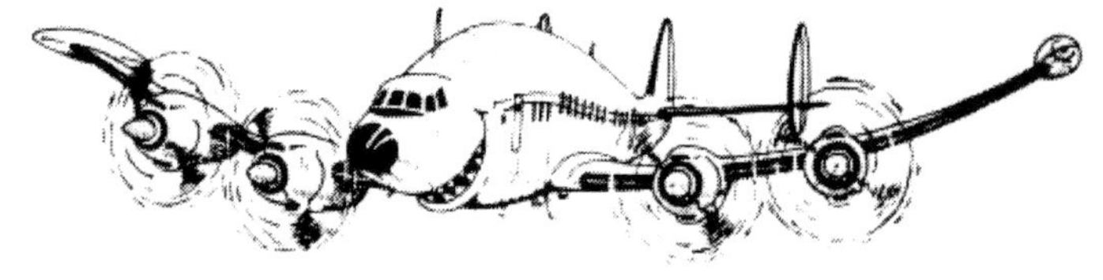

**Propliner Aviation Magazine**

*change. However, at eleven o'clock that morning Dr. Mayani called a meeting of the airline's staff to inform them that he had decided to stop flying the Britannia with immediate effect. He declared that he was not satisfied that he could continue a successful operation with the Britannia given the recent engine problems experienced by 9Q-CHY. This was a sad day indeed.'*

The 'Propliner' editor added:

*'The Britannia is now being offered for sale in the hope that there might still be someone out there who would like to operate the world's last airworthy Britannia. It seems a little ironic that Proteus engine problems, which delayed the aircraft's initial entry into service almost 40 years ago should now be the reason given for the grounding of the last example of the type.*

*'I would like to express Tony's immense appreciation of all those involved in providing him with one of the most enjoyable and memorable experiences of his life. In particular he would like to thank John Byrne, Technical Director BCF Aviation, Dr. Mayani owner of BCF Aviation, and the Airport Director of Kinshasa N'Djili Airport, Zaire.*

*'It should be emphasised that aircraft photography in Zaire is not approved of by the various airport authorities, and readers should not take this article as any sort of encouragement whatsoever for photography at Kinshasa or anywhere else in the country. You have been warned!'*

This is an amazing insight into how the 'Zaire Britannias' were heavily utilised - and the 'slender string' on which they were operated. So that was it.

**'Propliner'**

This article was first published in *'Propliner'* magazine. An aviation enthusiast has written thus of the magazine:

*''Propliner' magazine was founded by Stephen Piercey and first published in January 1979; he felt that vintage transports, affectionately known as 'propliners', deserved a magazine dedicated to them. He was right, as it is still around 20+ years later and widely respected by fans of the 'big, round engines'. The contents are dedicated to mostly civilian, propeller-driven transports still earning their keep or preserved in some way or another, but also looks back upon events and profiles airline companies when the aviation industry largely consisted of these prop-driven airliners or freighters. Tony Merton Jones joined 'Propliner' from the start and continues as the driving force behind this excellent magazine. 'Propliner' magazine is published four times each year and largely survives by the dedication of a small team and propliner fans from around the globe, providing articles, news and photographs.'*

Subscription enquiries to:
'New Roots', Sutton Green Road,
Sutton Green, Guildford,
Surrey, England GU4 7QD
Fax: +44 1725 513857

**The Phoenix arises**

The story above of the last flight of the Boscombe Down Britannia ended with, 'So that was it.' But it was not! It had been generally accepted that the last Britannia flight was this one by the old Boscombe aircraft, on 4 July 1991, in Zaire but on 16 September 1993, the purr of four Proteus engines was heard in the skies over Filton. The factory workers turned out to watch a ghostly white Britannia, registration 9Q-CM, fly up the runway and subsequently land. It was only on the ground a few hours before continuing its journey; this started in Cuba and was due to end in Zaire. What is of particular significance within these pages is that the aircraft was the old XM496. Ron King was there:

*'Although the Britannia that visited Filton was not actually built there, its visit was something of a triumph. Arthur Mitchell and I were indeed privileged and proud to attend. At Filton we were met by Peter Hicks and Duggie Dyson from the Rolls Royce Heritage Trust and our day of nostalgia began. The aircraft duly arrived*

*overhead (on time I might add) and, after a low-level flypast, did a 'silky' landing and the day began. We were escorted by coach over to the dispersal area in time for 'Doors Open'. We wandered about, poking and prying into everything; the old nostalgia returned. When was the last trip we did in her? Where did it go? We took loads of photographs, talked to many old friends and made many more. The crew were busy with the reason for their stop, to pick up all remaining spares so, whilst loading was going on, we walked all around her again, in and out, reliving those cherished memories; recalling accomplishments - and failures. It made you realise that this is what the Britannia Association is all about; this is the aircraft that generated this unique feeling of belonging.*

*'The coach then took the crew and the rest of our party to the staff canteen where we had an excellent repast after which we visited the Rolls Royce Heritage Trust for a conducted tour. We returned to the dispersal for the final preparations for the 1600 hours departure and the VIP arrival, Sir Archibald Russell, the designer of the Britannia, and his lady. TV and newsmen abounded and Sir Archibald gave an address. He made it clear that the aircraft had satisfied the design and performance standards but circumstances had overtaken the propjet with the arrival of the pure jet. He enthused about the affection that the Britannia had generated and agreed that she was a very gracious lady.*

*'We had the chance to talk to Walter Gibb, Bristol's ex-Chief Test Pilot who, with the great Bill Pegg, was responsible for the initial test flights and trials. It was time for 'turning and burning' and 496 left dispersal and lined up on the runway for 'stops and props' - and then she was away, smooth as silk and silent as a ghost. Around the circuit she went and then swooped low down the runway as in a final salute. Now gone, we were left highly elated and wished her 'God Speed' and 'Bon Voyage' and hoped to see her at a later date when she finally comes home.*

*'That's it, from not much of a literary giant, the King Bird, just a very faithful servant of a great aeroplane.'*

Sir Archibald and Lady Russell leave 496 after a nostalgic visit. (*Ron King*)

Ron expressed his gratitude to Ian Lansdowne 'who kept us posted and made things happen'. Roger Hargreaves met the aircraft at Shannon and his hope was that, at the end of its career in Zaire, it would be donated to the Britannia Aircraft Preservation Trust, 'who plan to restore her to former glory in RAF Transport Command colours as part of the Bristol Aero Collection.'

Author: Ron's questions, When? Where? sent me scurrying to my log book, hoping to find some exotic example with which to impress you readers. I went back three years and concluded that 496 must have lurked in the hangar a lot! In that time I only flew it four times. Where? Around Brize Norton local area on PRTs and co/captain conversions. Impressed?!

Perhaps, within my role of scribe, I could recover some credibility. I turned to my reference books. Yes!! XM496 was named after a star in the constellation Leo, 'Regulus'. A Roman general circa 200BC, Regulus was said to have been, to later Romans, 'a model of HEROIC ENDURANCE'. Bingo!!!!

More news of 496 follows.

So, in this account of the RAF Britannia and its people, we have reached the point where the engines are shut down, the parking brake is on .. the cabin lights are dimmed ...

... and the story is told ...

**SHUT-DOWN CHECKS**

| | | |
|---|---|---|
| Parking brake . . . | P | On. Pressure |
| Cabin lights . . . . | Q | DIM |
| Flight deck lighting . . | All | Minimum |
| Radios . . . . . . | C | All off |
| Landing lamps . . . | P | RETRACT and TAXY |
| Shut-off valves . . . | C | Shut |
| Cabin entry temperature controls . . . . . | C | OFF |
| Crash switch override switch . | C | NORMAL |
| Windscreen wipers . . . | P/C | Parked, FAST |
| Alternators . . . . . | E | All OFF |
| Inverters . . . . . | E | All OFF |
| Superfine . . . . . | E | OFF |
| HP cocks . . . . . | P | SHUT |
| Booster pumps . . . | C | OFF |
| Steering . . . . . | P | OFF |
| Compasses . . . . . | E | ISOLATE |
| Propeller brakes . . . | P | On below 100 PRPM |
| Navigation lights (night) . | E | ON/OFF |
| Leading edge lights (night) . | E | OFF |
| Flight deck lighting . . | P/C/E | Minimum |
| Hydraulics . . . . . | E | OFF-LOAD |
| Oxygen . . . . . . | P | Off |
| Gyro switches . . . | N | ISOLATE |
| Sextant mounting heater . | N | OFF |
| Oil cocks on F1 panel . . | E | SHUT |
| Anti-collision lights . . | E | OFF when propellers stopped |
| Radio supply switches and intercomm. . . . . | C/E | Off |
| LV and MV supply switches . | E | GROUND/OFF |
| Panel E7 . . . . . | E | Circuit breakers tripped |

RESTRICTED

APPENDIX TWO

# 496 - 'Regulus'

The last chapter ended with the news that the last flying Britannia, ex-RAF XM496 had passed through Filton on its way from Cuba to Zaire. The aircraft had joined the Cuban Britannia scene in the summer of 1984. It ceased flying in March 1990 when it suffered an engine failure on a Peru to Havana flight. It diverted to Guayaquil in Ecuador. The last flight was a three-engine ferry from there. Not following a traditional pattern, it wasn't broken up but lay at Havana until 1992. John Byrne, who had kept the Britannia aircraft in Zaire alive, visited Cuba and negotiated the purchase of 496. With a lot of persistence, it finally flew again in August 1993 prior to its ferry to Zaire in September.

**The task in Zaire?**

Amazingly the aircraft had a four year career there. Snippets of news filtered back including the fact that it had to land, main wheels only. The restoration involved the cannibalisation of XX367, the Boscombe Brit. So, it was repaired and went back into the air.

It might be as well not to enquire about some of its activities for those years in Zaire. It 'escaped' the country only just before the take-over by 'New Management'. It was then decided that it would be retired. The flight engineer, John Byrne, had enthusiastically kept 496 in the air. His keenness resulted in the aircraft being offered to the Britannia Aircraft Preservation Trust. Funds were raised for the flight to the UK and 'Regulus' duly arrived at ex-RAF Kemble on 14th October 1997.

**Press release**

More detail of the foregoing was given in a press release from the Britannia Aircraft Preservation Trust:

*'At 1300 GMT on the 14 October, The Britannia Aircraft Preservation Trust took delivery of the world's last airworthy Bristol Britannia aircraft. This marked the end of the types 45 years of flying, the prototype having flown on its maiden flight from Bristol Filton's runway on the 16 August 1952. This particular aircraft was built, under licence, by Shorts at Belfast as a 253 MkI aircraft, with constructor's number 13508, for Royal Air Force Transport Command. Delivered to RAF Lyneham on 17 September 1960, registered XM496 and named 'Regulus', it was operated jointly by*

The first of a series of photographs mapping out the life of XM496.

RAF life for '*Regulus*' - 17 Sep 60 to 2 Nov 75 - captain John Caskie and navigator Dave Smith.

The time in Athens - with Afrek - 21 May 76 to Jan 83 .
(*Tom Lowe*)

*99 and 511 Squadrons until withdrawn from RAF service on the 27 October 1975 and flown to RAF Kemble for storage. During its RAF career, the aircraft flew to South Africa from RAF Fairford, in September 1973, in support of Concorde 002's 'hot and high' trials.*

*'Purchased by Afrek on 21 May 1976, it was the last Britannia to leave No.5 Maintenance Unit at Kemble when it was flown to Luton for conversion by Monarch Aircraft Engineering to 253F all-cargo configuration. Delivered to Athens on 6 June 1976 as G-BDUR, it flew mainly to Nigeria carrying construction workers and equipment. After a period of storage in Greece, it was sold, along with its sister-ship, to the Cuban airline Aerocaribbean in August 1984. It was operated on the air-line's routes within the Americas and very occasionally to Europe until the 21 March 1990 when the aircraft suffered an engine*

Bristol

Britannias are 're-lifed'

New life has been breathed into three of the last of the famous Bristol Britannias still in airline service. Filton senior technical liaison engineer Mike Bowden, as part of his job, has been keeping a close eye on a Type 318 and two Type 253 Britannias which have been overhauled and resprayed by Monarch Engineering Limited at Luton Airport.

Three aircraft - one of them 496 - were refurbished at Filton for Aerocaribbean, Havana - 1984.
(*British Aerospace newsletter, November 1984*)

16 September 1993, 496 briefly visited Filton en route to its new owners in Zaire. (*British Aerospace*)

*failure whilst flying between Peru and Havana, thereby ending 30 years of Cuban Britannia operations.*

*'The aircraft remained in Havana until the 25 August 1993 when, having been sold to Transair Cargo Zaire, it was test flown, prior to being delivered to its new owners. Ironically this was the date in 1960 when this aircraft had first taken to the skies at the start of what was to become a long and varied flying career. Registered 9Q-C.111 and named 'Jack, in memory of Jack Horan, a well known and much respected Britannia flight engineer, it was delivered to Kinshasa via Gander, Dublin, Filton, Ostend and Cairo in September 1993. Since then the aircraft has flown over 1000 return flights mainly carrying fuel oil and supplies in Zaire and neighbouring countries.*

*'With the collapse this year of Mabut's government in Zaire, it was decided in early April to ferry 'Jack' and the other aircraft in the Transairfleet, south to Lanseria near Johannesburg. These plans seemed doomed to failure when one of the Britannia's engines failed. This coupled with other technical problems, meant the aircraft had to be abandoned in Kinshasa whilst a replacement engine was bought and flown to South Africa. The Britannia finally flew out of Kinshasa to Lanseria on 4 May on three engines, a mere 12 days before the rebel forces drove into Zaire's capital city. The replacement engine was installed and the other preparatory work completed over a period of months, culminating in a test flight on 21 September, in readiness for the aircraft's long ferry flight home to the UK.*

*'The aircraft, now registered EL-WXA, left South Africa to begin its final journey at 0558 GMT on Sunday 12 October, having been donated by Transair Cargo to The Britannia Aircraft Preservation Trust. It routed via Douala*

*(Cameroon) and Palma de Majorca to the, now former, RAF base at Kemble which it left over 20 years ago to start its new career in 'Civvy Street'.*

*'The aircraft will be kept in working order and regularly engine run and taxied as part of the growing Kemble aircraft preservation scene. The BAPT is to be supported by the Bristol Aero Collection, whose museum is based at Kemble, and the Britannia Association. It is planned to eventually restore the aircraft to its former glory by repainting in Royal Air Force Transport Command livery.'*

**The Kemble Arrival**

What was quite sensational was that arrival. The aircraft was 37 years-old. It had had a hard civil life with servicing done on a shoe string and spares being virtually non-existent. Yet the three flypasts at Kemble, prior to the very final landing were flown as if the aircraft was just off the production line! When a Britannia normally flew that low, its undercarriage would be down for landing!

**The preservation of 496**

Looking after an old aircraft in the open air is not an easy task. One only has to visit the outdoor elements of the museums at Duxford and Cosford to appreciate the difficulties - and these are organisations with large resources. So, the team at Kemble have a struggle on their hands and perhaps original ambitions will not come to fruition.

This report appeared in the Spring 2001 edition of the Britannia Association magazine:

*'The group of Kemble enthusiasts ... has held a meeting to establish some policy matters for 496. Ever since its arrival at Kemble, in a parlous flying condition, there has been the vain hope that, perhaps, the aircraft might fly again. This really was a pipe dream, as it would cost millions to achieve. Nevertheless, when jobs on restoration and preservation were being done, there often had to be duplication or unnecessary work with the faint possibility of eventual flight in mind. It was decided, at the meeting, that now the clear policy for all should be a concentration on that preservation. Mind you, if anyone wins the lottery and wants to put up the 'millions' then no doubt they would be accommodated!*

*'We won't make this too low - as it's the last flight.'* One of three flypast at Kemble - 14th October 1997. (*The Cheltenham Newspaper Company*)

*'That preservation and restoration have continued apace with the forward main cabin refurbishment nearly complete and, in early spring, Topper Brown and his 'Merry Men' will start on the next phase with the cabin. With a bit of luck, the preparation of the airframe ready for painting will also start. Derek Smith has been concentrating on the flight deck avionics and the ambition is to have all the 'rogue' equipment removed and the radios, instrumentation etc brought back to circa 1965 configuration. John Densem has been putting his carpentry skills to good use and is constructing a wooden mock-up of the galley. He continues to operate his radio station from the aircraft and, with the HF aerials, there is not a country in the world he cannot reach. A new member has joined the team, ex-Crew Chief George Holton. He brings the* **old** *Crew Chief line-up to three, the other two being Ian Lansdowne and Ron King.*

*'The day after the Britannia Aircraft Preservation Trust (BAPT) members' visit to Brize Norton on 12th January, a group assembled at Kemble. Wet runs were carried out on all four engines and Nos. 1 and 4 engines were 'turned and burned'.*

*'Many of you will know that the aircraft was moved to several different locations on the airfield before taking up permanent residence in its present place. It had to be positioned there rather hastily and a lot of ingenuity and good luck was required. This included taking a bit of a 'push back' run at it, as the port wheels had to go over grass. This now prevents an essential element of preservation, taking the aircraft 'walkies' every now and again - a tractor tow around the airfield - and the occasional taxy under its own power. There is a need to concrete over the grass area. This will cost £1500. BAPT are asking members of various organisations to sponsor a square metre of the concrete for £20 ...*

Further news of 496 appeared in the Winter 2002 edition. Firstly, Roger Hargreaves makes this report:

*'Under the leadership of Project Co-ordinator, Jim Cox, work on the aircraft has been making steady progress within our limited manpower resources. Early in the year it was decided not to remove No.2 engine for rectification of the parking brake problem. Instead it was decided to put the engine on care and maintenance and reassess the situation later in the year, as there were other priorities. Work has centred on checking out systems and making modifications to enable engine runs to be carried out again on a regular basis. The first engine runs should take place in the near future, once the VHF radios and a ground to flight deck wander lead have been installed. We now have an obligation to our landlords to adopt a more professional approach to the way in which we do things. This will become even more critical when Kemble Airfield becomes a fully licensed aerodrome towards the end of the year. We are therefore adopting new operating procedures in co-operation with the airfield management, which should allow us to taxy the aircraft on a regular basis next year. Four of the main wheel brake units have been removed and are in the process of being overhauled by our friends at Brize Norton. However, they are in poor condition and there is a distinct lack of spares available. This leaves us with the option of having replacement parts manufactured, which could prove expensive, or investigating the possibility of using an alternative type of brake unit. One thing for sure is that the brakes must be in full working order before we can taxy the aircraft.*

*'The main passenger door runners have given us a lot of problems as they and the runners have become worn. The problem has been resolved by using the runners off 'Charlie Fox' although we are having new runners manufactured. We are also hoping to get the overhauled rear passenger door back from Northbrook College in the near future. This will then allow the forward door to be sent away for overhaul. The overhauled nose wheels were fitted to the aircraft in early summer. John Densem has finished the replica main galley, although it still lacks some equipment such as boilers and catering canisters. With some help from Ron King and Derek Smith, John has now started rebuilding the signallers station and re-installing some of the navigators station instrumentation. John Fairbairne has been continuing with the task of replacing the cabin lighting and Topper along with Tony Reynolds are gradually getting the cabin looking more presentable. The aircraft had a wash in mid-September thanks to an agreement with Serco at Brize Norton arranged by Topper*

More shots of that flypast - from the airfield ...
(*David Berry*)

The crew: hedge-hopping captain Bob Sobek, the engineer who has kept the Zaire aircraft alive for the many years, John Byrne, and first officer Christian Vervaeke.
(*Cheltenhan Newspaper Co.*)

... and from the road.
(*Bob Henderson*)

The RAF News man, Terry Palin's version of the moment ...
(*Terry Palin, RAF News*)

The members of the Britannia Association who were there to greet the aircraft. L to R: the author, Dave Parfitt, Arthur Mitchell, Titus Oates, Ian Lansdowne, Ron Stubbs, Ron King and Tony Molland. Front pair: Bob Henderson and Curly Beauchamp. Note the battered leading edge and the improvised propeller brake!
(*RAF News*)

These photographs by Tony Cullum seem to show that the flight deck is in remarkably good condition. (*Tony Cullum*)

The aircraft arrived with this Liberian registration - a 'flag of convenience' for its flight from South Africa to the UK. (*David Berry*)

To end this miscellany - one of the most familiar of Britannia shots - from the forward passenger door. (*Tony Cullum*)

Many an ex-RAF Britannia person has sat in the captain's seat of 496 and pondered on how things were. Here ex-crew chief Ted Sharpe takes his turn.

*Brown. The aircraft's fin will now be repainted along with as much of the fuselage as time allows. The apron on the starboard side of the aircraft has been enlarged to allow the aircraft to be moved more easily. Funds permitting, the port side will be enlarged in the spring of 2003.*

*'Thanks to a small number of volunteer guides, we have managed to open the aircraft to the public on all Kemble event days. This has generated much-needed funds along with additional Society members and other useful contacts. We do however need more volunteers to act as guides. In addition we are constantly looking for new working volunteers to help with XM496. We don't just need skilled and experienced engineers. We need people to look after our ground equipment, help clean the aircraft, mow the grass, help put together display items etc. The tasks are endless.*

*'So if you are able to help, please call Roger Hargreaves on 01444 244613 or Derek Smith on 01793 814745'*

**The Radio Man**

John Densem is mentioned above as one of the stalwarts of 'The Team'. He was asked to write about his activities:

*'I did the Britannia course September 1965 and was posted to 99 Squadron around November. My first 'meeting' with Regulus was November 4th 1965, the captain was Fl/Lt Bayliss and the flying was an MCT detail. October 1997 via the grapevine, news spread that an ex-RAF Britannia was shortly to arrive at Kemble and on the appointed day I positioned myself on the lay-by opposite the airfield to await the arrival. I filmed the black Hunter as it took off; it was off to Filton to escort the Britannia back to Kemble. The rest is history but I did manage to film the arrival including most of the low-level flypast before the landing. I eventually visited the*

*aircraft later that day and was astonished to see what had been done to it, realising afterwards that the previous owners had to make it earn its living which it obviously had done. All I remember seeing was a GPS unit on the end of the navigator's equipment housing and an IF unit, an ICOM 707.*

*'There are ICOM 707s available in the amateur range but set up for different frequencies. During 1998 I flew into Kemble as a passenger in a light aircraft. On visiting the tower to pay the landing fee the controller told me he just obtained the radio telephony licence it is necessary to have to qualify for a private pilot's licence. When I told him I had one as well he recruited me as an air ground operator starting there about three weeks later, one day shift per week, UNPAID. I spent three years at the tower and enjoyed every minute including days when I used to drive the tractor cutting the grass on three runways and three parking areas. During 1998 I became a member of the Britannia Aircraft Preservation Trust and spent most Saturdays working in Regulus. The possibility of using amateur radio from the aircraft appealed to me so I spent some time, with permission of course, checking the HF aerials. To get to the connections meant removing a long metal tray approximately half way along the roof of the passenger compartment containing another piece of equipment which I removed, checked that the aerials were not earthed in any way and checked the co-axial cables that ran to the crew compartment.*

*'John Fairbairn, the Trust's electrician, installed a 13 amp socket for me in the signaller's position and I was then able to connect my amateur radio and started making contacts sat in the same place as I had when on 99 Squadron. I must add that the signaller's seat was missing so for quite some time it was a case of using a stool. Later I found that the equipment removed from the roof was an ICOM AH-3, an automatic aerial tuning unit. I managed to get some information about it from the ICOM dealers in Kent and as my transmitter is also ICOM was delighted to find that I could use the ATU as well. I suppose I must have spent some 30 hours working on the aerials but am delighted that they are still OK. I have also checked and used the VHF aerial, amateur radio has the use of VHF but different bands of frequencies of course, and I have made contact with an amateur*

Jock Manson, ex-Belfast captain sent an e-mail to the Britannia Association magazine editor: I was having a bit of a sort-out and came across a rather nice photograph of 496 taken as she was passing through Dublin en route from Cuba to Zaire. She is all-white with just the registration 9Q-CJH showing. Fairly typically, No.2 prop is feathered! I can well remember seeing her in the distance and thinking she was a CL44 and then being rather surprised as I taxied past to realise that she was the real thing. (My F/O didn't even know what a Britannia was!). Anyway, our ground engineer at Dublin knew that I was keen on such things and got me a copy of this rather nice photograph.

Corgi produced a superb model of a RAF Britannia. They were persuaded to use the registration XM496.

*using VHF. He was on holiday in the Brecon Beacons. Sometimes I use morse, still very popular with amateurs, voice of course which is upper or lower side band and have recently run a Special call to celebrate the reforming of 99 Squadron. I have also arranged another call to celebrate the first flight of the Britannia aircraft which was August 16th 1952, I operated that during August 2002 Countries worked included, Australia, New Zealand, Malaya, Japan, Brazil, Mauritius, the USA, Canada, Russia, and most of the European countries as well as many amateurs in the UK.*

*'Now that my job with the galley is complete I am working on the signaller's and navigator's positions. We don't have all the correct equipment so please, if and when you visit and see what has been and is being done, take all of our problems into account. But I'm sure we will get some smart-ass remarks, which we will accept graciously.*

*John Densem G4KJV (my amateur callsign) Choppy, radio operator, avionics, grass cutter, painter, tea/coffee maker etc. Cotswold, Startley, Chippenham. SN15 5HG Tel: 01249 720456*
*e-mail: G4kjv99sqn@supanet.com*

*'PS. Not many people know this but the STR18C radio complex in ATS at Lyneham, that most of the Britannia signallers used for training, was built by a member of the 216 Comet Squadron. Me!'*

**Visiting 496 has a strange effect on David Court-Smith ...**

*'Sitting in the tatty old navigator's seat in tatty old 496, on that May afternoon of the Association reunion weekend, brought memories flooding into my head - the fact of being back in the 'office' did things to me that reading logbooks or looking at pictures has never done. My senses rolled back the tide of time . . . further and further and further ....*

*'Looking out of my window I saw what appeared to be the Bristol Channel - yes, there was the muddy estuary of the Avon and a little inland a goodly gathering of houses around a large castle just where the Frome flowed into the Avon. Bristol? Indeed, but not the city I knew. We were flying eastwards on a bright but hazy morning in high summer; the countryside was vaguely familiar but there was much more woodland than I remembered, the fields were different, and - above all - no real roads, only myriads of tracks. There were people in the fields and on the tracks, going about their many chores and unaware that tomorrow they will have a new king, because today is Thursday the second of August 1100, and in*

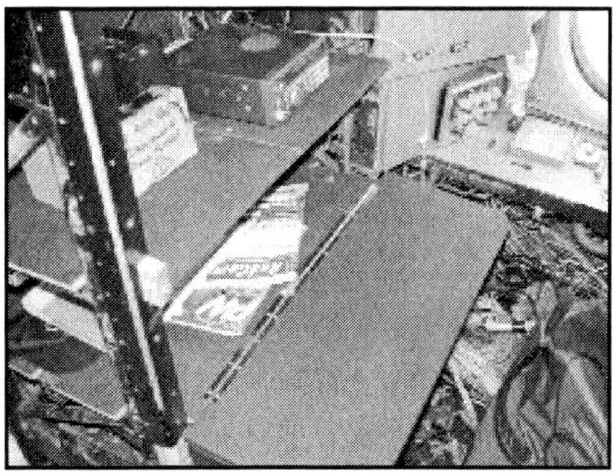

496's signaller's position from which ex-99 signaller John Densem speaks to the world. Below is the back of the card he sends to the people he contacts.

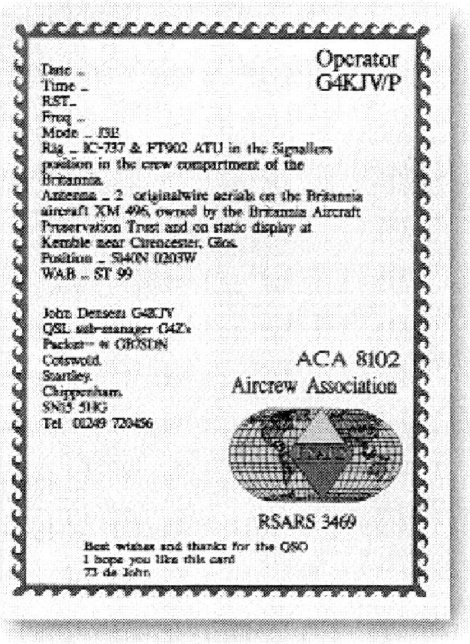

Operator
G4KJV/P

Date -
Time -
RST-
Freq -
Mode - J3E
Rig - IC-737 & FT902 ATU in the Signallers position in the crew compartment of the Britannia.
Antenna - 2 originalwire aerials on the Britannia aircraft XM 496, owned by the Britannia Aircraft Preservation Trust and on static display at Kemble near Cirencester, Glos.
Position - 5140N 0203W
WAB - ST 99

John Densem G4KJV
QSL sub-manager G4Z's
Packet - @ GB7SDN
Cotswold.
Startley.
Chippenham.
SN15 5HG
Tel 01249 720456

ACA 8102
Aircrew Association

RSARS 3469

Best wishes and thanks for the QSO
I hope you like this card
73 de John

The replica of the galley constructed by John Densem. (*David Berry*)

A lot of work has been done to the cabin - and a lot remains to be done. (*David Berry*)

*a few hours time William Rufus will lie dead on the sward of the New Forest.*

*'Ahead I can make out a settlement which must be Chippenham, and away to the northeast that familiar plateau, crowned not with runways but with a wispy blue carpet of flax, a very important cash crop for the lord of the manor of Bradenstoke, who holds this land. As yet, there is no name for this area but in the Charter Rolls of 1285 the place is referred to as Linham, 'the village where flax is grown' (Latin linumham). Passing on in time and place, we head northeast, across the Thames (the dark river) towards the little town of Bampton, with its fine castle rebuilt in the time of the Anarchy, when two cousins fought for the throne of England and 'Christ and his angels slept'. Just to the north of the town we see a tiny hamlet, Norton, i.e. the north settlement - a common enough name in medieval England. The ancient church there is unique in that it is the only one in the country dedicated to St Brice (or St Britius, as he is sometimes known), but it was the 19th century before the inhabitants incorporated his name into the village's - and the place became Brize Norton.*

*'Close by, the village of Black Bourton is remembered today for the Horse and Groom, a short stroll from the Britannia line and flying HQ, but as we turn gently over the 'settlement near a fortified*

Copilot wanted!
(*David Berry*)

*area' (burgh-tun) - probably Bampton again - several black-clad figures can be seen about their business. This manor has been gifted to the Augustinian canons of Oseney Abbey at Oxford, and their influence has probably given the place its prefix.*

*'I vaguely heard someone saying, 'Come on Dave, we're going now,' so I was obviously back in 1998, and a quick glance out of the window confirmed the fact that I was still at Kemble. Now there's an ancient name, first recorded in a Saxon charter of 682, British and possibly derived from a Celtic deity called Camulos; would not that have looked good on the side of a Britannia - much better than Argo!'*

**The future?**

Perhaps, from this chapter, it can be seen that the preservation of 496 is not a straightforward matter. There are peaks and troughs in the battle with preservation and it is hoped that there will be more highs than lows.

Another person was strangely affected by 496 - or, at least, Joe Belk's camera was! It has been suggested that this is how many a Britannia down the route might have appeared to some who had been 'tired and emotional' the night before.
(*Joe Belk*)

**Cheering news**

As it is, signs that the maintenance of 496 is on the 'up' this news at the end of 2004 is included here:

In time for the AGM, Roger Hargreaves reported to Chairman Fred Lace the plans for 496: It is widely known that the Bristol Aero Collection will eventually relocate to Filton where a new Aviation Heritage Centre is to be established in association with BAe, AirBus and Rolls Royce This is probably four or five years away and, although the lease on the Kemble hanger expires in December 2005, it is hoped that this can be extended until the Filton facility is ready,

After much deliberation, it has been decided that 496 will not go to Filton. The reasons for this being that we are unlikely to get a ferry flight permit even if we could get the aircraft into an airworthy condition. This would not be possible due to the lack of records for the aircraft. To dismantle the aircraft and reassemble it would cost in excess of £50k. Also, the Aero Collection already have Charlie Fox and RX as representative aircraft

We have had discussions with the Kemble Airfield Management and they are keen to retain the aircraft on site, possibly as part of a museum telling the story of Kemble. We have agreed, in principle, a number of points to secure the aircraft's future. When the aircraft is repainted this year, it will be painted overall in RAF Livery but only the starboard side will have Transport Command titles. This will allow the port side to be used by the airfield to advertise events etc and for the aircraft to be used more effectively for film work - something you cannot do with RAF titles emblazoned on the fuselage. We are also looking at the aircraft's interior being used for functions once the restoration work has been completed.

The aircraft will remain at its present location for the foreseeable future, with the dispersal being widened to allow it to be moved more easily. However a new security fence is to be built across the airfield which will mean 496 will not be easily accessible, but the intention is to build a picket gate in the fence, which will allow public access to the aircraft. The restoration of the interior is slowly progressing, under the leadership of John Densem, who has been a real stalwart amongst our small band of working volunteers.

The main issue facing us is the lack of working volunteers to help open the aircraft to the public, at weekends during the summer months, and to provide the manpower to work on the aircraft. Without this work force we are going to struggle to keep the aircraft live. On a brighter note, the Bristol Aero Collection have offered to open the aircraft for us when they can, which will obviously help us generate revenue from the public.

We have recently concluded an agreement to rent out our Douglas Tug to Chevron Technical Services who are establishing a BAe146 servicing facility at Kemble, Eventually there is a plan to build a hangar on the airfield which hopefully may be big enough to allow us to put 496 in there every now and again for servicing.

Martin and Ron take up the story of progress: On Tuesday 24th August 496 was successfully washed. This opened the door for some trials, on various parts of the aircraft, of the paint intended to be used and the method of application, prior to the Britannia Association purchasing the paint. White was applied to the fuselage window line above the port wing and around the port side of the cockpit windows. In addition, two areas were painted grey, these being the port lower fuselage just ahead of the wing and the top of the port wing adjacent to No.1 engine starboard bulkhead. Being a two-pack paint it wasn't the easiest to apply but it didn't seem to react with the existing colour scheme and has successfully 'gone off', looking very shiny. As expected, like the Belfast at Cosford, it exhibits a slight bubbly effect but this comes with roller application, so unless it is sprayed, which is out of the question, this will have to be lived with. With this satisfactory result the Britannia Association was asked to provide the previously agreed funds amounting to £1800.

Moving the aircraft was a further challenge. John Byrne, George Holton and Ron King changed three of the port main gear wheels. Having only three replacement wheels (tyres in better condition than those fitted), a decision was taken initially to change only two wheels on the port gear. However, when the gear was jacked up and after changing the rear inner wheel, it became clear that the two front wheels could not be turned as the brakes still fitted in these positions were seized. Therefore John, George and Ron decided to change both the wheels, removing the seized brakes in the process.

This should not cause a problem as, for the future, it is planned only to use the brakes on the rear of the main gear. Some of tyres fitted to the starboard main gear are not too healthy. With the problems encountered on the port gear, prior to any move attempt, it was thought advisable to check whether the forward brakes on the starboard gear were seized. Ron managed to get the 'cow shed' air compressor working and all 10 tyre pressures were checked and inflated as necessary so essentially, starboard gear wheel turning problems aside, the aircraft was ready for moving. This was planned for Thursday 9th September.

Team work really did work! Following a day's work to free the starboard gear forward wheels, the aircraft was moved over to Delta Jets on Thursday 9th September. We were conscious of the fact that it's been a long time since the engines were last run. The rest of the day was utilised to see if Nos.1,3 and 4 could be started. As we all know, there are problems with the No.2 so for the moment this cannot be started.. Regulus was successfully

Preservation is not confined to the aircraft - ground equipment is also required. (*John Densem*)

moved with the help of Chevron. It was towed out of her long term parking spot by Jamie in the white tug across the end of runway 08, past Delta Jets and to the new temporary spot at the end of the disused runway 31. Although there were a few anxious moments, it actually all seemed very easy and normal. So there we go, we've proved 496 does move! Alan Mutton the airfield manager commented on how pleased he was to see it in a different position.

Once over on the end of 31, John Byrne, George Holton and Ron King set about seeing how far they could get prior to attempting an engine run. Delta Jets had very kindly charged the 7 x 24v batteries that were in the aircraft with some success. The Vernon was used to provide the all important 112v/28v DC, and with the engine cowlings open and intakes checked for bird's nests, it was time to see if Regulus would provide a turn of any of the motors. Both John and George were extremely pleased with how many items they got live and on-line once the cockpit was powered up and this even included a successful deploy and retraction of the flaps and operational landing lights!!!

The really good news is that, with the exception of No.2, a wet run of all the engines was completed. Whilst it would be advisable to have indicated JPTs with some other items to be addressed (example - inoperation of some fuel cocks) it looks good for an attempted light up of the engines not too far in the future.

Both John and George are going to work on getting the aircraft ready for live engine running although before we do this it is going to be advisable to use some other form of ground power for the 112v DC. The Vernon is capable of supplying this but it wasn't easy to start and used £45 worth of fuel during its limited use to get us to the stage above. Therefore, as Rolls-Royce has said it is willing to donate its diesel-powered 112v/28v DC GPU (used for starting the Proteus at Hucknall) then ideally we need this in place before we do any more.

Above is the first wash time - note the dramatic 'before and after' effect. (*John Densem*)

More washing took place during the latter part of 2004 in hopeful anticipation of repainting.

2004 Kemble Air Day visitors view the piebald appearance of 496. This was the result of a painting trial...

... but for 2005 the repaint was completed and 496 looked quite splendid. (*Martin Fenner*)

APPENDIX THREE

# The Britannia Association

The Britannia Association exists for the benefit of members and ex-members of the Royal Air Force and Women's Royal Air Force whose service was associated with the Bristol Britannia. A reunion is held once a year and a magazine produced twice a year.

**The beginning**

Ex-AQM Ivan Burns provided this account:

*'I would like to describe the humble origins of the Association we have all come to know and take great pride in.*

*'On 1st January 1981, at 8 Cornfield Close, Witney, Oxfordshire, the home of David and Muriel Alexander, a party was being held. From somewhere in the crowd a voice was heard to say, 'You lot were on Brits. isn't it about time we had a Brit Doo?' As it was five years since the Brit. was disbanded, we did! A meeting was held later that month in the library of the Sergeants' Mess, RAF Brize Norton. The numbers present were four. Myself, Jack Moore, Tony Smith and John Browne. We held much discussion and were brave enough to form a committee. I was appointed Chairman as I bought the first round of drinks. A little later on we co-opted the late George Neilson on to the committee. We made progress and set a date for the very*

The Association committee in 1992. L to R: Arthur Mitchell, Fred Lace, the author, Tony Cullum, Bernie Burton, Len Shout, Jack Moore and a bit of Ron King. Absent from the photograph was Ted Sharpe ... and the photographer, Joy McArthur. (*Joy McArthur*)

This was the era of a large committee. At the time of writing the size is more modest - just five!

HIGH SOCIETY

# The Britannia Association

**The Britannia Association**

**Contact:** Arthur Mitchell, Secretary, The Britannia Association

**Membership:** 600 worldwide

**Subscription rates:**
Annual £3.00
Life £25.00

**What you get:** A twice-yearly magazine, 'The Whispering Giant', is posted free to all members. An annual reunion is held in the Swindon area, plus occasional additional social functions such as trips to former Britannia bases. With the advancing years of members, welfare support is also provided.

THE ROYAL AIR FORCE operated the Bristol Britannia for just 16 years, from 1959 to 1975, during the peak of RAF transport flying but at the twilight of the UK's global defence commitments. The scrapping of the aircraft marked the end of an era, but the ethos that surrounded the aircraft and the worldwide nature of its tasks created a tremendous camaraderie. Thus it was natural that, when the RAF fleet was disbanded, its crews wanted to stay in touch.

At a social gathering, a Sergeants' Mess group of groundcrew, air quartermasters and flight engineers decided that a bigger get-together should be organised, and a reunion was duly held on June 26, 1981.

From these beginnings the Britannia Association expanded to include people of all ranks and trades who served with Britannias, and membership has now stabilised at 600. An annual reunion in the Swindon area attracts an average attendance of 260.

A matter of pride for RAF Britannia enthusiasts was the fact that the very last Britannia to fly, XM496, was an RAF example. After finishing its lengthy and chequered subsequent civilian career in Cuba and Zaire, it flew into Kemble, Gloucestershire, on October 14, 1997. It is now preserved by the Britannia Aircraft Preservation Trust with the Association's support, and there is a plan to repaint it in its RAF Transport Command livery.

The relatively short — by RAF standards — life of the Britannia means that if someone served with the aircraft for any length of time at all then they will know a fair percentage of fellow members, which is not true of squadron associations and the like.

ABOVE Britannia Association Secretary Arthur Mitchell hands over a cheque to Roger Hargreaves of the Britannia Aircraft Preservation Trust as a contribution to the fuel costs of recovering XM496 to the UK. On the left is former crew chief Ron King, and on the right is Fred Lace, the Association's Chairman.

ABOVE Members in front of the plaque placed by the Association at RAF Lyneham to commemorate the type's service there during 1959–70.

**Society aims**

1 To exist for the benefit of members and ex-members of the RAF and WRAF whose service, both in the air and on the ground, was associated with the Bristol Britannia.
2 To support the preservation of Britannia XM496 by the Britannia Aircraft Preservation Trust at Kemble.

RIGHT A magnificent Charles E. Brown portrait of Bristol Britannia first prototype G-ALBO, which made its maiden flight from Filton on August 16, 1952, in the hands of A.J. "Bill" Pegg. The type went into service with airlines and the RAF, which operated Britannias from 1959 to 1975.

96 Aeroplane, January 2002

*first Reunion - 26th June 1981 and what a night it was - excellent!!! Because of its huge success, we continued to meet and laid plans to form a 'Britannia Association' from those who attended this first reunion. Volunteers were now forthcoming to join this 2nd year committee and the amount of effort and involvement they put in to achieve our Aim and write a Constitution was remarkable. The plans were finalised, the Constitution agreed upon and the second Reunion took place in the Gateway Hotel, once again at Brize Norton in May 1982.*

*'Prior to the fun part of the evening, a meeting was held of all those persons who wished to form a Britannia Association. The Aim and Constitution were read, discussed, amended and a vote taken. All agreed and the Britannia Association was born. The time had arrived to elect a future President of this new Association - any other title would have been well below the dignity of the Britannia. John J Browne was elected and formed the first Association Committee. He was succeeded, after two years by Tony Smith. Both have served the Association well and remained dedicated to its success. I must also mention Jack Moore without whose humour and drive we might easily have fallen by the wayside in that Spring of 1981.*

*'Thanks to all those involved then, now and best wishes for the future.'*

Publicity for the Association in 2001 - a feature in '*Aeroplane*'. Pity the photograph is BOAC!

Two eminent past members of the Association committee. Left is Jack Moore who took his turn as President and looked after 'Welfare', along with Joy McArthur, for many years. Ron King needs no introduction to Britannia people. An ex-President also, he was the Association's treasurer for a long, long time. (*David Berry*)

**The continuation**

From those beginnings the Association grew. As it was established by members of the Sergeants' Mess, membership was initially limited to AQMs, flight engineers and SNCO ground crew. Subsequently all ranks were invited to join and the numbers grew to around the 600 mark. Sadly death has taken its toll and there has been a falling off of interest by some. However, a trickle of new recruits who have just 'discovered' the Association helps to keep the numbers up. The total membership has been 500+ for a number of years now.

**The annual reunion**

This has been held at Blunsdon House Hotel for over 20 years. The date is equally well established - around the 3rd Saturday in May. The format has fluctuated but there has always been a meal. A variable

Britannia Association members in 'full flow' at a reunion: ex-ALM Joan Edwards (née Hisbent), ex-navigator Gerry Taylor and ex-captain (and route entertainer!) Dave Bridger. (*David Berry*)

has been music! This has recently been re-established with a live band, which has proved very popular. Attendance is now around 120 and the occasion is thoroughly enjoyed by this core of members.

**The magazine**

The author edits a twice-yearly, 16-page magazine for the Association. On the occasion of producing the 30th edition I wrote:

*'My trouble is that although I am well aware of the adage, 'Never volunteer!', it obviously slips my mind every now and then. This happened on 7th September 1984 when I attended my first Association committee meeting. The topic of a newsletter was raised - as, subsequently, was my hand. The result was a typewritten six-page production essentially concerned with the 1985 Reunion. The printing was done through the influence of the then Association president, Tony Smith. His wife, Marlene, worked in the Brize Norton printing section! Four more, twice-yearly, editions were produced this way with the contents and presentation becoming more ambitious within the confines of the method of reproduction. Then a*

Two Reunion stalwarts - ex-99 signaller Ken Heseltine and the ex-99 Squadron Adjutant Maurice Flynn MBE BEM. (*David Berry*)

Above is the setting of the memorial plaque at RAF Lyneham and below the detail. (*David Berry*)

*strange thing happened.*

*'At the time, I had resurrected the Boscombe Down magazine - must have volunteered again. This too was produced with local resources. Then I was approached by a company that had launched itself to professionally produce station magazines. The Service personnel would provide the content - the company would surround it with advertising, the revenue from which would cover production costs ... and provide a healthy commercial profit. The philosophy seemed quite sound. It was the early days of free newspapers and the like which had to be blanket distributed. A station magazine was a much more direct advertising weapon - or so potential advertisers would be persuaded. On the back of the Boscombe magazine, the company agreed to produce an Association one.*

*'This lasted for four editions before the publishers went out of business ... the philosophy was perhaps not so sound after all. So it was back to the DIY version, produced this time by the Lyneham printing section persuaded with some boxes of chocolates, flowers and smooth talking! But we had been spoilt by those professional editions and yours truly, with increasing computer facility, decided that a return could be made to that standard with me producing the camera ready copy and 'you' paying for the printing. Half the membership backed this idea with a payment of £10. This lasted three years - until Winter 1993. The committee then decided that the magazine should be financed out of Association funds and all members have received a copy, twice a year ever since. It is a slow drain on the funds but the feeling was that as we are not immortal, the situation was acceptable.*

*'The covers are historical - most in the sense that they recall past events - but others mark Britannia moments as they happened viz. the attempt to obtain a gate guard aircraft, the flight through Filton of 496 en route from Cuba to Zaire. This occurred when it had been believed that the very last Britannia flight had taken place some time earlier. Then there were the unveiling of the two memorial plaques to Britannia operations at Lyneham and Brize Norton, the publication of a RAF Britannia history and, finally, the return of 496 - the real 'last flight' - to the UK.'*

**RAF Britannia memorials**

Britannia Association members will recall the saga that led to the decision to install memorial plaques to our Britannia service at Lyneham and Brize Norton. The initial hope was to obtain an ex-RAF Britannia as a gate guard and many members contributed generously to the project. It became evident, as the years rolled by, that this ambition was not attainable - or sensible. With the decision to abandon it, the alternative of the memorial plaques was adopted and again generosity prevailed with many members allowing their gate guard

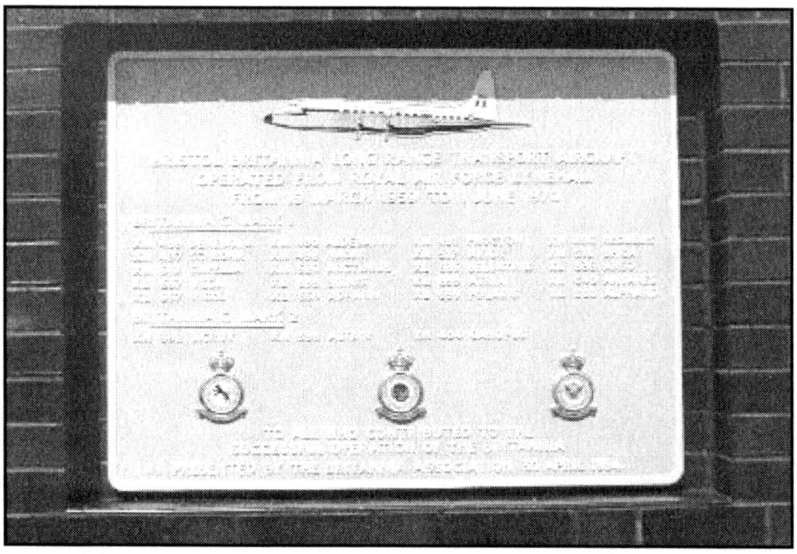

A photo of the limited edition print. (*David Berry*)

contributions to go towards this alternative. Also a substantial amount was raised with the sale of the Association's limited edition print of a painting by Bob Murray, signed by the Patrons and bought at its significant price by enthusiastic and supportive members of the Association.

Out of what might seem an anticlimax arises magnificence. The plaques now stand at Lyneham and Brize Norton in glory. They look tasteful and splendid and there is no fear that they are not an appropriate monument to those marvellous days of the Britannia fleet.

**That Limited Edition print**

The print was produced a number of years ago in support of the Gate Guard venture. They are from an original by Bob Murray, one time 99 flight engineer turned professional artist. Apart from aviation he also works in other fields, particularly automobiles. The print is entitled 'Climbing on Course' and the actual picture measures 18 x 12 inches. Each print is numbered and individually signed by the late Air Chief Marshal Sir Alasdair Steedman and Air Chief Marshal Sir Thomas Kennedy.

**Visits**

Although not a major feature of the Association, there have been a number of visits over the years. A group were invited to view the museum of the Rolls Royce Heritage Trust (Bristol Branch) at Filton. There have been two visits to Brize Norton and one to Lyneham. The latter one to Brize Norton marked an historic occasion in that No.99 Squadron was reformed as the unit to fly the new C-17 Globemasters on lease from the USA. Members were suitably impressed with the sophistication of this aircraft.

**Website**

The author puts Association information on the Internet via his website: www.keyhambooks.co.uk

**HM The Queen's Lyneham visit**

Her Majesty The Queen visited Royal Air Force Lyneham in May 1990. The Britannia Association was represented by, amongst others, ex-99 Flight Engineer Len Shout who writes about his day ...

'*When I left RAF Lyneham in 1966 after having served there for ten years, little*

The Association presented a copy of its Limited Edition print to the RAF Museum, Hendon. Air Commodore David Lawrence CBE RAF(retd), Keeper of Aircraft and Exhibits, accepts the print from Jack Moore, the author and Bob Murray, the artist.

On the Brize Norton visit Association members examine the cavernous interior of the C-17 Globemaster of 99 Squadron. (*Jimmy Kane-Smith*)

*did I realise that I would be returning nearly 25 years later to represent the Britannia Association at the 50th Anniversary of the Station and also at the Dedication of a window at the Parish Church of St Michael and All Angels in the village, in the presence of Her Majesty The Queen.*

*'On Thursday 17th May 1990, I arrived at the Station and having cleared the essential security, I was duly admitted. The Station was very impressive indeed with everything all spick and span. All the flowering shrubs were in full bloom and with the sun shining its very best, everything was set for a memorable day. After a pleasant walk through part of the Station and the village, I arrived at the church to be met by our esteemed President and Valerie, looking as charming as ever. And there was Jack McWicker who had flown over from the USA especially for the occasion.*

*'When Her Majesty arrived at the church, she was greeted by the Rt Revd J A Baker, Bishop of Salisbury, the Venerable John Smith, Archdeacon of Wiltshire, Group Captain The Reverend J Diamond and Wing Commander The Reverend R Resketh the Station's C of E padre.*

*'I found the Service of Dedication a very moving occasion, in particular the singing of the National Anthem in the presence of Her Majesty, just prior to her departure from the church.*

*'The stained glass window is a magnificent piece of work, depicting in montage the history of RAF Lyneham. It glows with vibrant colours with the Station crest prominent towards the bottom of the centre panel. This also features the main runway at night which takes the eye through the picture to the theme of St Michael portrayed above. There is so much to see and read in this work that I cannot attempt to describe it here; sufficient to say that if ever you are passing the door, you must enter the church and reflect on its magnificence.*

*'After Her Majesty had departed*

On the visit to Brize Norton, Association members admire the aircraft paintings in the Officers' Mess dining room. On the left are Bob Henderson and Dave Parfitt. On the right is ex-99 signaller Ian Partridge and his wife Ronnie. On leaving the RAF, Ian was ordained. (*David Berry*)

*the church for the Officers' Mess, I left, along with the President and his wife, for the buffet luncheon and drinks in the Sergeants' Mess. Of course, meeting a lot of old friends, the hangar doors were wide open and many a tale of yesterday was told! However, the moment for the departure of Her Majesty arrived and we all lined up beside the Comet Gate Guard to say farewell to such an honoured guest.*

*'It had been a really memorable day, one that I shall always treasure. It was a pity that it was not possible for all members of the Britannia Association to share in the enjoyment of such a Royal occasion. I was proud to be your representative.'*

**Association Information?**

If you are interested in finding out more about The Britannia Association then there are two avenues. You could go to www.keyhambooks.co.uk and follow the Britannia Association links.
Alternatively, write to:

The Britannia Association Secretary
15 Hayward Drive
Carterton,
Oxon OX18 3HX

The group photograph on the visit to RAF Lyneham. The author (extreme left) was still serving and hosted the visit.

The RAF Brize Norton visit. The Association's memorial plaque is on the wall of the Terminal Building behind the group.

Pride of place at reunions is given to the Association's model. Here it attempts to eclipse the good looks of two of the wives who used to run a small 'shop' - Valerie Berry and Jean Henderson. (*Maurice Flynn*)

During the afternoon tea break of the Association's visit to RAF Lyneham the group was joined by the RAF's first female pilot, Flt Lt Julie Gibson. The 'attraction' was Norman Rose whom she had met at a ceremony at The Imperial War Museum on the occasion of Norman presenting his medals, log books and model aircraft collecton for preservation. Julie is a Hercules captain on 24 Squadron. (*David Berry*)

APPENDIX FOUR

# Glossary

**A & AEE:** See Aeroplane and Armament Experimental Establishment.

**ADF:** Automatic Direction Finder; an outmoded navigation aid, sometimes called a radio compass. A transmitter on the ground sends out a signal rather the same way as a radio station. In the aircraft there is a receiver with an aerial which can be rotated. If a portable radio, with an internal aerial, is rotated then there is a point when the signal is at its best (maximum). It would be possible to determine the direction of the transmitter from this. The principle is the same in an aircraft except that it is better to detect the direction of the minimum signal. The equipment is subject to all the interferences associated with radio transmissions. The 'broadcasting station' is called an NDB (Non-directional Beacon). They have mostly been replaced with VORs (qv).

**advisory routes:** See airways.

**aeromed:** A colloquialism for aeromedical flights which can also go by the name of casualty evacuation or hospital flights. An important role for the Britannia, in all out war, would have been such flights. It was capable of being adapted to carry up to 53 stretchers and had the facility to operate two 'iron lungs'.

**Aeroplane and Armament Experimental Establishment:** When the Services order new equipment then a specification for its performance is drawn up for the eventual manufacturer. Before such equipment is released for Service use it needs to be checked to see that it meets the specification; also limits have to be decided for its use. In general terms, these are the tasks of A & AEE in relation to aircraft and associated equipment for the three Services. The document setting out the details of all this is known as the CA Release, CA standing for Controller Aircraft, the Service head of the controlling department. In the Britannia's days this was the Ministry of Supply. Now it is the MOD (Procurement Executive), MOD(PE).

**AIB:** The Accident Investigation Branch is an organisation that attempts to determine the cause of civilian flying accidents. Based at the Royal Aircraft Establishment Farnborough, it employs many sophisticated and painstaking methods with a reputation for considerable success.

**aileron:** A flying control (qv) on the wing of an aircraft that controls it in the rolling plane (left/right wing up/down).

**Air Ministry Operational Requirements (OR) Branch:** The branch in the Air Ministry (now Ministry of Defence (Air)) that determines the future equipment needs of the Royal Air Force and issues an initial outline of how this should be achieved.

**Air Clues:** An official magazine, circulated in the Royal Air Force, which is used as an organ for disseminating information associated with flying. It is, in the main, a 'serious' publication but does contain general interest articles viz the item on the withdrawal from Gan.

**Air Electronics Operator:** Since the earliest days of multi-crew aircraft, a radio specialist had been carried. With the increasing sophistication of airborne electronic equipment, which came within the province of these 'Signallers', it was decided to rename the aircrew trade to 'Air Electronics Operator' to better reflect their task.

**Air Support Command Examining Unit:** A considerable amount of training is carried out within the air transport force both at Operational Conversion Unit level and on the squadrons. It was the responsibility of the Air Support Command Examining (which, on the renaming of the Command, succeeded the Transport Command Examining Unit ) to oversee this training by checks and categorisations (qv) of the instructors involved.

**airspace:** Literally the air in which aircraft operate. There can be limitations on its use by legislation (controlled airspace) or by a country below it (see diplomatic clearance).

**airways:** An example of controlled airspace (qv). Air lanes are laid down by a controlling authority, generally defined by ground radio beacons, e.g.VORs (qv). Permission must be obtained to enter and fly along these lanes. Whilst in them, radio contact must be maintained with the appropriate air traffic control. That control will ensure that the traffic in the lanes is kept apart thus eliminating the risk of collision. This is the standard way that day-to-day commercial aircraft operate. Military air transport aircraft follow these procedures, when it is appropriate, which is most of the time.

The normal way to request permission to fly in the airway system is to submit a Flight Plan (qv) before the flight. Some lanes do not have the full power of being 'controlled' behind them. It is 'suggested' that they be flown in order to harmonise traffic. These are advisory routes.

**amsl:** Abbreviation for 'above mean sea level' which is appended to a height of an object, airfield, high ground etc to indicate the datum used. A value, known as the QNH (qv), can be set on an altimeter which makes it read the height of the aircraft amsl.

**AOC-in-C:** Air Officer Commanding-in-Chief.

**aquaplaning:** This is a phenomena associated with tyre behaviour on a wet surface. It can happen that a combination of conditions (depth of water, speed of tyre, weight of aircraft, type of tyre tread, tyre pressure etc) can cause the tyre not to be in total contact with the surface, a thin layer of water separating them. This can cause the aircraft to behave as if it were on ice.

This problem has not always been recognised. Now it is recommended that in wet conditions a firm touchdown is made to ensure that the water layer does not have a chance to be created.

**astro:** (astronavigation) As an aid to navigation, the angle of elevation of three stars in the sky is found with a sextant. From each angle it can be determined that the aircraft position is somewhere along a particular line. From the three 'shots', three 'position lines' can be drawn and where they intersect is the position of the aircraft. It would seem that two lines would suffice but accuracy is difficult to achieve. It is found that the lines produce a triangle (a 'cocked hat') and all that can be said is that the aircraft position lies somewhere within it.

**astro step:** A sextant is used to determine the angle of elevation of a star when carrying out 'astro' (qv). The sextant protrudes through a hole in the flight deck roof. In the Britannia, to allow the navigator's eye to reach the eyepiece, a platform was set in the flight deck floor. This could be raised and secured at a variety of heights.

**auto-feather:** See feather.

**avionics:** A convenient, manufactured word to describe aviation electronics. In the Britannia this would include all the navigation aids (qv), navigation equipment and the radios.

**B-Skin Jets:** A system fitted to civilian Britannia engines to overcome the engine icing problem. When required, jets of hot air were played on to the bend, where the air flow was reversed, to prevent the build up of ice there.

**ball and roller:** Equipment fitted to the cargo floor of the aircraft to assist the movement of freight. Boxes, pallets etc are slid in through the freight door on to the ball equipment. This is metal plates with cups holding 2 inch diameter steel balls at 9 inch grid intervals. On this, the freight can be slid in any direction, a facility required inside the door to transform sideways movement to aft. Once established in that direction, the freight runs on to rollers secured to the floor in frames for the push rearwards.

**BCARs:** British Civil Aviation Requirements - the rule book for those wishing to obtain a licence for their aircraft from the British authorities.

**Best Blue:** The Royal Air Force 'parade' uniform with brass buttons and full length jacket. A peaked cap is worn with it. The alternative was 'Working Blue' which had a jerkin style. A beret or forage cap was worn with this. 'Working Blue' is now a jersey.

**Britannia Freight Lift Platform:** The BFLP was a 12 feet x 12 feet platform that could be raised from ground level to a height of 10 feet in a framework with cables and pulleys. The platform was placed below the freight door and freight placed on it. This could then be raised to sill height and slid into the aircraft. Power for the electric motor could be provided from a ground power set or by running the No.3 engine. There was a power point for the platform in the starboard wheel bay. The platform could be dismantled for air transport. Its reliability record was not good and its use degenerated into it being permanently left in various locations as continual dismantling and reassembling did not improve its dependability.

**bone dome**: A colloquialism for the aircrew protective helmet. The inner blue cloth element of the 'bone dome' was the standard headgear for Britannia crews for many years.

**Boscombe Down:** The location, in South Wiltshire, of the Aeroplane and Armament Experimental Establishment (qv).

**brake dwell:** See full reverse.

**Britannia Association:** An organisation that exists for the benefit of members and ex-members of the Royal Air Force and Womens Royal Air Force whose service was associated with the Bristol Britannia. In 1995 there were over 500 members. An annual reunion is held and there is a magazine published twice a year. Details can be obtained from this book's publishers: Keyham Books, Startley, Chippenham SN15 5HG.

**C-in-C:** Commander-in-Chief.

**CA Release:** See Aeroplane and Armament Experimental Establishment.

**cabin altitude**: Transport aircraft of the Britannia era onwards are pressurised. High pressure air is bled from the engines into the air tight fuselage to maintain a higher pressure in there than exists outside the aircraft when it is flying at altitude. The thinner air at height contains less oxygen than at lower levels. Prolonged flying at heights above 12,000 feet would eventually result in unconsciousness and, higher still, death. By pressurising the aircraft, the inside of the cabin is kept at the pressure existing at lower levels. The height that the cabin pressure equates to is known as the cabin altitude.

**Cable Route:** A route flown that, at least initially and tokenly, followed the undersea route of the Cable & Wireless cable. By avoiding land it overcame all possible diplomatic objections to the flight. See diplomatic clearance.

**category:** In the transport aircrew sense, category refers to the level of competency of a crew member. This is determined by assessment. There are five levels: 'A', exceptional; 'B', above average; 'C', average; 'D', inexperienced; 'E', in need of further training.

**Cbs:** An abbreviation for cumulo-nimbus clouds (qv).

**CCWR:** An abbreviation for Cloud Collision Warning Radar (qv).

**Central Flying School:** The Central Flying School was the original Royal Flying Corps pilot training establishment. Later, and to this day, it specialised in the training of flying instructors. The graduates are known as QFIs (Qualified Flying Instructors).

**CFS:** Central Flying School (qv).

**Changi Slip:** Britannias on the route between Changi, Singapore and the UK used the 'slipping' (qv) procedure. The route therefore became known as the Changi Slip.

**chill factor:** A thermometer reading is not a complete guide to the effect of low temperatures on the human body. On two days with a similar temperature, the one with a strong wind will have a much greater cooling effect. In extremes this can be life threatening. This chill factor can be determined from tables which are entered with the temperature and wind speed.

**Cloud Collision Warning Radar:** Large cumulus (thunderstorm) type cloud are a danger to aircraft. Within them extreme turbulence can be experienced, even to the point of causing aircraft break up. Icing is also a danger. On the wings, this can spoil the lift providing shape and on the aircraft, as a whole, increase the weight. Lightning strikes can damage the aircraft, destroy aerials and make various pieces of navigation equipment unreliable. Such clouds should be avoided! A feature of them is that the amount of water they contain indicates the likely severity of the above effects. Water reflects radar signals so a special radar set is provided to look ahead for such clouds. This is the Cloud Collision Warning Radar (CCWR). Likely troublesome clouds will show up as white blobs. To assist differentiation between harmless clouds and threatening ones a device can be switched in which suppresses the strongest signals. This has the effect of the 'heavy' clouds showing up on the screen with black centres. Typically, on an Indian Ocean flight, a considerable amount of time could be spent weaving between these. It was exercise requiring some skill and a team effort between the pilots and the navigator.

**combustion chambers:** The air through the engine, having passed through the compressor (qv) enters the combustion chambers where the fuel is added and ignited. At this stage the air reaches a velocity of over 1,350 mph. It then passes to the turbines (qv).

**company messages:** As there is a discipline about transmissions from aircraft then their type falls into two categories: air traffic and 'company' messages. Examples of the former are the messages passed when flying in an airways (qv) system or those to an airfield air traffic control. It can be that, when operating a transport aircraft, there are administrative messages that need to be passed (how many passengers/how much freight on board/amount of fuel required on landing/details of unserviceabilities to be attended to etc.). These are labelled 'company' messages as they will generally be directed to the operating company's agents. Such messages cannot be allowed to clutter up the air traffic control frequencies so special arrangements are made. See Flight Watch.

**compressor:** The second engine component met by the air flow after passing the EGVs (qv). The compressor does just what it says; driven by a turbine (qv), it compresses the air with stages of rotating blades. The Proteus had the unusual feature here in that, after leaving the compressor, the air passed around an elbow, turning it through 180° before entering the combustion chambers (qv). It was this reversal that caused the Britannia's engine icing problem (see Cowl Heat and B-Skin Jets).

**Condecs:** A specially designed vehicle with a rising platform for loading aircraft. See also Britannia Freight Lift Platform.

**constituted crew:** A crew made up of individuals who always flew together. The alternative is to make a crew up from individuals from each 'section' (pilots', navigators', etc.) for each route flight.

**contingency plan:** Attempts are made to pre-empt the possible worldwide emergencies, crises, conflicts, evacuations etc by drawing up contingency plans for use in the possible event. These would outline the types and number of aircraft to be used, the support needed, timings, routings and so on. These plans, or something similar, might be rehearsed in an 'Exercise'.

**controlled air space**: Airspace (qv) which is reserved for use by aircraft with permission to enter it. Control can then be exercised to avoid collision. See airways.

**Country Club:** A colloquial term for the group on the squadron who, through length of service, experience, influence et al, were able to continually manoeuvre themselves on to the better route flights!

**coupled autopilot approaches:** The Britannia autopilot was capable of flying an ILS (qv) approach with the pilot only manipulating some flying instrument controls and autopilot switches. The autopilot could stay engaged right down to the minimum height permitted for an approach in cloud (typically 200 feet above runway level). Increased sophistication in modern aircraft has led to automatic landing equipment.

**cowl heat:** The system fitted to RAF Britannias to overcome the engine icing problem. When required the cowls and certain engine components were heated in an effort to prevent the formation of ice on the bend where the air flow through the engine was reversed.

**crew chief:** A technician who travelled with an aircraft on a route flight to attend to refuelling, routine inspections, unserviceabilities etc. Ground crew have a specialist trade (engines, airframes etc.). Crew chiefs had to extend their knowledge outside their own particular trade. They were also referred to as ground engineers.

**Critical Point:** A point, along with Point of No Return (PNR) and Last Point of Diversion (LPD), of particular significance on a flight with no airfields en route e.g.a long sea leg. On a flight from A to B there is going to a point where the time to fly back to A is equal to the time to fly on to B. This is the Critical Point (CP). If there was no wind (and ignoring the fact that as the aircraft gets lighter, with fuel burn-off, it will fly faster) that point would be half way in terms of distance. The actual calculation of the point is complicated by the wind (a head wind going from A to B becomes a tail wind if returning to A) and the reducing weight, allowing the aircraft to fly at a higher level for the second part of the flight. All this can be calculated by the navigator. A typical significance of the critical point would be if an emergency occurred requiring a landing as soon as possible; before CP turn back to A, after CP continue to B. The PNR between A and B is the point beyond which there is insufficient fuel to return to B. So, up to PNR there is the opportunity of going back; beyond it there is no choice but to go on. The application of this would be a situation arising in which it would be more judicious to return to A than continue to B. The LPD assumes that there an off-track diversion (qv) airfield (C) and the situation is such that a point is reached, on the track from A to B, beyond which it is impossible to reach C. All this certainly taxed the minds of navigators flying into the Indian Ocean island staging post of Gan.

**CRPM:** The Proteus was a turbo-prop engine. A jet engine drove a turbine which drove the propeller. The jet was produced by the combustion of fuel and compressed air. The air was compressed by multi-stage compressor. Each stage had a ring of aerodynamically shaped blades and when the compressor was rotating at high speed, driven by another jet turbine, the air was compressed. How much power was developed by the engine depended on how much air was compressed and how much fuel was added to it.

The speed at which the compressor rotated determined how much air was compressed. The speed at which the compressor rotates is CRPM, Compressor Revolutions Per Minute. At take-off power the Proteus CRPM was 11750.

**Cumulo-Nimbus:** Towering cloud that can reach 30,000 feet and produce thunderstorms and severe turbulence. A feature of the tropics.

**CuNim:** Cumulo-Nimbus (qv) by another name.

**diplomatic clearance:** Countries jealously guard the airspace (qv) above their land and territorial waters and wish to control who uses it. For civilian operators this probably is reflected in reciprocal flight arrangements, trade relationships etc. Military air transport movements are in a different category. By permitting such a flight, a country is tokenly endorsing the reason for it. If this is seen, even remotely, to be against their own interests or those of an ally, then that flight will be banned. To control all this a 'Diplomatic Clearance' system has evolved. At its extreme, all military flights are forbidden. The next degree is that permission must be sought for every flight giving such details as reason, load, route, maybe even crew names. Each flight is cleared individually; this is known as 'Positive Dip Clearance'. Time limits, perhaps only stretching to hours (only one hour in a classic case), might be set on this. A step down from 'Positive' is that it can be assumed that permission has been granted providing the country has been informed of the flight. It may be that a country will issue block clearances for certain types of flight. All this can change in a moment with a tricky diplomatic situation.

**diversion:** Before a large air transport aircraft can take-off it must have at least three airfields at which it can land taking into account the forecast weather. One of those must be the airfield from which it is departing or, if its weather is not 'landable', then one within 90 minutes flying time. This covers an emergency occurring just after take-off. The 90 minutes might seem excessive but it is taking into account the Performance 'A' standards (qv) of the aircraft. The second airfield, perhaps rather obviously, is the destination. The third is a diversion airfield which can be reached from the destination should a landing there not be possible. There is one exception to the 'three airfield' rule. There are destinations which, because of their remoteness, have no airfield within reasonable flying distance. The island of Gan in the Indian Ocean was the classic example. In this case extra fuel has to carried that would permit the aircraft to circle overhead for one hour. It is assumed that whatever problem is preventing the landing (weather, obstructed runway) will have cleared within that time. The weather is not such a gamble as it would appear to be as the rule is only applied to airfields which have a record for relatively short duration bad weather.

**DME:** Distance Measuring Equipment. The distance of the aircraft from a DME beacon is displayed by this device.

**Doors Open:** When a VIP flight is planned it is not the flight time that is important. The vital time for the despatchers of the VIP and the 'greeters' is the time that he/she steps into and out of the aircraft - the 'Doors Closed' and 'Doors Open' time. Having been planned, the crew will take great pride in trying to meet this to the second; not easy given the vagaries of in-flight winds and other factors. The principle of ground departure and arrival times being more important than take-off and landing times applies to all air transport work. It is for this reason that all scheduling is done on 'chock time' - the time the aircraft moves off from the departure parking slot and stops at the destination one.

**Doors Closed:** See 'Doors Open'.

**doppler:** The 'Doppler Effect' is responsible for the changing pitch of the sound of an approaching and receding train. Sound waves are 'compressed' as the train approaches and 'stretched' as it recedes. This effect can be used to determine how fast an aircraft is proceeding forwards over the ground (the Ground Speed). It will also detect sideways shift (the drift due to the wind). The signals can be fed into computing equipment and if information is also entered on the start position, intended track, number of miles to fly, then the Doppler will supply the aircraft's position, how far left or right of track it is and the distance to go. The Britannia's doppler navigation equipment went by the code name of 'Green Satin'.

**double crew:** Limits are imposed on how long a crew can operate. As their day starts with a good deal of preparation, the calculation starts from two hours before departure time. In the bulk of the Britannia years, 19 hours could then elapse before the final arrival. This was not generally planned but could come about through various circumstances. It is a wonder that no accident was caused when operating to this limit. In a military environment, even this length of day may not be enough to achieve an objective. In this case, two crews would be carried and an even longer 'day' could be operated. Double crews were sometimes used for less demanding reasons (training etc).

**EGVs:** Entry guide vanes were the first Proteus engine component met by the incoming air flow. They straightened, stabilised and directed the flow for the next component, the compressor (qv). As part of the battle against engine icing, the EGVs could be heated.

**elevators**: The horizontal flying controls (qv) on the tailplane which control the aircraft in the pitching plane (nose up and down).

**feather:** When an engine of a propeller driven aircraft fails then the propeller, instead of pulling the aircraft through the air, suddenly changes to behaving like a windmill i.e. it is rotated by the flow of air past it. This creates an enormous 'pull back' (drag) on the relevant side of the aircraft and thus a swing towards it. The swing can, generally, be counteracted by the pilot applying correcting rudder (qv). That having been done, the drag from the windmilling propeller must be reduced otherwise height and speed will be lost, perhaps to a dangerous degree. In the long term, fuel consumption will be greatly increased. These effects are countered, for the most part, by 'feathering' the propeller. For normal flight, the blades of a large aircraft's propeller can be twisted so that they meet the airflow at varying angles; this is the means by which the rpm is controlled. When the blades are feathered then they are twisted until they meet the airflow edge on. This reduces the drag to a minimum.

On some types of engine the onset of the drag from the windmilling propeller is so rapid at the low speeds associated with take-off, that the pilot would find it impossible to counteract it. It is necessary, therefore, to install an 'auto-feather' device. This immediately senses that the engine has failed and feathers the propeller which keeps the drag to a minimum. Control is thus maintained. Because of the free turbine (qv) principle of the Proteus engine, the Britannia did not require auto-feathering.

**feathering button:** The control on the flight deck to feather a propeller.

**FL:** See Flight Level.

**flaps:** A rear portion of the wing which can extended and lowered to increase the effective curvature of the wing and thus the lift it provides. They are used at the low speeds associated with take-off and landing.

**Flight Plan:** A form which is completed and submitted before a flight in controlled airspace (qv). It outlines the route required and flight levels (qv) and the associated timings. This will be analysed by air traffic control and form the initial basis for traffic separation.

**Flight Level:** When taking off or landing, it is critical to know the height in relation to the surrounding terrain. An altimeter measures such heights by using the principle that air pressure decreases with increase in height. Air pressure also varies with the changing weather situations (indeed they are cause of those varying conditions). This pressure (the QNH qv) can be forecast and is set on the altimeter. This will now read height above mean sea level, amsl (qv). The height of the airfield and the surrounding terrain will be known and safe flight conducted with those in mind. At higher altitudes such clearance is no longer critical. What is important is the separation from other traffic. For this reason, at a specified height in a region (typically 3000 feet) all aircraft in that area will reset their altimeters to a standard setting (1013 millibars). With all altimeters set the same, separation can be controlled. With this setting the altimeter is said to read Flight Levels (FL) e.g. 20,000 feet is FL200, 26,000 feet is FL260.

**flight director system:** Two of a pilot's basic flight instruments are the compass and the artificial horizon. The latter displays a model of the aircraft, as if viewed from the rear, and a line which is kept aligned with the horizon. When the aircraft climbs, descends or turns it will show up on this instrument. Other instruments on the flight deck display the location of various navigational aids (qv) in relation to the aircraft's position. A flight director system combines the compass and the artificial horizon with this navigational information and displays to the pilot his position in relationship to those aids and assists him in placing the aircraft into a different specified location required by air traffic control.

**flight idle:** The lowest engine power setting that can be used in flight. This will be given and controlled when the throttles are full retracted.

**Form 540:** Every RAF squadron is required to record its activities each month for historical record. The form used for this, in the numbering system for such things, is the Form 540.

**free turbine engine:** A turbo-prop engine has two turbines; one drives the propeller and the other the compressor (qv). On most engines these two are mechanically linked. On a free turbine engine they are independent. The Proteus was a free turbine engine. The shaft for the propeller passed inside that for the compressor. It was possible, though there was a time limit on it for reasons of lubrication, to allow the propeller to windmill (rotate in the airstream) with the engine shut down or, conversely, have the engine running with the propeller feathered (qv).

**freight bay:** A portion of the aircraft dedicated to the carriage of freight (typically passengers' suitcases). On the Britannia the cabin floor split the aircraft fuselage in two. Below it was the forward and aft freight bays and the electrical bays. Freight could also be carried on the strengthened cabin floor. A large freight door allowed access to the main cabin freight bay.

**fuel flow:** Carrying excess fuel does not give economical flight (more fuel is used the higher the weight, so you burn fuel to carry fuel). As, therefore, the amount of fuel required for a flight is carefully calculated and that, with safety margins, is all that is carried, it is important that the fuel consumption is monitored.

In addition to the fuel contents gauges, there are fuel flow gauges which give an instantaneous reading of the amount of fuel being used by each engine. With these two the fuel state, both present and anticipated, can be monitored. A graphical method is used by the navigator to calculate this which goes by the name of the 'Howgozit'.

**full reverse:** After touchdown an aircraft has to be slowed down; on a large aircraft using wheel brakes may not be sufficient. There is also a fire risk and wear and tear. To overcome this there is the facility of reversing the direction of the thrust of the engines. In a propeller driven aircraft this is done by altering the angle, from positive to negative, at which the propeller blades meet the airflow and then applying engine power. As it is important to check that the blades have assumed that negative angle before power is applied (otherwise the aircraft will be accelerated instead of retarded) there is position at which a pause is required for indications to be checked. On the Proteus this was known as Brake Dwell.

**Gateway Gazette:** The Station magazine of RAF Brize Norton.

**greaser:** A colloquialism for a smooth touchdown - not easily achieved in the Britannia.

**Green Satin:** See doppler.

**Green Island approaches:** Because of the terrain and location of the runway, the instrument approaches to runways at Hong Kong were very complex. One of these went by the name of Green Island approach.

**ground engineer:** Another name for a crew chief (qv).

**ground power unit:** The length of time that an aircraft's batteries can support the electrical loads before the engines are started is very limited. To overcome this, and have power available for pre-flight checking and engine starting, electricity is supplied from a ground power unit (GPU), an independent engine driven generator. This can be restrictive on aircraft operating and later generation aircraft than the Britannia had there own on-board power unit. If a GPU was not available then the Britannia's engines had to be started from the aircraft batteries. This was quite critical as the standing loads when the batteries were switched in were very high.

**headset:** The headphones and microphone worn for communication.

**height lock:** It was possible to make the Britannia's autopilot follow one of two parameters. Either the height could be specified, by engaging the height lock, or the airspeed with the airspeed lock.

**HF SSB:** Abbreviation for High Frequency Single Side Band, a type of powerful modern radio capable of long range communication capable of clearly carrying voice communications.

**HF AM:** Abbreviation for High Frequency Amplitude Modulation, a type of communication which preceded HF SSB (qv). Whilst it had a long range and speech capability it was subject to interference. To overcome this, the morse code was often used.

**Howgozit:** See Fuel Flow.

**HP bottles:** High pressure air containers for aircraft servicing.

**humidifier water tank:** A feature of the pressurisation (qv) of an aircraft is that the air inside the aircraft dries out. For comfort, water from the humidifier water tank is injected.

**IFR:** An element of air traffic control is the dividing line between weather conditions when flight by visual cues is possible and when flight has to be conducted by reference to flight instruments. When the latter situation exists, Instrument Meteorological Conditions (IMC), it is said that Instrument Flight Rules (IFR) apply. The converse is Visual Flight Rules (VFR) flown when Visual Meteorological Conditions (VMC) exist. Visibility and distance from cloud limits are laid down to define IMC and VMC. In controlled airspace (qv) it is assumed that IFR conditions always apply.

**ILS:** Abbreviation for Instrument Landing System (qv).

**IMC:** Instrument Meteorological Conditions. The weather conditions which dictate that IFR (qv) apply.

**indicated airspeed:** Aircraft speed is measured with a tubular device (a pitot head) with a hole in the end pointing into the airflow. The pressure generated in the hole is translated into a reading (the indicated airspeed) on the air speed indicator (ASI). The amount of lift generated by the wings is related to such pressure so the ASI is the ideal instrument for use in take-off, landing and in-flight control. As the density of the air reduces with altitude, then the higher an aircraft goes, the faster it must fly to generate the same pressure as at sea level, say. So, with increase in height, although the indicated airspeed (IAS) may remain the same, the true airspeed (TAS) increases. At sea level the two speeds will be the same but at height (say 25,000 feet) the TAS can be around 100 knots (qv) higher than the IAS. This is an important navigational consideration; with no wind, the speed at which the aircraft is going over the ground is equal to the true airspeed. If wind is taken into consideration the speed is known as the ground speed.

**Instrument Landing System:** An aid that allows a very precise approach to be made on to a runway in conditions of low cloud and/or low visibility. A radio beam is transmitted from the ground which is translated by the flight director system (qv) into demands for the pilot to follow.

**intercom:** The communication system between crew.

**introperiscope:** An optical device for inspecting the inside of the engine for damage, typically to the EGVs (qv) and compressor (qv) blades.

**J/T:** Junior Technician, a single stripe rank on the 'Technician' promotion ladder. A philosophy adopted in the 50s/60s for ground trades was that there should be two separate paths up through the ranks. The first should be the traditional one of Corporal, Sergeant, Flight Sergeant, Warrant Officer for men considered to have leadership, man management skills etc. Vacancies on this ladder would be limited so, to give men with technical skills a career pattern, the 'Technician' scheme was introduced.

The ranks were Junior Technician, Corporal Technician, Sergeant Technician and Chief Technician. The badges of rank were the appropriate number of stripes worn upside down. This rather ignominious label perhaps heralded that the scheme would not endure without much amendment. Out of it survived the ranks of Junior Technician (now with a four bladed propeller rank badge) and Chief Technician, three stripes the right way up plus a propeller symbol.

**jet pipe:** See turbine.

**JPT:** Jet pipe temperature. It is important that the temperatures in an engine are kept below imposed limits otherwise damage could ensue. Inside the Proteus, temperatures of up to nearly 900°C could be reached. Measuring this would be difficult so a reading is taken at a cooler spot using the principle that the temperatures through the engine are relative. The temperature monitored on the flight deck is the jet pipe temperature which reaches a mere 500° to 600°C.

**Judge Advocate:** Civilian legal adviser to the military trial officers at a court martial.

**Kai Tak:** The name of the Royal Air Force

station at Hong Kong.

**KD:** Khaki Drill. The traditional name, which has survived, for the military tropical uniform.

**knots:** The nautical measurement of speed which is also universally used in the air. One knot equals one nautical mile per hour. As the nautical mile is longer (6080 feet) than the statute (land) mile (5280 feet), a speed in knots has a smaller number designator than the same speed in mph.

Example: 200 knots = 230 mph.

**Last Point of Diversion:** See Critical Point.

**limiter:** In the Britannia this was a device to sense that the propeller turbine (qv) was overspeeding and shut that engine down.

**London Control Zone:** The very busy and critical controlled air space (qv) around London Heathrow.

**LPD:** Last Point of Diversion. See Critical Point.

**Lyneham Globe:** The excellent station newspaper of RAF Lyneham.

**Maintenance Unit:** Establishments in the RAF dedicated to back-up tasks such as aircraft and equipment storage, modification, special servicing and the like.

**Major Inspection:** Aircraft are subject to periodic inspections and servicings based either on hours flown or calendar months. The level of these inspections varies; the most comprehensive being the 'Major'. During this a considerable amount of dismantling is undertaken and component replacement.

**marshalling:** The guidance, by hand signals, of an aircraft on the ground.

**Master Signaller:** 'Master' is the senior non-commissioned aircrew rank and is the equivalent to Warrant Officer. It is a remnant from the aircrew rank structure introduced in the late 1940s. During the war normal NCO ranks had been used, Corporal Pilot, Sergeant Pilot, Flight Sergeant and Warrant Officer. Post-war it was decided that there should be a differentiation between air and ground ranks. The aircrew ranks were denoted by stars in a laurel leaf type surround. The ranks were the aircrew trade and the number of stars, perversely, were in reverse order e.g. a one star was a Pilot 4, the lowest. The senior rank was Master Pilot and the stars gave way to the Warrant Officer's Coat of Arms in the laurel leaves. The system only lasted a matter of a few years before reverting to the original structure except for the Master rank, which was retained. Typical ranks, to this day, are Sgt Engineer, Flt Sgt Engineer, Master Engineer. A brass albatross added to the normal rank badge distinguishes an aircrew rank.

**Maximum (Take-Off) Power:** Engine wear is directly related to the power used; also, beyond certain limits, failure could result. The maximum that can be used is dictated and a time limit (Britannia, five minutes) set. This is only generally required for the take-off and the initial part (400 feet) of the climb out. The power is then reduced to Maximum Continuous Power (MCP) on which there is no time limit.

**MCU:** Marine Craft Unit, established for seaborne Search and Rescue.

**middle airspace:** In between aircraft leaving airways (qv) control and reaching airfield control they pass through middle airspace.

**Military Operating Standards:** With the introduction of the civilian standards' Comet and Britannia into RAF service it became policy to operate them, whenever possible, to full civilian performance standards. However, there were going to be occasions where these standards could not be maintained if a particularly urgent military task was to be completed. At these times it was declared that the aircraft could operate to Military Operating Standards e.g. the maximum take-off weight for the Britannia was allowed to be 190,000lbs instead 185,000lbs. The increased risk was considered acceptable for military expediency.

**NDB:** Non-directional beacon. See ADF.

**OCU:** Abbreviation for Operational

Conversion Unit, a training organisation for converting crews to new types of aircraft.

**ODM:** Abbreviation for Operating Data Manual.

**Operating Data Manual (ODM):** A collection of facts and figures, mainly in graphical and tabular form, which spell out the capabilities of an aircraft and allows calculation so that it can operate within laid down limits.

**operation:** The highest priority of flight or set of flights in support of some actual emergency.

**Operational Conversion Unit:** See OCU.

**OR:** The Operational Requirements (OR) branch of MOD lays down the future equipment requirements of the Services to meet anticipated defence needs.

**patched through:** With modern HF radio transmissions (SSB) it is possible for the receiver to connect (patch through) the call into a switchboard situation so that it can be heard on the telephone. The person receiving this call can reply to the aircraft via the telephone. This system is known as a phone patch.

**PCF:** Passenger cum freight i.e. an aircraft layout/load split between the two.

**PCU:** Propeller Control Unit - a device for maintaining a constant propeller rpm despite changing conditions.

**Performance 'A' standards:** The full civilian performance standards.

**performance manuals:** The manuals that allowed Performance 'A' (qv) standards to be calculated.

**performance:** A general term that embraced all matters concerned with the take-off, en route and landing behaviour of a transport aircraft.

**Persons on Board:** The total number of people on board an aircraft on start-up. This is passed to air traffic control and is recorded by them in case of a subsequent accident and the need to account for number of people on board. The old term was SOB, Souls on Board.

**Pilot's Notes:** With each aircraft comes a set of notes setting out limitations and operating details. These were known as Pilot's Notes; the modern term is Aircrew Manual.

**pitch lock:** In order for the PCU (qv) to maintain a constant rpm the angle at which the propeller blade meets the airflow is varied. If there is a malfunction and this cannot be changed then the propeller is said to pitch locked.

**PNR:** Abbreviation for Point of No Return.

**Point of No Return:** See Critical Point.

**pressurisation:** Air density reduces with increase in height and with it the amount of oxygen. Human beings require oxygen to survive and the air above 12,000 feet does not contain sufficient oxygen for safe survival. Prolonged flight at that height would cause discomfort. As height is increased, signs of oxygen starvation would become increasingly apparent to the point where unconsciousness and death would eventually occur. This problem can be overcome by having a sealed aircraft fuselage in which a pressure can be maintained equivalent to that at sea level (or the lower levels of the atmosphere). With the maintenance of these pressures comes safe oxygen content. The system for maintaining this situation is known as the pressurisation. See also cabin altitude.

**propeller reduction gear:** If the propeller were connected directly to the engine it would rotate at far too high a speed. The propeller reduction gear reduces that speed to a safe and efficient level.

**propeller blade angle:** The angle at which the propeller blade meets the air flow.

**propeller control unit:** See PCU.

**propeller brake:** On the ground, with the engine shut down, the propeller of a free turbine engine (qv) would rotate in the wind. A propeller brake prevents this.

**PRPM:** Propeller revolutions per minute.

**QFE:** A barometric pressure in millibars

which, if set on the altimeter, makes it read zero when it is on the ground at a particular airfield. In flight the altimeter, with the QFE set, will read the height above that airfield.

**QFI:** Qualified flying instructor (see Central Flying School).

**QNH:** See amsl.

**QTR:** Quick turn round (qv).

**quick turn round:** Staging (qv) in the shortest time that is reasonably possible. It usually only involves a refuel.

**radio compass:** See ADF

**recat:** The aircrew categorisation process.

**reverse pitch:** The pitch of a propeller blade is the angle at which it meets the airflow. This is adjustable for different conditions. For flight this obviously has to be a positive angle to 'pull' the aircraft through the air. For landing, a braking effect is required so the blades are brought to a negative angle. This is reverse pitch.

**RFA:** Royal Fleet Auxiliary.

**roll-out:** The 'ceremony' when a new aircraft is towed out of its construction hangar for the first time.

**Romeo Yankee:** The letters R and Y, which might be a callsign, in the phonetic alphabet.

**route check:** Part of the procedure for determining aircrew category (qv). An instructor/examiner flies with the candidate on a route trip and observes and assesses his operating standard.

**RPM:** Revolutions per minute.

**Runway 04:** A way of identifying runways and indicating their approximate direction. Runway 04 would have a direction somewhere between 035° and 045° i.e. NE about.

**SASF:** Strategic Aircraft Servicing Flight: another term for TASS (qv).

**servo tabs:** Small control surfaces on the trailing edges of the control surfaces proper i.e. aileron, rudder, elevator. On a large aircraft these would be extremely heavy for the pilot to move directly. So it is arranged that the control column /rudder control moves the servo tabs and they, with the airflow acting on them, move the primary surface.

**sextant:** The optical device used by the navigator for determining the angle of elevation of selected heavenly bodies: see astro.

**Single Side Band HF:** See SSB HF.

**slipping:** In order that an aircraft can move along a route without delay for crew rest, crews are pre-positioned at suitable points along the intended route. The incoming 'tired' crew 'slips' to a fresh crew. The 'tired' crew can then rest ready for a later aircraft in the stream. By this method the aircraft is only on the ground for the 1½ hour refuelling stop.

**Smiths Flight System (SFS):** The make and model of flight director system (qv) fitted to the Britannia.

**snags:** Slang term for unserviceabilities.

**speed lock:** Autopilots, as well as maintaining the wings level, can hold a particular speed if the speed lock is engaged. This is useful for the climb and descent. The alternative, used in cruising flight, is to have the height lock engaged.

**SSB HF:** Abbreviation for single side band high frequency radio. This was a development from the old HF radios which used the whole of the transmission wave to carry the signal. SSB only uses half which greatly increases the power of the transmission.

**staging:** Air transport term for landing, refuelling, possibly reloading and then proceeding further along the route.

**Swan Song:** Popular term for one's 'special' last trip on a squadron before posting.

**T/R:** Transmitter/receiver.

**TACAN:** From Tactical Air Navigator; originally a military navigation aid which gives the bearing and distance of the aircraft from a ground source. It requires a ground transmitter/receiver which is 'interrogated' by the equipment in the aircraft and then transmits the range and bearing.

**tacho generator:** A tachometer indicates a speed of rotation (rpm). With a tacho generator that speed is transmitted by means of the engine or whatever driving a small generator.

**TASS:** Transport Aircraft Servicing Section. The section on a station responsible for the transport aircraft passing through.

**tech debrief:** At the conclusion of a flight it is important that the ground crew is fully debriefed on the aircraft faults. This is the tech debrief.

**toilet gate valve:** The valve through which the toilet tanks are drained during ground servicing.

**top of the descent:** Flying at lower levels in a large aircraft is 'expensive' in fuel. To minimise this the navigator calculates the shortest range from the destination at which to start the descent and be at a suitable height and range from the airfield for the approach to land.

**tour:** The period that a serviceman spends at a particular station/job. The standard time was 2½ years.

**tourex:** For tour (qv) expired i.e. due for posting.

**true air speed:** See indicated air speed.

**turbine:** After the engine air has exited the combustion chambers (qv) it passes through two turbines. On a turbo-prop aircraft, the first drives the compressor (qv), the second the propeller, through the propeller reduction gear (qv). If the shaft to the propeller passes inside the one to the compressor and is otherwise independent of it, the system is known as a 'free turbine engine' (qv). From the turbines the air leaves the engine through the jet pipe. This can provide a small amount of thrust.

**two engine approaches:** The essential element of having four engines on an aircraft is to develop sufficient power for efficient flight PLUS providing a safety factor. Should one engine fail then no danger will exist. In the unlikely event of two engines failing then flight can continue but, in view of the more critical situation, a landing needs to be carried out as soon as possible. Pilots practice this event, performing 'two engine approaches'.

**U/S:** Unserviceable.

**UDI:** Unilateral Declaration of Independence as proclaimed by Rhodesia in 1965.

**UHF:** Ultra High Frequency radio.

**VFR:** Visual Flight Rules. See IFR.

**VHF/UHF:** Combined Very High Frequency and Ultra High Frequency radios.

**VHF:** Very High Frequency radio.

**Victor Airways:** Airways in the USA based on VOR (qv) beacons.

**VMC:** Visual Meteorological Conditions. See IFR.

**VOR:** A VOR beacon is a ground transmitter which radiates a signal indicating bearing. This can be received by an aircraft's VOR receiver.

**VOR/DME:** Combined information on bearing and distance obtained from VOR (qv) and DME (qv) equipment.

**Westabout:** The name given to a flight indicating its general direction out of the UK i.e. a trip to the USA would be a 'Westabout'; one to Singapore, the shortest way, would be an 'Eastabout'.

**yaw:** An aircraft operates in three planes: rolling, pitching and yawing. Rolling is the wings rising and falling; pitching is the nose rising and falling and yawing is the nose being moved horizontally to the left and right. It is not a normal flying manoeuvre and the aircraft is generally kept in 'balanced flight', meaning that yaw is compensated out. It can happen when an engine failure occurs in a multi-engined aircraft and is compensated for by the use of rudder (qv).

APPENDIX 5

# Index

Items in the Glossary are not listed.

# B

# C

# D



# E

# F



# G

# H

# I

# J



# K

# L



# M

# N

# O



# P

# Q



# R

# S

# T



# U

# X



# Y

# Specialist Aircrew

**The life and times of a 1951 to 1991 RAF pilot**

**If you have enjoyed this book and would like to read more personal detail of Britannia life then 'Specialist Aircrew' is the book for you. The back cover spells out the content:**

**I hesitate to call this an autobiography after my daughter said, 'But, Dad, you're not famous enough!' Let it just be the reminiscences of a long serving, 1951 to 1991, Royal Air Force pilot. Through these, there is an insight into life in the peacetime Service.**
**There is a saying along the lines, 'Give me the boy until he is seven and I'll give you the man.' Believing this to be true, I have described my early years in some detail. What could be heavy going is relieved by the fact that my father was somewhat eccentric and provided me with some crazy memories!**

**In fact, there is a light hearted approach throughout. Service life is a breeding ground for natural humour and many amusing incidents are related.**
**For me, my journey through life has been interesting and enjoyable. I am sure that you will find interest and enjoyment on this guided trip, by my side, down my 'Memory Lane'.**

Published by and obtainable
from Keyham Books, Startley,
Chippenham SN15 5HG
Tel: 01249 720239
www.keyhambooks.co.uk

**Price: £10.99**
**inc. UK p&p**

Bill Robinson

The Royal Air Force only operated the elegant four turboprop Bristol Britannia for 16 years, 1959 to 1975. This was during the peak of RAF transport flying but at the twilight of our country's global defence commitment. The scrapping of the aircraft marked the end of an era; '*The RAF Britannia and its people*' is a record of those years. In its telling there is an insight into the peacetime activities of the Royal Air Force and of life at RAF Lyneham and RAF Brize Norton.

Military aircraft history books have a reputation for being a dull repetition of fact garnered from Service records. This book is different. There is historical detail but this is also a 'people' book and it has been broken up with asides which give a feel for what life was like for the air and ground crews. Details are given of how the aircraft was operated and difficulties encountered. Britannia complexities are explained and there is a comprehensive glossary - so it provides an interesting and enjoyable read for enthusiast and general reader alike.

Air Chief Marshal Sir Thomas Kennedy GCB AFC has written the foreword.

Using new material that has come to hand, this is a much expanded version of the original published in 1996 - an extra 350 pages and over 650 photographs! It is still the only RAF Britannia book!

Published by Keyham Books, Startley, Chippenham SN15 5HG
www.keyhambooks.co.uk

Barcode